The American Counties

Origins of County Names, Dates of Creation, Area, and Population Data, 1950–2010, 6th Edition

Charles Curry Aiken
Joseph Nathan Kane

The Scarecrow Press, Inc.
Lanham • Toronto • Plymouth, UK
2013

Published by Scarecrow Press, Inc.
A wholly owned subsidiary of The Rowman & Littlefield Publishing Group, Inc.
4501 Forbes Boulevard, Suite 200, Lanham, Maryland 20706
www.rowman.com

10 Thornbury Road, Plymouth PL6 7PP, United Kingdom

British Library Cataloguing in Publication Information Available

Library of Congress Cataloging-in-Publication Data

Aiken, Charles Curry, 1940–
  The American counties : origins of county names, dates of creation, area, and
population data, 1950–2010 / Charles Curry Aiken, Joseph Nathan Kane. — 6th ed.
    p. cm.
  Rev. ed. of: American counties / Joseph Nathan Kane. 5th ed. 2005.
  Includes bibliographical references.
  ISBN 978-0-8108-8761-9 (cloth : alk. paper) — ISBN 978-0-8108-8762-6 (ebook)
  1. United States—History, Local. 2. Counties—United States. I. Kane, Joseph
Nathan, 1899–2002. II. Kane, Joseph Nathan, 1899–2002. American counties. III. Title.
  E180.K3 2013
  973—dc23
                                                                    2012033701

∞™ The paper used in this publication meets the minimum requirements of American
National Standard for Information Sciences—Permanence of Paper for Printed Library
Materials, ANSI/NISO Z39.48-1992. Printed in the United States of America.

Contents

Preface

I have always had an interest in counties. It grew out of an interest in geography. As a child I would make lists of the states and their capitals; I ranked them by area, population, and order of admission. I did about all I could with the (then) forty-eight states. I did the same, except for order of admission, for the countries of the world which at the time amounted to not much more than fifty or sixty countries.

One day around the age of eleven I came across *The World Almanac and Book of Facts*. It contained an alphabetical listing of the counties for each state. My mind raced with the possibilities. First I combined them all into one national alphabetical list. Next I compiled state and national rankings based on area and population and alphabetical listings of county seats. All this was accomplished before computers. I never did much with these lists except when taking trips with family I could fascinate my parents and bore my brothers with national and state rankings as we entered a new county.

I forget the nature of the research project that led me to Joseph Kane's *The American Counties*. I remember the sensation of discovering Kane being similar to my first encounter with *The World Almanac*. Here was a wealth of information on counties; not just the information I had manipulated before but the date a county was created and the origin of the county's name. I was struck by the fact that here was an entire book devoted to counties—this meant that I was not alone in my interest with counties.

My interest in counties waned with college, career, and family responsibilities. My interest rekindled when I moved to Bloomington, Indiana. I was intrigued by the way county courthouses in southern Indiana were often massive structures plopped down on a square in the middle of town. I took pictures of some nearby courthouses on family drives around Bloomington.

My employer in Bloomington was the US Navy Safety School. My work as a safety instructor involved travel to naval bases on both coasts. These trips were usually for two weeks giving me an intervening weekend to kill. I hit on the idea of taking pictures of courthouses around the areas in which I was working as a good way to explore the surrounding territory. After getting pictures of most of the reachable courthouses around Norfolk, Charleston, Jacksonville, San Diego, San Francisco, etc., I realized that if I drove to these places from Bloomington, I could get courthouse pictures along the way. As often happens, a pastime had become an obsession. After retiring from the Civil Service, I became a safety-training consultant and continued to travel for other federal agencies that got me off the "Navy tour." Over the last thirty years, I have personally visited and taken pictures of 3,114 of the county courthouses in the United States—all except the twenty-nine boroughs and census areas of Alaska.

I bought a copy of the fourth edition of *The American Counties* (pub. 1983). I awaited the next edition that would include the 1990 census. When it was not forthcoming, I did not think much about it until the 2000 census was in progress. I thought it would be good to have *The American Counties* include the censuses from 1950 to 2000. Also, I had noted that some updating was required as some new counties were created and others were abolished. Some county seats had been relocated since the publication of Kane's first edition in 1953.

I contacted Scarecrow Press with a proposal to update *The American Counties*. The person I corresponded with said she would check with Mr. Kane for his concurrence to update his book. I was surprised to find that he was still alive (at 102!). I received Kane's approval through Scarecrow Press. I also received a letter from Kane's family saying he was very pleased that his book was going to be updated.

Joseph Kane has since died. I regret I did not conceive of this project earlier so I could possibly have met him. Mr. Kane did all the groundwork: the concept, researching the name origins, and tracking down the dates when counties were created. All I had to do was to verify some of them. This book is dedicated to Joseph Kane.

In compiling this sixth edition I have discovered sources of new information not included in previous editions. I found sources for dates of creation and more biographical information on persons for whom counties have been named. There are many people who helped make this edition what it is. The bibliography lists books and websites that provided information. I should also thank the numerous persons (usually library or county employees) who responded to my e-mails and letters as I tried to track down the proper spelling of a county or county seat or the date the county was created. The Government Documents Department of the Indiana University Library in Bloomington was also very helpful. I am, of course, responsible for any errors or omissions in this book. I would be remiss if I did not thank my wife for her patience during my many hours devoted to this project.

Charles C. Aiken
Bloomington, Indiana

Introduction

In 1634, twenty-seven years after the settlement of Jamestown, Virginia established seven counties. The need for localized government had become apparent as the colony spread out from Jamestown. These counties were patterned after those in seventeenth century England. This nascent idea for localized government in America expanded with the growth of the English colonies and spread with the expansion of the United States.

There are presently 3,143 counties in the United States. Everybody living in the United States lives in a county or "county equivalent." Counties and county equivalents are defined by the US Department of Commerce in *Federal Information Processing Standards Publication 6-4* as "first-order subdivisions of each State . . . regardless of local designations." This includes 3,007 counties in 48 states; 64 parishes in Louisiana; sixteen boroughs, eleven census areas, and two municipalities in Alaska; 39 independent cities in Virginia and one independent city in each of Maryland, Missouri, and Nevada. The District of Columbia is by default a county equivalent. (The five boroughs of New York City are counties.) As used herein, the term "county" includes all first-order subdivisions. To title this book *The American First-Order Subdivisions* would have been too unwieldy.

A county can be defined politically, geographically, historically, statistically, or by any number of adverbial categories. To many people their county is just another layer of government collecting taxes and otherwise not doing much. Many people think of their county only during the county fair or on visits to the courthouse. Travelers may notice highway signs announcing their passage from one county to another. In many rural areas, the high school carries the county name and is a focal point of local pride.

If anyone thinks about his or her county it is usually as something that has always been there and has always had a name that, unless named for a US president or a local geographic feature, has little, if any, significance. Most people for whom a county has been named have long since died, many in obscurity. This book offers a few facts about every county in the United States in hopes that it will spark the readers' interest to find out more about their county or other counties of interest. When was the county created? Who or what is it named for? Why? How does my county stack up against adjacent counties in area or population? Is my county older than the one next door? The bibliography lists sources that are dedicated solely to population data, or name origins, or areas, or dates of creation. But no other book has all this county data in one place.

The status of a county in this book is as it was on April 1, 2010, the official date of the 2010 Decennial Census. Since the 2000 Census there have been changes in the status of counties in Alaska, Colorado, and Virginia. In July 2001 the independent city of Clifton Forge, Virginia, returned to Alleghany County. In November 2001 the city of Broomfield, Colorado, became Broomfield County. The county was created to alleviate jurisdictional conflicts as the city had grown by several annexations to spread from Boulder County into Adams, Jefferson, and Weld Counties. In June 2007 Skagway Borough, Alaska, was separated from Skagway-Hoonah-Angoon Census Area. In June 2008 Prince of Wales-Outer Ketchikan Census Area, Alaska, became Prince of Wales-Hyder Census Area when Outer Ketchikan was annexed to Ketchikan Gateway Borough. Also in June 2008 Wrangell-Petersburg Census Area became Petersburg Census Area with the creation of Wrangell Borough. (In 2011 the city council of Bedford, Virginia, voted to return to Bedford County; the transition will occur in July 2013.) There have been minor boundary adjustments in almost every state, but these changes have not resulted in the addition or deletion of counties.

The counties of Connecticut and Rhode Island do not have governmental structures. They are geographical entities that are maintained for statistical, record keeping, and some judicial functions. Kalawao County, Hawaii, is included despite its dubious status as a county. It is administered by the Hawaii Department of Health as a leper colony. Any reader wishing to exclude Kalawao County can place its area and population in Maui County with simple arithmetic.

This book was prepared with the realization that each reader will turn first to his/her county. Some will find new information about their counties. Others will check this book to verify what they already know. Still other readers will be well versed in their county's history and will evaluate the veracity of the information included. Every effort has been made to verify the accuracy of the information in this book knowing that if readers find errors regarding their own counties, everything else in the book will be suspect. Readers are encouraged to inform the author of any errors or omissions.

This book is divided into five main sections. Following the introductory material is the heart of the book: "The American Counties," an alphabetical listing of the 3,143 counties in the United States. The arrangement and contents of each entry in this section are discussed below. Next is Appendix A, "Counties by State," a listing of counties in each state giving the county name, county seat, and the date of creation. A brief outline of the state's political history is provided so it may be determined under which government the county was created. Also included in this section are any county name changes. Appendix B is "Date of Creation," a list of counties in the order of their creation from 1634 to 2008. Appendix C ranks the 100 largest counties and the 100 smallest counties by their 2010 populations. Appendix D ranks the 100 largest counties and the 100 smallest counties by land area in square miles. Space considerations make it impractical to include all 3,143 counties in these two appendices. Appendix E is a list of counties that have been eliminated for various reasons. Last is a bibliography of the main sources used in verifying or compiling the information in this book.

In preparing this 6th edition, the organization of the previous editions has essentially been followed. The first line of each entry contains in bold type the name of the county and its state. The county seat and the county's area in square miles are on the second line. The third line gives the county's decennial census totals from 1950 to 2010. The fourth line begins with the date the county was created. Also included, as applicable, are the dates the county was renamed, abolished, recreated, organized, deorganized, and/or reorganized. Following the date(s) is a brief description of the origin of the county's name and, if named for a person, a brief sketch of biographical highlights of the person(s) so honored.

COUNTY NAME

The book's entries are arranged alphabetically by county and, if there is more than one county of the same name, by state. There are no known disputed spellings of any county name although some names are misspellings of their origins. For example, there are four counties named for Joseph Daveiss (including Jo Daviess, Illinois) and every one misspells the county name as "Daviess." Two of the three counties honoring John Stark spell his name correctly but Indiana added an *e* when creating Starke County. Once a misspelling is enacted into law by a legislature, it can only be corrected by a subsequent legislative action. Most states have not bothered to do this.

There is some confusion in the proper spacing of some county names. Are De Soto, La Salle, El Dorado, etc., one word or two? If one, is the third letter capitalized? An example is De Witt (two words) County, Illinois, and DeWitt (one word) County, Texas. Lagrange (lower case *g*) is the county seat of LaGrange (upper case *G*) County in Indiana. The first step in attempting to resolve these issues was to contact a county official or office listed on the National Association of Counties' (NACo) website (www.naco.org). The final arbiter was the Geographic Names Information System (GNIS) of the US Geological Survey, Department of the Interior (geonames.usgs.gov).

One hundred seventy-four counties have changed their names. Some have changed names more than once while others changed and then later reverted back to their original name. Often a change was made to honor a newly emerged hero or because the original honoree had fallen from favor. Some names are changed because the original was an Indian name that was too difficult to pronounce or spell, such as Warrosquyoake or Kautawubet. (In deciding whether to use "Indian" or "Native American" in referring to the native populations of America, guidance was taken from a note in David Fischer's *Champlain's Dream* [New York: Simon & Schuster, 2008, page 626, note 26]. Fischer asked a gathering of Indian leaders what term they preferred. They concurred that when referring to a certain nation or tribe the specific name should be used [i.e., Cherokee, Iroquois, Sisseton, etc.]. When referring to all Indians as a whole the leaders agreed "that Indian was as good as any other." As used in this book the term "Indian" also includes Alaskan natives and Polynesians unless otherwise specified.)

COUNTY SEAT

The county seat is the first item on the second line of each county's entry. During the nineteenth century many towns vied to be their county's center of government. Such status would usually make the town a center of growth and commerce in addition to being a source of local pride. Theft of county records, gunfights, and even burning down the courthouse were sometimes reverted to in order to encourage the relocation of a county seat. By the early twentieth century most counties had settled on their county seat, but county seats continue to be relocated although by more peaceful processes. County government centers are a fairly recent development in which a campus is built on an expanse of land outside the county seat. The cities or towns listed herein as county seats are consistent with NACo.

The cities or towns identified with Alaska's boroughs are not county seats but they serve the same function as administrative and judicial centers for their respective jurisdictions. Alaska's eleven census areas are administered by the state. Although there may be a locale within the census area from which a state official operates, none are listed as such. Shannon and Todd counties in South Dakota are not organized. They are attached to Fall River and Tripp Counties respectively.

Connecticut abolished county government in 1960. Rhode Island's counties emerged from judicial districts and never have had complete county governmental functions or structures. The cities named as county seats for these two states are judicial or record-keeping centers that are listed by NACo as functioning as county seats.

In previous editions of *The American Counties*, some listings had two county seats for some counties, most notably in Arkansas and Mississippi. It may be that the courthouse and county seat are in separate cities or that governmental offices are divided between the two cities. In this edition, only one county seat is listed for each county as named by the NACo and confirmed by *The Handybook for Genealogists* (10th edition, Everton Publishers, Draper, Utah, 2002).

AREA

The other item on the second line of each county's entry is its area in square miles. The figure given is for land area exclusive of any water areas in the county. The county areas given in this edition are the ones used by the US Census Bureau to compute population densities for the 2010 Census.

The area of a county changes more often than one would suspect. The square mileage of coastal or riverine counties can fluctuate as land is lost to or reclaimed from the water. Many coastal counties have lost land area. Most losses are less than five square miles, but the land area of Plaquemines Parish, Louisiana, at the mouth of the Mississippi River, has dropped from 845 to 780 square miles since 2000. The creation of reservoirs can also reduce a county's land area.

Boundary adjustments affect county areas. In Virginia, the establishment and growth of independent cities is done at the expense of surrounding counties. Alaska's boroughs are still evolving from census areas.

POPULATION

On the third line of each county's entry is the county's population from the last seven decennial censuses. The populations are listed from 2010 to 1950 reading left to right (2010, 2000, 1990, 1980, 1970, 1960, and 1950).

The population figures from 2000 are from the Census Bureau's 2000 Census. The figures from 1950 to 1980 are from Kane's previous editions verified against Richard L. Forstall, *Population of States and Counties of the United States: 1790–1990*, US Bureau of the Census, Washington, DC, 1996.

The 2010 populations of America's counties range from Los Angeles County, California, with 9,818,605 people to Loving County, Texas, with 82. Los Angeles County's population is over twice as large as every other county except Cook County, Illinois. Los Angeles has more people than all but eight states. Like most Western counties with large populations, Los Angeles is large enough, at 4,058 square miles, to include most if its own suburbs. If New York County were as large as Los Angeles County, it would have a population of 17,202,989. Such a county would consist of the five counties of New York City plus Nassau, Rockland, Suffolk, and Westchester Counties in New York State. Adjacent counties in New Jersey would include Bergen, Hudson, Middlesex, Monmouth, Passaic, and Union. Fairfield County, Connecticut would also be included. The total area would be 4,075 square miles, slightly larger than Los Angeles County.

DATE OF CREATION

The fourth line of each county's entry starts with the date the county was created. The six earliest counties were formed in Virginia in 1634; the last one, Wrangell Borough, Alaska, was created June 1, 2008. The various factors considered in determining the date a county was created are discussed at the beginning of Appendix B, "Dates of Creation."

For some counties the date the county was created is followed by the date the county was organized. Many counties on the frontier were created when there were few, if any, settlers within the county. This was sometimes done by the legislature just to be done with the business of establishing counties. Other times it was done at the behest of railroads so that maps of the empty territory would look settled. Some counties were abolished or deorganized after having been created or organized. This is noted in the date entry in "The American Counties" section along with the date of subsequent reorganization or recreation.

The date given for the creation of a county is the date it was established in its present location. If the county was abolished and subsequently recreated in its former location, the date given is the date the county was originally created.

Some counties were abolished and their names given to other counties elsewhere in the state. Seward County, Kansas, is a good example of a shifting county name. The first Seward County was created in 1855 in southeastern Kansas as Godfroy County, one of Kansas's original counties. Its name was changed to Seward in 1861. In 1867 Seward County, which was never organized, was abolished when it was merged with Butler County to create Howard County. In 1873 a new Seward County was created in the southwest corner of the state about 250 miles west of the first Seward County. In 1883 Seward absorbed two counties to its west: Kansas and Sumner. In 1886 Seward was organized and Morton and Stevens counties were created from where Kansas and Sumner had been. The result of all this is that, Seward County, Kansas, is listed as having been created in 1873 and organized in 1886. The first Seward County is listed in Appendix E, "Eliminated Counties" along with other counties that have been wiped off the map for various reasons.

In some states, the legislature specified the date the county would become effective. This is usually within a year of the creation date. The date listed is the date the legislation was passed creating the county. The effective date is included as applicable.

The date given for independent cities is the date the city became independent, not the date of its founding. Exceptions are Chesapeake, Hampton, Newport News, Suffolk, and Virginia Beach in Virginia, and Carson City, Nevada. These six cities merged with existing counties and the date given is the date the original county was created.

NAME ORIGIN

The last part of each entry is the origin of the county's name. Each name origin begins with the name of the person, river, mountain, battle, or whatever else the county may be named for. The immediate source of the name is printed in *italics*. Sometimes the origin of the county's name is unknown or there are a number of possibilities. There may be two or more persons with the same name with valid claims to be the source of a county's name. In some instances it is known that the county was named for a local mountain or river that has a foreign or Indian name but the origin of that name is unknown. Some consensus guesses are all that can be offered. These are indicated as "Uncertain." Unless otherwise noted, the possibilities are offered in the order of plausibility.

If a county is named for a person, a brief biographical sketch is included. The sketches given herein are not intended to portray the life of George Washington or Thomas Jefferson. They, and others of their stature, do not need much explanation as to why they were honored by namesake counties. The biographical entries attempt to list the military, business, and/or political highlights of the person's life that connect the person, if not of national stature, with the county or state. Because US presidents, especially, had counties named for them before they became president, the biographical sketch can indicate the position held at the time a county was named. In some instances, such as a private killed during the Civil War, little is known of the honoree's life other than the circumstances of his death.

The naming of a county was usually done by a gathering of settlers who petitioned for or otherwise sought the creation of the county. Sometimes the honoree has no discernible connection with the county or its state. This is usually the result of a prominent settler naming the county for a friend or relative who had no association with the new county. Often the name of the town or county the settlers had come from was chosen or the name was the former home of one of the more prominent persons among the settlers.

Legislatures usually went along with the wishes of the local citizens in naming counties. However, many counties, especially in the Great Plains, were created before anybody lived there so the legislators selected the names of new counties. A practice prevalent in Dakota Territory and Oklahoma—although it occurred in other states—was the naming of counties after persons who happened to be members of the legislature at the time counties were being named. Often such a person's life is unremarkable except for the happenstance of having been in the right place at the right time. Being on the committee that named counties was a virtual guarantee of eponymous immortality.

The meanings of Indian names are often unknown. The names we know today are often the result of being corrupted into whatever language was spoken by the Europeans who first encountered the Indians. Because the Europeans and Indians often had no idea what the other was saying, what was thought to be the name of the tribe could be almost anything the Indians thought the Europeans wanted to hear.

When more than one county is named for the same person, the first county in that series contains the biographical sketch. Subsequent counties named for the same person have an asterisk (*) after the name. The same system of italics and asterisks is used when counties are named for the same Indian group or geographical feature.

Most of Virginia's independent cities are within a county. In fact, some are the county seat of the county of which they are independent. At the end of the entries for Virginia's independent cities, the county(s) it is associated with is given and vice versa. This is so that readers who wish to may include the independent cities with their associated counties for statistical purposes.

THE NAMING OF COUNTIES

How does a county acquire its name? One can imagine a gathering of somber citizens carefully selecting an appropriate name for their new county. Should it be named for a president or general? How about the current governor, senator, or representative from the area? Perhaps a locally prominent merchant, educator, or clergyman should be honored. How about a name that might attract settlers to the county? Or should it be named for a prominent local geographic feature? Or a local Indian nation or tribe?

County names fall into three general categories: persons, geography, and descriptive. "Persons" includes presidents and kings as well as unknown, long-forgotten settlers or otherwise anonymous soldiers killed in battle. "Geographic features" include rivers, mountains, towns, and other counties. "Descriptive" is a miscellaneous category including names such as Elk, Coal, Fairfield, Union, etc., which are neither persons nor geographic. A county can be included in more than one category. Santa Barbara County, California, is counted among persons (saints and women), geographic (towns and missions), and descriptive (Spanish language).

Before discussing name origins it should be noted that the name origins of 176 counties are uncertain. The uncertainty may stem from two or more people of the same name. It may be a river named for a person but it is not clear if the county name is derived from the river or the person. If the uncertainty is between a geographic feature and a person, the person is included in the following discussions of counties named for persons and for geographic features. If the uncertainty is between two or more persons, or for two or more geographic features, they are listed in order of plausibility.

PERSONS

By far the largest source of county names is persons. There are 1,936 counties named for 1,464 persons. A factor in determining the source of a county's name is that some geographic features, including towns and forts within or near the county, were named for persons. Because these features associated with the new county were named to honor a person, these counties are included as a person's namesake county. For example, Churchill County, Nevada, is named for Fort Churchill which was named for General Sylvester Churchill, a hero of the Mexican War. There is a direct link between the man, fort, and county. Therefore, Sylvester Churchill is counted with having the county named for him.

A question arises when a county is named for another county or town that had been named for a person. It could be claimed that the second county was named for the first county and not necessarily for the person. Madison County, Arkansas, is named for a county in Alabama; Madison, Nebraska, is named for the Wisconsin city. These two counties were named to honor the former homes of settlers, not President Madison himself. The namers were from places that just happened to be named for Madison. However, since the citizens of the second county did not see fit to disavow Madison, these counties are included as being named for Madison.

The most popular or well-remembered person is not necessarily the person for whom a county is named. There are 24 counties named Lincoln. The supposition is that they were all named for President Abraham Lincoln. But there are five Lincoln counties that were named before or soon after Lincoln was born so it is obvious that another Lincoln was intended. The Lincoln for whom four of these counties were named was Benjamin Lincoln, a major general in the Continental Army. Two of Benjamin Lincoln's counties, Kentucky and North Carolina, gave their name to Lincoln County, Missouri, when proposed by a Missouri territorial legislator who had lived in both Lincoln counties. To further confuse matters, Lincoln County, Maine, was named for the town of Lincoln, England. Lincoln County, South Dakota, although named during Lincoln's presidency, was named for the county in Maine at the suggestion of a member of the Dakota Territorial Legislature from Lincoln County, Maine.

Counties may be named to gain favor with the honoree. Colonial counties were often named for British royalty or nobility. If a colony already had a county named for the reigning monarch, a member of his family could be honored. Eleven counties are named for James II and his immediate family. Seven are named for George II and his family. There are also seven counties named for William III. There are five named for George I, and three each for Charles I and Charles II and their families. There is one county, James City, Virginia, named for James I. Prince of Wales-Hyder, Alaska, is named for the future George IV. Hanover and New Hanover Counties were named for the British Royal Family.

There are eleven counties named for royalty other than British royalty. These counties were not named to gain favor but to honor the eponymous persons. Bourbon and Orleans counties were named for French royal families. Saint Louis County,

Minnesota, is named for French King Louis IX who was canonized by the Roman Catholic Church. Saint Louis city and county, Missouri, are named for King Louis XV and his patron saint, Louis IX. Dauphin County, Pennsylvania, is named from the title of the eldest son of Louis XVI. Isabella County, Michigan, is named for the Queen of Castile who sponsored Columbus' voyages. Saint Charles County, Missouri, is named for Spanish King Charles IV. King Haakon VII of Norway was honored by South Dakota in hopes of attracting Norwegian homesteaders. Haakon was the second to last surviving person to have a county named for him. He died in 1957.

Thirty-two counties were named for railroad executives in attempts to influence the routing of railroads through the county. In hopes of gaining favor for statehood, Michigan Territory named eight counties after President Jackson and members of his cabinet.

Many honorees had illustrious careers with many achievements. It is often difficult to determine which achievement led to a county being named for a person especially when different states honored different achievements. Lewis Cass had a varied career as evidenced by the different positions he held at the time counties were named for him. Indiana and Michigan named counties for him while he was the military governor of Michigan Territory. Illinois and Missouri named counties for Cass while he was Secretary of War. Iowa, Minnesota, Nebraska, and Texas named counties for him while he was a US Senator from Michigan in recognition of his advocacy for popular sovereignty. The reader can compare the date a county was created with the dates of the person's various achievements.

It is not always possible to determine whether counties have been named for certain areas or for the people who ruled them or those for whom the areas were named. For example, eight counties bear the name Cumberland. Disregarding whether these counties were named for the river, town, city, village, or other feature, one may claim that the counties named Cumberland were named for Cumberland, England. At the same time, it may be claimed that the counties were named for William Augustus, second son of George II, and third Duke of Cumberland, while others may insist they were named for previous or subsequent dukes.

In a similar vein, there are Essex Counties in Massachusetts, New Jersey, New York, Vermont, and Virginia. One may contend that these counties were named for Robert Devereux, Earl of Essex, but some may maintain that the counties were named for Essex, England, the earldom belonging to Devereux before he fell out of royal favor and was beheaded. Only rarely is the distinction made between the realm and the ruler as in the case of Norborne Berkeley, the Baron of Botetourt. The county of Berkeley, West Virginia, is named for him, and the county of Botetourt, Virginia, is named for his barony.

Although several counties have the same name, there are variations in spelling usually from names with Indian roots. There is an Allegany County in Maryland and New York, but North Carolina and Virginia have Alleghany Counties, and Pennsylvania has an Allegheny County. There is a Pottawatomie County in Kansas and Oklahoma, but the county in Iowa is Pottawattamie. Ohio has its Wyandot County whereas Kansas has Wyandotte County. Cheboygan County is in Michigan and Sheboygan County is in Wisconsin. Vermilion Counties are in Illinois and Louisiana; Vermillion County is in Indiana.

Some counties are named for persons who have only one claim to fame worthy of having a county named for them. Many in this category of singular accomplishments are state and territorial legislators who happened to be in the legislature when a county was named. These counties were often created when no one lived within their boundaries. Such counties, frequently evidenced on a map by their rectangular if not actually square boundaries, were created to give the impression that civilization had reached the region, usually in the Great Plains. (Texas legislator Collin McKinney [Collin County, Texas] insisted that counties in northern Texas have straight boundaries.) With no local citizens to request a name for an uninhabited county, legislators often named such counties for themselves. This practice was especially rampant in the Dakota Territorial Legislature during the 1870s and 1880s, and at the Oklahoma Constitutional Convention of 1907. Little is known of many of these eponymous legislators except that they happened to be in the legislature at the right time. Nothing is known about Norman Campbell except that Campbell County in what is now South Dakota was named for him. Edward McIntosh held up legislation until a county, now in North Dakota, was named for him. At the opposite end of the egotism spectrum is Thomas Craighead of Arkansas who did not want any county named for him but the legislature did so while Craighead was away from the legislature. George Henshaw, a delegate to the Oklahoma Constitutional Convention, had Marshall County named for his mother, Elizabeth Marshall Henshaw, a descendant of John Marshall. The reader can compare a person's tenure in the legislature against the date the county was created.

Other persons assured their immortality by naming counties for themselves. Ten of Maryland's 24 counties were named by and for members of the Calvert family and their estates: Anne Arundel, Baltimore (county and city), Calvert, Caroline, Cecil, Charles, Frederick, Harford, and Talbot. Sir William Gooch, a colonial governor of Virginia, assured his place on the map by naming Goochland County in his own honor.

Sixteen signers of the Declaration of Independence have 85 counties named for them. Thomas Jefferson and Benjamin Franklin lead the list with 26 and 22 respectively. Charles Carroll has 14. Carroll of Maryland had a flurry of counties named for him following his death in 1832 as the last surviving signer of the Declaration of Independence. John Hancock has ten and Thomas Nelson has two. The remaining eleven have one each. Twenty-five signers of the Texas Declaration Independence have counties named for them—all in Texas except for Caldwell Counties in Louisiana and Missouri.

Some counties are named for more than one person. Brown County, Nebraska, is named for any one or all five members of the legislature named Brown at the time of the county's creation. Some counties are named for two or more brothers. Texas has seven counties named for brothers all of whom were involved in the Texas Revolution. Taylor, Texas, is named for three brothers who died at the Alamo. Miner, South Dakota, is named for two brothers who were members of the legislature when the county was created.

Many fathers and sons have been honored by having counties named for them, the most prominent being the Adams family. John Adams, the second US President, has seven and his son, John Quincy Adams, the sixth US President, has three. Dodge County, Wisconsin, is named for Henry Dodge while Dodge County, Nebraska, is named for his son, Augustus Dodge. Dodge County, Minnesota, is named for both Henry and Augustus. Henry County, Iowa, used Henry Dodge's first name for its county. Robertson County, Tennessee, is named for James Robertson; Robertson County, Kentucky, is named for his son, George. George Clinton (two counties) was the uncle of De Witt Clinton (eight counties).

In some instances, counties have been named for both a person's first and last names, such as Charles Mix, Kit Carson, Roger Mills, Ben Hill, and Jo Daviess. This practice is most prevalent in Texas where counties have been named for Jim Wells, Jim Hogg, Tom Green, Deaf Smith, and Jeff Davis. There is also a Jeff Davis County in Georgia and Jefferson Davis Counties in both Louisiana and Mississippi.

Almost all counties were named between the late seventeenth and early twentieth centuries—a period of male dominance. Of the 1,465 persons who had counties named for them, only 49 were women. Most of these counties were named during the colonial period for feminine relatives of kings or noblemen. Of these 49 almost half—23—were the wife, daughter, mother, or sister of a man who already had a county named for him. Among the remaining 26 women for whom counties were named, nine were saints and six were characters from legends.

The eleven women for whom counties are named for their own accomplishments are certainly worthy of the honor. Clara Barton (Kansas) was a volunteer nurse during the Civil War; she was known as the "Angel of the Battlefield" and went on to be an organizer of the American Red Cross. Fredrika Bremer (Iowa) was a Swedish author whose popular novel *Herta* was published shortly before the county was organized. Doña Ana (New Mexico) was most probably a local widow celebrated for her charity. Francina Haines (Alaska) was the secretary of the Presbyterian Board of Home Missions that raised money for Haines Mission. Nancy Hart (Georgia) was a frontier settler renowned as a sharpshooter who captured some Tories; the local Indians called her *Wahatchee* or "war woman." Isabella (Michigan) is named for the Queen of Castile who financed Columbus' voyages. Louisa Massey (Louisa, Iowa) was a sixteen-year-old pioneer woman who gained local renown by killing her brother's murderer shortly before the county was created. Madame Montour (Pennsylvania), a woman of mixed Indian and French-Canadian parentage, was an interpreter for French and English settlers in the early eighteenth century. The fame of Pocahontas (Iowa and West Virginia) could be attributed to her being the daughter of Powhatan, a powerful chief, but the story of her saving the life of John Smith, whether or not apocryphal, gives her her own status. Queen Anne (Maryland) was the daughter of James II but she was the only queen in her own right during the colonial period of naming counties. Queen Anne can also be credited with Fluvanna County, Virginia, named from a river whose name was derived by combining Latin *fluvius* (river) with "anna." A tenuous case could be argued for Queen Mary II, also a daughter of James II, who reigned jointly with her husband William III following the Glorious Revolution. King and Queen County, Virginia, is partly named for her.

Four counties are named for children. Ada County, Idaho, is named for Ada Riggs, the daughter of one of the founders of Boise. Virginia Dare (North Carolina) was the first English child born in America. Dauphin, Pennsylvania, was named for Louis Joseph Xavier, Dauphin of France, the eldest son of Louis XVI and Marie Antoinette. He was a sickly child who died at the age of seven. Wayne, Utah, is named for Wayne Robison, the son of a Utah legislator, who was thrown from a horse and died at age eleven.

There are 1,464 persons who have counties named for them. The most prominent category of counties named for persons is US Presidents. There are 201 counties in 40 states named for 24 presidents. Every US President from George Washington to Theodore Roosevelt, except Andrew Johnson and Benjamin Harrison, has at least one county named for him. After Roosevelt, only Warren Harding has a county named for him. All subsequent presidents served after the heyday of county creation and naming. George Washington with 31 counties has more than any other person.

The fact that the name of a president is given to a county does not necessarily mean that it was his presidency being honored. The man did not just suddenly appear on the scene as president. Every man who became president had a notable political and/or military career prior to being president. Forty-three counties named for presidents were named before that person became president. For example, Andrew Jackson has 22 counties named for him but eight were named before his presidency. Jackson County, Tennessee, was created in 1801 when Jackson was a justice of the Tennessee Supreme Court. Counties in Alabama, Illinois, Indiana, Mississippi, and Ohio were created and named between 1812 and 1819 in honor of Jackson's military exploits during the War of 1812 and various Indian campaigns. Florida named its county after Jackson in 1822 while he was the military governor of Florida. Missouri created Jackson County in 1826 the year after he completed his service in the US Senate. The remaining fourteen counties were named for Jackson during or after his presidency (1829–37). Hickory County, Missouri, is included as one of Jackson's counties for honoring his nickname, "Old Hickory," Missouri already having a Jackson County.

The following list of counties named for US presidents includes all counties named for a president including those counties named before he became president.

Table I.1.   Presidential Counties

George Washington	31	John Quincy Adams	3
Thomas Jefferson	26	Millard Fillmore	3
Andrew Jackson	22	James Buchanan	3
James Madison	20	Grover Cleveland	2
James Monroe	17	Theodore Roosevelt	2
Abraham Lincoln	17	John Tyler	1
Ulysses Grant	12	Rutherford Hayes	1
James Polk	11	Chester Arthur	1
John Adams	7	William McKinley	1
James Garfield	6	Warren Harding	1
Martin Van Buren	4		
William Harrison	4		
Zachary Taylor	4		
Franklin Pierce	4		

Nebraska has the most presidential counties with twelve. Iowa is second with eleven. Arkansas has ten; Mississippi, Missouri, and Wisconsin have eight each. Florida, Georgia, Indiana, Ohio, Oklahoma, and Tennessee, have seven each followed by Illinois, Kentucky, Louisiana, Oregon, Texas, and Washington with six each. States with five counties named for presidents are Alabama, Colorado, Idaho, Kansas, Minnesota, Montana, New Mexico, and West Virginia. New York and Pennsylvania each has four presidential counties. Michigan, North Carolina, Utah, and Virginia have three each. States with one county named for a president are Maine, Maryland, Nevada, North Dakota, Rhode Island, South Dakota, Vermont, and Wyoming. The ten states with no counties named for any president are Alaska, Arizona, California, Connecticut, Delaware, Hawaii, Massachusetts, New Hampshire, New Jersey, and South Carolina.

Eight vice presidents of the United States who did not become president have 28 counties named for them, the most favored one being John Calhoun for whom eleven counties are named. Richard Johnson has five counties; George Dallas has four; George Clinton, Schuyler Colfax, and Charles Fairbanks have two each. Both of Fairbanks's counties are in Alaska: Fairbanks North Star and Southeast Fairbanks. Daniel Tompkins and Hannibal Hamlin each have one county. William King was the original honoree for King County, Washington, but in 1986 the King County Council voted to award the honor to the civil rights leader, Martin Luther King. (King is the last surviving person to have a county named for him having died in 1968.) Alexander Stephens was a vice president of the Confederacy. Kenneth Anderson, Edward Burleson, and David Burnet were vice presidents of the Republic of Texas.

There are fifteen persons other than presidents who have ten or more counties named for them:

Table I.2.   Other than Presidents

Benjamin Franklin	22
Nathanael Greene	18[1]
Anthony Wayne	17
Marquis de Lafayette	17
Henry Clay	16
Francis Marion	16
Richard Montgomery	15
Joseph Warren	15
Charles Carroll	12
Stephen Douglas	12
John Calhoun	11
Patrick Henry	11
Oliver Perry	10
Zebulon Pike	10
John Hancock	10

[1]Counties named for Greene include misspelled Green Counties in Kentucky and Wisconsin, Greensville County, Virginia, and Greenville County, South Carolina.

All but Clay, Calhoun, Douglas, Perry, and Pike are associated with American Independence. Greene, Lafayette, Wayne, Marion, Montgomery, and Warren gained renown in the Continental Army. Franklin, Carroll, and Hancock were signers of the Declaration of Independence. Henry gained fame as an ardent supporter of independence with his immortal peroration "Give me Liberty or give me Death." Clay, Calhoun, and Douglas were regional advocates of disparate positions in the debates concerning the expansion of slavery leading up to the Civil War. Pike gained fame as one of the first explorers of the West after Lewis and Clark but all of his counties came after his death during the War of 1812. Perry defeated a British squadron at the Battle of Lake Erie during the War of 1812. Lafayette is the only foreigner in this group. There are six counties named Lafayette and eleven, with American informality, named Fayette.

Four Americans, all military men, have nine counties named for them. Henry Knox, Daniel Morgan, and Isaac Shelby served in the Continental Army during the Revolutionary War. James Lawrence was killed in a naval engagement during the War of 1812; his dying words, "Don't give up the ship," became a rallying cry during the war.

Eleven people have eight counties named for them. Israel Putnam and William Jasper are the only two in this group honored for having been in the Continental Army. Alexander Hamilton was also in the Continental Army but gained his renown as the first Secretary of the Treasury. De Witt Clinton (including De Witt, Illinois) was the governor of New York who spearheaded the building of the Erie Canal which helped to open the West. Robert E. Lee commanded the Confederate Army of Northern Virginia during the Civil War. John Marshall was a Chief Justice of the United States. Daniel Webster was the North's spokesman in the US Senate prior to the Civil War. His relatively moderate views on slavery gained some favor in the South. In fact, six of the eight counties named for him are in former slave states. King James II of England has eight counties with four different names for his various duchies: Albany, York, Ulster, and Dukes. Christopher Columbus is honored with six counties named Columbia, one named Columbiana, and one simply named Columbus.

Nine persons have seven counties named for them. John Adams was the second US President. Hugh Mercer was in the Continental Army and was mortally wounded at Princeton. William Crawford was the Secretary of War under President Madison and of the Treasury under Monroe. Daniel Boone gained fame as a frontiersman leading parties of settlers to the Trans-Appalachian West. Thomas Benton was a senator from Missouri whose advocacy of Manifest Destiny was widely popular. (Benton, Tennessee, was originally named for Thomas Benton but in 1852 his moderate views on the expansion of slavery caused the county to transfer the honor to David Benton, a local veteran of the War of 1812.) Casimir Pulaski was a Polish nobleman who came to the aid of the American colonists. He was mortally wounded during the Siege of Savannah. The Duke of Cumberland, the second son of George II, has four counties named directly for him. In addition, there are Cumberland Counties named for a road, a river, and mountains. King William III, the Dutch Prince of Orange-Nassau, who ruled England jointly with his wife Mary II, has seven counties: three named Orange, two named Williamsburg; one Nassau; and one simply King William. (King and Queen County, Virginia, honors both William and Mary.)

Seven persons have six counties named for them. James Garfield was the twentieth US President. George Rogers Clark fought the Revolutionary War in the West. (His younger brother William Clark, of the Lewis and Clark Expedition, has three counties named for him.) Robert Fulton developed the steamboat which improved river travel in the West. Nathaniel Macon was an anti-Federalist who opposed ratification of the Constitution and spent his twelve terms in Congress—three as Speaker of the House—working to prevent the national government from becoming too strong. George Custer served admirably in the Civil War but all of his six counties were named following his massacre at the Battle of the Little Big Horn. Johann de Kalb, a German baron, was mortally wounded at Princeton while serving with the Continental Army.

Eight persons have five counties named for them. Stephen Decatur was a naval officer who defeated the Barbary Pirates and served during the War of 1812. Richard Johnson also served in the War of 1812 but gained fame as a senator from Kentucky and as Van Buren's Vice President. Meriwether Lewis was the nominal leader of the Lewis and Clark Expedition. John Logan was a senator from Illinois and a leader of the Republican Party who was nominated for vice president in 1884. Winfield Scott was an Army officer whose military career spanned the period from the War of 1812 to the Civil War. Philip Sheridan was a Union cavalry officer and later the Commander in Chief of the Army. John Newton was a sergeant in the Continental Army whose exploits were sensationalized enough to have five counties named for him. Queen Charlotte Sophia of Mecklenburg-Strelitz, wife of George III, has two counties named Charlotte, two named Mecklenburg, and one named Charlottesville. Her five counties are the most for any woman.

Nineteen persons have four counties named for them. Among this group are four US Presidents: Martin Van Buren, William Harrison, Zachary Taylor, and Franklin Pierce. Another president, Jefferson Davis, President of the Confederacy, is honored by Jeff Davis Counties in Georgia and Texas, and by Jefferson Davis Counties in Louisiana and Mississippi. Benjamin Lincoln was a Revolutionary War general. Thomas Sumter has four counties named for him for being the last surviving officer of the American Revolution at the time of his death in 1832. Four counties including Jo Daviess, Illinois, are named for Joseph Daveiss who was killed at the Battle of Tippecanoe. All four of his namesake counties use the alternate spelling of his name. There are two foreigners in this group. The Earl of Camden opposed the Stamp Act in the House of Lords. Hernando de Soto explored the southeastern US in the sixteenth century.

Twenty-eight persons have three counties named for them. John Quincy Adams, Millard Fillmore, and James Buchanan were US Presidents. William Clark was one of the leaders of the Lewis and Clark Expedition. Samuel Houston was the hero of the Battle of San Jacinto and the president of the Republic of Texas. Osceola, who was of mixed European and Indian parentage, led the Seminoles during the Second Seminole War. His capture by subterfuge raised enough sympathy to have three counties named for him, the most for any individual Indian. (Pocahontas, with two, is the only other Indian with more than one county namesake.) Arthur Saint Clair is deemed worthy of three counties in spite of surrendering Fort Ticonderoga to the British in 1777 and being defeated by the Miamis at the Battle of the Wabash (also known as St. Clair's Defeat) in 1791. Mathew Caldwell fought in the Texas Revolution and is honored by Louisiana and Missouri in addition to Texas. Six foreigners have three counties named for them: the Duke of Bedford, the Earl of Essex, King George I, Friedrich von Humboldt, the Sieur de la Salle, and the Marquess of Rockingham.

Sixty-three persons have two counties named for them. Grover Cleveland and Theodore Roosevelt were US Presidents. Twelve were US senators; eleven were governors; seven were in state or territorial legislatures; five were members of US cabinets; two each were vice presidents, congressmen, and ambassadors; and one was a member of the Continental Congress. Oklahoma Governor William "Alfalfa Bill" Murray has two Oklahoma counties named for him: Alfalfa and Murray. Nineteen foreign persons have two counties named for them. Sixteen were English, and one each was French, German, and Irish.

There are 1,055 persons who have one county named for them. Of these, 987 are Americans. Five were US Presidents. Almost two-thirds of these Americans (624) were officeholders at the state level or were senators or congressmen who were elected at the state level. Most of these were governors (167) or legislators (163). Sixty-one were US senators and 56 were US representatives including twelve territorial delegates to Congress. Not all of these 624 were from the state which honored them. Examples include Jonathon Trumbull (Ohio), who as the Governor of Connecticut ceded his state's Western Reserve to Ohio. Alabama named Blount County for Governor Willie Blount of Tennessee who had sent aid to Alabama during the Creek War. Senator William Clark of Montana won the gratitude of Nevada by supporting railroads in Southern Nevada. Senator John Clayton of Delaware won the favor of Iowa by advocating the creation of Wisconsin Territory which included Iowa. Massachusetts Senator Charles Sumner and South Carolina Representative Preston Brooks have counties named for them in Kansas and Georgia respectively from the 1856 incident in which Brooks severely caned Sumner on the floor of the Senate after Sumner had given an anti-slavery speech. Each was a hero in his respective region.

Many Virginians are honored by Kentucky and West Virginia. Kentucky was a part of Virginia until 1792 and West Virginia belonged to Virginia until 1863. Only five of West Virginia's 55 counties were created after 1863. Some counties in Tennessee honor North Carolinians. These counties were created before Tennessee separated from North Carolina in 1790.

Other single county honorees in the realm of government are 29 jurists. Nine were members of the US Supreme Court and three of these, John Jay, Roger Taney, and Samuel Chase were chief justices. Thirty-four single-county honorees were members of their respective state or territory supreme court. Nine of these served as chief justice of their state or territory.

Twenty-five single-county honorees were members of cabinets at the federal level. Twenty-nine were state-level cabinet members. Three were vice presidents of the US. Ten were lieutenant governors of their state or colony. Two were US ambassadors. Thirty-four were mayors.

Thirty-six Texas counties honor persons who served in various capacities in the government of the Republic of Texas. Sam Houston and Anson Jones served as presidents. Four were governors; 21 were in the legislature; eight were cabinet members; and one, James Henderson, was the Texas ambassador to the United States.

There are 126 foreign persons who have a single county named for them. Ninety-one are English; twelve are French; eight are Spanish; three are Irish. There are two Italians and two Mexicans with two counties named for each of them. There are eight nationalities represented by persons with one county named for them: German, Venezuelan, Swedish, Norwegian, Hungarian, Polish, Russian, and Portuguese.

Military service can lead to having a county named for a person. Of the 366 military personnel who have counties named for them only ten served in the navy. Forty-three were graduates of West Point; three graduated from Annapolis. Being killed in battle increased the possibility of having a namesake county. There are 147 counties named for persons killed in wars, revolutions, and skirmishes.

There are 327 counties named for 170 men who fought in the Revolutionary War. Forty-eight had counties named specifically for having fought in that war including eighteen who were killed in battle. The 152 who survived the war went on to careers that led to having counties named for them. For example, 40 became governors, 25 were US representatives, and 40 were US Senators. George Washington became US president after the war. Ten persons fought in both the Revolutionary War and the War of 1812.

William Jasper has six counties named for him. He was a sergeant who gained fame by rescuing a regimental flag that had been shot down during the defense of Fort Moultrie. Stories of Jasper's exploits with his friend John Newton (who has five counties named for him) in rescuing American prisoners during the Siege of Savannah were sensationalized in a popular tale by Parson Weems. This renown caused Jasper and Newton to become linked in the naming of counties. Jasper and Newton Counties are adjacent to each other in four states, Georgia, Indiana, Missouri, and Texas. (In Mississippi, Newton and Jasper Counties are contiguous but this Newton County is named for Sir Isaac Newton.) In both Illinois and Iowa, Newton is the county seat of Jasper County. In Arkansas Jasper is the county seat of Newton County although some sources attribute the county's name to Thomas Newton, a US representative from Arkansas.

There are 244 counties named for 132 men who fought in the War of 1812. Thirty-five had counties named specifically for having fought in that war including 23 who were killed in battle; eight in the River Raisin Massacre. The remaining 109 survived the war and went on to various careers that led to having counties named for them. Thirty became governors, 28 were US representatives, and eighteen were US Senators. Andrew Jackson, William Harrison, John Tyler, and James Buchanan became presidents of the US after serving in the War of 1812. Ten persons served in both the War of 1812 and the Mexican War. Winfield Scott served in the War of 1812, the Mexican War, and the Civil War.

There are 107 counties named for 67 men who fought in the Mexican War. Twenty had counties named specifically for having fought in that war ten of whom were killed in battle. The remaining 97 survived the war and went on to careers that led to having counties named for them. Fourteen became governors, nine were US representatives, and eight were US Senators. Zachary Taylor and Franklin Pierce became US presidents. Jefferson Davis became president of the Confederacy. Thirty persons with counties named for them served in both the Mexican War and the Civil War including Generals Ulysses Grant and Robert E. Lee.

The Civil War contributed 280 counties named for 160 persons. There are 165 counties named for 115 persons who were in the Union Army. Seventy-four persons from the Confederate Army gave their names to 86 counties. Twenty-eight of the Union soldiers were killed in battle—Kansas alone has 23 counties named for Union soldiers killed in Civil War battles. There are fifteen Confederate battle casualties that gave their names to counties. There were 117 persons from both sides who survived the war and went on to careers who led to having counties named for them. Thirty-five became governors, 29 were US senators, and 24 became US representatives. Ulysses Grant, Rutherford Hayes, James Garfield, Chester Arthur, and William McKinley became US presidents after the Civil War. Three persons served in both the Civil War and the Spanish-American War.

There are eight counties named for seven persons who served in the Spanish-American War. None were killed in battle. Two of these persons, George Dewey and Joseph Wheeler, were honored specifically for service in this war. Four later became governors and two were US representatives. Theodore Roosevelt, who had two counties named for him, became president of the US.

John Pershing is the only person from World War I to have a county named for him. Pershing had also served in the Spanish-American War. There are no military honorees after World War I.

There are 166 counties named for 120 men who had military service other than in US wars. (Many of them also had had military service during wars.) Some were members of local militias. Many of these were in campaigns against Indians. Among this group is George Custer who has no counties named to honor his service in the Union Cavalry during the Civil War but has six counties named for his having been massacred in the Battle of the Little Big Horn.

Fifty-three counties are named for persons who fought in the Texas Revolution or later served in the army or navy of the Republic of Texas. Thirteen were Texas Rangers. Six Texas counties are named for brothers who served in the Texas Revolution. Taylor County is named for three brothers who died at the Alamo. Twenty-one counties are named for persons killed during the Texas Revolution including twelve who died at the Alamo.

It was not only politicians or military men who had counties named for them. The following table lists the occupations or pursuits of men who had counties named for them and the number of counties so named.

Table I.3. Miscellaneous Occupations

Early settler	140
Trader/trapper	53
Educator	46
Explorer	46
Newspaperman	35
Surveyor	35
Landowner	33
Physician	30
Clergy	27
Lawyer	20
Author	15
Inventor	4

Settlers, trappers, traders, and explorers penetrated the wilderness. When a county was eventually created in the area, it was often named for the first person known to have been there. Educators, physicians (including dentists), lawyers, and the clergy were often leaders of the community and were honored by having a new county named for them. The 33 lawyers listed were persons who did not become judges. Newspapermen were often advocates for the creation of new counties. One newspaperman, Horace Greeley, had a national reputation aided by his popularization of the phrase, "Go West, young man." Landowners, including cattlemen and plantation owners, were men of substance worthy of having a namesake county. The work of surveyors indicated that civilization was approaching the area. Surveys were necessary to determine county boundaries and property boundaries. (George Washington is among the 35 surveyors.) Authors usually had regional, if not national, prominence. Some authors had international reputations. Joseph Addison wrote the tragedy *Cato*; he is also counted among the newspapermen in this group. Frederika Bremer—the only woman in this entire listing—was a Swedish author widely read in America. The four inventors contributed to progress. Robert Fulton developed the steamboat which advanced transportation of the nation's rivers. Cyrus McCormick perfected the reaper which led to settlement of the West; he is also counted as a landowner for extensive holdings in South Carolina. The contributions of Gail Borden and Joel Poinsett made life more pleasant. Borden, also a newspaperman and surveyor, invented condensed milk. Poinsett, an amateur botanist, developed the poinsettia flower while serving as US ambassador to Mexico.

There are 143 counties named for 103 Indian nations and tribes. The most frequent is Cherokee with eight followed by Ottawa with four. Cheyenne, Choctaw, Comanche, Delaware, Erie, Osage, Pawnee, Pottawatomie, Seminole, Sioux, and Winnebago have three each. Nations or tribes with two counties are Aleut, Chickasaw, Dakota, Huron, Kiowa, Menominee, Pend Oreille, Uinta, and Wyandotte. (Dakota and Sioux are names for the same nation; Sioux being a Chippewa-French derogatory name for the Dakotas.) The remaining 80 nations and tribes have one county each.

Indians could also be categorized by linguistic groups. For example, the Algonquin linguistic group includes Arapahoe, Cheyenne, Delaware, Menominee, Sac-Fox, Miami, Pottawatomie, and Shawnee. Uintah and Utah are tribes within the Shoshone linguistic group, a Uto-Aztecan language that includes Comanches and Paiutes. (The only examples given are those that have counties named for them.)

Most Indians had no written language so there are many variations in spelling: Muskogee/Muscogee, Uinta/Uintah, Wyandotte/Wyandot, Pend Oreille/Pondera, etc. Many of these variations can be attributed to the Europeans who wrote them down.

There are 47 counties named for individual Indians or families. The tribes or nations that these individuals are from are: Chickasaw, seven counties; Cherokee and Fox, six each; Choctaw five; Chippewa three; and Pottawatomie two. There are nineteen tribes or nations represented by one individual or family for whom a county is named. Twenty-two of these Indians were chiefs, eleven of whom signed treaties with the US ceding their tribal lands and emigrating, usually winding up in Indian Territory (Oklahoma). There is one emperor, Montezuma II of the Aztecs, among this group.

Fifteen Indians with counties named for them anglicized their names. Five of these were families: Adair, Carter, Colbert, Love, and McIntosh. Colbert County, Alabama, is named for the Colbert brothers, George and Levi; Itawamba County, Mississippi, carries Levi's Chickasaw name. Stanislaus County, California, is named for a neophyte from Mission San Jose who, at his baptism, was given the name of a Polish saint.

Five eponymous Indians are women. Madam Mountor was a French-Iroquois woman who served as an interpreter for French and English settlers on the Pennsylvania frontier. Pocahontas, the daughter of a powerful chief, gained renown for reputedly saving the life of Captain John Smith. Marinette, the daughter of a Menominee chief, was named for Marie Antoinette. Winona is the name traditionally given to the first-born daughter in a Dakota family. Winona is also the name of a princess in a Dakota legend. Leelanau is named for a legendary Chippewa maiden.

Pend Oreille County, Washington, and Pondera County, Montana, are both from the French rendering of *Pend d' Oreille* given to a local Indian tribe. Both counties are pronounced the same as "pon-der-AY." Montana sought to avoid confusion with the Washington county and its name is almost universally mispronounced as "pon-DER-ah."

The names of 30 saints have been given to 41 counties. The only one that might be named directly for a saint is Saint Mary's, Maryland. All of the other saints' counties were not named directly for the saint but are the names that have descended from towns, rivers, missions, parishes, etc. Many were named for geographic features that were named by early explorers and the name was passed on through missions and towns to the county. For example, San Diego Bay was entered and named on September 12, 1603, which happened to be San Diego's saint's day. Mission San Diego was founded and named for the bay in 1769; the town of San Diego grew up near the mission. When the county was created in 1850, it was named for the town.

The saint with the most counties is Saint John the Baptist with six: one Saint Johns, one Saint John the Baptist, and four San Juan Counties. Saint Francis has three: Saint Francis, Saint Francois, and San Francisco. Saint Louis, the canonized King Louis

IX of France, also has three counties: one in Minnesota, and the city and the county of Saint Louis, Missouri. Saint Joseph and Saint Mary each have two counties. The remaining 25 saints have one county each.

Other religious names for counties that are not actual persons are Sacramento, Santa Fe, and Santa Cruz. Two counties are named for Our Lady of Guadalupe in commemoration of the site at which the Virgin Mary is believed to have appeared to a Mexican peasant in 1531. Eight of the saints for whom counties are named are women including Our Lady of Guadalupe.

Quite frequently counties have used different names to honor the same person. The most conspicuous example of this is Fayette County (eleven counties) and Lafayette County (six counties), all of which are named for the Marquis de Lafayette. Nine counties are named Henry for Patrick Henry and one county is named Patrick for him. Two counties are named Dodge for Henry Dodge, and one county is named Henry in his honor. Three counties are named DeSoto for Hernando de Soto and one county is named Hernando. Seven counties are named Clinton for De Witt Clinton and one county is named De Witt. Two counties are named Fillmore and one county is named Millard to honor President Millard Fillmore.

There are ten counties named for fictitious or legendary characters. Six of them are named for women: Attala, Aurora, Evangeline, Minnehaha, Monona, and Winona. The three legendary males are El Dorado, Iosco, and Sanilac.

The names of 30 persons are misspelled by their counties. Some are attributable to the variations in spelling during colonial times when spelling was at best a casual endeavor. But most misspellings are from simple carelessness. The misspelling of the names of three of the defenders of the Alamo is carried over from the Alamo Monument. The Texas counties named Dickens, Kimbell, and Linn are named, respectively, for James Dimkins, George Kimble, and William Lynn.

Clerical errors account for most misspellings. Virginia added the letter *e* to the name of George Rogers Clark while Kansas deleted the letter *e* from Charles Clarke. Kentucky and Wisconsin dropped the final *e* from Nathanael Greene's name. Fourteen other persons had their names misspelled due to clerical errors. Not all clerical errors are misspellings. Possibly the most egregious error was committed by the Minnesota Territorial Legislature. Charles Stearns, a member of the legislature, sponsored the creation of a county to honor Isaac Stevens, but a clerical error named the county for Stearns. Stevens was later honored with a Minnesota county. The name for Nome, Alaska, resulted from a transcriptional error when a draftsman wrote the notation "? Name" on a manuscript chart for an unnamed cape on the south side of the Seward Peninsula; when transcribed to a British Admiralty chart in 1853, it was written as "C. Nome" which became Cape Nome on a subsequent chart.

Some counties have the same sound but are spelled differently because they are named for different people, such as Kearney County, Nebraska, and Kearny County, Kansas. Linn County, Iowa, and Lynn County, Texas, are similarly named for different people. There is a great diversity in the orthography of common names such as Smith and Smyth, Stanley and Stanly, Stephens and Stevens, Storey and Story, etc.

GEOGRAPHIC NAMES

The category of geographic names includes counties named for physical features and those named for places. "Physical features" includes streams, bodies of water, and landforms. "Streams" includes rivers, creeks, springs, falls, rapids, etc. "Land forms" includes mountains, mountain ranges, hills, prairies, valleys, islands, etc. "Bodies of water" includes lakes, oceans, bayous, etc. "Places" includes towns, cities, other counties, states, and countries.

There are 815 counties named for 737 geographic features or places; 413 named for 397 features and 365 named for 322 places. Some counties are named for two or more features of the same name. There are Beaver Counties in Oklahoma, Pennsylvania, and Utah named for three different Beaver Rivers. The same name may be given to different features that gave names to counties. Humboldt County, California, is named for a bay; Humboldt County, Nevada, named for a river. (There is also a Humboldt County, Iowa, named for the German explorer Friedrich von Humboldt after whom both the bay and river are named.)

Physical features are often named by the first persons to encounter them. Europeans did the best they could with Indian names for physical features. The names are sometimes difficult to account for because the Indians had no written language and many of the first Europeans to encounter the Indians were illiterate.

Determining the language from which a geographic feature and its namesake counties are named can be perplexing. Some are attempts by Europeans striving to approximate Indian names with varying degrees of futility. Some are translations of Indian names into a European language. Sometimes the process has been reversed. The name of Wakulla County, Florida, is from a Creek rendering of *guacara*, the name given to local springs by Spanish explorers based on what the Spaniards thought was the Creek name for the springs. The original Creek name and its meaning are lost.

There are 285 counties named for 268 streams. "Streams" include 229 rivers; 24 creeks; six falls, six springs; and one each of currents, rapids, and cut point (Pointe Coupee, Louisiana). The distinction between rivers, creeks, falls, rapids, and currents is often a matter of local usage. There are seven instances in which a name is common to two or three different rivers. In addition to the three counties named for three different Beaver Rivers mentioned above, there are two rivers each for counties named Alleghany, Chippewa, Clearwater, Nemaha, Platte, and Trinity. A Vermilion River has given its name to a Louisiana parish. A different river of the same name is shared by Illinois and Indiana. The Illinois county spells its name with one letter *l* and Indiana spells its county with two letters *l*. The Ohio and San Juan Rivers each have three namesake counties. There are ten rivers that have two namesake counties. There is a Hot Spring County in Arkansas and a Hot Springs County in Wyoming. Bath Counties in Kentucky and Virginia are named for two different springs.

There are 120 counties named for streams with Indian names; 74 English; 43 Spanish; 27 French; and one each from Dutch (Schuylkill), German (Humboldt River, Nevada), Hebrew (Dan [Danville]) and Polish (Stanislaus).

There are 66 counties named for 65 landforms. "Landforms" includes 16 mountain ranges; eleven islands and valleys; seven individual mountain peaks; three capes, buttes, passes, and prairies; two peninsulas and portages; and one each for bluffs, canyon, hills, park, and point. The only name of a landform given to two counties is Teton from the mountain range in Idaho and Wyoming. Teton, Montana, is named for a peak that is not a part of the Teton Range in Idaho and Wyoming. Other than "Teton" there are no other counties named for more than one landform.

There are 24 counties named for landforms with Indian names, including three Polynesian and one Aztec name; seventeen English, ten Spanish, nine French, and one each from Danish (Lassen) and Greek (Ida).

There are 63 counties named for bodies of water. "Bodies of water" includes 40 lakes, nine bays, three bayous and oceans; and counties named for one each for, anchorage, channel, everglades, gulf, harbor, marshlands, ox bow, and sound. New Jersey has two counties named for the Atlantic Ocean: Atlantic and Ocean.

There are 30 counties named for bodies of water with English names: 20 Indian including one Aztec, eight French, two Spanish, and one German (Humboldt Bay, California).

There are 378 counties named for 313 places. "Places" is divided into "populated places" and "sites and areas." Included in populated places are towns, cities, villages, townships, counties and shires, states, territories, municipalities, and countries. The distinction between cities, towns, and villages is a matter of local usage. At the time a county was named was the eponymous population center a town or city? In 1850 when California's first counties were created and named, San Francisco was definitely a city but were San Diego and Los Angeles towns or cities?

There are 118 counties named for cities and towns which were the leading population center in the new county at the time of its creation. These places usually became the county seat. Five counties are named for cities and towns in other states. Nineteen counties are named for foreign cities. Fifteen counties are named for twelve English cities; six are named for four French cities; Arabia, Greece, Ireland, Spain, and Switzerland, have one each. There are three counties named for states and two for territories. Four counties are named for five countries including the Republic of Texas which was an independent country at the time it was honored by a Missouri county. Counties named for locations in other states or foreign countries are usually named in honor of the former homes of settlers or at the behest of a leading citizen.

There are 110 counties named for 107 towns. Seventy-five counties are named for 55 counties and shires. This breaks down to 37 counties named for 34 US counties; seventeen are named for thirty English shires and counties; and four, all in Michigan, are named for Irish counties. Seventeen counties are named for villages; ten are Indian villages. There are ten counties which grew out of and retained the names of municipalities that were created while Texas was a Mexican province. Four counties, all in Missouri, grew out of Spanish political districts. Pushmataha County, Oklahoma, grew out of a district of the Choctaw Nation.

Included in "sites and areas" are regions, battle sites, ecclesiastical districts and parishes, churches and missions, forts, estates, and national parks. These "places" categories are arbitrary and readers may rearrange them as they see fit. There are 83 counties named for 79 "sites and areas." There are 22 counties named for forts. Eleven are named for battle sites. Four of these sites commemorate the sites of battles between Indians; three, all in Iowa, are from the Mexican War; two are from the Revolutionary War. There is only one county named for a Civil War battle site: Val Verde, Texas. Marengo County, Alabama, celebrates Napoleon's victory over Austria in 1800. Marathon County, Wisconsin, commemorates the Greek victory over Persia in 490 BCE.

Eight Louisiana parishes were created from and named for ecclesiastical districts. Six counties were named for missions. Acadia, Ionia, and Oregon Counties are named for regions. Ten counties are named for eight estates or plantations. Hopewell, Virginia, is named for a farm. Three counties are named for two national parks: Glacier and Yellowstone.

DESCRIPTIVE NAMES

There is much overlap between geographic names and descriptive names. Names conferred on a physical feature by Indians, explorers, and trappers were often descriptive. The most colorful example of a descriptive name is "Teton" bestowed by French trappers on the mountains for their supposed resemblance to female breasts.

There are 228 counties named from 141 descriptive words. The most commonly used word is "Union" which is used eighteen times. The next most popular word is "Lake" used twelve times. Richland has been used five times as has Saline. The words Carbon, Iron, Liberty, and Mineral have each been used four times. Each of the following descriptive words has been used three times as county names: Buffalo, Cedar, Delta, Fairfield, Orange, Rock, Summit, and Valley. Two counties have been named for each of the following words: Big Horn, Butte, Clearwater, Elk, Forest, Golden Valley, Grand, Highland, Limestone, and Midland.

There are 181 counties named for 157 Indian words. This does not include the names of tribes or individual Indians who are included above as persons. The tribes or nations that have contributed the most words are the Delawares with sixteen counties; Chippewas have fifteen; Choctaws have twelve. Dakotas and Iroquois each have eleven counties. There are ten counties named from unspecified Algonquin words. (Algonquin is a linguistic group rather than a tribe or nation.) There are nine counties from Ojibwa words; seven each from Cherokee and Pottawatomie. There are six Seneca and five Chinook and Tlingit words used as county names. There are six counties which have come from a single Allegewi word for "beautiful" first applied to the Potomac River. Variations on this word have led to Allegan, Allegany, Alleghany, and Allegheny Counties. Words from Creek, Miami, and Ute languages have been given to four counties each. Seven Indian groups, including Polynesian, each have three words applied to counties. Nine Indian groups, including Aztec, have two words applied to counties. Twenty-eight counties are named for a single word from Indian languages.

There are 245 counties named from 241 foreign words. Well over half of them, 152, are from Spanish. French is next with 58. Seven counties have Irish names and five have Greek names; four are from Latin and three are from Dutch. Hebrew and Swiss words are given to two counties each. Arabic, Italian, Semitic, and Welsh have each provided a single word to county names.

Henry Schoolcraft, explorer and author, combined various words or parts of words from Arabic, Latin, and Indian languages to come up with the names of six Michigan counties: Alcona, Allegan, Alpena, Arenac, Oscoda, and Tuscola. Schoolcraft also wrote two books whose fictitious protagonists had Michigan counties named for them: Iosco and Leelanau. There is also a Michigan county named for Schoolcraft himself.

Twenty-eight counties have been named for plants including Cedar and Orange with three each. Two counties are named Forest. Others, such as Garden, Sweet Grass, and Wheatland, were named in hopes of attracting settlers. Lonoke, Arkansas, was contrived from a lone oak tree used as a surveyor's mark in the area. Twenty-nine counties are named for rocks or minerals including four simply named Mineral, three named Rock, and one named Stone. Carbon, Coal, and Natrona refer to coal deposits. Five counties are named Saline for salt deposits in the area. Four counties are named Iron. El Dorado and Placer refer to gold deposits in California. Nine counties have been named for animals: Big Horn, Buffalo, Eagle, Elk, and Manatee. Bear Lake and Deer Lodge could also be added to this group.

Table I.4. Number of Counties per State

Alabama	67	Montana	56
Alaska[1]	29	Nebraska	93
Arizona	15	Nevada[5]	17
Arkansas	75	New Hampshire	10
California	58	New Jersey	21
Colorado	64	New Mexico	33
Connecticut	8	New York	62
Delaware	3	North Carolina	100
District of Columbia	1	North Dakota	53
Florida	67	Ohio	88
Georgia	159	Oklahoma	77
Hawaii[2]	5	Oregon	36
Idaho	44	Pennsylvania	67
Illinois	102	Rhode Island	5
Indiana	92	South Carolina	46
Iowa	99	South Dakota	66
Kansas	105	Tennessee	95
Kentucky	120	Texas	254
Louisiana	64	Utah	29
Maine	16	Vermont	14
Maryland[3]	24	Virginia[6]	134
Massachusetts	14	Washington	39
Michigan	83	West Virginia	55
Minnesota	87	Wisconsin	72
Mississippi	82	Wyoming	23
Missouri[4]	115		

[1]Alaska has 16 boroughs, 11 census areas, and 2 municipalities
[2]Kalawao County is sometimes included with Maui County, giving Hawaii 4 counties
[3]Maryland has 23 counties and one independent city
[4]Missouri has 114 counties and one independent city
[5]Nevada has 16 counties and one independent city
[6]Virginia has 95 counties and 39 independent cities

Table I.5.   States Ranked by Number of Counties

District of Columbia	1	Colorado	64
Delaware	3	Louisiana	64
Hawaii[2]	5	South Dakota	66
Rhode Island	5	Alabama	67
Connecticut	8	Florida	67
New Hampshire	10	Pennsylvania	67
Massachusetts	14	Wisconsin	72
Vermont	14	Arkansas	75
Arizona	15	Oklahoma	77
Maine	16	Mississippi	82
Nevada[5]	17	Michigan	83
New Jersey	21	Minnesota	87
Wyoming	23	Ohio	88
Maryland[3]	24	Indiana	92
Alaska[1]	29	Nebraska	93
Utah	29	Tennessee	95
New Mexico	33	Iowa	99
Oregon	36	North Carolina	100
Washington	39	Illinois	102
Idaho	44	Kansas	105
South Carolina	46	Missouri[4]	115
North Dakota	53	Kentucky	120
West Virginia	55	Virginia[6]	134
Montana	56	Georgia	159
California	58	Texas	254
New York	62		

[1]Alaska has 16 boroughs, 11 census areas, and 2 municipalities
[2]Kalawao County is sometimes included with Maui County, giving Hawaii 4 counties
[3]Maryland has 23 counties and one independent city
[4]Missouri has 114 counties and one independent city
[5]Nevada has 16 counties and one independent city
[6]Virginia has 95 counties and 39 independent cities

Table I.6. Largest and Smallest Counties in Land Area by State

State	County	Square Miles
Alabama	Baldwin	1,590
	Etowah	535
Alaska	Yukon-Koyukuk	145,505
	Skagway	452
Arizona	Coconino	18,619
	Santa Cruz	1,237
Arkansas	Union	1,039
	Lafayette	528
California	San Bernardino	20,057
	San Francisco	47
Colorado	Las Animas	4,773
	Broomfield	33
Connecticut	Litchfield	921
	Middlesex	369
Delaware	Sussex	936
	New Castle	426
District of Columbia		61
Florida	Collier	1,998
	Union	244
Georgia	Ware	892
	Clarke	119
Hawaii	Hawaii	4,028
	Kalawao	12
Idaho	Idaho	8,477
	Payette	407
Illinois	McLean	1,183
	Putnam	160
Indiana	Allen	657
	Ohio	86
Iowa	Kossuth	973
	Dickinson	381
Kansas	Butler	1,430
	Wyandotte	152
Kentucky	Pike	787
	Robertson	100
Louisiana	Vernon	1,328
	Orleans	169
Maine	Aroostook	6,671
	Sagadahoc	254
Maryland	Frederick	660
	Baltimore (City)	81
Massachusetts	Worcester	1,511
	Nantucket	45
Michigan	Marquette	1,808
	Benzie	320
Minnesota	Saint Louis	6,247
	Ramsey	152
Mississippi	Yazoo	923
	Alcorn	400
Missouri	Texas	1,177
	Saint Louis (City)	62
Montana	Beaverhead	5,542
	Silver Bow	718
Nebraska	Cherry	5,960
	Sarpy	239
Nevada	Nye	18,182
	Carson City (City)	145

State	County	Square Miles
New Hampshire	Coos	1,795
	Strafford	369
New Jersey	Burlington	799
	Hudson	46
New Mexico	Catron	6,924
	Los Alamos	109
New York	Saint Lawrence	2,680
	New York	23
North Carolina	Robeson	949
	Chowan	172
North Dakota	McKenzie	2,760
	Eddy	630
Ohio	Ashtabula	702
	Lake	227
Oklahoma	Osage	2,246
	Marshall	371
Oregon	Harney	10,133
	Multnomah	431
Pennsylvania	Lycoming	1,229
	Montour	130
Rhode Island	Providence	410
	Bristol	24
South Carolina	Horry	1,134
	McCormick	359
South Dakota	Meade	3,471
	Clay	412
Tennessee	Shelby	763
	Trousdale	114
Texas	Brewster	6,184
	Rockwall	127
Utah	San Juan	7,820
	Davis	299
Vermont	Windsor	969
	Grande Isle	82
Virginia	Pittsylvania	969
	Falls Church (City)	2
Washington	Okanogan	5,268
	San Juan	174
West Virginia	Randolph	1,040
	Hancock	83
Wisconsin	Marathon	1,545
	Pepin	232
Wyoming	Sweetwater	10,427
	Hot Springs	2,004

Table I.7. Largest and Smallest Counties By Population

State	County	Square Miles
Alabama	Jefferson	658,466
	Greene	9,045
Alaska	Anchorage	291,826
	Yakutat	662
Arizona	Maricopa	3,817,117
	Greenlee	8,437
Arkansas	Pulaski	382,748
	Calhoun	5,368
California	Los Angeles	9,818,605
	Alpine	1,175
Colorado	El Paso	622,263
	San Juan	699
Connecticut	Fairfield	916,829
	Windham	118,428
Delaware	New Castle	538,479
	Kent	162,310
District of Columbia		601,723
Florida	Miami-Dade	2,496,435
	Liberty	8,365
Georgia	Fulton	920,581
	Taliaferro	1,717
Hawaii	Honolulu	953,207
	Kalawao	90
Idaho	Ada	392,365
	Clark	982
Illinois	Cook	5,194,675
	Hardin	4,320
Indiana	Marion	903,393
	Ohio	6,128
Iowa	Polk	430,640
	Adams	4,029
Kansas	Johnson	544,179
	Greeley	1,247
Kentucky	Jefferson	741,096
	Robertson	2,282
Louisiana	East Baton Rouge	440,171
	Tensas	5,252
Maine	Cumberland	281,674
	Piscataquis	17,535
Maryland	Montgomery	971,777
	Kent	20,197
Massachusetts	Middlesex	1,503,085
	Nantucket	10,172
Michigan	Wayne	1,820,584
	Keweenaw	2,156
Minnesota	Hennepin	1,152,425
	Traverse	3,558
Mississippi	Hinds	245,285
	Issaquena	1,406
Missouri	Saint Louis	998,954
	Worth	2,171
Montana	Yellowstone	147,972
	Petroleum	494
Nebraska	Douglas	517,110
	Arthur	460
Nevada	Clark	1,951,269
	Esmeralda	783
New Hampshire	Hillsborough	400,721
	Coos	33,055

State	County	Square Miles
New Jersey	Bergen	905,116
	Salem	66,083
New Mexico	Bernalillo	662,564
	Harding	695
New York	Kings	2,504,700
	Hamilton	4,836
North Carolina	Mecklenburg	919,628
	Tyrrell	4,407
North Dakota	Cass	149,778
	Slope	727
Ohio	Cuyahoga	1,280,122
	Vinton	13,435
Oklahoma	Oklahoma	718,633
	Cimarron	2,475
Oregon	Multnomah	735,334
	Wheeler	1,441
Pennsylvania	Philadelphia	1,526,006
	Cameron	5,085
Rhode Island	Providence	626,667
	Bristol	49,875
South Carolina	Greenville	451,225
	McCormick	10,233
Tennessee	Shelby	927,644
	Pickett	5,077
Texas	Harris	4,092,459
	Loving	82
Utah	Salt Lake	1,029,655
	Daggett	1,059
Vermont	Chittenden	156,546
	Essex	6,306
Virginia	Fairfax	1,081,726
	Highland	2,321
Washington	King	1,931,249
	Garfield	2,266
West Virginia	Kanawha	193,063
	Wirt	5,717
Wisconsin	Milwaukee	947,735
	Menominee	4,232
Wyoming	Laramie	91,738
	Niobrara	2,484

The American Counties

The information in this section is arranged as follows:

County Name	State
County Seat	Area

Population:

2010	2000	1990	1980	1970	1960	1950

Date of creation; organization; name changes, etc. *Name Origin*

A

Abbeville **South Carolina**
Abbeville 490 sq. mi.

25,417	26,167	23,862	22,627	21,112	21,417	22,456

March 12, 1785; converted to judicial district January 1, 1800; redesignated as county April 16, 1868. *Town of Abbeville.* Named for Abbeville, France, origin of French Huguenot settlers.

Acadia **Louisiana**
Crowley 655 sq. mi.

61,773	58,861	55,882	56,427	52,109	49,931	47,050

October 2, 1886. *Acadia, Canada. Acadiens* settled in French Louisiana following expulsion from Canada by British during French and Indian War 1755.

Accomack **Virginia**
Accomac 450 sq. mi.

33,164	38,305	31,703	31,268	29,004	30,635	33,832

1661. *Accomac Indians.* Name meaning "on the other side;" applied to all Indians on Virginia's eastern shore.

Ada **Idaho**
Boise 1,053 sq. mi.

392,365	300,904	205,775	173,036	112,230	93,460	70,649

December 22, 1864. *Ada Riggs (1856–1909).* First American child born in Boise. Daughter of H. C. Riggs, one of original incorporators of Boise; erected first building in Boise; member of territorial legislature 1864.

Adair **Iowa**
Greenfield 569 sq. mi.

7,682	8,243	8,409	9,509	9,487	10,893	12,292

January 15, 1851; organized May 6, 1854. *John Adair (1757–1840).* Served in Revolutionary War; major of volunteers in expedition against Indians 1791–92; Kentucky legislature 1793–95; US senator 1805–06; aide to Governor Shelby at Battle of the Thames 1813; commanded Kentucky rifle brigade under Andrew Jackson 1814–15; governor of Kentucky 1820–24; US Representative 1831–33.

Adair   **Kentucky**
Columbia   405 sq. mi.
18,656   17,244   15,360   15,233   13,037   14,699   17,603
December 11, 1801; effective April 1, 1802. *John Adair.**

Adair   **Missouri**
Kirksville   567 sq. mi.
25,607   24,977   24,577   24,870   22,472   20,105   19,689
January 29, 1841. *John Adair.**

Adair   **Oklahoma**
Stilwell   573 sq. mi.
22,683   21,038   18,421   18,575   15,141   13,112   14,918
July 16, 1907. *Adair family.* Leading Cherokee family whose most prominent member was William P. Adair (?–1881); represented Cherokee Nation in Washington 1866–81; opposed influx of "boomers" into Oklahoma from Kansas.

Adams   **Colorado**
Brighton   1,168 sq. mi.
441,603   363,857   265,038   245,944   185,789   120,296   40,234
April 15, 1901. *Alva Adams (1850–1922).* Colorado legislature 1876; governor of Colorado, intermittently 1887–1905.

Adams   **Idaho**
Council   1,363 sq. mi.
3,976   3,476   3,254   3,347   2,877   2,978   3,347
March 3, 1911. *John Adams (1735–1826).* Continental Congress 1774; signer of Declaration of Independence 1776; commissioner to France 1777–78; negotiated peace treaty with England 1785–88; US vice president 1789–97; 2nd US president 1797–1801.

Adams   **Illinois**
Quincy   855 sq. mi.
67,103   68,277   66,090   71,622   70,861   68,467   64,690
January 13, 1825. *John Quincy Adams (1767–1848).* Massachusetts Senate 1802; US senator 1803–08; US minister to Russia 1809–14; negotiated treaty of Ghent ending War of 1812 1815; US minister to Great Britain 1815–17; US secretary of state 1817–25; 6th US president 1825–29; US representative 1831–48.

Adams   **Indiana**
Decatur   339 sq. mi.
34,387   33,625   31,095   29,619   26,871   24,643   22,393
February 7, 1835; organized January 23, 1836. *John Quincy Adams.**

Adams   **Iowa**
Corning   423 sq. mi.
4,029   4,482   4,866   5,731   6,322   7,468   8,753
January 15, 1851; organized January 12, 1853. *John Adams.**

Adams   **Mississippi**
Natchez   462 sq. mi.
32,297   34,340   35,356   38,035   37,293   37,730   32,256
April 2, 1799. *John Adams.**

Adams   **Nebraska**
Hastings   563 sq. mi.

| 31,364 | 31,151 | 29,625 | 30,656 | 30,553 | 28,944 | 28,855 |

February 16, 1867; organized January 2, 1872. *John Adams.**

Adams   **North Dakota**
Hettinger   988 sq. mi.

| 2,343 | 2,593 | 3,174 | 3,584 | 3,832 | 4,449 | 4,910 |

April 17, 1907. *John Quincy Adams (1848–1919)*. General land and town-site agent for Chicago, Milwaukee, St. Paul & Pacific Railway when county was created.

Adams   **Ohio**
West Union   584 sq. mi.

| 28,550 | 27,330 | 25,371 | 24,328 | 18,957 | 19,982 | 20,499 |

July 10, 1797. *John Adams.**

Adams   **Pennsylvania**
Gettysburg   519 sq. mi.

| 101,407 | 91,292 | 78,274 | 68,292 | 56,937 | 51,906 | 44,197 |

January 22, 1800. *John Adams.**

Adams   **Washington**
Ritzville   1,925 sq. mi.

| 18,728 | 16,428 | 13,603 | 13,267 | 12,014 | 9,929 | 6,584 |

November 28, 1883. *John Adams.**

Adams   **Wisconsin**
Friendship   646 sq. mi.

| 20,875 | 18,643 | 15,682 | 13,457 | 9,234 | 7,566 | 7,906 |

March 11, 1848. *Uncertain.* (1) *John Quincy Adams;** county was created two weeks after Adams' death. (2) *John Adams.** (3) Both John and John Quincy Adams.

Addison   **Vermont**
Middlebury   766 sq. mi.

| 36,821 | 35,974 | 32,953 | 29,406 | 24,266 | 20,076 | 19,442 |

October 18, 1785. *Joseph Addison (1672–1719)*. British essayist; under secretary of state 1706; member of Parliament 1708–19; editor of *The Spectator* 1711–12 and 1714; wrote tragic play *Cato* 1713; publisher of political newspaper *The Freeholder* 1715–16; buried in Westminster Abbey.

Aiken   **South Carolina**
Aiken   1,071 sq. mi.

| 160,099 | 142,552 | 120,940 | 105,625 | 91,023 | 81,038 | 53,137 |

March 10, 1871. *Town of Aiken*; named for William Aiken, Sr. (1779–1831); president of South Carolina Canal & Railway Company; built railroad to Charleston helping town become a popular summer resort.

Aitkin   **Minnesota**
Aitkin   1,822 sq. mi.

| 16,202 | 15,301 | 12,425 | 13,404 | 11,403 | 12,162 | 14,327 |

May 23, 1857, as Aiken; spelling corrected 1872; organized February 6, 1885. *William Alexander Aitkin (1787–1851)*. Fur trader; worked for the Fond du Loc department of the American Fur Company under John Jacob Astor.

Alachua   **Florida**
Gainesville   875 sq. mi.

| 247,336 | 217,955 | 181,956 | 151,348 | 104,764 | 74,074 | 57,026 |

December 29, 1824. *Town of Alachua*. From Creek word of uncertain meaning; most possibilities refer to the marshes and sinkholes in the area.

Alamance   **North Carolina**
Graham   424 sq. mi.

| 151,131 | 130,800 | 108,213 | 99,319 | 96,362 | 85,674 | 71,220 |

January 29, 1849. *Battle of Alamance.* Fought between Royal Governor William Tryon and the "Regulators," a group of settlers with various grievances against the Crown, May 16, 1771. Named for Alamance Creek, from a Sissipahau word for "blue clay."

Alameda   **California**
Oakland   739 sq. mi.

| 1,510,271 | 1,443,741 | 1,279,182 | 1,105,379 | 1,073,184 | 908,209 | 740,315 |

March 25, 1853. *Alameda Creek.* Principal stream in the area; Spanish for "poplar grove."

Alamosa   **Colorado**
Alamosa   723 sq. mi.

| 15,445 | 14,966 | 13,617 | 11,799 | 11,422 | 10,000 | 10,531 |

March 8, 1913. *Town of Alamosa.* Named for Alamosa Creek; Spanish for "cottonwood grove."

Albany   **New York**
Albany   523 sq. mi.

| 304,204 | 294,565 | 292,594 | 285,909 | 286,742 | 272,926 | 239,386 |

November 1, 1683. *King James II, Duke of York and Albany (1633–1701).* Second son of Charles I and Henrietta Maria; named Duke of York and Albany 1643; succeeded to throne on death of his brother, Charles II, 1685; King of England, Scotland (James VII), and Ireland 1685–88; escaped to France during Glorious Revolution 1688; defeated at Battle of the Boyne by William of Orange 1690 (see King William, Virginia).

Albany   **Wyoming**
Laramie   4,274 sq. mi.

| 36,299 | 32,014 | 30,797 | 29,062 | 26,431 | 21,290 | 19,055 |

December 16, 1868. *City of Albany, New York.* Former New Yorker, Charles Bradley, the area's territorial legislator, was asked to choose a name for the new county.

Albemarle   **Virginia**
Charlottesville   721 sq. mi.

| 98,970 | 79,236 | 68,040 | 55,783 | 37,780 | 30,969 | 26,662 |

October 16, 1744. *William Anne Kemple, Earl of Albemarle (1702–54).* Aide-de-camp to King George I 1727; absentee governor of Virginia 1737–54; brigadier general 1739; lieutenant general 1742; privy councilor 1751. (Associated independent city: Charlottesville.)

Alcona   **Michigan**
Harrisville   675 sq. mi.

| 10,942 | 11,719 | 10,145 | 9,740 | 7,113 | 6,352 | 5,856 |

April 1, 1840, as Negwegon; name changed March 8, 1843. *Contrived word.* Contrived by Henry Schoolcraft from Arabic *al* meaning "country," Ojibwa root word *co* which has no meaning, and Ojibwa interjection *na*. (See Schoolcraft, Michigan).

Alcorn   **Mississippi**
Corinth   400 sq. mi.

| 37,057 | 34,558 | 31,722 | 33,036 | 27,179 | 25,282 | 27,158 |

April 15, 1870. *James Lusk Alcorn (1816–94).* Kentucky House of Representatives 1843; Mississippi House of Representatives 1846 and 1856–57; Mississippi Senate 1848–54; opposed secession but served in Confederate Army 1864–65; elected US senator but not seated 1865; governor of Mississippi 1870–71; US senator 1871–77.

Aleutians East   **Alaska**
Sand Point   6,982 sq. mi.

3,141 2,697 2,464 (a) (a) (a) (b)

October 23, 1987. *Aleuts*. Eskimo word meaning "the people." [(a) Included in Aleutians Census Area; (b) included in 3rd Judicial District.]

Aleutians West **Alaska**
(Census Area) 4,390 sq. mi.
5,561 5,465 9,478 7,768[a] 8,057[a] 6,011[a] (b)

October 23, 1987. *Aleuts.** [(a) Aleutians Islands Census Area; (b) included in 3rd Judicial District.]

Alexander **Illinois**
Cairo 236 sq. mi.
8,238 9,590 10,626 12,264 12,015 16,061 20,316

March 4, 1819. *Dr. William Melville Alexander (?–?)*. Physician; early Illinois settler; Illinois House of Representatives 1820–24, Speaker 1822.

Alexander **North Carolina**
Taylorsville 260 sq. mi.
37,198 33,603 27,544 24,999 19,466 15,625 14,554

January 15, 1847. *Uncertain*. (1) *William Julius Alexander (1797–1857)*; North Carolina legislature. (2) *Abraham Alexander (1717–86)*; North Carolina Assembly. (3) *Nathaniel Alexander (1756–1808)*; US representative 1803–05; governor of North Carolina 1805–07.

Alexandria **Virginia**
(Independent City) 15 sq. mi.
139,966 128,283 111,183 103,217 110,938 91,023 61,787

1870. *John Alexander (1612–77)*. Acquired various land grants in Virginia including Howson Patent, site of Alexandria, 1669. (Associated counties: Arlington and Fairfax.)

Alfalfa **Oklahoma**
Cherokee 866 sq. mi.
5,642 6,105 6,416 7,077 7,224 8,445 10,699

July 16, 1907. *William Henry "Alfalfa Bill" Murray* (see Murray, Oklahoma).

Alger **Michigan**
Munising 915 sq. mi.
9,601 9,862 8,972 9,225 8,568 9,250 10,007

March 17, 1885. *Russell Alexander Alger (1836–1907)*. Private to captain, Michigan Volunteers 1861; major to major general 1862–64; governor of Michigan 1885–87; US secretary of war 1897–99; US senator 1902–07.

Allamakee **Iowa**
Waukon 639 sq. mi.
14,330 14,675 13,855 15,108 14,968 15,982 16,351

February 20, 1847; organized March 6, 1849. *Uncertain*. (1) *Allan Makee (?–?)*; Indian trader. (2) *Anameekee*; Sauk-Fox word for "thunder."

Allegan **Michigan**
Allegan 825 sq. mi.
111,408 105,665 90,509 81,555 66,575 57,729 47,493

March 2, 1831; organized September 7, 1835. *Contrived name*. One of many faux-Indian names contrived by Henry Schoolcraft by combining Arabic or Latin syllables with Indian words (see Schoolcraft, Michigan).

Allegany **Maryland**
Cumberland 424 sq. mi.
75,087 74,930 74,946 80,548 84,044 84,169 89,556

December 25, 1789. *Allegewi Indians.* Name of prehistoric people that became generally applied to all Indians in the Upper Ohio Valley; from *oolikjanna* meaning "beautiful river;" referring to the Potomac River in this instance. Applied with various spellings to geographic features throughout the region.

Allegany   **New York**
Belmont   1,029 sq. mi.
48,946   49,927   50,742   51,742   46,458   43,978   43,784
April 7, 1806. *Allegheny Trail.* Follows Allegheny River (see Allegany, Maryland).

Alleghany   **North Carolina**
Sparta   235 sq. mi.
11,155   10,677   9,590   9,587   8,134   7,734   8,155
1859. *Uncertain.* (1) *Alleghany Indians.* (2) *Allegheny River.* (See Allegany, Maryland.)

Alleghany   **Virginia**
Covington   445 sq. mi.
16,250   17,215   16,805   19,379   17,962   17,406   28,984
January 5, 1822. *Allegheny Mountains.* (See Allegany, Maryland.) (Associated independent city: Covington.) (Clifton Forge ended its independent status and reverted back to being a part of Alleghany County July 1, 2001. Populations shown above include the City of Clifton Forge.)

Allegheny   **Pennsylvania**
Pittsburgh   730 sq. mi.
1,223,348   1,281,666   1,336,449   1,450,085   1,605,016   1,628,587   1,515,237
September 24, 1788. *Allegheny River.* (See Allegany, Maryland.)

Allen   **Indiana**
Fort Wayne   657 sq. mi.
355,329   331,849   300,836   294,335   280,455   232,196   182,722
December 17, 1823; effective April 1, 1824. *John Allen (1772–1813).* Kentucky Senate; lieutenant colonel 1812; killed in River Raisin Massacre, January 1813.

Allen   **Kansas**
Iola   500 sq. mi.
13,371   14,385   14,638   15,654   15,043   16,369   18,187
August 25, 1855; organized May 7, 1856. *William Allen (1803–79).* US representative from Ohio 1833–35; US senator 1837–49; declined Democratic presidential nomination 1848; governor of Ohio 1874–76. Anti-free-soil position popular in Kansas territorial legislature.

Allen   **Kentucky**
Scottsville   344 sq. mi.
19,956   17,800   14,628   14,128   12,598   12,269   13,787
January 11, 1815. *John Allen.**

Allen   **Louisiana**
Oberlin   762 sq. mi.
25,764   25,440   21,226   21,390   20,794   19,867   18,835
June 12, 1912. *Henry Watkins Allen (1820–66).* Louisiana legislature 1853; enlisted as private in Confederate Army; elected to lieutenant colonel 1861; wounded at Shiloh and Baton Rouge 1862; brigadier general 1863; governor of the portion of Louisiana not under Union control 1864–65; moved to Mexico to escape Reconstruction 1865.

Allen   **Ohio**
Lima   403 sq. mi.
106,331   108,473   109,755   112,241   111,144   103,691   88,183

February 12, 1820. *Ethan Allen (1738–89)*. Leader of Vermont's resistance against New York; leader of militia group Green Mountain Boys 1770; captured Fort Ticonderoga May 10, 1775; captured at Montreal 1775; exchanged 1778; led movement for Vermont statehood.

Allendale   **South Carolina**
Allendale   408 sq. mi.
10,419   11,211   11,722   10,700   9,692   11,362   11,773
February 6, 1919. *Town of Allendale*. Named for *Paul H. Allen (c1800–?)*, local landowner and first postmaster of Allendale 1849.

Alpena   **Michigan**
Alpena   572 sq. mi.
29,598   31,314   30,605   32,315   30,708   28,556   22,189
April 1, 1840, as Anamickee; name changed March 8, 1843; organized February 7, 1857. *Contrived word*. Contrived by Henry Schoolcraft by combining Arab *al* meaning "country" and Ojibwa *pena* meaning "partridge" to arrive at "partridge country." (See Schoolcraft, Michigan.)

Alpine   **California**
Markleeville   738 sq. mi.
1,175   1,208   1,113   1,097   484   397   241
March 16, 1864. *Descriptive*. Refers to county's location in Sierra Nevada Mountains.

Amador   **California**
Jackson   595 sq. mi.
38,091   35,100   30,039   19,314   11,821   9,990   9,151
May 10, 1854. *Josef María Amador (1794–1883)*. Majordomo of Mission San Jose; early settler and miner.

Amelia   **Virginia**
Amelia Court House   355 sq. mi.
12,690   11,400   8,787   8,405   7,592   7,815   7,908
September 30, 1734. *Princess Amelia Sophia Eleanor (1711–86)*. Second daughter of King George II.

Amherst   **Virginia**
Amherst   474 sq. mi.
32,353   31,894   28,578   29,122   26,072   22,953   20,332
April 7, 1761. *Jeffrey Amherst (1717–97)*. War of Austrian Succession (King George's War) 1741–48; aide to Duke of Cumberland 1745; French and Indian War; Siege of Louisbourg 1758; captured Montreal 1760; governor-general of Canada 1760–63; approved unsuccessful plan to infect Indians with Smallpox during Pontiac's Rebellion 1763; nominal governor of Virginia 1759–68; rejected field command during American Revolution; advocated limited war against American colonists.

Amite   **Mississippi**
Liberty   730 sq. mi.
13,131   13,599   13,328   13,369   13,763   15,573   19,261
February 24, 1809. *Amite River*. French *amité* meaning "friendship."

Anchorage   **Alaska**
Anchorage   1,705 sq. mi.
291,826   260,283   226,338   174,431   124,542   82,833   (a)
September 13, 1963. *Knik Anchorage*. Ships' anchorage in Cook Inlet serving an Alaskan Railroad construction camp at Ship Creek 1915. [(a) Part of 3rd Judicial District.]

Anderson   **Kansas**
Garnett   580 sq. mi.
8,102   8,110   7,803   8,749   8,501   9,035   10,267

August 25, 1855; organized January 7, 1856. *Joseph C. Anderson (?–?)*. Elected to first Kansas territorial legislature by pro-slavery residents of Missouri who crossed border to vote in Kansas election; Speaker of the legislature.

Anderson   **Kentucky**
Lawrenceburg   202 sq. mi.

| 21,421 | 19,111 | 14,571 | 12,567 | 9,358 | 8,618 | 8,984 |

January 16, 1827. *Richard Clough Anderson (1788–1826)*. Kentucky legislature 1815, 1821–22, Speaker 1822; US representative 1817–21; US minister to Colombia 1823; appointed envoy extraordinary and minister plenipotentiary to Panama Congress of Nations but died en route.

Anderson   **South Carolina**
Anderson   715 sq. mi.

| 187,126 | 165,740 | 145,196 | 133,235 | 105,474 | 98,478 | 90,664 |

December 20, 1826. *Robert Anderson (1741–1813)*. Captain, 3rd South Carolina Rangers 1775–79; major to colonel 1781; adjutant general South Carolina Militia; South Carolina legislature.

Anderson   **Tennessee**
Clinton   337 sq. mi.

| 75,129 | 71,330 | 68,250 | 67,346 | 60,300 | 60,032 | 59,407 |

November 6, 1801. *Joseph Inslee Anderson (1757–1837)*. Revolutionary War brevet major; US judge Territory South of the Ohio (Tennessee) 1791; US Senate 1797–1815; first comptroller of the US treasury 1815–36.

Anderson   **Texas**
Palestine   1,063 sq. mi.

| 58,458 | 55,109 | 48,024 | 38,381 | 27,789 | 28,162 | 31,875 |

March 24, 1846; organized July 13, 1846. *Kenneth Lewis Anderson (1805–45)*. Sheriff, Bedford County, Tennessee 1830; sheriff, San Augustine 1838; Republic of Texas legislature 1841–42; Texas vice president 1844–45.

Andrew   **Missouri**
Savannah   433 sq. mi.

| 17,291 | 16,492 | 14,632 | 13,980 | 11,913 | 11,062 | 11,727 |

January 29, 1841. *Andrew Jackson Davis (?–?)*. Lawyer in St. Louis and Savannah, Missouri.

Andrews   **Texas**
Andrews   1,501 sq. mi.

| 14,786 | 13,004 | 14,338 | 13,323 | 10,372 | 13,450 | 5,002 |

August 21, 1876; organized 1910. *Richard "Big Dick" Andrews (1814–1835)*. Wounded at Battle of Gonzales October 2, 1835; only Texan killed in Battle of Concepción making him the first Texan killed in Texas Revolution October 28, 1835.

Androscoggin   **Maine**
Auburn   468 sq. mi.

| 107,702 | 103,793 | 105,259 | 99,657 | 91,279 | 86,312 | 83,594 |

March 18, 1854. *Uncertain.* (1) *Arosaguntacooks*; name was applied by British to all tribes in the area; name refers to curing and drying of fish. (2) *Edmund Andros (1637–1714)*; British major, fought Dutch in West Indies; royal governor of New England 1686. (3) *Androscoggin River*; named for Arsoguntacook Indians.

Angelina   **Texas**
Lufkin   798 sq. mi.

| 86,771 | 80,130 | 69,884 | 64,172 | 49,349 | 39,814 | 36,032 |

April 22, 1846. *Angelina River*. Name given to neophyte girl at Mission San Francisco de los Tejas; Spanish for "little angel."

Anne Arundel   **Maryland**
Annapolis   415 sq. mi.

| 537,656 | 489,656 | 427,239 | 370,775 | 297,539 | 206,634 | 117,392 |

July 30, 1650; name changed to Providence 1654; original name restored 1658. *Anne Arundell Calvert (1616–49)*. Daughter of Thomas, Lord Arundell of Wardour; wife of Cecilius Calvert, 2nd Lord Baltimore (see Cecil, Maryland); mother of Charles Calvert (see Charles, Maryland).

Anoka	Minnesota					
Anoka	423 sq. mi.					
330,844	298,084	243,641	195,998	154,556	85,916	35,579

May 23, 1857. *Town of Anoka*. Dakota word for "on both sides of the river."

Anson	North Carolina					
Wadesboro	531 sq. mi.					
26,948	25,275	23,474	25,649	23,488	24,962	26,781

1750. *George Lord Anson (1697–1762)*. Joined British Navy at age 15, 1712; captain of naval ship at age 27, 1725; North American station 1724–30 and 1733–35; voyage of circumnavigation 1740–44; defeated French off Cape Finisterre 1747; full admiral 1748; first lord of the admiralty 1748; admiral of the fleet, highest rank in British Navy 1761.

Antelope	Nebraska					
Neligh	857 sq. mi.					
6,685	7,452	7,965	8,675	9,047	10,176	11,624

March 1, 1871; organized October 1872. *Descriptive* of an individual antelope killed for food by Leander Gerrard who later proposed this name while a member of the Nebraska legislature.

Antrim	Michigan					
Bellaire	476 sq. mi.					
23,580	23,110	18,185	16,194	12,612	10,373	10,721

April 1, 1840, as Meegisee; name changed March 8, 1843. *County Antrim, Ireland*. Michigan legislature renamed several counties after Irish counties March 8, 1843.

Apache	Arizona					
Saint Johns	11,198 sq. mi.					
71,518	69,423	61,591	52,108	32,298	30,438	27,767

February 24, 1879. *Apache Indians*. Name of uncertain origin applied to several southwestern tribes. (1) *Apa-ahwa-tche*, combining Yuman word for "men" with "fight" or "battle." (2) *Apachu*, Zuni word meaning "enemy."

Appanoose	Iowa					
Centerville	497 sq. mi.					
12,887	13,721	13,743	15,511	15,007	16,015	19,683

February 17, 1843; organized January 3, 1846; effective August 3, 1846. *Appanoose (?–1845)*. Sauk-Fox chief; leader of peace faction during Black Hawk War 1832; name means "little child" or "chief when child."

Appling	Georgia					
Baxley	509 sq. mi.					
18,236	17,419	15,744	15,565	12,726	13,246	14,003

December 15, 1818. *Daniel Appling (1787–1818)*. Lieutenant colonel, US Army 1805; War of 1812; defeated British at Battle of Sandy Creek, New York, 1814; awarded sword by Georgia legislature but died before presentation.

Appomattox	Virginia					
Appomattox	333 sq. mi.					
14,973	13,705	12,298	11,971	9,784	9,148	8,764

February 8, 1845. *Appomattox River*. Algonquin word describing "sinuous tidal estuary."

Aransas	Texas					
Rockport	252 sq. mi.					
23,158	22,497	17,892	14,260	8,902	7,006	4,252

September 18, 1871. *Aransas River*. Named for a river in Spain: *Rio Nuestra Señora de Aranzazu* (Our Lady of Aranzazu). Also possibly named for Aransas Bay or Aransas Pass.

Arapahoe   **Colorado**
Littleton   798 sq. mi.
572,003   487,967   391,511   293,621   161,142   113,426   52,125
November 1, 1861. *Arapahoe Indians*. From Pawnee *tirapihu* or *larapihu* meaning "trader."

Archer   **Texas**
Archer City   903 sq. mi.
9,054   8,854   7,973   7,266   5,759   6,110   6,816
January 22, 1858; organized July 27, 1880. *Dr. Branch Turner Archer (1790–1856)*. One of three commissioners from Republic of Texas sent to Washington to solicit US aid 1835; Speaker, Texas House of Representatives 1836; Texas secretary of war 1836–42.

Archuleta   **Colorado**
Pagosa Springs   1,350 sq. mi.
12,084   9,898   5,345   3,664   2,733   2,629   3,030
April 14, 1885. *Uncertain*. (1) *Antonio D. Archuleta (1855–?)*; Colorado legislature 1876; Colorado Senate 1885. (2) *José M. Archuleta (?–?)*; head of prominent Colorado family. (3) Both Antonio and José Archuleta.

Arenac   **Michigan**
Standish   363 sq. mi.
15,899   17,269   14,931   14,706   11,149   9,860   9,644
March 2, 1831; abolished April 20, 1857; reestablished April 1, 1883. *Contrived word*. Contrived by Henry Schoolcraft from Latin *arena* meaning "sand" and Algonquin *akee* meaning "land." (See Schoolcraft, Michigan.)

Arkansas   **Arkansas**
De Witt   989 sq. mi.
19,019   20,749   21,653   24,175   23,347   23,355   23,665
December 31, 1813. *Arkansas Indians*. French corruption of Sioux word *quopaw* or *ugakhpa* meaning "downstream people."

Arlington   **Virginia**
Arlington   26 sq. mi.
207,627   189,453   170,936   152,599   174,284   163,401   135,449
March 13, 1847, as Alexandria; name changed March 16, 1920. *Arlington Estate*. Home of George Washington Parke Custis, adopted grandson of George and Martha Custis Washington; named for Custis ancestral home in England. (Associated independent city: Alexandria.)

Armstrong   **Pennsylvania**
Kittanning   653 sq. mi.
68,941   73,392   73,478   77,768   75,590   79,524   80,842
May 12, 1800. *John Armstrong (1758–1843)*. On staffs of Generals Gates and Mercer during Revolutionary War; carried wounded Mercer from Princeton battlefield 1776; Continental Congress 1778–80 and 1787–88; Pennsylvania secretary of state 1783–87; US senator from New York 1800–02 and 1803–04 (resigned both terms); US minister to France 1804–10; US minister to Spain 1806; brigadier general 1812; US secretary of war 1813–14.

Armstrong   **Texas**
Claude   909 sq. mi.
1,901   2,148   2,021   1,994   1,895   1,966   2,215
August 21, 1876; organized March 8, 1890. *Armstrong family*. Any one or a combination of six Texas pioneer families named Armstrong.

Aroostook   **Maine**
Houlton   6,671 sq. mi.

| 71,870 | 73,938 | 86,936 | 91,331 | 92,463 | 106,064 | 96,039 |

March 16, 1839. *Aroostook River*. Algonquin word of uncertain origin referring to a clear, smooth, or beautiful river.

Arthur   **Nebraska**
Arthur   715 sq. mi.

| 460 | 444 | 462 | 513 | 606 | 680 | 803 |

March 31, 1887; organized 1913. *Chester Allen Arthur (1830–86)*. Brigadier general and quartermaster general Union Army 1860–62; collector of Port of New York 1871–78; US vice president 1881; 21st president of US 1881–85.

Ascension   **Louisiana**
Donaldsonville   290 sq. mi.

| 107,215 | 76,627 | 58,214 | 50,068 | 37,086 | 27,927 | 22,387 |

March 31, 1807. *Ascension Ecclesiastical District*. Named for ascension of Jesus into heaven.

Ashe   **North Carolina**
Jefferson   426 sq. mi.

| 27,281 | 24,384 | 22,209 | 22,325 | 19,571 | 19,768 | 21,878 |

1799. *Samuel Ashe (1725–1813)*. Member of North Carolina Council of Thirteen, president 1776; Halifax Convention 1776; North Carolina Constitutional Convention 1776; chief justice 1777–95; governor 1795–98.

Ashland   **Ohio**
Ashland   423 sq. mi.

| 53,139 | 52,523 | 47,507 | 46,178 | 43,303 | 38,771 | 33,040 |

February 24, 1846. *Ashland*. Henry Clay's estate near Lexington, Kentucky.

Ashland   **Wisconsin**
Ashland   1,045 sq. mi.

| 16,157 | 16,866 | 16,307 | 16,783 | 16,743 | 17,375 | 19,461 |

March 27, 1860. *Village of Ashland*. Named for Ashland, Henry Clay's estate near Lexington, Kentucky.

Ashley   **Arkansas**
Hamburg   925 sq. mi.

| 21,853 | 24,209 | 24,319 | 26,538 | 24,976 | 24,220 | 25,660 |

November 30, 1848. *Chester Ashley (1790–1848)*. Practiced law in Hudson, New York; moved to Little Rock 1820; US senator 1844–48.

Ashtabula   **Ohio**
Jefferson   702 sq. mi,

| 101,497 | 102,728 | 99,821 | 104,215 | 98,237 | 93,067 | 78,695 |

February 20, 1807. *Ashtabula River*. European rendering of Delaware word meaning "fish river."

Asotin   **Washington**
Asotin   636 sq. mi.

| 21,623 | 20,551 | 17,605 | 16,823 | 13,799 | 12,909 | 10,878 |

October 27, 1883. *Town of Asotin City*. Named for Asotin Creek from Nez Perce word meaning "eel creek."

Assumption   **Louisiana**
Napoleonville   339 sq. mi.

| 23,421 | 23,388 | 22,753 | 22,084 | 19,654 | 17,991 | 17,278 |

March 31, 1807. *Church of the Assumption*. Oldest church in Louisiana, built in Plattenville 1793; named for the festival of the Assumption of the Virgin Mary.

Atascosa   **Texas**
Jourdanton   1,220 sq. mi.

44,911   38,628   30,533   25,055   18,696   18,828   20,048
January 25, 1856; organized August 4, 1856. *Atascosa River*. Spanish word for "boggy."

Atchison   **Kansas**
Atchison   431 sq. mi.
16,924   16,774   16,932   18,397   19,165   20,898   21,496
August 25, 1855; organized September 17, 1855. *David Rice Atchison (1807–86)*. Missouri legislature 1834 and 1838; Platte District circuit court judge 1841; US senator 1843–55, president pro tempore 1845–49 and 1852–54; pro-slavery sentiments made him popular with Kansas Territory legislature.

Atchison   **Missouri**
Rock Port   547 sq. mi.
5,685   6,430   7,457   8,605   9,240   9,213   11,127
February 23, 1843, as Allen; name changed and organized February 14, 1845. *David Rice Atchison.**

Athens   **Ohio**
Athens   504 sq. mi.
64,757   62,223   59,549   56,399   54,889   46,998   45,839
February 20, 1805. *Town of Athens*. Named for Athens, Greece, as a suitably classical name for the location of newly founded Ohio University.

Atkinson   **Georgia**
Pearson   339 sq. mi.
8,375   7,609   6,213   6,141   5,879   6,188   7,362
August 15, 1917. *William Yates Atkinson (1854–99)*. Georgia Assembly 1886–94; governor of Georgia 1894–99.

Atlantic   **New Jersey**
Mays Landing   556 sq. mi.
274,549   252,552   224,327   194,119   175,043   160,880   132,399
February 17, 1837. *Atlantic Ocean*. County fronts on the ocean.

Atoka   **Oklahoma**
Atoka   976 sq. mi.
14,182   13,879   12,778   12,748   10,972   10,352   14,269
July 16, 1907. *Charles Atoka (?–?)*. Choctaw chief; signed Treaty of Dancing Rabbit Creek leading to removal of Choctaw Nation from southeastern US to Oklahoma 1830; member of Choctaw Council. *Atoka* resembles Choctaw word for "ball ground" and may have been given to Atoka in recognition of his prowess as a ballplayer.

Attala   **Mississippi**
Kosciusko   735 sq. mi.
19,564   19,661   18,481   19,865   19,570   21,335   26,652
December 23, 1833. *Atala*. Fictitious Indian heroine in *The Interesting History of Atala, the Beautiful Indian of the Mississippi* by Francois René 1801. Extra *t* added to county name.

Audrain   **Missouri**
Mexico   692 sq. mi.
25,529   25,853   23,599   26,458   25,362   26,079   23,829
January 12, 1831; organized December 17, 1836. *Uncertain*. (1) *James H. Audrain (1782–1831)*; Missouri legislature 1830–31. (2) *Samuel Audrain (?–?)*; first settler in the area.

Audubon   **Iowa**
Audubon   443 sq. mi.
6,119   6,830   7,334   8,559   9,595   10,919   11,579
January 15, 1851; organized July 9, 1855. *John James Audubon (1785–1851)*. Naturalist, ornithologist, and artist; *Birds of America* 1839.

Auglaize **Ohio**
Wapakoneta 401 sq. mi.
45,949   46,611   44,585   42,554   38,602   36,147   30,637
February 14, 1848. *Auglaize River*. European rendering of Shawnee word meaning "fallen timbers."

Augusta **Virginia**
Staunton 967 sq. mi.
73,750   65,615   54,677   53,732   44,220   37,363   34,154
December 15, 1738. *Augusta of Saxe-Gotha (1719–72)*. Wife of Frederick, Prince of Wales; mother of King George III. (Associated independent cities: Staunton and Waynesboro.)

Aurora **South Dakota**
Plankinton 708 sq. mi.
2,170   3,058   3,135   3,638   4,183   4,749   5,020
February 22, 1879; organized August 29, 1881. *Aurora*. Roman goddess of dawn; name suggested by literary club composed of early settlers' wives.

Austin **Texas**
Bellville 647 sq. mi.
28,417   23,590   19,832   17,726   13,831   13,777   14,663
March 17, 1836. *Stephen Fuller Austin (1793–1836)*. Missouri territorial legislature 1814–20; judge for 1st District of Arkansas 1820; surveyed and explored Texas for colonization 1822; defeated by Sam Houston for president of the Republic of Texas 1836; appointed Texas secretary of state 1836.

Autauga **Alabama**
Prattville 594 sq. mi.
54,571   43,671   34,222   32,259   24,460   18,739   18,186
November 21, 1818. *Autauga Creek*. Autauga word *atagi* meaning "land of plenty."

Avery **North Carolina**
Newland 247 sq. mi.
17,797   17,167   14,867   14,409   12,655   12,009   13,352
February 11, 1911. *Waightstill Avery (1741–1821)*. Mecklenburg Convention 1775; North Carolina legislature 1776; attorney general of North Carolina 1777–79; colonel of Jones County Militia 1779; North Carolina House of Commons 1782–83 and 1793; fought duel with Andrew Jackson 1788; North Carolina Senate 1796.

Avoyelles **Louisiana**
Marksville 832 sq. mi.
42,073   41,481   39,159   41,393   37,751   37,606   38,031
March 31, 1807. *Avoyels*. Indian word of uncertain meaning; possibilities include "flint people" and "nation [or people] of the rocks."

B

Baca **Colorado**
Springfield 2,555 sq. mi.
3,788   4,517   4,556   5,419   5,674   6,310   7,964
April 16, 1889. *Baca family*. Early settlers in southeast Colorado; Felipe Baca (1828–74) donated land for town site of Trinidad, Colorado.

Bacon **Georgia**
Alma 259 sq. mi.
11,096   10,103   9,566   9,379   8,233   8,359   8,940
July 27, 1914. *Augustus Octavius Bacon (1839–1914)*. Adjutant, 9th Georgia Regiment in Army of Northern Virginia 1861–62; captain, Confederate Army 1862–65; Georgia legislature 1871–86; US Senate 1895–1914.

Bailey **Texas**
Muleshoe 827 sq. mi.
7,165   6,594   7,064   8,168   8,487   9,090   7,592
August 21, 1876; organized 1917. *Peter James Bailey III (1812–36)*. Private from Springfield, Kentucky; died at the Alamo March 6, 1836.

Baker **Florida**
Macclenny 585 sq. mi.
27,115   22,259   18,486   15,289   9,242   7,363   6,313
February 8, 1861. *James McNair Baker (1821–92)*. Solicitor of Eastern Circuit 1859–62; Confederate Senate 1862–64; associate justice of Florida Supreme Court 1866; judge, 4th Judicial Circuit 1881.

Baker **Georgia**
Newton 342 sq. mi.
3,451   4,074   3,615   3,808   3,875   4,543   5,952
December 12, 1825. *John Baker (?–1792)*. Lieutenant to colonel in British army; Georgia Provisional Congress; served with colonists during American Revolution.

Baker **Oregon**
Baker City 3,068 sq. mi.
16,134   16,741   15,317   16,134   14,919   17,295   16,175
September 22, 1862. *Edward Dickinson Baker (1811–61)*. Private in Black Hawk War 1832; Illinois House of Representatives 1837; Illinois Senate 1840–44; colonel in 4th Illinois Volunteer Infantry in Mexican War 1846; US senator from Oregon 1860–61; major general of volunteers 1861; killed at Battle of Balls Bluff, October 21, 1861.

Baldwin **Alabama**
Bay Minette 1,590 sq. mi.
182,265   140,415   98,280   78,556   59,382   49,088   40,997
December 21, 1809. *Abraham Baldwin (1754–1807)*. Tutor at Yale University 1775–79; Chaplain 2nd Continental Brigade 1777–83; Georgia legislature 1785; Continental Congress 1785–88; president, University of Georgia 1786–1801; federal Constitutional Convention 1787; US representative from Georgia 1789–99; US senator 1799–1807.

Baldwin **Georgia**
Milledgeville 258 sq. mi.
45,720   44,700   39,530   34,686   34,240   34,064   29,706
May 11, 1803; organized 1807. *Abraham Baldwin.**

Ballard **Kentucky**
Wickliffe 247 sq. mi.
8,249   8,286   7,902   8,798   8,276   8,291   8,545
February 15, 1842. *Bland Williams Ballard (1761–1853)*. Scout for George Rogers Clark on Piqua Expedition 1782; Battle of Fallen Timbers 1794; Battle of Tippecanoe 1811; wounded and captured at River Raisin, escaped massacre 1813; Kentucky legislature.

Baltimore **Maryland**
Towson 598 sq. mi.
805,029   754,292   692,134   655,615   621,077   492,428   270,273
June 30, 1695. *Baltimore, Ireland*. Irish barony of the Calvert family; George Calvert (c1580–1632) made 1st Lord Baltimore by James I 1625; Cecilius Calvert, 2nd Baron of Baltimore, granted colony in Maryland by Charles I 1632. (See Calvert and Cecil, Maryland.)

Baltimore **Maryland**
(Independent City) 81 sq. mi.
620,961   651,154   736,014   786,775   905,759   939,024   949,708
July 4, 1851. *Baltimore, Ireland.**

Bamberg   **South Carolina**
Bamberg   393 sq. mi.

15,987	16,658	16,902	18,118	15,950	16,274	17,533

February 25, 1897. *Town of Bamberg*. Grew from station owned by Bamberg family on stage line between Charleston, South Carolina, and Augusta, Georgia.

Bandera   **Texas**
Bandera   791 sq. mi.

20,485	17,645	10,562	7,084	4,747	3,892	4,410

January 25, 1856. *Uncertain*. (1) *Bandera Mountains*. (2) *Bandera Pass*; in Bandera Mountains; strategic pass on a route to San Antonio; Spanish for "flag" in honor of some event in which a flag was probably erected in the pass. (3) Both the mountains and the pass.

Banks   **Georgia**
Homer   232 sq. mi.

18,395	14,422	10,308	8,702	6,833	6,497	6,935

December 11, 1858. *Richard E. Banks*. Popular itinerant physician in the area.

Banner   **Nebraska**
Harrisburg   746 sq. mi.

690	819	852	918	1,034	1,269	1,325

November 6, 1888. *Hyperbole*. County's founders sought to give the impression that their county would be the foremost (banner) county in Nebraska.

Bannock   **Idaho**
Pocatello   1,112 sq. mi.

82,839	75,565	66,026	65,421	52,200	49,342	41,745

March 6, 1893. *Bannack Indians*. From Shoshone words *bamp* meaning "hair," and *nack* meaning "backward;" describing Bannack practice of wearing hair pulled back in tufts.

Baraga   **Michigan**
L'Anse   898 sq. mi.

8,860	8,746	7,954	8,484	7,789	7,151	8,037

February 19, 1875. *Irenaeus Frederich Baraga (1791–1868)*. Austrian missionary; ordained priest 1823; arrived in US 1830; wrote Chippewa grammar 1850 and Chippewa dictionary 1853; consecrated bishop 1853; established schools in Ohio and Michigan for Chippewas and Ottawas 1830–68.

Barber   **Kansas**
Medicine Lodge   1,134 sq. mi.

4,861	5,307	5,874	6,548	7,016	8,713	8,521

February 26, 1867, as Barbour; organized July 7, 1873; spelling changed March 1, 1883. *Thomas W. Barber (?–1855)*. Free-state martyr murdered near Lawrence, Kansas, December 6, 1855.

Barbour   **Alabama**
Clayton   885 sq. mi.

27,457	29,038	25,417	24,756	22,543	24,700	28,892

December 18, 1832. *James Barbour (1775–1842)*. Virginia House of Delegates 1796–1812, Speaker 1809–12; governor of Virginia 1812–14; US senator 1815–25; US secretary of war 1825–28; US minister to England 1828–29; strong pro-slavery stand was popular throughout South.

Barbour   **West Virginia**
Philippi   341 sq. mi.

16,589	15,557	15,699	16,639	14,030	15,474	19,745

March 3, 1843. *Philip Pendleton Barbour (1783–1841)*. Virginia House of Delegates 1812–14; US representative 1814–24 and 1827–30, Speaker 1821–22; Virginia general court judge 1826–27; US circuit judge 1830–36; US Supreme Court justice 1836–41.

Barnes **North Dakota**
Valley City 1,492 sq. mi.
11,066 11,775 12,545 13,960 14,669 16,719 16,884
January 4, 1873, as Burbank; name changed January 14, 1875; organized January 6, 1879. *Alanson H. Barnes (1818–90).* Justice of Dakota Territory Supreme Court 1873–81.

Barnstable **Massachusetts**
Barnstable 394 sq. mi.
215,888 222,230 186,605 147,925 96,656 70,286 46,805
June 2, 1685. *Town of Barnstable.* Named with variant spelling for Barnstaple, Devonshire, England.

Barnwell **South Carolina**
Barnwell 548 sq. mi.
22,621 23,478 20,293 19,868 17,176 17,659 17,266
March 12, 1785, as Winton; deorganized 1791; reorganized as judicial district and name changed January 1, 1800; redesignated as county April 16, 1868. *Uncertain.* (1) *John Barnwell (?–?)*; provisional congress 1775–76; general in South Carolina Militia; elected to US Congress but declined to serve 1795. (2) *Robert Barnwell (1761–1814)*; lieutenant in Revolutionary War; captured by British 1780; released 1781; US representative 1791–93. (3) *Village of Barnwell*; named for John Barnwell (c1671–1724); immigrated to Carolina from Ireland 1701; active in colonial government.

Barren **Kentucky**
Glasgow 488 sq. mi.
42,173 38,033 34,001 34,009 28,677 28,303 28,461
December 20, 1798. *Descriptive.* Refers to "Kentucky barrens," a treeless prairie amidst forests.

Barron **Wisconsin**
Barron 863 sq. mi.
45,870 44,963 40,750 38,730 33,955 34,270 34,703
March 19, 1859, as Dallas; name changed March 4, 1869. *Henry D. Barron (1833–82).* Waukesha postmaster 1853–57; Wisconsin legislature, Speaker 1866 and 1873; declined appointment as chief justice of Dakota Territory Supreme Court 1869; judge of circuit court 1876–82.

Barrow **Georgia**
Winder 160 sq. mi.
69,367 46,144 29,721 21,354 16,859 14,485 13,115
July 7, 1914. *Dr. David Crenshaw Barrow (1852–1929).* Adjunct professor of mathematics, University of Georgia 1878 and 1899; professor of engineering 1883; chancellor of University of Georgia 1907–25.

Barry **Michigan**
Hastings 553 sq. mi.
59,173 56,755 50,057 45,781 36,166 31,738 26,183
October 29, 1829; organized March 5, 1839. *William Taylor Barry (1784–1835).* Kentucky House of Representatives 1807 and 1814; US representative 1810–11; aide de camp to General Shelby during War of 1812; Battle of the Thames 1813; US senator 1814–16; Kentucky Senate 1817–21; Kentucky secretary of state 1824; US postmaster general 1829–35; appointed envoy extraordinary and minister plenipotentiary to Spain but died en route 1835. Michigan Territory named seven counties after members of Jackson's first cabinet in hopes of promoting statehood.

Barry **Missouri**
Cassville 778 sq. mi.
35,597 34,010 27,547 24,408 19,597 18,921 21,755
January 5, 1835. *Uncertain.* (1) *William Taylor Barry.** (2) *John Barry (?–1803)*; merchant seaman; captain, Continental Navy; captured British tender *Essex*, first British ship captured by a commissioned American ship 1776.

Bartholomew   **Indiana**
Columbus   407 sq. mi.

76,794	71,435	63,657	65,088	57,022	48,198	36,108

January 8, 1821; effective February 12, 1821. *Joseph Bartholomew (1766–1840)*. Revolutionary War; served with General Wayne in Northwest Territory 1792; lieutenant colonel Indiana Militia; wounded at Battle of Tippecanoe 1811; major general War of 1812; Indiana legislature 1819.

Barton   **Kansas**
Great Bend   895 sq. mi.

27,674	28,205	29,382	31,343	30,663	32,368	29,909

February 26, 1867; organized May 16, 1872. *Clara H. Barton (1821–1912)*. Volunteer nurse in Civil War; called "Angel of the Battlefield;" Superintendent of Nurses for the Army of the James 1864; organizer of American Red Cross 1881; urged US ratification of Geneva Convention 1882.

Barton   **Missouri**
Lamar   592 sq. mi.

12,402	12,541	11,312	11,292	10,431	11,113	12,678

December 12, 1855. *David Barton (1783–1837)*. Attorney general of Missouri 1813; Howard County circuit judge 1815–16; territorial legislature 1818; president of Missouri Constitutional Convention 1820; US senator 1821–31; Missouri Senate 1834; Boonville circuit judge 1835.

Bartow   **Georgia**
Carterville   460 sq. mi.

100,157	76,019	55,911	40,760	32,663	28,267	27,230

December 3, 1832, as Cass; name changed December 6, 1861. *Francis S. Bartow (1816–61)*. Georgia legislature; Confederate Congress; Confederate brigadier general; killed at Manassas Plains July 21, 1861.

Bastrop   **Texas**
Bastrop   888 sq. mi.

74,171	57,733	38,263	24,726	17,297	16,925	19,622

March 17, 1836, as Mina; name changed December 18, 1837. *Felipe Enrique Neri, Baron of Bastrop (1759–1827)*. Founded unsuccessful German colony in Spanish Louisiana 1795; assisted Moses and Stephen Austin in establishing Anglo-American colony in Spanish Texas 1820.

Bates   **Missouri**
Butler   837 sq. mi.

17,049	16,653	15,025	15,873	15,468	15,905	17,534

January 29, 1841. *Uncertain*. One of two brothers. (1) *Edward Bates (1793–1869)*; War of 1812; Missouri Constitution Convention 1820; Missouri legislature 1822; US representative 1827–29; US attorney general 1861–64. (2) *Frederick Bates (1777–1825)*; judge of Michigan Territory 1805; secretary of Louisiana Territory 1806; Missouri territorial governor 1809–10; governor of Missouri 1824–25.

Bath   **Kentucky**
Owingsville   279 sq. mi.

11,591	11,085	9,692	10,025	9,235	9,114	10,410

January 15, 1811. *Descriptive*. Refers to local medicinal bathing springs.

Bath   **Virginia**
Warm Springs   529 sq. mi.

4,731	5,048	4,799	5,860	5,192	5,335	6,296

December 14, 1790. *Descriptive*. Refers to local sulfur bathing springs.

Baxter   **Arkansas**
Mountain Home   554 sq. mi.

41,513   38,386   31,186   27,409   15,319   9,943   11,683

March 24, 1873. *Elisha Baxter (1827–99)*. Arkansas legislature 1854–55; raised mounted infantry for Union Army 1861; chief justice of Arkansas 1864; circuit judge 1868–72; governor of Arkansas 1872–74.

Bay   **Florida**
Panama City   758 sq. mi.
168,852   148,217   126,994   97,740   75,283   67,131   42,689

April 24, 1913. *Saint Andrew's Bay*. Bay on Gulf of Mexico. Named by Spanish explorers.

Bay   **Michigan**
Saginaw   442 sq. mi.
107,771   110,157   111,723   119,881   117,339   107,042   88,461

April 20, 1857. *Saginaw Bay*. Bay on Lake Huron; from Ojibwa *saging* meaning "at the mouth."

Bayfield   **Wisconsin**
Washburn   1,478 sq. mi.
15,014   15,013   14,008   13,822   11,683   11,910   13,760

February 19, 1845, as La Pointe; name changed April 12, 1866. *Town of Bayfield*. Named for Henry W. Bayfield (1795–1885); admiral, British Royal Navy; surveyed Lakes Superior, Erie, and Huron 1822–23.

Baylor   **Texas**
Seymour   867 sq. mi.
3,726   4,093   4,385   4,919   5,221   5,893   6,875

February 1, 1858; organized April 12, 1879. *Henry Weidner Baylor (1818–54)*. Comanche Campaign 1840; surgeon, 1st Regiment of Texas Mounted Riflemen during Mexican War.

Beadle   **South Dakota**
Huron   1,259 sq. mi.
17,398   17,023   18,253   19,195   20,877   21,682   21,082

February 22, 1879; organized July 9, 1880. *William Henry Harrison Beadle (1838–1915)*. From private to captain with Indiana Volunteer Infantry during Civil War; lieutenant colonel, Michigan Sharpshooters; brevet colonel of volunteers; government surveyor 1869–99; territorial legislature 1877; private secretary to Dakota territorial governor 1878; superintendent of public instruction 1879–86; president of South Dakota State normal school 1899–1905; professor emeritus of history 1905–11.

Bear Lake   **Idaho**
Paris   975 sq. mi.
5,986   6,411   6,084   6,931   5,801   7,148   6,834

January 5, 1875. *Bear Lake*. Named "Black Bear Lake" by Donald McKenzie for numerous bears in the area 1818.

Beaufort   **North Carolina**
Washington   827 sq. mi.
47,759   44,958   42,283   40,355   35,980   36,014   37,134

December 3, 1705, as Pamptecough; name changed 1712. *Henry Somerset, 2nd Duke of Beaufort (1684–1714)*. One of several lords proprietor of Carolina; inherited proprietorship from his mother, Lady Rebecca Granville.

Beaufort   **South Carolina**
Beaufort   576 sq. mi.
162,233   120,937   86,425   65,364   51,136   44,187   26,993

1769 as a judicial district; designated as county April 16, 1868. *Town of Beaufort*. Named for Henry Somerset, 2nd Duke of Beaufort.*

Beauregard   **Louisiana**
DeRidder   1,157 sq. mi.
36,654   32,986   30,083   29,692   22,888   19,191   17,766

June 12, 1912. *Pierre Gustave Toutant Beauregard (1818–93)*. Graduated West Point 1838; Army engineering department 1840–45; wounded twice during Mexican War 1846; superintendent of West Point, resigned to join Confederate Army 1861; directed bombardment of Fort Sumter April 12, 1861; Battle of Bull Run 1861; promoted to general 1862; president of New Orleans, Jackson, & Mississippi Railroad Company; adjutant general of Louisiana; manager of Louisiana Lottery.

Beaver **Oklahoma**
Beaver 1,815 sq. mi.

5,636	5,857	6,023	6,806	6,282	6,965	7,411

May 2, 1890, as County 7; name changed July 16, 1907. *Beaver River*. Descriptive of numerous beaver dams in the area.

Beaver **Pennsylvania**
Beaver 435 sq. mi.

170,539	181,412	186,093	204,441	208,418	206,948	175,192

March 12, 1800. *Beaver River*. Descriptive of numerous beaver dams in the area.

Beaver **Utah**
Beaver 2,590 sq. mi.

6,629	6,005	4,765	4,378	3,800	4,331	4,856

January 5, 1856. *Beaver River*. Descriptive of numerous beaver dams in the area.

Beaverhead **Montana**
Dillon 5,542 sq. mi.

9,246	9,202	8,424	8,186	8,187	7,194	6,671

February 2, 1865. *Beaverhead River*. Descriptive of a rock in the river resembling the head of a beaver.

Becker **Minnesota**
Detroit Lakes 1,315 sq. mi.

32,504	30,000	27,881	29,336	24,372	23,959	24,836

March 18, 1858; organized March 1, 1871. *George Loomis Becker (1829–1904)*. Brigadier general 1858; mayor of St. Paul 1856; land commissioner of St. Paul & Pacific Railroad Company; Minnesota legislature 1868–71; Minnesota Railroad and Warehouse Commission 1885–1901.

Beckham **Oklahoma**
Sayre 902 sq. mi.

22,119	19,799	18,812	19,243	15,754	17,782	21,627

July 16, 1907. *John Crepps Wickliffe Beckham (1869–1940)*. Kentucky House of Representatives 1899; governor of Kentucky 1900–07; US senator 1815–21. Name was suggested by a member of the Oklahoma Constitutional Convention from Kentucky.

Bedford **Pennsylvania**
Bedford 1,012 sq. mi.

49,762	49,984	47,919	46,784	42,353	42,451	40,775

March 9, 1771. *Uncertain*. (1) *Town of Bedford*. (2) *Fort Bedford*. Both town and fort are named for John Russell II, Duke of Bedford (see Bedford County, Virginia).

Bedford **Tennessee**
Shelbyville 474 sq. mi.

45,058	37,586	30,411	27,916	25,039	23,150	23,627

December 3, 1807. *Thomas Bedford (1758–1804)*. Captain in Continental Army; Virginia House of Delegates 1788; moved to Tennessee 1795.

Bedford **Virginia**
Bedford 753 sq. mi.

68,676	60,371	45,656	34,927	26,728	31,028	29,627

December 13, 1753. *John Russell II, Duke of Bedford (1710–71)*. First lord of the admiralty 1744; privy councilor 1744; major general 1755; lord lieutenant of Ireland 1755–61; chancellor of University of Dublin 1765. (Associated independent city: Bedford.)

Bedford	**Virginia**					
(Independent City)	7 sq. mi.					
6,222	6,299	6,073	5,991	6,011	(a)	(a)

August 30, 1968. *John Russell II, Duke of Bedford.** [(a) Included in Bedford County] (Associated county: Bedford) [Bedford City Council voted to return to Bedford County September 14, 2011; transition to occur in July 2013.]

Bee	**Texas**					
Beeville	880 sq. mi.					
31,861	32,359	25,135	26,030	22,737	23,755	18,174

December 8, 1857. *Bernard E. Bee, Sr. (1787–1853)*. Texas Army; secretary of treasury in Texas ad interim government 1836; Republic of Texas secretary of war 1836–38; Texas minister to US 1838–41; opposed US annexation of Texas.

Belknap	**New Hampshire**					
Laconia	400 sq. mi.					
60,088	56,325	49,216	42,884	32,267	28,912	26,632

December 22, 1840. *Jeremy Belknap (1744–98)*. Congregational pastor, Dover, New Hampshire; Federal Street Church, Boston 1787–98; founded Massachusetts Historical Society 1792; wrote 3–volume *History of New Hampshire*, published 1784 and 1792.

Bell	**Kentucky**					
Pineville	359 sq. mi.					
28,691	30,060	31,506	34,330	31,087	35,336	47,602

February 28, 1867, as Josh Bell; name changed 1873. *Joshua Fry Bell (1811–70)*. US representative 1845–47; Kentucky secretary of state 1849; Kentucky House of Representatives 1862–67; declined Union Democrat nomination for governor 1863.

Bell	**Texas**					
Belton	1,051 sq. mi.					
310,235	237,974	191,088	157,889	124,483	94,097	73,824

January 22, 1850; organized August 1, 1850. *Peter Hansborough Bell (1812–98)*. Battle of San Jacinto 1836; Texas assistant adjutant general 1837; Texas inspector general 1839; captain to colonel in Mexican War 1845–49; governor of Texas 1849–53; US representative 1853–57; moved to new wife's home in North Carolina 1857; declined rank of colonel in North Carolina Regiment 1861.

Belmont	**Ohio**					
Saint Clairsville	532 sq. mi.					
70,400	70,226	71,074	82,569	80,917	83,864	87,740

September 7, 1801. *Descriptive*. French combination of poetic contractions *bel* meaning "beautiful" and *mont* meaning "mountain" or "hills."

Beltrami	**Minnesota**					
Bemidji	2,505 sq. mi.					
44,442	39,650	34,384	30,982	26,373	23,425	24,962

February 28, 1866; organized April 6, 1897. *Giacomo Constantino Beltrami (1779–1855)*. Exiled from Italy and migrated to US 1821; explored Mississippi River and incorrectly believed he found its source.

Benewah	**Idaho**					
Saint Maries	777 sq. mi.					
9,285	9,171	7,937	8,292	6,230	6,036	6,173

January 25, 1915. *Benewah (?–?)*. Coeur d'Alene chief.

Ben Hill　　　　　　**Georgia**
Fitzgerald　　　　　　250 sq. mi.

17,634	17,484	16,245	16,000	13,171	13,633	14,879

July 31, 1906. *Benjamin Harvey Hill (1823–82)*. Georgia House of Representatives 1851; Georgia Senate 1859–60; delegate to Confederate Provisional Congress 1861; Confederate senator 1861–65; US representative 1875–77; US senator 1877–82.

Bennett　　　　　　**South Dakota**
Martin　　　　　　1,185 sq. mi.

3,431	3,574	3,206	3,044	3,088	3,053	3,396

March 9, 1909; organized April 27, 1912. *Granville G. Bennett (1833–1910)*. Union Army 1861–65; Iowa legislature 1865–71; associate judge, Dakota Territory Supreme Court 1875–78; territorial delegate to Congress 1879–81; practiced law in Yankton and Deadwood.

Bennington　　　　　　**Vermont**
Bennington　　　　　　675 sq. mi.

37,125	36,994	35,845	33,345	29,282	25,088	24,115

1779. *Town of Bennington*. Named for Benning Wentworth (1696–1770); royal governor of New Hampshire 1741–66; granted land for town of Bennington 1749; donated 500 acres to Dartmouth College 1768.

Benson　　　　　　**North Dakota**
Minnewaukan　　　　　　1,389 sq. mi.

6,660	6,694	7,198	7,944	8,245	9,435	10,675

March 9, 1883; organized June 4, 1884. *Bertil W. Benson (?–c1907)*. Land agent for Northern Pacific Railroad; Dakota territorial legislature at time of county's creation 1883–84.

Bent　　　　　　**Colorado**
Las Animas　　　　　　1,513 sq. mi.

6,499	5,998	5,048	5,945	6,493	7,419	8,775

February 11, 1870. *Bents Fort*. The four Bent brothers were involved in trapping and trading and built three forts in Colorado; the last and biggest was on the Arkansas River 1853: Charles (1799–1847), William (1809–69), George (1814–47) and Robert (1816–41). William was the most responsible for the forts.

Benton　　　　　　**Arkansas**
Bentonville　　　　　　847 sq. mi.

221,339	156,406	97,499	78,115	50,476	36,272	38,076

September 30, 1830. *Thomas Hart Benton (1782–1858)*. Tennessee Senate 1809–11; colonel, Tennessee volunteers 1812–13; colonel US infantry 1813–15; US senator from Missouri 1821–51; advocate of westward expansion and Manifest Destiny.

Benton　　　　　　**Indiana**
Fowler　　　　　　406 sq. mi.

8,854	9,421	9,441	10,218	11,262	11,912	11,462

February 18, 1840. *Thomas Hart Benton.**

Benton　　　　　　**Iowa**
Vinton　　　　　　716 sq. mi.

26,076	25,308	22,429	23,649	22,885	23,422	22,656

December 21, 1837; organized January 17, 1845. *Thomas Hart Benton.**

Benton　　　　　　**Minnesota**
Foley　　　　　　408 sq. mi.

38,451	34,226	30,185	25,187	20,841	17,287	15,911

October 27, 1849; effective March 31, 1851. *Thomas Hart Benton.**

Benton　　　　　　**Mississippi**
Ashland　　　　　　407 sq. mi.

8,729   8,026   8,046   8,153   7,505   7,723   8,793

July 21, 1870. *Samuel Benton (1820–64)*. Mississippi legislature; Mississippi Secession Convention 1861; rose from captain to colonel in Confederate Army 1861–64; died from wounds in Battle of Atlanta July 22, 1864.

Benton   **Missouri**
Warsaw   704 sq. mi.
19,056   17,180   13,859   12,183   9,695   8,737   9,080
January 3, 1835. *Thomas Hart Benton.**

Benton   **Oregon**
Corvallis   676 sq. mi.
85,579   78,153   70,811   68,211   53,776   39,165   31,570
December 23, 1847. *Thomas Hart Benton.**

Benton   **Tennessee**
Camden   394 sq. mi.
16,489   16,537   14,524   14,901   12,126   10,662   11,495
December 19, 1835; effective January 1, 1836. *David Benton (1779–1860)*. War of 1812; active in creation of Benton County. Originally named for Thomas Hart Benton* who became unpopular in Tennessee for his moderate position on slavery and abolition. On January 26, 1852, the Tennessee legislature retained the name of Benton for the county but changed the honoree to David Benton, a local veteran of the War of 1812.

Benton   **Washington**
Prosser   1,700 sq. mi.
175,177   142,475   112,560   109,444   67,540   62,070   51,370
March 8, 1905. *Thomas Hart Benton.**

Benzie   **Michigan**
Beulah   320 sq. mi.
17,525   15,998   12,200   11,205   8,593   7,834   8,306
February 27, 1863; organized March 30, 1869. *Uncertain.* (1) *Betsie River* from French *bec scies* referring to the saw-bill ducks in the area. (2) *Village of Benzonia*; disputed origin: either Hebrew or Greek-Latin meaning "sons of light," or "life," or "toil," or "Zion." (3) Coined word from "Benzonia" and "Betsie."

Bergen   **New Jersey**
Hackensack   233 sq. mi.
905,116   884,118   825,380   845,385   898,012   780,255   539,139
March 7, 1683. *Village of Bergen.* Named for city of Bergen-op-zoom, Holland, origin of early settlers.

Berkeley   **South Carolina**
Moncks Corner   1,099 sq. mi.
177,843   142,651   128,776   94,727   56,199   38,196   30,251
January 31, 1882. *Proprietary county of Berkeley (1682–1798)*. Named for one of two brothers both of whom were among eight original lords proprietor of Carolina. (1) John Berkeley (1607–78); special ambassador to Sweden; member of Parliament; lord lieutenant of Ireland; proprietor of New Jersey. (2) William Berkeley (1606–77); royal governor of Virginia 1641–52 and 1660–77; put down Bacon's Rebellion 1676.

Berkeley   **West Virginia**
Martinsburg   321 sq. mi.
104,169   75,905   59,253   46,775   36,356   33,791   30,359
March 24, 1772. *Norborne Berkeley, Lord Botetourt (1718–70)*. Member of Parliament 1741–63; admitted to peerage 1764; colonial governor of Virginia 1768–70; favored colonists cause but dissolved colonial legislature 1769.

Berks   **Pennsylvania**
Reading   857 sq. mi.

411,422   373,638   336,523   312,509   286,382   275,414   255,740
March 11, 1752. *Berkshire, England.* Origin of early settlers.

Berkshire   **Massachusetts**
Pittsfield   927 sq. mi.
131,219   134,953   139,352   145,110   149,402   142,135   132,966
April 24, 1761. *Berkshire County, England.* Origin of early settlers.

Bernalillo   **New Mexico**
Albuquerque   1,161 sq. mi.
662,564   556,678   480,577   419,700   315,774   262,199   145,673
January 9, 1852. *Town of Bernalillo.* Named for any one of six members of the Gonzales-Bernal family that settled in New Mexico in the 17th Century; *illo* is a Spanish diminutive suffix that may have been applied to a "junior" member of the Bernal family.

Berrien   **Georgia**
Nashville   452 sq. mi.
19,286   16,235   14,153   13,525   11,556   12,038   13,966
February 25, 1856. *John McPherson Berrien (1781–1856).* Solicitor general for Eastern Circuit of Georgia 1809; judge, Eastern Judicial Circuit 1810–21; colonel of cavalry 1810; Georgia Senate 1822–23; US senator 1825–29 and 1841–52; US attorney general 1829–31.

Berrien   **Michigan**
Saint Joseph   568 sq. mi.
156,813   162,453   161,378   171,276   163,875   149,865   115,702
October 29, 1829; organized September 1, 1831. *John McPherson Berrien.** Michigan Territory named seven counties after members of Jackson's first cabinet in hopes of promoting statehood.

Bertie   **North Carolina**
Windsor   699 sq. mi.
21,182   19,773   20,388   21,024   20,528   24,350   26,439
August 2, 1722. *Uncertain.* Either *James Bertie (1673–1735)* or his brother *Henry Bertie (1675–1735)*; both were lords proprietor of Carolina.

Bethel   **Alaska**
(Census Area)   40,570 sq. mi.
17,013   16,006   13,656   10,999   9,885[a]   7,838[a]   (b)
Bethel Mission. Hebrew "house of God" (Genesis 35:1); name of Moravian church mission 1884. [(a) Includes Kuskokwin Census Division; (b) part of 4th Judicial District.]

Bexar   **Texas**
San Antonio   1,240 sq. mi.
1,714,773   1,392,931   1,185,394   988,800   830,460   687,151   500,460
March 17, 1836. *Presidio, village or municipality of San Antonio de Bexar.* Named for Baltazar Manuel de Zuñiga (1658–1727); second son of the Duke of Bexar; viceroy of New Spain (Mexico) 1716–22 when presidio was founded 1718.

Bibb   **Alabama**
Centreville   623 sq. mi.
22,915   20,826   16,576   15,723   13,812   14,357   17,987
February 7, 1818, as Cahawba; name changed December 2, 1820. *William Wyatt Bibb (1781–1820).* Physician; Georgia House of Representatives 1803–05; US representative 1807–13; US senator 1813–16; governor of Alabama Territory 1817–19; 1st governor of Alabama 1819–20.

Bibb   **Georgia**
Macon   250 sq. mi.

| 155,547 | 153,887 | 149,967 | 150,256 | 143,418 | 141,249 | 114,079 |

December 9, 1822. *William Wyatt Bibb.**

Bienville   **Louisiana**
Arcadia   811 sq. mi.

| 14,353 | 15,752 | 15,979 | 16,387 | 16,024 | 16,726 | 19,105 |

March 14, 1848. *Jean Babtiste le Moyne, Sieur de Bienville (1680–1765).* Explored mouth of the Mississippi River with his brother 1699 (see Iberville, Louisiana); French governor of Louisiana intermittingly 1706–40; founded Mobile, 1702, and New Orleans, 1718; returned to France 1743.

Big Horn   **Montana**
Hardin   4,995 sq. mi.

| 12,865 | 12,671 | 11,337 | 11,096 | 10,057 | 10,007 | 9,824 |

January 13, 1913. *Descriptive.* Refers to big horn sheep in the area.

Big Horn   **Wyoming**
Basin   3,137 sq. mi.

| 11,668 | 11,461 | 10,525 | 11,896 | 10,202 | 11,898 | 13,176 |

March 12, 1890. *Uncertain.* (1) *Descriptive* of big horn sheep. (2) *Big Horn Mountains*; named for the sheep.

Big Stone   **Minnesota**
Ortonville   499 sq. mi.

| 5,269 | 5,820 | 6,285 | 7,716 | 7,941 | 8,954 | 9,607 |

February 20, 1862; organized February 8, 1881. *Big Stone Lake.* Translation of Dakota word referring to granite outcrops near the lake.

Billings   **North Dakota**
Medora   1,149 sq. mi.

| 783 | 888 | 1,108 | 1,138 | 1,198 | 1,513 | 1,777 |

February 10, 1879; organized May 4, 1886. *Frederick Billings (1823–90).* Original partner of Northern Pacific Railroad 1870; president of railroad 1879; resigned 1881.

Bingham   **Idaho**
Blackfoot   2,094 sq. mi.

| 45,607 | 41,735 | 37,583 | 36,489 | 29,167 | 28,218 | 23,271 |

January 13, 1885. *Henry Harrison Bingham (1841–1912).* From lieutenant to brigadier general 1862–65; Congressional Medal of Honor 1864; Philadelphia postmaster 1867–72; US representative from Pennsylvania 1879–1912; friend of Idaho Territorial Governor William Bunn.

Blackford   **Indiana**
Hartford City   165 sq. mi.

| 12,766 | 14,048 | 14,067 | 15,570 | 15,888 | 14,792 | 14,026 |

February 15, 1838; effective April 2, 1838; organized January 29, 1839. *Isaac Newton Blackford (1786–1859).* Clerk and recorder of Washington County 1813; clerk of Indiana territorial legislature 1814; district court judge 1814; Speaker, Indiana legislature 1816; Indiana Supreme Court judge 1817–52; US Court of Claims judge 1855–59.

Black Hawk   **Iowa**
Waterloo   566 sq. mi.

| 131,090 | 128,012 | 123,798 | 137,961 | 132,916 | 122,482 | 100,448 |

February 17, 1843; organized August 17, 1853. *Black Hawk (1767–1838).* Chief of Sauk-Fox alliance; warrior at age 17; sided with British in War of 1812; leader in Black Hawk War 1832; captured at Battle of Bad Axe 1832; toured eastern cities with other captured chiefs 1833.

Bladen   **North Carolina**
Elizabethtown   874 sq. mi.

35,190	32,278	28,663	30,491	26,477	28,881	29,703

November 11, 1734. *Martin Bladen (1680–1746)*. English colonel in Europe; comptroller of the mint 1714; member of Parliament 1715–46; supervised colonial affairs as commissioner of trade and plantations 1717–46.

Blaine **Idaho**
Hailey 2,644 sq. mi.

21,376	18,991	13,552	9,841	5,749	4,598	5,384

March 5, 1895. *James Gillespie Blaine (1830–93)*. Maine House of Representatives 1859–62, Speaker 1861–62; US representative 1863–76, Speaker 1869–71; US senator 1876–81; US secretary of state 1881 and 1889–92; Republican candidate for President 1884.

Blaine **Montana**
Chinook 4,228 sq. mi.

6,491	7,009	6,728	6,999	6,727	8,091	8,516

February 29, 1912. *James Gillespie Blaine.**

Blaine **Nebraska**
Brewster 711 sq. mi.

478	583	675	867	847	1,016	1,203

March 5, 1885; organized June 24, 1886. *James Gillespie Blaine.**

Blaine **Oklahoma**
Watonga 928 sq. mi.

11,943	11,976	11,470	13,443	11,794	12,077	15,049

April 19, 1892, as County "C"; name changed July 16, 1907. *James Gillespie Blaine.**

Blair **Pennsylvania**
Hollidaysburg 526 sq. mi.

127,089	129,144	130,542	136,621	135,356	137,270	139,154

February 26, 1846. *John Blair (?–1832)*. Pennsylvania legislature; supported building of canals and railroads.

Blanco **Texas**
Johnson City 709 sq. mi.

10,497	8,418	5,972	4,681	3,567	3,657	3,780

February 12, 1858. *Blanco River*. Spanish for "white"; named for white, chalky limestone in the region that colors the river.

Bland **Virginia**
Bland 358 sq. mi.

6,824	6,871	6,514	6,349	5,423	5,982	6,436

March 30, 1861. *Richard Bland (1710–76)*. Virginia House of Burgesses 1742–75; Continental Congress 1774–75; Virginia House of Delegates 1776.

Bleckley **Georgia**
Cochran 216 sq. mi.

13,063	11,666	10,430	10,767	10,291	9,642	9,218

July 30, 1912. *Logan Edwin Bleckley (1827–1907)*. Solicitor general of Atlanta 1852–56; Confederate Army private 1861; Georgia Supreme Court reporter 1864–67; associate justice Georgia Supreme Court 1875–87; chief justice of Georgia Supreme Court 1887–94.

Bledsoe **Tennessee**
Pikeville 406 sq. mi.

12,876	12,367	9,669	9,478	7,643	7,811	8,561

November 30, 1807. *Uncertain*. One or more members of pioneer Bledsoe family: (1) *Abraham Bledsoe (?–?)*; major Continental Army. (2) *Anthony Bledsoe (1733–88)*; father of Abraham. (3) *Isaac Bledsoe (1735–93)*; brother of Anthony. (4) *Thomas, Anthony, Jr., and/or Henry Bledsoe*; sons of Anthony and nephews of Isaac.

Blount   **Alabama**
Oneonta   645 sq. mi.
57,322   51,024   39,248   36,459   26,853   25,449   28,975
February 6, 1818. *Willie G. Blount (1768–1835)*. Tennessee legislature; governor of Tennessee 1809–15; sent aid to eastern Mississippi Territory (Alabama) during Creek wars.

Blount   **Tennessee**
Maryville   559 sq. mi.
123,010   105,823   85,969   77,770   63,744   57,525   54,691
July 11, 1795. *William Blount (1749–1800)*. North Carolina House of Commons 1780–89; Continental Congress intermittently 1782–87; federal Constitutional Convention 1787; North Carolina Senate 1788–90; only governor of Territory South of the Ohio (Tennessee) 1790–96; superintendent of Indian Affairs 1790–96; North Carolina Constitutional Convention 1796; US senator from Tennessee 1796–97, president.

Blue Earth   **Minnesota**
Mankato   748 sq. mi.
64,013   55,941   54,044   52,314   52,322   44,385   38,327
March 5, 1853. *Blue Earth River*. English translation of *mahkahto*, a Sisseton word describing the color of the river caused by deposits of blue-green clay.

Boise   **Idaho**
Idaho City   1,899 sq. mi.
7,028   6,670   3,509   2,999   1,763   1,646   1,776
February 4, 1864. *Boise River*. Descriptive from French *bois* meaning "woods."

Bolivar   **Mississippi**
Cleveland   877 sq. mi.
34,145   40,633   41,875   45,965   49,409   54,464   63,004
February 9, 1836. *Simón Bolívar y Ponte (1783–1830)*. Defeated Spain in South America, leading to independence for Bolivia, Colombia, Ecuador, Peru, and Venezuela; "The George Washington of South America."

Bollinger   **Missouri**
Marble Hill   618 sq. mi.
12,363   12,029   10,619   10,301   8,820   9,167   11,019
March 1, 1851. *George F. Bollinger (1770–1842)*. Early settler; led twenty families from North Carolina to Missouri 1799; Missouri senate president pro tempore 1828.

Bond   **Illinois**
Greenville   380 sq. mi.
17,768   17,633   14,991   16,224   14,012   14,060   14,157
January 4, 1817. *Shadrach Bond (1773–1832)*. Legislative counsel for Indiana Territory 1805–08; congressional delegate from Illinois Territory 1812–14; land office receiver of public moneys 1814–18; 1st governor of Illinois 1818–22; Kaskaskia land office registrar 1823–32.

Bon Homme   **South Dakota**
Tyndall   564 sq. mi
7,070   7,260   7,089   8,059   8,577   9,229   9,440
April 5, 1862. *Town of Bon Homme*. Named from an island in the Missouri River; from French phrase *bon homme Jacques* meaning "good man Jack" or "good fellow;" originally a derisive reference to peasants but became adopted as a source of pride.

Bonner   **Idaho**
Sandpoint   1,735 sq. mi.
40,877   36,835   26,622   24,163   15,560   15,587   14,853
February 21, 1907. *Edwin L. Bonner (?–?)*. Established a ferry across the Kootenai River 1864.

Bonneville   **Idaho**
Idaho Falls   1,866 sq. mi.

104,234	82,522	72,207	65,980	51,250	46,906	30,210

February 7, 1911. *Benjamin Louis Eulalie de Bonneville (1796–1878)*. Graduated West Point 1815; captain of infantry 1825; explored California and Rocky Mountains on military leave of absence 1831–36; major to colonel 1845–55; retired as brevet brigadier general 1865.

Boone   **Arkansas**
Harrison   590 sq. mi.

36,903	33,948	28,297	26,067	19,073	16,116	16,260

April 9, 1869. *Daniel Boone (1734–1820)*. Explorer; member of American militia under British General Braddock during French and Indian War 1755; developed Wilderness Road to Kentucky 1775.

Boone   **Illinois**
Belvidere   281 sq. mi.

54,165	41,786	30,806	28,630	25,440	20,326	17,070

March 4, 1837. *Daniel Boone.**

Boone   **Indiana**
Lebanon   423 sq. mi.

56,640	46,107	38,147	36,446	30,870	27,543	23,993

January 29, 1830; effective April 1, 1830. *Daniel Boone.**

Boone   **Iowa**
Boone   572 sq. mi.

26,306	26,224	25,186	26,184	26,470	28,037	28,139

January 13, 1846; organized October 1, 1849. *Nathan Boone (1780–?)*. Youngest son of Daniel Boone*; captain Missouri Militia 1808; major 1815; Missouri Constitutional Convention 1820; captain Black Hawk War 1832; lieutenant colonel 1835.

Boone   **Kentucky**
Burlington   246 sq. mi.

118,811	85,991	57,589	45,842	32,812	21,940	13,015

December 13, 1798; effective June 1, 1799. *Daniel Boone.**

Boone   **Missouri**
Columbia   685 sq. mi.

162,642	135,454	112,379	100,376	80,911	55,202	48,432

November 16, 1820; effective January 1, 1821. *Daniel Boone.**

Boone   **Nebraska**
Albion   687 sq. mi.

5,505	6,259	6,667	7,391	8,190	9,134	10,721

March 1, 1871. *Daniel Boone.**

Boone   **West Virginia**
Madison   502 sq. mi.

24,629	25,535	25,870	30,447	25,118	28,764	33,173

March 11, 1847. *Daniel Boone.**

Borden   **Texas**
Gail   897 sq. mi.

641	729	799	859	888	1,076	1,106

August 21, 1876; organized March 17, 1891. *Gail Borden, Jr. (1801–74)*. Surveyor of Stephen Austin's colony 1830; newspaper publisher of *Telegraph* and *Texas Register* 1835; collector for Port of Galveston; received patent for invention of condensed milk 1856.

Bosque **Texas**
Meridian 983 sq. mi.
18,212 17,204 15,125 13,401 10,966 10,809 11,836
February 4, 1854; organized August 7, 1854. *Bosque River*. Spanish word meaning "forest" or "woodland"; descriptive of thick vegetation along the river.

Bossier **Louisiana**
Benton 840 sq. mi.
116,979 98,310 86,088 80,721 64,519 57,622 40,139
February 24, 1843. *Pierre Evariste John Baptiste Bossier (1797–1844)*. Louisiana Senate 1833–43; US representative 1843–44.

Botetourt **Virginia**
Fincastle 541 sq. mi.
33,148 30,496 24,992 23,270 18,193 16,715 15,766
November 28, 1769. *Norborne Berkeley, Lord Botetourt*. (See Berkeley, West Virginia.)

Bottineau **North Dakota**
Bottineau 1,668 sq. mi.
6,429 7,149 8,011 9,239 9,496 11,315 12,140
January 4, 1873; organized July 17, 1884. *Pierre Bottineau (?–1895)*. French-Canadian scout, guide, translator, and fur trader; assisted US Army against Sioux 1863; guided railroad survey party 1869.

Boulder **Colorado**
Boulder 726 sq. mi.
294,567 291,288 225,339 189,625 131,889 74,254 48,296
November 1, 1861. *Town of Boulder*. Named for Boulder Creek; descriptive of large rocks in the area.

Boundary **Idaho**
Bonners Ferry 1,269 sq. mi.
10,972 9,871 8,332 7,289 6,371 5,809 5,908
January 23, 1915. *International boundary*. Descriptive of being the only Idaho county bordering on Canada.

Bourbon **Kansas**
Fort Scott 635 sq. mi.
15,173 15,379 14,966 15,969 15,215 16,090 19,153
August 25, 1855. *Bourbon County, Kentucky*. Name suggested by Samuel A. Williams, a member of the Kansas territorial legislature from Kentucky.

Bourbon **Kentucky**
Paris 290 sq. mi.
19,985 19,360 19,236 19,405 18,476 18,178 17,752
December 29, 1785; effective May 1, 1786. *French royal family*. Ruled France from 1589 (Henry IV) to 1792 (Louis XV); county's name celebrated French support during American Revolution.

Bowie **Texas**
New Boston 885 sq. mi.
92,565 89,306 81,665 75,301 67,813 59,971 61,966
December 17, 1840; organized 1846. *James Bowie (1795–1836)*. Colonel of Texas volunteers; Battle of Concepción 1835; killed at the Alamo, March 6, 1836; developed Bowie knife.

Bowman **North Dakota**
Bowman 1,162 sq. mi.
3,151 3,242 3,596 4,229 3,901 4,154 4,001
March 8, 1883; abolished November 30, 1896; recreated May 24, 1901; organized July 5, 1907. *Edward M. Bowman (?–?)*. Dakota Territorial legislature at time of county's creation 1883.

Box Butte **Nebraska**
Alliance 1,075 sq. mi.
11,308 12,158 13,130 13,696 10,094 11,688 12,279
November 2, 1886; organized April 23, 1887. *Box Butte*. Natural landmark shaped like a box; French *butte* means "mound" or "isolated elevation."

Box Elder **Utah**
Brigham City 5,746 sq. mi.
49,975 42,745 36,485 33,222 28,129 25,061 19,734
January 5, 1856. *Box elder trees*. Prevalent in settled parts of the county.

Boyd **Kentucky**
Catlettsburg 160 sq. mi.
49,542 49,752 51,150 55,513 52,376 52,163 49,949
April 25, 1860. *Linn Boyd (1800–59)*. Kentucky legislature 1827–30; US representative 1835–37 and 1839–55, Speaker 1852–55; elected lieutenant governor but was too ill to serve 1859.

Boyd **Nebraska**
Butte 540 sq. mi.
2,099 2,438 2,835 3,331 3,752 4,513 4,911
March 20, 1891; organized August 29, 1891. *James E. Boyd (1834–1906)*. Nebraska legislature 1866, president, Omaha Board of Trade 1868–69; Nebraska Constitutional Convention 1871 and 1875; mayor of Omaha 1881–82 and 1885–87; governor of Nebraska 1891, removed because of contested citizenship 1892, declared citizen and resumed governorship 1892–93.

Boyle **Kentucky**
Danville 180 sq. mi.
28,432 27,697 25,641 25,066 21,090 21,257 20,352
February 15, 1842. *John Boyle (1774–1834)*. Kentucky legislature 1800; US representative 1803–09; declined appointment to governorship of Illinois Territory 1809; judge, Kentucky court of appeals 1809–26, chief justice 1810–26; US judge for District of Kentucky 1826–34.

Bracken **Kentucky**
Brooksville 206 sq. mi.
8,488 8,279 7,766 7,738 7,227 7,422 8,424
June 1, 1796. *Uncertain*. (1) *William Bracken (?–?)*; Member of survey parties of Kentucky River and Falls of the Ohio; early settler in Kentucky. (2) *Big and Little Bracken Creeks*; named for William Bracken.

Bradford **Florida**
Starke 294 sq. mi.
28,520 20,088 22,515 20,023 14,625 12,446 11,457
December 21, 1858, as New River; name changed December 6, 1861. *Richard Bradford (c1839–61)*. First Confederate officer from Florida killed in Civil War, Battle of Santa Rosa Island, October 9, 1861.

Bradford **Pennsylvania**
Towanda 1,147 sq. mi.
62,622 62,761 60,967 62,919 57,962 54,925 51,722
February 21, 1810, as Ontario; name changed March 24, 1812. *William Bradford (1755–95)*. Revolutionary War private to colonel 1776–77; resigned 1779; Pennsylvania attorney general 1780–91; associate justice Pennsylvania Supreme Court 1791; US attorney general 1794–95.

Bradley **Arkansas**
Warren 649 sq. mi.
11,508 12,600 11,793 13,803 12,778 14,029 15,987
December 18, 1840. *Hugh Bradley (?–?)*. Captain under Andrew Jackson at Battle of New Orleans; Arkansas territorial legislature.

Bradley   **Tennessee**
Cleveland   329 sq. mi.
98,963   87,965   73,712   67,547   50,686   38,324   32,338
February 10, 1836. *Edward Bradley (?–1829)*. Lieutenant colonel, 1st Regiment, Tennessee Volunteers 1812–15; wounded during Creek War 1813; Tennessee legislature 1813–15.

Branch   **Michigan**
Coldwater   506 sq. mi.
45,248   45,787   41,502   40,188   37,906   34,903   30,202
October 29, 1829; organized March 1, 1833. *John Branch (1782–1863)*. North Carolina Senate 1811–17 and 1822, Speaker 1815–17; governor of North Carolina 1817–20; US senator 1823–29; secretary of the Navy 1829–31; US representative 1831–33; governor of Florida Territory 1844–45. Michigan Territory named seven counties after members of Jackson's first cabinet in hopes of promoting statehood.

Brantley   **Georgia**
Nahunta   442 sq. mi.
18,411   14,629   11,077   8,701   5,940   5,891   6,387
August 14, 1920. *Uncertain.* (1) *Benjamin D. Brantley (1832–91)*; Confederate army 1861–65; Georgia house of representatives 1873; Pierce County treasurer 1876–94. (2) *William G. Brantley (1860–1934)*; son of Benjamin; Georgia House of Representatives 1884–85; Georgia Senate 1886–87; US representative 1897–1913.

Braxton   **West Virginia**
Sutton   511 sq. mi.
14,523   14,702   12,998   13,894   12,666   15,152   18,082
January 15, 1836. *Carter Braxton (1736–97)*. Virginia House of Burgesses 1761–71 and 1775; Continental Congress intermittently 1775–85; signer of Declaration of Independence 1776; Virginia Council of State 1786–91 and 1794–97.

Brazoria   **Texas**
Angleton   1,358 sq. mi.
313,166   241,767   191,707   169,587   108,312   76,204   46,549
March 17, 1836. *Brazos River.* Spanish *Rio de los Brazos de Dios* (Arms of God River); longest river in Texas.

Brazos   **Texas**
Bryan   585 sq. mi.
194,851   152,415   121,862   93,588   57,978   44,985   38,390
January 30, 1841, as Navasota; name change January 28, 1842. *Brazos River.**

Breathitt   **Kentucky**
Jackson   492 sq. mi.
13,878   16,100   15,703   17,004   14,221   15,490   19,964
February 8, 1839. *John Breathitt (1786–1834)*. Kentucky legislature 1811; lieutenant governor 1828–32; governor of Kentucky 1832–34.

Breckinridge   **Kentucky**
Hardinsburg   567 sq. mi.
20,059   18,648   16,312   16,861   14,789   14,734   15,528
December 9, 1799. *John Breckinridge (1760–1806)*. Elected to Virginia house of Burgesses but denied seat because of age (19) 1780; Virginia Militia during Revolutionary War; Kentucky attorney general 1795–97; Kentucky House of Representatives 1798–1800, Speaker 1799–1800; US senator 1801–05; US attorney general 1805–06.

Bremer   **Iowa**
Waverly   435 sq. mi.
24,276   23,325   22,813   24,820   22,737   21,108   18,884
January 15, 1821; organized August 15, 1853. *Fredrika Bremer (1801–65)*. Swedish traveler and author of novels similar to Jane Austen; first book published 1823; most popular novel *Herta* published 1856.

Brevard **Florida**
Titusville 1,016 sq. mi.
543,376 476,230 398,978 272,959 230,006 111,435 23,653
March 14, 1844, as Saint Lucie; name changed January 6, 1855. *Theodore Washington Brevard (1804–77)*. Lawyer; judge, Macon County, Alabama, 1847; Florida comptroller 1855–61.

Brewster **Texas**
Alpine 6,184 sq. mi.
9,232 8,866 8,681 7,573 7,780 6,434 7,309
February 2, 1887. *Henry Percy Brewster (1816–84)*. Private secretary to General Houston 1836; Texas secretary of war 1836; district attorney, 2nd judicial district 1840–43; Texas attorney general 1847–49; adjutant general and chief of staff under Confederate General Albert Johnston; Texas commissioner of insurance, statistics and history 1883.

Briscoe **Texas**
Silverton 900 sq. mi.
1,637 1,790 1,971 2,579 2,794 3,577 3,528
August 21, 1876; organized January 11, 1892. *Andrew Briscoe (1810–49)*. Captain at Battle of Concepción 1835; signer, Texas Declaration of Independence 1836; captain at Battle of San Jacinto 1836; chief justice of Harrisburg, Texas, 1836–39; railroad builder and promoter 1840–41.

Bristol **Massachusetts**
Taunton 563 sq. mi.
548,285 534,678 506,325 474,641 444,301 398,488 381,569
June 2, 1685. *Town of Bristol, Rhode Island*. Named for Bristol, England; boundary change moved the town from Massachusetts to Rhode Island 1746.

Bristol **Rhode Island**
Bristol 24 sq. mi.
49,875 50,648 48,859 46,942 45,937 37,146 29,079
February 17, 1747. *Town of Bristol*. Named for Bristol, England.

Bristol **Virginia**
(Independent City) 13 sq. mi.
17,835 17,367 18,426 19,042 14,857 17,144 15,954
February 12, 1890. *Bristol, England*. Named for Bristol, England. (Associated county: Washington.)

Bristol Bay **Alaska**
Naknek 504 sq. mi.
997 1,258 1,410 1,094 1,147 (a) (b)
October 1962. *Bristol Bay*. Named by Captain James Cook (1778) for Admiral Augustus John Hervey, 2nd Earl of Bristol (1724–79); served with distinction with Admiral Rodney in West Indies; member of Parliament 1757–63 and 1768–75; commander in chief of Mediterranean Fleet 1763; lord of the admiralty 1771–75. [(a) part of Bristol Bay (Dillingham) Census Area; (b) part of 4th Judicial; District].

Broadwater **Montana**
Townsend 1,193 sq. mi.
5,612 4,385 3,318 3,267 2,526 2,804 2,922
February 9, 1897. *Charles Arthur Broadwater (1840–92)*. Livestock trader 1862; James Hill's manager in Montana during construction of St. Paul, Minneapolis & Manitoba Railway (Great Northern) 1870s; Helena banker; assumed honorific title of "Colonel."

Bronx **New York**
Bronx 42 sq. mi.
1,385,108 1,332,650 1,203,789 1,168,972 1,471,701 1,424,815 1,451,277

April 19, 1912. *Bronx Borough of New York City*. Named from Bronx River; corruption of "Bronck's River," a small stream named for Jonas Bronck (?–1643); first settler north of Harlem River 1641.

Brooke   **West Virginia**
Wellsburg   89 sq. mi.
24,069   25,447   26,992   31,117   29,685   28,940   26,904
November 30, 1796. *Robert Brooke (1751–99)*. Captured twice during Revolutionary War; Virginia House of Delegates 1791–94; governor of Virginia 1794–96; Virginia attorney general 1798.

Brookings   **South Dakota**
Brookings   792 sq. mi.
31,965   28,220   25,207   24,332   22,158   20,046   17,851
April 5, 1862; organized January 13, 1871. *Wilmont Wood Brookings (1833–1905)*. Pioneer settler 1857; lost both feet to frostbite 1858; Dakota territorial legislature 1862–65, Speaker 1864–65; superintendent in charge of building road from Minnesota boundary to Crow Creek Agency 1865–68; associate justice of Dakota Territory supreme court 1869–73; constitutional convention 1883 and 1885.

Brooks   **Georgia**
Quitman   493 sq. mi.
16,243   16,243   15,398   15,255   13,739   15,292   18,169
December 11, 1858. *Preston Smith Brooks (1819–57)*. South Carolina legislature; captain in Mexican War 1846; US representative from South Carolina 1853–57; severely caned Senator Charles Sumner of Massachusetts because of anti-Southern speech 1856; caning attack made Brooks a hero in antebellum South.

Brooks   **Texas**
Falfurrias   943 sq. mi.
7,233   7,976   8,204   8,428   8,005   8,609   9,195
March 11, 1911; organized 1912. *James Abijah Brooks (1855–1944)*. Cattleman 1876–80; Texas Ranger 1882–1906, resigned; Texas House of Representatives 1909–11; Brooks County judge 1911–39.

Broome   **New York**
Binghamton   706 sq. mi.
200,600   200,536   212,160   213,648   221,815   212,661   184,698
March 28, 1806. *John Broome (1738–1810)*. New York Constitutional Convention 1777; president of New York City chamber of commerce 1794; New York Senate; lieutenant governor 1804–10.

Broomfield   **Colorado**
Broomfield   33 sq. mi.
55,889   38,272[a]   24,638[a]   (a)   (a)   (a)   (a)
November 15, 2001. *City of Broomfield*. Named for broom corn growing in the area. Problems caused by city's spreading from Boulder County into Adams, Jefferson, and Weld counties resolved by creating separate county. [(a) Population included in Adams, Boulder, Jefferson, and Weld counties; 2000 and 1990 populations listed for these four counties also include Bloomfield's population.]

Broward   **Florida**
Fort Lauderdale   1,210 sq. mi.
1,748,066   1,623,018   1,255,488   1,018,200   620,100   333,946   83,933
April 30, 1915. *Napoleon Bonaparte Broward (1857–1910)*. Smuggled arms to Cuban revolutionaries fighting Spain; sheriff of Duval County, Florida, 1887–1900; Florida legislature 1900; Florida Board of Health 1900–04; governor of Florida 1905–09.

Brown   **Illinois**
Mount Sterling   306 sq. mi.
6,937   6,950   5,836   5,411   5,586   6,210   7,132

February 1, 1839. *Jacob Jennings Brown (1775–1828).* Brigadier general, New York Volunteers 1813; brigadier general US Army 1813; major general 1814; army commander in chief 1821–28; received thanks of Congress and gold medal for actions at Chippewa, Niagara, and Erie during War of 1812.

Brown   **Indiana**
Nashville   312 sq. mi.

15,242	14,957	14,080	12,377	9,057	7,024	6,209

February 4, 1836; effective April 1, 1836. *Jacob Jennings Brown.**

Brown   **Kansas**
Hiawatha   571 sq. mi.

9,984	10,724	11,128	11,955	11,685	13,229	14,651

August 25, 1855. *Uncertain.* (1) *Albert Gallatin Brown (1813–80)*; Mississippi house of representatives 1835–39; US representative 1839–41 and 1847–53; circuit superior court judge 1842–43; governor of Mississippi 1844–48; US senator 1854–61; captain, Mississippi infantry 1861; Confederate Senate 1862; brigadier general, Mississippi Militia; pro-slavery record was popular in Kansas Territorial legislature. (2) *Orville H. Browne (?–?)*; Kansas territorial legislature. County was created as "Browne" but the *e* was omitted from the county seal and never replaced. Some sources maintain that adding the *e* was a mistake rather than dropping it later.

Brown   **Minnesota**
New Ulm   611 sq. mi.

25,893	26,911	26,984	28,645	28,887	27,676	25,895

February 20, 1855; organized February 11, 1856. *Joseph Renshaw Brown (1805–70).* Drummer boy at age 14 at Fort St. Anthony (Snelling); trader with Sioux; negotiated treaties with Chippewas and Sioux; secretary, Minnesota Territorial Council 1849–51; Minnesota territorial printer 1853–54; chief clerk, Minnesota House of Representatives 1853; Minnesota council 1854–55; Minnesota Territory House of Representative 1857.

Brown   **Nebraska**
Ainsworth   1,221 sq. mi.

3,145	3,525	3,657	4,377	4,021	4,436	5,164

February 19, 1883. Any one or more of five members of Nebraska legislature named Brown at time of county's creation.

Brown   **Ohio**
Georgetown   490 sq. mi.

44,846	42,285	34,966	31,920	26,635	25,178	22,221

December 17, 1817; effective March 1, 1818. *Jacob Jennings Brown.**

Brown   **South Dakota**
Aberdeen   1,713 sq. mi.

36,531	35,460	35,580	36,962	36,920	34,106	32,617

February 22, 1879; organized September 14, 1880. *Alfred Brown (1836–1919).* Arrived in Dakota Territory from Canada 1874; Dakota territorial legislature at time of county's creation 1879.

Brown   **Texas**
Brownwood   944 sq. mi.

38,106	37,674	34,371	33,057	25,877	24,728	28,607

August 27, 1856; organized March 2, 1857. *Henry Stevenson Brown (1793–1834).* War of 1812; operated keel boats to New Orleans 1814–24; settled in Texas 1824; traded with Indians and Mexicans 1824–32; fought Waco Indians 1825; captured Mexican fort at Velasco 1832; delegate to Texas Convention 1832–33.

Brown   **Wisconsin**
Green Bay   530 sq. mi.

248,007	226,778	194,594	175,280	158,244	125,082	98,314

October 26, 1818. *Jacob Jennings Brown.**

Brule   **South Dakota**
Chamberlain   817 sq. mi.

| 5,255 | 5,364 | 5,485 | 5,245 | 5,870 | 6,319 | 6,076 |

January 14, 1875. *Brule Sioux*. Derisively called *sicangu* by Pawnees meaning "burned people," possibly the result of a prairie fire set by Pawnees; translated to French *brulé* (burned).

Brunswick   **North Carolina**
Bolivia   847 sq. mi.

| 107,431 | 73,143 | 50,985 | 35,777 | 24,223 | 20,278 | 19,218 |

March 9, 1764. *Town of Brunswick*. Named for *George I, Duke of Brunswick-Lunenburg*. (See King George, Virginia.)

Brunswick   **Virginia**
Lawrenceville   566 sq. mi.

| 17,434 | 18,419 | 15,987 | 15,632 | 16,172 | 17,779 | 20,316 |

December 17, 1720. *House of Brunswick*. Named for *George I, Duke of Brunswick-Lunenburg*. (See King George, Virginia.)

Bryan   **Georgia**
Pembroke   436 sq. mi.

| 30,233 | 23,417 | 15,438 | 10,175 | 6,539 | 6,226 | 5,965 |

December 19, 1793. *Jonathon Bryan (1708–88)*. Established colony of Georgia with George Oglethorpe 1732; King's council of Georgia; became active opponent of England; suspended from council by George III 1769; Georgia Provincial Congress 1775; prisoner for two years following capture by British on Long Island.

Bryan   **Oklahoma**
Durant   904 sq. mi.

| 42,416 | 36,534 | 32,089 | 39,535 | 25,552 | 24,252 | 28,999 |

July 16, 1907. *William Jennings Bryan (1860–1925)*. US representative from Nebraska 1891–95; unsuccessful Democratic presidential candidate 1896, 1900, and 1908; assisted in developing Oklahoma constitution 1907; US secretary of state 1913–15.

Buchanan   **Iowa**
Independence   571 sq. mi.

| 20,958 | 21,093 | 20,844 | 22,900 | 21,746 | 22,293 | 21,297 |

December 21, 1837; organized October 4, 1847. *James Buchanan (1791–1868)*. War of 1812; Pennsylvania House of Representatives 1814–15; US representative 1821–34; US senator 1834–45; US secretary of state 1845–49; minister to Great Britain 1853–56; 15th president of the US 1857–61. While a senator, Buchanan advocated creation of Wisconsin Territory from which Iowa Territory was created.

Buchanan   **Missouri**
Saint Joseph   408 sq. mi.

| 89,201 | 85,998 | 83,083 | 87,888 | 86,915 | 90,581 | 96,826 |

December 31, 1838. *James Buchanan.**

Buchanan   **Virginia**
Grundy   503 sq. mi.

| 24,098 | 26,978 | 31,333 | 37,989 | 32,071 | 36,724 | 35,748 |

February 13, 1858. *James Buchanan.**

Buckingham   **Virginia**
Buckingham   580 sq. mi.

| 17,146 | 15,623 | 12,873 | 11,751 | 10,597 | 10,877 | 12,288 |

April 7, 1761. *Uncertain*. (1) *Buckinghamshire, England*. (2) *John Sheffield, 1st Duke of Buckingham and Normandy (?–1721)*; court favorite of Charles II, James II, William and Mary, and Anne; suitor to Queen Anne; made duke on first day of Anne's reign 1702.

Bucks   **Pennsylvania**

Doylestown 604 sq. mi.

625,249	597,635	541,174	479,211	415,056	308,567	144,620

March 10, 1682. *Buckinghamshire, England.* Home of William Penn, founder of Pennsylvania.

Buena Vista **Iowa**
Storm Lake 575 sq. mi.

20,260	20,411	19,965	20,774	20,693	21,189	21,113

January 15, 1851; organized November 20, 1858. *Battle of Buena Vista.* US victory under Zachary Taylor against much larger Mexican force led by General Santa Ana, February 22–23, 1847.

Buena Vista **Virginia**
(Independent City) 7 sq. mi.

6,650	6,349	6,406	6,717	6,425	6,300	5,214

February 15, 1892. *Buena Vista Furnace.* Provided cannon balls used at Battle of Buena Vista.* (Associated county: Rockbridge.)

Buffalo **Nebraska**
Kearney 968 sq. mi.

46,102	42,259	37,447	34,797	31,222	26,236	25,134

March 14, 1855. *Descriptive.* Named for bison herds in the area.

Buffalo **South Dakota**
Gannvalley 471 sq. mi.

1,912	2,032	1,759	1,795	1,739	1,547	1,615

January 6, 1864; organized January 13, 1873. *Descriptive.* Named for bison herds in the area.

Buffalo **Wisconsin**
Alma 672 sq. mi.

13,587	13,804	13,584	14,309	13,743	14,202	14,719

July 6, 1853. *Buffalo River.* Named for bison herds in the area.

Bullitt **Kentucky**
Shepherdsville 297 sq. mi.

74,319	61,236	47,567	43,346	26,090	15,726	11,349

December 13, 1796. *Alexander Scott Bullitt (c1761–1816).* Virginia legislature 1782; Kentucky statehood convention 1788; Kentucky constitutional conventions 1796 and 1799; Kentucky Senate 1792–1800 and 1804–08; lieutenant governor 1800–04.

Bulloch **Georgia**
Statesboro 673 sq. mi.

70,217	55,983	43,125	35,785	31,585	24,263	24,740

February 8, 1796. *Archibald Bulloch (1730–77).* Speaker, Georgia Royal Assembly 1775–76; president, Georgia Provisional Congress 1775–76; Continental Congress 1775–76; commander in chief of Georgia forces 1776–77; governor of Georgia 1776–77.

Bullock **Alabama**
Union Springs 623 sq. mi.

10,914	11,714	11,042	10,596	11,824	13,462	16,054

December 5, 1866. *Edward C. Bullock (1825–61).* Alabama Senate; colonel, Confederate Army; died of typhoid fever at Mobile 1861.

Buncombe **North Carolina**
Asheville 657 sq. mi.

238,318	206,330	174,821	160,934	145,056	130,074	124,403

January 14, 1792; organized April 1792. *Edward Buncombe (1742–78)*. Colonel, North Carolina Militia 1771; colonel North Carolina Minute Men 1775; joined General Washington 1777; wounded at Germantown, October 4, 1777; recovered but died after falling down stairs while sleepwalking which reopened his wounds causing him to bleed to death.

Bureau   **Illinois**
Princeton   869 sq. mi.
34,978   35,503   35,688   39,114   38,541   37,594   37,711
February 28, 1837. *Bureau Creek*. Named for *Pierre de Buero (?–?)*; French trader; established trading post on Illinois River 1818.

Burke   **Georgia**
Waynesboro   827 sq. mi.
23,316   22,243   20,579   19,349   18,255   20,596   23,458
February 5, 1777. *Edmund Burke (1729–97)*. Whig member of Parliament 1765–94; urged repeal of the Stamp Act and advocated conciliation with American colonies.

Burke   **North Carolina**
Morgantown   507 sq. mi.
90,912   89,148   75,744   72,504   60,364   52,701   45,518
April 8, 1777. *Uncertain*. (1) *Edmund Burke*.* (2) *Thomas Burke (c1747–83)*; North Carolina Provisional Congress 1774–76; Continental Congress 1776–81; volunteer at Battle of Brandywine 1777; governor of North Carolina 1781–82; British prisoner for four months before escaping.

Burke   **North Dakota**
Bowbells   1,104 sq. mi.
1,968   2,242   3,002   3,822   4,739   5,886   6,621
July 12, 1910. *John Burke (1859–1937)*. North Dakota House of Representatives 1891–92; North Dakota Senate 1893–95; governor of North Dakota 1907–13; US treasurer 1913; North Dakota Supreme Court 1924–37.

Burleigh   **North Dakota**
Bismarck   1,633 sq. mi.
81,308   69,416   60,131   54,811   40,714   34,016   25,673
January 4, 1873; organized July 16, 1873. *Walter A. Burleigh (1820–96)*. Physician in Maine and Pennsylvania; Indian agent at Yankton Sioux Agency 1863; Dakota Territory congressional delegate 1865–69; Dakota territorial legislature 1877–78; South Dakota Senate 1893.

Burleson   **Texas**
Caldwell   659 sq. mi.
17,187   16,470   13,625   12,313   9,999   11,177   13,000
March 24, 1846; organized July 13, 1846. *Edward Burleson (1798–1852)*. War of 1812, battles of Horseshoe Bend and New Orleans; commander, Texas Army, major 1835; Battle of San Jacinto 1836; Texas Republic senator 1836; vice president of Republic of Texas 1841; brigadier general of Texas troops 1838–41; Texas state senate 1848–52, president 1852.

Burlington   **New Jersey**
Mount Holly   799 sq. mi.
448,734   423,394   395,066   362,542   323,132   224,499   135,910
May 17, 1694. *Town of Burlington*. Corruption of Bridlington, England; origin of Quaker settlers.

Burnet   **Texas**
Burnet   994 sq. mi.
42,750   34,147   22,677   17,803   11,420   9,265   10,356
February 5, 1852; organized August 7, 1854. *David Gouverneur Burnet (1788–1870)*. Lieutenant in Venezuelan liberation forces 1806; district judge in Mexican Texas 1834–36; president, Texas colonial government 1836; Republic of Texas vice president 1838–41; elected to US Senate but denied seat 1866.

Burnett   **Wisconsin**
Siren   822 sq. mi.
15,457   15,674   13,084   12,340   9,276   9,214   10,236
March 31, 1856. *Thomas Pendleton Burnett (1800–46)*. Indian agent Prairie du Chien 1830; district attorney for western Michigan Territory 1835; reporter, Wisconsin territorial supreme court 1835; territorial legislature; Wisconsin Constitutional Convention 1846.

Burt   **Nebraska**
Tekamah   492 sq. mi.
6,858   7,791   7,868   8,813   9,247   10,192   11,536
November 23, 1854. *Francis Burt (1807–54)*. South Carolina nullification convention 1832; South Carolina legislature 1832–44; South Carolina treasurer 1844; editor Pendleton *Messenger* 1847–51; South Carolina Constitutional Convention 1852; auditor of US treasury 1853; territorial governor of Nebraska, served for two days before his death.

Butler   **Alabama**
Greenville   777 sq. mi.
20,947   21,399   21,892   21,680   22,007   24,560   29,228
December 13, 1819. *William Butler (?–1818)*. Georgia legislature; Georgia Militia; early settler in county's area; killed by Indians at Butler Springs, March 20, 1818.

Butler   **Iowa**
Allison   580 sq. mi.
14,867   15,305   15,731   17,668   16,953   17,467   17,394
January 15, 1851; organized October 2, 1854. *William Orlando Butler (1791–1880)*. Private, Kentucky volunteers; wounded at Battle of the Thames October 6, 1813; imprisoned in Canada, returned as captain; brevet major at Battle of New Orleans 1815; aide to General Jackson 1816–17; Kentucky House of Representatives 1817–18; US representative 1839–43; major general Kentucky Volunteers 1846; received thanks of Congress and a sword for gallantry at Monterey, Mexico; unsuccessful candidate for US vice president 1848; declined appointment as governor of Nebraska Territory.

Butler   **Kansas**
El Dorado   1,430 sq. mi.
65,880   59,482   50,580   44,782   38,658   38,395   31,001
August 25, 1855; organized February 11, 1859. *Andrew Pickens Butler (1796–1857)*. South Carolina legislature 1824–33; judge, South Carolina court of common pleas 1835–46; US senator 1846–57; pro-slavery views popular in Kansas territorial legislature.

Butler   **Kentucky**
Morgantown   426 sq. mi.
12,690   13,010   11,245   11,064   9,723   9,586   11,309
January 18, 1810. *Richard Butler (1743–91)*. Major to colonel in Pennsylvania regiment 1776–77; fought at Saratoga and Stony Point 1779; negotiated treaty with Iroquois 1783; northern district superintendent of Indian affairs; Pennsylvania Senate 1790; major general under General Saint Clair in Northwest Territory; died in Battle of the Wabash, November 3, 1791.

Butler   **Missouri**
Poplar Bluff   695 sq. mi.
42,794   40,867   38,765   37,693   33,529   34,656   37,707
February 27, 1849. *William Orlando Butler.**

Butler   **Nebraska**
David City   585 sq. mi.
8,395   8,767   8,601   9,330   9,461   10,312   11,432
January 26, 1856; organized October 21, 1868. *William Orlando Butler.**

Butler   **Ohio**

Hamilton		467 sq. mi.				
368,130	332,807	291,479	258,787	236,207	199,076	147,203

March 24, 1803. *Richard Butler.**

Butler **Pennsylvania**
Butler 789 sq. mi.

183,862	174,083	152,013	142,912	127,941	114,639	97,320

March 12, 1800. *Richard Butler.**

Butte **California**
Oroville 1,636 sq. mi.

220,000	203,171	182,120	143,851	101,969	82,030	64,930

February 18, 1850. *Sutter Buttes*. From French word for "isolated hill" or "mound." Sutter Buttes is a landmark in Sacramento Valley. (See Sutter, California.)

Butte **Idaho**
Arco 2,232 sq. mi.

2,891	2,899	2,918	3,342	2,925	3,498	2,722

February 6, 1917. *Uncertain*. (1) *Descriptive* of buttes in general in the area. (2) *Three Buttes*; local landmark from French *trios buttes*. (3) *Big Butte*; largest of the Three Buttes. (See Butte, California.)

Butte **South Dakota**
Belle Fourche 2,250 sq. mi.

10,110	9,094	7,914	8,372	7,825	8,592	8,161

March 2, 1883. *Descriptive* of numerous buttes in the area. (See Butte, California.)

Butts **Georgia**
Jackson 184 sq. mi.

23,655	19,522	15,326	13,665	10,560	8,976	9,079

December 24, 1825. *Samuel Butts (1777–1814)*. Private in Georgia regiment 1812; elected captain; killed at Battle of Chillabee January 27, 1814.

C

Cabarrus **North Carolina**
Concord 362 sq. mi.

178,011	131,063	98,935	85,895	74,629	68,137	63,783

1792. *Stephen Cabarrus (1754–1808)*. North Carolina House of Commons 1784–1805; first board of trustees, University of North Carolina 1789.

Cabell **West Virginia**
Huntington 281 sq. mi.

96,319	96,784	96,827	106,835	106,918	108,202	108,035

January 2, 1809. *William H. Cabell (1772–1853)*. Virginia Assembly 1795 and 1798; governor of Virginia 1805–08; judge of general court 1808; judge, circuit court of appeals 1811; judge, court of appeals 1830.

Cache **Utah**
Logan 1,165 sq. mi.

112,656	91,391	70,183	57,176	42,331	35,788	33,536

January 5, 1856. *Cache Valley*. From French *cacher* meaning "to hide"; refers to trappers' practice of hiding pelts for later retrieval.

Caddo **Louisiana**
Shreveport 879 sq. mi.

254,969	252,161	248,253	252,358	230,184	223,859	176,547

January 18, 1838. *Caddo Indians*. Contraction of *Kadohadacho* meaning "real chiefs."

Caddo   **Oklahoma**
Anadarko   1,278 sq. mi.

29,600	30,150	29,550	30,905	28,931	28,621	34,913

July 4, 1901, as County "I"; organized and name changed November 8, 1902. *Caddo Indians.**

Calaveras   **California**
San Andreas   1,020 sq. mi.

45,578	40,554	31,998	20,710	13,585	10,289	9,902

February 18, 1850. *Calaveras River.* Spanish word for "skulls"; possibly from skeletal remains found at site of an Indian battle.

Calcasieu   **Louisiana**
Lake Charles   1,064 sq. mi.

192,768	183,577	168,134	167,223	134,415	145,475	89,635

March 24, 1840. *Calcasieu River.* Uncertain origin may have derived from either of two possibilities. (1) Atakapa chief; war cry was likened to a crying eagle; translated to French as *calcasieu.* (2) Colloquial French *quelques chaux* meaning "some cabbages" referring to cabbages grown by local settlers.

Caldwell   **Kentucky**
Princeton   345 sq. mi.

12,984	13,060	13,232	13,473	13,179	13,073	13,199

January 13, 1809. *John W. Caldwell (1757–1804).* Major general; served with George Rogers Clark 1786; Kentucky conventions 1787–89; Kentucky Senate 1792–93; lieutenant governor 1804; died while presiding over senate.

Caldwell   **Louisiana**
Columbia   529 sq. mi.

10,132	10,560	9,810	10,761	9,354	9,004	10,293

March 6, 1838. *Mathew Caldwell (1798–1842).* Battle of San Jacinto 1836; signer of Texas Declaration of Independence 1836; commanded Texas Rangers 1838–39; captured by Mexico while scouting for Santa Fe expedition 1841; released 1842.

Caldwell   **Missouri**
Kingston   426 sq. mi.

9,424	8,969	8,380	8,660	8,351	8,830	9,929

December 29, 1836. *Uncertain.* (1) *John Caldwell.** (2) *Mathew Caldwell.**

Caldwell   **North Carolina**
Lenoir   472 sq. mi.

83,029	77,415	70,709	67,746	56,699	49,552	43,352

January 11, 1841. *Joseph Caldwell (1773–1835).* Professor of mathematics; first president of University of North Carolina 1804–12 and 1817–35.

Caldwell   **Texas**
Lockhart   545 sq. mi.

38,066	32,194	26,392	23,637	21,178	17,222	19,350

March 6, 1848; organized August 7, 1848. *Mathew Caldwell.**

Caledonia   **Vermont**
Saint Johnsbury   649 sq. mi.

31,227	29,702	27,846	25,808	22,789	22,786	24,049

November 5, 1792. *Scotland.* Latin name for Scotland; many settlers in the area were Scots.

Calhoun   **Alabama**
Anniston   606 sq. mi.

118,572	112,249	116,034	119,761	103,092	95,878	79,539

December 18, 1832, as Benton; name changed January 29, 1856. *John Caldwell Calhoun (1782–1850)*. South Carolina House of Representatives 1808–09; US representative 1811–17; US secretary of war 1817–25; US vice president 1825–32; US senate 1832–43 and 1848–50; US secretary of state 1844–45; leading pro-slavery spokesman.

Calhoun   **Arkansas**
Hampton   629 sq. mi.

5,368	5,744	5,826	6,079	5,573	5,991	7,132

December 6, 1850. *John Caldwell Calhoun.**

Calhoun   **Florida**
Blountstown   567 sq. mi.

14,625	13,017	11,011	9,294	7,624	7,422	7,922

January 26, 1838. *John Caldwell Calhoun.**

Calhoun   **Georgia**
Morgan   280 sq. mi.

6,694	6,320	5,013	5,717	6,606	7,341	8,578

February 20, 1854. *John Caldwell Calhoun.**

Calhoun   **Illinois**
Hardin   254 sq. mi.

5,089	5,084	5,322	5,867	5,675	5,933	6,898

January 10, 1825. *John Caldwell Calhoun.**

Calhoun   **Iowa**
Rockwell City 570 sq. mi.

9,670	11,115	11,508	13,542	14,287	15,923	16,925

January 15,1851, as Fox; name changed January 22, 1853; organized November 7, 1855. *John Caldwell Calhoun.**

Calhoun   **Michigan**
Marshall   706 sq. mi.

136,146	137,985	135,982	141,557	141,963	138,858	120,813

October 29, 1829; organized April 11, 1833. *John Caldwell Calhoun.** In an attempt to gain favor for Michigan statehood, the territorial legislature named counties for members of President Jackson's cabinet, including Vice President Calhoun.

Calhoun   **Mississippi**
Pittsboro   587 sq. mi.

14,962	15,069	14,908	15,664	14,623	15,941	18,369

March 8, 1852. *John Caldwell Calhoun.**

Calhoun   **South Carolina**
Saint Matthews 381 sq. mi.

15,175	15,185	12,753	12,206	10,780	12,256	14,753

February 14, 1908. *John Caldwell Calhoun.**

Calhoun   **Texas**
Port Lavaca   507 sq. mi.

21,381	20,647	19,053	19,574	17,831	16,592	9,222

April 4, 1846. *John Caldwell Calhoun.**

Calhoun   **West Virginia**
Grantsville   279 sq. mi.

7,627	7,582	7,885	8,250	7,046	7,948	10,259

March 5, 1856. *John Caldwell Calhoun.**

Callahan   **Texas**
Baird   899 sq. mi.

| 13,544 | 12,905 | 11,859 | 10,992 | 8,205 | 7,929 | 9,087 |

February 1, 1858; organized July 3, 1877. *James Hughes Callahan (1814–56)*. Texas volunteer; captured at Goliad 1836, escaped massacre; captain, Texas Rangers; killed in a feud.

Callaway   **Missouri**
Fulton   835 sq. mi.

| 44,332 | 40,766 | 32,809 | 32,252 | 25,850 | 23,858 | 23,316 |

November 25, 1820. *James Callaway (1783–1815)*. Grandson of Daniel Boone; organized company of rangers to protect against Indians; killed in battle with Indians.

Calloway   **Kentucky**
Murray   385 sq. mi.

| 37,191 | 34,177 | 30,735 | 30,031 | 27,692 | 20,972 | 20,147 |

December 19, 1821; organized 1823. *Richard Callaway (c1722–80)*. Major, French and Indian War; constructed fort at Boonesborough 1775; represented Kentucky County in Virginia House of Burgesses; killed by Indians while building ferry across Kentucky River. (Variation in spelling due to uncorrected clerical error.)

Calumet   **Wisconsin**
Chilton   318 sq. mi.

| 48,971 | 40,631 | 34,291 | 30,867 | 27,604 | 22,268 | 18,840 |

December 7, 1836; organized 1850. *Menominee village*. From French word for "shepherd's pipe"; name given to Indian pipes.

Calvert   **Maryland**
Prince Frederick   213 sq. mi.

| 88,737 | 74,563 | 51,372 | 34,638 | 20,682 | 15,826 | 12,100 |

July 3, 1654; name changed to Patuxent, October 31, 1654; renamed Calvert, December 31, 1658. *Uncertain*; any one of three or all three members of Calvert family. (1) *George Calvert, 1st Baron of Baltimore (c1580–1632)*; knighted 1617; secretary of state for James I 1619; resigned 1624; raised to Irish peerage as Baron of Baltimore 1625; petitioned James I for land grant in North America as a haven for Catholics; died before charter was signed for Maryland tract. (2) *Cecilius Calvert*, son of George (see Cecil, Maryland). (3) *Leonard Calvert (1606–47)*; second son of George; lieutenant-general (governor) of Maryland 1633–43 and 1644–47, appointed by his brother, Cecilius.

Camas   **Idaho**
Fairfield   1,074 sq. mi.

| 1,117 | 991 | 727 | 818 | 728 | 917 | 1,079 |

February 6, 1917. *Big Camas Prairie*. From Chinook *kamas* meaning "sweet"; name of a root prized by local Indians for food.

Cambria   **Pennsylvania**
Ebensburg   688 sq. mi.

| 143,679 | 152,598 | 163,029 | 183,263 | 186,785 | 203,283 | 209,541 |

March 26, 1804; organized 1807. *Cambria Township*. Medieval name for Wales; first settlers in area were Welsh.

Camden   **Georgia**
Woodbine   613 sq. mi.

| 50,513 | 43,664 | 30,167 | 13,371 | 11,334 | 9,975 | 7,322 |

February 5, 1777. *Charles Pratt, Earl of Camden (1714–94)*. British attorney general 1757; chief justice, court of common pleas 1761–66; House of Lords 1766; opposed Stamp Act and tax on American colonies as unconstitutional; lord chancellor 1766–70; lord president of council 1782 and 1784–94.

Camden   **Missouri**
Camdenton   656 sq. mi.

| 44,002 | 37,051 | 27,495 | 20,017 | 13,315 | 9,116 | 7,861 |

January 29, 1841, as Kinderhook; name changed February 23, 1843. *Camden County, North Carolina*.

Camden   **New Jersey**
Camden   221 sq. mi.
513,657   508,932   502,824   471,650   456,291   392,035   300,743
March 13, 1844. *Village of Camden*. Named for *Charles Pratt, Earl of Camden*.*

Camden   **North Carolina**
Camden   241 sq. mi.
9,980   6,885   5,904   5,829   5,453   5,598   5,223
April 8, 1777. *Charles Pratt, Earl of Camden*.*

Cameron   **Louisiana**
Cameron   1,285 sq. mi.
6,839   9,991   9,260   9,336   8,194   6,909   6,244
March 15, 1870. *Simon Cameron (1799–1889)*. US senator from Pennsylvania intermittently 1845–77; US secretary of war 1861–62; organized Union forces 1862; US minister to Russia 1862; county named by Louisiana's Reconstruction government.

Cameron   **Pennsylvania**
Emporium   396 sq. mi.
5,085   5,974   5,913   6,674   7,096   7,586   7,023
March 29, 1860. *Simon Cameron*.*

Cameron   **Texas**
Brownsville   891 sq. mi.
406,220   335,227   260,120   209,727   140,368   151,098   125,170
February 12, 1848; organized August 7, 1858. *Ewen Cameron (1811–43)*. Kentucky volunteer in Texas Revolution; leader in Mier expedition to Mexico 1842; captured 1842; led prison escape but recaptured and executed by order of Santa Ana.

Camp   **Texas**
Pittsburg   196 sq. mi.
12,401   11,549   9,904   9,275   8,005   7,849   8,740
April 6, 1874. *John Lafayette Camp (1828–91)*. Captain, Upshur County Militia 1861; colonel Texas Regulars, Confederate Army 1861; twice wounded and captured during Civil War; elected US representative but was refused a seat 1866; Texas Senate 1874; district judge 1878.

Campbell   **Kentucky**
Newport   151 sq. mi.
90,336   88,616   83,866   83,317   88,501   86,803   76,196
December 17, 1794. *John Campbell (c1735–99)*. Served under British General Braddock in French and Indian War; fur trader; taken prisoner by British during Revolutionary War; represented Jefferson County (Kentucky) in Virginia legislature; Kentucky Constitutional Convention 1792; Kentucky legislature; died on floor of Kentucky Senate chamber.

Campbell   **South Dakota**
Mound City   734 sq. mi.
1,466   1,782   1,965   2,243   2,966   3,351   4,046
January 8, 1873; organized April 17, 1884. *Norman B. Campbell (?–?)*. Dakota territorial legislature 1872–73 when county was created.

Campbell   **Tennessee**
Jacksboro   480 sq. mi.
40,716   39,854   35,079   34,923   26,045   27,936   34,369
September 11, 1806. *Uncertain*. (1) *Arthur Campbell (c1742–1811)*; volunteered for militia at age 15; captured by Indians and taken to Great Lakes area; commander of frontier militia units during Revolutionary War; leader in State of Franklin (Tennessee) movement. (2) *George Washington Campbell (1769–1848)*; US representative 1803–09; judge, Tennessee Supreme Court of errors and appeals 1809–11; US senator 1811–14 and 1815–18; US treasury secretary 1814; US minister to Russia 1818–21.

Campbell   **Virginia**
Rustburg   504 sq. mi.
54,842   51,078   47,572   45,424   43,319   32,958   28,877
December 15, 1781. *William Campbell (1745–81)*. Captain, 1st Virginia Regiment 1775; resigned 1776; colonel Virginia Militia 1777–80; battles of Kings Mountain, 1780, and Guilford Courthouse, 1781; died during Siege of Yorktown. (Associated independent city: Lynchburg.)

Campbell   **Wyoming**
Gillette   4,803 sq. mi.
46,133   33,698   29,370   24,367   12,957   5,861   4,839
February 13, 1911. *Uncertain*; either John Campbell or both John and Robert Campbell. (1) *John Allen Campbell (1835–80)*; from 2nd lieutenant to brevet major general, Union Army 1861–65, mustered out 1865; officer in regular army 1867; assistant secretary of war 1869; first territorial governor of Wyoming 1869–75. (2) *Robert Campbell (1804–79)*; trapper in northern Rocky Mountains.

Canadian   **Oklahoma**
El Reno   897 sq. mi.
115,541   87,697   74,409   56,452   32,245   24,727   25,644
May 2, 1890. *North and South Canadian Rivers*. Uncertain origins of rivers' name. (1) From French-Canadian trappers. (2) Spanish *cañada* for "canyon." (3) From Caddoan name meaning "red river."

Candler   **Georgia**
Metter   243 sq. mi.
10,998   9,577   7,744   7,518   6,412   6,672   8,063
November 3, 1914. *Allen Daniel Chandler (1834–1910)*. From private to colonel in Confederate Army 1861–65; wounded at Kennesaw Mountain; lost eye at Jonesboro; administrator at various schools 1865–71; mayor of Jonesboro, Tennessee 1866; mayor of Gainesville, Georgia 1872; Georgia House of Representatives 1873–77; Georgia Senate 1878–79; US representative 1883–91; Georgia secretary of state 1894–98; governor of Georgia 1899–1902.

Cannon   **Tennessee**
Woodbury   266 sq. mi.
13,801   12,826   10,467   10,234   8,467   8,537   9,174
January 31, 1836. *Newton Cannon (1781–1842)*. Tennessee legislature 1811; from private to colonel, Tennessee Mounted Rifles 1813; US representative 1814–17 and 1819–23; negotiated treaty with Chickasaws 1819; governor of Tennessee 1836–39.

Canyon   **Idaho**
Caldwell   587 sq. mi.
188,923   131,441   90,076   83,756   61,288   57,662   53,597
March 7, 1891. *Uncertain*. (1) *Snake River Canyon*. (2) *Boise River Canyon*.

Cape Girardeau   **Missouri**
Jackson   579 sq. mi.
75,674   68,693   61,633   58,837   49,350   42,020   38,397
October 1, 1812. *Spanish district of Cape Girardeau*. Name of a promontory on the Mississippi River; named for *Jean B. Girardeau (?–?)*; French soldier stationed at Kaskaskia, Illinois 1704–20; established trading post at Cape Girardeau 1733; resigned from French military 1735.

Cape May   **New Jersey**
Cape May Court House   251 sq. mi.
97,265   102,326   95,089   82,266   59,554   48,555   37,131
November 12, 1692. *Cape May*. Named for *Cornelius Jacobsen Mey (?–?)*; navigator in exploration of North America 1614; explored Delaware River for Dutch West India Company 1623; first director general of New Netherlands (New York) 1624–25.

Carbon   **Montana**
Red Lodge   2,049 sq. mi.

10,078   9,552   8,080   8,099   7,080   8,317   10,241
March 4, 1895. *Descriptive*. Refers to local coal deposits.

Carbon   **Pennsylvania**
Jim Thorpe   381 sq. mi.
65,249   58,802   56,846   53,285   50,573   52,889   57,558
March 13, 1843. *Descriptive*. Refers to local coal deposits.

Carbon   **Utah**
Price   1,478 sq. mi.
21,403   20,422   20,228   22,179   15,647   21,135   24,901
March 8, 1894. *Descriptive*. Refers to local coal deposits.

Carbon   **Wyoming**
Rawlins   7,898 sq. mi.
15,885   15,639   16,659   21,896   13,354   14,937   15,742
December 16, 1868. *Descriptive*. Refers to local coal deposits.

Caribou   **Idaho**
Soda Springs   1,764 sq. mi.
6,963   7,304   6,963   8,695   6,534   5,976   5,576
February 11, 1919. *Caribou Mountains*. Named for Caribou City which flourished near site of gold discovery by prospector "Cariboo" Fairchild (or Fairbanks) who arrived in Idaho from Caribou, British Columbia, 1860.

Carlisle   **Kentucky**
Bardwell   189 sq. mi.
5,104   5,351   5,238   5,487   5,354   5,608   6,206
April 3, 1886. *John Griffin Carlisle (1835–1910)*. Kentucky House of Representatives 1859–61; Kentucky Senate 1866–71; lieutenant governor 1871–75; US representative 1877–93, speaker 1877–93; US senator 1890–93; US treasury secretary 1893–97.

Carlton   **Minnesota**
Carlton   861 sq. mi.
35,386   31,671   29,259   29,936   28,072   27,932   24,584
May 23, 1857; organized February 18, 1870. *Reuben B. Carlton (1812–63)*. Indian agent at Fond du Lac; Minnesota Senate 1858; promoted transportation improvements to attract settlers.

Caroline   **Maryland**
Denton   319 sq. mi.
33,066   29,772   27,035   23,143   19,781   19,462   18,234
December 5, 1773. *Caroline Calvert Eden (c1734–84)*. Daughter of Charles Calvert, 5th Lord Baltimore; sister of Frederick Calvert, last Lord Baltimore; wife of Robert Eden, last colonial governor of Maryland.

Caroline   **Virginia**
Bowling Green   528 sq. mi.
28,545   22,121   19,217   17,904   13,925   12,725   12,471
March 15, 1727. *Princess Wilhelmina Caroline of Anspach (1683–1737)* Daughter of John Frederick, Margrave of Brandenburg-Anspach; married George Augustus, Prince of Hanover 1705; became Princess of Wales when father-in-law became George I of England 1714; became queen when husband became George II 1727.

Carroll   **Arkansas**
Berryville   630 sq. mi.
27,446   25,357   18,654   16,203   12,301   11,284   13,244
November 1, 1833. *Charles Carroll (1737–1832)*. Continental commissioner to Canada 1776; Continental Congress 1776–78; signer of Declaration of Independence 1776; Maryland Senate 1777–1800; US senator 1789–92; last surviving signer of Declaration of Independence.

Carroll   **Georgia**
Carrollton   499 sq. mi.

110,527	87,268	71,422	56,346	45,404	36,451	34,112

December 11, 1826. *Charles Carroll.**

Carroll   **Illinois**
Mount Carroll   445 sq. mi.

15,387	16,674	16,805	18,779	19,276	19,507	18,976

February 22, 1839. *Charles Carroll.**

Carroll   **Indiana**
Delphi   372 sq. mi.

20,155	20,165	18,809	19,722	17,734	16,934	16,010

January 7, 1828; effective May 1, 1828. *Charles Carroll.**

Carroll   **Iowa**
Carroll   569 sq. mi.

20,816	21,421	21,423	22,951	22,912	23,431	23,065

January 15, 1851; organized August 17, 1855. *Charles Carroll.**

Carroll   **Kentucky**
Carrollton   129 sq. mi.

10,811	10,155	9,292	9,270	8,523	7,978	8,517

February 9, 1838. *Charles Carroll.**

Carroll   **Maryland**
Westminster   448 sq. mi.

167,134	150,897	123,372	96,356	69,006	52,785	44,907

January 19, 1837. *Charles Carroll.**

Carroll   **Mississippi**
Carrollton   628 sq. mi.

10,597	10,769	9,237	9,776	9,397	11,177	15,499

December 23, 1833. *Charles Carroll.**

Carroll   **Missouri**
Carrollton   695 sq. mi.

9,295	10,285	10,748	12,131	12,565	13,847	15,589

January 2, 1833. *Charles Carroll.**

Carroll   **New Hampshire**
Ossipee   931 sq. mi.

47,818	43,666	35,410	27,931	18,548	15,829	15,868

December 22, 1840. *Charles Carroll.**

Carroll   **Ohio**
Carrollton   395 sq. mi.

28,836	28,836	26,521	25,598	21,579	20,857	19,039

December 25, 1832. *Charles Carroll.**

Carroll   **Tennessee**
Huntingdon   599 sq. mi.

28,522	29,475	27,514	28,285	25,741	23,476	26,553

November 7, 1821. *William Carroll (1788–1844).* General with Andrew Jackson at Battle of New Orleans 1815; governor of Tennessee 1821–27 and 1829–35.

Carroll **Virginia**
Hillsville 475 sq. mi.
30,042 29,245 26,594 27,270 23,092 23,178 26,695
January 17, 1842. *Charles Carroll.** (Associated independent city: part of Galax.)

Carson **Texas**
Panhandle 920 sq. mi.
6,182 6,516 6,576 6,672 6,358 7,781 6,852
August 21, 1876; organized June 26, 1888. *Samuel Price Carson (1798–1838)*. North Carolina Senate 1822–24 and 1834; US representative 1825–33; North Carolina Constitutional Convention 1835; signer, Texas Declaration of Independence 1836; Texas Constitutional Convention 1836; Texas Republic secretary of state 1836–38; commissioner to Washington to intercede for Texas 1838.

Carson City **Nevada**
(Independent City) 145 sq. mi.
55,274 52,457 40,443 32,022 15,468 8,063[a] 4,172[a]
November 25, 1861, as Ormsby County; city and county consolidated 1969. *Christopher "Kit" Carson (1809–68)*. Guide on Fremont's expeditions 1842–43 and 1845; Indian agent 1853–61; fought against southwest Indians during Civil War; brevet brigadier general 1865. [(a) Ormsby County].

Carter **Kentucky**
Grayson 410 sq. mi.
27,720 26,889 24,340 25,060 19,850 20,817 22,559
February 9, 1838. *William G. Carter (?–1850)*. Kentucky Senate 1834–38; large landowner.

Carter **Missouri**
Van Buren 507 sq. mi.
6,265 5,941 5,515 5,428 3,878 3,973 4,777
March 10, 1859. *Zimri A. Carter (1794–1870)*. First settler in county; judge of county court.

Carter **Montana**
Ekalaka 3,341 sq. mi.
1,160 1,360 1,503 1,799 1,956 2,493 2,798
February 22, 1917. *Thomas Henry Carter (1854–1911)*. Congressional delegate to Congress from Montana Territory 1889; US representative 1889–91; commissioner of general land office 1891–93; US senator 1895–1901 and 1905–11.

Carter **Oklahoma**
Ardmore 822 sq. mi.
47,557 45,621 42,919 43,610 37,349 39,040 36,455
July 16, 1907. *Uncertain*. (1) *Benjamin Wisner Carter (1837–94)*; Cherokee; superintendent of Chickasaw Male Academy; captain in Confederate Army; Oklahoma territorial judge. (2) *Charles David Carter (1868–1929)*; son of Benjamin Carter; mineral trustee for Choctaw and Chickasaw nations; US representative 1907–27. (3) *Carter family*; includes Benjamin and Charles as well as *Nathaniel G. Carter (c1770–?)* and *David Carter (1812–67)*; grandfather and father respectively of Benjamin.

Carter **Tennessee**
Elizabethtown 341 sq. mi.
57,424 56,742 51,505 50,205 42,575 41,578 42,432
April 9, 1796. *Landon Carter (1760–1800)*. Active in Watauga settlements and Revolutionary War; North Carolina legislature; advocate for State of Franklin (Tennessee).

Carteret **North Carolina**
Beaufort 506 sq. mi.
66,469 59,383 52,556 41,092 31,603 30,940 23,059
August 8, 1722. *John Carteret, Earl of Granville (1690–1763)*. House of Lords 1711; British ambassador to Sweden 1719; lord lieutenant of Ireland 1724–30; one of lords proprietor of Carolina, refused to sell his share to King George II 1728; became Earl of Granville 1744; lord president of council 1751–63.

Carver **Minnesota**
Chaska 354 sq. mi.
91,042 70,205 47,915 37,046 28,310 21,358 18,155
February 20, 1855. *Jonathon Carver (1710–80)*. Captain in French and Indian War 1755; wintered in Minnesota 1766–67; explored Upper Midwest region; moved to England 1767; wrote *Travels through the Interior Parts of North America, in the Years 1766, 1767, and 1768*; published in England 1778.

Cascade **Montana**
Great Falls 2,698 sq. mi.
81,327 80,357 77,691 80,696 81,804 73,418 53,027
September 12, 1887. *Great Falls of the Missouri River*. A series of five cascades and waterfalls in which the Missouri River drops 612 feet; discovered by Lewis and Clark June 13,1805; only one of the five waterfalls has not been submerged by reservoirs.

Casey **Kentucky**
Liberty 444 sq. mi.
15,955 15,447 14,211 14,818 12,930 14,327 17,446
November 14, 1806. *William Casey (1754–1816)*. Revolutionary War; lieutenant colonel of Kentucky Militia 1792; Kentucky legislature; 2nd Kentucky Constitutional Convention 1799.

Cass **Illinois**
Virginia 376 sq. mi.
13,642 13,695 13,437 15,084 14,219 14,539 15,097
March 3, 1837. *Lewis Cass (1782–1866)*. Ohio House of Representatives 1806; US marshal, Ohio district 1807–12; colonel to brigadier general, US Infantry 1813; military and civil governor of Michigan Territory 1813–31; US secretary of war 1831–36; US minister to France 1836–42; US senator from Michigan 1845–46 and 1849–57; Democratic nominee lost to Zachary Taylor 1848; US secretary of state 1857–60.

Cass **Indiana**
Logansport 412 sq. mi.
38,966 40,930 38,413 40,936 40,456 40,931 38,793
December 18, 1828; effective April 14, 1829. *Lewis Cass.**

Cass **Iowa**
Atlantic 564 sq. mi.
13,956 14,684 15,128 16,932 17,007 17,919 18,532
January 15, 1851; organized March 7, 1853. *Lewis Cass.**

Cass **Michigan**
Cassopolis 490 sq. mi.
52,293 51,104 49,477 49,499 43,312 36,932 28,185
October 29, 1829. *Lewis Cass.**

Cass **Minnesota**
Walker 2,022 sq. mi.
28,567 27,150 21,791 21,050 17,323 16,720 19,468
March 31, 1851; organized May 4, 1872; deorganized 1876; reorganized 1897. *Lewis Cass.**

Cass **Missouri**
Harrisonville 697 sq. mi.
99,478 82,092 63,808 51,029 39,448 29,702 19,325
March 3, 1835, as Van Buren; name changed February 19, 1849. *Lewis Cass.**

Cass **Nebraska**
Plattsmouth 557 sq. mi.

25,241   24,334   21,318   20,297   18,076   17,281   16,361
November 23, 1854; organized 1857. *Lewis Cass.**

Cass   **North Dakota**
Fargo   1,765 sq. mi.
149,778   123,138   102,874   88,247   73,653   66,947   58,877
January 4, 1873; organized October 27, 1873. *George W. Cass (1810–88)*. West Point 1832; assisted building of Cumberland Road 1832–36; president of Northern Pacific Railroad when construction reached Dakota Territory 1873.

Cass   **Texas**
Linden   937 sq. mi.
30,464   30,438   29,982   29,430   24,133   23,496   26,732
April 25, 1846, as Cass; organized July 13, 1846; name changed to Davis, December 17, 1861; renamed Cass, May 16, 1871. *Lewis Cass.**

Cassia   **Idaho**
Burley   2,565 sq. mi.
22,952   21,416   19,532   19,427   17,017   16,121   14,629
February 20, 1879. *Cassia Creek*. Named for cassia plant (wild senna), a variety of cinnamon.

Castro   **Texas**
Dimmitt   894 sq. mi.
8,062   8,285   9,070   10,556   10,394   8,923   5,417
August 21, 1876; organized 1891. *Henri Castro (1786–1865)*. Republic of Texas counsel general in Paris; established Castro's Colony for French immigrants 1842; founded other French colonies in Texas 1844–47.

Caswell   **North Carolina**
Yanceyville   425 sq. mi.
23,719   23,501   20,693   20,705   19,055   19,912   20,870
April 8, 1777. *Richard Caswell (1729–89)*. North Carolina assembly 1769–71; continental congress 1774–76; brigadier general 1776; Halifax convention 1776; governor of North Carolina 1775–79; Battle of Camden 1780; North Carolina senate 1788.

Catahoula   **Louisiana**
Harrisonburg   708 sq. mi.
10,407   10,920   11,065   12,287   11,769   11,421   11,834
March 23, 1808. *Catahoula Lake*. Named for Catahoula Indians; meaning of name is uncertain, most suggestions refer to lake or water.

Catawba   **North Carolina**
Newton   399 sq. mi.
154,358   141,685   118,412   105,208   90,873   73,191   61,794
December 12, 1842. *Uncertain*. (1) *Catawba Indians*; sided with colonists in Revolutionary War; uncertain origin of name. (2) *Catawba River*; named for Catawba Indians.

Catoosa   **Georgia**
Ringgold   162 sq. mi.
63,942   53,282   42,464   36,991   28,271   12,202   15,146
December 5, 1853. *Catoosa Springs*. From Cherokee *gatusi* meaning "hill" or "small mountain."

Catron   **New Mexico**
Reserve   6,924 sq. mi.
3,725   3,543   2,563   2,720   2,198   2,773   3,553
February 25, 1921. *Thomas Benton Catron (1840–1921)*. Confederate army 1860–64; district attorney, 3rd District of New Mexico Territory 1866–68; attorney general of New Mexico Territory 1869; US attorney 1870; territorial council intermittently 1884–1909; congressional delegate from New Mexico Territory 1894–97; US senator 1912–17.

Cattaraugus   **New York**
Little Valley   1,308 sq. mi.

80,317	83,955	84,234	85,697	81,666	80,187	77,901

March 11, 1808; organized 1817. *Cattaraugus Creek*. Seneca word meaning "bad-smelling banks"; refers to gas deposits in the area.

Cavalier   **North Dakota**
Langdon   1,489 sq. mi.

3,993	4,831	6,064	7,636	8,213	10,064	11,840

January 4, 1873; organized July 8, 1884. *Charles Turner Cavaleer (1818–1902)*. Fur trader; Minnesota territorial librarian 1849; collector of customs for Minnesota Territory at Pembina 1851; postmaster Pembina, Dakota Territory, 1864–84; mayor of Pembina; credited with being first settler in the area. (Surname usually spelled with double *e*.)

Cayuga   **New York**
Auburn   692 sq. mi.

80,026	81,963	82,313	79,894	77,439	73,942	70,136

March 8, 1799. *Cayuga Indians*. Members of Iroquois League; name may mean "where they haul boats out" or "from the water to the shore."

Cecil   **Maryland**
Elkton   346 sq. mi.

101,108	85,951	71,347	60,430	53,291	48,408	33,356

December 31, 1674. *Cecilius Calvert, 2nd Lord Baltimore (1605–75)*. Son of George Calvert (see Calvert, Maryland); received grant originally requested by his father from James I following his father's death 1632; never visited Maryland but managed tract from England; father of Charles Calvert (see Charles, Maryland).

Cedar   **Iowa**
Tipton   579 sq. mi.

18,499	18,187	17,381	18,635	17,655	17,791	16,910

December 21, 1837. *Cedar River*. Also called Red Cedar River for trees in area.

Cedar   **Missouri**
Stockton   474 sq. mi.

13,982	13,733	12,093	11,894	9,424	9,185	10,663

February 14, 1845. *Descriptive*. Refers to trees in the area.

Cedar   **Nebraska**
Hartington   740 sq. mi.

8,852	9,615	10,131	11,375	12,192	13,368	13,843

February 12, 1857. *Descriptive*. Refers to trees in the area.

Centre   **Pennsylvania**
Bellefonte   1,110 sq. mi.

153,990	135,758	123,786	112,760	99,267	78,580	65,922

February 13, 1800. *Descriptive*. Refers to county's location in the center of the state.

Cerro Gordo   **Iowa**
Mason City   568 sq. mi.

44,151	46,447	46,733	48,458	49,335	49,894	46,053

January 15, 1851; organized December 29, 1855. *Battle of Cerro Gordo*. US victory under General Scott in Mexican War, April 17–18, 1847.

Chaffee   **Colorado**
Salida   1,013 sq. mi.

17,809	16,242	12,684	13,227	10,162	8,298	7,168

November 1, 1861, as Lake; name changed February 10, 1879. *Jerome Bunty Chaffee (1825–86).* One of the founders of Denver; Colorado Territory House of Representatives 1861–63, speaker 1863; president of First National Bank of Denver 1865–80; territorial delegate to Congress 1871–76; US senator 1876–79.

Chambers   **Alabama**
Lafayette   597 sq. mi.

34,215	36,583	36,876	39,191	36,356	37,828	39,528

December 18, 1832. *Henry H. Chambers (1790–1826).* Physician; surgeon on staff of General Jackson; Alabama Constitutional Convention 1819; Alabama legislature 1820; US senator 1825–26.

Chambers   **Texas**
Anahuac   597 sq. mi.

35,096	26,031	20,088	18,538	12,187	10,379	7,871

February 12, 1858; organized August 2, 1858. *Thomas Jefferson Chambers (1802–65).* Surveyor general of Mexican Texas 1829; attorney general of Mexican State of Coahuila and Texas 1834; major general of reserves in Texas Army 1836; Texas Secession Convention 1861; unsuccessful attempt to raise a Texas company for the Confederate Army 1862; volunteer in Hood's Texas Brigade 1862–63; assassinated in his home, March 15, 1865.

Champaign   **Illinois**
Urbana   996 sq. mi.

201,081	179,669	173,025	166,392	163,281	132,436	106,100

February 20, 1833. *Champaign County, Ohio.* County surveyor waived fee in lieu of being able to name new county for his wife who died and was buried in Champaign County, Ohio.

Champaign   **Ohio**
Urbana   429 sq. mi.

40,097	38,890	36,019	33,649	30,491	29,714	26,793

February 20, 1805. *Descriptive.* From French *champagne* meaning "open, level country."

Chariton   **Missouri**
Keytesville   751 sq. mi.

7,831	8,438	9,202	10,489	11,084	12,270	14,944

November 16, 1820. *Uncertain.* (1) *Chariton River*; named for one of two trappers; John Chariton (?–?) or John Chorette (?–1795). (2) *Town of Chariton*; named for Chariton River; flooded 1824; abandoned 1832.

Charles   **Maryland**
La Plata   458 sq. mi.

146,551	120,546	101,154	72,751	47,678	35,572	23,415

July 10, 1658. *Charles Calvert, 3rd Lord Baltimore (1637–1715).* Son of Cecilius Calvert (see Cecil, Maryland) and Anne Arundell (see Anne Arundel, Maryland); governor of Maryland 1660–84; retained proprietary rights after Maryland became royal colony.

Charles City   **Virginia**
Charles City   183 sq. mi.

7,256	6,926	6,282	6,692	6,158	5,492	4,676

1634. *Charles City.* Named for *King Charles I (1600–49).* Duke of Albany 1600; Duke of York 1605; became Prince of Wales on death of older brother Henry Frederick 1612; King of England 1625–49; beheaded during English Civil War, January 30, 1649.

Charles Mix   **South Dakota**
Lake Andes   1,097 sq. mi.

9,129	9,350	9,131	9,680	9,994	11,785	15,558

May 8, 1862; deorganized 1864; reorganized 1879. *Charles H. Mix (1833–1909).* Indian agent 1858; 1st lieutenant, 1st Minnesota Cavalry; commandant of Fort Abercrombie, Dakota Territory, 1864.

Charleston   **South Carolina**
Charleston   916 sq. mi.
350,209   309,969   295,039   276,974   247,650   216,382   164,856
1769 as judicial district; designated as county April 16, 1868. *City of Charleston.* Named for *King Charles II (1630–85).* Prince of Wales from birth; led Royalists during English Civil War; defeated by Cromwell at Battle of Worcester 1651; exiled to Europe during the Commonwealth 1651–60; invited to restore monarchy after death of Cromwell 1660; King of England 1660–85.

Charlevoix   **Michigan**
Charlevoix   416 sq. mi.
25,949   26,090   21,468   19,907   16,541   13,421   13,475
April 1, 1840, as Reshkauko; name changed March 8, 1843; abolished January 29, 1853; recreated April 1, 1869. *Pierre Francois de Charlevoix (1682–1761).* Jesuit historian and explorer; traveled through Great Lakes and Illinois and Mississippi Rivers to New Orleans 1720–22.

Charlotte   **Florida**
Port Charlotte   680 sq. mi.
159,978   141,627   110,975   58,460   27,559   12,594   4,286
April 23, 1921. *Charlotte Harbor.* A corruption of *Calus*, a local tribe. Changed to "Carlos" by the Spanish and later to "Charlotte" by the English in honor of Charlotte Sophia of Mecklenburg-Strelitz. (See Charlotte, Virginia.)

Charlotte   **Virginia**
Charlotte Court House   475 sq. mi.
12,586   12,472   11,688   12,266   11,551   13,368   14,057
November 27, 1764. *Charlotte Sophia of Mecklenburg-Strelitz (1744–1818).* Married King George III of England 1761; mother of kings George IV and William IV.

Charlottesville   **Virginia**
(Independent City)   10 sq. mi.
43,475   45,049   40,341   39,916   38,880   29,427   25,969
March 2, 1888. *Charlotte Sophia of Mecklenburg-Strelitz.** (Associated county: Albemarle.)

Charlton   **Georgia**
Folkston   774 sq. mi.
12,171   10,282   8,496   7,343   5,680   5,313   4,821
February 18, 1854. *Uncertain.* (1) *Robert Milledge Charlton (1807–54)*; Georgia legislature 1829; US district attorney 1830; judge, superior court for eastern district of Georgia 1832; US senator 1851–52. (2) *Thomas U. P. Charlton (1779–1835)*; Georgia legislature 1800; attorney general of Georgia; mayor of Savannah 1815–17 and 1819–21.

Chase   **Kansas**
Cottonwood Falls   773 sq. mi.
2,790   3,030   3,021   3,309   3,408   3,921   4,831
February 11, 1859. *Samuel Portland Chase (1808–73).* Cincinnati City Council 1840; US senator 1849–53 and two days in 1861; governor of Ohio 1855–59; US treasury secretary 1861–64; chief justice of US 1864–73; presided over impeachment trial of President Johnson 1868.

Chase   **Nebraska**
Imperial   894 sq. mi.
3,966   4,068   4,381   4,758   4,129   4,317   5,176
February 27, 1873; organized April 24, 1886. *Champion Spalding Chase (1820–98).* Paymaster in Union Army; attorney general of Nebraska 1867–69; mayor of Omaha intermittently 1874–84; member, first board of regents, University of Nebraska.

Chatham   **Georgia**
Savannah   426 sq. mi.
265,128   232,048   216,935   202,226   187,767   188,299   151,481

February 5, 1777. *William Pitt, 1st Earl of Chatham (1708–78)*. English statesman; member of Parliament 1735–61; secretary of state 1756; strengthened British Fleet during Seven Years' War 1756–63; opposed British policies in America; prime minister 1766–67.

Chatham   **North Carolina**
Pittsboro   682 sq. mi.
63,505   49,329   38,759   33,415   29,554   26,785   25,392
April 1, 1771. *William Pitt, 1st Earl of Chatham.**

Chattahoochee   **Georgia**
Cusseta   249 sq. mi.
11,267   14,882   16,934   21,732   25,813   13,011   12,149
February 13, 1854. *Chattahoochee River*. From Muskogean *chatto hoche* meaning "painted stone" referring to red and pink stones along the river.

Chattooga   **Georgia**
Summerville   313 sq. mi.
26,015   25,470   22,242   21,856   20,541   19,954   21,197
December 28, 1838. *Chattooga River*. Possible Cherokee borrowing of Creek *tsatu gi*, *chato-algi*, or *chato-agi* meaning "full of rocks."

Chautauqua   **Kansas**
Sedan   639 sq. mi.
3,669   4,359   4,407   5,016   4,642   5,956   7,376
March 25, 1875; effective June 1, 1875. *Chautauqua County, New York*. Proposed by Kansas legislator from New York.

Chautauqua   **New York**
Mayville   1,060 sq. mi.
134,905   139,750   141,895   146,925   147,305   145,377   135,189
March 11, 1808; organized 1811. *Chautauqua Lake*. Contraction of Seneca phrase of unknown origin; most suggestions pertain to lakes or fish.

Chaves   **New Mexico**
Roswell   6,065 sq. mi.
65,645   61,382   57,849   51,103   43,335   57,649   40,605
February 25, 1889. *José F. Chaves (1833–1904)*. New Mexico territorial legislature; lieutenant colonel in Union Army; New Mexico territorial delegate 1865–67 and 1869–71; Superintendent of Public Instruction 1903–04; assassinated.

Cheatham   **Tennessee**
Ashland City   302 sq. mi.
39,105   35,912   27,140   21,616   13,199   9,428   9,167
February 28, 1856. *Edwin Saunders Cheatham (1818–78)*. President of Louisville & Nashville Railroad; Tennessee legislature under both Union and Confederacy; Speaker of Tennessee Senate during Confederacy.

Cheboygan   **Michigan**
Cheboygan   715 sq. mi.
26,152   26,448   21,398   20,649   16,573   14,550   13,731
April 1, 1840; organized January 29, 1853. *Cheboygan River*. Being named for the river is only the best of many possibilities. *He* is Ojibwa word for "big" and *boygan* means "pipe"; may refer to a geographic feature or a specific body of water.

Chelan   **Washington**
Wenatchee   2,921 sq. mi.
72,453   66,616   52,250   45,061   41,355   40,744   39,301
March 13, 1899. *Lake Chelan*. From Salish word *tsill-ane* meaning "deep water."

Chemung   **New York**
Elmira   407 sq. mi.

| 88,830 | 91,070 | 95,195 | 97,656 | 101,537 | 98,706 | 86,827 |

March 29, 1836. *Chemung River*. Named for Delaware village; word for "big horn."

Chenango   **New York**
Norwich   894 sq. mi.

| 50,477 | 51,401 | 51,768 | 49,344 | 46,368 | 43,243 | 39,138 |

March 15, 1798. *Uncertain*. (1) *Chenango River*. (2) *Chenango Lake*. (3) *Onondaga village* on Lake Chenango. Onondaga word meaning "large bull-thistle."

Cherokee   **Alabama**
Centre   554 sq. mi.

| 25,989 | 23,988 | 19,543 | 18,760 | 15,606 | 16,303 | 17,634 |

January 9, 1836. *Cherokee Indians*. Cherokee word *chera* meaning "fire" or Chickasaw word *chiluk-ki* for "cave people." Moved from Great Lakes area to the Southeast US in pre-Columbian period; part of Iroquois linguistic family; one of Five Civilized Tribes; forcibly moved to Indian Territory (Oklahoma) in 1830s.

Cherokee   **Georgia**
Canton   422 sq. mi.

| 214,316 | 141,903 | 90,204 | 51,699 | 31,059 | 23,001 | 20,750 |

December 26, 1831. *Cherokee Indians*.*

Cherokee   **Iowa**
Cherokee   577 sq. mi.

| 12,072 | 13,035 | 14,098 | 16,238 | 17,269 | 18,598 | 19,052 |

January 15, 1851; organized October 2, 1858. *Cherokee Indians*.*

Cherokee   **Kansas**
Columbus   588 sq. mi.

| 21,603 | 22,605 | 21,374 | 22,304 | 21,549 | 22,279 | 25,144 |

August 25, 1855, as McGee; name changed and organized February 18, 1860. *Cherokee Indians*.*

Cherokee   **North Carolina**
Murphy   455 sq. mi.

| 27,444 | 24,298 | 20,170 | 18,933 | 16,330 | 16,335 | 18,294 |

January 4, 1839. *Cherokee Indians*.*

Cherokee   **Oklahoma**
Tahlequah   749 sq. mi.

| 46,987 | 42,521 | 34,049 | 30,684 | 23,174 | 17,762 | 18,989 |

July 16, 1907. *Cherokee Indians*.*

Cherokee   **South Carolina**
Gaffney   393 sq. mi.

| 55,342 | 52,537 | 44,506 | 40,983 | 36,791 | 35,205 | 34,992 |

February 25, 1897. *Cherokee Indians*.*

Cherokee   **Texas**
Rusk   1,053 sq. mi.

| 50,845 | 46,659 | 41,049 | 38,127 | 32,008 | 33,120 | 38,694 |

April 11, 1846. *Cherokee Indians*.*

Cherry   **Nebraska**
Valentine   5,960 sq. mi.

5,713   6,148   6,307   6,758   6,846   8,218   8,397

February 23, 1883. *Samuel A. Cherry (1850–81)*. Graduate of West Point; lieutenant, 5th Cavalry; murdered near Rock Creek, Dakota Territory.

Chesapeake   **Virginia**
(Independent City)   341 sq. mi.
222,209   191,184   151,976   114,486   89,580   73,647[a]   110,371[b]

May 16, 1691, as Norfolk County; consolidation of City of South Norfolk and Norfolk County into independent city of Chesapeake January 1, 1963. *Chesapeake Bay*. Algonquin word meaning "mother of waters" or "great salt bay"; compounded from *kitschi* meaning "highly salted" and *peek* meaning "body of water." [(a) Norfolk County (51,612) and City of South Norfolk (22,035). (b) Norfolk County (99,937) and City of South Norfolk (10,434).]

Cheshire   **New Hampshire**
Keene   707 sq. mi.
77,117   73,825   70,121   62,116   52,364   43,342   38,811

April 29, 1769. *Cheshire County, England*. Name chosen by King George III possibly to honor an admiral from Cheshire County.

Chester   **Pennsylvania**
West Chester   751 sq. mi.
498,886   433,501   379,396   316,660   278,311   210,608   159,141

March 10, 1682. *City of Chester, England*. Origin of many early settlers. Named by William Penn.

Chester   **South Carolina**
Chester   581 sq. mi.
33,140   34,068   32,170   30,148   29,811   30,888   32,597

March 12, 1785; converted to judicial district January 1, 1800; redesignated as county April 16, 1868. *Chester County, Pennsylvania*. Area was settled by Scotch-Irish immigrants from Chester County, Pennsylvania.

Chester   **Tennessee**
Henderson   286 sq. mi.
17,131   15,540   12,819   12,727   9,927   9,569   11,149

March 4, 1879. *Robert I. Chester (1793–1892)*. Postmaster of Jackson, Tennessee; quartermaster, 4th Tennessee Regiment, War of 1812; Tennessee legislature; US marshal.

Chesterfield   **South Carolina**
Chesterfield   799 sq. mi.
46,734   42,768   38,577   38,161   33,667   33,717   36,236

March 12, 1785; converted to judicial district January 1, 1800; redesignated as county April 16, 1868. *Philip Dormer Stanhope, 4th Earl of Chesterfield (1694–1773)*. Whig Member of House of Commons 1715–26; House of Lords 1726–73; ambassador to The Hague 1728–32 and 1744; lord lieutenant of Ireland 1745–46; daily letters to his son on conduct and etiquette published in 1774 by his son's widow were popular in America.

Chesterfield   **Virginia**
Chesterfield   423 sq. mi.
316,236   259,903   209,274   141,372   76,855   71,197   40,400

May 1, 1749. *Philip Dormer Stanhope, 4th Earl of Chesterfield*.* (Associated independent cities: Colonial Heights and part of Richmond.)

Cheyenne   **Colorado**
Cheyenne Wells   1,778 sq. mi.
1,836   2,231   2,397   2,153   2,396   2,789   3,453

March 25, 1889. *Cheyenne Indians*. Sioux word for "aliens" or possibly "scarred arms" from Cheyenne warrior practice of scarring left arm. Originally in Great Lakes area c1500; pushed out of Black Hills area by Sioux and settled in Plains; divided into northern and southern branches; constant warfare with other Indians and US Army; Northern Cheyennes fought Custer at Little Big Horn 1876; resettled in Indian Territory (Oklahoma).

Cheyenne   **Kansas**
Saint Francis   1,020 sq. mi.

2,726	3,165	3,243	3,678	4,256	4,708	5,668

March 20, 1873; organized April 1, 1886. *Cheyenne Indians.**

Cheyenne   **Nebraska**
Sidney   1,196 sq. mi.

9,998	9,830	9,494	10,057	10,778	14,848	12,081

June 22, 1867; organized December 17, 1870. *Cheyenne Indians.**

Chickasaw   **Iowa**
New Hampton   504 sq. mi.

12,439	13,095	13,295	15,437	14,969	15,034	15,228

January 15, 1851; organized September 12, 1853. *Chickasaw Indians.* Origin of tribal name is unknown; lived in southeastern US and had no known association with Iowa.

Chickasaw   **Mississippi**
Houston   502 sq. mi.

17,392	19,440	18,085	17,853	16,805	16,891	18,951

February 9, 1836. *Chickasaw Indians.**

Chicot   **Arkansas**
Lake Village   644 sq. mi.

11,800	14,117	15,713	17,793	18,164	18,990	22,306

October 25, 1823. *Point Chicot.* Former bend in Mississippi River; now an ox-bow lake. Name origin is uncertain; (1) French word for "stub"; (2) Indian village named Chiska.

Childress   **Texas**
Childress   696 sq. mi.

7,041	7,688	5,953	6,950	6,605	8,421	12,123

August 21, 1876; organized April 11, 1877. *George Campbell Childress (1804–41).* One of five commissioners who drafted Texas Declaration of Independence 1836; Texas Constitutional Convention 1836; committed suicide after several unsuccessful attempts to establish law practice.

Chilton   **Alabama**
Clanton   693 sq. mi.

43,643	39,593	32,458	30,612	25,180	25,693	26,922

December 30, 1868, as Baker; name changed December 17, 1874. *William Parish Chilton (1810–71).* Alabama Legislature 1839; Alabama Supreme Court 1847–56, chief justice 1852–56; Alabama Senate 1859; provisional Confederate Congress 1860; Confederate Congress 1861–65.

Chippewa   **Michigan**
Sault Sainte Marie   1,558 sq. mi.

38,520	38,543	34,604	29,029	32,412	32,655	29,206

December 22, 1826; effective February 1, 1827. *Chippewa Indians.* Name is a corruption of *Objibwa,* another name for the tribe. Algonquin linguistic family; controlled much of western Great Lakes area.

Chippewa   **Minnesota**
Montevideo   581 sq. mi.

12,441	13,088	13,228	14,941	15,109	16,320	16,739

February 20, 1862; organized January 9, 1869. *Chippewa River.* Named for Chippewa Indians.*

Chippewa   **Wisconsin**
Chippewa Falls   1,008 sq. mi.
62,415   55,195   52,360   52,127   47,717   45,096   42,439
February 3, 1845; organized 1852; *Chippewa River.**

Chisago   **Minnesota**
Center City   415 sq. mi.
53,887   41,101   30,521   25,717   17,492   13,419   12,669
March 31, 1851; organized January 1, 1852. *Chisago Lake.* American coinage from Ojibwa words *kichi* meaning "large" and *saga* meaning "beautiful."

Chittenden   **Vermont**
Burlington   537 sq. mi.
156,545   146,571   131,761   115,534   99,131   74,425   62,570
October 22, 1787. *Thomas Chittenden (1730–97).* 14th Connecticut Regiment 1767–73, colonel 1773; moved to New Hampshire Grants (Vermont) 1774; unofficial governor of Vermont while seeking independence from New Hampshire; first governor of Vermont 1791–97.

Choctaw   **Alabama**
Butler   914 sq. mi.
13,859   15,922   16,018   16,839   16,589   17,870   19,152
December 29, 1847. *Choctaw Indians.* Large nation in southern Mississippi and Alabama; ceded lands in 1830s and moved to Indian Territory (Oklahoma).

Choctaw   **Mississippi**
Ackerman   418 sq. mi.
8,547   9,758   9,071   8,996   8,440   8,423   11,009
December 23, 1833. *Choctaw Indians.**

Choctaw   **Oklahoma**
Hugo   770 sq. mi.
15,205   15,342   15,302   17,203   15,141   16,637   20,405
July 16, 1907. *Choctaw Indians.**

Chouteau   **Montana**
Fort Benton   3,972 sq. mi.
5,813   5,970   5,452   6,092   6,473   7,348   6,974
February 2, 1865. *Chouteau family.* Fur traders; most likely Pierre Chouteau (1789–1865); Missouri Constitutional Convention 1820; headed western department of American Fur Company for John Jacob Astor; bought out Astor; first fur company to take steamboat up Missouri River to Montana.

Chowan   **North Carolina**
Edenton   172 sq. mi.
14,793   14,526   13,506   12,558   10,764   11,729   12,540
1671, as Shaftesbury; name changed 1684. *Uncertain.* (1) *Chowan River*; named for Chowanoc Indians. (2) *Chowanoc Indians*; name means "people of the south."

Christian   **Illinois**
Taylorville   709 sq. mi.
34,800   35,372   34,418   36,446   35,948   37,207   38,816
February 15, 1839, as Dane; name changed February 1, 1840. *Christian County, Kentucky.* Origin of early settlers.

Christian   **Kentucky**
Hopkinsville   718 sq. mi.
73,955   72,265   68,941   66,878   56,224   56,904   42,359

December 13, 1796; effective March 1, 1797. *William Christian (?–1786)*. Officer in French and Indian War; colonel of militia 1774; Virginia legislature; moved to Kentucky 1785; killed by Indians.

Christian   **Missouri**
Ozark   563 sq. mi.
77,422   54,285   32,644   22,402   15,124   12,359   12,412
March 8, 1859. *Christian County, Kentucky*. Name suggested by resident from Kentucky.

Churchill   **Nevada**
Fallon   4,930 sq. mi.
24,877   23,982   17,938   13,917   10,513   8,452   6,161
November 25, 1861; organized February 19, 1864. *Fort Churchill*. Named for Sylvester Churchill (1783–1862); commissioned 1812; Inspector General of the Army 1841; cited for valor at Battle of Buena Vista 1847, promoted to brigadier general.

Cibola   **New Mexico**
Grants   4,539 sq. mi.
27,213   25,595   23,794   (a)   (a)   (a)   (a)
June 19, 1981. *Seven Cities of Cibola*. Fabled cities of great wealth believed to be in southwestern US; sought by Francisco Coronado 1540–42. [(a) Part of Valencia County.]

Cimarron   **Oklahoma**
Boise City   1,835 sq. mi.
2,475   3,148   3,301   3,648   4,145   4,496   4,589
July 16, 1907. *Cimarron River*. Spanish for "wild."

Citrus   **Florida**
Inverness   582 sq. mi.
141,236   118,085   93,515   54,703   19,196   9,268   6,111
June 2, 1887. *Descriptive*. Refers to citrus fruit grown in the area.

Clackamas   **Oregon**
Oregon City   1,870 sq. mi.
375,992   338,391   278,850   241,919   166,088   113,038   86,716
July 5, 1843. *Clackamas Indians*. Chinookan tribe living at lower end of Clackamas River; encountered by Lewis and Clark 1806.

Claiborne   **Louisiana**
Homer   755 sq. mi.
17,195   16,851   17,405   17,095   17,024   19,407   25,063
March 13, 1828. *William Charles Coles Claiborne (1775–1817)*. Tennessee Constitutional Convention 1796; superior court judge 1796; US representative 1791–1801; governor of Mississippi Territory 1801–05; commissioner to accept Louisiana from France 1803; governor of Orleans Territory 1804–12; first governor of Louisiana 1812–16; US senator 1817.

Claiborne   **Mississippi**
Port Gibson   487 sq. mi.
9,604   11,831   11,370   12,279   10,086   10,845   11,944
January 27, 1802. *William Charles Coles Claiborne.**

Claiborne   **Tennessee**
Tazewell   435 sq. mi.
32,213   29,862   26,137   24,595   19,420   19,067   24,788
October 29, 1801. *William Charles Coles Claiborne.**

Clallam   **Washington**
Port Angeles   1,738 sq. mi.

71,404   64,525   56,464   51,648   34,770   30,022   26,396
April 26, 1854. *Clallam Indians*. Name means "brave people"; lived on Strait of Juan de Fuca.

Clare   **Michigan**
Harrison   564 sq. mi.
30,926   31,252   24,952   23,822   16,695   11,647   10,253
April 1, 1840, as Kaykakee; name changed March 8, 1843; organized March 13, 1871. *County Clare, Ireland*. On March 8, 1843, the Michigan legislature changed some Indian-based names to Irish counties.

Clarendon   **South Carolina**
Manning   607 sq. mi.
34,971   32,502   28,450   27,464   25,604   29,490   32,215
March 12, 1785; abolished 1800; recreated 1855. *Edward Hyde, 3rd Earl of Clarendon (1609–74)*. Colonel, Royal Regiment of Dragoons 1685–88; civil and military governor of New York and East and West Jersey 1701–08; privy councilor 1711; envoy extraordinary to Hanover on ascension of George I 1714; one of eight original lords proprietor of Carolina.

Clarion   **Pennsylvania**
Clarion   601 sq. mi.
39,988   41,765   41,699   43,362   38,414   37,408   38,344
March 11, 1839. *Clarion River*. French for "clear sounding."

Clark   **Arkansas**
Arkadelphia   866 sq. mi.
22,995   23,456   21,437   23,326   21,537   20,950   22,998
December 15, 1818; effective March 1, 1819. *William Clark (1770–1838)*. Fought Indians on frontier 1791–96; co-leader of Lewis and Clark Expedition 1804–07; brigadier general of Louisiana Territory Militia and Superintendent of Indian Affairs at St. Louis 1807; governor of Missouri Territory 1813–20; surveyor general for Illinois, Missouri, and Arkansas. Brother of George Rogers Clark.

Clark   **Idaho**
Dubois   1,764 sq. mi.
982   1,022   762   798   741   915   918
February 1, 1919. *Sam K. Clark (?–?)*. Pioneer cattleman; Idaho legislature; first state senator from the county.

Clark   **Illinois**
Marshall   501 sq. mi.
16,335   17,008   15,921   16,913   16,216   16,546   17,362
March 22, 1819. *George Rogers Clark (1752–1818)*. Frontier leader; surveyor; volunteer under Virginia Governor Dunmore against Shawnee Indians; major of militia 1776; lieutenant colonel 1777; captured British garrison at Vincennes 1779; brigadier general of Continental Army. Brother of William Clark.

Clark   **Indiana**
Jeffersonville   373 sq. mi.
110,232   96,472   87,777   88,838   75,876   62,795   48,330
February 3, 1801. *George Rogers Clark*.*

Clark   **Kansas**
Ashland   975 sq. mi.
2,215   2,390   2,418   2,599   2,896   3,396   3,946
February 26, 1867; abolished 1883; recreated March 7, 1885; organized May 5, 1885. *Charles F. Clarke (?–1862)*. Captain, 6th Kansas Cavalry; died at Memphis December 10, 1862. Final letter *e* dropped by legislature.

Clark   **Kentucky**
Winchester   252 sq. mi.
35,613   33,144   29,496   28,322   24,090   21,075   18,898
December 6, 1792; effective February 1, 1793. *George Rogers Clark*.*

Clark **Missouri**
Kahoka 505 sq. mi.
7,139 7,416 7,547 8,493 8,260 8,725 9,003
December 16, 1836. *William Clark.**

Clark **Nevada**
Las Vegas 7,891 sq. mi.
1,951,269 1,375,765 741,459 463,087 273,288 127,016 48,289
February 5, 1909; effective July 1, 1909. *William Andrews Clark (1839–1925)*. Placer miner in Montana; major in battalion pursuing Chief Joseph 1877; president of Montana Constitutional Conventions 1884 and 1889; US senator from Montana 1899–1900 and 1901–07; advocated railroad through southern Nevada.

Clark **Ohio**
Springfield 397 sq. mi.
138,333 144,742 147,548 150,236 157,115 131,440 111,661
December 26, 1817. *George Rogers Clark.**

Clark **South Dakota**
Clark 958 sq. mi.
3,961 4,143 4,403 4,894 5,515 7,134 8,369
January 18, 1873; organized May 2, 1881. *Newton Clark (?–?)*. First schoolteacher in Sioux Falls; Dakota Territorial legislature when county was created.

Clark **Washington**
Vancouver 629 sq. mi.
425,363 345,238 238,053 192,227 128,454 93,809 85,307
June 27, 1844, as Vancouver; name changed to Clarke September 3, 1849; spelling corrected 1925. *William Clark.**

Clark **Wisconsin**
Neillsville 1,210 sq. mi.
34,690 33,557 31,647 32,910 30,361 31,527 32,459
July 6, 1853; organized 1857. *George Rogers Clark.**

Clarke **Alabama**
Grove Hill 1,238 sq. mi.
25,833 27,867 27,240 27,702 26,724 25,738 26,548
December 10, 1812. *Uncertain.* (1) *Elijah Clarke (1733–99)*; general, Continental Army; Siege of Augusta 1781. (2) *John Clark (1766–1832)*; son of Elijah; Revolutionary War; general, War of 1812; Georgia legislature; governor of Georgia 1819–23; dropped *e* from family name.

Clarke **Georgia**
Athens 119 sq. mi.
116,714 101,489 87,594 74,498 65,177 45,363 36,550
December 5, 1801. *Elijah Clarke.**

Clarke **Iowa**
Osceola 431 sq. mi.
9,286 9,133 8,287 8,612 7,581 8,222 9,369
January 13, 1846; organized August 21, 1851. *James Clarke (1812–50)*. Printer, first Wisconsin Territorial Legislature 1836; established Burlington, Iowa, *Gazette* 1837; secretary of Iowa Territory; governor of Iowa Territory 1845–46.

Clarke **Mississippi**
Quitman 692 sq. mi.
16,732 17,955 17,313 16,945 15,049 16,493 19,362
December 23, 1833. *Joshua G. Clarke (?–1828)*. Mississippi Territorial Legislature; Mississippi Constitutional Convention 1817; Mississippi Supreme Court 1818; chancellor of Mississippi Supreme Court of Chancery 1821–28.

Clarke   **Virginia**
Berryville   176 sq. mi.
14,034   12,652   12,101   9,965   8,102   7,942   7,074
March 8, 1836. *George Rogers Clark.** (Uncorrected spelling error from legislation.)

Clatsop   **Oregon**
Astoria   829 sq. mi.
37,039   35,630   33,301   32,489   28,473   27,380   30,776
June 22, 1844. *Clatsop Indians.* Chinook group, northwestern Oregon; Lewis and Clark wintered with the Clatsops 1805–06.

Clay   **Alabama**
Ashland   604 sq. mi.
13,932   14,254   13,252   13,703   12,636   12,400   13,929
December 7, 1866. *Henry Clay (1777–1852).* Kentucky House of Representatives 1803 and 1808–09; US senator, intermittently 1806–52; US representative, intermittently 1811–25; unsuccessful Whig presidential candidate 1824, 1832, and 1844; US secretary of state 1825–29; fought duel with John Randolph (see Randolph, Alabama) 1826; crafted Compromise of 1850.

Clay   **Arkansas**
Piggott   639 sq. mi.
16,083   17,609   18,107   20,616   18,771   21,258   26,674
March 24, 1873, as Clayton; name changed December 6, 1875. *Uncertain.* (1) Continued to be named for *John Middleton Clayton* (see Clayton, Iowa). (2) *Henry Clay.**

Clay   **Florida**
Green Cove Springs   604 sq. mi.
190,865   140,814   105,986   67,052   32,059   19,535   14,323
December 31, 1858. *Henry Clay.**

Clay   **Georgia**
Fort Gaines   195 sq. mi.
3,183   3,357   3,364   3,553   3,636   4,551   5,844
February 16, 1854. *Henry Clay.**

Clay   **Illinois**
Louisville   468 sq. mi.
13,815   14,560   14,460   15,283   14,735   15,815   17,445
December 23, 1824. *Henry Clay.**

Clay   **Indiana**
Brazil   358 sq. mi.
26,890   26,556   24,705   24,862   23,933   24,207   23,918
February 12, 1825; effective April 1, 1825. *Henry Clay.**

Clay   **Iowa**
Spencer   567 sq. mi.
16,667   17,372   17,585   19,576   18,464   18,504   18,103
January 15, 1851; organized October 15, 1858. *Henry Clay, Jr. (1807–47).* Graduated West Point 1831; brevet 2nd lieutenant 1831; resigned 1831; lieutenant colonel, 2nd Kentucky Volunteers 1846; killed at Battle of Buena Vista February 23, 1847.

Clay   **Kansas**
Clay Center   645 sq. mi.
8,535   8,822   9,158   9,802   9,890   10,675   11,697
February 20, 1857; organized July 26, 1866. *Henry Clay.**

Clay   **Kentucky**
Manchester   469 sq. mi.

| 21,730 | 24,556 | 21,746 | 22,752 | 18,481 | 20,748 | 23,116 |

December 2, 1806; effective April 1, 1807. *Green Clay (1757–1826)*. Surveyor in Kentucky 1777; Virginia legislature 1788–89; Kentucky legislature 1793–94; Kentucky Senate 1795–98 and 1807; Kentucky Constitutional Convention 1799; War of 1812, led 3,000 volunteers to aid Fort Meigs 1813; commanded Fort Meigs 1813; major general, Kentucky Militia.

Clay   **Minnesota**
Moorhead   1,045 sq. mi.

| 58,999 | 51,229 | 50,422 | 49,327 | 46,585 | 39,080 | 30,363 |

March 18, 1858, as Breckinridge; name changed March 6, 1862; organized February 27, 1872. *Henry Clay.**

Clay   **Mississippi**
West Point   410 sq. mi.

| 20,634 | 21,979 | 21,120 | 21,082 | 18,840 | 18,933 | 17,757 |

May 12, 1871, as Colfax; name changed April 10, 1876. *Henry Clay.**

Clay   **Missouri**
Liberty   397 sq. mi.

| 221,939 | 184,006 | 153,411 | 136,488 | 123,322 | 87,474 | 45,221 |

January 2, 1822. *Henry Clay.**

Clay   **Nebraska**
Clay Center   572 sq. mi.

| 6,542 | 7,039 | 7,123 | 8,106 | 8,266 | 8,717 | 8,700 |

February 16, 1867. *Henry Clay.**

Clay   **North Carolina**
Hayesville   215 sq. mi.

| 10,587 | 8,775 | 7,155 | 6,619 | 5,180 | 5,526 | 6,006 |

February 20, 1861. *Henry Clay.**

Clay   **South Dakota**
Vermillion   412 sq. mi.

| 13,864 | 13,537 | 13,186 | 13,689 | 12,923 | 10,810 | 10,993 |

April 10, 1862. *Henry Clay.**

Clay   **Tennessee**
Celina   237 sq. mi.

| 7,861 | 7,976 | 7,238 | 7,676 | 6,624 | 7,289 | 8,701 |

June 16, 1870. *Henry Clay.**

Clay   **Texas**
Henrietta   1,089 sq. mi.

| 10,752 | 11,006 | 10,024 | 9,582 | 8,079 | 8,351 | 9,896 |

December 24, 1857; organized 1861; deorganized 1862; reorganized May 27, 1873. *Henry Clay.**

Clay   **West Virginia**
Clay   342 sq. mi.

| 9,386 | 10,330 | 9,983 | 11,265 | 9,330 | 11,942 | 14,961 |

March 29, 1858. *Henry Clay.**

Clayton   **Georgia**
Jonesboro   142 sq. mi.

| 259,424 | 236,517 | 182,052 | 150,357 | 98,043 | 46,365 | 22,872 |

November 30, 1858. *Augustin Smith Clayton (1783–1839)*. Georgia legislature 1810–12; clerk, Georgia House of Representatives 1813–15; Georgia Senate 1826–27; judge, Georgia Superior Court 1819–31; US representative 1832–35.

Clayton   **Iowa**
Elkader   779 sq. mi.
18,129   18,678   19,054   21,098   20,606   21,962   22,522
December 21, 1837. *John Middleton Clayton (1796–1856)*. Delaware House of Representatives 1824; Delaware secretary of state 1826–28; US senator intermittently 1845–56; US secretary of state 1849–50. While a senator, Clayton worked for creation of Wisconsin Territory which included Iowa.

Clear Creek   **Colorado**
Georgetown   395 sq. mi.
9,088   9,322   7,619   7,308   4,819   2,793   3,289
November 1, 1861. *Clear Creek*. Descriptive.

Clearfield   **Pennsylvania**
Clearfield   1,145 sq. mi.
81,642   83,382   78,097   83,578   74,619   81,534   85,957
March 26, 1804. *Descriptive*. Refers to area cleared by Indians.

Clearwater   **Idaho**
Orofino   2,457 sq. mi.
8,761   8,930   8,505   10,390   10,871   8,548   8,217
February 27, 1911. *Clearwater River*. Translation of *koos-koos-kia*; Nez Perce name for the river.

Clearwater   **Minnesota**
Bagley   999 sq. mi.
8,695   8,423   8,309   8,761   8,013   8,864   10,204
December 20, 1902. *Clearwater River and Clearwater Lake*. Translation of Chippewa name for the river and lake.

Cleburne   **Alabama**
Heflin   560 sq. mi.
14,972   14,123   12,730   12,595   10,996   10,911   11,904
December 6, 1866. *Patrick Ronayne Cleburne (1828–64)*. Arrived in New Orleans from Ireland 1849; captain to colonel, 15th Arkansas Infantry; brigadier and major general 1862; Battle of Shiloh 1862; battles of Missionary Ridge, Ringgold, Resaca, and New Hope Church; killed at Battle of Franklin, November 30, 1864.

Cleburne   **Arkansas**
Heber Springs   554 sq. mi.
25,970   24,046   19,411   16,909   10,349   9,059   11,487
February 20, 1883. *Patrick Ronayne Cleburne*.*

Clermont   **Ohio**
Batavia   452 sq. mi.
197,363   177,977   150,187   128,483   95,725   80,530   42,182
December 6, 1800. *Uncertain*. (1) *City of Clermont-Ferrand, France*. Possibly named as tribute to recent French assistance during American Revolution. (2) Combination of French *cler*, approximating "clear," and *mont* meaning "mount."

Cleveland   **Arkansas**
Rison   598 sq. mi.
8,689   8,571   7,781   7,868   6,605   6,944   8,956
April 17, 1873, as Dorsey; name changed March 5, 1885. *Steven Grover Cleveland (1837–1908)*. Sheriff of Erie County, New York 1870–73; mayor of Buffalo 1881–82; governor of New York 1883–85; 22nd and 24th Presidents of the US 1885–89 and 1893–97.

Cleveland   **North Carolina**
Shelby   464 sq. mi.
98,078   96,287   84,714   83,435   72,556   66,048   64,357

January 11, 1841, as Cleaveland; spelling changed to more familiar spelling of President Cleveland's name 1887. *Benjamin Cleaveland (1738–1806)*. Ensign, 2nd North Carolina Regiment 1775; lieutenant and captain 1776; retired 1778; colonel, North Carolina Militia 1778; hero at Battle of King's Mountain 1780.

Cleveland **Oklahoma**
Norman 539 sq. mi.
255,755 208,016 174,253 133,173 81,839 47,600 41,443
May 2, 1890. *Steven Grover Cleveland.**

Clinch **Georgia**
Homerville 800 sq. mi.
6,798 6,878 6,160 6,660 6,405 6,545 6,007
February 14, 1850. *Duncan Lamont Clinch (1787–1849)*. Infantry lieutenant, US Army 1808; captain to colonel 1810–19; brevetted brigadier general for ten year's service 1829; Seminole Wars 1835; resigned 1836; US representative from Georgia 1844–45.

Clinton **Illinois**
Carlyle 474 sq. mi.
37,762 35,535 33,944 32,617 28,315 24,029 22,594
December 27, 1824. *De Witt Clinton (1769–1828)*. Secretary to his uncle New York Governor George Clinton (see Clinton, New York); New York Assembly 1798; New York Senate 1798–1802 and 1806–11; US senator 1802–03; mayor of New York City intermittently 1803–15; governor of New York 1817–21 and 1825–28; led development of Erie Canal.

Clinton **Indiana**
Frankfort 405 sq. mi.
33,224 33,866 30,974 31,545 30,547 30,765 29,734
January 29, 1830; effective March 1, 1830. *De Witt Clinton.**

Clinton **Iowa**
Clinton 695 sq. mi.
49,116 50,149 51,040 57,122 56,749 55,060 49,664
December 21, 1837; organized January 5, 1841. *De Witt Clinton.**

Clinton **Kentucky**
Albany 197 sq. mi.
10,272 9,634 9,135 9,321 8,174 8,886 10,605
February 20, 1836. *De Witt Clinton.**

Clinton **Michigan**
Saint Johns 566 sq. mi.
75,382 64,753 57,883 55,893 48,492 37,696 31,195
March 2, 1831; organized March 12, 1839. *De Witt Clinton.**

Clinton **Missouri**
Plattsburg 419 sq. mi.
20,743 18,979 16,595 15,916 12,462 11,588 11,726
January 2, 1833. *De Witt Clinton.**

Clinton **New York**
Plattsburg 1,038 sq. mi.
82,128 79,894 85,969 80,750 72,934 72,722 53,622
March 7, 1788. *George Clinton (1739–1812)*. Clerk, New York Court of Common Pleas 1759; New York Assembly 1768; Continental Congress 1775–76; brigadier general 1777; governor of New York 1777–95 and 1801–04; US vice president 1805–12; uncle of De Witt Clinton.*

Clinton   **Ohio**
Wilmington   409 sq. mi.
42,040   40,543   35,415   34,603   31,464   30,004   25,572
February 19, 1810. *George Clinton.**

Clinton   **Pennsylvania**
Lock Haven   888 sq. mi.
39,238   37,914   37,182   38,971   37,721   37,619   36,532
June 21, 1839. *De Witt Clinton.**

Cloud   **Kansas**
Concordia   715 sq. mi.
9,533   10,268   11,023   12,494   13,466   14,407   16,104
February 9, 1860, as Shirley; abolished 1865; recreated 1866; name changed February 26, 1867. *William F. Cloud (1825–1905)*. Mexican War; captain, Ohio Volunteer Militia 1848; Union Army 1861; Battle of Wilson's Creek 1861; Battle of Cane Hill 1862; colonel, 2nd Kansas Cavalry.

Coahoma   **Mississippi**
Clarksdale   552 sq. mi.
26,151   30,622   31,665   36,918   40,447   46,212   49,361
February 9, 1836. *Uncertain*. (1) *Coahoma (c1750–c1840)*; Chickasaw chief also known as William McGillivray; captain under Washington. (2) *Sweet Coahoma*, Indian princess, daughter of a chief from a family named Sheriff. Name is Choctaw word for "red panther."

Coal   **Oklahoma**
Coalgate   517 sq. mi.
5,925   6,031   5,780   6,041   5,525   5,546   8,056
July 16, 1907. *Descriptive*. Refers to coal deposits in the area.

Cobb   **Georgia**
Marietta   340 sq. mi.
688,078   607,751   447,745   297,718   196,793   114,174   61,830
December 3, 1832. *Thomas Willis Cobb (1784–1830)*. US representative from Georgia 1817–21 and 1823–24; US senator 1824–28; judge, Georgia Superior Court 1828.

Cochise   **Arizona**
Bisbee   6,166 sq. mi.
131,346   117,755   97,624   85,686   61,910   55,039   31,488
February 1, 1881. *Cochise (?–1874)*. Chief of Chiracahua Apaches; fought against US Army 1861–71; moved tribe to reservation 1871.

Cochran   **Texas**
Morton   775 sq. mi.
3,127   3,730   4,377   4,825   5,326   6,417   5,928
August 21, 1876; organized 1924. *Robert Cochran (1810–36)*. Settled in Texas 1835; private, Texas Army; killed at Alamo March 6, 1836.

Cocke   **Tennessee**
Newport   435 sq. mi.
35,662   33,565   29,141   28,792   25,283   23,390   22,991
October 9, 1797; name changed to Union January 28, 1846; renamed Cocke January 3, 1850. *William Cocke (1748–1828)*. Explored Tennessee with Daniel Boone; Virginia House of Burgesses 1776; Tennessee Constitutional Convention 1796; US senator 1796–97 and 1799–1805; Mississippi legislature 1813; served with Andrew Jackson in War of 1812; Chickasaw Indian agent 1814.

Coconino   **Arizona**
Flagstaff   18,619 sq. mi.

134,421	116,320	96,591	75,008	48,326	41,857	23,910

February 19, 1891. *Havasupai and Yavapai Indians*. Corruption of Hopi name for their neighboring tribes; most suggested translations are derogatory or refer to water.

Codington   **South Dakota**
Watertown   689 sq. mi.

27,227	25,897	22,698	20,885	19,140	20,220	18,944

February 15, 1877; organized August 7, 1878. *G. S. Codington (?–?)*. Circuit riding Protestant clergyman; member of Dakota territorial legislature at time county was created.

Coffee   **Alabama**
Elba   679 sq. mi.

49,948	43,615	40,240	38,533	34,872	30,583	30,720

December 29, 1841. *John Coffee (1772–1833)*. Business partner of Andrew Jackson; Tennessee Volunteers 1812–13; brigadier general, Tennessee Mounted Riflemen 1813; wounded at Battle of New Orleans 1815; public lands surveyor 1815. Cousin of John Coffee listed below.

Coffee   **Georgia**
Douglas   575 sq. mi.

42,356	37,413	29,592	26,894	22,828	21,953	23,961

February 9, 1854. *John Coffee (1782–1836)*. General of Georgia Militia, Creek War 1814; Georgia Senate 1819–27; US representative 1833–36. Cousin of John Coffee.*

Coffee   **Tennessee**
Manchester   429 sq. mi.

52,796	48,014	40,339	38,311	32,572	28,603	23,049

January 8, 1836. *John Coffee (1772–1833)*.*

Coffey   **Kansas**
Burlington   627 sq. mi.

8,601	8,865	8,404	9,370	7,397	8,403	10,408

August 30, 1855; organized February 17, 1859. *Asbury M. Coffey (1804–79)*. Osage River Indian Agency; Kansas Territorial legislature 1855–56; advocated preservation of the Union but favored slavery and served as a colonel in Confederate Army in Indian Territory (Oklahoma).

Coke   **Texas**
Robert Lee   911 sq. mi.

3,320	3,864	3,424	3,196	3,087	3,589	4,045

March 13, 1889. *Richard Coke (1829–97)*. Texas Secession Convention 1861; private to captain in Confederate Army 1861–65; district judge at Waco 1865; associate justice of Texas Supreme Court 1866; removed by military governor 1867; governor of Texas 1874–76; US senator 1877–85.

Colbert   **Alabama**
Tuscumbia   593 sq. mi.

54,428	54,984	51,666	54,519	49,632	46,506	39,561

February 6, 1867; abolished 1867; recreated 1869. *George Colbert (1744–1839) and Levi Colbert (1759–1834)*. Brothers; Chickasaw chiefs *Tootemastubie* (George) and *Itawamba Mingo* (Levi; see Itawamba, Mississippi); George owned ferry on Natchez Trace.

Cole   **Missouri**
Jefferson City   394 sq. mi.

75,990	71,397	63,579	56,663	46,228	40,761	35,464

November 16, 1820. *Stephen Cole (c1792–1822)*. Early settler in central Missouri; traded on Santa Fe Trail; killed by Indians on Rio Grande.

Coleman   **Texas**
Coleman   1,262 sq. mi.
8,895   9,235   9,710   10,439   10,288   12,458   15,503
February 1, 1858; organized October 6, 1864. *Robert M. Coleman (1797–1837)*. Aide-de-camp to General Houston at Battle of San Jacinto 1836; signer, Texas Declaration of Independence 1836; Texas Ranger 1836–37; drowned in Brazos River.

Coles   **Illinois**
Charleston   508 sq. mi.
53,873   53,196   51,644   52,260   47,815   42,860   40,328
December 25, 1830. *Edward Coles (1786–1868)*. Private secretary to President Madison 1809–15; special envoy to Russia 1816; emancipated his slaves and gave each 160 acres of land. 1818; governor of Illinois 1822–26.

Colfax   **Nebraska**
Schuyler   412 sq. mi.
10,515   10,441   9,139   9,890   9,498   9,595   10,010
February 15, 1869. *Schuyler Colfax (1823–85)*. Editor, *Valley Register*, St. Joseph, Indiana, 1845; Indiana Constitutional Convention 1850; US representative 1855–69; US vice president 1869–73.

Colfax   **New Mexico**
Raton   3,758 sq. mi.
13,750   14,189   12,925   13,667   12,170   13,806   16,761
January 25, 1869. *Schuyler Colfax.**

Colleton   **South Carolina**
Walterboro   1,056 sq. mi.
38,892   38,264   34,377   31,676   27,622   27,816   28,242
1682; abolished 1769; recreated 1785; converted to judicial district January 1, 1800; redesignated as county April 16, 1868. *John Colleton (1608–66)*. Loyalist during English Civil War; lived in Barbados during Interregnum; one of eight original lords proprietor of Carolina 1663.

Collier   **Florida**
Naples   1,998 sq. mi.
321,520   251,377   152,099   85,971   38,040   15,733   6,488
May 8, 1923. *Barron Gift Collier (1873–1939)*. Industrialist; owned Florida real estate and hotels; reclaimed sections of the Everglades.

Collin   **Texas**
McKinney   841 sq. mi.
782,341   491,675   264,036   144,576   66,920   41,247   41,692
April 3, 1846. *Collin McKinney (1766–1861)*. Texas Constitutional Convention 1836; one of five commissioners to draft Texas Declaration of Independence 1836; Republic of Texas legislature; insisted that counties in northern Texas have rectangular boundaries.

Collingsworth   **Texas**
Wellington   918 sq. mi.
3,057   3,206   3,573   4,648   4,755   6,276   9,139
August 1, 1876; organized September 30, 1890. *James T. Collinsworth (1806–38)*. Texas Constitutional Convention 1836; major and aide-de-camp to General Houston 1836; Texas Senate 1836; first chief justice, Republic of Texas 1837; drowned in Galveston Bay. Uncorrected error added letter *g* to county's name.

Colonial Heights   **Virginia**
(Independent City)   8 sq. mi.

17,411   16,897   16,064   16,509   15,097   9,587   6,077

1948. *Descriptive.* Refers to elevated position where Lafayette placed his field pieces, known as "colonials," to bombard Petersburg 1781. (Associated county: Chesterfield.)

Colorado   **Texas**
Columbus   960 sq. mi.
20,874   20,390   18,383   18,823   17,638   18,463   17,576

March 17, 1836; organized 1837. *Colorado River.* Spanish for "colored"; refers to reddish silt in river.

Colquitt   **Georgia**
Moultrie   544 sq. mi.
45,498   42,053   36,645   35,376   32,200   34,048   33,999

February 25, 1856. *Walter Terry Colquitt (1799–1855).* Methodist preacher; judge of Chattahoochee Circuit 1826; Georgia Senate 1834 and 1837; US representative 1839–42; US senator 1843–48.

Columbia   **Arkansas**
Magnolia   766 sq. mi.
24,552   25,063   25,691   26,644   25,952   26,400   28,770

December 17, 1852. *Columbia.* Goddess of liberty.

Columbia   **Florida**
Lake City   798 sq. mi.
67,531   56,513   42,613   35,399   25,250   20,077   18,216

February 4, 1832. *Christopher Columbus (1451–1506).* Italian navigator serving Spain; sailed from Palos, Spain, August 3, 1492; discovered San Salvador Island in Bahamas October 12, 1492; made three more voyages to Americas; died believing he had reached Asia. "Columbia" is Latinized form of "Columbus."

Columbia   **Georgia**
Appling   290 sq. mi.
124,053   89,288   66,031   40,118   22,327   13,423   9,525

December 10, 1790. *Christopher Columbus.**

Columbia   **New York**
Hudson   635 sq. mi.
63,096   63,094   62,982   59,487   51,519   47,322   43,182

April 4, 1786. *Christopher Columbus.**

Columbia   **Oregon**
Saint Helens   657 sq. mi.
49,351   43,560   37,557   35,646   28,790   22,379   22,967

January 16, 1854. *Columbia River.* Named for the ship *Columbia* on which Captain Robert Gray sailed up the river 1792. (See Grays Harbor, Washington.)

Columbia   **Pennsylvania**
Bloomsburg   483 sq. mi.
67,295   64,151   63,202   61,967   55,114   53,489   53,460

March 22, 1813. *Christopher Columbus.**

Columbia   **Washington**
Dayton   869 sq. mi.
4,078   4,064   4,024   4,057   4,439   4,569   4,860

November 11, 1875. *Columbia River.**

Columbia   **Wisconsin**
Portage   766 sq. mi.

| 56,833 | 52,468 | 45,088 | 43,222 | 40,150 | 36,708 | 34,023 |

February 3, 1846. *Town of Columbus*. Named for Christopher Columbus.*

Columbiana   **Ohio**
Lisbon   532 sq. mi.

| 107,841 | 112,075 | 108,276 | 113,572 | 108,310 | 107,004 | 98,920 |

March 25, 1803. *Contrived*. Combines *Christopher Columbus** with an unknown Anna.

Columbus   **North Carolina**
Whitesville   937 sq. mi.

| 58,098 | 54,749 | 49,587 | 51,037 | 46,937 | 48,973 | 50,621 |

December 15, 1808. *Christopher Columbus*.*

Colusa   **California**
Colusa   1,151 sq. mi.

| 21,419 | 18,804 | 16,275 | 12,791 | 12,430 | 12,075 | 11,651 |

February 18, 1850, as Colusi; organized 1851; name changed 1854. *Colus Indians*. Name may mean "scratch" or "scratcher."

Comal   **Texas**
New Braunfels   559 sq. mi.

| 108,472 | 78,021 | 51,832 | 36,446 | 24,165 | 19,844 | 16,357 |

March 24, 1846. *Comal River*. Spanish for "griddle"; describes flat surrounding landscape.

Comanche   **Kansas**
Coldwater   788 sq. mi.

| 1,891 | 1,967 | 2,313 | 2,554 | 2,702 | 3,271 | 3,888 |

February 26, 1867; organized February 27, 1885. *Comanche Indians*. From Ute word meaning "enemy." Southern Shoshone group driven southward from Wyoming by Sioux; nomadic horsemen ranged from Kansas into Mexico; agreed to move to Indian Territory (Oklahoma) by Treaty of Medicine Lodge 1867.

Comanche   **Oklahoma**
Lawton   1,069 sq. mi.

| 124,098 | 114,996 | 111,486 | 112,456 | 108,144 | 90,803 | 55,165 |

August 6, 1901. *Comanche Indians*.*

Comanche   **Texas**
Comanche   938 sq. mi.

| 13,974 | 14,026 | 13,381 | 12,617 | 11,898 | 11,865 | 15,516 |

January 25, 1856. *Comanche Indians*.*

Concho   **Texas**
Paint Rock   984 sq. mi.

| 4,087 | 3,966 | 3,044 | 2,915 | 2,937 | 3,672 | 5,078 |

February 1, 1858; organized March 11, 1879. *Concho River*. Spanish for "shell"; may be from mussel shells found in the area.

Concordia   **Louisiana**
Vidalia   697 sq. mi.

| 20,822 | 20,247 | 20,828 | 22,981 | 22,578 | 20,467 | 14,398 |

April 10, 1805. *New Concordia*. Spanish military post 1768; named for good relations (concord) between Spanish and American settlers.

Conecuh   **Alabama**
Evergreen   850 sq. mi.

| 13,228 | 14,089 | 14,054 | 15,884 | 15,645 | 17,762 | 21,776 |

February 13, 1818. *Conecuh River*. Uncertain origin; (1) Muskogee word for "crooked"; (2) corruption of Creek word *econneka* meaning "land of cane."

Conejos **Colorado**
Conejos 1,287 sq. mi.

8,256	8,400	7,453	7,794	7,846	8,428	10,171

November 1, 1861, as Guadalupe; name changed after six days, November 7, 1861. *Conejos River*. Spanish for "rabbit."

Contra Costa **California**
Martinez 716 sq. mi.

1,049,025	948,816	803,732	656,380	558,389	409,030	298,984

February 18, 1850. *Descriptive*. Spanish for "opposite coast"; refers to county's location across San Francisco Bay; opposite City of San Francisco.

Converse **Wyoming**
Douglas 4,255 sq. mi.

13,833	12,052	11,128	14,069	5,938	6,366	5,933

March 9, 1888. *Amasa R. Converse (1842–85)*. Merchant, stockman, and banker; treasurer, Wyoming Territory 1875–76 and 1877–79.

Conway **Arkansas**
Morrilton 552 sq. mi.

21,273	20,336	19,151	19,505	16,805	15,430	18,137

October 20, 1825; effective January 1, 1826. *Henry Wharton Conway (1793–1827)*. Navy ensign and lieutenant 1813; clerk, US Treasury 1817; congressional delegate from Arkansas Territory 1823–27; killed in duel by Robert Crittenden (see Crittenden, Arkansas).

Cook **Georgia**
Adel 227 sq. mi.

17,212	15,771	13,456	13,490	12,129	11,822	12,201

July 30, 1918. *Philip Cook (1817–94)*. Georgia Senate 1859–60 and 1863–64; Confederate Army 1861, brigadier general 1863; US representative 1873–83; Georgia secretary of state 1890–94.

Cook **Illinois**
Chicago 945 sq. mi.

5,194,675	5,376,741	5,105,067	5,253,655	5,492,369	5,129,725	4,508,792

January 15, 1831. *Daniel Pope Cook (1794–1827)*. Editor, Edwardsville *Illinois Intelligencer* 1816; advocated Illinois statehood; first attorney general of Illinois for 11 days 1819; US representative 1819–27.

Cook **Minnesota**
Grand Marais 1,452 sq. mi.

5,176	5,168	3,868	4,092	3,423	3,377	2,900

November 3, 1874; organized April 6, 1897. *Michael Cook (1828–64)*. Minnesota territorial and state senator 1857–62; major, 10th Minnesota Regiment 1864; died from wounds received at Battle of Nashville December 16, 1864.

Cooke **Texas**
Gainesville 875 sq. mi.

38,437	36,363	30,777	27,656	23,471	22,560	22,146

March 20, 1848; organized March 10, 1849. *William G. Cooke (1808–47)*. Captain, Texas Rangers 1835; Battle of San Jacinto 1836; quartermaster general, Texas Army 1839.

Cooper **Missouri**
Boonville 565 sq. mi.

17,601	16,670	14,835	14,643	14,732	15,448	16,608

December 17, 1818. *Uncertain.* (1) *Benjamin Cooper (1784–1867)*; early settler; Missouri Senate 1820. (2) *Sarshall (or Sarshel) Cooper (1762–1815)*; built Cooper's Fort on Missouri River; War of 1812; killed by Indians.

Coos   **New Hampshire**
Lancaster   1,795 sq. mi.

33,055	33,111	34,828	35,147	34,291	37,140	35,932

December 24, 1803; effective March 1, 1805. *Uncertain.* (1) Algonquin word meaning "crooked river"; refers to Connecticut River. (2) Corruption of Algonquin word *cohos* meaning "pines."

Coos   **Oregon**
Coquille   1,596 sq. mi.

63,043	62,779	60,273	64,047	56,515	54,955	42,265

December 22, 1853. *Kusan Indians.* Meaning of name unknown; inhabited area around Coos Bay.

Coosa   **Alabama**
Rockford   651 sq. mi.

11,539	12,202	11,063	11,377	10,662	10,726	11,766

December 18, 1832. *Coosa River.* Cherokee word for "rippling."

Copiah   **Mississippi**
Hazlehurst   777 sq. mi.

29,449	28,757	27,592	26,503	24,749	27,051	30,493

January 21, 1823. *Combined words.* Choctaw words *koi* (panther) and *panya* (screaming).

Corson   **South Dakota**
McIntosh   2,470 sq. mi.

4,050	4,181	4,195	5,196	4,994	5,798	6,168

March 2, 1909. *Dighton Corson (c1827–1915)*, Wisconsin legislature 1857–58; Nevada state attorney; Nevada Constitutional Conventions 1885 and 1889; South Dakota Supreme Court 1889–1913.

Cortland   **New York**
Cortland   499 sq. mi.

49,336	48,599	48,963	48,820	45,894	41,113	37,158

April 8, 1808. *Pierre van Cortlandt (1721–1814).* Revolutionary War; Provincial Legislature of New York 1777; New York Constitutional Convention; first lieutenant governor of New York 1777–95.

Coryell   **Texas**
Gatesville   1,052 sq. mi.

75,388	74,978	64,213	56,767	35,311	23,961	16,284

February 4, 1854. *James Coryell (1803–37).* Explored for silver mines with James Bowie 1831 (see Bowie, Texas); Texas Ranger 1836; killed by Indians while raiding a bee hive.

Coshocton   **Ohio**
Coshocton   564 sq. mi.

36,901	36,655	35,427	36,024	33,486	32,224	31,141

January 31, 1810; organized 1811. *Delaware village.* From Delaware word *koshachkink* (one of many variations) meaning "union of waters" or "ferry."

Costilla   **Colorado**
San Luis   1,227 sq. mi.

3,524	3,663	3,190	3,071	3,091	4,219	6,067

November 1, 1861. *Costilla River.* Spanish for "rib" possibly for a long, sweeping curve in the river.

Cottle   **Texas**
Paducah   901 sq. mi.

1,505	1,904	2,247	2,947	3,204	4,207	6,099

August 21, 1876; organized January 1892. *George Washington Cottle (1798–1836)*. Private, Texas Army; killed at Alamo March 6, 1836.

Cotton   **Oklahoma**
Walters   633 sq. mi.

6,193	6,614	6,651	7,338	6,832	8,031	10,180

August 27, 1912. *Descriptive*. Refers to cotton growing in the area; name drawn from a hat by citizens of the county.

Cottonwood   **Minnesota**
Windom   639 sq. mi.

11,687	12,167	12,694	14,854	14,887	16,166	15,763

May 23, 1857; organized July 4, 1873. *Cotton River*. English translation of *waraju*, Dakota name for trees along the river.

Covington   **Alabama**
Andalusia   1,030 sq. mi.

37,765	37,631	36,478	36,850	34,079	35,631	40,373

December 7, 1821. *Leonard Covington (1768–1813)*. US Army 1792, lieutenant of dragoons 1793, served with General Wayne 1794, resigned 1795; Maryland House of Delegates; US representative 1805–07; lieutenant colonel to brigadier general 1809–13; mortally wounded at Battle of Chrysler's Field, November 11, 1813.

Covington   **Mississippi**
Collins   414 sq. mi.

19,568	19,407	16,527	15,927	14,002	13,637	16,036

January 5, 1819. *Leonard Covington.**

Covington   **Virginia**
(Independent City)   5 sq. mi.

5,961	6,303	6,991	9,063	10,060	11,062	(a)

1952. *Uncertain*. (1) *Peter Covington (?–?)*; early settler. (2) *Leonard Covington.** [(a) Part of Alleghany County] (Associated county: Alleghany.)

Coweta   **Georgia**
Newnan   441 sq. mi.

127,317	89,215	53,853	39,268	32,310	28,893	27,786

June 9, 1826. *Coweta Indians*. Named from Creek word *kawita*, possibly meaning "falls" on the Chattahoochee River.

Cowley   **Kansas**
Winfield   1,126 sq. mi.

36,311	36,291	36,915	36,824	35,012	37,861	36,905

August 30, 1835, as Hunter; abolished 1864; recreated and name changed February 26, 1867, organized 1870. *Matthew Cowley (?–1864)*. 1st lieutenant, Company I, 9th Kansas Cavalry; died at Little Rock, October 7, 1864.

Cowlitz   **Washington**
Kelso   1,140 sq. mi.

102,410	92,948	82,119	79,548	68,616	57,801	53,369

April 21, 1854. *Uncertain*. (1) *Cowlitz Indians*; from Cowlitz word meaning "capturing the medicine spirit"; refers to practice of young Cowlitz braves communing with spirits. (2) *Cowlitz River*; named for Cowlitz Indians.

Craig   **Oklahoma**
Vinita   761 sq. mi.

15,029	14,950	14,104	15,014	14,722	16,303	18,263

July 16, 1907. *Granville C. Craig (1849–?)*. Cherokee merchant and stockman.

Craig   **Virginia**
New Castle   330 sq. mi.

5,190	5,091	4,372	3,948	3,524	3,356	3,452

March 21, 1851. *Robert Craig (1792–1852)*. Virginia House of Delegates, intermittently 1817–52; US representative 1829–33 and 1835–41.

Craighead   **Arkansas**
Jonesboro   707 sq. mi.

96,443	82,148	68,956	63,239	52,068	47,303	50,613

February 19, 1859. *Thomas B. Craighead (1800–?)*. Arkansas Senate; opposed creation of the county which was approved and named for him while he was absent from the senate.

Crane   **Texas**
Crane   785 sq. mi.

4,375	3,996	4,652	4,600	4,172	4,699	3,965

February 26, 1887; organized 1927. *William Carey Crane (1816–85)*. Ordained Baptist minister 1838; president of Mississippi Female College 1851–57; president of Baylor University 1863–85.

Craven   **North Carolina**
New Bern   709 sq. mi.

103,505	91,436	81,613	71,043	62,554	58,773	48,823

December 3, 1705, as Archdale; name changed 1712. *Uncertain*. (1) *William Craven, Earl of Craven (1606–97)*; military officer; knighted 1627; supporter of Charles I; one of eight original lords proprietor of Carolina 1663; made 1st Earl of Craven 1664. (2) *William, Lord Craven (1668–1711)*; grand nephew or distant cousin of William Craven; inherited proprietorship and title as 2nd Lord Craven; Lord Lieutenant of Berkshire 1702. (3) *William, 3rd Lord Craven (1700–39)*; inherited Carolina proprietorship on death of his father, the 2nd Lord Craven 1711; sold proprietorship to crown 1729.

Crawford   **Arkansas**
Van Buren   593 sq. mi.

61,948	53,247	42,493	36,892	25,677	21,318	22,727

October 18, 1820. *William Harris Crawford (1772–1834)*. Georgia House of Representatives 1803–07; US senator 1807–13, president pro tempore 1812; US minister to France 1813–15; US secretary of war 1815–16; US treasury secretary 1816–25; Georgia circuit judge 1827–34.

Crawford   **Georgia**
Knoxville   325 sq. mi.

12,630	12,495	8,991	7,684	5,748	5,816	6,080

December 9, 1822. *William Harris Crawford.*

Crawford   **Illinois**
Robinson   444 sq. mi.

19,817	20,452	19,464	20,818	19,824	20,751	21,137

December 31, 1816. *William Harris Crawford.*

Crawford   **Indiana**
English   306 sq. mi.

10,713	10,743	9,914	9,820	8,033	8,379	9,289

January 29, 1818; effective February 15, 1818. *Uncertain*. (1) *William Crawford (1732–82)*; surveyor; captain under General Braddock 1761; Pontiac's War 1763–64; colonel, Revolutionary War battles of Long Island, Trenton, and Princeton, resigned 1781; fought Wyandot and Delaware Indians on Sandusky River; captured, tortured, and burned at the stake. (2) *William Harris Crawford.*

Crawford   **Iowa**
Denison   714 sq. mi.

17,096	16,942	16,775	18,935	18,780	18,569	19,741

January 15, 1851; organized September 3, 1855. *William Harris Crawford.*

Crawford   **Kansas**
Girard   590 sq. mi.

39,134	38,242	35,568	37,916	37,850	37,032	40,231

February 13, 1867; organized March 3, 1868. *Samuel J. Crawford (1835–1913)*. Kansas legislature 1861; organized company of volunteers, captain to brevet brigadier general 1864; governor of Kansas 1865–68; resigned to command 19th Kansas Cavalry 1868, joined Custer-Sheridan winter campaign 1868–69.

Crawford   **Michigan**
Grayling   556 sq. mi.

14,074	14,273	12,260	9,465	6,482	4,971	4,151

April 1, 1840, as Shawano; name changed March 8, 1843; organized March 22, 1879. *William Crawford (1732–82)*.*

Crawford   **Missouri**
Steelville   743 sq. mi.

24,696	22,804	19,173	18,300	14,828	12,647	11,615

January 23, 1829. *William Harris Crawford*.*

Crawford   **Ohio**
Bucyrus   402 sq. mi.

43,784	46,966	47,870	50,075	50,364	46,775	38,738

February 12, 1820. *William Harris Crawford*.*

Crawford   **Pennsylvania**
Meadville   1,012 sq. mi.

88,765	90,366	86,169	88,869	81,342	77,956	78,948

March 12, 1800. *William Crawford (1732–82)*.*

Crawford   **Wisconsin**
Prairie du Chien   571 sq. mi.

16,644	17,243	15,940	16,556	15,252	16,351	17,652

October 1, 1818. *Fort Crawford*. Named for William Harris Crawford.*

Creek   **Oklahoma**
Sapulpa   950 sq. mi.

69,967	67,367	60,915	59,016	45,532	40,495	43,143

July 16, 1907. *Creek Indians*. Occupied most of Alabama and Georgia; defeated in Creek War 1813–14; removed to Indian Territory (Oklahoma) by 1841.

Crenshaw   **Alabama**
Luverne   609 sq. mi.

13,906	13,665	13,635	14,110	13,188	14,909	18,981

November 24, 1866. *Anderson Crenshaw (1786–1847)*. Alabama circuit court judge 1821–38; Alabama Supreme Court 1838; Court of Chancery 1838–47.

Crisp   **Georgia**
Cordele   273 sq. mi.

23,439	21,996	20,011	19,489	18,087	17,768	17,663

August 17, 1905. *Charles Frederick Crisp (1845–96)*. Confederate Army 1861–64, lieutenant; prisoner of war 1864, released 1865; solicitor general of Southwestern Judicial Circuit 1872–77; superior court judge 1877–82; US representative from Georgia 1883–96.

Crittenden   **Arkansas**
Marion   610 sq. mi.

50,902	50,866	49,939	49,499	48,106	47,564	47,184

October 22, 1825; effective January 1, 1826. *Robert Crittenden (1797–1834)*. War of 1812; secretary of Arkansas Territory; mortally wounded Congressman Henry Conway in a duel. (See Conway, Arkansas.)

Crittenden	**Kentucky**					
Marion	360 sq. mi.					
9,315	9,384	9,196	9,207	8,493	8,648	10,818

January 26, 1842. *John Jordan Crittenden (1787–1863)*. Attorney general of Illinois Territory 1809–10; War of 1812; Kentucky legislature 1811–17, Speaker 1817; Kentucky Senate 1817–19; Kentucky House of Representatives 1825 and 1829–32; US district attorney 1827–29; US senator 1835–48 and 1855–61; US attorney general 1841 and 1850–53; governor of Kentucky 1848–50; US representative 1861–63.

Crockett	**Tennessee**					
Alamo	266 sq. mi.					
14,586	14,532	13,378	14,941	14,402	14,594	16,624

December 20, 1845; abolished 1846; recreated November 23, 1871. *David "Davey" Crockett (1786–1836)*. Creek Indian campaign 1813–14; Tennessee House of Representatives 1821–25; US representative 1827–31 and 1833–35; aided Texas independence; killed at Alamo March 6, 1836.

Crockett	**Texas**					
Ozona	2,807 sq. mi.					
3,719	4,099	4,078	4,608	3,885	4,209	3,981

January 22, 1875; organized July 14, 1891. *David "Davey" Crockett.**

Crook	**Oregon**					
Prineville	2,979 sq. mi.					
20,978	19,182	14,111	13,091	9,985	9,430	8,991

October 24, 1882. *George Crook (1829–90)*. Graduated West Point 1852; lieutenant to major general in serving Oregon Territory 1852–60; captain to major general 1861–65; battles of Antietam, Chickamauga, and South Mountain; commander of Arizona and Idaho districts 1866–72.

Crook	**Wyoming**					
Sundance	2,854 sq. mi.					
7,083	5,887	5,294	5,308	4,535	4,691	4,738

December 8, 1875. *George Crook.**

Crosby	**Texas**					
Crosbyton	900 sq. mi.					
6,059	7,072	7,304	8,859	9,085	10,347	9,582

August 21, 1876; organized September 11, 1886. *Stephen Crosby (1808–69)*. Steamboat captain; chief clerk in Texas Land Office 1853–57 and 1859–67.

Cross	**Arkansas**					
Wynne	616 sq. mi.					
17,870	19,526	19,225	20,434	19,783	19,551	24,757

November 15, 1862. *Uncertain.* (1) *David Cross (?–1874)*; colonel, Confederate Army 1861, resigned for poor health 1862. (2) *Edward Cross (1798–1887)*; US judge for Arkansas Territory 1830; surveyor general of Arkansas Territory 1836–38; US representative 1839–45; Arkansas Supreme Court 1845–55; attorney general of Arkansas 1874.

Crowley	**Colorado**					
Ordway	787 sq. mi.					
5,823	5,518	3,946	2,988	3,086	3,978	5,222

May 29, 1911. *John H. Crowley (1849–?)*. Colorado House of Representatives 1893–94 and 1897–98; Colorado Board of Horticulture 1899–1905; Colorado Senate 1911.

Crow Wing	**Minnesota**
Brainerd	999 sq. mi.

| 62,500 | 55,099 | 44,249 | 41,722 | 34,826 | 32,134 | 30,875 |

May 23, 1857; deorganized 1858; reorganized March 3, 1870. *Crow Wing River*. Translation of Chippewa name *kayaugewe-guan*, meaning "crow's wing" or "crow's feather."

Culberson   **Texas**
Van Horn   3,813 sq. mi.

| 2,398 | 2,975 | 3,407 | 3,315 | 3,429 | 2,794 | 1,825 |

March 10, 1911; organized 1912. *David Browning Culberson (1830–1900)*. Texas legislature 1859–60; opposed secession but joined Confederate Army as a private, rose to colonel; Texas House of Representatives 1864; Texas Senate 1873–75; US representative 1875–97; commissioner to codify US laws 1897–1900.

Cullman   **Alabama**
Cullman   735 sq. mi.

| 80,406 | 77,483 | 67,613 | 61,642 | 52,445 | 45,572 | 49,046 |

January 24, 1877. *John Gottfried Cullman (c1825–95)*. Emigrated from Germany to US 1866; founded town of Cullman as a German colony 1873.

Culpeper   **Virginia**
Culpeper   379 sq. mi.

| 46,689 | 34,262 | 27,791 | 22,620 | 18,218 | 15,088 | 13,242 |

March 23, 1748. *Thomas Culpeper, Lord Culpeper (1635–89)*. Received 31–year grant from Charles II for entire Virginia Colony 1673; proclaimed governor of Virginia for life 1675; commission declared forfeit 1683.

Cumberland   **Illinois**
Toledo   346 sq. mi.

| 11,048 | 11,253 | 10,670 | 11,062 | 9,772 | 9,936 | 10,496 |

March 2, 1843. *Cumberland Road*. First national thoroughfare; from Cumberland, Maryland, to Wheeling, Virginia (West Virginia) 1818. (See Cumberland, Maine.)

Cumberland   **Kentucky**
Burkesville   305 sq. mi.

| 6,856 | 7,147 | 6,784 | 7,289 | 6,850 | 7,835 | 9,309 |

December 14, 1798. *Cumberland River*. Named for William Augustus, Duke of Cumberland (see Cumberland, Maine).

Cumberland   **Maine**
Portland   835 sq. mi.

| 281,674 | 265,612 | 253,135 | 215,789 | 192,528 | 182,751 | 169,201 |

June 19, 1760; effective November 1, 1760. *William Augustus, Duke of Cumberland (1721–65)*. Second son of King George II and Queen Caroline; privy councilor 1742; major general 1742; lieutenant general 1743; captain general of the army 1745–57; commanded English troops in defeat of Jacobites at Battle of Culloden, Scotland, 1745.

Cumberland   **New Jersey**
Bridgeton   484 sq. mi.

| 156,898 | 146,438 | 138,053 | 132,866 | 121,374 | 106,850 | 88,597 |

January 19, 1748. *William Augustus, Duke of Cumberland.**

Cumberland   **North Carolina**
Fayetteville   652 sq. mi.

| 319,431 | 302,963 | 274,566 | 247,160 | 212,042 | 148,418 | 96,006 |

1754. *William Augustus, Duke of Cumberland.**

Cumberland   **Pennsylvania**
Carlisle   545 sq. mi.

| 235,406 | 213,674 | 195,257 | 178,541 | 158,177 | 124,816 | 94,457 |

January 27, 1750. *Cumberlandshire, England*. "Land of Cumbri" (Wales).

Cumberland   **Tennessee**
Crossville   681 sq. mi.
56,053   46,802   34,736   28,676   20,733   19,135   18,877
November 16, 1855. *Cumberland Mountains*. Named for William Augustus, Duke of Cumberland.*

Cumberland   **Virginia**
Cumberland   297 sq. mi.
10,052   9,017   7,825   7,881   6,179   6,360   7,252
March 23, 1748. *William Augustus, Duke of Cumberland.**

Cuming   **Nebraska**
West Point   571 sq. mi.
9,139   10,203   10,117   11,664   12,034   12,435   12,994
March 16, 1855. *Thomas B. Cuming (1828–58)*. Secretary of Nebraska Territory 1854–58; acting governor of Nebraska Territory 1854–55.

Currituck   **North Carolina**
Currituck   262 sq. mi.
23,547   18,190   13,736   11,089   6,976   6,601   6,201
1668. *Currituck Indians*. An Algonquin tribe; traditional translation of name is "wild geese."

Curry   **New Mexico**
Clovis   1,405 sq. mi.
48,376   45,044   42,207   42,019   39,517   32,691   23,251
February 25, 1909. *George Curry (1861–1947)*. Officer in Roosevelt's Rough Riders during Spanish-American War 1898; sheriff, Otero County 1899; provost marshal and provost judge of provinces in Philippine Islands 1899–1907; territorial governor of New Mexico 1907–11; US representative 1912–13; International Boundary Commission 1922–26; New Mexico Sate Historian 1945–47.

Curry   **Oregon**
Gold Beach   1,627 sq. mi.
22,364   21,137   19,327   16,992   13,006   13,983   6,048
December 18, 1855. *George Law Curry (1820–78)*. Oregon territorial legislature 1848–49 and 1851; editor of *Oregon Spectator*, first newspaper west of the Rockies 1846; governor of Oregon Territory 1853–59.

Custer   **Colorado**
Westcliffe   739 sq. mi.
4,255   3,503   1,926   1,528   1,120   1,305   1,573
March 9, 1877. *George Armstrong Custer (1839–76)*. Graduated West Point 1851; 2nd lieutenant to brevet brigadier general of cavalry 1861–65; led campaign against Cheyennes 1868; killed with entire command at Little Big Horn, June 25, 1876.

Custer   **Idaho**
Challis   4,921 sq. mi.
4,368   4,342   4,133   3,385   2,967   2,996   3,318
January 8, 1881; effective April 2, 1882. *General Custer Mine*. Named for George Armstrong Custer.*

Custer   **Montana**
Miles City   3,783 sq. mi.
11,699   11,696   11,697   13,109   12,174   13,227   12,661
February 2, 1865, as Big Horn; name changed February 16, 1877. *George Armstrong Custer.**

Custer   **Nebraska**
Broken Bow   2,576 sq. mi.
10,939   11,793   12,270   13,877   14,092   16,517   19,170
February 17, 1877; organized June 27, 1877. *George Armstrong Custer.**

Custer   **Oklahoma**
Arapaho   989 sq. mi.

27,469	26,142	26,897	25,995	22,665	21,040	21,097

April 19, 1892, as County G; name changed November 8, 1892; organized 1898. *George Armstrong Custer.**

Custer   **South Dakota**
Custer   1,557 sq. mi.

8,216	7,275	6,179	6,000	4,698	4,906	5,517

January 11, 1875; organized April 26, 1877. *George Armstrong Custer.**

Cuyahoga   **Ohio**
Cleveland   457 sq. mi.

1,280,122	1,393,978	1,412,140	1,498,400	1,721,300	1,647,895	1,389,532

February 10, 1807; organized February 10, 1808. *Cuyahoga River.* Iroquois word meaning "crooked."

D

Dade   **Georgia**
Trenton   174 sq. mi.

16,633	15,154	13,147	12,318	9,910	8,666	7,364

December 25, 1837. *Francis Longhorn Dade (1793–1835).* US Infantry, lieutenant to brevet major 1813–28; killed in Seminole ambush.

Dade   **Missouri**
Greenfield   490 sq. mi.

7,883	7,923	7,449	7,383	6,850	7,577	9,324

January 29, 1841. *Francis Longhorn Dade.**

Daggett   **Utah**
Manila   697 sq. mi.

1,059	921	690	769	666	1,164	364

March 4, 1917; organized March 4, 1919. *Ellsworth Daggett (1845–1923).* Surveyor-general of Utah Territory 1888; surveyor for canal system in Daggett section of Utah.

Dakota   **Minnesota**
Hastings   562 sq. mi.

398,552	355,904	275,227	194,279	139,808	78,303	49,019

October 27, 1849; organized March 5, 1853. *Dakota Indians.* Commonly known as "Sioux" which is an Ojibwa derogatory name meaning "little snakes" (see Sioux, Iowa). The Sioux called themselves *Lakota* or *Dakota* meaning "friends" or "allies."

Dakota   **Nebraska**
Dakota City   264 sq. mi.

21,006	20,253	16,742	16,573	13,137	12,168	10,401

March 7, 1855; organized January 5, 1857. *Dakota Indians.**

Dale   **Alabama**
Ozark   561 sq. mi.

50,251	49,129	49,633	47,821	52,938	31,066	20,828

December 22, 1824; effective October 1825. *Samuel Dale (1772–1841).* Indian scout; militia officer; Alabama legislature 1819–20; Mississippi legislature 1836.

Dallam   **Texas**
Dalhart   1,503 sq. mi.

6,703	6,222	5,461	6,531	6,012	6,302	7,640

August 21, 1876; organized September 8, 1891. *James Wilmer Dallam (1818–47).* Legal scholar and publisher; compiler of *A Digest of the Laws of Texas* 1845; *Opinions of the Supreme Court of Texas from 1840–44,* 1845; died while preparing to establish a newspaper in Indianola, Texas.

Dallas   **Alabama**
Selma   979 sq. mi.
43,820   46,365   48,130   53,981   55,296   56,667   56,270
February 9, 1818. *Alexander James Dallas (1759–1817).* US district attorney in Pennsylvania 1810–14; US treasury secretary 1814–15; US secretary of war 1815.

Dallas   **Arkansas**
Fordyce   667 sq. mi.
8,116   9,210   9,614   10,515   10,022   10,522   12,416
January 1, 1845. *George Mifflin Dallas (1792–1864).* Solicitor of the US Bank 1815–17; mayor of Philadelphia 1829; US district attorney 1829–31; US senator 1831–33; attorney general of Pennsylvania 1833–35; US minister to Russia 1837–39; US vice president 1845–49; US minister to Great Britain 1856–61.

Dallas   **Iowa**
Adel   588 sq. mi.
66,135   40,750   29,755   29,513   26,085   24,123   23,661
January 13, 1846; organized March 1, 1847. *George Mifflin Dallas.**

Dallas   **Missouri**
Buffalo   541 sq. mi.
16,777   15,661   12,646   12,096   10,054   9,314   10,392
January 29, 1841, as Niangua; name changed December 16, 1844. *George Mifflin Dallas.**

Dallas   **Texas**
Dallas   871 sq. mi.
2,368,139   2,218,899   1,852,810   1,556,390   1,327,321   951,527   614,799
March 30, 1846; organized July 10, 1846. *Uncertain.* Most probably named for *George Mifflin Dallas.** Other suggestions include (1) either Walter R. or James L. Dallas, soldiers in Texas Army; (2) US Navy commander A. J. Dallas; (3) Alexander James Dallas*; (4) Joseph Dallas, an early settler in the area.

Dane   **Wisconsin**
Madison   1,197 sq. mi.
488,073   426,526   367,085   323,545   290,272   222,095   169,357
December 7, 1836; organized 1839. *Nathan Dane (1752–1835).* Massachusetts House of Representatives 1782–85; Continental Congress 1785–88; Massachusetts Senate 1790–91 and 1794–97; author of 8–volume *Abridgement and Digest of American Law* 1829. Only connection with Wisconsin is having written the article in the Northwest Ordnance of 1787 which prohibited slavery in the region.

Daniels   **Montana**
Scobey   1,426 sq. mi.
1,751   2,017   2,266   2,835   3,083   3,755   3,946
August 30, 1920. *Mansfield A. Daniels (1858–1919).* Pioneer rancher; one of first settlers in the area.

Danville   **Virginia**
(Independent City)   43 sq. mi.
43,055   48,411   53,056   45,642   36,391   46,577   35,006
1890. *Dan River.* Origin of name is uncertain; possibly from Dan River, Israel, source of the Jordan River. (Associated county: Pittsylvania.)

Dare   **North Carolina**
Manteo   383 sq. mi.

| 33,920 | 29,967 | 22,746 | 13,377 | 6,995 | 5,935 | 5,405 |

February 2, 1870. *Virginia Dare (1587–?)*. First English child born in America, August 18, 1587; granddaughter of John White, governor of Virginia Colony on Roanoke Island; vanished with Roanoke Colony before 1590.

Darke   **Ohio**
Greenville   598 sq. mi.

| 52,959 | 53,309 | 53,619 | 55,096 | 49,141 | 45,612 | 41,799 |

January 3, 1809; organized 1817. *William Darke (1736–1801)*. Served under General Braddock at Fort Duquesne 1755; Indian fighter 1755–70; Continental Army, captain to brigadier general 1775–83; wounded and captured at Germantown 1777; exchanged 1780; retired as brigadier general 1783; Constitutional Convention 1788; lieutenant colonel at St. Clair's defeat in Battle of the Wabash 1791.

Darlington   **South Carolina**
Darlington   561 sq. mi.

| 68,681 | 67,394 | 61,851 | 62,717 | 53,442 | 52,928 | 50,016 |

March 12, 1785; converted to judicial district January 1, 1800; redesignated as county April 16, 1868. *Darlington, England*. Traditional supposition of county's name origin with no solid proof.

Dauphin   **Pennsylvania**
Harrisburg   525 sq. mi.

| 268,100 | 251,798 | 237,813 | 232,317 | 222,834 | 220,255 | 197,784 |

March 4, 1785. *Louis Joseph Xavier, Dauphin of France (1781–1789)*. Eldest son of Louis XVI and Marie Antoinette; a sickly child; died at age seven. *Dauphin* has been the hereditary title of the eldest son of the King of France since 1349. County was named to honor French alliance during American Revolution.

Davidson   **North Carolina**
Lexington   553 sq. mi.

| 162,878 | 147,246 | 126,677 | 113,162 | 95,627 | 79,493 | 62,244 |

December 9, 1822. *William Lee Davidson (1746–81)*. Major to brigadier general in Continental Army 1776–80; wounded at Battle of Camden 1780; killed at Battle of Cowan's Pass, January 17, 1781.

Davidson   **Tennessee**
Nashville   504 sq. mi.

| 626,681 | 569,891 | 510,748 | 477,811 | 448,003 | 399,743 | 321,758 |

October 6, 1783. *William Lee Davidson.**

Davie   **North Carolina**
Mocksville   264 sq. mi.

| 41,240 | 34,835 | 27,859 | 24,599 | 18,855 | 16,728 | 15,420 |

December 20, 1836. *William Richardson Davie (1756–1820)*, Captain to brigadier general 1779–97; North Carolina Cavalry 1780; federal Constitutional Convention 1787; US Army 1797; governor of North Carolina 1798–99; peace commissioner to France 1799.

Daviess   **Indiana**
Washington   429 sq. mi.

| 31,648 | 29,820 | 27,533 | 27,836 | 26,602 | 26,636 | 26,762 |

December 24, 1816; effective February 15, 1817. *Joseph Hamilton Daveiss (1774–1811)*. US district attorney for Kentucky, prosecuted Aaron Burr for treason 1807; killed at Battle of Tippecanoe, November 7, 1811. (All five counties named for Daveiss [including Jo Daviess, Illinois] use the alternative spelling for his name.)

Daviess   **Kentucky**
Owensboro   458 sq. mi.

| 96,656 | 91,545 | 87,189 | 85,949 | 79,486 | 70,588 | 57,241 |

January 14, 1815. *Joseph Hamilton Daveiss.**

Daviess   **Missouri**
Gallatin   563 sq. mi.
8,433   8,016   7,865   8,905   8,420   9,502   11,180
December 29, 1836. *Joseph Hamilton Daveiss.**

Davis   **Iowa**
Bloomfield   502 sq. mi.
8,753   8,541   8,312   9,104   8,207   9,199   9,959
February 17, 1843; organized March 1, 1844. *Garrett Davis (1801–72)*. Kentucky House of Representatives 1833–35; US representative 1839–47; US senate 1861–72. Davis' primary connection with Iowa is that as a Congressman, he chaired the Committee on Territories while Iowa was a territory.

Davis   **Utah**
Farmington   299 sq. mi.
306,479   238,994   187,941   146,540   99,028   64,670   30,867
October 5, 1850. *Daniel C. Davis (1804–50)*. Captain, Mormon Battalion 1846; mustered out of army 1847; opened wagon road from Utah to California 1848.

Davison   **South Dakota**
Mitchell   436 sq. mi.
19,504   18,741   17,503   17,820   17,319   16,681   16,522
January 8, 1873; organized July 31, 1874. *Henry C. Davison (?–1874)*. Merchant; one of first homesteaders in the area 1869.

Dawes   **Nebraska**
Chadron   1,396 sq. mi.
9,182   9,060   9,021   9,609   9,693   9,536   9,708
February 19, 1885. *James William Dawes (1845–87)*. Nebraska Constitutional Convention 1875; Nebraska Senate 1876; governor of Nebraska 1883–87.

Dawson   **Georgia**
Dawsonville   211 sq. mi.
22,330   15,999   9,429   4,774   3,639   3,590   3,712
December 3, 1857. *William Crosby Dawson (1798–1856)*. Clerk, Georgia House of Representatives; compiler of Georgia laws 1820–30; volunteer in Creek War 1836; US representative 1836–41; circuit court judge 1845; US senator 1849–55.

Dawson   **Montana**
Glendive   2,372 sq. mi.
8,966   9,059   9,505   11,805   11,269   12,314   9,092
January 15, 1869. *Andrew Dawson (1817–71)*. Trapper and trader for American Fur Company.

Dawson   **Nebraska**
Lexington   1,013 sq. mi.
24,326   24,365   19,940   22,304   19,467   19,405   19,393
January 11, 1860; organized 1871. *Jacob Dawson (?–?)*. Newspaper publisher; postmaster of Lancaster (now Lincoln) 1864–68.

Dawson   **Texas**
Lamesa   900 sq. mi.
13,833   14,985   14,349   16,184   16,604   19,185   19,113
August 21, 1876; organized February 13, 1905. *Nicholas Mosby Dawson (1808–42)*. Second lieutenant to captain in Texas Army, 1836–42; Battle of San Jacinto 1836; killed by Mexican cavalry in Dawson Massacre near San Antonio, September 8, 1842.

Day   **South Dakota**
Webster   1,028 sq. mi.

5,710   6,267   6,978   8,133   8,713   10,516   12,294
October 1, 1879; organized January 2, 1882. *Merritt H. Day (1844–1900)*. Dakota Territorial legislature 1879–89; commander, South Dakota State Militia in Messiah War against Dakotas 1890.

Deaf Smith   **Texas**
Hereford   1,497 sq. mi.
19,372   18,561   19,153   21,165   18,999   13,187   9,111
August 21, 1876; organized December 1, 1890. *Erastus "Deaf Smith" Smith (1787–1837)*. Scout for General Houston at Battle of Concepción 1835; destroyed Vince's Bridge before Battle of San Jacinto 1836; captain, Texas Rangers 1837; lost hearing from childhood disease.

Dearborn   **Indiana**
Lawrenceburg   305 sq. mi.
50,047   46,109   38,835   34,291   29,430   28,674   25,141
March 7, 1803. *Henry Dearborn (1751–1829)*. Fought at Bunker Hill and Quebec (1775), Stillwater and Saratoga (1777), Monmouth (1778), and Newton (1779); colonel to major general 1781–89; US representative from Massachusetts 1793–97; US secretary of war 1801–09; collector of Port of Boston 1809–12; US Army senior major general 1812; US minister to Portugal 1822–24.

De Baca   **New Mexico**
Fort Sumner   2,323 sq. mi.
2,022   2,240   2,252   2,454   2,547   2,991   3,464
February 18, 1917. *Ezequiel Cabeza de Baca (1864–1917)*. Publisher and business manager of Spanish-language newspaper; lieutenant governor of New Mexico 1911–16; governor of New Mexico 1917, died six weeks after taking office.

Decatur   **Georgia**
Bainbridge   597 sq. mi.
27,842   28,240   25,511   24,495   22,310   25,203   23,620
December 8, 1823. *Stephen Decatur (1779–1820)*. Commanded schooner USS *Enterprise* in Tripolitan War 1804; War of 1812; forced Barbary pirates to submit to terms; commissioner of the Navy 1815; killed in a duel with Commodore James Barron, March 20, 1820.

Decatur   **Indiana**
Greensburg   373 sq. mi.
25,740   24,555   23,645   23,841   22,738   20,019   18,218
December 31, 1821. *Stephen Decatur.**

Decatur   **Iowa**
Leon   532 sq. mi.
8,457   8,689   8,338   9,794   9,737   10,539   12,601
January 13, 1846; organized May 6, 1850. *Stephen Decatur.**

Decatur   **Kansas**
Oberlin   894 sq. mi.
2,961   3,472   4,021   4,509   4,988   5,778   6,185
March 20, 1873; organized December 15, 1879. *Stephen Decatur.**

Decatur   **Tennessee**
Decaturville   334 sq. mi.
11,757   11,731   10,472   10,857   9,457   8,324   9,442
November 1845; organized March 6, 1846. *Stephen Decatur.**

Deer Lodge   **Montana**
Anaconda   737 sq. mi.
9,298   9,417   10,278   12,518   15,652   18,640   16,553

February 2, 1865. *Town of Deer Lodge*. Descriptive of a site where deer were frequently seen, near a landmark resembling an Indian lodge.

Defiance   **Ohio**
Defiance   411 sq. mi.
39,037   39,500   39,350   39,987   36,949   31,508   25,925
March 4, 1845. *Fort Defiance*. Established by General Anthony Wayne 1794.

DeKalb   **Alabama**
Fort Payne   777 sq. mi.
71,109   64,452   54,651   53,658   41,981   41,417   45,048
January 9, 1836. *Johann Kalb, Baron de Kalb (1721–80)*. Brigadier in French Army 1764; aided American colonists; commissioned major general in Continental Army 1777; mortally wounded at Battle of Camden, August 16, 1780.

DeKalb   **Georgia**
Decatur   268 sq. mi.
691,893   665,865   545,837   483,024   415,387   256,782   136,395
December 9, 1822. *Johann Kalb, Baron de Kalb*.*

DeKalb   **Illinois**
Sycamore   631 sq. mi.
105,160   88,969   77,932   74,624   71,654   51,714   40,781
March 4, 1837. *Johann Kalb, Baron de Kalb*.*

DeKalb   **Indiana**
Auburn   363 sq. mi.
42,223   40,285   35,324   33,606   30,837   28,271   26,023
February 7, 1835; organized January 14, 1837; effective May 1, 1837. *Johann Kalb, Baron de Kalb*.*

DeKalb   **Missouri**
Maysville   421 sq. mi.
12,892   11,597   9,967   8,222   7,305   7,226   8,047
February 25, 1845. *Johann Kalb, Baron de Kalb*.*

DeKalb   **Tennessee**
Smithville   304 sq. mi.
18,723   17,423   14,360   13,589   11,151   10,774   11,680
December 11, 1837. *Johann Kalb, Baron de Kalb*.*

Delaware   **Indiana**
Muncie   392 sq. mi.
117,671   118,769   119,659   128,587   129,219   110,938   90,252
January 26, 1827; effective April 1, 1827. *Delaware Indians*. Named for Delaware River (see Delaware, New York). Originally lived in New Jersey and Pennsylvania; migrated west 1720–70.

Delaware   **Iowa**
Manchester   578 sq. mi.
17,764   18,404   18,035   18,933   18,770   18,483   17,734
December 21, 1837; organized November 19, 1841. *Uncertain*. (1) *State of Delaware* in appreciation of services of Senator John Clayton of Delaware in creation of Wisconsin Territory which included Iowa (see Clayton, Iowa). (2) *Delaware County, New York*.

Delaware   **New York**
Delhi   1,442 sq. mi.
47,980   48,055   47,225   46,824   44,718   43,540   44,420

March 10, 1797. *Delaware River.* Named for Tomas West, 3rd Baron De La Warr (1577–1618); first colonial governor of Virginia 1609; resided in Virginia 1610; returned to England 1611; died on second voyage to Virginia 1618.

Delaware   **Ohio**
Delaware   443 sq. mi.

174,214	109,989	66,929	53,840	42,908	36,107	30,278

February 10, 1808. *Delaware Indians.**

Delaware   **Oklahoma**
Jay   738 sq. mi.

41,487	37,077	28,070	23,946	17,767	13,198	14,734

July 16, 1907. *Delaware Indians.**

Delaware   **Pennsylvania**
Media   184 sq. mi.

558,979	550,864	547,651	555,007	600,035	553,154	414,234

September 26, 1789. *Delaware River.**

Del Norte   **California**
Crescent City   1,006 sq. mi.

28,610	27,507	23,460	18,217	14,580	17,771	8,078

March 7, 1857. *Descriptive.* Spanish for "northern"; refers to county's location in northwest corner of the state.

Delta   **Colorado**
Delta   1,142 sq. mi.

30,952	27,834	20,980	21,225	15,286	15,602	17,365

February 11, 1883. *Town of Delta.* Descriptive of the city's location at the Uncompahgre River delta with the Gunnison River.

Delta   **Michigan**
Escanaba   1,171 sq. mi.

37,069	38,520	37,780	38,947	35,924	34,298	32,913

March 9, 1843; organized March 12, 1861. *Descriptive.* Refers to county's original shape roughly resembling the Greek letter "delta."

Delta   **Texas**
Cooper   257 sq. mi.

5,231	5,327	4,857	4,839	4,927	5,860	8,964

July 29, 1870. *Descriptive.* Refers to county's triangular shape similar to the Greek letter "delta."

Denali   **Alaska**
Healy   12,751 sq. mi.

1,826	1,893	(a)	(a)	(a)	(a)	(b)

December 7, 1990. *Denali Mountain.* Tanana name for Mount McKinley; means "the big one" or "the high one." [(a) Part of Yukon-Koyukuk Censes Area; (b) part of 4th Judicial District.]

Dent   **Missouri**
Salem   753 sq. mi.

15,657	14,927	13,702	14,517	11,457	10,445	10,936

February 10, 1851. *Lewis Dent (1808–80).* Early settler; elected to Missouri legislature after the county was named for him.

Denton   **Texas**
Denton   878 sq. mi.

622,614	432,976	273,525	143,126	75,633	47,432	41,365

April 11, 1846; organized July 13, 1846. *John B. Denton (1806–41).* Itinerant minister; lawyer, missionary; Texas Army captain, aide to Colonel Tarrant (see Tarrant, Texas); killed near Fort Worth while fighting Indians.

Denver   **Colorado**
Denver   153 sq. mi.

600,158	554,636	467,610	492,365	514,678	493,887	415,786

March 18, 1901. *City of Denver*. Named for James William Denver (1817–92); Mexican War; California Senate 1851; California secretary of state 1852; US representative from California 1855–57; commissioner of Indian Affairs 1857–59; governor of Kansas Territory which included Colorado 1857–58; brigadier general, Union Army 1861; resigned 1863.

Deschutes   **Oregon**
Bend   3,018 sq. mi.

157,733	115,367	74,958	62,142	30,442	23,100	21,812

December 13, 1916. *Deschutes River*. From French *Riviére des Chutes* meaning "river of the falls."

Desha   **Arkansas**
Arkansas City   768 sq. mi.

13,008	15,341	16,798	19,760	18,761	20,770	25,155

December 12, 1838. *Benjamin Desha (c1790–1835)*. Third lieutenant of Light Dragoons, 1813; captain of US Rifles 1814.

Des Moines   **Iowa**
Burlington   416 sq. mi.

40,325	42,351	42,614	46,203	46,982	44,605	42,056

September 6, 1834. *Des Moines River*. From Moingwena Indians, possibly referring to the loon that is one of their totems; rendered by French as *riviére des moines*.

DeSoto   **Florida**
Arcadia   637 sq. mi.

34,862	32,209	23,865	19,039	13,060	11,683	9,242

May 19, 1887. *Hernando de Soto (1496–1542)*. Spanish conqueror and explorer; served under Francisco Pizarro in conquest of Peru 1532; governor of Cuba 1537; explored southeastern US 1539–42; discovered Mississippi River 1541; buried in Mississippi River after dying from fever.

De Soto   **Louisiana**
Mansfield   876 sq. mi.

26,656	25,494	25,346	25,727	22,764	24,248	24,398

April 1, 1843. *Hernando de Soto*.* (Louisiana spelling maintains space in name.)

DeSoto   **Mississippi**
Hernando   476 sq. mi.

161,252	107,199	67,910	53,930	35,885	23,891	24,599

February 9, 1836. *Hernando de Soto*.*

Deuel   **Nebraska**
Chappell   440 sq. mi.

1,941	2,098	2,237	2,462	2,717	3,125	3,330

November 6, 1888; organized January 21, 1889; *Henry Porter Deuel (1836–1914)*. Agent, Kansas City & St. Joseph Railroad 1888, Omaha passenger agent 1888–96; Chicago, Burlington & Quincy station agent in Omaha 1896; auditor, Douglas County 1899–1901.

Deuel   **South Dakota**
Clear Lake   623 sq. mi.

4,364	4,498	4,522	5,289	5,686	6,782	7,689

April 5, 1862; organized May 20, 1878. *Jacob Smith Deuel (1830–98)*. Dakota Territorial legislature 1862–63 at time of county's creation; owned small store and sawmill in Vermillion; moved to Nebraska 1863.

Dewey   **Oklahoma**
Taloga   999 sq. mi.

| 4,810 | 4,743 | 5,551 | 5,922 | 5,656 | 6,051 | 8,789 |

April 19, 1892, as County D; name changed November 8, 1898. *George Dewey (1837–1917).* Graduated Annapolis 1858; served under Admiral Farragut during Civil War 1861; commanded Asiatic Squadron in Spanish-American War 1897; won Battle of Manila Bay, May 1, 1898; First Admiral of the Navy 1899.

Dewey   **South Dakota**
Timber Lake   2,302 sq. mi.

| 5,301 | 5,972 | 5,523 | 5,366 | 5,170 | 5,257 | 4,916 |

January 8, 1873, as Rusk; name changed March 9, 1883; organized December 3, 1910. *William Pitt Dewey (1833–1900).* Surveyor general of Dakota Territory 1873–77; Dakota Territorial legislature at time of county's name change 1883.

DeWitt   **Illinois**
Clinton   398 sq. mi.

| 16,561 | 16,798 | 16,516 | 18,108 | 16,975 | 17,253 | 16,894 |

March 1, 1839. *De Witt Clinton.* (See Clinton, Illinois.)

DeWitt   **Texas**
Cuero   909 sq. mi.

| 20,097 | 20,013 | 18,840 | 18,903 | 18,660 | 20,693 | 22,973 |

March 24, 1846; organized July 13, 1846. *Green C. De Witt (1787–1835).* Captain, War of 1812; awarded Mexican grant to establish colony on the Guadalupe River 1825.

Dickens   **Texas**
Dickens   902 sq. mi.

| 2,444 | 2,762 | 2,571 | 3,539 | 3,737 | 4,963 | 7,177 |

August 21, 1876; organized March 14, 1891. *James R. Dimpkins (?–1836).* Englishman; Siege of Bexar, first campaign of Texas Revolution 1835; killed at Alamo March 6, 1836; listed on Alamo Monument as "J. Dickens."

Dickenson   **Virginia**
Clintwood   331 sq. mi.

| 15,903 | 16,395 | 17,620 | 19,806 | 16,077 | 20,211 | 23,393 |

March 3, 1880. *William J. Dickenson (1828–1907).* Virginia legislature; one of the founders of Virginia's Readjuster Party concerned with economic issues following Reconstruction.

Dickey   **North Dakota**
Ellendale   1,131 sq. mi.

| 5,289 | 5,757 | 6,107 | 7,207 | 6,976 | 8,147 | 9,121 |

March 5, 1881; organized August 18, 1882. *George H. Dickey (1858–1923).* Attorney; Dakota Territorial legislature at time of county's creation 1881.

Dickinson   **Iowa**
Spirit Lake   381 sq. mi.

| 16,667 | 16,424 | 14,909 | 15,629 | 12,565 | 12,574 | 12,756 |

January 15, 1851; organized August 3, 1857. *Daniel Stevens Dickinson (1800–66).* New York Assembly 1837–40; lieutenant governor 1842–44; US senator 1844–51, anti-slavery support for the Compromise of 1850 was popular in Iowa; attorney general of New York 1861; US attorney 1865–66.

Dickinson   **Kansas**
Abilene   847 sq. mi.

| 19,754 | 19,344 | 18,958 | 20,175 | 19,993 | 21,572 | 21,190 |

February 20, 1857. *Daniel Stevens Dickinson.** Anti-slavery support for the Compromise of 1850 was popular in Kansas.

Dickinson   **Michigan**
Iron Mountain   761 sq. mi.

| 26,168 | 24,472 | 26,831 | 25,341 | 23,753 | 23,917 | 24,844 |

May 21, 1891. *Donald McDonald Dickinson (1846–1917).* Chairman, Michigan Democratic state committee; US postmaster general 1887–89.

Dickson   **Tennessee**
Charlotte   490 sq. mi.

49,666	43,156	35,061	30,037	21,977	18,839	18,805

October 25, 1803. *William Dickson (1770–1816).* Physician; Tennessee House of Representatives 1799–1803; US representative 1801–07; trustee, University of Nashville 1806–16.

Dillingham   **Alaska**
(Census Area)   18,569 sq. mi.

4,847	4,922	4,012	4,616	3,385[a]	4,024[a]	(b)

April 24, 1989. *William Paul Dillingham (1843–1923).* Governor of Vermont 1888–90; US senator 1903–23; led Senate subcommittee tour of Alaska 1903; Senate's "authority" on Alaska. [(a) Bristol Bay Census Area; (b) part of 3rd Judicial District.]

Dillon   **South Carolina**
Dillon   405 sq. mi.

32,062	30,722	29,114	31,083	28,838	30,584	30,930

February 15, 1910. *Town of Dillon.* Named for James W. Dillon (1826–1913); merchant; persuaded Florence Southern Railroad to build station on site that became Dillon.

Dimmitt   **Texas**
Carrizo Springs   1,329 sq. mi.

9,996	10,248	10,433	11,367	9,039	10,095	10,654

February 1, 1858; organized November 2, 1880. *Philip Dimmitt (1801–41).* Merchant; captain of troops at Goliad after its capture 1835–36; captured during Siege of Bexar, took poison rather than go to Mexican prison 1841.

Dinwiddie   **Virginia**
Dinwiddie   504 sq. mi.

28,001	24,533	20,960	22,602	25,406	22,183	18,839

March 9, 1752. *Robert Dinwiddie (1693–1770).* Lieutenant governor of Royal Province of Virginia 1751–58; sent George Washington to western frontier to check French, led to French and Indian War 1753; returned to England 1758. (Associated independent city: Petersburg)

District of Columbia   **(Federal District)**
Washington   61 sq. mi.

601,723	572,059	606,900	638,333	756,510	763,956	802,178

July 16, 1790. *Christopher Columbus.* (See Columbia, Florida.)

Divide   **North Dakota**
Crosby   1,261 sq. mi.

2,071	2,283	2,899	3,494	4,564	5,566	5,967

December 6, 1910. *Uncertain.* (1) Descriptive of divide between Missouri and Red Rivers which runs through the county. (2) In honor of vote to divide county from Williams County.

Dixie   **Florida**
Cross City   705 sq. mi.

16,422	13,827	10,585	7,751	5,480	4,479	3,928

April 25, 1921. *Nickname for the South.* Derived from French *dix* meaning "ten"; refers to $10.00 bank notes issued by Citizens Bank of New Orleans which were used throughout the South.

Dixon   **Nebraska**
Ponca   476 sq. mi.

6,000	6,339	6,143	7,137	7,453	8,106	9,129

January 26, 1856; organized November 1, 1858. *Uncertain.* (1) *Town of Dixon.* (2) Unknown settler of the area named Dixon; town may have been named after him.

Doddridge   **West Virginia**
West Union   320 sq. mi.

| 8,202 | 7,403 | 6,994 | 7,433 | 6,389 | 6,970 | 9,026 |

February 4, 1845. *Philip Doddridge (1773–1832)*. Virginia House of Delegates, intermittently 1815–29; Virginia Constitutional Convention 1829. US Representative 1829–32.

Dodge   **Georgia**
Eastman   496 sq. mi.

| 21,796 | 19,171 | 17,607 | 16,955 | 15,658 | 16,483 | 17,865 |

October 26, 1870. *William Earle Dodge (1805–83)*. New York City merchant; founded Phelps-Dodge mining company with father-in-law Anson Phelps 1833; purchased large tracts of Georgia pine lands; president, National Temperance Society 1865–83.

Dodge   **Minnesota**
Mantorville   439 sq. mi.

| 20,087 | 17,731 | 15,731 | 14,773 | 13,037 | 13,259 | 12,624 |

February 20, 1855. *Henry Dodge (1782–1867)* and *Augustus Caesar Dodge (1812–83)*. (1) Henry served in War of 1812 and Black Hawk War; US Rangers 1832; governor of Wisconsin Territory 1836–41 and 1845–48; congressional delegate from Wisconsin Territory 1841–45; US senator 1848–57; declined appointment as governor of Washington Territory. (2) Augustus was son of Henry; congressional delegate from Iowa Territory 1840–48; US senator 1848–55; US minister to Spain 1855.

Dodge   **Nebraska**
Fremont   529 sq. mi.

| 36,691 | 36,160 | 34,500 | 35,847 | 34,782 | 32,471 | 26,265 |

November 23, 1854; organized January 6, 1857. *Augustus Caesar Dodge.**

Dodge   **Wisconsin**
Juneau   876 sq. mi.

| 88,759 | 85,897 | 76,559 | 75,064 | 69,004 | 63,170 | 57,611 |

December 7, 1836; organized 1844. *Henry Dodge.**

Dolores   **Colorado**
Dove Creek   1,067 sq. mi.

| 2,064 | 1,844 | 1,504 | 1,658 | 1,641 | 2,196 | 1,966 |

February 19, 1881. *Dolores River*. From Spanish *Rio de Nuestra Señora de los Dolores* (River of Our Lady of Sorrows); named when a member of a Spanish exploration party drowned in the river.

Doña Ana   **New Mexico**
Las Cruces   3,808 sq. mi.

| 209,233 | 174,682 | 135,510 | 96,340 | 69,773 | 59,948 | 39,557 |

January 9, 1852. *Village of Dona Ana*. Origin of name is unknown. Possibilities include: (1) Doña Ana Robledo (?–?), a local widow known for her charity; (2) Señorita Ana, a legendary maiden captured by Indians; (3) Doña Ana María, Niña de Córdeba (?–?), sheep rancher in the area.

Doniphan   **Kansas**
Troy   393 sq. mi.

| 7,945 | 8,249 | 8,134 | 9,268 | 9,107 | 9,574 | 10,499 |

August 25, 1855. *Alexander William Doniphan (1808–87)*. Missouri legislature intermittently 1836–54; brigadier general in Missouri Militia formed to drive Mormons out of Missouri 1838; colonel of mounted volunteers in Mexican War 1846; Battles of Chihuahua and Saltillo.

Donley   **Texas**
Clarendon   927 sq. mi.

| 3,677 | 3,828 | 3,696 | 4,075 | 3,641 | 4,449 | 6,216 |

August 21, 1876; organized March 22, 1882. *Stockton P. Donley (1821–71)*. District attorney, 6th Texas Judicial District 1852; private to lieutenant Confederate Army 1861; captured at Fort Donelson, exchanged for poor health 1862; Texas Supreme Court 1867, removed by Reconstruction military commandant.

Dooly   **Georgia**
Vienna   392 sq. mi.
14,918   11,525   9,901   10,826   10,404   11,474   14,159
May 15, 1821. *John Dooly (1740–80)*. Captain, 1st Georgia Regiment 1775; resigned 1776; colonel Georgia Militia; murdered in home by Tories August 1780.

Door   **Wisconsin**
Sturgeon Bay   482 sq. mi.
27,785   27,961   25,690   25,029   20,106   20,685   20,870
February 11, 1851; organized 1861. *Death's Door*. From French *Porte du Morte*; name for hazardous currents flowing between islands and Door Peninsula at entrance to Green Bay.

Dorchester   **Maryland**
Cambridge   541 sq. mi.
32,618   30,674   30,236   30,623   29,405   29,666   27,815
February 16, 1669. *Uncertain.* (1) *Edward Sackville, 4th Earl of Dorset (1591–1652)*; member of Parliament; British ambassador to France; governor of Bermuda Islands Company; lord chamberlain to Queen Henrietta Maria, wife of Charles I. (2) *Richard Sackville, 5th Earl of Dorset (1622–77)*; friend of Calverts (see Calvert, Maryland); member of Parliament 1640–43; court favorite of Charles II.

Dorchester   **South Carolina**
Saint George   573 sq. mi.
136,555   96,413   83,060   58,761   32,276   24,383   22,601
February 25, 1897. *Town of Dorchester*. Named for Dorchester, Massachusetts, by early settlers from New England 1696.

Dougherty   **Georgia**
Albany   329 sq. mi.
94,565   96,065   96,311   100,718   89,639   75,680   43,617
December 15, 1853. *Charles Dougherty (1801–53)*. Judge of Western Circuit; leader of Georgia's Whig Party.

Douglas   **Colorado**
Castle Rock   840 sq. mi.
285,465   175,766   60,391   25,153   8,407   4,816   3,507
November 1, 1861. *Stephen Arnold Douglas (1813–61)*. Illinois House of Representatives 1836–37; Illinois secretary of state 1840–41; US representative 1843–47; US senator 1847–61; Lincoln-Douglas Debates 1858; Democratic nominee for president 1860; advocate of "popular sovereignty" related to expansion of slavery into the Western territories.

Douglas   **Georgia**
Douglasville   200 sq. mi.
132,403   92,174   71,120   54,573   28,659   16,741   12,173
October 17, 1870. *Stephen Arnold Douglas.**

Douglas   **Illinois**
Tuscola   417 sq. mi.
19,980   19,992   19,464   19,774   18,997   19,243   16,706
February 8, 1859. *Stephen Arnold Douglas.**

Douglas   **Kansas**
Lawrence   456 sq. mi.
110,826   99,962   81,798   67,640   57,932   43,720   34,086
August 25, 1855. *Stephen Arnold Douglas.**

Douglas   **Minnesota**
Alexandria   637 sq. mi.
36,009   32,821   28,674   27,839   22,892   21,313   21,304
March 8, 1858. *Stephen Arnold Douglas.**

Douglas   **Missouri**
Ava   814 sq. mi.
13,684   13,084   11,876   11,594   9,268   9,653   12,638
October 29, 1857. *Stephen Arnold Douglas.**

Douglas   **Nebraska**
Omaha   328 sq. mi.
517,110   463,585   416,444   397,038   389,455   343,490   281,020
November 23, 1854. *Stephen Arnold Douglas.**

Douglas   **Nevada**
Minden   710 sq. mi.
46,997   41,259   27,637   19,421   6,882   3,481   2,029
November 25, 1861. *Stephen Arnold Douglas.**

Douglas   **Oregon**
Roseburg   5,036 sq. mi.
107,667   100,399   94,649   93,748   71,743   68,458   54,549
January 7, 1852. *Stephen Arnold Douglas.**

Douglas   **South Dakota**
Armour   432 sq. mi.
3,002   3,458   3,746   4,181   4,569   5,113   5,636
January 8, 1873; organized June 7, 1882. *Stephen Arnold Douglas.**

Douglas   **Washington**
Waterville   1,819 sq. mi.
38,431   32,603   26,205   22,144   16,787   14,890   10,817
November 28, 1883. *Stephen Arnold Douglas.**

Douglas   **Wisconsin**
Superior   1,304 sq. mi.
44,159   43,287   41,758   44,421   44,657   45,008   46,715
February 9, 1854. *Stephen Arnold Douglas.**

Drew   **Arkansas**
Monticello   828 sq. mi.
18,509   18,723   17,369   17,910   15,157   15,213   17,959
November 26, 1846. *Thomas Stevenson Drew (1802–79).* Merchant; schoolteacher; county clerk 1823–25; Arkansas Constitutional Convention 1836; governor of Arkansas 1844–49.

Dubois   **Indiana**
Jasper   427 sq. mi.
41,889   39,674   36,616   34,238   30,934   27,463   23,785
December 20, 1817; effective February 1, 1818. *Toussaint Dubois (1764–1816).* French soldier; Indian trader; Battle of Tippecanoe 1811; drowned in Little Wabash River.

Dubuque   **Iowa**
Dubuque   608 sq. mi.
93,653   89,143   86,403   93,745   90,609   80,048   71,337

September 6, 1834; effective October 1, 1834. *Julien Dubuque (1762–1810)*. First settler in Iowa; received option from Indians to operate lead mines.

Duchesne	**Utah**
Duchesne	3,241 sq. mi.

| 18,607 | 14,371 | 12,645 | 12,565 | 7,299 | 7,179 | 8,134 |

March 3, 1913. *Duchesne River*. Origin of name is unknown; possibilities include: (1) French trapper named Du Chasne or Du Chesne; (2) Mother Rose Philippine Duchesne (1769–1852), founder of US branch of Society of the Sacred Heart; (3) André Duchesne (1584–1640), French geographer and historian; (4) Ute word meaning "dark canyon."

Dukes	**Massachusetts**
Edgartown	103 sq. mi.

| 16,535 | 14,987 | 11,639 | 8,942 | 6,117 | 5,829 | 5,633 |

June 22, 1695. *King James II, Duke of York and Albany*. (See Albany, New York.)

Dundy	**Nebraska**
Benkelman	920 sq. mi.

| 2,008 | 2,292 | 2,582 | 2,861 | 2,926 | 3,570 | 4,354 |

February 27, 1873; organized June 12, 1884. *Elmer S. Dundy (1830–96)*. Nebraska territorial legislature 1858–61; Nebraska Territorial Supreme Court 1863–67; US Circuit Court 1867–96.

Dunklin	**Missouri**
Kennett	541 sq. mi.

| 31,953 | 33,155 | 33,112 | 36,324 | 33,742 | 39,139 | 45,329 |

February 14, 1845. *Daniel Dunklin (1790–1844)*. Sheriff, Washington County, Missouri; Missouri Constitutional Convention 1820; lieutenant governor 1828; governor of Missouri 1833–36; surveyor general of Missouri, Illinois, and Arkansas 1836.

Dunn	**North Dakota**
Manning	2,008 sq. mi.

| 3,536 | 3,600 | 4,005 | 4,627 | 4,895 | 6,360 | 7,212 |

March 9, 1883; abolished 1896; recreated May 24, 1901; organized February 10, 1908. *John Piatt Dunn (1839–1917)*. Homesteaded 1873; merchant; mayor of Bismarck 1884–85.

Dunn	**Wisconsin**
Menominee	850 sq. mi.

| 43,857 | 39,858 | 35,909 | 34,314 | 29,154 | 26,156 | 27,341 |

February 3, 1854; organized 1857. *Charles Dunn (1799–1872)*. Illinois legislature; first chief justice of Wisconsin Territory 1836; Wisconsin Senate 1853–56.

DuPage	**Illinois**
Wheaton	328 sq. mi.

| 916,924 | 904,161 | 781,666 | 658,835 | 491,882 | 313,459 | 154,599 |

February 9, 1839. *Du Page River*. Named for unknown French trader who had trading posts on the banks of the river c1800.

Duplin	**North Carolina**
Kenansville	816 sq. mi.

| 58,505 | 49,063 | 39,995 | 40,952 | 38,015 | 40,270 | 41,074 |

April 7, 1750. *George Henry Hay, Viscount Dupplin and Earl of Kinnoull (1710–87)*. English nobleman; made Viscount Dupplin 1627; member of Parliament 1741–58; commissioner of Irish revenue; ambassador extraordinary to Portugal. (County name misspelled at creation.)

Durham	**North Carolina**
Durham	286 sq. mi.

| 267,587 | 223,314 | 181,835 | 152,785 | 132,681 | 111,995 | 101,639 |

February 28, 1881. *Town of Durham*. Named for *Dr. Bartlett Durham (1822–58)*; donated land for railroad station which became Durhamville.

Dutchess   **New York**
Poughkeepsie   796 sq. mi.

297,488	280,150	259,462	245,055	222,295	176,008	136,781

November 1, 1683; organized 1713. *Mary Beatrice Modena, Duchess of York and Albany (1658–1718)*. Daughter of Alfonso IV, Duke of Modena; second wife of James II, Duke of York and Albany (see Albany, New York); Queen Consort of England 1685–88; fled to France with husband during Glorious Revolution; died in exile. ("Dutchess" is 18th-century spelling.)

Duval   **Florida**
Jacksonville   762 sq. mi.

864,263	778,879	672,971	571,003	528,865	455,411	304,029

August 12, 1822. *William Pope DuVal (1784–1854)*. Captain of Kentucky Mounted Rangers 1812; US representative from Kentucky 1813–15; judge, East Florida District 1821; governor of Florida Territory 1822–34.

Duval   **Texas**
San Diego   1,793 sq. mi.

11,782	13,120	12,918	12,517	11,722	11,398	15,643

February 1, 1858; organized November 7, 1876. *Uncertain*. (1) *Three Duval brothers*, sons of William Pope DuVal*; (a) *Burr H. Duval (1809–36)*, captain of Kentucky Mustangs, massacred at Goliad, Texas, March 27, 1836; (b) *John Crittenden Duval (1816–96)*, escaped Goliad Massacre; surveyor; Texas Ranger; writer of Texas frontier books; (c) *Thomas Howard Duval (1813–80)*, federal judge, Texas secretary of state 1851–55, only member of Duval family to support Union during Civil War. (2) *Burr Duval* specifically.

Dyer   **Tennessee**
Dyersburg   512 sq. mi.

38,335	37,279	34,854	34,663	30,427	29,537	33,473

October 16, 1823. *Robert Henry Dyer (c1774–1826)*. Lieutenant to lieutenant colonel 1807–12; served under General Jackson, War of 1812; Battle of New Orleans 1815; colonel, Seminole Campaign 1818.

E

Eagle   **Colorado**
Eagle   1,685 sq. mi.

52,197	41,659	21,928	13,320	7,498	4,677	4,488

February 11, 1883. *Eagle River*. Uncertain derivation. (1) Name of Ute chief. (2) Descriptive of numerous eagles in the area.

Early   **Georgia**
Blakely   513 sq. mi.

11,008	12,354	11,854	13,158	12,682	13,151	17,413

December 15, 1818; organized December 24, 1825. *Peter Early (1773–1817)*. US representative from Georgia 1803–07; first judge, Superior Court of Ocmulgee Circuit 1807–13; governor of Georgia 1813–15; Georgia Senate 1815–17.

East Baton Rouge   **Louisiana**
Baton Rouge   455 sq. mi.

440,171	412,852	380,105	366,191	185,167	230,058	158,236

December 22, 1810. *Town of Baton Rouge*. French for "red stick"; French-Canadian explorer Pierre le Moyne, Sieur d'Iberville (see Iberville, Louisiana), noted a "reddened maypole" marking the boundary between two Indian hunting areas 1699; the pole may also have had some religious significance.

East Carroll   **Louisiana**
Lake Providence   421 sq. mi.

7,759   9,421   9,709   11,772   12,884   14,333   16,302
March 28, 1877. *Carroll Parish*. Named for Charles Carroll (see Carroll, Arkansas); Carroll Parish was established March 14, 1832, and divided into east and west parishes 1877.

East Feliciana   **Louisiana**
Clinton   453 sq. mi.
20,267   21,360   19,211   19,015   17,657   20,198   19,133
February 17, 1824. *Feliciana Parish*. Named for Spanish *Distrito de Feliciana* in West Florida; claimed by US 1810. Origin of name is uncertain; possibilities include: (1) Spanish for "land of happiness"; (2) Maria Feliciana de Saint-Maxent (?–?), French wife of Bernardo de Gálvez, Spanish governor of Louisiana. Feliciana Parish was established December 7, 1810, and divided into east and west parishes 1824.

Eastland   **Texas**
Eastland   926 sq. mi.
18,583   18,297   18,488   19,480   18,092   19,526   23,942
February 1, 1858; organized December 2, 1873. *William Mosby Eastland (1806–43)*. Texas Army, 1st lieutenant; fought Waco Indians 1835; Battle of San Jacinto 1836; captain, Texas Rangers 1836–38; captured after Meir Expedition and taken to Mexico; one of every ten prisoners was to be executed as determined by drawing a white or black bean; Eastland drew a black bean and was executed.

Eaton   **Michigan**
Charlotte   575 sq. mi.
107,759   103,655   92,879   88,337   68,892   49,684   40,023
October 29, 1829; organized December 29, 1837. *John Henry Eaton (1790–1856)*. Tennessee House of Representatives 1815–16; US senator 1818–29; US secretary of war 1829–31; governor of Florida Territory 1834–36; envoy extraordinary and minister plenipotentiary to Spain 1836–40. Michigan Territory named seven counties after members of Jackson's first cabinet in hopes of promoting statehood.

Eau Claire   **Wisconsin**
Eau Claire   638 sq. mi.
98,736   93,142   85,183   78,805   67,219   58,300   54,187
October 6, 1856. *Eau Claire River*. French for "clear water."

Echols   **Georgia**
Statenville   415 sq. mi.
4,034   3,754   2,334   2,297   1,924   1,876   2,494
December 13, 1858. *Robert M. Echols (c1800–47)*. Georgia Assembly; colonel, 13th US Infantry Regiment 1847; brevet brigadier general 1847; mortally injured when thrown from his horse during a dress parade at Natural Bridge, Mexico, December 3, 1847.

Ector   **Texas**
Odessa   898 sq. mi.
137,130   121,123   118,934   115,374   91,805   90,995   42,102
February 26, 1887; organized January 6, 1891. *Mathew Duncan Ector (1822–79)*. Georgia legislature 1841; 3rd Texas Cavalry; private to brigadier general 1861–62; lost left leg to wounds at Atlanta 1864; judge, Court of Appeals 1875.

Eddy   **New Mexico**
Carlsbad   4,176 sq. mi.
53,829   51,658   48,605   47,855   41,119   50,783   40,640
February 25, 1889. *Charles B. Eddy (1857–?)*. Cattleman; manager of Carlsbad Irrigation Project in Pecos Valley 1889–94.

Eddy   **North Dakota**
New Rockford   630 sq. mi.
2,385   2,757   2,951   3,554   4,103   4,936   5,732
March 31, 1885. *Ezra B. Eddy (1830–85)*. 1st lieutenant, Minnesota Volunteer Infantry, 1861; founder of First National Bank, Fargo, 1878.

Edgar   **Illinois**
Paris   623 sq. mi.
18,576   19,704   19,595   21,725   21,591   22,550   23,407
January 3, 1823. *John Edgar (c1750–1832)*. British naval officer on Great Lakes during American Revolution; deserted to American side; judge, Common Pleas Court; Illinois delegate to the legislature of the Northwest Territories; major general of militia; wealthy merchant reputed to have bought and sold the entire county.

Edgecombe   **North Carolina**
Tarboro   505 sq. mi.
56,552   55,606   56,558   55,988   52,341   54,226   51,634
April 4, 1741. *Richard Edgcumbe, Baron Edgcumbe (1680–1758)*. British Parliament 1701–42; Lord of English Treasury; treasurer and paymaster of His Majesty's Services in Ireland 1724–42; made 1st Baron Edgcumbe 1742. (Trans-Atlantic spelling variations were common in 18th Century.)

Edgefield   **South Carolina**
Edgefield   500 sq. mi.
26,985   24,595   18,375   17,528   15,692   15,735   16,591
March 12, 1785; converted to judicial district January 1, 1800; redesignated as county April 16, 1868. *Descriptive* of county's location on the western edge of the state.

Edmonson   **Kentucky**
Brownsville   303 sq. mi.
12,161   11,644   10,357   9,962   8,751   8,085   9,376
January 12, 1825. *John Edmonson 1813*. Virginia Militia; Battle of King's Mountain 1780; raised company of volunteer riflemen, commissioned colonel 1812; killed at River Raisin January 18, 1813.

Edmunds   **South Dakota**
Ipswich   1,126 sq. mi.
4,071   4,367   4,356   5,159   5,548   6,079   7,275
January 8, 1873; organized July 27, 1883. *Newton Edmunds (1819–1908)*. Banker; governor of Dakota Territory 1863–66; sought peace with Indians.

Edwards   **Illinois**
Albion   222 sq. mi.
6,721   6,971   7,440   7,961   7,090   7,940   9,056
November 28, 1814. *Ninian Edwards (1775–1833)*. Kentucky House of Representatives 1796–97; judge, of various Kentucky courts 1803–08; Kentucky chief justice 1808; governor of Illinois Territory 1808–18; US senator from Illinois 1818–24; governor of Illinois 1826–30.

Edwards   **Kansas**
Kinsley   622 sq. mi.
3,037   3,449   3,787   4,271   4,581   5,118   5,936
March 18, 1874. *William Corydon Edwards (1846–1922)*. Banking and railroad executive; Kansas legislature 1885–87; Kansas Secretary of State 1895–93.

Edwards   **Texas**
Rocksprings   2,118 sq. mi.
2,002   2,162   2,266   2,033   2,107   2,317   2,908
February 1, 1858; organized April 10, 1883. *Hayden (or Haden) Edwards (1771–1849)*. Founded colony at Nacagdoches 1825; expelled by Mexican governor 1826; leader of settlers in Fredonia Rebellion against Mexico 1826.

Effingham   **Georgia**
Springfield   478 sq. mi.
52,250   37,535   25,687   18,327   13,632   10,144   9,133

February 5, 1777. *Thomas Howard, 3rd Earl of Effingham (1746–91)*. 1st Regiment of Foot Guards 1766; captain, 22nd Regiment 1772; deputy earl marshal of England 1777–82; lieutenant colonel British Army 1782; resigned commission rather than fight American colonists; governor of Jamaica 1790–91.

Effingham   **Illinois**
Effingham   479 sq. mi.

34,242	34,264	31,704	30,944	24,608	23,107	21,675

February 15, 1831; organized 1833. *Uncertain.* (1) *Edward Effingham (?–?)*; general, Black Hawk War 1832; US surveyor, surveyed county. (2) *Thomas Howard, 3rd Earl of Effingham.**

Elbert   **Colorado**
Kiowa   1,851 sq. mi.

23,086	19,872	9,646	6,850	3,903	3,708	4,477

February 2, 1874. *Samuel Hitt Elbert (1833–1907)*. Secretary of Colorado Territory 1862; Colorado territorial legislature 1869; governor of Colorado Territory 1873–74; justice, Colorado Supreme Court 1876–80, chief justice 1880–83.

Elbert   **Georgia**
Elberton   351 sq. mi.

20,166	20,511	18,949	18,758	17,262	17,835	18,585

December 10, 1790. *Samuel Elbert (1740–88)*. Captain to brevet brigadier general 1774–82 Georgia Council of Safety 1775; expedition against British in East Florida 1777; wounded and imprisoned at Briar Creek 1779; governor of Georgia 1785–86.

El Dorado   **California**
Placerville   1,708 sq. mi.

181,058	156,299	125,995	85,812	43,833	29,390	16,207

February 18, 1850. *Descriptive.* Refers to gold in the area; Spanish for "gilded one," from mythical king covered in gold dust each day.

Elk   **Kansas**
Howard   644 sq. mi.

2,882	3,261	3,327	3,918	3,858	5,048	6,679

March 25, 1875; effective June 1, 1875. *Elk River.* Descriptive of elk in the area.

Elk   **Pennsylvania**
Ridgway   827 sq. mi.

31,946	35,112	34,878	38,338	37,770	37,328	34,503

April 18, 1843. *Descriptive.* Refers for numerous elk in the area.

Elkhart   **Indiana**
Goshen   463 sq. mi.

197,559	182,791	156,198	137,330	126,529	106,790	84,512

January 29, 1830; effective April 1, 1830. *Chief Elkhart (?–?)*. Shawnee chief named for Elkhart River which had been named by Miami Indians for a heart-shaped island in the river.

Elko   **Nevada**
Elko   17,170 sq. mi.

48,818	45,291	33,530	17,269	13,958	12,011	11,654

March 5, 1869. *Town of Elko.* Name of uncertain origin and meaning; possibly Shoshone for "white woman." At least seven different towns were named "Elko" by railroads.

Elliott   **Kentucky**
Sandy Hook   234 sq. mi.

7,852	6,748	6,455	6,908	5,933	6,330	7,085

April 1, 1869. *Uncertain.* (1) *John L. Elliott (1794–1855)*; ran away to Virginia as a youth and assumed the name Isaac Lowe; War of 1812; returned to Kentucky and resumed true name 1825; Kentucky House of Representatives 1836–37; Kentucky

Senate 1851–53. (2) *John Milton Elliott (1820–79)*; son of John L.; Kentucky House of Representatives 1847 and 1861; US representative 1853–59; Confederate Congresses 1861–65; judge 1868–79; assassinated in Frankfort 1879.

Ellis   **Kansas**
Hays   900 sq. mi.

28,452	27,507	26,004	26,098	24,730	21,270	19,043

February 26, 1867. *George Ellis (?–1864)*. 1st lieutenant, Company I, 12th Kansas Infantry; killed at Jenkins Ferry, Arkansas, April 30, 1864.

Ellis   **Oklahoma**
Arnett   1,232 sq. mi.

4,151	4,075	4,497	5,596	5,129	5,457	7,326

July 16, 1907. *Albert H. Ellis (c1876–?)*. Oklahoma Constitutional Convention which named the county after him 1907.

Ellis   **Texas**
Waxahachie   935 sq. mi.

149,610	111,360	85,167	59,743	46,638	43,395	45,645

December 20, 1849; organized August 5, 1850. *Richard Ellis (1781–1846)*. Alabama Constitutional Convention 1819; Alabama Supreme Court 1819–25; president, Texas Convention 1836; signer, Texas Declaration of Independence 1836; Texas Republic Senate 1836–40.

Ellsworth   **Kansas**
Ellsworth   716 sq. mi.

6,497	6,525	6,586	6,640	6,146	7,677	8,465

February 26, 1867. *Fort Ellsworth*. Named for Allen Ellsworth (c1831–?); 2nd lieutenant, Company H, 7th Iowa Cavalry 1863; supervised construction of fort later named for him.

Elmore   **Alabama**
Wetumpka   618 sq. mi.

79,303	65,874	49,210	43,390	33,535	30,524	31,649

February 15, 1866. *John Archer Elmore (1762–1834)*. Continental Army; Battle of Yorktown 1781; South Carolina legislature; Alabama legislature 1821.

Elmore   **Idaho**
Mountain Home   3,075 sq. mi.

27,038	29,130	21,205	21,565	17,479	16,719	6,687

February 7, 1889. *Ida Elmore Mine*. Most productive gold and silver mine in the region. Name origin unknown.

El Paso   **Colorado**
Colorado Springs   2,127 sq. mi.

622,263	516,929	397,014	309,424	235,972	143,742	74,523

November 1, 1861. *Ute Pass*. Spanish for "pass"; Ute Pass is near Pikes Peak.

El Paso   **Texas**
El Paso   1,013 sq. mi.

800,647	679,622	591,610	479,899	359,921	314,070	194,968

January 3, 1850; organized March 7, 1871. *City of El Paso*. From Spanish *El Paso del Norte* (Northern Pass) or *El Paso del Rio del Norte* (Northern Pass River). Both names refer to the Rio Grande's passage through local mountains.

Emanuel   **Georgia**
Swainsboro   681 sq. mi.

22,598	21,837	20,546	20,795	18,189	17,815	19,789

December 10, 1812. *David Emmanuel (1742–1808)*. Burke County Militia 1775; Georgia legislature 1783–1808; governor of Georgia 1801; first Jewish governor of any US state.

Emery   **Utah**
Castle Dale   4,462 sq. mi.

| 10,976 | 10,860 | 10,332 | 11,451 | 5,137 | 5,546 | 6,304 |

February 12, 1880. *George W. Emery (1830–1909)*. Governor of Utah Territory 1875–80.

Emmet   **Iowa**
Estherville   396 sq. mi.

| 10,302 | 11,027 | 11,569 | 13,336 | 14,009 | 14,871 | 14,102 |

January 15, 1851; organized February 7, 1859. *Robert Emmet (1778–1803)*. Irish patriot and fighter; captured and executed for his participation in the Irish Rebellion, September 20, 1803.

Emmet   **Michigan**
Petoskey   467 sq. mi.

| 32,694 | 31,437 | 25,040 | 22,992 | 18,331 | 15,904 | 16,534 |

April 1, 1840, as Tonedagana; name changed March 8, 1843; organized January 29, 1853. *Robert Emmet*.*

Emmons   **North Dakota**
Linton   1,510 sq. mi.

| 3,550 | 4,331 | 4,830 | 5,877 | 7,200 | 8,462 | 9,715 |

February 10, 1879; organized November 9, 1883. *James A. Emmons (1845–1919)*. Steamboat operator on Missouri River; Bismarck merchant.

Emporia   **Virginia**
(Independent City)   7 sq. mi.

| 5,927 | 5,665 | 5,306 | 4,840 | 5,300 | (a) | (a) |

July 31, 1967. *Town of Emporia*. Latin for "trade center." [(a) Part of Greensville County] (Associated county: Greensville.)

Erath   **Texas**
Stephenville   1,083 sq. mi.

| 37,890 | 33,001 | 27,991 | 22,560 | 18,141 | 16,236 | 18,434 |

January 25, 1856; organized August 4, 1856. *George Bernard Erath (1813–91)*. Arrived in Texas from Austria 1833; Battle of San Jacinto 1836; captain, Texas Rangers 1839; Somervell Expedition 1842; Republic of Texas legislature 1843–45; Texas legislature 1846; Texas Senate 1857–61 and 1874; 15th Texas Infantry Regiment 1861–64.

Erie   **New York**
Buffalo   1,043 sq. mi.

| 919,040 | 950,265 | 968,532 | 1,015,472 | 1,113,491 | 1,064,688 | 899,238 |

April 2, 1821. *Erie Indians*. Unknown origin of name; may be Iroquois for "long tail" or "cat people." Lived between Lake Erie and Ohio River; eradicated by Iroquois 1655.

Erie   **Ohio**
Sandusky   252 sq. mi.

| 77,079 | 79,551 | 76,779 | 79,655 | 75,909 | 68,000 | 52,565 |

March 15, 1838. *Erie Indians*.*

Erie   **Pennsylvania**
Erie   799 sq. mi.

| 280,566 | 280,843 | 275,572 | 279,280 | 263,654 | 250,682 | 219,388 |

March 12, 1800; organized 1803. *Lake Erie*. Named for Erie Indians.*

Escambia   **Alabama**
Brewton   945 sq. mi.

| 38,319 | 38,440 | 35,518 | 38,440 | 34,906 | 33,511 | 31,443 |

December 10, 1868. *Escambia River*. Name of unknown origin; possible from Spanish *cambiar*, meaning "to exchange."

Escambia   **Florida**
Pensacola   656 sq. mi.

| 297,619 | 294,410 | 262,798 | 233,794 | 205,334 | 173,829 | 112,707 |

July 21, 1821. *Escambia River.**

Esmeralda   **Nevada**
Goldfield   3,582 sq. mi.

| 783 | 971 | 1,344 | 777 | 929 | 619 | 614 |

November 25, 1861. *Esmeralda Mining District*. From Spanish for "emerald."

Essex   **Massachusetts**
Salem   493 sq. mi.

| 743,159 | 723,419 | 670,080 | 633,632 | 637,887 | 568,831 | 522,384 |

May 10, 1643. *Essex County, England*. Located in southeastern England; origin of many early American colonists.

Essex   **New Jersey**
Newark   126 sq. mi.

| 783,969 | 793,633 | 778,206 | 851,116 | 929,986 | 923,545 | 905,949 |

March 1, 1683. *Essex County, England.**

Essex   **New York**
Elizabethtown   1,794 sq. mi.

| 39,370 | 38,851 | 37,152 | 36,176 | 34,631 | 35,300 | 35,036 |

March 1, 1799. *Uncertain*. (1) *Town of Essex*, (2) *Essex County, Massachusetts*.

Essex   **Vermont**
Guildhall   664 sq. mi.

| 6,306 | 6,459 | 6,405 | 6,313 | 5,416 | 6,083 | 6,257 |

November 5, 1792; organized 1800, *Uncertain*. (1) *Essex County, England.** (2) *Robert Devereux, 2nd Earl of Essex (1567–1601)*; court favorite of Elizabeth I; lord lieutenant of Ireland 1599; fell out of favor and executed for treason.

Essex   **Virginia**
Tappahannock   257 sq. mi.

| 11,151 | 9,989 | 8,689 | 8,864 | 7,099 | 6,690 | 6,530 |

April 26, 1692. *Uncertain*. (1) *Essex County, England.** (2) *Robert Devereux.**

Estill   **Kentucky**
Irvine   253 sq. mi.

| 14,672 | 15,307 | 14,614 | 14,495 | 12,752 | 12,466 | 14,677 |

February 19, 1808; effective April 1, 1808. *James Estill (1750–82)*. Militia captain; killed by Indians while on a mission to punish Indians for raids on settlements.

Etowah   **Alabama**
Gadsden   535 sq. mi.

| 104,430 | 103,459 | 99,840 | 103,057 | 94,144 | 96,980 | 93,892 |

December 6, 1866, as Baine; abolished December 3, 1867; recreated and name changed December 3, 1868. *Cherokee word* of unknown meaning; may mean "pine tree."

Eureka   **Nevada**
Eureka   4,176 sq. mi.

| 1,987 | 1,651 | 1,547 | 1,198 | 948 | 767 | 896 |

March 1, 1873. *Town of Eureka*. Greek for "I have found it!;" an exclamation associated with mining discoveries.

Evangeline   **Louisiana**
Ville Platte   662 sq. mi.

| 33,984 | 35,434 | 33,274 | 33,343 | 31,932 | 31,639 | 31,629 |

June 15, 1910. *Evangeline*. Legendary heroine of Longfellow's poem *Evangeline*.

Evans   **Georgia**
Claxton   183 sq. mi

| 11,000 | 10,495 | 8,724 | 8,428 | 7,290 | 6,952 | 6,653 |

August 11, 1914. *Clement Anselm Evans (1833–1911)*. Judge, Stewart County Court; Georgia Senate 1859; private to brigadier general in Confederate Army 1861–63; wounded at Battles of Gettysburg (1863) and the Wilderness (1864); Methodist minister 1866.

F

Fairbanks North Star   **Alaska**
Fairbanks   7,338 sq. mi.

| 97,581 | 82,840 | 77,720 | 53,983 | 45,864 | 43,412 | (a) |

January 1, 1964. *City of Fairbanks*. Named for Charles Warren Fairbanks (1852–1918); US senator from Indiana 1897–1905; headed US delegation to joint high commission with Canada; US vice president 1905–09. "North Star" was selected by school children in a contest to name the borough. [(a) Part of 4th Judicial District.]

Fairfax   **Virginia**
Fairfax   391 sq. mi.

| 1,081,726 | 969,749 | 818,584 | 596,901 | 455,021 | 275,002 | 98,557 |

May 27, 1742. *Thomas Fairfax, 6th Baron Fairfax of Cameron (1692–1782)*. Inherited his title from his father and extensive land holdings in America from his mother. (Associated independent cities: Fairfax and Falls Church.)

Fairfax   **Virginia**
(Independent City)   6 sq. mi.

| 22,565 | 21,498 | 19,622 | 19,390 | 21,970 | (a) | (a) |

July 30, 1961. *Fairfax County, Virginia*. [(a) Part of Fairfax County] (Associated county: Fairfax.)

Fairfield   **Connecticut**
Bridgeport   625 sq. mi.

| 916,829 | 882,567 | 827,645 | 807,143 | 792,814 | 653,589 | 504,342 |

May 10, 1666. *City of Fairfield*. Named for area's topography.

Fairfield   **Ohio**
Lancaster   504 sq. mi.

| 146,156 | 122,759 | 103,461 | 93,678 | 73,301 | 63,912 | 52,130 |

December 9, 1800. *Descriptive*. Refers to rolling farm land.

Fairfield   **South Carolina**
Winnsboro   686 sq. mi.

| 23,956 | 23,454 | 22,295 | 20,700 | 19,999 | 20,713 | 21,780 |

March 12, 1785; converted to judicial district January 1, 1800; redesignated as county April 16, 1868. *Uncertain*. Most suggestions concern the nature of the landscape.

Fallon   **Montana**
Baker   1,621 sq. mi.

| 2,890 | 2,837 | 3,103 | 3,763 | 4,050 | 3,997 | 3,660 |

December 9, 1913. *Benjamin O'Fallon (1793–1842)*. Indian agent for Missouri River tribes; explored Yellowstone River 1825.

Fall River   **South Dakota**
Hot Springs   1,740 sq. mi.

| 7,094 | 7,453 | 7,353 | 8,439 | 7,505 | 10,688 | 10,439 |

April 3, 1883. *Fall River*. Descriptive of falls and rapids; translation of Sioux name.

Falls   **Texas**
Marlin   765 sq. mi.

17,866	18,576	17,712	17,946	17,300	21,263	26,724

January 28, 1850; organized August 5, 1850. *Falls of the Brazos River.*

Falls Church   **Virginia**
(Independent City)   2 sq. mi.

12,332	10,377	9,578	9,515	10,722	10,192	7,535

1948. *Anglican church.* Built near Falls of the Potomac 1734. (Associated county: Fairfax.)

Fannin   **Georgia**
Blue Ridge   387 sq. mi.

23,682	19,798	15,992	14,748	13,357	13,620	15,192

January 21, 1854. *James Walker Fannin (1805–36),* Native of Georgia; joined Texas Revolution; hero at Concepción 1835; captured at Goliad and executed.

Fannin   **Texas**
Bonham   891 sq. mi.

33,915	31,242	24,804	24,285	22,705	23,880	31,253

December 14, 1837. *James Walker Fannin.**

Faribault   **Minnesota**
Blue Earth   712 sq. mi.

14,553	16,181	16,937	19,714	20,896	23,685	23,879

February 20, 1855; organized May 1, 1857, *Jean Baptiste Faribault (1774–1860).* French-Canadian fur trapper; agent in northwest for American Fur Company 1796–1806; taught agriculture to Indians.

Faulk   **South Dakota**
Faulkton   982 sq. mi.

2,364	2,640	2,744	3,327	3,893	4,397	4,752

January 8, 1873; organized November 5, 1883. *Andrew Jackson Faulk (1814–98).* Post trader to Yankton Indians 1861; oil business at Oil City, Pennsylvania, 1864–66; governor of Dakota Territory and superintendent of Indian affairs 1866–69; mayor of Yankton; clerk of federal and territorial courts.

Faulkner   **Arkansas**
Conway   648 sq. mi.

113,237	86,014	60,006	46,192	31,572	24,303	25,289

April 12, 1873. *Sanford C. Faulkner (1803–74).* Composer of *Arkansas Traveler* 1847; colonel in Confederate Army, commanded Little Rock Arsenal 1861–63.

Fauquier   **Virginia**
Warrenton   647 sq. mi.

65,203	55,139	48,741	35,889	26,375	24,006	21,248

April 5, 1759. *Francis Fauquier (1704–68).* Royal Society 1754; lieutenant governor of Virginia 1758–68; opposed colonial attempts of government and self-expression; defended western frontier during French and Indian War.

Fayette   **Alabama**
Fayette   628 sq. mi.

17,241	18,495	17,962	18,809	16,252	16,148	19,338

December 20, 1824. *Marquis de Lafayette (1757–1834).* Resigned from French military service to aid American cause for independence; commissioned as major general in Continental Army 1777; served with General Washington; Battle of Yorktown 1781; returned to France 1781; commander in chief of French National Guard 1789; captured by Austria during Napoleonic Wars 1792; revisited and toured US 1824–25. (Full name is Marie Jean Paul Roch Yves Gilbert Motier.)

Fayette   **Georgia**
Fayetteville   194 sq. mi.

106,567   91,263   62,415   29,043   11,364   8,199   7,978
May 15, 1821. *Marquis de Lafayette.**

Fayette   **Illinois**
Vandalia   716 sq. mi.
22,140   21,802   20,893   22,167   20,752   21,946   24,582
February 15, 1821. *Marquis de Lafayette.**

Fayette   **Indiana**
Connersville   215 sq. mi.
24,277   25,588   26,015   28,272   26,216   24,454   23,391
December 28, 1818. *Marquis de Lafayette.**

Fayette   **Iowa**
West Union   731 sq. mi.
20,880   22,008   21,843   25,488   26,898   28,581   28,294
December 21, 1837; organized August 26, 1850. *Marquis de Lafayette.**

Fayette   **Kentucky**
Lexington   284 sq. mi.
295,803   260,512   225,366   204,165   174,323   131,906   100,746
June 30, 1780; effective November 1, 1780. *Marquis de Lafayette.**

Fayette   **Ohio**
Washington Court House 406 sq. mi.
29,030   28,433   27,466   27,467   25,461   24,775   22,554
February 19, 1810. *Marquis de Lafayette.**

Fayette   **Pennsylvania**
Uniontown   790 sq. mi.
136,606   148,644   145,351   159,417   154,667   169,340   189,899
September 26, 1783. *Marquis de Lafayette.**

Fayette   **Tennessee**
Somerville   705 sq. mi.
38,413   28,806   25,559   25,305   22,692   24,577   27,535
September 29, 1824. *Marquis de Lafayette.**

Fayette   **Texas**
La Grange   950 sq. mi.
24,554   21,804   20,095   18,832   17,650   20,384   24,176
December 14, 1837. *Marquis de Lafayette.**

Fayette   **West Virginia**
Fayetteville   662 sq. mi.
46,039   47,579   47,952   57,863   49,332   61,731   82,443
February 28, 1831. *Marquis de Lafayette.**

Fentress   **Tennessee**
Jamestown   499 sq. mi.
17,959   16,625   14,669   14,826   12,593   13,288   14,917
November 28, 1823. *James Fentress (1763–1843).* Tennessee House of Representatives 1809–23, speaker 1820–23.

Fergus   **Montana**
Lewistown   4,340 sq. mi.

| 11,586 | 11,893 | 12,083 | 13,076 | 12,611 | 14,018 | 14,015 |

March 12, 1885. *John Fergus (1813–1902)*. Montana Territorial legislature; initiated idea for Yellowstone National Park; Montana Constitutional Convention 1889.

Ferry   **Washington**
Republic   2,203 sq. mi.

| 7,551 | 7,260 | 6,295 | 5,811 | 3,655 | 3,889 | 4,096 |

February 18, 1899. *Elisha Peyre Ferry (1825–95)*. Illinois Constitutional Convention 1861; surveyor general of Washington Territory 1869; governor of Washington Territory 1872–80; governor of Washington 1889–93.

Fillmore   **Minnesota**
Preston   861 sq. mi.

| 20,866 | 21,122 | 20,777 | 21,930 | 21,916 | 23,768 | 24,465 |

March 5, 1853. *Millard Fillmore (1800–74)*. New York Assembly 1829–31; US representative 1833–35 and 1837–43; New York comptroller 1847–49; US vice president 1849–50; 13th president of US 1850–53.

Fillmore   **Nebraska**
Geneva   575 sq. mi.

| 5,890 | 6,634 | 7,103 | 7,920 | 8,137 | 9,425 | 9,610 |

January 26, 1856; organized April 21, 1871. *Millard Fillmore.**

Finney   **Kansas**
Garden City   1,302 sq. mi.

| 36,776 | 40,523 | 33,070 | 23,825 | 18,947 | 16,093 | 15,092 |

March 20, 1873, as Sequoyah; name changed February 22, 1883. *David W. Finney (1839–1916)*. Union private to sergeant 1861–65; Kansas legislature 1876–80; Kansas lieutenant governor 1881–85.

Fisher   **Texas**
Roby   899 sq. mi.

| 3,974 | 4,344 | 4,842 | 5,891 | 6,344 | 7,865 | 11,023 |

August 21, 1876; organized April 27, 1886. *Samuel Rhoads Fisher (1794–1839)*. Republic of Texas Constitutional Convention 1836; signer, Texas Declaration of Independence 1836; Texas secretary of navy 1836–37.

Flagler   **Florida**
Bunnell   485 sq. mi.

| 95,696 | 49,832 | 28,701 | 10,913 | 4,454 | 4,566 | 3,367 |

April 28, 1917. *Henry Morrison Flagler (1830–1913)*. Capitalist and industrialist; made fortune in oil industry; developed railroads and hotels in Florida.

Flathead   **Montana**
Kalispell   5,088 sq. mi.

| 90,928 | 74,471 | 59,218 | 51,966 | 39,460 | 32,965 | 31,495 |

February 6, 1893. *Salish Indians*. Named Flatheads by Lewis and Clark, although they did not flatten heads as did tribes farther west; Lewis and Clark may have noticed flat-headed captives among the Salish.

Fleming   **Kentucky**
Flemingsburg   349 sq. mi.

| 14,348 | 13,792 | 12,292 | 12,323 | 11,366 | 10,890 | 11,962 |

February 10, 1798; effective March 1, 1798. *John Fleming (1735–?)*. Surveyor; explored Ohio River 1776.

Florence   **South Carolina**
Florence   800 sq. mi.

| 136,885 | 125,761 | 114,344 | 110,163 | 89,636 | 84,438 | 79,710 |

December 22, 1888. *City of Florence*. Named for Florence Harllee (1848–?); daughter of General W. W. Harllee, president of Wilmington and Manchester Railroad.

Florence   **Wisconsin**
Florence   488 sq. mi.

4,423	5,088	4,590	4,172	3,298	3,437	3,756

March 18, 1882. *Mine and Town of Florence.* Named for Florence Hulst (?–?), wife of Nelson P. Hulst; first American woman to settle in the region. The town and mine were originally named Eagle but were renamed because there already was a town of Eagle in Wisconsin.

Floyd   **Georgia**
Rome   510 sq. mi.

96,317	90,565	81,251	79,800	73,742	69,130	62,899

December 3, 1832. *John Floyd (1769–1839).* Brigadier general, Georgia Militia 1813–15; fought against Creeks and Choctaws; Georgia House of Representatives 1820–27; US representative 1827–29.

Floyd   **Indiana**
New Albany   148 sq. mi.

74,578	70,823	64,404	61,169	55,622	51,397	43,955

January 2, 1819; effective February 1, 1819. *Uncertain.* (1) *Davis Floyd (1772–?)*; Indiana territorial legislature 1805–06; indicted for association with Aaron Burr in his conspiracy with Spain, sentenced to a half-hour in jail. (2) *James Floyd* (see Floyd, Kentucky).

Floyd   **Iowa**
Charles City   501 sq. mi.

16,303	16,900	17,058	19,597	19,860	21,102	21,505

January 15, 1851; organized September 4, 1854. *Uncertain.* (1) *Charles Floyd (?–1804)*; sergeant on Lewis and Clark Expedition; only fatality (from disease) on expedition; buried in what is now Sioux City, Iowa. (2) *William Floyd (1734–1821)*; New York Colonial Senate; Continental Congress 1774–77 and 1778–83; signer, Declaration of Independence; major general, New York Militia; US representative 1789–91; New York Senate 1803.

Floyd   **Kentucky**
Prestonsburg   393 sq. mi.

39,451	42,441	43,586	48,764	35,889	41,642	53,500

December 13, 1799. *James John Floyd (1751–83).* Surveyor in Kentucky 1774; commanded USS *Phoenix* as privateer 1776; captured by British but escaped; settled in Louisville 1779; killed by Indians.

Floyd   **Texas**
Floydada   992 sq. mi.

6,446	7,771	8,497	9,834	11,044	12,369	10,535

August 21, 1876; organized May 28, 1890. *Dolphin Ward Floyd (1804–36).* Texas Revolution; killed at the Alamo, March 6, 1836.

Floyd   **Virginia**
Floyd   380 sq. mi.

15,279	13,874	12,005	11,563	9,775	10,462	11,351

January 15, 1831. *John Floyd (1783–1837).* Major to brigadier general in Virginia Militia 1807–13; Virginia House of Delegates 1814–15; US representative 1817–29; governor of Virginia 1830–34.

Fluvanna   **Virginia**
Palmyra   286 sq. mi.

25,691	20,047	12,429	10,244	7,621	7,227	7,121

June 3, 1777. *Fluvanna River.* Name is combined from Latin *fluvius* meaning "river," and "anna" for Queen Anne (see Queen Anne's, Maryland).

Foard   **Texas**
Crowell   704 sq. mi.

1,336	1,622	1,794	2,158	2,211	3,125	4,216

March 3, 1891; organized April 27, 1891. *Robert Levi Foard (1831–98)*. Maryland attorney; moved to Texas 1852; 1st lieutenant to major, 13th Texas Infantry 1861–63.

Fond du Lac	**Wisconsin**					
Fond du Lac	720 sq. mi.					
101,633	97,296	90,083	88,964	84,567	75,085	67,829

December 7, 1836; organized 1844. *Town of Fond du Lac*. French for "end of the lake"; describes town's location at the southern end of Lake Winnebago.

Ford	**Illinois**					
Paxton	486 sq. mi.					
14,081	14,241	14,275	15,265	16,382	16,606	15,901

February 17, 1859. *Thomas Ford (1800–50)*. Illinois state attorney 1829–33; judge, 6th Circuit 1836; Chicago Municipal Court 1837; Illinois Supreme Court 1840; governor of Illinois 1842–46.

Ford	**Kansas**					
Dodge City	1,098 sq. mi.					
33,848	32,458	27,463	24,315	22,587	20,938	19,670

February 26, 1867; organized April 1, 1873. *James Hobart Ford (?–1867)*. Captain to brevet brigadier general 1861–64; relocated Fort Dodge 1867.

Forest	**Pennsylvania**					
Tionesta	427 sq. mi.					
7,716	4,946	4,802	5,072	4,926	4,485	4,944

April 11, 1848; organized 1857. *Descriptive*. Refers to extensive forests in the area.

Forest	**Wisconsin**					
Crandon	1,014 sq. mi.					
9,304	10,024	8,776	9,044	7,691	7,542	9,437

April 11, 1885. *Descriptive*. Refers to extensive forests in the area.

Forrest	**Mississippi**					
Hattiesburg	466 sq. mi.					
74,934	72,604	68,314	66,018	57,849	52,722	45,055

April 19, 1906; organized January 6, 1908. *Nathan Bedford Forrest (1821–77)*. Enlisted in Confederate mounted rifle company 1861; lieutenant to brigadier general 1861–65; twenty-nine horses were shot from under him during his numerous engagements.

Forsyth	**Georgia**					
Cumming	224 sq. mi.					
175,511	98,407	44,083	27,958	16,928	12,170	11,005

December 3, 1832. *John Forsyth (1780–1841)*. Georgia attorney general 1808; US representative 1813–18 and 1823–27; US senator 1818–19 and 1829–34; US minister to Spain 1819–23; governor of Georgia 1827–29; US secretary of state 1834–41.

Forsyth	**North Carolina**					
Winston-Salem	408 sq. mi.					
350,670	306,067	265,878	243,683	214,348	189,428	146,135

January 16, 1849. *Benjamin Forsyth (c1775–1814)*. 2nd lieutenant, North Carolina Infantry 1800; captain of riflemen 1808; North Carolina legislature 1807–08; commanded assault on Gananoque, Upper Canada, 1812; brevet lieutenant colonel at Elizabethtown 1813; killed near Odellltown, New York.

Fort Bend	**Texas**					
Richmond	861 sq. mi.					
585,375	354,452	225,421	130,846	52,314	40,527	31,056

December 29, 1837. *Fort Bend*. Named for its location on a bend of the Brazos River 1821.

Foster   **North Dakota**
Carrington   635 sq. mi.

| 3,343 | 3,759 | 3,983 | 4,611 | 4,832 | 5,361 | 5,337 |

January 4, 1873; organized October 11, 1883. *James S. Foster (1828–90)*. Established colony in Dakota Territory 1864; Dakota Territory commissioner of immigration.

Fountain   **Indiana**
Covington   396 sq. mi.

| 17,240 | 17,954 | 17,808 | 19,033 | 18,257 | 18,706 | 17,836 |

December 30, 1825; effective April 1, 1826. *James Fountain (?–1790)*. Militia major; killed in Battle of Maumee 1790. (Name is also spelled Fontaine.)

Franklin   **Alabama**
Russellville   634 sq. mi.

| 31,704 | 31,223 | 27,814 | 28,350 | 23,933 | 21,988 | 25,705 |

February 6, 1818; effective June 1, 1818. *Benjamin Franklin (1706–90)*. Printer and editor; founded *Pennsylvania Gazette* 1728; Pennsylvania General Assembly 1736–50; Philadelphia postmaster 1737; provincial assembly 1744–45; deputy postmaster general of the British North American colonies 1753–74; Continental Congress 1775–76; signer, Declaration of Independence 1776; Pennsylvania Constitutional Convention 1776; commissioner and minister to France 1776–85; governor of Pennsylvania 1785–88; federal Constitutional Convention 1787.

Franklin   **Arkansas**
Ozark   609 sq. mi.

| 18,125 | 17,771 | 14,897 | 14,705 | 11,301 | 10,213 | 12,358 |

December 19, 1837. *Benjamin Franklin.**

Franklin   **Florida**
Apalachicola   535 sq. mi.

| 11,549 | 11,057 | 8,967 | 7,661 | 7,065 | 6,576 | 5,814 |

February 8, 1832. *Benjamin Franklin.**

Franklin   **Georgia**
Carnesville   262 sq. mi.

| 22,084 | 20,285 | 16,650 | 15,185 | 12,784 | 13,274 | 14,446 |

February 25, 1784. *Benjamin Franklin.**

Franklin   **Idaho**
Preston   664 sq. mi.

| 12,786 | 11,329 | 9,232 | 8,895 | 7,353 | 8,457 | 9,867 |

January 20, 1913. *Town of Franklin*. Named for Franklin Dewey Richards (1821–99); high priest, Church of Latter-Day Saints 1844; led settlers to Salt Lake Valley 1848; ordained one of twelve Mormon apostles 1849; Utah legislature 1849; regent, University of Deseret; historian, Mormon Church 1889–99; president of the Quorum of the Twelve Apostles 1898.

Franklin   **Illinois**
Benton   409 sq. mi.

| 39,561 | 39,018 | 40,319 | 43,201 | 38,329 | 39,281 | 48,685 |

January 2, 1818. *Benjamin Franklin.**

Franklin   **Indiana**
Brookville   384 sq. mi.

| 23,087 | 22,151 | 19,580 | 19,612 | 16,943 | 17,015 | 16,034 |

February 11, 1811. *Benjamin Franklin.**

Franklin   **Iowa**
Hampton   582 sq. mi.

10,680   10,074   11,364   13,036   13,255   15,472   16,268
January 15, 1851; organized March 3, 1856. *Benjamin Franklin.**

Franklin   **Kansas**
Ottawa   572 sq. mi.
25,992   24,784   21,994   22,062   20,007   19,548   19,928
August 25, 1855. *Benjamin Franklin.**

Franklin   **Kentucky**
Frankfort   208 sq. mi.
49,285   47,687   43,781   41,830   34,481   29,421   25,933
December 7, 1794; effective May 10, 1795. *Benjamin Franklin.**

Franklin   **Louisiana**
Winnsboro   625 sq. mi.
20,767   21,263   22,387   24,141   23,946   26,088   29,376
March 1, 1843. *Benjamin Franklin.**

Franklin   **Maine**
Farmington   1,697 sq. mi.
30,768   29,467   29,008   27,098   22,444   20,069   20,682
March 20, 1838; effective May 9, 1838. *Benjamin Franklin.**

Franklin   **Massachusetts**
Greenfield   699 sq. mi.
71,372   71,535   70,092   64,317   59,210   54,864   52,747
June 24, 1811; effective December 2, 1811. *Benjamin Franklin.**

Franklin   **Mississippi**
Meadville   564 sq. mi.
8,118   8,448   8,377   8,208   8,011   9,286   10,929
December 21, 1809. *Benjamin Franklin.**

Franklin   **Missouri**
Union   923 sq. mi.
101,492   93,807   80,603   71,233   55,116   44,566   36,046
December 11, 1818. *Benjamin Franklin.**

Franklin   **Nebraska**
Franklin   576 sq. mi.
3,225   3,574   3,938   4,377   4,566   5,449   7,096
February 16, 1867; organized June 21, 1871. *Benjamin Franklin.**

Franklin   **New York**
Malone   1,629 sq. mi.
51,599   51,134   46,540   44,929   43,931   44,742   44,830
March 11, 1808. *Benjamin Franklin.**

Franklin   **North Carolina**
Louisburg   492 sq. mi.
60,619   47,260   36,414   30,055   26,820   28,755   31,341
1779. *Benjamin Franklin.**

Franklin   **Ohio**
Columbus   532 sq. mi.

1,163,414   1,068,978   961,437   869,132   833,249   682,962   503,410
March 30, 1803. *Benjamin Franklin.**

Franklin   **Pennsylvania**
Chambersburg   772 sq. mi.
149,618   129,313   121,082   113,629   100,833   88,172   75,927
September 9, 1784. *Benjamin Franklin.**

Franklin   **Tennessee**
Winchester   555 sq. mi.
41,052   39,270   34,725   31,983   27,244   25,528   25,431
December 3, 1807. *Benjamin Franklin.**

Franklin   **Texas**
Mount Vernon   284 sq. mi.
10,605   9,458   7,802   6,893   5,291   5,101   6,257
March 6, 1875; organized April 30, 1875. *Benjamin Cromwell Franklin (1805–73)*. First judge in Republic of Texas 1836; captain, Texas Army 1836; Battle of San Jacinto 1836; Texas legislature 1845.

Franklin   **Vermont**
Saint Albans   634 sq. mi.
47,746   45,417   39,980   34,788   31,282   29,474   29,894
November 5, 1792; organized 1796. *Benjamin Franklin.**

Franklin   **Virginia**
Rocky Mount   692 sq. mi.
56,159   47,286   39,549   35,740   26,858   25,925   24,560
November 29, 1785. *Benjamin Franklin.**

Franklin   **Virginia**
(Independent City)   8 sq. mi.
8,582   8,346   7,864   7,308   6,880   (a)   (a)
December 21, 1961. *Uncertain*. (1) *Benjamin Franklin.** (2) Early storekeeper named Franklin in Franklin Depot, the original name of the town. [(a) Part of Southampton County] (Associated county: Southampton.)

Franklin   **Washington**
Pasco   1,242 sq. mi.
78,163   49,347   37,473   35,025   25,816   23,342   13,563
November 28, 1883. *Benjamin Franklin.**

Frederick   **Maryland**
Frederick   660 sq. mi.
233,385   195,277   150,028   114,792   84,927   71,930   62,287
June 10, 1748. *Uncertain*. (1) *Frederick Calvert (1731–71)*; 6th and last Baron Baltimore 1751; tried to pass title to Henry Harford, his illegitimate son (see Harford, Maryland). (2) *Frederick Louis (1707–51)*; eldest son of King George II; Duke of Gloucester 1717; Duke of Edinburgh 1727; Prince of Wales 1729; father of King George III.

Frederick   **Virginia**
Winchester   414 sq. mi.
78,305   59,209   45,723   34,150   28,893   21,941   17,537
December 15, 1738. *Frederick Louis.** (Associated independent city: Winchester.)

Fredericksburg   **Virginia**
(Independent City)   10 sq. mi.

24,286	19,279	19,027	15,322	14,450	13,639	12,158

1879. *Frederick Louis.** (Associated county: Spotsylvania.)

Freeborn   **Minnesota**
Albert Lea   707 sq. mi.

31,255	32,584	33,060	36,329	38,064	37,891	34,517

February 20, 1855; organized March 6, 1857. *William Freeborn (1816–1900)*. Minnesota territorial legislature 1854–57; mayor of Red Wing 1858; emigrated to Montana 1864 and to California 1868.

Freestone   **Texas**
Fairfield   878 sq. mi.

19,816	17,867	15,818	14,830	11,116	12,525	15,696

September 6, 1850; organized July 6, 1851. *Descriptive*. Refers to local stone deposits.

Fremont   **Colorado**
Cañon City   1,533 sq. mi.

46,824	46,145	32,273	28,676	21,942	20,196	18,366

November 1, 1861. *John Charles Fremont (1813–90)*. "The Pathfinder"; led five explorations of the Far West 1842–49; lieutenant colonel, US Mounted Rifles 1846; governor of California Republic 1849; US senator 1850–51; major general, Union Army, commanded Western District 1861; governor of Arizona Territory 1878–81.

Fremont   **Idaho**
Saint Anthony   1,864 sq. mi.

13,242	11,819	10,937	10,813	8,710	8,679	9,351

March 4, 1893. *John Charles Fremont.**

Fremont   **Iowa**
Sidney   511 sq. mi.

7,441	8,010	8,226	9,401	9,282	10,282	12,323

February 24, 1847; organized September 10, 1849. *John Charles Fremont.**

Fremont   **Wyoming**
Lander   9,184 sq. mi.

40,123	35,804	33,662	38,992	28,352	26,128	19,580

March 5, 1884. *John Charles Fremont.**

Fresno   **California**
Fresno   5,958 sq. mi.

930,450	799,407	667,490	514,621	413,053	365,945	276,515

April 19, 1856. *Descriptive*. Refers to ash trees (Spanish: *fresno*) in the area.

Frio   **Texas**
Pearsall   1,134 sq. mi.

17,217	16,252	13,472	13,785	11,159	10,112	10,357

February 1, 1858; organized July 20, 1871. *Frio River*. Spanish for "cold"; tributary of the Nueces River.

Frontier   **Nebraska**
Stockville   975 sq. mi.

2,756	3,099	3,101	3,647	3,982	4,311	5,282

January 17, 1872; organized February 5, 1872. *Descriptive*. Refers to county's location at the time it was created.

Fulton   **Arkansas**
Salem   618 sq. mi.

12,245	11,642	10,037	9,975	7,699	6,657	9,187

December 21, 1842; effective January 1, 1843. *William Savin Fulton (1795–1844)*. Defense of Fort McHenry 1813; private secretary to General Jackson 1818; editor of Florence, Alabama, *Gazette* 1821; judge of county court 1822; secretary of Arkansas Territory 1829–35; governor of Arkansas Territory 1835–36; US senator 1836–44.

Fulton   **Georgia**
Atlanta   527 sq. mi.
920,581   816,006   648,951   589,904   607,592   556,326   473,572
December 20, 1853. *Uncertain.* (1) *Hamilton Fulton (?–1834)*; chief engineer of Georgia; proposed and surveyed railroad through northwest Georgia. (2) *Robert Fulton* (see Fulton, Illinois).

Fulton   **Illinois**
Lewistown   866 sq. mi.
37,069   38,250   38,080   43,687   41,890   41,954   43,716
January 28, 1823. *Robert Fulton (1765–1815)*. Inventor; experimented with submarines in France 1801; developed naval mines; built the first steam-powered boat, *Clermont*, which steamed up the Hudson River 1807.

Fulton   **Indiana**
Rochester   368 sq. mi.
20,836   20,511   18,840   19,335   16,984   16,957   16,565
February 7, 1835; organized January 23, 1836; effective April 1, 1836. *Robert Fulton.**

Fulton   **Kentucky**
Hickman   206 sq. mi.
6,813   7,752   8,271   8,971   10,183   11,256   13,668
January 15, 1845. *Robert Fulton.**

Fulton   **New York**
Johnstown   495 sq. mi.
55,531   55,073   54,191   55,153   52,637   51,304   51,021
April 18, 1838. *Robert Fulton.**

Fulton   **Ohio**
Wauseon   405 sq. mi.
42,698   42,084   38,498   37,751   33,071   29,301   25,580
February 20, 1850. *Robert Fulton.**

Fulton   **Pennsylvania**
McConnellsburg   438 sq. mi.
14,845   14,261   13,837   12,842   10,776   10,597   10,387
April 19, 1850. *Robert Fulton.**

Furnas   **Nebraska**
Beaver City   719 sq. mi.
4,959   5,324   5,553   6,486   6,897   7,711   9,385
February 27, 1873. *Robert Wilkinson Furnas (1824–1905)*. Editor, Troy, Ohio, *Times* 1826–31; editor, *Nebraska Advertiser* 1855–61; Nebraska legislature 1856–60; colonel, Union Army 1861–62; governor of Nebraska 1873–75; regent, University of Nebraska 1875–81; author of numerous agricultural and horticultural reports.

G

Gadsden   **Florida**
Quincy   516 sq. mi.
46,389   45,807   41,105   41,565   39,184   41,989   36,457

June 24, 1823. *James Gadsden (1788–1858)*. War of 1812; aide-de-camp to General Jackson during Seminole Wars 1818; led removal of Seminoles from Florida to Indian Territory (Oklahoma) 1820; US minister to Mexico 1853; negotiated Gadsden Purchase with Mexico 1854.

Gage   **Nebraska**
Beatrice   851 sq. mi.

| 22,311 | 22,993 | 22,794 | 24,456 | 25,719 | 26,818 | 28,052 |

March 16, 1855; organized March 13, 1858. *William D. Gage (1803–85)*. Methodist clergyman; chaplain of Nebraska territorial legislature; treasurer of Otoe County 1855–56; Cass County commissioner 1857.

Gaines   **Texas**
Seminole   1,502 sq. mi.

| 17,526 | 14,467 | 14,123 | 13,150 | 11,593 | 12,267 | 8,909 |

August 21, 1876; organized October 24, 1905. *James Gaines (1776–1856)*. Mexican Army 1813; signer, Texas Declaration of Independence 1836; Texas Senate 1838–42; California Gold Rush 1849.

Galax   **Virginia**
(Independent City)   8 sq. mi.

| 7,042 | 6,837 | 6,670 | 6,524 | 6,278 | 5,254 | (a) |

November 30, 1953. *Descriptive*. Refers to a native decorative evergreen tree. [(a) Part of Carroll and Grayson counties] (Associated counties: Carroll and Grayson.)

Gallatin   **Illinois**
Shawneetown   323 sq. mi.

| 5,589 | 6,445 | 6,909 | 7,590 | 7,418 | 7,638 | 9,818 |

September 14, 1812. *Abraham Alfonse Gallatin (1761–1849)*. Native of Switzerland; Pennsylvania Constitutional Convention 1789; Pennsylvania legislature 1790–92; election to US Senate voided by party-line vote challenging citizenship 1794; US representative 1795–1801; US secretary of the treasury 1802–14; US minister to France 1815–23; US minister to Great Britain 1826–27.

Gallatin   **Kentucky**
Warsaw   101 sq. mi.

| 8,589 | 7,870 | 5,393 | 4,842 | 4,134 | 3,867 | 3,969 |

December 14, 1798. *Abraham Alfonse Gallatin.**

Gallatin   **Montana**
Bozeman   2,603 sq. mi.

| 89,513 | 67,831 | 50,463 | 42,865 | 32,505 | 26,045 | 21,902 |

February 2, 1865. *Gallatin River*. Named for Abraham Alfonse Gallatin* by Lewis and Clark 1805.

Gallia   **Ohio**
Gallipolis   467 sq. mi.

| 30,934 | 31,069 | 30,954 | 30,098 | 25,239 | 26,120 | 24,910 |

March 25, 1803. *France*. From *Gaul*, Latin name for France; land in Ohio was granted by US to a group of French immigrants who had been defrauded of land 1803.

Galveston   **Texas**
Galveston   378 sq. mi.

| 291,309 | 250,158 | 217,399 | 195,940 | 169,812 | 140,364 | 113,006 |

May 15, 1838; organized 1839. *Bernardo de Gálvez y Madrid (1746–86)*. Spanish Army service in Portugal, Mexico, and Algiers 1762–75; governor of Spanish Louisiana 1777; fought British 1783; captain at Baton Rouge, Mobile, and Pensacola 1780–81; viceroy of New Spain (Mexico) 1785–86.

Garden   **Nebraska**
Oshkosh   1,704 sq. mi.

2,057   2,292   2,460   2,802   2,929   3,472   4,114
November 2, 1909. *Descriptive*. Refers to hoped-for future as "The Garden Spot of the West."

Garfield   **Colorado**
Glenwood Springs   2,948 sq. mi.
56,389   43,791   29,974   22,514   14,821   12,017   11,625
February 10, 1883. *James Abram Garfield (1831–81)*. President, Hiram College 1857–61; Ohio Senate 1859; lieutenant colonel to major general 1861–63; US representative 1863–80; 20th president of US 1881; assassinated July 2, 1881, died September 19.

Garfield   **Montana**
Jordan   4,675 sq. mi.
1,206   1,279   1,589   1,656   1,796   1,981   2,172
February 7, 1919. *James Abram Garfield*.*

Garfield   **Nebraska**
Burwell   570 sq. mi.
2,049   1,902   2,141   2,363   2,411   2,699   2,912
November 8, 1884. *James Abram Garfield*.*

Garfield   **Oklahoma**
Enid   1,058 sq. mi.
60,580   57,813   56,735   62,820   55,365   52,975   52,820
August 21, 1893, as County O; name changed November 6, 1894. *James Abram Garfield*.*

Garfield   **Utah**
Panguitch   5,175 sq. mi.
5,172   4,735   3,980   3,673   3,157   3,577   4,151
March 9, 1882. *James Abram Garfield*.*

Garfield   **Washington**
Pomeroy   711 sq. mi.
2,266   2,397   2,248   2,468   2,911   2,976   3,204
November 29, 1881. *James Abram Garfield*.*

Garland   **Arkansas**
Hot Springs   678 sq. mi.
96,024   88,068   73,397   70,531   54,131   46,697   47,102
April 5, 1873. *Augustus Hill Garland (1832–99)*. Confederate Congress 1861; elected US senator from Arkansas, denied seat 1867; governor of Arkansas 1874–76; US senator 1877–85; US attorney general 1885–89.

Garrard   **Kentucky**
Lancaster   230 sq. mi.
16,912   14,792   11,579   10,853   9,457   9,747   11,029
December 17, 1796; effective June 1, 1797. *James Garrard (1749–1822)*, Captain, Virginia Militia 1776–77; Virginia legislature 1779; Kentucky Constitutional Convention 1792; governor of Kentucky 1796–1804.

Garrett   **Maryland**
Oakland   647 sq. mi.
30,097   29,846   28,138   26,498   21,476   20,420   21,259
April 1, 1872. *John Work Garrett (1820–84)*. Industrialist and financier; director of Baltimore & Ohio Railroad 1858–84.

Garvin   **Oklahoma**
Pauls Valley   802 sq. mi.
27,576   27,210   26,605   27,856   24,874   28,290   29,500

July 16, 1907. *Samuel Garvin (1844–1908)*. Merchant; member of Chickasaw tribal organization after marrying a Chickasaw wife 1870; ran freight caravans on Santa Fe Trail and through Indian Territory (Oklahoma).

Garza   **Texas**
Post   893 sq. mi.
6,461   4,872   5,143   5,336   5,289   6,611   6,281
August 21, 1876; organized June 15, 1907. *Garza Family*. One of the first families to arrive in Texas from the Canary Islands 1731; settled in San Antonio.

Gasconade   **Missouri**
Hermann   518 sq. mi.
15,222   15,342   14,006   13,181   11,478   12,195   12,342
November 25, 1820. *Gasconade River*. French *gascon* meaning "braggart" or "boaster" applied to local Indians or perhaps to an individual settler from Gascony, France.

Gaston   **North Carolina**
Gastonia   356 sq. mi.
206,086   190,365   175,093   162,568   148,415   127,074   110,836
December 21, 1846. *William Gaston (1778–1844)*. North Carolina legislature intermittently 1800–31; North Carolina Supreme Court 1833–44; wrote state song "The Old North State."

Gates   **North Carolina**
Gatesville   340 sq. mi.
12,197   10,516   9,305   8,875   8,524   9,254   9,555
1779. *Horatio Gates (1728–1806)*. Served with General Cornwallis in Nova Scotia 1749–50; wounded at Fort Duquesne while with General Braddock 1755; adjutant general and brigadier general Continental Army 1775; major general 1776; defeated General Burgoyne at Saratoga 1777; Battle of Camden 1780; New York legislature 1800–01.

Geary   **Kansas**
Junction City   385 sq. mi.
34,362   27,947   30,453   29,852   28,111   28,779   21,671
August 25, 1855, as Davis; organized 1857; name changed February 28, 1889. *John White Geary (1819–73)*. Mexican War, wounded at Chapultepec 1846; postmaster of San Francisco 1849; mayor of San Francisco 1850; governor of Kansas Territory 1856–57; brigadier general, Union army 1862; military governor of Savannah 1864; governor of Pennsylvania 1867–73.

Geauga   **Ohio**
Chardon   400 sq. mi.
93,389   90,895   81,129   74,474   62,977   47,573   26,646
December 31, 1805. *Grand River*. Indian name for the river was *Sheauga sepe* meaning "Raccoon River"; modern name for the river is Grand River.

Gem   **Idaho**
Emmett   561 sq. mi.
16,719   11,844   11,972   9,387   9,127   8,730
March 15, 1915. *Uncertain*. Best guess is from Idaho's motto: "Gem of the Mountains."

Genesee   **Michigan**
Flint   637 sq. mi.
425,790   436,141   430,459   450,449   444,341   374,313   270,963
March 28, 1835; organized April 4, 1836. *Genesee County, New York*.

Genesee   **New York**
Batavia   493 sq. mi.

60,079   60,370   60,060   59,400   58,722   53,994   47,584
March 30, 1802; organized 1803. *Genesee River Valley.* Seneca word for "beautiful valley."

Geneva   **Alabama**
Geneva   574 sq. mi.
26,790   25,764   23,647   24,253   21,924   22,310   25,899
December 26, 1868. *Town of Geneva.* The town was named for Geneva, Switzerland.

Gentry   **Missouri**
Albany   491 sq. mi.
6,738   6,861   6,848   7,887   8,060   8,793   11,036
February 12, 1841; organized 1843. *Richard Gentry (1788–1837).* Militia captain; Missouri Senate 1826 and 1828; major general 1832; commander of Missouri troops in Black Hawk War 1832; killed in Seminole War at Okeechobee, Florida, December 25, 1837.

George   **Mississippi**
Lucedale   479 sq. mi.
22,578   19,144   16,673   15,297   12,459   11,098   10,012
March 16, 1910. *James Zachariah George (1826–97).* Mexican War 1846; reporter, Mississippi Supreme Court 1854; Mississippi Secession Convention 1861; captain to brigadier general, Confederate Army 1861–63; prisoner of war 1863–65; chief justice of Mississippi Supreme Court 1879–81; US senator 1881–97; Mississippi Constitutional Convention 1890.

Georgetown   **South Carolina**
Georgetown   814 sq. mi.
60,158   55,797   46,302   42,461   33,500   34,798   31,762
1769 as judicial district; designated as county April 16, 1868. *Town of Georgetown.* Named for George II (1683–1760); Prince of Hanover; made Prince of Wales when his father became George I 1714; succeeded to throne 1727; last British monarch to lead troops in battle at Dettingen during War of Austrian Succession, 1743.

Gibson   **Indiana**
Princeton   487 sq. mi.
33,503   32,500   31,913   33,156   30,444   29,949   30,720
March 9, 1813. *John Gibson (1740–1822).* Soldier in French and Indian War 1756; colonel and general, Continental Army 1777; judge, court of common pleas; secretary of Indiana Territory 1800–16.

Gibson   **Tennessee**
Trenton   603 sq. mi.
49,683   48,152   46,315   49,467   47,871   44,699   48,132
October 21, 1823; organized January 5, 1825. *John H. Gibson (?–1823).* Lieutenant, Tennessee Militia 1811; major in General Jackson's Natchez expedition 1812–13.

Gila   **Arizona**
Globe   4,758 sq. mi.
53,597   51,335   40,216   37,080   29,255   25,745   24,158
February 8, 1881. *Gila River.* Uncertain origin of name; (1) Spansh expression *de gila* meaning "steady flowing"; (2) Spanish corruption of Yuman *Hah-quah-sa eel* "salty river," describing river's alkalinity at junction with Colorado River.

Gilchrist   **Florida**
Trenton   350 sq. mi.
16,939   14,437   9,667   5,767   3,551   2,868   3,499
December 4, 1925. *Albert Waller Gilchrist (1858–1926).* Florida House of Representatives 1893–1903; colonel in Spanish-American War 1898–99; governor of Florida 1909–13.

Giles   **Tennessee**
Pulaski   611 sq. mi.

| 29,485 | 29,447 | 25,741 | 24,625 | 22,138 | 22,410 | 26,961 |

November 14, 1809. *William Branch Giles (1762–1830)*. US representative from Virginia 1790, supported Tennessee statehood; US senator 1804–05; governor of Virginia 1827–30.

Giles   **Virginia**
Pearisburg   356 sq. mi.

| 17,286 | 16,657 | 16,366 | 17,810 | 16,741 | 17,219 | 18,956 |

January 16, 1806; effective May 1, 1806. *William Branch Giles.**

Gillespie   **Texas**
Fredericksburg   1,058 sq. mi.

| 24,837 | 20,814 | 17,204 | 13,532 | 10,553 | 10,048 | 10,520 |

February 23, 1848; organized June 3, 1848. *Robert Addison Gillespie (1815–46)*. Somervell expedition 1842; Texas Ranger 1844; Mexican War, killed at Monterrey September 21, 1846.

Gilliam   **Oregon**
Condon   1,205 sq. mi.

| 1,871 | 1,915 | 1,717 | 2,057 | 2,342 | 3,069 | 2,817 |

February 25, 1885. *Cornelius Gilliam (1798–1848)*. Sheriff, Clay County, Missouri, 1830; Black Hawk War 1832; captain, Seminole War 1837; led wagon train to Oregon 1844; colonel of volunteers to avenge murders of Marcus and Narcissa Whitman (see Whitman, Washington); died from accidental discharge of his rifle.

Gilmer   **Georgia**
Ellijay   427 sq. mi.

| 28,292 | 23,456 | 13,268 | 11,110 | 8,956 | 8,922 | 9,963 |

December 3, 1832. *George Rockingham Gilmer (1790–1859)*. 1st lieutenant in campaign against Creeks 1813–15; Georgia House of Representatives 1821–23; trustee, University of Georgia 1826–27; US representative 1827–20 and 1833–35; governor of Georgia 1829–31 and 1837–39.

Gilmer   **West Virginia**
Glenville   339 sq. mi.

| 8,693 | 7,160 | 7,669 | 8,334 | 7,782 | 8,050 | 9,746 |

February 3, 1854. *Thomas Walker Gilmer (1802–44)*. Virginia House of Delegates 1829–36 and 1839–40, speaker 1834–36; governor of Virginia 1840–41; US, representative 1841–44; secretary of the Navy 1844; killed in explosion aboard USS *Princeton* during demonstration of naval guns in presence of President Tyler, September 28, 1844 (see Upshur, Texas).

Gilpin   **Colorado**
Central City   150 sq. mi.

| 5,441 | 4,757 | 3,070 | 2,441 | 1,272 | 685 | 850 |

November 1, 1861. *William Gilpin (1815–94)*. Member of Fremont's 1843 expedition; major in Mexican War 1846; first governor of Colorado Territory 1861; raised regiment of Union volunteers to check Confederate operations in the West 1861; dismissed as territorial governor by President Lincoln for spending unauthorized funds in support of volunteer regiment 1861.

Glacier   **Montana**
Cut Bank   2,996 sq. mi.

| 13,399 | 13,247 | 12,121 | 10,628 | 10,783 | 11,565 | 9,645 |

February 17, 1919. *Glacier National Park*. Descriptive of numerous glaciers in the park.

Glades   **Florida**
Moore Haven   806 sq. mi.

| 12,884 | 10,576 | 7,591 | 5,992 | 3,669 | 2,950 | 2,199 |

April 23, 1921. *Florida Everglades*.

Gladwin   **Michigan**
Gladwin   502 sq. mi.

| 25,692 | 26,023 | 21,896 | 19,957 | 13,471 | 10,769 | 9,451 |

March 2, 1831; organized April 18, 1875. *Henry Gladwin (1729–91)*. British officer during French and Indian War; defended Fort Detroit during Pontiac's Rebellion 1763; returned to England before American Revolution.

Glascock   **Georgia**
Gibson   144 sq. mi.

| 3,082 | 2,556 | 2,357 | 2,382 | 2,280 | 2,672 | 3,579 |

December 19, 1857. *Thomas Glascock (1790–1841)*. Georgia Constitutional Convention 1798; captain of volunteers, War of 1812; Georgia House of Representatives intermittently 1821–39; US representative 1835–39.

Glasscock   **Texas**
Garden City   900 sq. mi.

| 1,226 | 1,406 | 1,447 | 1,304 | 1,155 | 1,118 | 1,089 |

April 4, 1887; organized March 28, 1893. *George Washington Glasscock (1810–68)*. Flatboating partner on the Sangamon River with Abraham Lincoln 1832; Black Hawk War 1832; Siege of Bexar 1835; Texas legislature 1866–72.

Glenn   **California**
Willows   1,314 sq. mi.

| 28,122 | 26,453 | 24,798 | 21,350 | 17,521 | 17,245 | 15,448 |

March 11, 1891. *Hugh James Glenn (1824–83)*. Dentist; Mexican War 1846–47; hauled freight to California gold miners; one of largest landowners in Northern California; California Board of Agriculture; murdered by an employee.

Gloucester   **New Jersey**
Woodbury   322 sq. mi.

| 288,288 | 254,673 | 230,082 | 199,917 | 172,681 | 134,840 | 91,727 |

May 26, 1686. *Uncertain*. (1) *Gloucester, England*. (2) *Gloucestershire, England*. Possible origin of early settlers or named for the home of a prominent settler.

Gloucester   **Virginia**
Gloucester   218 sq. mi.

| 36,858 | 34,780 | 30,131 | 20,107 | 14,059 | 11,919 | 10,343 |

1651. *Uncertain*. (1) *Gloucester, England*.* (2) *Gloucestershire, England*.* (3) *Henry, Duke of Gloucester (1640–60)*; son of King Charles I and Henrietta Maria; younger brother of Charles II and James II; died of smallpox.

Glynn   **Georgia**
Brunswick   420 sq. mi.

| 79,626 | 67,568 | 62,496 | 54,981 | 50,528 | 41,954 | 29,046 |

February 5, 1777. *John Glynn (1722–79)*. Member of British Parliament; supported American colonists.

Gogebic   **Michigan**
Bessemer   1,102 sq. mi.

| 16,427 | 17,370 | 18,052 | 19,686 | 20,676 | 24,370 | 27,053 |

February 7, 1887. *Uncertain*. (1) *Lake Gogebic*. (2) *Gogebic Iron Mining District*. The name is from a European rendering of the Chippewa name for the lake.

Golden Valley   **Montana**
Ryegate   1,175 sq. mi.

| 884 | 1,042 | 912 | 1,026 | 931 | 1,203 | 1,337 |

October 4, 1920. *Descriptive*. Promotional name in hopes of attracting settlers to the region.

Golden Valley   **North Dakota**
Beach   1,001 sq. mi.

| 1,680 | 1,924 | 2,108 | 2,391 | 2,611 | 3,100 | 3,499 |

November 11, 1912. *Golden Valley Land and Cattle Company*. Extensive Northern Plains landholding company; named for golden appearance of wheat in the area.

Goliad   **Texas**
Goliad   852 sq. mi.
7,210   6,928   5,980   5,193   4,869   5,429   6,219
March 17, 1836; organized 1837. *Municipality of Goliad*. Name derived from an anagram of [H]idalgo, Mexican Independence leader (see Hidalgo, Texas).

Gonzales   **Texas**
Gonzales   1,067 sq. mi.
19,807   18,628   17,205   16,883   16,375   17,845   21,164
March 17, 1836; organized 1837. *Municipality of Gonzales*. Named for Rafael Gonzales (1789–1857); 2nd lieutenant to lieutenant colonel in Spanish Army 1814–21; governor of Coahuila and Texas Province 1824.

Goochland   **Virginia**
Goochland   281 sq. mi.
27,717   16,863   14,163   11,761   10,069   9,206   8,934
March 6, 1727. *Sir William Gooch (1681–1751)*. Lieutenant colonel; governor of Virginia 1727–40 and 1741–49; commanded British assault on Cartagena, New Grenada (Colombia) 1741. Gooch named the county for himself during first year as governor.

Goodhue   **Minnesota**
Red Wing   757 sq. mi.
46,183   44,127   40,690   38,749   34,763   33,035   32,118
March 5, 1853; organized June 15, 1854. *James Madison Goodhue (1810–52)*. Owned *Wisconsin Herald* 1845–49; published *Minnesota Pioneer*, first newspaper in Minnesota 1849.

Gooding   **Idaho**
Gooding   729 sq. mi.
15,464   14,155   11,633   11,874   8,645   9,544   11,101
January 29, 1913. *Frank Robert Gooding (1859–1929)*. Idaho senate 1898–1902; governor of Idaho 1905–09; US senator 1921–28.

Gordon   **Georgia**
Calhoun   356 sq. mi.
55,186   44,104   35,072   30,070   23,570   19,228   18,922
February 13, 1850. *William Washington Gordon (1796–1842)*. Graduated West Point 1814; 3rd lieutenant 1815; aide to General Gaines, resigned 1815; president of Georgia Central Railroad 1836–42.

Goshen   **Wyoming**
Torrington   2,225 sq. mi.
13,249   12,538   12,373   12,040   10,885   11,941   12,634
February 9, 1911. *Uncertain*. (1) *Land of Goshen*; area allotted to Joseph by the King of Egypt; Genesis 45:10. (2) *Goshen Hole*; livestock and oil region named for any one of an Assiniboine trapper, or one of two French trappers, or a local cowboy.

Gosper   **Nebraska**
Elwood   458 sq. mi.
2,044   2,143   1,928   2,140   2,178   2,489   2,734
November 26, 1873. *John J. Gosper (1841–1913)*. Cavalry lieutenant, Union army; Nebraska secretary of state 1873–75; secretary of Arizona Territory 1877.

Gove   **Kansas**
Gove City   1,072 sq. mi.
2,695   3,068   3,231   3,726   3,940   4,107   4,447
March 11, 1868; organized September 2, 1886. *Grenville L. Gove (c1841–64)*. Cavalry private to captain, Union army 1861–64; died of illness.

Grady   **Georgia**
Cairo   455 sq. mi.
25,011   23,659   20,279   19,845   17,826   18,015   18,928
August 17, 1905; effective January 1, 1906. *Henry Woodfin Grady (1850–89)*. Newspaperman; correspondent for *New York Herald* in Georgia 1871; editor and part owner of *Atlanta Constitution* 1880; nationally recognized advocate for the South during Reconstruction.

Grady   **Oklahoma**
Chickasha   1,101 sq. mi.
52,431   45,516   41,747   39,490   29,354   29,590   34,872
July 16, 1907. *Henry Woodfin Grady.**

Grafton   **New Hampshire**
North Haverhill   1,709 sq. mi.
89,118   81,743   74,929   65,806   54,914   48,857   47,923
April 29, 1769; organized 1773. *Augustus Henry Fitzroy, 3rd Duke of Grafton (1735–1811)*. Member of Parliament 1756–57; House of Lords 1757; Privy Councilor 1765–66; prime minister 1768–70; favored conciliation with American colonists.

Graham   **Arizona**
Safford   4,623 sq. mi.
37,220   33,489   26,554   22,862   16,578   14,045   12,985
March 10, 1881. *Graham Mountain*. Named for James Duncan Graham (1799–1865); graduate of West Point 1817; topographical engineer; lieutenant to major 1817–38; surveyed US-Mexico boundary 1851.

Graham   **Kansas**
Hill City   899 sq. mi.
2,597   2,946   3,543   3,995   4,751   5,586   5,020
February 26, 1867; organized 1880. *John L. Graham (1832–63)*. Captain, 8th Kansas Regiment; killed at Chickamauga, September 9, 1863.

Graham   **North Carolina**
Robbinsville   292 sq. mi.
8,861   7,993   7,196   7,217   6,562   6,432   6,886
January 30, 1872. *William Alexander Graham (1804–75)*. North Carolina House of Commons 1836–40, speaker, 1838 and 1840; US senator 1840–43; governor of North Carolina 1845–49; US secretary of the Navy 1850–52; North Carolina Senate intermittently 1854–65; Confederate Senate 1863; elected to US Senate but credentials not presented 1866; arbiter in Virginia-Maryland boundary dispute 1873–75.

Grainger   **Tennessee**
Rutledge   281 sq. mi.
22,657   20,659   17,095   16,751   13,948   12,506   13,086
April 22, 1796. *Mary Grainger Blount (?–1802)*. Daughter of Caleb Grainger; married William Blount (see Blount, Tennessee), only governor of the Territory South of the Ohio.

Grand   **Colorado**
Hot Sulphur Springs   1,846 sq. mi.
14,843   12,442   7,966   7,475   4,107   3,557   3,963
February 2, 1874. *Grand River*. Alternative name for the Colorado River until Congress chose "Colorado" to be the river's official name 1921.

Grand   **Utah**
Moab   3,672 sq. mi.
9,225   8,485   6,620   8,241   6,688   6,345   1,903
March 13, 1890. *Grand River.**

Grand Forks   **North Dakota**
Grand Forks   1,436 sq. mi.

| 66,861 | 66,109 | 70,683 | 66,100 | 61,102 | 48,677 | 39,443 |

January 4, 1873; organized March 2, 1875. *Town of Grand Forks*. Named for location at junction of Red River and Red Lake River.

Grand Isle   **Vermont**
North Hero   82 sq. mi.

| 6,970 | 6,901 | 5,318 | 4,613 | 3,574 | 2,927 | 3,406 |

November 9, 1802; organized November 2, 1805; effective December 1, 1805. *Grand Isle*. Largest island in Lake Champlain.

Grand Traverse   **Michigan**
Traverse City   464 sq. mi.

| 86,986 | 77,654 | 64,273 | 54,899 | 39,175 | 33,490 | 28,598 |

April 7, 1851. *Grand Traverse Bay*. From French phrase meaning "long crossing"; applied to the larger of two openings crossed in navigating northeastern Lake Michigan.

Granite   **Montana**
Philipsburg   1,727 sq. mi.

| 3,079 | 2,830 | 2,548 | 2,700 | 2,737 | 3,014 | 2,773 |

March 2, 1893. *Granite Mountain Silver Mine*. Mountain was named for its granite content.

Grant   **Arkansas**
Sheridan   632 sq. mi.

| 17,853 | 16,464 | 13,948 | 13,008 | 9,711 | 8,294 | 9,024 |

February 4, 1869. *Ulysses S. Grant (1822–85)*. Graduated West Point 1843; opposed Mexican War but served with distinction 1846–48; resigned from Army 1854; reenlisted as colonel 1861; brigadier general to lieutenant general 1861–63; Commanding General of the US Army 1864–65; received General Lee's surrender April 9, 1865; 18th president of the US 1869–77.

Grant   **Indiana**
Marion   414 sq. mi.

| 70,061 | 73,403 | 74,169 | 80,934 | 83,955 | 74,741 | 62,156 |

February 10, 1831; effective April 1, 1831. *Samuel Grant (1762–89) and Moses Grant (1768–89)*. Brothers from Kentucky killed in skirmish with Indians in Switzerland County, Indiana.

Grant   **Kansas**
Ulysses   575 sq. mi.

| 7,829 | 7,909 | 7,159 | 6,977 | 5,961 | 5,269 | 4,638 |

March 20, 1873; organized 1889. *Ulysses S. Grant.**

Grant   **Kentucky**
Williamstown   258 sq. mi.

| 24,662 | 22,384 | 15,737 | 13,308 | 9,999 | 9,489 | 9,809 |

February 12, 1820. *Uncertain.* (1) *John Grant (1754–1826)*; pioneer salt producer. (2) *Samuel Grant.** (3) *Squire Grant (1764–1833)*; surveyor; Kentucky Senate 1801–06.

Grant   **Louisiana**
Colfax   643 sq. mi.

| 22,309 | 18,698 | 17,526 | 16,703 | 13,671 | 13,330 | 14,263 |

March 4, 1869. *Ulysses S. Grant.**

Grant   **Minnesota**
Elbow Lake   548 sq. mi.

| 6,018 | 6,289 | 6,246 | 7,171 | 7,462 | 8,870 | 9,542 |

March 6, 1868; organized March 1, 1883. *Ulysses S. Grant.**

Grant   **Nebraska**
Hyannis   776 sq. mi.
614   747   769   877   1,019   1,009   1,057
March 31, 1887; organized May 13, 1888. *Ulysses S. Grant.**

Grant   **New Mexico**
Silver City   3,962 sq. mi.
29,514   31,002   27,676   26,204   22,030   18,700   21,649
January 30, 1868. *Ulysses S. Grant.**

Grant   **North Dakota**
Carson   1,659 sq. mi.
2,394   2,841   3,549   4,274   5,009   6,248   7,114
November 25, 1916. *Ulysses S. Grant.**

Grant   **Oklahoma**
Medford   1,001 sq. mi.
4,527   5,144   5,689   6,518   7,117   8,140   10,461
August 21, 1893, as County L; name changed November 6, 1894. *Ulysses S. Grant.**

Grant   **Oregon**
Canyon City   4,529 sq. mi.
7,445   7,935   7,853   8,210   6,996   7,726   8,329
October 14, 1864. *Ulysses S. Grant.**

Grant   **South Dakota**
Milbank   681 sq. mi.
7,356   7,847   8,372   9,013   9,005   9,913   10,233
January 8, 1873; organized June 17, 1878. *Ulysses S. Grant.**

Grant   **Washington**
Ephrata   2,680 sq. mi.
89,120   74,698   54,758   48,522   41,881   46,477   24,346
February 24, 1909. *Ulysses S. Grant.**

Grant   **West Virginia**
Petersburg   477 sq. mi.
11,937   11,299   10,428   10,210   8,607   8,304   8,756
February 14, 1866. *Ulysses S. Grant.**

Grant   **Wisconsin**
Lancaster   1,147 sq. mi.
51,208   49,597   49,264   51,736   48,398   44,419   41,460
December 8, 1836; effective March 4, 1837. *Uncertain.* (1) *Cuthbert Grant (c1791–1854)*; fur trapper. (2) *Grant River*; named for Cuthbert Grant or his father, James Grant (?–?).

Granville   **North Carolina**
Oxford   532 sq. mi.
59,916   48,498   36,345   34,043   32,762   33,110   31,793
1746. *John Carteret, Earl of Granville.* (See Carteret, North Carolina.)

Gratiot   **Michigan**
Ithaca   568 sq. mi.
42,476   42,285   38,982   40,448   39,246   31,012   33,429

March 2, 1831; organized February 3, 1855. *Uncertain.* (1) *Charles Gratiot (1786–1855)*; graduated West Point 1806; chief engineer of US Army 1812 and 1828–38; attack on Fort Meigs 1813; brevet colonel 1814; directed construction of Fort Gratiot 1814; brevet brigadier general 1828. (2) *Fort Gratiot*; named for Charles Gratiot; located at head of St. Clair River on Lake Huron.

Graves   **Kentucky**
Mayfield   552 sq. mi.

37,121	37,028	33,550	34,049	30,939	30,021	31,364

December 19, 1821; organized 1824. *Benjamin Graves (1771–1813).* Major to colonel; killed at Battle of River Raisin 1813.

Gray   **Kansas**
Cimarron   869 sq. mi.

6,006	5,904	5,396	5,138	4,516	4,380	4,894

March 13, 1881; abolished February 21, 1883; recreated March 5, 1887; organized July 20, 1887. *Alfred Gray (1830–80).* Kansas legislature 1861; Union Army quartermaster 1862–64; secretary, Kansas Board of Agriculture 1873–80.

Gray   **Texas**
Pampa   926 sq. mi.

22,535	22,744	23,967	26,386	26,949	31,535	24,728

August 21, 1876; organized May 27, 1902. *Peter W. Gray (1819–74).* Captain, Texas Army 1840; Texas legislature 1846; Texas Secession Convention 1861; district judge 1861–64; Confederate Congress 1861–65; justice, Texas Supreme Court 1874.

Grays Harbor   **Washington**
Montesano   1,902 sq. mi.

72,797	67,194	64,175	66,314	59,553	54,465	53,644

April 14, 1854, as Chehalis; name changed March 15, 1915. *Grays Harbor.* Named for Robert Gray (1755–1806); Boston trader; commanded first American circumnavigation 1787–90; entered Columbia River and named it after his ship *Columbia* 1792.

Grayson   **Kentucky**
Leitchfield   497 sq. mi.

25,746	24,053	21,050	20,854	16,445	15,834	17,063

January 25, 1810; effective April 1, 1810. *William Grayson (c1736–90).* Captain of independent company of cadets, Prince William County, Virginia, 1774; aide-de-camp to General Washington 1776; organized Grayson's Continental Regiment 1777; colonel 1777; Battle of Monmouth 1778; Continental Congress 1784–87; Virginia Constitutional Convention 1788; US senator 1789–90.

Grayson   **Texas**
Sherman   933 sq. mi.

120,877	110,595	95,021	89,796	83,225	73,043	70,467

March 17, 1846; organized July 13, 1846. *Peter Wagener Grayson (1788–1838).* Aide-de-camp to Stephen Austin 1835; Republic of Texas attorney general 1836–37; mediator between Mexico and Texas at Washington, DC, 1836; committed suicide.

Grayson   **Virginia**
Independence   442 sq. mi.

15,533	17,917	16,278	16,579	15,439	17,390	21,379

November 7, 1792. *William Grayson.** (Associated independent city: part of Galax.)

Greeley   **Kansas**
Tribune   778 sq. mi.

1,247	1,534	1,774	1,845	1,819	2,087	2,010

March 20, 1873; organized July 9, 1888. *Horace Greeley (1811–72).* Founded *New York Tribune* 1841; US representative 1848–49; defeated for US presidency 1872; popularized phrase "Go West, young man."

Greeley   **Nebraska**
Greeley   570 sq. mi.
2,538   2,714   3,006   3,462   4,000   4,595   5,575
March 1, 1871; organized January 20, 1873. *Horace Greeley.**

Green   **Kentucky**
Greensburg   286 sq. mi.
11,258   11,518   10,371   11,043   10,350   11,249   11,261
December 20, 1792. *Nathanael Greene.* No explanation for difference in spelling. (See Greene, Alabama.)

Green   **Wisconsin**
Monroe   584 sq. mi.
36,842   33,647   30,339   30,012   26,714   25,851   24,172
December 8, 1836; organized 1838. *Uncertain.* (1) *Nathanael Greene*; letter *e* dropped by legislative error (see Greene, Alabama). (2) *Descriptive*; refers to local forests.

Greenbrier   **West Virginia**
Lewisburg   1,020 sq. mi.
35,480   34,453   34,693   37,665   32,090   34,446   39,295
January 12, 1778. *Greenbrier River.* Translation of French name *Ronceverte*, from *ronce* meaning "brier" or "bramble" and *verte* meaning "green."

Greene   **Alabama**
Eutaw   647 sq. mi.
9,045   9,974   10,153   11,021   10,650   13,600   16,842
December 13, 1819. *Nathanael Greene (1742–86).* Rhode Island Volunteers 1775; brigadier general to major general in Continental Army 1775–80; commanded Army of the South 1780; president of the court of inquiry for British spy Major André 1780; resigned from army 1783.

Greene   **Arkansas**
Paragould   578 sq. mi.
42,090   37,331   31,804   30,744   24,765   25,198   29,149
November 5, 1833; effective November 1, 1834. *Nathanael Greene.**

Greene   **Georgia**
Greensboro   387 sq. mi.
15,994   14,406   11,793   11,391   10,212   11,193   12,843
February 3, 1786. *Nathanael Greene.**

Greene   **Illinois**
Carrollton   543 sq. mi.
13,886   14,761   15,317   16,661   17,014   17,460   18,852
January 20, 1821. *Nathanael Greene.**

Greene   **Indiana**
Bloomfield   542 sq. mi.
33,165   33,157   30,410   30,416   26,894   26,327   27,886
January 5, 1821. *Nathanael Greene.**

Greene   **Iowa**
Jefferson   570 sq. mi.
9,336   10,366   10,045   12,119   12,716   14,379   15,544
January 15, 1851; organized August 25, 1853. *Nathanael Greene.**

Greene   **Mississippi**
Leakesville   713 sq. mi.
14,400   13,299   10,220   9,827   8,545   8,366   8,215
December 9, 1811. *Nathanael Greene.**

Greene   **Missouri**
Springfield   675 sq. mi.
275,174   240,391   207,949   185,302   152,929   126,276   104,823
January 2, 1833. *Nathanael Greene.**

Greene   **New York**
Catskill   647 sq. mi.
49,221   48,195   44,739   40,861   33,136   31,372   28,745
March 25, 1800. *Nathanael Greene.**

Greene   **North Carolina**
Snow Hill   266 sq. mi.
21,362   19,974   15,384   16,117   14,967   16,741   18,024
1799. *Nathanael Greene.**

Greene   **Ohio**
Xenia   414 sq. mi.
161,573   147,886   136,731   129,769   125,057   94,642   58,892
March 24, 1803. *Nathanael Greene.**

Greene   **Pennsylvania**
Waynesburg   576 sq. mi.
38,686   40,672   39,550   40,476   36,090   29,424   45,394
February 9, 1796. *Nathanael Greene.**

Greene   **Tennessee**
Greenville   622 sq. mi.
68,831   62,909   55,853   54,422   47,630   42,163   41,048
1783. *Nathanael Greene.**

Greene   **Virginia**
Stanardsville   156 sq. mi.
18,403   15,244   10,297   7,625   5,248   4,715   4,745
January 24, 1838. *Nathanael Greene.**

Green Lake   **Wisconsin**
Green Lake   349 sq. mi.
19,051   19,105   18,651   18,370   16,878   15,418   14,749
March 5, 1858. *Green Lake*. Translation of Indian name describing the lake's appearance.

Greenlee   **Arizona**
Clifton   1,843 sq. mi.
8,437   8,547   8,008   11,406   10,330   11,509   12,805
March 10, 1909. *Mason Greenlee (1835–1903)*. Early prospector and mineral surveyor in Eastern Arizona.

Greensville   **Virginia**
Emporia   295 sq. mi.
12,243   11,560   8,853   10,903   9,604   16,155   16,319

November 28, 1780. *Uncertain.* (1) *Richard Grenville (1542–91)*; member of Parliament 1571–84; established colony at Roanoke 1585; died in a naval engagement against Spain 1591. (2) *Nathanael Greene* (see Greene, Alabama). (Associated independent city: Emporia.)

Greenup   **Kentucky**
Greenup   344 sq. mi.

36,910	36,891	36,742	39,132	33,192	29,238	24,887

December 12, 1803. *Christopher Greenup (1750–1818).* Colonel, Revolutionary War; Virginia House of Delegates 1785; member of conventions to consider separating Kentucky from Virginia 1785 and 1788; US representative from Kentucky 1792–97; Kentucky House of Representatives 1798 and 1809; clerk of Kentucky Senate 1799–1802; circuit court judge 1802; Franklin County justice of the peace 1812.

Greenville   **South Carolina**
Greenville   785 sq. mi.

451,225	379,616	320,167	287,913	240,546	209,776	168,152

March 22, 1786; converted to judicial district January 1, 1800; redesignated as county April 16, 1868. *Uncertain.* (1) *Nathanael Greene* (see Greene, Alabama). (2) *Isaac Green (1762–?)*; early settler; established grist mill on Reedy River. (3) *Descriptive*; referring to local foliage.

Greenwood   **Kansas**
Eureka   1,143 sq. mi.

6,689	7,673	7,847	8,764	9,141	11,253	13,574

August 25, 1855; organized February 27, 1860. *Alfred Burton Greenwood (1811–89).* Arkansas House of Representatives 1842–45; Arkansas prosecuting attorney 1845–51; circuit judge 1851–53; US representative from Arkansas 1853–59; US commissioner of Indian affairs 1859–61; Confederate House of Representatives 1862–65. Pro-slavery Kansas territorial legislature named many counties for prominent Southerners.

Greenwood   **South Carolina**
Greenwood   455 sq. mi.

69,661	66,271	59,567	57,847	49,686	44,346	41,628

March 2, 1897. *City of Greenwood.* Named for local foliage.

Greer   **Oklahoma**
Mangum   639 sq. mi.

6,239	6,061	6,559	7,028	7,979	8,877	11,749

February 8, 1860 as part of Texas; organized July 1886; declared belonging to Oklahoma by US Supreme Court May 4, 1896. *John Alexander Greer (1802–55).* Republic of Texas legislature 1837–45; Republic of Texas secretary of treasury 1845; Texas lieutenant governor 1845–51; died while campaigning for governor.

Gregg   **Texas**
Longview   273 sq. mi.

121,730	111,379	104,948	99,487	75,929	69,436	61,258

April 12, 1873. *John Gregg (1828–64).* District judge 1856–60; delegate to Provincial Congress of the Confederacy 1860; organized regiment of volunteers 1861; brigadier general 1862; killed near Fort Harrison, Virginia, October 7, 1864.

Gregory   **South Dakota**
Burke   1,015 sq. mi.

4,271	4,792	5,359	6,015	6,710	7,399	8,556

May 8, 1862; organized September 5, 1898. *John Shaw Gregory (1829–81).* Graduated Annapolis; Dakota territorial council 1862–66; US Indian agent for Poncas.

Grenada   **Mississippi**
Grenada   422 sq. mi.

21,906	23,263	21,555	21,043	19,854	18,409	18,830

May 9, 1870. *Town of Grenada.* Named for city and province of Granada, Spain. Variation in spelling is most likely a clerical error.

Griggs **North Dakota**
Cooperstown 709 sq. mi.
2,420 2,754 3,303 3,714 4,184 5,023 5,460
February 18, 1881; organized June 16, 1882. *Alexander Griggs (1838–1903)*. Steamboat pilot on Mississippi River; moved to Red River; one of founders of Grand Forks; North Dakota Constitutional Convention 1889.

Grimes **Texas**
Anderson 787 sq. mi.
26,604 23,552 18,828 13,580 11,855 12,709 15,135
April 6, 1846. *Jesse Grimes (1788–1866)*. Elected 1st lieutenant in Mexican-Texas Militia 1829; signer, Texas Declaration of Independence 1836; Texas Senate 1836–37; Texas legislature 1841–45.

Grundy **Illinois**
Morris 418 sq. mi.
50,063 37,535 32,337 30,582 26,535 22,350 19,217
February 17, 1841; organized May 24, 1841. *Felix Grundy (1777–1840)*. Kentucky House of Representatives 1800–05; judge, Kentucky Supreme Court 1806–07, chief justice 1807; US representative from Tennessee 1811–14; Tennessee House of Representatives 1819–25; US senator 1829–40; US attorney general 1838–40.

Grundy **Iowa**
Grundy Center 502 sq. mi.
12,453 12,369 12,029 14,366 14,119 14,132 13,722
January 15, 1851; organized December 25, 1856. *Felix Grundy*.*

Grundy **Missouri**
Trenton 435 sq. mi.
10,261 10,432 10,536 11,959 11,819 12,220 13,220
January 29, 1841. *Felix Grundy*.*

Grundy **Tennessee**
Altamont 361 sq. mi.
13,703 14,332 13,362 13,787 10,631 11,512 12,558
January 29, 1844. *Felix Grundy*.*

Guadalupe **New Mexico**
Santa Rosa 3,030 sq. mi.
4,687 4,640 4,156 4,496 4,969 5,610 6,772
February 26, 1891, as Guadalupe; name changed to Leonard Wood 1903; renamed Guadalupe 1905. *Our Lady of Guadalupe*. Patron saint of Mexico. Spanish rendering of the name the Virgin Mary called herself when she appeared to a Mexican peasant 1531.

Guadalupe **Texas**
Seguin 711 sq. mi.
131,533 89,023 64,873 46,708 33,554 29,107 25,392
March 30, 1846. *Guadalupe River*. Named for Our Lady of Guadalupe.*

Guernsey **Ohio**
Cambridge 522 sq. mi.
40,087 40,792 39,024 42,024 37,665 38,579 39,452
January 31, 1810. *Isle of Guernsey, England*. One of the Channel Islands; source of early settlers.

Guilford **North Carolina**
Greensboro 646 sq. mi.
488,406 421,048 347,420 316,154 288,590 246,520 191,057
April 1, 1771. *Francis North, Earl of Guilford (1704–90)*. Member of Parliament 1727; governor to the royal princes Edward Augustus and George William Frederick, the future George III; personal court favorite of George III and Queen Charlotte Sophia.

Gulf   **Florida**
Port Saint Joe   564 sq. mi.
15,863   13,332   11,504   10,658   10,096   9,937   7,460
June 6, 1925. *Gulf of Mexico*. Descriptive of county's location on the Gulf of Mexico.

Gunnison   **Colorado**
Gunnison   3,239 sq. mi.
15,324   13,956   10,273   10,689   7,578   5,477   5,716
March 9, 1877. *The Gunnison Country*. Area of western Colorado named for John William Gunnison (1812–53); West Point 1837; 2nd lieutenant, 2nd Cavalry 1837; Cherokee War 1837–38; Seminole campaign 1839; 1st lieutenant to captain 1846–53; killed by Indians near Sevier Lake, Utah, while surveying Pacific railroad route.

Guthrie   **Iowa**
Guthrie Center   591 sq. mi.
10,954   11,353   10,935   11,983   12,243   13,607   15,197
January 15, 1851. *Edwin Guthrie (1806–47)*. Captain, Iowa Volunteers during Mexican War; died of wounds received at La Hoya.

Gwinnett   **Georgia**
Lawrenceville   430 sq. mi.
805,321   588,448   352,910   166,903   72,349   43,541   32,320
December 15, 1818. *Button Gwinnett (1732–77)*. President, Georgia Provisional Council; Continental Congress 1776–77; signer, Declaration of Independence 1776; acting president and commander in chief for Georgia 1777; killed in duel by General Lachlan McIntosh (see McIntosh [3], Georgia).

H

Haakon   **South Dakota**
Philip   1,811 sq. mi.
1,937   2,196   2,624   2,794   2,802   3,303   3,167
November 3, 1914; organized February 8, 1915. *King Haakon II of Norway (1872–1957)*. Second son of Frederick VIII of Denmark; married Princess Maud, youngest daughter of Edward VII of England 1896; chosen as King of Norway after independence from Sweden 1905; crowned King of Norway 1906; headed government-in-exile during World War II 1940–45. Name was proposed to garner local Norwegian support for the new county.

Habersham   **Georgia**
Clarkesville   277 sq. mi.
43,041   35,902   27,621   25,020   20,691   18,116   16,553
December 15, 1818. *Joseph Habersham (1751–1815)*. Major to colonel, 1st Georgia Regiment 1776; resigned 1778; Continental Congress 1785–86; US postmaster general 1795–1801.

Haines   **Alaska**
Haines   2,319 sq. mi.
2,508   2,392   2,117   1,680   1,504   (a)   (b)
August 1968. *Haines Mission*. Named for Francina Haines (1819–?), secretary of the Presbyterian mission board that had raised money for the mission; mission founded by Reverend Eugene S. Willard 1881. [(a) Part of Lynn Canal-Icy Straits Census District; (b) Part of 1st Judicial District.]

Hale   **Alabama**
Greensboro   644 sq. mi.
15,760   17,185   15,498   15,604   15,888   19,537   20,832
January 30, 1867. *Stephen F. Hale (1816–62)*. Mexican War 1846–48; lieutenant colonel, 11th Alabama Infantry Regiment 1861; died in combat near Richmond.

Hale   **Texas**
Plainview   1,005 sq. mi.

36,273	36,602	34,671	37,592	34,137	36,798	28,211

August 21, 1876; organized August 4, 1888. *John C. Hale (1806–36)*. Lieutenant in Captain Benjamin Bryant's volunteer company; killed at Battle of San Jacinto April 21, 1836.

Halifax   **North Carolina**
Halifax   724 sq. mi.

54,691	57,370	55,516	55,286	53,884	58,956	58,377

January 1, 1759. *George Montagu Dunk, 2nd Earl of Halifax (1716–71)*. President, Board of Trade 1748; one of founders of Halifax, Nova Scotia, 1749; lord lieutenant of Ireland 1761; first lord of the admiralty.

Halifax   **Virginia**
Halifax   818 sq. mi.

36,241	37,355	36,030[a]	37,692[a]	36,965[a]	39,611[a]	41,442

April 17, 1752. *George Montagu Dunk, 2nd Earl of Halifax.** [[a] Includes independent city of South Boston: 1990, 6,997; 1980, 7,093; 1970, 6,889; 1960, 5,974.]

Hall   **Georgia**
Gainesville   393 sq. mi.

179,684	139,277	95,428	75,649	59,405	49,739	40,113

December 5, 1818. *Lyman Hall (1731–90)*. Physician; Provisional Council of Georgia 1774–75; Continental Congress 1774–80; signer, Declaration of Independence 1776; governor of Georgia 1783–84.

Hall   **Nebraska**
Grand Island   546 sq. mi.

58,607	53,534	48,925	47,960	42,851	35,757	32,186

November 4, 1858; organized January 7, 1867. *Augustus Hall (1814–61)*. Assistant US marshal in Ohio 1839; US representative from Iowa 1855–57; chief justice, Nebraska Territory 1858–61.

Hall   **Texas**
Memphis   883 sq. mi.

3,353	3,782	3,905	5,594	6,015	7,322	10,930

August 21, 1876; organized June 23, 1890. *Warren D. C. Hall (1788–1867)*. Mexican Army 1812, resigned 1814; Texas committee of safety 1835; adjutant general, Republic of Texas 1835; Texas secretary of war 1836.

Hamblen   **Tennessee**
Morristown   161 sq. mi.

62,544	58,128	50,480	49,300	38,696	33,092	23,976

June 8, 1870. *Hezekiah Hamblen (1775–1855)*. Lawyer and local landowner.

Hamilton   **Florida**
Jasper   514 sq. mi.

14,799	13,327	10,930	8,761	7,787	7,705	8,981

December 26, 1827. *Alexander Hamilton (1757–1804)*. Captain of artillery, Continental Army 1776; aide-de-camp to General Washington 1777–81; Continental Congress 1782–83 and 1787–88; federal Constitutional Convention 1788; co-author of *The Federalist* Papers 1787–88; US secretary of the treasury 1789–95; mortally wounded in duel with Aaron Burr, July 11, 1804.

Hamilton   **Illinois**
Jasper   435 sq. mi.

8,457	8,621	8,499	9,172	8,665	10,010	12,356

February 8, 1821. *Alexander Hamilton.**

Hamilton   **Indiana**
Noblesville   394 sq. mi.

274,569   182,740   108,936   82,027   54,532   40,132   28,491
January 8, 1823; effective April 7, 1823. *Alexander Hamilton.**

Hamilton   **Iowa**
Webster City   577 sq. mi.
15,673   16,438   16,071   17,862   18,383   20,032   19,660
December 22, 1856. *William H. Hamilton (c1816–?)*. Probate judge of Dubuque County; president of Iowa Senate 1856–57.

Hamilton   **Kansas**
Syracuse   997 sq. mi.
2,690   2,670   2,388   2,514   2,747   3,144   3,696
March 20, 1873; organized January 29, 1886. *Alexander Hamilton.**

Hamilton   **Nebraska**
Aurora   543 sq. mi.
9,124   9,403   8,862   9,301   8,867   8,714   8,778
February 16, 1867; organized October 1870. *Alexander Hamilton.**

Hamilton   **New York**
Lake Pleasant   1,717 sq. mi.
4,836   5,379   5,279   5,034   4,714   4,367   4,105
April 12, 1816; organized 1847. *Alexander Hamilton.**

Hamilton   **Ohio**
Cincinnati   406 sq. mi.
802,374   845,303   866,228   873,224   924,018   864,121   723,952
January 2, 1790. *Alexander Hamilton.**

Hamilton   **Tennessee**
Chattanooga   542 sq. mi.
336,463   307,896   285,536   287,740   254,236   237,905   208,255
October 25, 1819. *Alexander Hamilton.**

Hamilton   **Texas**
Hamilton   836 sq. mi.
8,517   8,229   7,733   8,297   7,198   8,488   10,660
January 22, 1858. *James Hamilton (1786–1857)*. Major, War of 1812; mayor of Charleston, South Carolina, 1822–24; US representative from South Carolina 1822–29; governor of South Carolina 1830–32; brigadier general of South Carolina troops 1833; Republic of Texas diplomatic agent in Europe; drowned in Gulf of Mexico shipwreck.

Hamlin   **South Dakota**
Hayti   507 sq. mi.
5,903   5,540   4,974   5,261   5,172   6,303   7,058
January 8, 1873; organized September 10, 1878. *Hannibal Hamlin (1809–91)*. US representative from Maine 1843–47; US senator intermittently 1848–81; governor of Maine 1857; US vice president 1861–65; enlisted in Maine State Guards for sixty days 1864; US minister to Spain 1881–82.

Hampden   **Massachusetts**
Springfield   617 sq. mi.
463,490   456,228   456,310   444,018   459,050   429,353   367,971
February 12, 1812; effective August 1, 1812. *John Hampden (1594–1643)*. Member of Parliament 1621; resisted attempt by Charles I to force loans and raise taxes; member of Short Parliament 1640; involved in lawsuit against Charles I; impeached by attorney general 1642; mortally wounded during English Civil War.

Hampshire   **Massachusetts**
Northampton   527 sq. mi.

| 158,080 | 152,251 | 146,568 | 138,813 | 123,981 | 103,229 | 87,594 |

May 7, 1662. *Hampshire County, England.* Origin of many early Puritan settlers.

Hampshire   **West Virginia**
Romney   640 sq. mi.

| 23,964 | 20,203 | 16,498 | 14,867 | 11,710 | 11,705 | 12,577 |

December 13, 1753. *Hampshire County, England.* Name chosen by Thomas Fairfax (see Fairfax, Virginia) for hogs in the area which reminded him of hogs in Hampshire County, England.

Hampton   **South Carolina**
Hampton   560 sq. mi.

| 21,090 | 21,386 | 18,191 | 18,159 | 15,878 | 17,425 | 18,027 |

February 18, 1878. *Wade Hampton (1818–1902).* South Carolina legislature; colonel, Confederate Army; lieutenant general 1864; governor of South Carolina 1877–79; US senator 1879–91.

Hampton   **Virginia**
(Independent City)   51 sq. mi.

| 137,436 | 146,437 | 133,793 | 122,617 | 120,797 | 89,258 | 60,994[a] |

1634 concurrently with Elizabeth City County; merged with Elizabeth City County July 1, 1952. *Henry Wriothesley, 3rd Earl of Southampton* (see Southampton, Virginia). [(a) includes Elizabeth City County (55,028).]

Hancock   **Georgia**
Sparta   472 sq. mi.

| 9,429 | 10,076 | 8,908 | 9,466 | 9,019 | 9,979 | 11,052 |

December 17, 1793. *John Hancock (1737–93).* Massachusetts provisional legislature 1766–72; Continental Congress 1775–80 and 1785–86, president 1775–77; first signer of Declaration of Independence 1776; major general, Massachusetts militia; Massachusetts Constitutional Convention 1780; governor of Massachusetts 1780–85 and 1787–93.

Hancock   **Illinois**
Carthage   794 sq. mi.

| 19,104 | 20,121 | 21,373 | 23,877 | 23,645 | 24,574 | 25,790 |

January 13, 1825; organized 1829. *John Hancock.**

Hancock   **Indiana**
Greenfield   306 sq. mi.

| 70,022 | 55,391 | 45,527 | 43,939 | 35,096 | 26,665 | 20,332 |

January 26, 1827; organized March 1, 1828. *John Hancock.**

Hancock   **Iowa**
Garner   571 sq. mi.

| 11,341 | 12,100 | 12,638 | 13,833 | 13,227 | 14,604 | 15,077 |

January 15, 1851; organized November 25, 1858. *John Hancock.**

Hancock   **Kentucky**
Hawesville   188 sq. mi.

| 8,565 | 8,392 | 7,864 | 7,742 | 7,080 | 5,330 | 6,009 |

January 3, 1829. *John Hancock.**

Hancock   **Maine**
Ellsworth   1,587 sq. mi.

| 54,418 | 51,791 | 46,948 | 41,781 | 34,590 | 32,293 | 32,105 |

June 25, 1789; effective May 1, 1790. *John Hancock.**

Hancock   **Mississippi**
Bay Saint Louis   474 sq. mi.
43,929   42,967   31,760   24,537   17,387   14,039   11,891
December 14, 1812. *John Hancock.**

Hancock   **Ohio**
Findlay   531 sq. mi.
74,782   71,295   65,536   64,581   61,217   53,686   44,280
February 12, 1820; organized 1828. *John Hancock.**

Hancock   **Tennessee**
Sneedville   222 sq. mi.
6,819   6,786   6,739   6,887   6,719   7,757   9,116
January 7, 1844. *John Hancock.**

Hancock   **West Virginia**
New Cumberland   83 sq. mi.
30,676   32,667   35,233   40,418   39,749   39,615   34,388
January 15, 1848. *John Hancock.**

Hand   **South Dakota**
Miller   1,437 sq. mi.
3,431   3,741   4,272   4,948   5,883   6,712   7,149
January 8, 1873; organized September 1, 1882. *George H. Hand (1837–91).* Union Army 1864; US attorney for Dakota Territory 1866–69; secretary of Dakota Territory 1874–83.

Hanover   **Virginia**
Hanover   469 sq. mi.
99,863   86,320   63,306   50,398   37,479   27,550   21,985
November 26, 1720. *George I, Duke of Hanover* (see King George, Virginia).

Hansford   **Texas**
Spearman   920 sq. mi.
5,613   5,369   5,848   6,209   6,351   6,208   4,202
August 21, 1876; organized March 11, 1889. *John M. Hansford (?–1844).* Republic of Texas legislature 1838–40; district judge 1840–42; murdered by Regulators during the Regulator-Moderator War which raged in East Texas 1839–44.

Hanson   **South Dakota**
Alexandria   435 sq. mi.
3,331   3,139   2,994   3,415   3,781   4,584   4,896
January 13, 1871; organized August 16, 1873. *Joseph R. Hanson (1837–1917).* Dakota Territory legislature 1864–65; territorial auditor; judge advocate; Sioux agent 1865–70.

Haralson   **Georgia**
Buchanan   282 sq. mi.
28,780   25,690   21,966   18,422   15,927   14,543   14,663
January 26, 1856. *Hugh Anderson Haralson (1805–54).* Georgia House of Representatives 1831–32; Georgia Senate 1837–38; major general, Georgia militia 1838–50; US representative 1843–51.

Hardee   **Florida**
Wauchula   638 sq. mi.
27,731   26,938   19,499   19,379   14,889   12,370   10,073
April 23, 1921. *Cary Augustus Hardee (1876–1957).* Florida attorney, 3rd judicial circuit 1905–13; speaker, Florida House of Representatives 1915–17; governor of Florida 1921–25.

Hardeman　　　　**Tennessee**
Bolivar　　　　668 sq. mi.
27,253　　28,105　　23,377　　23,873　　22,435　　21,517　　23,311
October 16, 1823. *Thomas Jones Hardeman (1788–1854)*. Captain, War of 1812; active in creation of Hardeman County and its seat of Bolivar 1823; member of Republic of Texas Congress 1837–39; Texas legislature 1847–51; suggested name of "Austin" for state capital. Brother of Bailey Hardeman (see Hardeman, Texas).

Hardeman　　　　**Texas**
Quanah　　　　695 sq. mi.
4,139　　4,724　　5,283　　6,368　　6,795　　8,275　　10,212
February 1, 1858; organized December 1, 1884. *Bailey Hardeman (1795–1836)*. Tennessee volunteer, War of 1812; lieutenant 1813; Santa Fe trader and trapper 1824–25; signer, Texas Declaration of Independence 1836; ad interim treasury secretary, Republic of Texas 1836. Brother of Thomas Hardeman (see Hardeman, Tennessee).

Hardin　　　　**Illinois**
Elizabethtown　　　　178 sq. mi.
4,320　　4,800　　5,189　　5,383　　4,914　　5,879　　7,530
March 2, 1839. *Hardin County, Kentucky*.

Hardin　　　　**Iowa**
Eldora　　　　569 sq. mi.
17,534　　18,812　　19,094　　21,776　　22,248　　22,533　　22,218
January 15, 1851; organized March 2, 1853. *John J. Hardin (1810–47)*. Colonel, Mexican War, killed in Battle of Buena Vista.

Hardin　　　　**Kentucky**
Elizabethtown　　　　623 sq. mi.
105,543　　94,174　　89,240　　88,917　　78,421　　67,789　　50,312
December 15, 1792; effective February 20, 1793. *John Hardin (1753–92)*. Governor Dunmore's expedition 1774; 2nd lieutenant, 8th Pennsylvania, Continental Army 1777; Indian fighter; brigadier general, Kentucky Militia 1792; killed by Indians while on a peace mission.

Hardin　　　　**Ohio**
Kenton　　　　470 sq. mi.
32,058　　31,945　　31,111　　32,719　　30,813　　29,633　　28,673
February 12, 1820; organized 1833. *John Hardin.*

Hardin　　　　**Tennessee**
Savannah　　　　577 sq. mi.
26,026　　25,578　　22,633　　22,280　　18,212　　17,397　　16,908
November 13, 1819. *Joseph Hardin (1734–1801)*. North Carolina Minutemen; Continental Army; legislature, Territory South of the Ohio (Tennessee) 1794–95, speaker 1795.

Hardin　　　　**Texas**
Kountze　　　　891 sq. mi.
54,635　　48,073　　41,320　　40,721　　29,996　　24,629　　19,535
January 22, 1858; organized August 2, 1858. *Hardin brothers*. Five brothers were all active in Texas independence movement: Benjamin (1796–1850), Augustine (1797–1871), William (1801–39), Franklin (1803–78), and Milton (1813–94).

Harding　　　　**New Mexico**
Mosquero　　　　2,125 sq. mi.
695　　810　　987　　1,090　　1,348　　1,874　　3,013
March 4, 1921. *Warren Gamaliel Harding (1865–1923)*. Editor, Marion, Ohio, *Star* 1884; Ohio Senate 1899–1903; governor of Ohio 1904–05; US senator 1915–21; 29th US president 1921–23.

Harding   **South Dakota**
Buffalo   2,671 sq. mi.

1,255	1,353	1,669	1,700	1,855	2,371	2,289

March 5, 1881; abolished November 8, 1898; recreated November 3, 1908; organized January 30, 1911. *John A. Harding (?–?)*. Miner in Black Hills; speaker, Dakota territorial legislature when county was created 1881.

Hardy   **West Virginia**
Moorefield   582 sq. mi.

14,025	12,669	10,977	10,030	8,855	9,308	10,032

December 10, 1785. *Samuel Hardy (1758–85)*. Virginia House of Delegates 1780; executive council 1781; Continental Congress 1783–85.

Harford   **Maryland**
Bel Air   437 sq. mi.

244,826	218,590	182,132	145,930	115,378	76,722	51,782

March 2, 1774. *Henry Harford (1758–1834)*. Last proprietor of Maryland; illegitimate son of Frederick, 6th Lord Baltimore (see Frederick, Maryland); did not inherit title because of illegitimacy.

Harlan   **Kentucky**
Harlan   466 sq. mi.

29,278	33,202	36,574	41,889	37,370	51,107	71,751

January 28, 1819. *Silas Harlan (1753–82)*. Major, served with George Rogers Clark; killed at Battle of Blue Licks, last Battle of the American Revolution, August 19, 1782.

Harlan   **Nebraska**
Alma   553 sq. mi.

3,423	3,786	3,810	4,292	4,357	5,081	7,189

June 3, 1871; organized July 29, 1872. *Uncertain.* (1) *James Harlan (1820–99)*; US senator from Iowa 1855–65 and 1867–72; supported development of the West by homesteads, college land grants, and railroads; US secretary of interior 1865–66. (2) *Thomas Harlan (?–?);* founded settlement on Republican River. (3) Unidentified nephew of James Harlan.

Harmon   **Oklahoma**
Hollis   537 sq. mi.

2,922	3,283	3,793	4,519	5,136	5,852	8,079

June 2, 1909. *Judson Harmon (1846–1927)*. Judge of Common Pleas Court, Ohio, 1876; judge of Superior Court of Cincinnati 1878–87; US attorney general 1895–97; participated in Oklahoma's winning of Greer County from Texas 1896; governor of Ohio 1909–13.

Harnett   **North Carolina**
Lillington   595 sq. mi.

114,678	91,025	67,822	59,570	49,667	48,236	47,605

February 7, 1855. *Cornelius Harnett (1723–81)*. North Carolina legislature 1770–71; Wilmington Committee of Safety 1774; author of Halifax Resolves advocating independence from England 1776; Continental Congress 1777–80.

Harney   **Oregon**
Burns   10,133 sq. mi.

7,422	7,609	7,060	8,314	7,215	6,744	6,113

February 25, 1889. *William Selby Harney (1800–89)*. Cavalry officer; 2nd lieutenant to brigadier general 1818–58; Black Hawk War 1832; 2nd Seminole War 1835–42; Mexican War 1847; Battle of Ash Hollow 1858; commanded Department of Oregon 1858–60; commanded Department of the West 1861–63.

Harper   **Kansas**
Anthony   801 sq. mi.

6,034	6,536	7,124	7,778	7,871	9,541	10,263

February 26, 1867; organized 1873. *Marion Harper (?–1863)*. Enlisted in Union Army 1861; 1st sergeant, Company E, 2nd Kansas; died of wounds at Waldron, Arkansas, December 30, 1863.

Harper   **Oklahoma**
Buffalo   1,039 sq. mi.

3,685	3,562	4,063	4,715	5,151	5,956	5,977

July 16, 1907. *Oscar G. Harper (1874–?)*. Postmaster of Brule (later Buffalo) 1899; clerk, Oklahoma Constitutional Convention 1907.

Harris   **Georgia**
Hamilton   464 sq. mi.

32,024	23,695	17,788	15,464	11,250	11,167	11,265

December 14, 1827. *Charles Harris (1772–1827)*. Lawyer, alderman, and mayor (first alderman) of Savannah, Georgia, intermittently 1802–27; offered many judicial posts but declined them all.

Harris   **Texas**
Houston   1,703 sq. mi.

4,092,459	3,400,578	2,818,199	2,409,547	1,741,912	1,243,158	806,701

March 17, 1836, as Harrisburg; organized 1837; name changed December 28, 1839. *Community of Harrisburg*. Named for John Richardson Harris (1790–1829); established trading post 1824; operated boats between Texas and New Orleans; died of yellow fever at New Orleans.

Harrison   **Indiana**
Corydon   485 sq. mi.

39,364	34,325	29,890	27,276	20,423	19,207	17,858

October 11, 1808; effective December 1, 1808. *William Henry Harrison (1773–1841)*. Indian wars; captain, commanding Fort Washington 1797; secretary of Northwest Territory 1798–99; congressional delegate from Northwest Territory 1799–1800; governor of Indiana Territory 1800–11; defeated Tecumseh at Battles of Tippecanoe (1811) and the Thames (1813); major general US Army 1813; US, representative from Ohio 1816–19; Ohio Senate 1819–21; US senator 1825–28; US minister to Colombia 1828–29; retired to farming in Ohio; 9th President of US for one month, March 4 to April 4, 1841.

Harrison   **Iowa**
Logan   697 sq. mi.

14,928	15,666	14,730	16,348	16,240	17,600	19,560

January 15, 1851; organized March 7, 1853. *William Henry Harrison.**

Harrison   **Kentucky**
Cynthiana   306 sq. mi.

18,846	17,983	16,248	15,166	14,158	13,704	13,736

December 21, 1793; effective February 1, 1794. *Benjamin Harrison (c1745–1808)*. Colonel, Continental Army; Kentucky Constitutional Convention 1792; general, Kentucky Militia; Kentucky legislature 1793.

Harrison   **Mississippi**
Gulfport   574 sq. mi.

187,105	189,601	165,365	157,665	134,582	119,489	84,073

February 5, 1841. *William Henry Harrison.**

Harrison   **Missouri**
Bethany   723 sq. mi.

8,957	8,850	8,469	9,890	10,257	11,603	14,107

February 14, 1845. *Albert Gallatin Harrison (1800–39)*. Board of Visitors, US Military Academy 1828; commissioner to adjust land title of Spanish grants 1829–35; US representative from Missouri 1835–39.

Harrison   **Ohio**
Cadiz   402 sq. mi.

15,864   15,856   16,085   18,152   17,013   17,995   19,054
January 2, 1813. *William Henry Harrison.**

Harrison   **Texas**
Marshall   900 sq. mi.
65,631   62,110   47,483   52,265   44,841   45,594   47,745
January 28, 1839; organized June 18, 1842. *Jonas Harrison (1777–1837)*. Lawyer and banker in Michigan Territory 1807; ruined in Panic of 1819; migrated to Texas 1820; active in Texas independence movement.

Harrison   **West Virginia**
Clarksburg   416 sq. mi.
69,099   68,652   69,371   77,710   73,028   77,856   85,296
June 4, 1784. *Benjamin Harrison (1726–91)*. Virginia House of Burgesses intermittently 1749–75; Continental Congress 1774–77; signer, Declaration of Independence 1776; Virginia House of Delegates 1778–81 and 1785; Virginia Constitutional Convention 1788; governor of Virginia 1781–84. Father of President William Henry Harrison and great-grandfather of President Benjamin Harrison.

Harrisonburg   **Virginia**
(Independent City)   17 sq. mi.
48,914   40,468   30,707   19,671   14,605   11,916   10,810
1916. *Thomas Harrison (1704–85)*. Early settler; donated land for courthouse and county seat for Rockbridge County. (Associated county: Rockbridge.)

Hart   **Georgia**
Hartwell   232 sq. mi.
25,213   22,997   19,712   18,585   15,814   15,229   14,495
December 7, 1853. *Nancy Morgan Hart (1735–1830)*. Settled in frontier Georgia with husband, Benjamin Hart c1773; she was a sharpshooter reputed to have captured many Tories; credited with other legendary exploits; local Indians named her *Wahatchee* (War Woman).

Hart   **Kentucky**
Munfordville   412 sq. mi.
18,199   17,445   14,890   15,402   13,980   14,119   15,321
January 28, 1819. *Nathaniel G. S. Hart (?–1813)*. Captured and massacred at River Raisin, June 18, 1813.

Hartford   **Connecticut**
Hartford   735 sq. mi.
894,014   857,183   851,783   807,766   816,737   689,555   539,661
May 10, 1666. *City of Hartford*. Named for Hertford, Hertfordshire, England; birthplace of Reverend Samuel Stone, one of the founders of Hartford.

Hartley   **Texas**
Channing   1,462 sq. mi.
6,062   5,537   3,634   3,987   2,782   2,171   1,913
August 21, 1876; organized February 9, 1891. *Hartley Brothers*. (1) Oliver Cromwell Hartley (1823–59); private to lieutenant in Mexican War; reporter, Texas Supreme Court 1846–59; compiled *A Digest of Laws of Texas*, published 1850; Texas legislature 1851–52. (2) Rufus K. Hartley (?–?); like his brother, Rufus was a court reporter, Texas Supreme Court 1846–59.

Harvey   **Kansas**
Newton   540 sq. mi.
34,684   32,869   31,028   30,531   27,236   25,865   21,698
March 7, 1872. *James Madison Harvey (1833–94)*. Government surveyor in Southwest; enlisted in Union Army 1861; mustered out of Kansas Volunteer Infantry as captain 1864; Kansas House of Representatives 1865–66; Kansas Senate 1867–68; governor of Kansas 1869–73; US senator 1874–77.

Haskell   **Kansas**
Sublette   578 sq. mi.
4,256   4,307   3,886   3,814   3,672   2,990   2,606
March 23, 1887. *Dudley Chase Haskell (1842–83)*. Miner in Colorado 1859–61; declined Prohibition Party nomination for US presidency 1874; Kansas House of Representatives 1872, 1875, speaker 1876; US representative 1877–83.

Haskell   **Oklahoma**
Stigler   577 sq. mi.
12,769   11,792   10,940   11,010   9,578   9,121   13,313
July 16, 1907. *Charles Nathaniel Haskell (1860–1933)*. Oklahoma Constitutional Convention 1906; governor of Oklahoma 1907–11.

Haskell   **Texas**
Haskell   903 sq. mi.
5,899   6,093   6,820   7,725   8,512   11,174   13,736
February 1, 1858; organized January 13, 1885. *Charles Ready Haskell (1817–36)*. Moved from Tennessee to volunteer in Texas Army 1835; Battle of Coleto 1836; killed in Goliad Massacre, March 27, 1836.

Hawaii   **Hawaii**
Hilo   4,028 sq. mi.
185,079   148,677   120,317   92,053   63,468   61,332   68,350
July 1905. *Island of Hawaii*. Possible origins of name include: (1) Hawaiki, legendary home of Hawaiians near Tahiti; (2) Hawaii-Loa, legendary Polynesian fisherman who discovered Hawaii; (3) reference to a Polynesian mythical land.

Hawkins   **Tennessee**
Rogersville   487 sq. mi.
56,833   53,563   44,565   43,751   33,726   30,468   30,494
January 6, 1787. *Benjamin Hawkins (1754–1816)*. French interpreter for General Washington during Revolutionary War; North Carolina House of Commons 1778–79 and 1784; Continental Congress 1781–84 and 1786–87; negotiated treaties with Creeks and Cherokees 1789; delegate to state convention that ratified Federal Constitution 1789; US senator 1789–95; Indian agent for all tribes south of the Ohio River 1796–1816.

Hayes   **Nebraska**
Hayes Center   713 sq. mi.
967   1,068   1,222   1,356   1,530   1,919   2,404
February 19, 1877. *Rutherford Birchard Hayes (1822–93)*. Cincinnati city solicitor 1857–59; major to brevet major general in Union Army 1861–65; US representative 1865–67; governor of Ohio 1868–72 and 1876–77; 19th President of US 1877–81.

Hays   **Texas**
San Marcos   678 sq. mi.
157,107   97,589   65,614   40,594   27,642   19,934   17,840
March 1, 1848; organized August 7, 1848. *John Coffee Hays (1817–83)*. Surveyor; captain, Texas Rangers 1837; colonel, 1st Regiment Mounted Troops under General Taylor in Mexican War; Battles of Monterrey and Mexico City 1846; sheriff of San Francisco County, California 1850–53; one of the founders of Oakland, California 1852; surveyor general of California 1859.

Haywood   **North Carolina**
Waynesville   554 sq. mi.
59,036   54,033   46,942   46,495   41,710   39,711   37,631
December 15, 1808. *John Haywood (1755–1827)*. Clerk of North Carolina Senate 1781–86; treasurer of North Carolina 1787–1827; one of the original trustees of University of North Carolina 1789–1827.

Haywood   **Tennessee**
Brownsville   533 sq. mi.
18,787   19,797   19,437   20,318   19,596   23,393   26,212

November 3, 1823. *John Haywood (1753–1826)*. Attorney general of North Carolina 1791–94; judge, Superior Court of North Carolina 1794–1800; settled in Tennessee 1810; judge, Tennessee Supreme Court 1816–26.

Heard **Georgia**
Franklin 296 sq. mi.
11,834 11,012 8,628 6,520 5,354 5,333 6,975
December 20, 1830. *Stephen Heard (1740–1815)*. Served under Washington in French-Indian War 1754–63; Battle of Kettle Creek 1779; governor of Georgia 1780; president, Georgia Council 1794–95; Georgia Constitutional Convention 1795.

Hemphill **Texas**
Canadian 906 sq. mi.
3,807 3,351 3,720 5,304 3,084 3,185 4,123
August 21, 1876; organized July 5, 1887. *John Hemphill (1803–62)*. 2nd lieutenant, Seminole War 1836; moved to Texas 1838; district judge 1840–42; chief justice, Texas Supreme Court 1846–58; US senator 1859–61, expelled; Provisional Congress of Confederate States 1861.

Hempstead **Arkansas**
Hope 728 sq. mi.
22,609 23,587 21,621 23,635 19,308 19,661 25,080
December 15, 1818; effective March 1, 1819. *Edward Hempstead (1780–1817)*. Attorney general, Territory of Upper Louisiana 1809–11; speaker, territorial legislature 1812; congressional delegate from Missouri Territory 1812–14; died of injuries from being thrown by his horse.

Henderson **Illinois**
Oquawka 379 sq. mi.
7,331 8,213 8,096 9,114 8,451 8,237 8,416
January 20, 1841. *Uncertain*. (1) *Henderson River*. (2) *Henderson County, Kentucky*. Both are named for Richard Henderson (see Henderson, Kentucky).

Henderson **Kentucky**
Henderson 437 sq. mi.
46,250 44,829 43,044 40,849 36,031 33,519 30,715
December 21, 1798; effective May 15, 1799. *Richard Henderson (1735–85)*. Attorney; judge of Superior Court in North Carolina 1769; purchased land from Cherokees which comprised half of present-day Kentucky to create Transylvania 1775; hired Daniel Boone to develop Wilderness Road to facilitate immigration to Transylvania (see Boone (1), Arkansas).

Henderson **North Carolina**
Hendersonville 373 sq. mi.
106,740 89,173 69,285 58,580 42,804 36,163 30,921
December 15, 1838. *Leonard Henderson (1772–1833)*. Judge, North Carolina Appellate Court 1808–18; North Carolina Supreme Court 1818–29, chief justice 1829.

Henderson **Tennessee**
Lexington 520 sq. mi.
27,769 25,522 21,844 21,390 17,291 16,115 17,173
November 7, 1821. *James Henderson (?–1815)*. Colonel, Tennessee Militia; quartermaster on staff of General Jackson during Natchez expedition 1812–13; killed at Battle of New Orleans, January 8, 1815.

Henderson **Texas**
Athens 874 sq. mi.
78,532 73,277 58,543 42,606 24,466 21,786 23,405
April 26, 1846; organized July 13, 1846. *James Pinckney Henderson (1808–58)*. Brigadier general, Texas Army 1836; attorney general Republic of Texas 1836; Texas secretary of state 1837; Texas representative in Europe 1838; Texas minister to US 1844; Texas Constitutional Convention 1845; governor of Texas 1846–47; major general, US Army, voted sword by Congress for bravery at Monterrey; US senator 1857–58.

Hendricks   **Indiana**
Danville   407 sq. mi.

145,448	104,093	75,717	69,804	53,974	40,896	24,594

December 20, 1823; effective April 1, 1824. *William Hendricks (1782–1850)*. Indiana Territory legislature 1813–14, speaker 1814; secretary, Indiana Constitutional Convention 1816; US representative 1816–22; governor of Indiana 1822–25; US senator 1825–37; trustee, Indiana University 1829–40.

Hendry   **Florida**
LaBelle   1,153 sq. mi.

39,140	36,210	25,773	18,599	11,859	8,119	6,051

May 11, 1923. *Francis Asbury Hendry (1833–1917)*. Private in 3rd Seminole War 1856; opposed secession but served as captain in Confederate Cavalry 1861; 2nd Florida Constitutional Convention 1865; Florida legislature 1866; cattleman with huge landholdings in South Florida.

Hennepin   **Minnesota**
Minneapolis   554 sq. mi.

1,152,425	1,116,200	1,032,431	941,411	960,080	842,854	676,570

March 6, 1852. *Louis Hennepin (1640–1701)*. Franciscan priest and missionary; explored Great Lakes with La Salle 1679 (see LaSalle, Illinois); explored upper Mississippi River 1680.

Henrico   **Virginia**
Henrico   234 sq. mi.

306,935	262,300	217,881	180,735	154,364	117,339	57,340

1634. *Settlement of Henrico*. Named for Henry Frederick, Prince of Wales (1594–1612); eldest son of James I; made Earl of Gloucester and Prince of Wales 1610; died before becoming king. (Associated independent city: Richmond.)

Henry   **Alabama**
Abbeville   562 sq. mi.

17,302	16,310	15,374	15,302	13,254	15,286	18,674

December 13, 1819. *Patrick Henry (1736–99)*. Virginia House of Burgesses 1765; Continental Congress 1774–76; speech before Virginia Provincial Congress "Give me liberty or give me death" 1775; governor of Virginia 1776–79 and 1784–86; Constitutional Convention 1788; opposed US Constitution; elected to Virginia Senate but died before taking office 1799.

Henry   **Georgia**
McDonough   322 sq. mi.

203,922	119,341	58,741	36,309	23,724	17,619	15,387

May 15, 1821. *Patrick Henry.*

Henry   **Illinois**
Cambridge   823 sq. mi.

50,486	51,020	51,159	57,968	53,217	49,317	46,492

January 13, 1825; organized 1837. *Patrick Henry.*

Henry   **Indiana**
New Castle   392 sq. mi.

49,462	48,508	48,139	53,336	52,603	48,899	45,505

December 31, 1821; effective June 1, 1822. *Patrick Henry.*

Henry   **Iowa**
Mount Pleasant   434 sq. mi.

20,145	20,336	19,226	18,890	18,114	18,187	18,708

December 7, 1836. *Henry Dodge*. (See Dodge, Minnesota.)

Henry   **Kentucky**
New Castle   286 sq. mi.

| 15,416 | 15,060 | 12,823 | 12,740 | 10,910 | 10,987 | 11,394 |

December 14, 1798; effective June 1, 1799. *Patrick Henry.**

Henry   **Missouri**
Clinton   697 sq. mi.

| 22,272 | 21,997 | 20,044 | 19,672 | 18,451 | 19,226 | 20,043 |

December 13, 1834, as Rives; name changed February 15, 1841. *Patrick Henry.**

Henry   **Ohio**
Napoleon   416 sq. mi.

| 28,215 | 29,210 | 29,108 | 28,383 | 27,058 | 25,392 | 22,423 |

February 12, 1820; organized 1834. *Patrick Henry.**

Henry   **Tennessee**
Paris   562 sq. mi.

| 32,330 | 31,115 | 27,888 | 28,656 | 23,749 | 22,275 | 23,828 |

November 7, 1821. *Patrick Henry.**

Henry   **Virginia**
Martinsville   382 sq. mi.

| 54,151 | 57,390 | 56,942 | 57,654 | 50,901 | 40,335 | 31,219 |

October 23, 1776. *Patrick Henry.** (Associated independent city: Martinsville.)

Herkimer   **New York**
Herkimer   1,411 sq. mi.

| 64,519 | 64,427 | 65,797 | 66,714 | 67,633 | 66,370 | 61,407 |

February 16, 1791. *Nicholas Herkimer (1728–77).* Brigadier general, New York Militia 1775; mortally wounded at Battle of Oriskany, August 6, 1777.

Hernando   **Florida**
Brooksville   473 sq. mi.

| 172,778 | 130,802 | 101,115 | 44,469 | 17,004 | 11,205 | 6,693 |

February 24, 1843; name changed to Benton March 6, 1844; renamed Hernando, December 24, 1850. *Hernando de Soto.* See DeSoto, Florida.

Hertford   **North Carolina**
Winton   353 sq. mi.

| 24,669 | 22,601 | 22,523 | 23,368 | 23,529 | 22,718 | 21,453 |

May 1, 1760. *Francis Seymour Conway, Earl of Hertford (1719–94).* Became Earl of Hertford 1736; privy councilor of Ireland 1749; ambassador extraordinary to Paris 1763–65; lord-lieutenant of Ireland 1765–66; lord chamberlain of the household 1766–82.

Hettinger   **North Dakota**
Mott   1,132 sq. mi.

| 2,477 | 2,715 | 3,445 | 4,275 | 5,075 | 6,317 | 7,100 |

March 9, 1883; organized April 19, 1907. *Mathias Hettinger (1810–90).* Banker and brewer in Illinois; name proposed by his father-in-law Erastus Williams, a member of Dakota territorial legislature (see Williams, North Dakota).

Hickman   **Kentucky**
Clinton   242 sq. mi.

| 4,902 | 5,262 | 5,566 | 6,065 | 6,264 | 6,747 | 7,778 |

December 19, 1821. *Paschal Hickman (c1778–1813).* Private, Battle of Fallen Timbers 1794; ensign to lieutenant, Kentucky Militia 1802–03; captured and massacred at River Raisin, January 23, 1813.

Hickman **Tennessee**
Centerville 613 sq. mi.
24,690   22,295   16,754   15,151   12,096   11,862   13,353
December 3, 1807. *Edwin (or Edmund) Hickman (?–1785)*. Captain, Revolutionary War; murdered by Indians while surveying Duck River.

Hickory **Missouri**
Hermitage 399 sq. mi.
9,627   8,940   7,335   6,367   4,481   4,516   5,387
February 14, 1845. *Andrew Jackson*. From Jackson's nickname "Old Hickory"; (see Jackson, Alabama).

Hidalgo **New Mexico**
Lordsburg 3,437 sq. mi.
4,894   5,932   5,958   6,049   4,734   4,961   5,095
February 25, 1919. *Uncertain*. (1) *Treaty of Guadalupe Hidalgo*; ended Mexican War 1848. (2) *Miguel Hidalgo y Castilla* (see Hidalgo, Texas).

Hidalgo **Texas**
Edinburg 1,571 sq. mi.
774,769   569,463   383,545   283,229   181,535   180,904   160,446
January 24, 1852; organized August 7, 1852. *Miguel Hidalgo y Castilla (1753–1811)*; Mexican parish priest at Dolores; began movement of Mexican independence from Spain by leading parishioners to seize prison at Dolores 1810; captured and executed August 1, 1811.

Highland **Ohio**
Hillsboro 553 sq. mi.
43,589   40,875   35,728   33,477   28,996   29,716   28,188
February 18, 1805. *Descriptive*. Refers to elevated land between Scioto and Little Miami Rivers.

Highland **Virginia**
Monterey 415 sq. mi.
2,321   2,536   2,635   2,937   2,529   3,221   4,069
March 19, 1847. *Descriptive*. Refers to location in Allegheny Mountains.

Highlands **Florida**
Sebring 1,017 sq. mi.
98,786   87,366   68,432   47,526   29,507   21,338   13,636
April 23, 1921. *Descriptive*. Refers to area's relatively hilly landscape.

Hill **Montana**
Havre 2,899 sq. mi.
16,096   16,673   17,654   17,985   17,358   18,653   14,285
February 28, 1912. *James Jerome Hill (1838–1916)*. Railroad builder and philanthropist; vice president of St. Paul & Manitoba Railway Company 1882, president 1883; founded Great Northern Railway 1893.

Hill **Texas**
Hillsboro 959 sq. mi.
35,089   32,321   27,146   25,024   22,596   23,650   31,982
February 7, 1853. *George Washington Hill (1814–60)*. Surgeon at Fort Houston 1836–37; Texas legislature 1838–40 and 1842; Republic of Texas secretary of war and navy 1843–44.

Hillsborough **Florida**
Tampa 1,020 sq. mi.
1,229,226   998,948   834,054   646,960   490,265   397,788   249,894
January 25, 1834. *Hillsborough Bay*. Named for Wills Hill, Earl of Hillsborough (see Hillsborough, New Hampshire).

Hillsborough   **New Hampshire**
Nashua   876 sq. mi.
400,721   380,841   336,073   276,608   223,941   178,161   156,987
April 29, 1769; organized March 19, 1771. *Wills Hill, Earl of Hillsborough (1718–93).* Privy councilor of Ireland 1746; became Earl of Hillsborough 1751; comptroller of the household 1754–56; president, Board of Trade and Colonies 1763–65; secretary of state for the colonies 1768–72.

Hillsdale   **Michigan**
Hillsdale   598 sq. mi.
46,688   46,527   43,431   42,071   37,171   34,742   31,916
October 29, 1829; organized February 11, 1835. *Descriptive.* Refers to hilly landscape.

Hinds   **Mississippi**
Jackson   870 sq. mi.
245,285   250,800   254,441   250,998   214,973   187,045   142,164
February 12, 1821. *Thomas Hinds (1780–1840).* Major of cavalry, War of 1812; brevetted for gallantry at New Orleans; US representative from Mississippi 1828–31.

Hinsdale   **Colorado**
Lake City   1,117 sq. mi.
843   790   467   408   202   208   263
February 10, 1874. *George Hinsdale (1826–74).* Nebraska territorial legislature; lieutenant governor of Colorado Territory 1865; Territorial Council 1868, president 1870.

Hitchcock   **Nebraska**
Trenton   710 sq. mi.
2,908   3,111   3,750   4,079   4,051   4,829   5,867
February 27, 1873; organized August 30, 1873. *Phineas Warrener Hitchcock (1831–81).* US marshal 1861–64; congressional delegate from Nebraska Territory 1865–67; surveyor general of Nebraska and Iowa 1867–69; US senator from Nebraska 1871–77.

Hocking   **Ohio**
Logan   421 sq. mi.
29,380   28,241   25,533   24,304   20,322   20,168   19,520
January 3, 1818. *Hocking River.* Named from Delaware words *hockhock* for "gourd" or "bottle" and *ing* meaning "place"; describes a wide section of the river.

Hockley   **Texas**
Levelland   908 sq. mi.
22,935   22,716   24,199   23,230   20,396   22,340   20,407
August 21, 1876; organized February 1921. *George Washington Hockley (1802–54).* Chief of staff under Sam Houston 1835; Battle of San Jacinto 1836; colonel of ordnance 1836; Republic of Texas secretary of war 1838–41.

Hodgeman   **Kansas**
Jetmore   860 sq. mi.
1,916   2,085   2,177   2,269   2,662   3,115   3,310
February 26, 1867, as Hageman; name changed 1868; organized March 29, 1879. *Amos Hodgman (c1826–1863).* Captain, Company H, 7th Kansas Cavalry; mortally wounded at Wyatt, Mississippi. Inclusion of letter *e* is uncorrected spelling error of county's name.

Hoke   **North Carolina**
Raeford   391 sq. mi.
46,952   33,646   22,856   20,383   16,436   16,356   15,756
February 7, 1911. *Robert Frederick Hoke (1837–1912).* Private, 1st Carolina Volunteers 1861; Confederate Army, major to major general 1861–64; surrendered with Johnston's army at Durham Station, May 1, 1865; president, Georgia, Carolina & Northern Railway Company.

Holmes   **Florida**
Bonifay   479 sq. mi.

19,927	18,564	15,778	14,723	10,720	10,844	13,988

January 8, 1848. *Holmes Creek*. Uncertain origin: (1) Thomas J. Holmes (?–?), moved from North Carolina to Florida c1830; (2) Anglo-Indian named Holmes, killed by Andrew Jackson's troops.

Holmes   **Mississippi**
Lexington   757 sq. mi.

19,198	21,609	21,604	22,970	23,120	27,096	33,301

February 19, 1833. *David Holmes (1770–1832)*. US representative from Virginia 1797–1809; governor of Mississippi Territory 1809–17; governor of Mississippi 1817–20 and 1826; US senator 1820–25. Brother of Andrew Holmes (see Holmes, Ohio).

Holmes   **Ohio**
Millersburg   423 sq. mi.

42,366	38,943	32,849	29,416	23,024	21,591	18,760

January 20, 1824; organized 1825. *Andrew Hunter Holmes (1780–1814)*. Captain, 24th Mississippi Infantry, War of 1812; major 1813; Battle of the Thames 1813; commanded American victory at Battle of Longwoods 1814; killed at Battle of Mackinac Island, August 4, 1814. Brother of David Holmes.*

Holt   **Missouri**
Oregon   463 sq. mi.

4,912	5,351	6,034	6,882	6,654	7,885	9,833

January 29, 1841, as Nodaway; name changed February 15, 1841. *David Rice Holt (1803–40)*. Minister and physician; Missouri legislature 1840.

Holt   **Nebraska**
O'Neill   2,412 sq. mi.

10,435	11,551	12,599	13,552	12,933	13,722	14,859

January 13, 1860, as West; name changed January 9, 1862; organized July 13, 1876. *Joseph Holt (1807–94)*. US commissioner of patents 1857; US postmaster general 1859–61; US secretary of war 1861; US Army judge advocate general 1862–75; headed prosecution of Lincoln assassination conspirators 1865.

Honolulu   **Hawaii**
Honolulu   601 sq. mi.

953,207	876,156	836,231	762,565	629,176	500,409	353,020

July 1905. *City of Honolulu*. Most suggestions of name's origin refer to Hawaiian word meaning "sheltered bay" or "harbor."

Hood   **Texas**
Granbury   421 sq. mi.

51,182	41,100	29,981	17,714	6,368	5,443	5,287

November 2, 1866. *John Bell Hood (1831–79)*. Graduated West Point 1853; 3rd to 1st lieutenant 1855–58; resigned to join Confederate Army 1861; commanded 4th Texas Infantry 1861; brigadier general to lieutenant general 1862–64; lost right leg at Chickamauga 1863; commanded Army of Tennessee 1864; defeated at Nashville and relieved of command 1865; died of yellow fever in New Orleans.

Hood River   **Oregon**
Hood River   522 sq. mi.

22,346	20,411	16,903	15,835	13,187	13,395	12,740

June 23, 1908. *Hood River*. Named for its source on Mount Hood; named for Samuel Hood (1724–1816), commanded British North American Fleet 1767–70; vice admiral; lord of the admiralty 1788–93; admiral 1794; made Viscount Hood 1796.

Hooker   **Nebraska**
Mullen   721 sq. mi.

736	783	793	990	939	1,130	1,061

March 29, 1889; organized April 13, 1899. *Joseph Hooker (1814–79)*. Graduated West Point 1837; 1st lieutenant to lieutenant colonel 1838–47; resigned 1853; rejoined Union Army 1861; brigadier general to major general of volunteers 1862; brigadier general US Army 1862; commander, Army of the Potomac 1863; retired 1865.

Hoonah-Angoon	**Alaska**					
(Census Area)	7,525 sq. mi.					
2,150	(a)	(b)	(b)	(b)	(c)	(d)

June 20, 2007. "Hoonah" is from *Huna*, Tlingit village; "Angoon" is from Tligit village *Augoon*. [(a) Part of Skagway-Hoonah-Angoon Census Area; (b) part of Skagway-Yakutat-Angoon Census Area; (c) part of Lynn Canal-Icy Straits Census Area; (d) part of 1st Judicial Division.]

Hopewell	**Virginia**					
(Independent City)	10 sq. mi.					
22,591	22,354	23,101	23,397	23,471	17,895	10,219

July 1, 1916. *Hopewell Farm*. Named for ship *Hopewell* that brought Francis Eppes (1627–1678), an early settler, to Virginia. (Associated county: Prince George.)

Hopkins	**Kentucky**					
Madisonville	542 sq. mi.					
46,920	46,519	46,126	46,174	38,167	38,458	38,815

December 9, 1806; effective May 1, 1807. *Samuel Hopkins (1753–1819)*. Captain to lieutenant general 1776–78; wounded at Germantown 1777; taken prisoner at Charleston 1780, exchanged 1781; Kentucky House of Representatives, intermittently 1800–06; Kentucky Senate 1809–13; major general, commander in chief of Western Frontier 1812; US representative 1813–15.

Hopkins	**Texas**					
Sulphur Springs	767 sq. mi.					
35,161	31,960	28,833	25,247	20,710	18,594	23,490

March 25, 1846; organized July 13, 1846. *David Hopkins (1825–1906) and his family*. Early settlers in the area.

Horry	**South Carolina**					
Conway	1,134 sq. mi.					
269,291	196,629	144,053	101,419	69,992	68,247	59,820

December 19, 1801. *Peter Horry (c1747–1815)*. Captain to colonel, 2nd South Carolina Regiment 1775–81; wounded at Eutaw Springs 1781.

Hot Spring	**Arkansas**					
Malvern	615 sq. mi.					
32,923	30,353	26,115	26,819	21,963	21,893	22,181

November 2, 1829. *Descriptive*. Refers to local hot springs in what is now Garland County.

Hot Springs	**Wyoming**					
Thermopolis	2,004 sq. mi.					
4,812	4,882	4,809	5,710	4,952	6,365	5,250

February 9, 1911. *Descriptive*. Refers to mineral springs in the area.

Houghton	**Michigan**					
Houghton	1,009 sq. mi.					
36,628	36,016	35,446	37,872	34,652	35,654	39,771

March 19, 1845; organized May 18, 1846. *Douglas Houghton (1809–45)*. Professor of chemistry and natural history, Rensselaer Polytechnic Institute, Troy, New York, 1828–30; Michigan state geologist 1838–41; drowned in Lake Superior.

Houston	**Alabama**					
Dothan	580 sq. mi.					
101,547	88,787	81,331	74,632	56,574	50,718	46,522

February 9, 1903. *George Smith Houston (1808–79)*. Alabama House of Representatives 1832; Alabama state attorney 1836; US representative 1841–49 and 1851–61, resigned 1861, reelected but not allowed to take seat 1866; governor of Alabama 1874–78; US senate 1879.

Houston   Georgia
Perry   376 sq. mi.

139,900	110,765	89,208	77,605	62,924	39,154	20,964

May 15, 1821. *John Houston (1744–96)*. Chairman, Georgia Sons of Liberty 1774; Continental Congress 1775–76; Georgia Executive Council 1777; governor of Georgia 1778–79 and 1784–85.

Houston   Minnesota
Caledonia   552 sq. mi.

19,207	19,718	18,497	18,382	17,556	16,588	14,435

April 4, 1854. *Samuel Houston (1793–1863)*. Sergeant under General Jackson during Creek War; lieutenant 1812; Tennessee adjutant general 1820; major general 1821; US representative 1823–27; governor of Tennessee 1827–29; member of Texas Constitutional Convention 1835; signed Texas Declaration of Independence 1836; commander in chief, Republic of Texas Army, defeated Santa Ana at San Jacinto 1836; president, Republic of Texas 1836–38 and 1841–44; US senator 1846–49; governor of Texas 1860–61, deposed after refusing to take oath of allegiance to Confederate States.

Houston   Tennessee
Erin   200 sq. mi.

8,426	8,088	7,018	6,871	5,845	4,794	5,318

January 21, 1871. *Samuel Houston.**

Houston   Texas
Crockett   1,231 sq. mi.

23,732	23,185	21,375	22,299	17,855	19,376	22,825

June 12, 1871. *Samuel Houston.**

Howard   Arkansas
Nashville   589 sq. mi.

13,789	14,300	13,569	13,459	11,412	10,878	13,342

April 17, 1873. *James Howard (1838–?)*. Pike County clerk 1862–68; Arkansas Senate 1871–73.

Howard   Indiana
Kokomo   293 sq. mi.

82,752	84,964	80,827	86,896	83,198	69,509	54,498

January 15, 1844, as Richardville; effective May 1, 1844; name changed December 28, 1846. *Tilghman Ashurst Howard (1797–1844)*. Tennessee Senate 1824; Indiana district attorney 1833–37; US representative 1839–40; US charge d' affaires to Republic of Texas 1844, died soon after arriving in Texas.

Howard   Iowa
Cresco   473 sq. mi.

9,566	9,932	9,809	11,114	11,442	12,734	13,105

January 15, 1851; organized September 15, 1855. *Tilghman Ashurst Howard.**

Howard   Maryland
Ellicott City   251 sq. mi.

287,085	247,842	187,328	118,572	61,911	36,152	23,119

July 4, 1851. *John Edgar Howard (1752–1827)*. Commanded company at Battle of White Plains 1776; captain to colonel 1776–78; received thanks and medal from Congress for gallantry at Cowpens 1781; wounded at Eutaw Springs 1781; retired 1783; Continental Congress 1784–88; governor of Maryland 1788–91; Maryland Senate 1791–95; US senator 1796–1803.

Howard   Missouri
Fayette   464 sq. mi.

| 10,144 | 10,212 | 9,631 | 10,008 | 10,561 | 10,859 | 11,857 |

January 13, 1816. *Benjamin Howard (1760–1814)*. Kentucky House of Representatives 1800; US representative 1807–10; governor of Louisiana Territory 1810–12; appointed brigadier general 1813; commanded Military Department West of the Mississippi River.

Howard   **Nebraska**
Saint Paul   569 sq. mi.

| 6,274 | 6,567 | 6,055 | 6,773 | 6,807 | 6,541 | 7,226 |

March 1, 1871. *Oliver Otis Howard (1830–1909)*. Graduated West Point 1854; colonel, 3rd Maine Volunteer Regiment 1861; brigadier general, first Battle of Bull Run 1861; lost right arm at Seven Pines 1862; Antietam 1862; Chancellorsville and Gettysburg 1863; commissioner of Freedmen's Bureau 1865; active in establishment of Howard University 1867; president, Howard University 1869–73.

Howard   **Texas**
Big Spring   901 sq. mi.

| 35,012 | 33,267 | 32,343 | 33,142 | 37,796 | 40,139 | 26,722 |

August 21, 1876; organized June 15, 1882. *Volney Erskine Howard (1809–89)*. Mississippi House of Representatives 1836; injured in duel with Hiram Runnels 1840 (see Runnels, Texas); Texas Constitutional Convention 1845; US representative from Texas 1849–53; Los Angeles, California, district attorney 1861–70; Los Angeles Superior Court judge 1878–79.

Howell   **Missouri**
West Plains   927 sq. mi.

| 40,400 | 37,238 | 31,447 | 28,807 | 23,521 | 22,027 | 22,725 |

March 2, 1857. *Uncertain*. (1) *James (or Josiah) Howell (?–?)*; first settler in the area 1832. (2) *Howell Valley*; named for James Howell.

Hubbard   **Minnesota**
Park Rapids   926 sq. mi.

| 20,428 | 18,376 | 14,939 | 14,098 | 10,583 | 9,962 | 11,085 |

February 26, 1883. *Lucius Frederick Hubbard (1836–1913)*. Established Red Wing, Minnesota, *Republican* 1857; private, 5th Minnesota Infantry 1861; captain to colonel 1862; wounded at Corinth (1862) and Nashville (1864); Minnesota Senate 1872–76; governor of Minnesota 1882–87; brigadier general in Spanish-American War with service in Florida 1898.

Hudson   **New Jersey**
Jersey City   46 sq. mi.

| 634,266 | 608,975 | 553,099 | 556,972 | 609,266 | 610,734 | 647,437 |

February 22, 1840. *Henry Hudson (c1570–c1611)*. English navigator and explorer; sought Northwest Passage; explored Hudson River for Dutch East India Company 1609; set adrift in Hudson Bay by mutinous crew 1611.

Hudspeth   **Texas**
Sierra Blanca   4,571 sq. mi.

| 3,476 | 3,344 | 2,915 | 2,728 | 2,392 | 3,343 | 4,298 |

February 16, 1917. *Claude Benton Hudspeth (1877–1941)*. Texas House of Representatives 1902–06; Texas Senate 1906–18; US representative 1919–31.

Huerfano   **Colorado**
Walsenburg   1,591 sq. mi.

| 6,711 | 7,862 | 6,009 | 6,440 | 6,590 | 7,867 | 10,549 |

November 1, 1861. *Huerfano River*. Spanish word for "orphan"; refers to an isolated butte near the river.

Hughes   **Oklahoma**
Holdenville   805 sq. mi.

| 14,003 | 14,154 | 13,023 | 14,338 | 13,228 | 15,144 | 20,664 |

July 16, 1907. *William C. Hughes (1869–1938)*. Oklahoma Constitutional Convention 1907; chairman, State Board of Affairs 1931–35.

Hughes   **South Dakota**
Pierre   742 sq. mi.

17,022	16,481	14,817	14,220	11,632	12,725	8,111

January 8, 1873; organized November 26, 1880. *Alexander Hughes (1846–1907).* Joined Union Army at age 15, 1861; president, Dakota territorial legislature 1872–73; attorney general of Dakota Territory 1883–85; attorney for Northern Pacific Railroad.

Humboldt   **California**
Eureka   3,568 sq. mi.

134,623	126,518	119,118	108,514	99,692	104,892	69,241

May 22, 1853. *Humboldt Bay.* Named for Friedrich Heinrich Alexander von Humboldt. (See Humboldt, Iowa.)

Humboldt   **Iowa**
Dakota City   434 sq. mi.

9,815	10,381	10,756	12,246	12,519	13,156	13,117

January 15, 1851; abolished January 24, 1855; recreated August 31, 1857. *Friedrich Heinrich Alexander von Humboldt (1769–1859).* German naturalist, explorer, and statesman; explored Latin America 1799–1804; extensive writings were popular in America.

Humboldt   **Nevada**
Winnemucca   9,641 sq. mi.

16,528	16,106	12,844	9,434	6,375	5,708	4,838

November 25, 1861. *Humboldt River.* Named for Friedrich Heinrich Alexander von Humboldt.*

Humphreys   **Mississippi**
Belzoni   418 sq. mi.

9,375	11,206	12,134	13,931	14,601	19,093	23,115

March 28, 1918. *Benjamin Gruff Humphreys (1808–82).* Dismissed from West Point for discipline 1828; Mississippi House of Representatives 1837; Mississippi Senate 1840–44; captain to colonel, 21st Mississippi Regiment; wounded at Gettysburg and promoted to brigadier general for gallantry 1863; governor of Mississippi 1866–68, forced to resign for not following federal Reconstruction plan.

Humphreys   **Tennessee**
Waverly   531 sq. mi.

18,538	17,929	15,795	15,957	13,560	11,511	11,030

October 18, 1809. *Parry Wayne Humphreys (1778–1839).* Tennessee superior court judge 1807–09; circuit court judge 1809–13 and 1818–36; US representative 1813–15.

Hunt   **Texas**
Greenville   840 sq. mi.

86,129	76,596	64,343	55,248	47,948	39,399	42,731

April 11, 1846; organized July 12, 1846. *Memucan Hunt (1807–56).* Republic of Texas minister to US to secure recognition of Texas 1836; Texas secretary of navy 1838–39; US-Texas boundary commission 1839; Texas legislature 1852; US-Mexico boundary commission 1853.

Hunterdon   **New Jersey**
Flemington   428 sq. mi.

128,349	121,989	107,776	87,361	69,718	54,107	42,736

March 13, 1714. *Robert Hunter (1664–1734).* Major general, British Army; appointed governor of Virginia, captured at sea by French and never reached Virginia 1707; exchanged for French Bishop of Quebec; governor of New York, and East and West Jersey 1710–19; governor of Jamaica 1727–34.

Huntingdon   **Pennsylvania**
Huntingdon   875 sq. mi.

45,913	45,586	44,164	42,253	39,108	39,457	40,872

September 20, 1787. *Town of Huntingdon*. Named for Selina Shirley Hastings, Countess of Huntingdon (1707–91); pursued religion and missionary work; daughter of Washington Shirley, 2nd Earl of Huntingdon; married Theophilus Hastings, 9th Earl of Huntingdon 1728.

Huntington   **Indiana**
Huntington   383 sq. mi.

37,124	38,075	35,427	35,596	34,970	33,814	31,400

February 2, 1832; effective April 1, 1832; organized February 1, 1834. *Samuel Huntington (1731–96)*. Continental Congress from Connecticut 1776–84, president 1779–81; signer, Declaration of Independence 1776; chief justice, Connecticut Superior Court 1784; lieutenant governor 1785; governor of Connecticut 1786–96. Name suggested by legislator from Connecticut.

Huron   **Michigan**
Bad Axe   836 sq. mi.

33,118	36,079	34,951	36,459	34,083	34,006	33,149

April 1, 1840; organized January 25, 1859. *Uncertain*. (1) *Huron Indians*; from French *hures* meaning "wild boar," or *huron* meaning "knave" or "ruffian"; Iroquois linguistic family; moved to Ohio and Michigan from Georgian Bay, Canada, c1650; ceded lands in Ohio to US 1805; moved to Kansas 1842; moved to Indian Territory (Oklahoma) 1867. (2) *Lake Huron*; named for Huron Indians.

Huron   **Ohio**
Norwalk   491 sq. mi.

59,626	59,487	56,420	54,608	49,587	47,326	39,353

February 7, 1809; organized 1815. *Huron Indians*.*

Hutchinson   **South Dakota**
Olivet   813 sq. mi.

7,343	8,075	8,262	9,350	10,379	11,085	11,423

May 8, 1862; organized January 13, 1871. *John S. Hutchinson (1829–89)*. Secretary of Dakota Territory 1861–65, acting governor of Dakota Territory 1861–63.

Hutchinson   **Texas**
Stinnett   887 sq. mi.

22,150	23,857	25,689	26,304	24,443	34,419	31,580

August 21, 1876; organized May 13, 1901. *Anderson Hutchinson (1798–1853)*. Mississippi attorney; co-authored *A Digest of the Laws of Mississippi* 1840; Republic of Texas district judge 1841; captured and imprisoned by Mexican Army while presiding in court in San Antonio 1842; released and returned to Mississippi 1843.

Hyde   **North Carolina**
Swanquarter   613 sq. mi.

5,810	5,826	5,411	5,873	5,571	5,765	6,479

December 3, 1705, as Wickham, name changed 1712. *Edward Hyde (1667–1712)*. Cousin of Queen Anne; provost marshal of Jamaica 1701; deputy governor of Carolina Colony 1710; governor of North Carolina 1711–12.

Hyde   **South Dakota**
Highmore   861 sq. mi.

1,420	1,671	1,696	2,069	2,515	2,602	2,811

January 8, 1873; organized October 1, 1883. *James Hyde (1842–1902)*. Union soldier; imprisoned at Libby Prison and Andersonville; honorable discharge 1865; Dakota territorial legislature at time of county's creation.

I

Iberia   **Louisiana**
New Iberia   574 sq. mi.

73,420	73,266	68,297	63,752	57,397	51,657	40,059

October 30, 1868. *Town of New Iberia*. Named for the Iberian Peninsula (Spain and Portugal).

Iberville   **Louisiana**
Plaquemine   619 sq. mi.

| 33,387 | 33,320 | 31,049 | 32,159 | 30,746 | 29,939 | 26,750 |

April 10, 1805. *Pierre le Moyne, Sieur d'Iberville (1661–1706)*. French Navy; assisted in capture of English forts at Hudson Bay 1686; captured Fort Albany against a superior British force 1687; destroyed British settlements on Newfoundland 1696–97; defeated British in Battle of Hudson Bay 1697; sent to Louisiana to secure mouth of the Mississippi River from the British 1697; built fort at Biloxi 1699; left his brother, Jean Baptiste, as second-in-command in Louisiana and returned to France 1699 (see Bienville, Louisiana).

Ida   **Iowa**
Ida Grove   432 sq. mi.

| 7,089 | 7,837 | 8,365 | 8,908 | 9,190 | 10,269 | 10,697 |

January 15, 1851; organized January 1, 1859. *Mount Ida*. Mountain on the island of Crete; Indian fires on a nearby hill reminded surveyors of stories of the vestal fires on Mount Ida.

Idaho   **Idaho**
Grangeville   8,477 sq. mi.

| 16,267 | 15,511 | 13,783 | 14,769 | 12,891 | 13,542 | 11,423 |

February 4, 1864. *Uncertain*. (1) *Contrived name*; made up by lobbyist George Willing as a practical joke while Congress was considering a name for what became Colorado Territory; name spread throughout Northern Rocky Mountains 1861. (2) *Steamboat "Idaho;"* operated on Columbia and Snake Rivers. (3) Shoshone phrase *ee-da-how* roughly equivalent to "good morning."

Imperial   **California**
El Centro   4,177 sq. mi.

| 174,528 | 142,361 | 109,303 | 92,110 | 74,492 | 72,105 | 62,975 |

August 6, 1907. *Imperial Valley*. Named for Imperial Land Company that sold land in the Colorado Desert.

Independence   **Arkansas**
Batesville   764 sq. mi.

| 36,647 | 34,233 | 31,192 | 30,147 | 22,723 | 20,048 | 23,488 |

October 23, 1820. *Declaration of Independence*. Proclaimed separation of American colonies from England, July 4, 1776.

Indiana   **Pennsylvania**
Indiana   827 sq. mi.

| 88,880 | 89,605 | 89,994 | 92,281 | 79,451 | 75,366 | 77,106 |

March 30, 1803. *Uncertain*. (1) *American Indians*; Latin construction for "Land of Indians." (2) *Indiana Territory*; popular name for area ceded by the Iroquois Confederation in Treaty of Fort Stanwix 1768; Indiana Territory created from Northwest Territory 1787.

Indian River   **Florida**
Vero Beach   503 sq. mi.

| 138,028 | 112,947 | 90,208 | 59,896 | 35,992 | 25,309 | 11,872 |

May 30, 1925. *Indian River*. Named for local Ays Indians.

Ingham   **Michigan**
Mason   556 sq. mi.

| 280,895 | 279,320 | 281,912 | 275,520 | 261,039 | 211,296 | 172,941 |

October 29, 1829; organized June 14, 1838. *Samuel Delucenna Ingham (1779–1860)*. Pennsylvania House of Representatives 1806–08; US representative 1813–18 and 1822–29; Secretary of the Commonwealth of Pennsylvania 1819–20; US secretary of the treasury 1829–31. Michigan Territory named seven counties after members of Jackson's first cabinet in hopes of promoting statehood.

Inyo   **California**
Independence   10,181 sq. mi.

18,546   17,945   18,281   17,895   15,571   11,68   11,658
March 22, 1866. *Inyo Mountains*. From Paiute word for "dwelling place of great spirit."

Ionia   **Michigan**
Ionia   571 sq. mi.
63,905   61,518   57,024   51,815   45,848   43,132   38,158
March 2, 1831; organized April 3, 1837. *Ionia, Asia Minor*. Ancient Greek district of Ionia, Asia Minor (Turkey); probably suggested by Henry Schoolcraft (see Schoolcraft, Michigan).

Iosco   **Michigan**
Tawas City   549 sq. mi.
25,887   27,339   30,209   28,349   24,905   16,505   10,906
April 1, 1840, as Kanotin; name changed March 8, 1843; organized February 16, 1857. *Fictional character*. Fictional Indian hero in *Algic Researches* by Henry Rowe Schoolcraft 1839 (see Schoolcraft, Michigan).

Iowa   **Iowa**
Marengo   586 sq. mi.
16,355   15,671   14,630   15,429   15,419   16,396   15,835
February 17, 1843; organized July 1, 1845. *Iowa River*. Named for Iowa Indians (see Iowa, Wisconsin).

Iowa   **Wisconsin**
Dodgeville   763 sq. mi.
23,687   22,780   20,150   19,802   19,306   19,631   19,610
October 9, 1829. *Iowa Indians*. From French rendering of Dakota name *Ouauiatonon* that eventually evolved into "Iowa"; may mean "sleepy ones."

Iredell   **North Carolina**
Statesville   574 sq. mi.
159,437   122,660   92,931   82,538   72,197   62,526   56,303
1788. *James Iredell (1751–99)*. Collector for Port of Edenton, North Carolina 1768–76; superior court judge 1777; attorney general of North Carolina 1779–81; influential in ratification of US Constitution 1789; justice, US Supreme Court 1790–99.

Irion   **Texas**
Mertzon   1,052 sq. mi.
1,599   1,771   1,629   1,386   1,070   1,183   1,590
March 7, 1889. *Robert Anderson Irion (1804–61)*. Physician and surveyor; Republic of Texas Senate 1836–37; Texas secretary of state 1837–38.

Iron   **Michigan**
Crystal Falls   1,166 sq. mi.
11,817   13,138   13,175   13,635   13,813   17,184   17,692
April 3, 1885. *Descriptive*. Refers to iron ore deposits in the area.

Iron   **Missouri**
Ironton   550 sq. mi.
10,630   10,697   10,726   11,084   9,529   8,041   9,458
February 17, 1857. *Descriptive*. Refers to iron ore deposits in the area.

Iron   **Utah**
Parowan   3,297 sq. mi.
46,163   33,779   20,789   17,349   12,177   10,795   9,642
January 31, 1850, as Little Salt Lake; name changed December 3, 1850. *Descriptive*. Refers to iron ore deposits in the area.

Iron   **Wisconsin**
Hurley   758 sq. mi.

| 5,916 | 6,861 | 6,153 | 6,730 | 6,533 | 7,830 | 8,714 |

March 1, 1893. *Gogebic Iron District*. (See Gogebic, Michigan.)

Iroquois **Illinois**
Watseka 1,117 sq. mi.

| 29,718 | 31,334 | 30,787 | 32,976 | 33,532 | 33,562 | 32,348 |

February 26, 1833. *Iroquois River*. Named for Iroquois Indians after a battle with Illinois Indians; French rendering of Huron derogatory word *innakhoiw* meaning "black snake" or "red adder." Confederation of tribes in New York; allied with British during American Revolution.

Irwin **Georgia**
Ocilla 354 sq. mi.

| 9,538 | 9,931 | 8,649 | 8,988 | 8,036 | 9,211 | 11,973 |

December 15, 1818. *Jared Irwin (c1751–1818)*. Brigadier general, Georgia Militia; Georgia Constitutional Conventions 1789, 1795, and 1798; governor of Georgia 1796–98 and 1806–09; president, Georgia Senate 1804–06.

Isabella **Michigan**
Mount Pleasant 573 sq. mi.

| 70,311 | 63,351 | 54,624 | 54,110 | 44,594 | 35,348 | 28,964 |

March 2, 1831; organized February 11, 1859. *Queen Isabella of Castile and León (1451–1504)*. Created a united Spain with husband, King Ferdinand of Aragón and Catalonia; financed Columbus' voyage of discovery 1492.

Isanti **Minnesota**
Cambridge 436 sq. mi.

| 37,816 | 31,287 | 25,921 | 23,600 | 16,560 | 13,530 | 12,123 |

February 13, 1857; deorganized 1858; reorganized 1871. *Izaty Indians*. Members of Dakota Alliance; name may translate to "dwell at Knife Lake."

Island **Washington**
Coupeville 208 sq. mi.

| 78,506 | 71,558 | 60,195 | 44,048 | 27,011 | 19,638 | 11,079 |

January 6, 1853. *Islands of Puget Sound*.

Isle of Wight **Virginia**
Isle of Wight 316 sq. mi.

| 35,270 | 29,728 | 25,053 | 21,603 | 18,285 | 17,164 | 14,906 |

1634, as Warrosquyoake; name changed 1637. *Isle of Wight, England*. Island in the English Channel. Name possibly from Welsh *gwyth* meaning "channel."

Issaquena **Mississippi**
Mayersville 413 sq. mi.

| 1,406 | 2,274 | 1,909 | 2,513 | 2,737 | 3,576 | 4,966 |

January 23, 1844. *Deer Creek*. From Choctaw words *isi* meaning "deer" and *okhina* meaning "stream."

Itasca **Minnesota**
Grand Rapids 2,668 sq. mi.

| 45,058 | 43,992 | 40,863 | 43,069 | 35,530 | 38,006 | 33,321 |

October 27, 1849; organized March 6, 1857; deorganized 1858; reorganized 1891. *Lake Itasca*. Contrived word from last two syllables of Latin *veritas* (truth) and first syllable of *caput* (head) signifying the lake as the true source of the Mississippi River.

Itawamba **Mississippi**
Fulton 533 sq. mi.

| 23,401 | 22,770 | 20,017 | 20,518 | 16,847 | 15,080 | 17,216 |

February 9, 1836. *Itawamba Mingo (1759–1834)*. Leader of Chickasaws; mixed English and Chickasaw ancestry; was called Itawamba Mingo (Bench Chief) for leading Chickasaw resistance to a Choctaw raid. English name was Levi Colbert. (See Colbert, Alabama.)

Izard   **Arkansas**
Melbourne   581 sq. mi.
13,696   13,249   11,364   10,768   7,381   6,766   9,953
October 27, 1825; effective January 1, 1826. *George Izard (1776–1828)*. Lieutenant of artillery 1794; commanded Charleston Harbor fortifications 1798; colonel to major general of artillery 1812–14; governor of Arkansas Territory 1825–28.

J

Jack   **Texas**
Jacksboro   911 sq. mi.
9,044   8,763   6,981   7,408   6,711   7,418   7,755
August 27, 1856; organized July 1, 1857. *Jack Brothers*. (1) William Houston Jack (1806–44); Alabama legislature 1829; major, Texas Army 1835; volunteer private at Battle of San Jacinto 1836; Republic of Texas secretary of state 1836; Texas House of Representatives 1839–40; Texas Senate 1842–43. (2) Patrick Churchill Jack (1808–44); Texas House of Representatives 1837–38; district attorney 1840–41.

Jackson   **Alabama**
Scottsboro   1,078 sq. mi.
53,227   53,926   47,796   51,407   39,202   36,681   38,998
December 12, 1819. *Andrew Jackson (1767–1845)*. Tennessee Constitutional Convention 1788; US representative 1796–97; US senator 1797–98 and 1823–25; judge, Tennessee Supreme Court 1798–1804; major general of volunteers 1812–14; Creek War 1813; major general, US Army 1814; defeated British at Battle of New Orleans 1815; captured Florida 1817; military governor of Florida 1821–22; 7th US president 1829–37.

Jackson   **Arkansas**
Newport   634 sq. mi.
17,997   18,418   18,944   21,646   20,452   22,843   25,912
November 5, 1829; effective December 25, 1829. *Andrew Jackson.*

Jackson   **Colorado**
Walden   1,614 sq. mi.
1,394   1,577   1,605   1,863   1,811   1,758   1,976
May 5, 1909. *Andrew Jackson.*

Jackson   **Florida**
Marianna   918 sq. mi.
49,746   46,755   41,375   39,154   34,434   36,208   34,645
August 12, 1822. *Andrew Jackson.*

Jackson   **Georgia**
Jefferson   340 sq. mi.
60,485   41,589   30,005   25,343   21,093   18,499   18,997
February 11, 1796. *James Jackson (1757–1806)*. Georgia Constitutional Convention 1777; colonel, Continental Army 1778; lieutenant colonel to major general, Georgia Militia 1781–92; elected governor of Georgia but declined claiming he was too young and inexperienced 1788; US representative 1789–91; US senator 1793–95, resigned, and 1801–06; Georgia legislature 1796–97; governor of Georgia 1798–1801.

Jackson   **Illinois**
Murphysboro   584 sq. mi.
60,218   59,612   61,067   61,522   55,008   42,151   38,124
January 10, 1816. *Andrew Jackson.*

Jackson   **Indiana**
Brownstown   509 sq. mi.

42,376   41,335   37,730   36,523   33,187   30,556   28,237
December 18, 1815. *Andrew Jackson.**

Jackson   **Iowa**
Maquoketa   636 sq. mi.
19,848   20,296   19,950   22,503   20,839   20,754   18,622
December 21, 1837. *Andrew Jackson.**

Jackson   **Kansas**
Holton   656 sq. mi.
13,462   12,657   11,525   11,644   10,342   10,309   11,098
August 25, 1855, as Calhoun; name changed February 11, 1859. *Andrew Jackson.**

Jackson   **Kentucky**
McKee   345 sq. mi.
13,494   13,495   11,955   11,996   10,005   10,677   13,101
February 2, 1858. *Andrew Jackson.**

Jackson   **Louisiana**
Jonesboro   569 sq. mi.
16,274   15,397   15,705   17,321   15,963   15,828   15,434
February 27, 1845. *Andrew Jackson.**

Jackson   **Michigan**
Jackson   702 sq. mi.
160,248   158,422   149,756   151,495   143,274   131,994   107,925
October 29, 1829; organized August 1, 1832. *Andrew Jackson.** Michigan Territory named seven counties after Jackson and members of his first cabinet in hopes of promoting statehood.

Jackson   **Minnesota**
Jackson   703 sq. mi.
10,266   11,268   11,677   13,690   14,352   15,501   16,306
May 23, 1857; deorganized 1862; reorganized 1866. *Uncertain.* (1) *Andrew Jackson.** (2) *Henry Jackson (1811–57)*; one of five merchants in St. Paul 1842; justice of the peace 1843; postmaster 1846–49; Wisconsin territorial legislature 1847–48; Minnesota territorial legislature 1849–50.

Jackson   **Mississippi**
Pascagoula   723 sq. mi.
139,668   131,420   115,243   118,015   87,975   55,522   31,401
December 18, 1812. *Andrew Jackson.**

Jackson   **Missouri**
Kansas City   604 sq. mi.
674,158   654,880   633,232   629,266   654,558   622,732   541,035
December 15, 1826. *Andrew Jackson.**

Jackson   **North Carolina**
Sylva   491 sq. mi.
40,271   33,121   26,846   25,811   21,593   17,780   19,261
January 29, 1851. *Andrew Jackson.**

Jackson   **Ohio**
Jackson   420 sq. mi.
33,225   32,641   30,230   30,592   27,174   29,372   27,767
January 12, 1816. *Andrew Jackson.**

Jackson   **Oklahoma**
Altus   803 sq. mi.
26,446   28,439   28,764   30,356   30,902   29,736   20,082
July 16, 1907. *Uncertain.* (1) *Andrew Jackson.** (2) *Tomas Jonathon "Stonewall" Jackson* (see Stonewall, Texas).

Jackson   **Oregon**
Medford   2,784 sq. mi.
203,206   181,269   146,389   132,456   94,533   73,962   58,310
January 12, 1852. *Andrew Jackson.**

Jackson   **South Dakota**
Kadoka   1,864 sq. mi.
3,031   2,930   2,811   3,437   2,920[a]   3,027[a]   3,319[a]
March 8, 1883; abolished June 3, 1909; recreated November 3, 1914; organized February 9, 1915. *John R. Jackson (?–?).* Dakota territorial legislature at time of county's creation 1879 and 1883. [(a) Includes Washabaugh County: 1970, 1,389; 1960, 1,042; 1950, 1,551.]

Jackson   **Tennessee**
Gainesboro   308 sq. mi.
11,638   10,984   9,297   9,398   8,141   9,233   12,348
November 6, 1801. *Andrew Jackson.**

Jackson   **Texas**
Edna   829 sq. mi.
14,075   14,391   13,039   13,352   12,975   14,040   12,916
March 17, 1836; organized 1837. *Municipality of Jackson.* Named for Andrew Jackson.*

Jackson   **West Virginia**
Ripley   464 sq. mi.
29,211   28,000   25,938   25,794   20,903   18,541   15,299
March 1, 1831. *Andrew Jackson.**

Jackson   **Wisconsin**
Black River Falls   988 sq. mi.
20,449   19,100   16,588   16,831   15,325   15,151   16,073
February 11, 1853. *Andrew Jackson.**

James City   **Virginia**
Williamsburg   142 sq. mi.
67,009   48,102   34,859   22,763   17,853   11,539   6,317
1634. *Town of Jamestown.* Named for King James I of England (1566–1625); became James VI of Scotland as an infant on death of his mother, Mary, Queen of Scots 1567; chosen as successor of cousin Elizabeth I 1603; King of England 1603–25; sponsored King James version of the Bible 1611. (Associated independent city: part of Williamsburg.)

Jasper   **Georgia**
Monticello   368 sq. mi.
13,900   11,426   8,453   7,553   5,760   6,135   7,473
December 10, 1807, as Randolph; name changed December 10, 1812. *William Jasper (c1750–79).* Private and sergeant, Moultrie's 2nd South Carolina Infantry 1775; made heroic rescue of flag at Fort Moultrie 1775; linked with friend John Newton (see Newton, Georgia) by a sensationalized story by Parson Weems of their exploits during Siege of Savannah 1775; killed while planting South Carolina flag at Battle of Savannah, October 9, 1779.

Jasper   **Illinois**
Newton   495 sq. mi.

9,698   10,117   10,609   11,318   10,741   11,346   12,266
February 15, 1821; organized 1835. *William Jasper.**

Jasper   **Indiana**
Rensselaer   560 sq. mi.
33,478   30,043   24,960   26,138   20,429   18,842   17,031
February 7, 1835; organized February 17, 1838. *William Jasper.**

Jasper   **Iowa**
Newton   730 sq. mi.
36,842   37,213   34,795   36,425   35,425   35,282   32,305
January 13, 1846. *William Jasper.**

Jasper   **Mississippi**
Bay Springs   676 sq. mi.
17,062   18,149   17,114   17,265   15,994   16,909   18,912
December 23, 1833. *William Jasper.**

Jasper   **Missouri**
Carthage   638 sq. mi.
117,404   104,686   90,465   86,958   79,852   78,863   79,106
January 29, 1841. *William Jasper.** One of three counties, with McDonald and Newton, in southwestern Missouri named for South Carolina soldiers who served with General Marion.

Jasper   **South Carolina**
Ridgeland   655 sq. mi.
24,777   20,678   15,487   14,504   11,885   12,237   10,995
January 30, 1912. *William Jasper.**

Jasper   **Texas**
Jasper   939 sq. mi.
35,710   35,604   31,102   30,781   24,692   22,100   20,049
March 17, 1836. *William Jasper.**

Jay   **Indiana**
Portland   384 sq. mi.
21,253   21,806   21,512   23,239   23,575   22,572   23,157
February 7, 1835; organized January 30, 1836; effective March 1, 1836. *John Jay (1745–1829).* Continental Congress intermittently 1774–79, president 1778–79; New York Supreme Court 1777–78; US minister to Spain 1779; one of negotiators of Treaty of Paris with England ending the Revolutionary War 1781–83; co-author of *The Federalist* Papers 1787–88; first chief justice of the US 1789–95; US minister to Great Britain 1794–95; Jay Treaty with Great Britain 1794; governor of New York 1795–1801.

Jeff Davis   **Georgia**
Hazlehurst   331 sq. mi.
15,068   12,684   12,032   11,473   9,425   8,914   9,299
August 18, 1905; effective January 1, 1906. *Jefferson Davis (1808–89).* Graduated West Point 1828; Black Hawk War 1832; US representative from Mississippi 1845–46; commanded Mississippi Riflemen under General Taylor during Mexican War 1846; declined appointment to brigadier general 1847; US senator 1847–51 and 1857–61, resigned; US secretary of war 1853–57; major general of Mississippi Militia 1861; president, Provisional Confederate Congress 1861; president of the Confederate States of America 1861–65; captured by Union forces 1865; tried for treason 1866, paroled 1867.

Jeff Davis   **Texas**
Fort Davis   2,265 sq. mi.

2,342   2,207   1,946   1,647   1,527   1,582   2,090
March 15, 1887. *Jefferson Davis.**

Jefferson   **Alabama**
Birmingham   1,111 sq. mi.
658,466   662,047   651,525   671,324   644,991   634,864   558,928
December 13, 1819. *Thomas Jefferson (1743–1826)*. Virginia House of Burgesses 1769–74; Continental Congress 1775–76 and 1783–85; author of Declaration of Independence 1776; governor of Virginia 1779–81; Virginia House of Delegates 1782; US minister to France 1784–87; US secretary of state 1790–93; US vice president 1797–1801; 3rd president of US 1801–09.

Jefferson   **Arkansas**
Pine Bluff   871 sq. mi.
77,435   84,278   85,487   90,718   85,329   81,373   76,075
November 2, 1829; effective January 1, 1830. *Thomas Jefferson.**

Jefferson   **Colorado**
Golden   764 sq. mi.
534,543   527,026   438,430   371,753   233,031   127,520   55,687
November 1, 1861. *Jefferson Territory*. Name of provisional government until Congress chose "Colorado"; named for Thomas Jefferson.*

Jefferson   **Florida**
Monticello   598 sq. mi.
14,761   12,902   11,296   10,703   8,778   9,543   10,413
January 6, 1827. *Thomas Jefferson.**

Jefferson   **Georgia**
Louisville   526 sq. mi.
16,930   17,266   17,408   18,403   17,174   17,468   18,855
February 20, 1796. *Thomas Jefferson.**

Jefferson   **Idaho**
Rigby   1,094 sq. mi.
26,140   19,155   16,543   15,304   11,619   11,672   10,495
February 18, 1913. *Thomas Jefferson.**

Jefferson   **Illinois**
Mount Vernon   571 sq. mi.
38,827   40,045   37,020   36,522   31,446   32,315   35,892
March 26, 1819. *Thomas Jefferson.**

Jefferson   **Indiana**
Madison   361 sq. mi.
32,428   31,705   29,797   30,419   27,006   24,061   21,613
November 23, 1810; effective February 1, 1811. *Thomas Jefferson.**

Jefferson   **Iowa**
Fairfield   436 sq. mi.
16,843   16,181   16,310   16,316   15,774   15,818   15,696
January 21, 1839. *Thomas Jefferson.**

Jefferson   **Kansas**
Oskaloosa   533 sq. mi.
19,126   18,426   15,905   15,207   11,945   11,252   11,084
August 25, 1855. *Thomas Jefferson.**

Jefferson   **Kentucky**
Louisville   380 sq. mi.

741,096	693,694	664,937	685,004	695,055	610,947	484,615

June 30, 1780; effective November 1, 1780. *Thomas Jefferson.**

Jefferson   **Louisiana**
Gretna   296 sq. mi.

432,552	455,466	448,306	454,592	337,568	208,769	103,873

February 11, 1825. *Thomas Jefferson.**

Jefferson   **Mississippi**
Fayette   520 sq. mi.

7,726	9,740	8,653	9,181	9,295	10,142	11,306

April 2, 1799, as Pickering; name changed January 11, 1802. *Thomas Jefferson.**

Jefferson   **Missouri**
Hillsboro   657 sq. mi.

218,733	198,099	171,380	146,183	105,248	66,377	38,007

December 8, 1818. *Thomas Jefferson.**

Jefferson   **Montana**
Boulder   1,656 sq. mi.

11,406	10,049	7,939	7,019	5,238	4,297	4,014

February 2, 1865. *Jefferson River.* Named by Lewis and Clark for Thomas Jefferson* 1805.

Jefferson   **Nebraska**
Fairbury   570 sq. mi.

7,547	8,333	8,759	9,817	10,436	11,620	13,623

January 26, 1856, as Jones; organized October 23, 1865; name changed 1867. *Thomas Jefferson.**

Jefferson   **New York**
Watertown   1,269 sq. mi.

116,229	111,738	110,943	88,151	88,508	87,835	85,521

March 28, 1805. *Thomas Jefferson.**

Jefferson   **Ohio**
Steubenville   408 sq. mi.

69,709	73,894	80,298	91,564	96,193	99,201	96,495

July 29, 1797. *Thomas Jefferson.**

Jefferson   **Oklahoma**
Waurika   759 sq. mi.

6,472	6,818	7,010	8,183	7,125	8,192	11,122

July 16, 1907. *Thomas Jefferson.**

Jefferson   **Oregon**
Madras   1,781 sq. mi.

21,720	19,009	13,676	11,599	8,548	7,130	5,536

December 12, 1914. *Mount Jefferson.* Named by Lewis and Clark for Thomas Jefferson* 1806.

Jefferson   **Pennsylvania**
Brookville   652 sq. mi.

45,200	45,932	46,083	48,303	43,695	46,792	49,147

March 26, 1804; organized 1830. *Thomas Jefferson.**

Jefferson   **Tennessee**
Dandridge   274 sq. mi.
51,407   44,294   33,016   31,284   24,940   21,493   19,667
June 11, 1792. *Thomas Jefferson.**

Jefferson   **Texas**
Beaumont   876 sq. mi.
252,273   252,051   239,397   250,938   244,773   245,659   195,083
March 17, 1836; organized 1837. *Municipality of Jefferson.* Named for Thomas Jefferson.*

Jefferson   **Washington**
Port Townsend   1,804 sq. mi.
29,872   25,953   20,146   15,965   10,661   9,639   11,618
December 22, 1852. *Thomas Jefferson.**

Jefferson   **West Virginia**
Charles Town   210 sq. mi.
53,498   42,190   35,926   30,032   21,280   18,665   17,184
January 8, 1801. *Thomas Jefferson.**

Jefferson   **Wisconsin**
Jefferson   556 sq. mi.
83,686   74,021   67,783   66,152   60,060   50,094   43,069
December 7, 1836; organized 1839. *Thomas Jefferson.**

Jefferson Davis   **Louisiana**
Jennings   651 sq. mi.
31,594   31,435   30,722   32,168   29,554   29,825   26,298
June 12, 1912. *Jefferson Davis.* (See Jeff Davis, Georgia.)

Jefferson Davis   **Mississippi**
Prentiss   408 sq. mi.
12,487   13,962   14,051   13,846   12,936   13,540   15,500
March 31, 1906. *Jefferson Davis.* (See Jeff Davis, Georgia.)

Jenkins   **Georgia**
Millen   347 sq. mi.
8,340   8,575   8,247   8,841   8,332   9,148   10,264
August 17, 1905. *Charles Jones Jenkins (1805–83).* Georgia House of Representatives 1830 and 1836–49, speaker four times 1840–47; US vice presidential candidate for National Constitutional Union Party 1852; Georgia Senate 1856; Georgia Supreme Court 1860–65; governor of Georgia 1865–67; trustee, University of Georgia 1871–83; president, Georgia Constitutional Convention 1877.

Jennings   **Indiana**
Vernon   377 sq. mi.
28,525   27,554   23,661   22,854   19,454   17,267   15,250
December 27, 1816. *Jonathon Jennings (1784–1834).* Clerk, Indiana territorial legislature 1807; congressional delegate from Indiana Territory 1809–16; Indiana Constitutional Convention 1816; first governor of Indiana 1816–22; US representative 1822–31; one of three commissioners appointed by President Jackson to settle Indian claims 1833.

Jerauld   **South Dakota**
Wessington Springs   526 sq. mi.
2,071   2,295   2,425   2,929   3,310   4,048   4,476
March 9, 1883. *H. A. Jerauld (?–?).* Dakota territorial legislature when county was created 1883–84.

Jerome   **Idaho**
Jerome   597 sq. mi.

22,374	18,342	15,138	14,840	10,253	11,712	12,080

February 8, 1919. *Uncertain*. (1) *Jerome Hill (?–?)*; developer of Twin Falls North Side Irrigation Project. (2) *Jerome Kuhn (?–?)*; son-in-law of Jerome Hill. (3) *Jerome Kuhn Jr. (?–?)*; grandson of Jerome Hill and nephew of Jerome Kuhn. (4) *Village of Jerome*; named for Jerome Kuhn.

Jersey   **Illinois**
Jerseyville   369 sq. mi.

22,985	21,668	20,539	20,538	18,492	17,023	15,264

February 28, 1839. *Town of Jerseyville*. Named for state of New Jersey.

Jessamine   **Kentucky**
Nicholasville   172 sq. mi.

48,586	39,041	30,508	26,146	17,430	13,625	12,458

December 19, 1798; effective February 1, 1799. *Uncertain*. (1) *Jessamine flower*; a type of jasmine that grows in the area. (2) *Jessamine River*; named for the flower. (3) Both the flower and the river.

Jewell   **Kansas**
Mankato   910 sq. mi.

3,077	3,791	4,251	5,241	6,099	7,217	9,698

February 26, 1867; organized July 14, 1870. *Lewis R. Jewell (1822–1862)*. Lieutenant colonel, 6th Kansas Cavalry; died of wounds at Cane Hill, Arkansas, November 30, 1862.

Jim Hogg   **Texas**
Hebbronville   1,136 sq. mi.

5,300	5,281	5,109	5,168	4,654	5,022	5,389

March 31, 1913. *James Stephen Hogg (1851–1906)*. Established *Longview News* 1871; district attorney 1880–84; attorney general of Texas 1886–90; governor of Texas 1891–95.

Jim Wells   **Texas**
Alice   865 sq. mi.

40,838	39,326	37,679	36,498	33,032	34,548	27,991

March 25, 1911; organized 1912. *James Babbidge Wells (1850–1923)*. Brownsville lawyer 1878; specialized in defending Spanish and Mexican land titles in southern Texas.

Jo Daviess   **Illinois**
Galena   601 sq. mi.

22,678	22,289	21,821	23,520	21,766	21,821	21,459

February 17, 1827. *Joseph Hamilton Daveiss*. (See Daviess, Indiana.)

Johnson   **Arkansas**
Clarksville   660 sq. mi.

25,540	22,781	18,221	17,423	13,630	12,421	16,138

November 16, 1833; effective December 25, 1833. *Benjamin Johnson (1784–1849)*. Judge, Arkansas territorial Supreme Court; judge, District of Arkansas 1836–49.

Johnson   **Georgia**
Wrightsville   303 sq. mi.

9,980	8,560	8,329	8,660	7,727	8,048	9,893

December 11, 1858. *Herschel Vespasian Johnson (1812–80)*. US senator from Georgia 1848–49; judge, Superior Court of Okmulgee Circuit 1849–53; governor of Georgia 1853–57; Confederate Senate 1862–65; president, Georgia Constitutional Convention 1865; elected US senator but failed to qualify 1866; judge, Middle Circuit of Georgia 1873–80.

Johnson   **Illinois**
Vienna   344 sq. mi.

| 12,582 | 12,878 | 11,347 | 9,624 | 7,550 | 6,928 | 8,729 |

September 14, 1812. *Richard Mentor Johnson (1780–1850)*. Kentucky House of Representatives intermittently 1804–42; US representative 1807–19 and 1829–37; colonel, Kentucky Volunteers; Battle of the Thames 1813; presented sword for heroism by Congress; US senator 1819–29; vice president of US 1837–41.

Johnson   **Indiana**
Franklin   320 sq. mi.

| 139,654 | 115,209 | 88,109 | 77,240 | 61,138 | 43,704 | 26,183 |

December 31, 1822; effective May 5, 1823. *John Johnson (1776–1816)*. Indiana territorial legislature 1805–09; member of board to establish Vincennes University; Indiana Supreme Court 1816; Indiana Constitutional Convention 1816.

Johnson   **Iowa**
Iowa City   614 sq. mi.

| 130,882 | 111,006 | 96,119 | 81,717 | 72,127 | 53,663 | 45,756 |

December 21, 1837; organized July 4, 1838. *Richard Mentor Johnson.**

Johnson   **Kansas**
Olathe   473 sq. mi..

| 544,179 | 451,086 | 355,054 | 270,269 | 217,662 | 143,792 | 62,783 |

August 25, 1855. *Thomas Johnson (1802–65)*. Shawnee Manual Training School 1838; missionary to Shawnees 1829–58; Kansas territorial legislature 1855; robbed and murdered for pro-Unionist sympathies.

Johnson   **Kentucky**
Paintsville   262 sq. mi.

| 23,356 | 23,445 | 23,248 | 24,432 | 17,539 | 19,748 | 23,846 |

February 24, 1843. *Richard Mentor Johnson.**

Johnson   **Missouri**
Warrensburg   829 sq. mi.

| 52,595 | 48,258 | 42,514 | 39,059 | 34,172 | 28,981 | 20,716 |

December 13, 1834. *Richard Mentor Johnson.**

Johnson   **Nebraska**
Tecumseh   376 sq. mi.

| 5,217 | 4,488 | 4,673 | 5,285 | 5,743 | 6,281 | 7,251 |

March 2, 1855. *Richard Mentor Johnson.**

Johnson   **Tennessee**
Mountain City   298 sq. mi.

| 18,244 | 17,499 | 13,766 | 13,745 | 11,569 | 10,765 | 12,278 |

January 2, 1836. *Thomas Johnson (?–?)*; early settler; justice of the peace.

Johnson   **Texas**
Cleburne   725 sq. mi.

| 150,934 | 126,811 | 97,165 | 67,649 | 45,769 | 34,720 | 31,390 |

February 13, 1854; organized August 7, 1854. *Middleton Tate Johnson (1810–66)*. Arkansas territorial legislature 1832; Alabama legislature 1842; Republic of Texas legislature 1844–45; Texas Mounted Volunteers 1846; Battle of Monterrey 1846; commanded Texas Rangers 1848–50; surveyed Southern Pacific Railroad west of Fort Worth 1851; opposed secession but raised 14th Texas Confederate Cavalry Regiment 1861–65.

Johnson   **Wyoming**
Buffalo   4,154 sq. mi.

| 8,569 | 7,075 | 6,145 | 6,700 | 5,587 | 5,475 | 4,707 |

December 8, 1875, as Pease; name changed December 13, 1879; organized 1881. *Edward P. Johnson (1842–79)*. Union Army; US attorney for Wyoming Territory.

Johnston   **North Carolina**
Smithfield   791 sq. mi.

168,878	121,965	81,306	70,599	61,737	62,936	65,906

1746. *Gabriel Johnston (1699–1752)*. Colonial governor of North Carolina 1734–52; encouraged settlement of Scottish immigrants in North Carolina.

Johnston   **Oklahoma**
Tishomingo   643 sq. mi.

10,957	10,513	10,032	10,356	7,870	8,517	10,608

July 16, 1907. *Douglas Hancock Cooper Johnston (1856–1939)*. Superintendent of Bloomfield Academy, Indian Territory, 1882–98; governor of Chickasaw Nation 1898–1939.

Jones   **Georgia**
Gray   394 sq. mi.

28,669	23,639	20,739	16,579	12,218	8,468	7,538

December 10, 1807. *James Jones (?–1801)*. 1st lieutenant, Georgia Militia 1790; Georgia House of Representatives 1796–98; Georgia Constitutional Convention 1798; US representative 1799–1801.

Jones   **Iowa**
Anamosa   576 sq. mi.

20,638	20,221	19,444	20,401	19,868	20,693	19,401

December 21, 1837; organized January 24, 1839; effective June 1, 1839. *George Wallace Jones (1804–96)*. Clerk of US courts in Missouri 1830; Black Hawk War 1832; congressional delegate from Wisconsin Territory 1835–38; surveyor of public lands for Wisconsin and Iowa Territories 1840; US senator from Iowa 1848–59.

Jones   **Mississippi**
Laurel   695 sq. mi.

67,761	64,958	62,031	61,912	56,357	59,542	57,235

January 24, 1826; name changed to Davis 1865; renamed Jones 1869. *John Paul Jones (1747–92)*. Born in Scotland as John Paul; 3rd mate on a ship engaged in slave trade; as a passenger, brought a ship to port after captain died 1766; fled to America to avoid murder charge on British merchantman and added "Jones" to his name from his friend Willie Jones (see Jones North Carolina) 1773; 1st lieutenant in Continental Navy aboard *Alfred* 1775; captain of *Bonhomme Richard*, captured British ship *Serapis* 1779; admiral in Russian Navy 1788.

Jones   **North Carolina**
Trenton   471 sq. mi.

10,153	10,381	9,414	9,705	9,779	11,005	11,004

January 19, 1779. *Willie Jones (1741–1801)*. North Carolina legislature, intermittently 1766–88; Continental Congress 1780; opposed ratification of US Constitution; leading founder of Raleigh 1792.

Jones   **South Dakota**
Murdo   970 sq. mi.

1,006	1,193	1,324	1,463	1,882	2,006	2,281

January 15, 1916; organized January 16, 1917. *Jones County, Iowa*.

Jones   **Texas**
Anson   929 sq. mi.

20,202	20,785	16,490	17,268	16,106	19,299	22,147

February 1, 1858; organized June 13, 1881. *Anson Jones (1798–1858)*. Army surgeon at Battle of San Jacinto 1836; Texas Army; Republic of Texas Congress 1836–37; Texas secretary of state 1841–44; last president of Republic of Texas 1844.

Josephine   **Oregon**
Grants Pass   1,640 sq. mi.

82,713	75,726	62,649	58,855	35,746	29,917	26,542

January 22, 1856. *Josephine Creek*. Named for Virginia Josephine Rollins (also Rawlings) (1833–?); daughter of a local miner; first American woman in the county 1850.

Juab   **Utah**
Nephi   3,392 sq. mi.
10,246   8,238   5,817   5,530   4,574   4,597   5,981
March 3, 1852. *Uncertain*. (1) Ute word *yoab* meaning "thirsty plain." (2) An Indian friendly to settlers in the area.

Judith Basin   **Montana**
Stanford   1,870 sq. mi.
2,072   2,329   2,282   2,646   2,667   3,085   3,200
December 10, 1920. *Judith Basin River*. Named for Julia "Judith" Hancock Clark (1791–1820); wife of William Clark who named the river after his wife 1805.

Juneau   **Alaska**
Juneau   2,702 sq. mi.
31,275   30,711   26,751   19,528   13,556   9,745   (a)
December 1971. *Joseph Juneau (1826–99)*. Discovered gold on Gold Creek 1880; co-founder of Juneau 1880. [(a) Part of 1st Judicial District.]

Juneau   **Wisconsin**
Mauston   767 sq. mi.
26,664   24,316   21,650   21,039   18,455   17,490   18,930
October 13, 1856. *Solomon Juneau (1793–1856)*. Agent of Northwest Fur Company and the American Fur Company; a founder of Milwaukee 1818; established *Milwaukee Sentinel* 1837; first mayor of Milwaukee 1846–47.

Juniata   **Pennsylvania**
Mifflintown   391 sq. mi.
24,636   22,821   20,625   19,188   16,712   15,874   15,243
March 2, 1831. *Juniata River*. Corruption of a Seneca word meaning "projecting rock"; from a prominent rock on the river.

K

Kalamazoo   **Michigan**
Kalamazoo   562 sq. mi.
250,331   238,603   223,411   212,378   201,550   169,712   126,707
October 29, 1829; organized October 1, 1830. *Kalamazoo River*. From Pottawatomie word meaning "boiling pot"; named for rapids in the river.

Kalawao   **Hawaii**
(Administered by State)   12 sq. mi.
90   147   130   144   172   279   340
July 1905. *Descriptive*. Hawaiian word for "mountain area." (Kalawao County is a leper colony administered by the Hawaiian State Department of Health. It is usually included in Maui County for statistical purposes.)

Kalkaska   **Michigan**
Kalkaska   560 sq. mi.
17,153   16,571   13,497   10,952   5,272   4,382   4,597
April 1, 1840, as Wabassee; name changed to Kalcasca March 8, 1843; organized and spelling changed January 27, 1871. *Uncertain*. (1) Chippewa word for "burned over." (2) Name contrived by Henry Schoolcraft and Lewis Cass from elements of both their names (see Cass, Illinois, and Schoolcraft, Michigan).

Kanabec   **Minnesota**
Mora   522 sq. mi.

| 16,239 | 14,996 | 12,802 | 12,161 | 9,775 | 9,007 | 9,192 |

October 12, 1858; organized November 4, 1881. *Snake River*. From Ojibwa name for the river meaning "snake."

Kanawha   **West Virginia**
Charleston   902 sq. mi.

| 193,063 | 200,073 | 207,619 | 231,414 | 229,515 | 252,925 | 239,629 |

November 14, 1788. *Kanawha River*. Named for Kanawha Indians, an Algonquin tribe.

Kandiyohi   **Minnesota**
Willmar   797 sq. mi.

| 42,239 | 41,203 | 38,761 | 36,763 | 30,548 | 29,987 | 28,644 |

March 20, 1858; deorganized 1866; reorganized 1871. *Kandiyohi Lakes*. Dakota name for a group of lakes, meaning "where the buffalo-fish come."

Kane   **Illinois**
Geneva   520 sq. mi.

| 515,269 | 404,119 | 317,471 | 278,405 | 251,005 | 208,246 | 150,388 |

January 16, 1836. *Elias Kent Kane (1794–1835)*. Illinois territorial judge 1816; Illinois Constitutional Convention 1818; Illinois secretary of state 1818–21; Illinois House of Representatives 1824; US senator 1825–35.

Kane   **Utah**
Kanab   3,990 sq. mi.

| 7,125 | 6,046 | 5,169 | 4,024 | 2,421 | 2,667 | 2,299 |

January 16, 1864. *Thomas Leiper Kane (1822–83)*. Colonel, Mormon Battalion during Mexican War; Brigham Young's representative during Mormon War 1858; lieutenant colonel, 13th Pennsylvania 1861; wounded at Dranesville (1861) and Harrisburg (1862); brigadier general of volunteers 1862; brevet major general for bravery at Gettysburg 1865.

Kankakee   **Illinois**
Kankakee   677 sq. mi.

| 113,449 | 103,933 | 96,255 | 102,926 | 97,250 | 92,063 | 73,254 |

February 11, 1853. *Kankakee River*. Corruption of Pottawatomie word meaning "low land" or "swampy country."

Karnes   **Texas**
Karnes City   748 sq. mi.

| 14,824 | 15,446 | 12,455 | 13,593 | 13,462 | 14,995 | 17,139 |

February 4, 1854. *Henry Wax Karnes (1812–40)*. Private to colonel in Texas Army 1836; imprisoned while negotiating with Mexico for release of prisoners, escaped 1836; Texas Ranger 1838; wounded fighting Comanches 1839.

Kauai   **Hawaii**
Lihue   620 sq. mi.

| 67,091 | 58,463 | 51,177 | 39,082 | 29,761 | 28,176 | 29,905 |

July 1905. *Island of Kauai*. Polynesian word of unknown origin; possibilities range from "drying place" to "source of water."

Kaufman   **Texas**
Kaufman   781 sq. mi.

| 103,350 | 71,313 | 52,220 | 39,015 | 32,392 | 29,931 | 31,170 |

February 26, 1848; organized August 7, 1848. *David Spangler Kaufman (1813–51)*. Texas House of Representatives 1843–45; Republic of Texas charge d'affaires to US 1845; US representative 1846–51.

Kay   **Oklahoma**
Newkirk   920 sq. mi.

| 48,562 | 48,080 | 48,056 | 49,852 | 48,791 | 51,042 | 48,892 |

August 21, 1893 as County K; organized and spelled out 1895. *The letter "K."* Some early Oklahoma districts were identified by letters. All were renamed except Kay County.

Kearney   **Nebraska**
Minden   516 sq. mi.
6,489   6,882   6,629   7,053   6,707   6,580   6,409
January 10, 1860; organized June 17, 1872. *Fort Kearney*. Named for Stephen Watts Kearny (1794–1848); 1st lieutenant to brevet major general 1812–46; Battle of Queenstown Heights 1812; twice wounded at San Pascual 1846; proclaimed himself governor of California 1847; military and civil governor of Veracruz 1848; died of yellow fever. Misspelling with the additional letter *e* reportedly originated in War Department.

Kearny   **Kansas**
Lakin   871 sq. mi.
3,977   4,531   4,027   3,435   3,047   3,108   3,492
March 20, 1873, as Kearney; abolished 1883; recreated and spelling corrected March 5, 1887; organized February 25, 1889. *Philip Kearny (1815–62)*. Inherited a fortune from his grandfather 1836; 2nd lieutenant of cavalry 1837, resigned; studied cavalry tactics in France, fought in Algiers 1839–40; lost left arm in Battle of Churubusco, Mexico, 1847; resigned and returned to France; first US citizen to receive French Legion of Honor for bravery at Battle of Solferino 1859; brigadier general, 1st New Jersey Brigade 1861; major general of volunteers 1862; killed at Battle of Chantilly, September 1, 1862.

Keith   **Nebraska**
Ogallala   1,062 sq. mi.
8,368   8,875   8,584   9,364   8,487   7,958   7,449
February 27, 1873; organized June 9, 1873. *Morell C. Keith (1824–99)*. Cattleman; promoted railroads and irrigation projects.

Kemper   **Mississippi**
De Kalb   766 sq. mi.
10,456   10,453   10,356   10,148   10,233   12,277   15,893
December 23, 1833. *Reuben Kemper (1770–1827)*. Adventurer; made filibuster raids into Spanish Florida with his brothers Nathan and Samuel 1804–10.

Kenai Peninsula **Alaska**
Soldotna   16,075 sq. mi.
55,400   49,691   40,802   25,282   16,586[a]   9,053[a]   (b)
September 13, 1963; effective January 1, 1964. *Kenaitze Indians*. From *Kenayskaya*, Russian name for Cook Inlet. [(a) Includes Seward: 1970, 2,336; 1960, 2,956. (b) Part of 3rd Judicial District.]

Kendall   **Illinois**
Yorkville   320 sq. mi.
114,736   54,544   39,413   37,202   26,374   17,540   12,115
February 19, 1841. *Amos Kendall (1789–1869)*. Editor of *Washington Globe*, organ for the Jackson Administration; US postmaster general 1835–40; established Columbia Institution for the Deaf and Dumb 1857, which became Gallaudet University 1894.

Kendall   **Texas**
Boerne   662 sq. mi.
33,410   23,743   14,589   10,635   6,964   5,889   5,423
January 10, 1862. *George Wilkins Kendall (1809–67)*. One of the founders of New Orleans *Picayune* newspaper 1837; captain, Santa Fe expedition 1841, captured and imprisoned 1841–43; wrote *The War Between the United States and Mexico* 1851.

Kenedy   **Texas**
Sarita   1,458 sq. mi.
416   414   460   543   678   884   632
April 2, 1921. *Mifflin Kenedy (1818–95)*. Steamship clerk and captain 1834–50; shipping business 1850–74; half interest in King Ranch 1860–68; part owner of a Texas narrow-gauge railroad 1876–81.

Kennebec   **Maine**
Augusta   868 sq. mi.

122,151   117,114   115,904   109,889   95,247   89,150   83,881
February 20, 1799; effective April 1, 1799. *Kennebec River*. Abnaki name meaning "long reach."

Kenosha   **Wisconsin**
Kenosha   272 sq. mi.
166,426   149,577   128,181   123,137   117,917   100,615   75,238
January 30, 1850. *City of Kenosha*. From Ojibwa name for the Pike River; translates to "fish."

Kent   **Delaware**
Dover   586 sq. mi.
162,310   126,697   110,993   98,219   81,892   65,651   37,870
June 21, 1680, as Saint Jones; name changed December 31, 1683. *Kent County, England*. Named by William Penn.

Kent   **Maryland**
Chestertown   277 sq. mi.
20,197   19,197   17,842   16,695   16,146   15,481   13,677
August 2, 1642. *Kent Island*. Named for Kent County, England; former home of early settler.

Kent   **Michigan**
Grand Rapids   847 sq. mi.
602,622   574,335   500,631   444,506   411,044   363,187   288,292
March 2, 1831; organized April 4, 1836. *James Kent (1763–1847)*. New York legislature 1796; New York City recorder 1791; New York Supreme Court 1798–1814, chief justice 1804–14; chancellor of New York 1814–23; New York Constitutional Convention 1821; represented Michigan Territory in boundary dispute with Ohio 1835.

Kent   **Rhode Island**
Warwick   169 sq. mi.
166,158   167,090   161,135   154,163   142,382   112,619   77,763
June 11, 1750, *Kent County, England*.

Kent   **Texas**
Jayton   903 sq. mi.
808   859   1,010   1,145   1,434   1,727   2,249
August 21, 1876; organized November 8, 1892. *Andrew Kent (1798–1836)*. Private, Texas Army; killed at Alamo, March 6, 1836.

Kenton   **Kentucky**
Covington   160 sq. mi.
159,720   151,464   142,031   137,058   129,440   120,700   104,254
January 29, 1840. *Simon Kenton (1755–1836)*. Pioneer scout; served with Daniel Boone and George Rogers Clark; Indian fighter; joined Kentucky troops in Battle of the Thames 1813.

Keokuk   **Iowa**
Sigourney   579 sq. mi.
10,511   11,400   11,624   12,921   13,943   15,492   16,797
February 17, 1843. *Keokuk (?–1848)*. Name is a French approximation of *Kiyo'kaga*; Sauk leader of part French ancestry; ally of US in War of 1812 and in Black Hawk War 1832; appointed chief of Sauks by General Winfield Scott 1832. Year of birth varies from 1780 to 1810.

Kern   **California**
Bakersfield   8,132 sq. mi.
839,631   661,645   543,477   403,089   329,162   291,984   228,309
April 2, 1866. *Kern River*. Named for Edward M. Kern (1823–63); topographer and artist; served with Fremont 1845–48; California Bear Flag Revolt 1846; participated in relief of Donner Party 1847.

Kerr   **Texas**
Kerrville   1,103 sq. mi.

49,625	43,653	36,304	28,780	19,454	16,800	14,022

January 26, 1856. *James Kerr (1790–1850).* Lieutenant, War of 1812; Republic of Texas Constitutional Convention 1836; Texas legislature 1838.

Kershaw   **South Carolina**
Camden   727 sq. mi.

61,697	52,647	43,599	39,015	34,727	33,585	32,287

February 19, 1791; converted to judicial district January 1, 1800; redesignated as county April 16, 1868. *Joseph Kershaw (1727–91).* Early settler c1758; colonel, South Carolina Militia 1777–80; died impoverished having given his wealth and property to finance the American Revolution.

Ketchikan Gateway   **Alaska**
Ketchikan   4,858 sq. mi.

13,477	14,070	13,828	11,316	10,041	11,746[a]	(b)

September 13, 1963. *Ketchikan River.* Tlingit word believed to mean "eagle wing river," referring to water spray over a boulder in the river. "Gateway" refers to the borough's location as the first stop in Alaska for ferries and ships arriving from the south on the Inward Passage. [(a) Includes Outer Ketchikan: 1960, 1,676. (b) Part of 1st Judicial District.]

Kewaunee   **Wisconsin**
Kewaunee   343 sq. mi.

20,574	20,187	18,878	19,539	18,961	18,282	17,366

April 16, 1852; organized 1859. *Kewaunee River.* From Chippewa word meaning "prairie hen" or "wild duck."

Keweenaw   **Michigan**
Eagle River   540 sq. mi.

2,156	2,301	1,701	1,963	2,264	2,417	2,918

March 11, 1861; organized August 1, 1861. *Keweenaw Peninsula.* From Ojibwa word for "portage" or "detour" referring to how the peninsula juts into Lake Superior causing travelers following shoreline to go around it or walk across it.

Keya Paha   **Nebraska**
Springview   773 sq. mi.

824	983	1,029	1,301	1,340	1,672	2,160

November 4, 1884; organized February 9, 1885. *Keya Paha River.* Dakota phrase meaning "turtle hill"; refers to small, round hills in the area.

Kidder   **North Dakota**
Steele   1,351 sq. mi.

2,435	2,753	3,332	3,833	4,362	5,386	6,168

January 4, 1873; organized March 22, 1881. *Jefferson Parish Kidder (1815–83).* Vermont Constitutional Convention 1843; Vermont state's attorney 1843–47; Vermont Senate 1847–48; lieutenant governor of Vermont 1853–54; Minnesota House of Representatives 1863–64; associate justice, Dakota Territory Supreme Court 1865–75 and 1879–83; congressional delegate from Dakota Territory 1875–79.

Kimball   **Nebraska**
Kimball   952 sq. mi.

3,821	4,089	4,108	4,882	6,009	7,975	4,283

November 6, 1888; organized January 22, 1889. *Town of Kimball.* Named for Thomas Lord Kimball (1831–99); jeweler in Maine; worked for Pennsylvania Railroad Company; general ticket and passenger agent for Union Pacific Railroad 1871.

Kimble   **Texas**
Junction   1,251 sq. mi.

4,607	4,468	4,122	4,063	3,904	3,943	4,619

January 22, 1858; organized January 3, 1876. *George C. Kimbell (1803–36)*. Resident of Gonzales; lieutenant of mounted volunteers; died at Alamo, March 6, 1836. Misspelled name on the Alamo Monument was carried over to legislation creating the county.

King   **Texas**
Guthrie   911 sq. mi.

286	356	354	425	464	640	870

August 21, 1876; organized 1891. *William P. King (1820–36)*. Resident of Gonzales; youngest defender killed at the Alamo, March 6, 1836.

King   **Washington**
Seattle   2,166 sq. mi.

1,931,249	1,737,034	1,507,319	1,269,749	1,156,633	935,014	732,992

December 22, 1852. *Martin Luther King (1929–68)*. Leading civil rights advocate; followed nonviolent tactics; assassinated April 4, 1968. County originally named for William Rufus de Vane King (1786–1853); North Carolina House of Commons 1807–09; US representative 1811–16; US senator from Alabama 1819–44 and 1848–52; US minister to France 1844–46; US vice president March 4 to April 18, 1853. King County Council voted February 24, 1986, to make Martin Luther King the honoree of the county's name.

King and Queen   **Virginia**
King and Queen Court House   315 sq. mi.

6,945	6,630	6,289	5,968	5,491	5,889	6,299

May 12, 1691. *King William III (1650–1702) and Queen Mary II (1662–94)*. (1) William III (see King William, Virginia). (2) Mary II was eldest surviving child of James II; married her Protestant cousin William of Orange 1677. Both ruled jointly 1689–94.

Kingfisher   **Oklahoma**
Kingfisher   898 sq. mi.

15,034	13,926	13,212	14,187	12,857	10,635	12,860

May 2, 1890. *Town of Kingfisher*. Named for Kingfisher River; origin of name is uncertain; (1) belted kingfisher bird, common in area; (2) King Fisher (?–?), early settler, operated stagecoach on the Chisholm Trail; (3) King Fisher (?–?), local cattleman and rancher.

King George   **Virginia**
King George   180 sq. mi.

23,584	16,803	13,527	10,543	8,039	7,243	6,710

November 24, 1720. *King George I (1660–1727)*. German Duke of Brunswick-Lunenburg; Elector of Hanover 1698; great-grandson of James I of England; ascended English throne on death of heirless Queen Anne 1714.

Kingman   **Kansas**
Kingman   863 sq. mi.

7,858	8,673	8,292	8,960	8,886	9,958	10,324

March 7, 1872; organized February 27, 1874. *Samuel Austin Kingman (1818–1904)*. Kentucky legislature 1849–50 and 1851; Kansas Constitutional Convention 1857; associate justice Kansas Supreme Court 1861–65, chief justice 1866–77.

Kings   **California**
Hanford   1,389 sq. mi.

152,982	129,461	101,469	73,738	64,610	49,954	46,768

March 22, 1893. *Kings River*. Named by Spanish explorers *Rio de los Santos Reyes* (River of the Holy Kings) for the Three Wise Men.

Kings   **New York**
Brooklyn   71 sq. mi.

2,504,700	2,465,326	2,300,664	2,230,936	2,602,012	2,627,319	2,738,175

November 1, 1683. *King Charles II (1630–85)*. See Charleston, South Carolina.

Kingsbury   **South Dakota**
De Smet   832 sq. mi.
5,148   5,815   5,925   6,679   7,657   9,227   9,962
January 8, 1783; organized February 18, 1880. *Kingsbury Brothers*. (1) George Washington Kingsbury (1837–1925); Dakota territorial legislature 1872–73; one of the founders of Yankton *Press and Dakotan* 1861; South Dakota Board of Charities and Corrections 1897–1901; wrote *History of Dakota Territory* 1915. (2) T. A. Kingsbury (?–?); Dakota territorial legislature.

King William   **Virginia**
King William   274 sq. mi.
15,935   13,146   10,913   9,334   7,497   7,563   7,589
September 12, 1701. *King William III (1650–1702)*. William Nassau, Prince of Orange; nephew of Charles II; married his cousin Mary, daughter of James II, presumptive heir of British throne 1677; invaded England during Glorious Revolution 1688; ruled England jointly with Mary until her death 1689–94; ruled alone 1694–1702.

Kinney   **Texas**
Brackettville   1,360 sq. mi.
3,598   3,379   3,119   2,279   2,006   2,452   2,668
January 28, 1850; organized February 7, 1874. *Henry Lawrence Kinney (1814–62)*. Land speculator and probable smuggler; founder of Corpus Christi 1839; Republic of Texas legislature 1844; Texas Senate 1845–53; proposed colony in Nicaragua abandoned under pressure from US; returned to Texas legislature but resigned in opposition to secession 1861.

Kiowa   **Colorado**
Eads   1,768 sq. mi.
1,398   1,622   1,688   1,936   2,029   2,425   3,003
April 11, 1889. *Kiowa Indians*. From Kiowa phrase *ka-i-gwu* meaning "principal people."

Kiowa   **Kansas**
Greensburg   723 sq. mi.
2,553   3,278   3,660   4,046   4,088   4,626   4,743
February 26, 1867; abolished 1875; recreated February 10, 1886; organized March 23, 1886. *Kiowa Indians*.*

Kiowa   **Oklahoma**
Hobart   1,015 sq. mi.
9,446   10,227   11,347   12,711   12,532   14,825   18,926
1901. *Kiowa Indians*.*

Kit Carson   **Colorado**
Burlington   2,161 sq. mi.
8,270   8,011   7,140   7,599   7,530   6,957   8,600
April 11, 1889. *Christopher "Kit" Carson*. See Carson City, Nevada.

Kitsap   **Washington**
Port Orchard   395 sq. mi.
251,133   231,969   189,731   147,152   101,732   84,176   75,724
January 16, 1857, as Slaughter; name changed July 13, 1857. *Kitsap (?–1860)*. Suquamish chief; name means "brave"; formed confederation to oppose Cowichan raids from Vancouver Island; defeated Cowichans 1825.

Kittitas   **Washington**
Ellensburg   2,297 sq. mi.
40,915   33,362   26,725   24,877   25,039   20,467   22,235
November 24, 1883. *K'tatas Indians*. Name has many suggested meanings; leading suggestions refer to geographic features such as "shale rock," "white chalk," "shoal people," or "land of plenty."

Kittson   **Minnesota**
Hallock   1,099 sq. mi.
4,552   5,285   5,767   6,672   6,853   8,343   9,649

October 27, 1849, as Pembina; organized March 4, 1852; deorganized March 5, 1853; name changed March 9, 1878; reorganized April 6, 1897. *Norman Wolford (or Wolfred) Kittson (1814–88)*. Fur trader; manager, American Fur Company 1843–52; Minnesota territorial legislature 1851–55; mayor of St. Paul 1858–59.

Klamath **Oregon**
Klamath Falls 5,941 sq. mi.
66,380 63,775 57,702 59,117 50,021 47,475 42,150
October 17, 1882. *Uncertain.* (1) *Klamath Indians*; name derived from *Tlamatl*, the Chinook name for a Modoc tribe. (2) *Klamath Lakes*; named for Klamath Indians.

Kleberg **Texas**
Kingsville 881 sq. mi.
32,061 31,549 30,274 33,358 33,166 30,052 21,991
February 27, 1913. *Robert Justus Kleberg (1803–88)*. German immigrant; Battle of San Jacinto 1836; chief justice of Austin County 1846; raised a company of Confederate Militia 1861, but did not see active service because of his advanced age.

Klickitat **Washington**
Goldendale 1,871 sq. mi.
20,318 19,161 16,616 15,822 12,138 13,455 12,049
December 20, 1859. *Klickitat Indians*. Chinook name meaning "beyond," i.e. on the other side of the Cascade Mountains; may also mean "robber."

Knott **Kentucky**
Hindman 352 sq. mi.
16,346 17,649 17,906 17,940 14,698 17,362 20,320
May 5, 1884. *James Proctor Knott (1830–1911)*. Missouri House of Representatives 1857–59; Missouri attorney general 1859–60; US representative from Kentucky 1867–71 and 1875–83; governor of Kentucky 1883–87; Kentucky Constitutional Convention 1891; professor of civics and economics, Centre College, 1892–94, Dean of Law School 1894–1901.

Knox **Illinois**
Galesburg 716 sq. mi.
52,919 55,836 56,393 61,607 61,280 61,280 54,366
January 13, 1825; organized 1830. *Henry Knox (1750–1806)*. Continental Army; Battle of Bunker Hill 1775; colonel, continental regiment of artillery 1775; brigadier general and chief of artillery 1776; major general 1782; West Point commandant 1782; commander in chief of the Army 1783–84; first US secretary of war 1789–95.

Knox **Indiana**
Vincennes 516 sq. mi.
38,440 39,256 39,884 41,838 41,546 41,561 43,415
June 20, 1790. *Henry Knox.**

Knox **Kentucky**
Barbourville 386 sq. mi.
31,883 31,795 29,676 30,239 23,689 25,258 30,409
December 19, 1799; effective June 2, 1800. *Henry Knox.**

Knox **Maine**
Rockland 265 sq. mi.
39,736 39,618 36,310 32,941 29,013 28,575 28,121
March 9, 1860; effective April 1, 1860. *Henry Knox.**

Knox **Missouri**
Edina 504 sq. mi.
4,131 4,361 4,482 5,508 5,692 6,558 7,617
February 14, 1845. *Henry Knox.**

Knox   **Nebraska**
Center   1,108 sq. mi.

| 8,701 | 9,374 | 9,534 | 11,457 | 11,723 | 13,300 | 14,820 |

February 10, 1857, as L'eau qui Court; name changed to Emmett, February 18, 1867; organized and name changed to Knox, February 21, 1873. *Henry Knox.**

Knox   **Ohio**
Mount Vernon   525 sq. mi.

| 60,921 | 54,500 | 47,473 | 46,304 | 41,795 | 38,808 | 35,287 |

January 30, 1808. *Henry Knox.**

Knox   **Tennessee**
Knoxville   508 sq. mi.

| 432,226 | 382,032 | 335,749 | 319,694 | 276,293 | 250,523 | 223,007 |

June 11, 1792. *Henry Knox.**

Knox   **Texas**
Benjamin   851 sq. mi.

| 3,719 | 4,253 | 4,837 | 5,329 | 5,972 | 7,857 | 10,082 |

February 1, 1858; organized March 20, 1886. *Henry Knox.**

Kodiak Island   **Alaska**
Kodiak   6,550 sq. mi.

| 13,592 | 13,913 | 13,309 | 9,939 | 9,409 | 7,174 | (a) |

September 1963. *Kodiak Island*. From Inuit word *kaniag* or *kikhtak* meaning "island." [(a) Part of 3rd Judicial District.]

Koochiching   **Minnesota**
International Falls   3,104 sq. mi.

| 13,311 | 14,355 | 16,299 | 17,571 | 17,131 | 18,190 | 16,910 |

December 19, 1906. *Falls of the Rainy River*. From Cree name for the river; refers to mist over the falls.

Kootenai   **Idaho**
Coeur d'Alene   1,244 sq. mi.

| 138,494 | 108,685 | 69,795 | 59,770 | 35,332 | 29,556 | 24,947 |

December 22, 1864; organized 1881. *Kutenai Indians*. Most sources agree the name means "water people."

Kosciusko   **Indiana**
Warsaw   531 sq. mi.

| 77,358 | 74,057 | 65,294 | 59,555 | 48,127 | 40,373 | 33,002 |

February 7, 1835; organized February 4, 1836; effective June 1, 1836. *Thaddeus Andrzji Bonawentura Kosciusko (1746–1817)*. Polish patriot; immigrated to America to assist colonists in American Revolution 1776; colonel of engineers 1776; brevet brigadier general 1783; returned to Poland 1786; major general and commander in chief of Polish insurgent army; captured by Russians 1794; released and returned to hero's welcome in US 1797; buried among Polish kings in Wawel Castle, Krakow, Poland.

Kossuth   **Iowa**
Algona   973 sq. mi.

| 15,543 | 17,163 | 18,591 | 21,891 | 22,937 | 25,314 | 26,241 |

January 15, 1851; organized March 1, 1856. *Lajos Kossuth (1802–94)*. Member of Hungarian Diet 1847–49; leader of Hungarian Revolution against Austria 1848–49; Hungarian minister of finance 1848; issued Hungarian Declaration of Independence from Austria 1849; exiled to Turkey after Russia intervened on the side of Austria 1849; visited US and lived with Hungarian political refugees in Iowa 1851.

L

Labette   **Kansas**
Oswego   645 sq. mi.
21,607   22,835   23,693   25,682   25,775   26,805   29,285
February 26, 1867. *Labette River*. Uncertain origin; suggestions include (1) Pierre Labette (?–?), local trapper and guide; (2) corruption of French *la bête*, meaning "beast" or "skunk."

Lackawanna   **Pennsylvania**
Scranton   459 sq. mi.
214,437   213,295   219,039   227,908   234,107   234,531   257,396
August 21, 1878. *Lackawanna River*. Uncertain origin; most likely a Delaware word *lechauhanne* meaning "stream that forks."

Laclede   **Missouri**
Lebanon   765 sq. mi.
35,571   32,513   27,158   24,323   19,944   18,991   19,010
February 24, 1849. *Pierre Lacléde Liguest (1724–78)*. French fur trader on the Missouri River; established trading post that became St. Louis 1764.

Lac qui Parle   **Minnesota**
Madison   765 sq. mi.
7,259   8,067   8,924   10,592   11,164   13,330   14,545
November 7, 1871; organized January 7, 1873. *Lac qui Parle*. French for "lake which talks"; possibly refers to an echo.

La Crosse   **Wisconsin**
La Crosse   452 sq. mi.
144,638   107,120   97,904   91,056   80,468   72,465   67,587
March 1, 1851. *City of La Crosse*. French word meaning "crosier," the name given to an Indian game played with a long, hooked stick.

Lafayette   **Arkansas**
Lewisville   528 sq. mi.
7,645   8,559   9,643   10,213   10,018   11,030   13,203
October 15, 1827; effective February 1, 1828. *Marquis de Lafayette*. (See Fayette, Alabama.)

Lafayette   **Florida**
Mayo   543 sq. mi.
8,870   7,022   5,578   4,035   2,892   2,889   3,440
December 23, 1856. *Marquis de Lafayette*. (See Fayette, Alabama.)

Lafayette   **Louisiana**
Lafayette   269 sq. mi.
221,578   190,503   164,762   150,017   109,716   84,656   57,743
January 17, 1823. *Marquis de Lafayette*. (See Fayette, Alabama.)

Lafayette   **Mississippi**
Oxford   632 sq. mi.
47,351   38,744   31,826   31,030   24,181   21,355   22,798
February 9, 1836. *Marquis de Lafayette*. (See Fayette, Alabama.)

Lafayette   **Missouri**
Lexington   628 sq. mi.
33,381   32,960   31,107   29,925   26,626   25,274   25,272
November 16, 1820, as Lillard; name changed February 16, 1825. *Marquis de Lafayette*. (See Fayette, Alabama.)

Lafayette   **Wisconsin**
Darlington   634 sq. mi.
16,836   16,137   16,076   17,412   17,456   18,142   18,137
January 31, 1846. *Marquis de Lafayette.* (See Fayette, Alabama.)

Lafourche   **Louisiana**
Thibodaux   1,068 sq. mi.
96,318   89,974   85,860   82,483   68,941   55,381   42,209
April 10, 1805, as Interior; name changed to Lafourche Interior 1812; name changed to Lafourche 1853. *Bayou Lafourche.* French for "the fork."

LaGrange   **Indiana**
Lagrange   380 sq. mi.
37,128   34,909   29,477   25,550   20,890   17,380   15,347
February 2, 1832; effective April 1, 1832. *La Grange.* Home of Marquis de Lafayette near Paris, France (see Fayette, Alabama). (County has upper case *G*; county seat has lower case *g*.)

Lake   **California**
Lakeport   1,256 sq. mi.
64,665   58,309   50,631   36,366   19,548   13,768   11,481
May 20, 1861. *Clear Lake.* Largest freshwater lake entirely within California.

Lake   **Colorado**
Leadville   377 sq. mi.
7,310   7,812   6,077   8,830   8,282   7,101   6,150
November 1, 1861, as Carbonate; name changed February 10, 1879. *Twin Lakes.* Lakes located in the county.

Lake   **Florida**
Tavares   938 sq. mi.
297,052   210,528   152,104   104,870   69,305   57,383   36,340
May 27, 1887. *Descriptive.* Refers to numerous lakes in the area.

Lake   **Illinois**
Waukegan   444 sq. mi.
703,462   644,356   516,418   440,372   382,638   293,656   179,097
March 1, 1839. *Uncertain.* (1) *Lake Michigan.* (2) *Descriptive* of numerous lakes in the area.

Lake   **Indiana**
Crown Point   499 sq. mi.
496,005   484,564   475,594   522,965   546,253   513,269   368,152
January 28, 1836; organized January 16, 1837; effective February 15, 1837. *Lake Michigan.*

Lake   **Michigan**
Baldwin   567 sq. mi.
11,539   11,333   8,583   7,711   5,661   5,338   5,257
April 1, 1840, as Aischum; name changed March 8, 1843; organized May 1, 1871. *Descriptive.* Refers to numerous lakes in the area.

Lake   **Minnesota**
Two Harbors   2,109 sq. mi.
10,866   11,058   10,415   13,043   13,351   13,702   7,781
February 20, 1855, as Superior; name changed to St. Louis March 3, 1855; name changed to Lake March 1, 1856; organized February 27, 1891. *Lake Superior.*

Lake   **Montana**
Polson   1,490 sq. mi.

28,746	26,507	21,401	19,056	14,445	13,104	13,835

May 11, 1923. *Flathead Lake*. Named for Flathead Indians (see Flathead, Montana).

Lake   **Ohio**
Painesville   227 sq. mi.

230,041	227,511	215,499	212,801	197,200	148,700	75,979

March 6, 1840. *Lake Erie*. Named for Erie Indians (see Erie, New York).

Lake   **Oregon**
Lakeview   8,139 sq. mi.

7,895	7,422	7,186	7,532	6,343	7,158	6,649

October 24, 1874. *Descriptive*. Refers to numerous lakes in the area.

Lake   **South Dakota**
Madison   563 sq. mi.

11,200	11,276	10,550	10,724	11,456	11,764	11,792

January 8, 1873. *Descriptive*. Refers to numerous lakes in the area.

Lake   **Tennessee**
Tiptonville   166 sq. mi.

7,832	7,954	7,129	7,455	7,896	9,572	11,655

June 24, 1870. *Reelfoot Lake*. Formed by Mississippi River following New Madrid earthquakes 1811–12. Named for Choctaw chief with deformed foot.

Lake and Peninsula   **Alaska**
King Salmon   23,652 sq. mi.

1,631	1,823	1,668	(a)	(b)	(b)	(c)

April 24, 1989. "Lake" from *Lake Iliamna*, largest lake in Alaska. "Peninsula" from *Alaskan Peninsula*. [(a) Part of Dillingham Census Area; (b) part of Bristol Bay Census Area; (c) part of 3rd and 4th Judicial Districts.]

Lake of the Woods   **Minnesota**
Baudette   1,298 sq. mi..

4,045	4,522	4,076	3,764	3,987	4,304	4,955

November 28, 1922. *Lake of the Woods*. Translation of French *Lac de Bois*; describes the lake surrounded by trees in an otherwise open prairie region.

Lamar   **Alabama**
Vernon   605 sq. mi.

14,564	15,904	15,715	16,453	14,335	14,271	16,441

February 4, 1867, as Jones; abolished November 3, 1867; recreated as Sanford, October 8, 1868; name changed February 8, 1877. *Lucius Quintis Cincinnatus Lamar (1825–93)*. Georgia House of Representatives 1853; US representative from Mississippi 1857–60, resigned, and 1873–77; lieutenant colonel and colonel 18th Mississippi Regiment 1861–63; Confederate diplomat to Russia, France, and England 1863; University of Mississippi professor of metaphysics, social science, and law 1866–67; US senator 1877–85; US secretary of interior 1885–88; justice, US Supreme Court 1888–93.

Lamar   **Georgia**
Barnesville   184 sq. mi.

18,317	15,912	13,038	12,215	10,688	10,240	10,242

August 17, 1920. *Lucius Quintis Cincinnatus Lamar*.*

Lamar   **Mississippi**
Purvis   497 sq. mi.

55,658   39,070   30,424   22,821   15,209   13,675   13,225
March 13, 1904. *Lucius Quintis Cincinnatus Lamar.**

Lamar   **Texas**
Paris   907 sq. mi.
49,793   48,499   43,949   42,156   36,062   34,234   43,033
December 17, 1840. *Mirabeau Buonaparte Lamar (1798–1859)*. Editor, Columbus, Georgia, *Enquirer* 1826; Georgia legislature 1829; commanded cavalry at Battle of San Jacinto 1836; Republic of Texas attorney general, secretary of war, vice president, and president 1836–41; favored expanding an independent Texas to the Pacific Ocean rather than being annexed by US.

Lamb   **Texas**
Littlefield   1,016 sq. mi.
13,977   14,709   15,072   18,669   17,770   21,896   20,015
August 21, 1876; organized June 20, 1908. *George A. Lamb (1814–36)*. 2nd lieutenant, Texas Volunteers; killed at Battle of San Jacinto, April 21, 1836.

Lamoille   **Vermont**
Hyde Park   459 sq. mi.
24,475   23,233   19,735   16,767   13,309   11,027   11,388
October 26, 1835; organized 1836. *Lamoille River*. Named *La Mouette* (the seagull) by French explorer Champlain 1609; name erroneously transcribed as *La Mouelle* and later corrupted to Lamoille.

LaMoure   **North Dakota**
LaMoure   1,146 sq. mi.
4,139   4,701   5,383   6,473   7,117   8,705   9,498
January 4, 1873; organized October 17, 1881. *Judson La Moure (1839–1918)*. Dakota territorial legislature 1872–88 at time of county's creation; North Dakota Senate 1889–1913.

Lampasas   **Texas**
Lampasas   713 sq. mi.
19,677   17,762   13,521   12,005   9,323   9,418   9,929
February 1, 1856. *Lampasas River*. Origin is uncertain; may be from Mexican village of Lampazos.

Lancaster   **Nebraska**
Lincoln   838 sq. mi.
285,407   250,291   213,641   192,884   167,972   155,272   119,742
March 6, 1855. *Lancaster city and county, Pennsylvania*. Most likely the former home of a prominent settler.

Lancaster   **Pennsylvania**
Lancaster   944 sq. mi.
519,445   470,658   422,822   362,346   319,693   279,359   234,717
May 10, 1729. *Lancashire, England*. Name suggested by a settler from Lancashire.

Lancaster   **South Carolina**
Lancaster   549 sq. mi.
76,652   61,351   54,516   53,361   43,328   39,352   37,071
March 12, 1785; converted to judicial district January 1, 1800; redesignated as county April 16, 1868. *Lancaster city and county, Pennsylvania*. Named by settlers from Pennsylvania.

Lancaster   **Virginia**
Lancaster   133 sq. mi.
11,391   11,567   10,896   10,129   9,126   9,174   8,640
1651. *Lancaster and Lancashire, England*. Named by early settlers from Lancashire.

Lander   **Nevada**
Battle Mountain   5,490 sq. mi.

5,775	5,794	6,266	4,076	2,666	1,566	1,850

December 19, 1862. *Frederick West Lander (1821–62)*. Participated in five transcontinental railroad surveys; constructed Lander Road between Oregon and Wyoming territories 1859; one of the first volunteer generals in the Union Army 1861; wounded at Edwards' Ferry 1861; died of pneumonia.

Lane   **Kansas**
Dighton   717 sq. mi.

1,750	2,155	2,375	2,472	2,707	3,060	2,808

March 20, 1873; organized June 3, 1886. *James Henry Lane (1814–66)*. Colonel, 3rd Indiana Volunteers 1846–47; 5th Indiana Infantry 1847–48; lieutenant governor of Indiana 1849; US representative 1853–55; vote for Kansas-Nebraska Bill was unpopular in Indiana, moved to Kansas 1855; Kansas Constitutional Convention 1855; US senator from Kansas 1861–66; brigadier general of volunteers 1861–62.

Lane   **Oregon**
Eugene   4,553 sq. mi.

351,715	322,959	282,912	275,226	213,358	162,890	125,776

January 28, 1851. *Joseph Lane (1801–81)*. Indiana House of Representatives, intermittently 1822–39; Indiana Senate 1844–46; colonel to brevet major general, Indiana Volunteers 1846–48; governor of Oregon Territory 1849–50 and 1853; congressional delegate from Oregon Territory 1851–59; US senator 1859–61.

Langlade   **Wisconsin**
Antigo   871 sq. mi.

19,977	20,740	19,505	19,978	19,220	19,916	21,975

February 27, 1879, as New; name changed February 19, 1880. *Charles Michel Mouet de Langlade (1729–1801)*. Established trading post at Green Bay 1745; sided with French in the French and Indian War; fought against Washington in Battle of the Monongahela 1755; served with General Montcalm at Quebec 1759; warned English colonists of Pontiac's Rebellion 1763; led Indians and Loyalists against George Rogers Clark during Revolutionary War.

Lanier   **Georgia**
Lakeland   185 sq. mi.

10,078	7,241	5,531	5,654	5,031	5,097	5,151

November 2, 1920. *Sidney C. Lanier (1842–81)*. Tutor, Oglethorpe College 1860–61; private in Macon Volunteers 1861; captured as blockade runner, contracted tuberculosis while in prison 1864; lecturer in English literature at Johns Hopkins University; wrote numerous poems about Georgia and the South.

La Paz   **Arizona**
Parker   4,500 sq. mi.

20,489	19,715	13,844	(a)	(a)	(a)	(a)

November 2, 1982. *Town of La Paz*. Named for early settlement on the Colorado River, now a ghost town; Spanish for "peace." [(a) Part of Yuma County.]

Lapeer   **Michigan**
Lapeer   643 sq. mi.

88,319	87,904	74,768	70,038	52,317	41,926	35,794

September 10, 1822; organized February 2, 1835. *Flint River*. Refers to deposits of flint near the river; French translated Indian word for flint as "La Pierre" which was corrupted by English into "Lapeer."

La Plata   **Colorado**
Durango   1,692 sq. mi.

51,334	43,941	32,284	27,424	19,199	19,225	14,880

February 10, 1874. *La Plata River and Mountains*. Spanish for "silver"; describes rich deposits in the area.

LaPorte   **Indiana**
LaPorte   598 sq. mi.

111,467	110,106	107,066	108,632	105,342	95,111	76,808

January 9, 1832; effective April 1, 1832. *Descriptive*. French for "door" or "portal"; describes a natural opening in the forest connecting two open prairies.

Laramie	**Wyoming**					
Cheyenne	2,686 sq. mi.					
91,738	81,607	73,142	68,649	56,360	60,149	47,662

January 9, 1867. *Jacques la Ramee (c1784–1821)*. French-Canadian trapper; killed by Indians near Laramie River.

Larimer	**Colorado**					
Fort Collins	2,596 sq. mi.					
299,630	251,494	186,136	149,184	89,900	53,343	43,554

November 1, 1861. *William Larimer (1809–75)*. Founder of Denver 1858; colonel, 3rd Colorado Volunteers, 1861–63; captain, 14th Kansas Cavalry Regiment 1863–65; Kansas Senate 1867–70.

Larue	**Kentucky**					
Hodgenville	262 sq. mi.					
14,193	13,373	11,679	11,922	10,672	10,346	9,956

March 1, 1843. *John P. La Rue (1746–92)*. Revolutionary War; settled in Kentucky 1779; large landowner.

LaSalle	**Illinois**					
Ottawa	1,135 sq. mi.					
113,924	111,509	106,913	112,033	111,409	110,800	100,610

January 15, 1831. *Rene Robert Cavalier, Sieur de la Salle (1643–87)*. French explorer; explored Mississippi River from Great Lakes area to Gulf of Mexico 1681–82; claimed interior of North America for France; stranded in Texas, killed by mutineers. (Illinois' name is one word.)

La Salle	**Louisiana**					
Jena	625 sq. mi.					
14,890	14,282	13,662	17,004	13,295	13,011	12,717

July 3, 1908. *Rene Robert Cavalier, Sieur de la Salle.**

La Salle	**Texas**					
Cotulla	1,487 sq. mi.					
6,886	5,866	5,254	5,514	5,014	5,972	7,485

February 1, 1858; organized November 2, 1880. *Rene Robert Cavalier, Sieur de la Salle.**

Las Animas	**Colorado**					
Trinidad	4,773 sq. mi.					
15,507	15,207	13,765	14,897	15,744	19,983	25,902

February 9, 1866; effective November 1, 1866; *Purgatoire River*. Spanish for "souls"; translation of Spanish name for the river; *El Rio de las Animas Perdidas en Purgatoria*, "River of the Souls Lost in Purgatorie."

Lassen	**California**					
Susanville	4,541 sq. mi.					
34,895	33,828	27,598	21,661	14,960	13,597	18,474

April 1, 1863. *Mount Lassen*. Named for Peter Lassen (1793–1859); Danish pioneer; led immigrant party to Sacramento Valley 1848; killed by Indians near Pyramid Lake, Nevada.

Latah	**Idaho**					
Moscow	1,076 sq. mi.					
37,244	34,935	30,617	28,749	24,891	21,170	20,971

May 14, 1888. *Latah Creek*. Coined word from first syllable of Nez Perce words *la-kah* (pine tree) and *taho* (pestle).

Latimer	**Oklahoma**
Wilburton	722 sq. mi.

| 11,154 | 10,692 | 10,333 | 9,840 | 8,601 | 7,738 | 9,690 |

July 16, 1907. *James S. Latimer (1855–1941).* Station agent for Choctaw, Oklahoma & Gulf Railroad; Oklahoma Constitutional Convention 1907.

Lauderdale   **Alabama**
Florence   668 sq. mi.

| 92,709 | 87,996 | 79,661 | 80,546 | 68,111 | 61,622 | 54,179 |

February 6, 1818; effective June 1, 1818. *James Lauderdale (1780–1814).* Major, volunteer cavalry 1813; wounded in Battle of Talladega 1813; colonel with General Jackson, killed in first Battle of New Orleans December 23, 1814.

Lauderdale   **Mississippi**
Meridian   704 sq. mi.

| 80,261 | 78,161 | 75,555 | 77,285 | 67,087 | 67,119 | 64,171 |

December 23, 1833. *James Lauderdale.**

Lauderdale   **Tennessee**
Ripley   472 sq. mi.

| 27,815 | 27,101 | 23,491 | 24,555 | 20,271 | 21,844 | 25,047 |

November 24, 1835. *James Lauderdale.**

Laurel   **Kentucky**
London   434 sq. mi.

| 58,849 | 52,715 | 43,438 | 38,982 | 27,386 | 24,901 | 25,797 |

December 12, 1825. *Uncertain.* (1) *Descriptive* of mountain laurel flowers. (2) *Laurel River*; named for the flowers.

Laurens   **Georgia**
Dublin   807 sq. mi.

| 48,434 | 44,874 | 39,988 | 36,990 | 32,738 | 32,313 | 33,123 |

December 10, 1807. *John Laurens (1754–82).* Lieutenant colonel, aide-de-camp to Washington; wounded at Battle of Germantown 1777; envoy extraordinary to France 1780–81; captured British redoubt at Yorktown 1781; killed in skirmish at Combahee River, South Carolina, August 27, 1782. Son of Henry Laurens (see Laurens, South Carolina.)

Laurens   **South Carolina**
Laurens   714 sq. mi.

| 66,537 | 69,567 | 58,092 | 52,214 | 49,713 | 47,609 | 46,974 |

March 12, 1785; converted to judicial district January 1, 1800; redesignated as county April 16, 1868. *Henry Laurens (1724–92).* South Carolina Provisional Congress 1776–77; President of Continental Congress 1777–78; appointed minister to Holland but ship was captured by British and Laurens was imprisoned in Tower of London 1779; exchanged for Lord Cornwallis 1781; signed preliminary version of Treaty of Paris before returning to South Carolina 1782. Father of John Laurens.*

Lavaca   **Texas**
Hallettsville   970 sq. mi.

| 19,263 | 19,210 | 18,690 | 19,004 | 17,903 | 20,174 | 22,159 |

April 6, 1846; organized 1852. *Lavaca River.* Spanish translation of original French name *Les Veches* meaning "the cows"; named for bison in the area.

Lawrence   **Alabama**
Moulton   691 sq. mi.

| 34,339 | 34,803 | 31,513 | 30,170 | 27,281 | 24,501 | 27,128 |

February 6, 1818; effective June 1, 1818. *James Lawrence (1781–1813).* American naval commander; fought against Tripolitan pirates 1804; captain 1812; commanded USS *Chesapeake*; mortally wounded in battle with British frigate *Shannon*, June 1, 1813; while dying, gave order, "Don't give up the ship."

Lawrence   **Arkansas**
Walnut Ridge   588 sq. mi.

17,415   17,774   17,457   18,447   16,320   17,267   21,303
January 15, 1815; effective March 1, 1815. *James Lawrence.**

Lawrence   **Illinois**
Lawrenceville   372 sq. mi.
16,833   15,452   15,972   17,807   17,522   18,540   20,539
January 16, 1821. *James Lawrence.**

Lawrence   **Indiana**
Bedford   449 sq. mi.
46,134   45,922   42,836   42,472   38,038   36,564   34,346
January 7, 1818; effective March 16, 1818. *James Lawrence.**

Lawrence   **Kentucky**
Louisa   416 sq. mi.
15,860   15,569   13,998   14,121   10,726   12,134   14,418
December 14, 1821. *James Lawrence.**

Lawrence   **Mississippi**
Monticello   431 sq. mi.
12,929   13,258   12,458   12,518   11,137   10,215   12,639
December 22, 1814. *James Lawrence.**

Lawrence   **Missouri**
Mount Vernon   612 sq. mi.
38,634   35,204   30,236   28,973   24,585   23,260   23,420
February 14, 1845. *James Lawrence.**

Lawrence   **Ohio**
Ironton   453 sq. mi.
62,450   62,319   61,834   63,849   56,868   55,438   49,115
December 21, 1815; organized March 4, 1817. *James Lawrence.**

Lawrence   **Pennsylvania**
New Castle   358 sq. mi.
91,108   94,643   96,246   107,150   107,374   112,965   105,120
March 20, 1849. USS *Lawrence*. Flagship of Oliver Hazard Perry (see Perry, Alabama) at Battle of Lake Erie 1813; named for James Lawrence.*

Lawrence   **South Dakota**
Deadwood   800 sq. mi.
24,097   21,802   20,655   19,339   17,453   17,075   16,648
January 11, 1875; organized March 5, 1877. *John Lawrence (?–1889)*. Early settler in Sioux Falls 1858; 2nd lieutenant, Dakota Militia; Dakota territorial House of Representatives 1863–64; Dakota territorial council 1872–75; superintendent of Sioux Falls-Fort Randall wagon road 1868; county treasurer 1877–78.

Lawrence   **Tennessee**
Lawrenceburg   617 sq. mi.
41,869   39,926   35,303   34,101   29,097   28,049   28,818
October 21, 1817. *James Lawrence.**

Lea   **New Mexico**
Lovington   4,391 sq. mi.
64,727   55,511   55,765   55,993   49,554   53,429   30,717

March 7, 1917. *Joseph C. Lea (1841–1904)*. Colonel, Confederate Army; pioneer of Chaves County 1876; Board of Regents, New Mexico Military Institute 1891; elected mayor of Roswell 1903, died two months after taking office.

Leake   **Mississippi**
Carthage   583 sq. mi.

23,805	20,940	18,436	18,790	17,085	18,660	21,610

December 23, 1833. *Walter Leake (1762–1825)*. Revolutionary War; Virginia legislature 1805; chief judge, Mississippi Territory 1807; Mississippi Constitutional Convention 1817; US senator 1817–20; US marshal for Mississippi District 1820; governor of Mississippi 1822–25.

Leavenworth   **Kansas**
Leavenworth   463 sq. mi.

76,227	68,691	64,371	54,809	53,340	48,524	42,361

August 25, 1855. *Fort Leavenworth*. Named for Henry Leavenworth (1783–1834); captain to colonel 1812–25; brevet lieutenant colonel for distinguished service at Niagara Falls 1814; brevet brigadier general for ten years of service 1824; built Fort Leavenworth 1827.

Lebanon   **Pennsylvania**
Lebanon   362 sq. mi.

133,568	120,327	113,744	108,582	99,665	90,853	81,683

February 16, 1813. *Lebanon Township (or Borough)*. Named for Mount Lebanon, Lebanon; name suggested because of cedar trees in the area.

Lee   **Alabama**
Opelika   608 sq. mi.

140,247	115,092	87,146	76,283	61,268	49,754	45,073

December 5, 1866. *Robert Edward Lee (1807–70)*. Graduated from West Point 1829; wounded at Chapultepec, Mexico, 1847; captured John Brown 1859; resigned from US Army after being offered command of the Union Army 1861; commanded Confederate Army of Northern Virginia 1861–65; surrendered to Grant at Appomattox Court House 1865; granted amnesty pardon 1865; president of Washington College (Washington and Lee) 1865–70; US citizenship officially restored 1975.

Lee   **Arkansas**
Marianna   603 sq. mi.

10,424	12,580	13,053	15,539	18,884	21,001	24,322

April 17, 1873. *Robert Edward Lee.**

Lee   **Florida**
Fort Myers   785 sq. mi.

618,754	440,888	335,113	205,266	105,216	54,539	23,404

May 13, 1887. *Robert Edward Lee.**

Lee   **Georgia**
Leesburg   356 sq. mi.

28,298	24,757	16,250	11,684	7,044	6,204	6,674

December 11, 1826. *Richard Henry Lee (1732–94)*. Virginia House of Burgesses 1758–75; Continental Congress 1774–80 and 1784–87, introduced independence resolution 1776; signer of Declaration of Independence 1776; Virginia House of Delegates, intermittently 1777–85; US senator 1789–92.

Lee   **Illinois**
Dixon   725 sq. mi.

36,031	36,062	34,392	36,328	37,947	38,749	36,451

February 27, 1839. *Uncertain*. (1) *Henry Lee (1756–1818)*; captain, Virginia Dragoons 1776; nicknamed "Light Horse Henry"; lieutenant colonel to major general 1780–1800; Continental Congress 1785–88; governor of Virginia 1791–94; commanded US troops during Whiskey Rebellion 1794; US representative 1799–1801; wrote Washington's funeral oration "first in war, first in peace . . ." 1799. (2) *Richard Henry Lee.**

Lee   **Iowa**
Fort Madison   518 sq. mi.
35,862   38,052   38,687   43,106   42,996   44,207   43,102
December 7, 1836. *Uncertain.* (1) *Albert Miller Lea (1808–?)*; graduate of West Point 1831; topographer with Stephen Kearny, explored Iowa for fort sites 1835; Albert Lea Lake and the town of Albert Lea, Minnesota, are named for him; wrote *Notes on the Wisconsin Territory* that applied name "Iowa" to the region 1836; acting secretary of war 1841; Confederate Army engineer 1861–65; name misspelled by transcription error. (2) *William E. Lee (?–?)*; New York land speculator with large holdings in Iowa.

Lee   **Kentucky**
Beattyville   209 sq. mi.
7,887   7,916   7,422   7,754   6,587   7,420   8,739
January 29, 1870. *Uncertain.* (1) *Robert Edward Lee.** (2) *Lee County, Virginia.*

Lee   **Mississippi**
Tupelo   450 sq. mi.
82,910   75,755   65,581   57,061   46,148   40,589   38,237
October 26, 1866. *Robert Edward Lee.**

Lee   **North Carolina**
Sanford   255 sq. mi.
57,866   49,040   41,374   36,718   30,467   26,561   23,522
March 6, 1907. *Robert Edward Lee.**

Lee   **South Carolina**
Bishopville   410 sq. mi.
19,220   20,119   18,437   18,929   18,323   21,832   23,173
February 25, 1902. *Robert Edward Lee.**

Lee   **Texas**
Giddings   629 sq. mi.
16,612   15,657   12,854   10,952   8,048   8,949   10,144
April 14, 1874; organized June 2, 1874. *Robert Edward Lee.**

Lee   **Virginia**
Jonesville   436 sq. mi.
25,587   23,589   24,496   25,956   20,321   25,824   36,106
October 25, 1792. *Henry Lee.**

Leelanau   **Michigan**
Suttons Bay   347 sq. mi.
21,708   21,119   16,527   14,007   10,872   9,321   8,647
April 1, 1840; organized February 27, 1863. *Leelinau.* Fictitious Chippewa maiden; recorded as "Leelanau" in Henry Schoolcraft's *Algic Researches*, a collection of Indian tales, 1839 (see Schoolcraft, Michigan).

Leflore   **Mississippi**
Greenwood   593 sq. mi.
32,317   37,947   37,341   41,525   42,111   47,142   51,813
March 15, 1871. *Greenwood Le Flore (1800–65).* Choctaw chief; owned large cotton plantation; oversaw removal of Choctaws to Indian Territory (Oklahoma) 1830; Mississippi Senate 1841–44; opposed secession 1861.

Le Flore   **Oklahoma**
Poteau   1,589 sq. mi.
50,384   48,109   43,270   40,698   32,137   29,106   35,276
July 16, 1907. *Greenwood Le Flore.**

Lehigh   **Pennsylvania**
Allentown   345 sq. mi.
349,497   312,090   291,130   272,349   255,304   227,536   198,207
March 6, 1812. *Lehigh River.* From Delaware word *lechauwekenk*, meaning "at the forks"; shortened to *lecha* and further corrupted to "lehigh."

Lemhi   **Idaho**
Salmon   4,563 sq. mi.
7,936   7,806   6,899   7,460   5,566   5,816   6,278
January 9, 1869. *Fort Lemhi.* Established by Mormons 1855; abandoned 1858; named for King Lemhi from the *Book of Mormon.*

Lenawee   **Michigan**
Adrian   750 sq. mi.
99,892   98,890   91,476   89,948   81,609   77,789   64,629
September 10, 1822; organized November 20, 1826. Shawnee word meaning "man" or "people."

Lenoir   **North Carolina**
Kinston   401 sq. mi.
59,495   59,648   52,274   59,819   55,204   55,276   45,953
1791. *William Lenoir (1751–1839).* Captain, wounded at Battle of Kings Mountain 1780; North Carolina legislature 1781–95, speaker of Senate 1790–95; founding member and first president of Board of Trustees, University of North Carolina, 1795.

Leon   **Florida**
Tallahassee   667 sq. mi.
275,487   239,452   192,493   148,655   103,047   74,225   51,590
December 29, 1824. *Ponce de León (1460–1521).* Spanish explorer; second voyage of Columbus 1493–94, remained in Santo Domingo; colonized Puerto Rico 1508; governor of Puerto Rico 1510; first European to visit Continental US 1513; died in Cuba from poisoned-arrow wound during second expedition to Florida 1521.

Leon   **Texas**
Centerville   1,073 sq. mi.
16,801   15,335   12,665   9,594   8,738   9,951   12,024
March 17, 1846; organized July 13, 1846. *Uncertain.* (1) *Alonso de León (1637–91)*; Spanish explorer in Texas; checked French advances into Texas. (2) *Martín de León (1765–1833)*; pioneer rancher; established colony with settlers from Mexico, Ireland, and US. (3) *Leon Prairie*; commemorates the killing of a lion (Spanish *león*) or, more likely, a yellow wolf.

Leslie   **Kentucky**
Hyden   401 sq. mi.
11,310   12,401   13,642   14,882   11,623   10,941   15,537
March 29, 1878. *Preston Hopkins Leslie (1819–1907).* Kentucky House of Representatives 1844–50; Kentucky Senate 1851–55 and 1867–71, president 1869–71; governor of Kentucky 1871–75; circuit judge 1881; governor of Montana Territory 1887–89; US district attorney for Montana 1894–98.

Le Sueur   **Minnesota**
Le Center   449 sq. mi.
27,703   25,426   23,239   23,434   21,332   19,906   19,088
March 5, 1853. *Pierre Charles le Sueur (1657–1704).* Fur trader; built fort on Prairie Island near Red Wing 1695; ascended Mississippi River to Mankato and built a fort 1700.

Letcher   **Kentucky**
Whitesburg   338 sq. mi.
24,519   25,277   27,000   30,687   23,165   30,012   39,522
March 3, 1842. *Robert Perkins Letcher (1788–1861).* Kentucky House of Representatives, intermittently 1813–38; US representative 1823–33 and 1834–35; governor of Kentucky 1840–44; US minister to Mexico 1849–52.

Levy   **Florida**
Bronson   1,118 sq. mi.
40,801   34,450   25,923   19,870   12,756   10,364   10,637
March 10, 1845. *David Levy (1810–86)*. Florida Constitutional Convention 1838; congressional delegate from Florida 1841–45; US senator 1845–51 and 1855–61, resigned; changed name to David Levy Yulee 1846; railroad executive 1853–66, "Father of Florida's railroads."

Lewis   **Idaho**
Nezperce   479 sq. mi.
3,821   3,747   3,516   4,118   3,867   4,423   4,208
March 3, 1911. *Meriwether Lewis (1774–1809)*. Served in US Army during Whiskey Rebellion 1794; lieutenant to captain 1795–97; private secretary to President Jefferson (see Jefferson, Alabama) 1801–03; commanded expedition to the Pacific Ocean with Captain William Clark (see Clark, Arkansas) 1803–06; governor of Louisiana Territory 1807–09; died under mysterious circumstances at Hohenwald, Tennessee, October 10, 1809.

Lewis   **Kentucky**
Vanceburg   483 sq. mi.
13,870   14,092   13,029   14,545   12,355   13,115   13,520
December 2, 1806; effective April 1, 1807. *Meriwether Lewis*.*

Lewis   **Missouri**
Monticello   505 sq. mi.
10,211   10,494   10,233   10,901   10,993   10,984   10,733
January 2, 1833. *Meriwether Lewis*.*

Lewis   **New York**
Lowville   1,275 sq. mi.
27,087   26,944   26,796   25,035   23,644   23,249   22,521
March 28, 1805. *Morgan Lewis (1754–1844)*. Colonel, Continental Army 1776–83, chief of staff to General Gates; quartermaster for Northern New York 1779; New York legislature 1789; attorney general of New York 1791–92; justice, New York Supreme Court 1801; governor of New York 1804–07; major general, War of 1812.

Lewis   **Tennessee**
Hohenwald   282 sq. mi.
12,161   11,367   9,247   9,700   6,761   6,269   6,078
December 23, 1843. *Meriwether Lewis*.*

Lewis   **Washington**
Chehalis   2,403 sq. mi.
75,455   68,600   59,358   56,025   45,467   41,858   43,755
December 21, 1845. *Meriwether Lewis*.*

Lewis   **West Virginia**
Weston   385 sq. mi.
16,372   16,919   17,223   18,813   17,847   19,711   21,074
December 18, 1816. *Charles Lewis (1736–74)*. Virginia House of Burgesses 1773–74; colonel in Revolutionary War; killed at Battle of Point Pleasant, October 10, 1774.

Lewis and Clark   **Montana**
Helena   3,459 sq. mi.
63,395   55,716   47,495   43,039   33,281   28,006   24,540
February 2, 1865, as Edgerton; name changed December 20, 1867; effective March 1, 1868. *Lewis and Clark Expedition*. Corps of Discovery; explored from St. Louis to the mouth of the Columbia River 1803–06; led by Meriwether Lewis (see Lewis, Idaho) and William Clark (see Clark, Arkansas).

Lexington   **South Carolina**
Lexington   699 sq. mi.

262,391	216,014	167,611	140,353	89,012	60,726	44,279

March 12, 1785; abolished 1800; recreated 1804 as judicial district; redesignated as county April 16, 1868. *Battle of Lexington.* Opening battle of the American Revolution, April 19, 1775.

Lexington   **Virginia**
(Independent City)   3 sq. mi.

7,042	6,867	6,959	7,292	7,597	(a)	(a)

January 1, 1966. *Battle of Lexington.* [(a) Part of Rockbridge County] (Associated County: Rockbridge.)

Liberty   **Florida**
Bristol   836 sq. mi.

8,365	7,021	5,569	4,260	3,397	3,138	3,182

December 15, 1855. *Descriptive* of American ideal of freedom.

Liberty   **Georgia**
Hinesville   490 sq. mi.

63,453	61,610	52,745	37,583	17,569	14,487	8,444

February 5, 1777. *Descriptive* of local residents' participation in American independence movement.

Liberty   **Montana**
Chester   1,430 sq. mi.

2,339	2,158	2,295	2,329	2,359	2,624	2,180

February 11, 1920. *Descriptive* of patriotic feelings following US victory in World War I.

Liberty   **Texas**
Liberty   1,158 sq. mi.

75,643	70,154	52,726	47,088	33,014	31,595	26,729

March 17, 1836. *Villa de Santissima Trinidad de la Libertad.* Mexican municipality established in 1831; name translates to "Town of the Most Holy Trinity of Liberty"; shortened to "Liberty" which was also the name of a Mississippi town many of the settlers had come from.

Licking   **Ohio**
Newark   683 sq. mi.

166,492	145,491	128,300	120,981	107,799	90,242	70,645

January 30, 1808. *Licking River.* Named for numerous salt licks in the area.

Limestone   **Alabama**
Athens   560 sq. mi.

82,782	65,676	54,135	46,005	41,699	36,513	35,766

February 6, 1818. *Limestone Creek.* Refers to local limestone deposits.

Limestone   **Texas**
Groesbeck   905 sq. mi.

23,384	22,051	20,946	20,224	18,100	20,413	25,251

April 11, 1846; organized August 18, 1846. *Descriptive.* Refers to local limestone deposits.

Lincoln   **Arkansas**
Star City   562 sq. mi.

14,134	14,492	13,690	13,369	12,913	14,447	17,079

March 21, 1871. *Abraham Lincoln (1809–65).* Captain, Sangamon County Rifles in Black Hawk War 1832; postmaster New Salem, Illinois 1833–36; deputy county surveyor 1834–36; Illinois House of Representatives 1834–41; US representative 1847–49; Lincoln-Douglas debates 1858; 16th President of US 1861–65; assassinated April 14, 1865.

Lincoln   **Colorado**
Hugo   2,578 sq. mi.
5,467   6,087   4,529   4,663   4,836   5,310   5,909
April 11, 1889. *Abraham Lincoln.**

Lincoln   **Georgia**
Lincolnton   210 sq. mi.
7,996   8,348   7,442   6,716   5,895   5,906   6,462
February 20, 1796. *Benjamin Lincoln (1733–1810).* Major general, Continental Army 1776; Battle of White Plains 1776; wounded at Saratoga 1777; Siege of Yorktown, received Cornwallis's sword from surrogate in surrender 1781; secretary of war 1781–83; put down Shay's Rebellion 1787; lieutenant governor of Massachusetts 1788; collector of the Port of Boston 1789–1808.

Lincoln   **Idaho**
Shoshone   1,201 sq. mi.
5,208   4,044   3,308   3,436   3,057   3,686   4,256
March 18, 1895. *Abraham Lincoln.**

Lincoln   **Kansas**
Lincoln   719 sq. mi.
3,241   3,578   3,653   4,145   4,582   5,556   6,643
February 26, 1867. *Abraham Lincoln.**

Lincoln   **Kentucky**
Stanford   334 sq. mi.
24,742   23,361   20,045   19,053   16,663   16,503   18,668
June 30, 1780. *Benjamin Lincoln.**

Lincoln   **Louisiana**
Ruston   472 sq. mi.
46,735   42,509   41,745   39,763   33,800   28,535   25,782
February 27, 1873. *Abraham Lincoln.**

Lincoln   **Maine**
Wiscasset   456 sq. mi.
34,457   33,616   30,357   25,691   20,537   18,497   18,004
June 19, 1760; effective November 1, 1760. *Town of Lincoln, England.* Tribute to birthplace of Thomas Pownall (1722–1805) royal governor of Massachusetts Bay Colony 1757–60.

Lincoln   **Minnesota**
Ivanhoe   537 sq. mi.
5,896   6,429   6,890   8,207   8,143   9,651   10,150
November 4, 1873; organized February 9, 1881. *Abraham Lincoln.**

Lincoln   **Mississippi**
Brookhaven   586 sq. mi.
34,869   33,166   30,278   30,174   26,198   26,759   27,899
April 7, 1870. *Abraham Lincoln.**

Lincoln   **Missouri**
Troy   627 sq. mi.
52,566   38,944   28,892   22,193   18,041   14,783   13,478
December 14, 1818. *Lincoln Counties, Kentucky and North Carolina.* Both named for Benjamin Lincoln.* Prominent settler Christopher Clark was born in Lincoln County, North Carolina, and had lived in Lincoln County, Kentucky.

Lincoln   **Montana**
Libby   3,613 sq. mi.
19,687   18,837   17,481   17,752   18,063   12,537   8,693
March 9, 1909. *Abraham Lincoln.**

Lincoln   **Nebraska**
North Platte   2,564 sq. mi.
36,288   34,632   32,508   36,455   29,538   28,491   27,380
January 7, 1860, as Shorter; name changed December 11, 1861; organized October 1, 1866. *Abraham Lincoln.**

Lincoln   **Nevada**
Pioche   10,633 sq. mi.
5,345   4,165   3,775   3,732   2,557   2,431   3,837
February 25, 1866. *Abraham Lincoln.**

Lincoln   **New Mexico**
Carrizozo   4,831 sq. mi.
20,497   19,411   12,219   10,997   7,560   7,744   7,409
January 16, 1869. *Abraham Lincoln.**

Lincoln   **North Carolina**
Lincolnton   298 sq. mi.
78,265   63,780   50,319   42,372   32,682   28,814   27,459
1779. *Benjamin Lincoln.**

Lincoln   **Oklahoma**
Chandler   952 sq. mi.
34,273   32,080   29,216   26,601   19,482   18,783   22,102
September 18, 1891. *Abraham Lincoln.**

Lincoln   **Oregon**
Newport   980 sq. mi.
46,034   44,479   38,889   35,264   25,755   24,635   21,308
February 20, 1893. *Abraham Lincoln.**

Lincoln   **South Dakota**
Canton   577 sq. mi.
44,828   24,131   15,427   13,942   11,761   12,371   12,767
April 5, 1862; organized December 30, 1867. *Lincoln County, Maine.* Name suggested by Maine native Wilmot Brookings (see Brookings, South Dakota), a member of the Dakota territorial legislature; some legislators thought the name was honoring President Abraham Lincoln.*

Lincoln   **Tennessee**
Fayetteville   570 sq. mi.
33,361   31,340   28,157   26,483   24,318   23,829   25,624
November 14, 1809. *Benjamin Lincoln.**

Lincoln   **Washington**
Davenport   2,310 sq. mi.
10,570   10,184   8,864   9,604   9,572   10,919   10,970
November 24, 1883. *Abraham Lincoln.**

Lincoln   **West Virginia**
Hamlin   437 sq. mi.
21,720   22,108   21,382   23,675   18,912   20,267   22,466
February 23, 1867. *Abraham Lincoln.**

Lincoln   **Wisconsin**
Merrill   879 sq. mi.
28,743   29,641   26,993   26,555   23,499   22,338   22,235
March 4, 1874; organized 1875. *Abraham Lincoln.**

Lincoln   **Wyoming**
Kemmerer   4,076 sq. mi.
18,106   14,573   12,625   12,177   8,640   9,018   9,023
February 20, 1911. *Abraham Lincoln.**

Linn   **Iowa**
Cedar Rapids   717 sq. mi.
211,226   191,801   168,767   169,775   163,213   136,899   104,274
December 21, 1837; organized January 15, 1839; effective June 1, 1839. *Lewis Fields Linn (1795–1843)*. Army surgeon, War of 1812; received medical degree 1816; combated two cholera epidemics in Missouri; Missouri Senate 1827; US senator 1833–43, advocated acquisition of Oregon.

Linn   **Kansas**
Mound City   594 sq. mi.
9,656   9,570   8,254   8,234   7,770   8,274   10,053
August 25, 1855. *Lewis Fields Linn.**

Linn   **Missouri**
Linneus   616 sq. mi.
12,761   13,754   13,885   15,495   15,125   16,815   18,865
January 6, 1837. *Lewis Fields Linn.**

Linn   **Oregon**
Albany   2,290 sq. mi.
116,672   103,069   91,227   89,495   71,914   58,867   54,317
December 28, 1847. *Lewis Fields Linn.**

Lipscomb   **Texas**
Lipscomb   932 sq. mi.
3,302   3,057   3,143   3,766   3,486   3,406   3,658
August 21, 1876; organized June 6, 1887. *Abner Smith Lipscomb (1789–1856)*. Creek Indian Wars 1813–14; Alabama territorial legislature 1818; circuit judge 1819; Alabama Supreme Court 1820–35, chief justice 1823–35, resigned; Alabama legislature 1838; Republic of Texas secretary of state 1839–40; Texas Constitutional Convention 1845; Texas Supreme Court 1846–56.

Litchfield   **Connecticut**
Litchfield   921 sq. mi.
189,927   182,193   174,092   156,769   144,091   119,856   98,872
October 9, 1751. *Town of Litchfield*. Named for Litchfield, England.

Little River   **Arkansas**
Ashdown   532 sq. mi.
13,171   13,628   13,966   13,952   11,194   9,211   11,690
March 5, 1867. *Little River*. Forms northern boundary of the county.

Live Oak   **Texas**
George West   1,040 sq. mi.
11,531   12,309   9,556   9,606   6,697   7,846   9,054
February 2, 1856; organized August 4, 1856. *Descriptive*. Refers to trees in the area.

Livingston   **Illinois**
Pontiac   1,044 sq. mi.

| 38,950 | 39,678 | 39,301 | 41,381 | 40,690 | 40,341 | 37,809 |

February 27, 1837. *Edward Livingston (1764–1836)*. US representative from New York 1795–1801; US district attorney 1801–03; mayor of New York City 1801–03; staff of General Jackson at Battle of New Orleans 1815; Louisiana House of Representatives 1820; US representative from Louisiana 1823–29; US senator 1829–31; US secretary of state 1829–31; US minister to France 1833–35. Brother of Robert Livingston (see Livingston, Kentucky).

Livingston   **Kentucky**
Smithland   313 sq. mi.

| 9,519 | 9,804 | 9,062 | 9,219 | 7,596 | 7,029 | 7,184 |

December 13, 1798. *Robert R. Livingston (1746–1813)*. New York City recorder 1773–75; Continental Congress 1775–77 and 1779–81; New York Constitutional Convention 1777; secretary of foreign affairs under Articles of Confederation 1781–83; chancellor of New York 1783–1801; administered oath of office to President Washington 1789; US minister to France 1801–04, negotiated Louisiana Purchase 1803. Brother of Edward Livingston.*

Livingston   **Louisiana**
Livingston   648 sq. mi.

| 128,026 | 91,814 | 70,526 | 58,806 | 36,511 | 26,974 | 20,054 |

February 10, 1832. *Edward Livingston.*

Livingston   **Michigan**
Howell   565 sq. mi.

| 180,967 | 156,951 | 115,645 | 100,239 | 58,967 | 38,233 | 26,725 |

March 21, 1833; organized March 24, 1836. *Edward Livingston.*

Livingston   **Missouri**
Chillicothe   532 sq. mi.

| 15,195 | 14,558 | 14,592 | 15,739 | 15,368 | 15,771 | 16,532 |

January 6, 1837. *Edward Livingston.*

Livingston   **New York**
Geneseo   632 sq. mi.

| 65,393 | 64,328 | 62,372 | 57,006 | 54,041 | 44,053 | 40,257 |

February 23, 1821. *Robert R. Livingston.*

Llano   **Texas**
Llano   934 sq. mi.

| 19,301 | 17,044 | 11,631 | 10,144 | 6,979 | 5,240 | 5,377 |

February 1, 1856; organized August 4, 1856. *Llano River*. From Spanish *Río de los Llanos*; "River of the Plains."

Logan   **Arkansas**
Paris   708 sq. mi.

| 22,353 | 22,486 | 20,557 | 20,144 | 16,789 | 15,957 | 20,260 |

March 22, 1871, as Slater; name changed December 14, 1875. *James Logan (1791–1859)*. Early settler in western Arkansas c1829; Arkansas legislature 1836.

Logan   **Colorado**
Sterling   1,839 sq. mi.

| 22,709 | 20,504 | 17,567 | 19,800 | 18,852 | 20,302 | 17,187 |

February 25, 1887. *John Alexander Logan (1826–86)*. Mexican War, 2nd lieutenant, 1st Illinois Infantry 1847; Illinois House of Representatives 1852–53 and 1856–57; US representative 1859–62 and 1867–71; colonel to major general 1862–65; US senator 1871–77 and 1879–86; Republican nominee for US vice president 1884.

Logan   **Illinois**
Lincoln   618 sq. mi.

| 30,305 | 31,183 | 30,798 | 31,802 | 33,538 | 33,656 | 30,671 |

February 15, 1839. *John Logan (1788–1852)*. Corporal, Black Hawk War 1832; Illinois legislature; father of John Alexander Logan.*

Logan   **Kansas**
Oakley   1,073 sq. mi.

2,756	3,046	3,081	3,478	3,814	4,036	4,206

March 13, 1881, as Saint John; name changed February 24, 1887; organized September 17, 1887. *John Alexander Logan.**

Logan   **Kentucky**
Russellville   552 sq. mi.

26,835	26,573	24,416	23,138	21,793	20,896	22,335

September 1, 1792. *Benjamin Logan (c1742–1802)*. Indian fighter; built fort at Stanford, Kentucky, 1776; Virginia legislature 1781–87; Kentucky Constitutional Convention 1792; Kentucky legislature 1792–95.

Logan   **Nebraska**
Stapleton   571 sq. mi.

763	774	878	983	991	1,108	1,357

February 24, 1885. *John Alexander Logan.**

Logan   **North Dakota**
Napoleon   993 sq. mi.

1,990	2,308	2,847	3,493	4,245	5,369	6,357

January 4, 1873; organized September 1, 1884. *John Alexander Logan.**

Logan   **Ohio**
Bellefontaine   458 sq. mi.

45,858	46,005	42,310	39,155	35,072	34,803	31,329

December 30, 1817. *Benjamin Logan.**

Logan   **Oklahoma**
Guthrie   744 sq. mi.

41,848	33,924	29,011	26,881	19,645	18,662	22,170

May 2, 1890. *John Alexander Logan.**

Logan   **West Virginia**
Logan   454 sq. mi.

36,743	37,710	43,032	50,679	46,269	61,570	77,391

January 12, 1824. *John Logan (c1725–80)*. Mingo chief named *Tah-gah-jute*, took name of friend, John Logan*; friendly to settlers until family was massacred by settlers 1774; led Indians in Lord Dunmore's War 1774; raided settlements during American Revolution.

Long   **Georgia**
Ludowici   400 sq. mi.

14,464	10,304	6,202	4,524	3,746	3,874	3,598

August 14, 1920. *Crawford Williamson Long (1815–78)*. First physician to use ether as anesthetic during surgery, Jefferson, Georgia, 1842.

Lonoke   **Arkansas**
Lonoke   771 sq. mi.

68,356	52,828	39,268	34,518	26,249	24,551	27,278

April 16, 1873. *Descriptive*. Contraction of "lone oak," after a tree used in early surveys.

Lorain   **Ohio**
Elyria   491 sq. mi.

301,356	284,664	271,126	274,909	256,483	217,500	148,162

December 26, 1822; organized January 21, 1824. *Lorraine, France*. Suggested by Judge Herman Ely who has visited Lorraine and liked it; Ely donated land for courthouse.

Los Alamos   **New Mexico**
Los Alamos   109 sq. mi.

17,950	18,343	18,115	17,599	15,198	13,037	10,746

March 16, 1949. *City of Los Alamos*. Spanish for "cottonwood trees" in the area.

Los Angeles   **California**
Los Angeles   4,058 sq. mi.

9,818,605	9,519,338	8,863,164	7,477,503	7,032,075	6,038,771	4,151,687

February 15, 1850. *City of Los Angeles*. Named for *El Río de Nuestra Señora la Reina de los Ángeles de Portiúncula* (River of Our Lady, Queen of the Angels of Portiuncula); Portiuncula is the site of a shrine to the Virgin Mary in Assisi, Italy.

Loudon   **Tennessee**
Loudon   229 sq. mi.

48,556	39,086	31,255	28,553	24,266	23,757	23,182

June 2, 1870, as Christiana; name changed July 7, 1870. *Fort Loudoun*. Named for John Campbell, Earl of Loudoun (see Loudoun, Virginia). Uncorrected spelling error in legislation.

Loudoun   **Virginia**
Leesburg   516 sq. mi.

312,311	169,599	86,129	57,427	37,150	24,549	21,147

May 17, 1757. *John Campbell, 4th Earl of Loudoun (1705–82)*. Commander in chief and governor of Virginia 1756; lost Fort William Henry during French and Indian War, recalled 1757; commanded British troops in Portugal 1762–63.

Louisa   **Iowa**
Wapello   402 sq. mi.

11,387	12,183	11,592	12,055	10,682	10,290	11,101

December 7, 1836. *Louisa Massey (c1817–?)*. Sixteen-year-old pioneer woman who gained local renown by shooting and killing her brother's murderer shortly before the county was created.

Louisa   **Virginia**
Louisa   496 sq. mi.

33,153	25,627	20,325	17,825	14,004	12,959	12,826

June 2, 1742. *Princess Louise (1724–51)*. Eighth and youngest child of King George II (see Georgetown, South Carolina) and Queen Caroline (see Caroline, Virginia); married Frederick V of Denmark 1744.

Loup   **Nebraska**
Taylor   568 sq. mi.

632	712	683	859	854	1,097	1,348

February 23, 1883. *North Loup River*. French for "wolf."

Love   **Oklahoma**
Marietta   514 sq. mi.

9,423	8,831	8,157	7,469	5,637	5,862	7,721

July 16, 1907. *Love Family*. Prominent Chickasaw family; most notably Overton Love (1820–1907); represented Chickasaw Nation in dealings with US.

Loving   **Texas**
Mentone   669 sq. mi.

82	67	107	91	164	226	227

February 26, 1887; organized 1931. *Oliver Loving (1812–67)*. Cattleman and trail driver; supplied cattle and hogs to Confederate government; developed Goodnight-Loving Trail 1866; killed by Indians.

Lowndes   **Alabama**
Hayneville   716 sq. mi.
11,299   13,473   12,658   13,253   12,897   15,417   18,018
January 20, 1857. *William Jones Lowndes (1782–1822)*. South Carolina House of Representatives 1806–10; captain of militia 1807; US representative 1811–22, resigned.

Lowndes   **Georgia**
Valdosta   496 sq. mi.
106,233   92,115   75,981   67,972   55,112   49,270   35,211
December 23, 1825. *William Jones Lowndes.**

Lowndes   **Mississippi**
Columbus   506 sq. mi.
59,779   61,586   59,308   57,304   49,700   46,639   37,852
January 30, 1830. *William Jones Lowndes.**

Lubbock   **Texas**
Lubbock   896 sq. mi.
278,831   242,628   222,636   211,651   179,295   156,271   101,048
August 21, 1876; organized March 10, 1891. *Thomas Saltus Lubbock (1817–62)*. Member of New Orleans Grays during Texas Revolution; Siege of Bexar 1835; strong secessionist; lieutenant colonel, Texas 8th Cavalry, 1861.

Lucas   **Iowa**
Charlton   431 sq. mi.
8,898   9,422   9,070   10,313   10,163   10,923   12,069
January 13, 1846; organized January 15, 1849; effective July 4, 1849. *Robert Lucas (1781–1853)*. Scioto County, Ohio, surveyor; major general Ohio Militia; Ohio House of Representatives 1808–09 and 1831–32; captain US Army 1812; Ohio Senate 1814–22 and 1824–30; governor of Ohio 1832–36; governor of Iowa Territory 1838–41.

Lucas   **Ohio**
Toledo   341 sq. mi.
441,815   455,054   462,361   471,741   484,370   456,931   395,551
June 20, 1835. *Robert Lucas.**

Luce   **Michigan**
Newberry   899 sq. mi.
6,631   7,024   5,763   6,659   6,789   7,827   8,147
March 1, 1887. *Cyrus Gray Luce (1824–1905)*. Michigan House of Representatives 1855–56; Michigan Senate 1865–68; Michigan Constitutional Convention 1867; governor of Michigan 1887–91.

Lumpkin   **Georgia**
Dahlonega   283 sq. mi.
29,966   21,016   14,573   10,762   8,728   7,241   6,574
December 3, 1832. *Wilson Lumpkin (1783–1870)*. Georgia House of Representatives 1808–12; Georgia Senate 1812–15; US representative 1815–17 and 1827–31; governor of Georgia 1831–35; US senator 1837–41.

Luna   **New Mexico**
Deming   2,965 sq. mi.
25,095   25,016   18,110   15,585   11,706   9,839   8,753
March 16, 1901. *Solomon Luna (1858–1912)*. Largest sheep rancher in the Southwest; richest man in New Mexico; New Mexico Constitutional Convention 1910.

Lunenburg   **Virginia**
Lunenburg   432 sq. mi.

12,914   13,146   11,419   12,124   11,687   12,523   14,116
April 1, 1746. *King George II, Duke of Brunswick-Lunenburg.* (See Georgetown, South Carolina.)

Luzerne   **Pennsylvania**
Wilkes-Barre   890 sq. mi.
320,918   319,250   328,149   343,079   342,301   346,972   392,241
September 25, 1786. *Anne Cesar, Chevalier de la Luzerne (1741–91).* French Army during Seven Years War; French minister to US 1779; raised money for American independence cause.

Lycoming   **Pennsylvania**
Williamsport   1,229 sq. mi.
116,111   120,044   118,710   118,416   113,296   109,367   101,249
April 13, 1795. *Lycoming Creek.* Corruption of Delaware word meaning "sandy creek."

Lyman   **South Dakota**
Kennebec   1,642 sq. mi.
3,755   3,895   3,638   3,864   4,060   4,428   4,572
January 8, 1873; organized May 21, 1893. *William P. Lyman (c1833–c1880).* Served with General Harney (see Harney, Oregon) in punitive expedition against Indians 1855; early settler in Dakota Territory; operated ferry and trading post on James River; Dakota territorial legislature 1873 at time of county's creation.

Lynchburg   **Virginia**
(Independent City)   49 sq. mi.
75,568   65,269   66,049   66,743   54,083   54,790   47,727
1895. *John Lynch (c1740–1820).* Built ferry landing on James River; city grew from the landing. (Associated counties: Bedford and Campbell.)

Lynn   **Texas**
Tahoka   892 sq. mi.
5,915   6,550   6,758   8,605   9,107   10,914   11,030
August 21, 1876; organized 1903. *William Linn (?–1836).* Private under Captain Blazeby's infantry company; killed at Alamo, March 6, 1836. Name is misspelled on the Alamo Monument.

Lyon   **Iowa**
Rock Rapids   588 sq. mi.
11,581   11,763   11,952   12,896   13,340   14,468   14,697
January 15, 1851, as Buncombe; name changed September 11, 1862; organized January 1, 1872. *Nathaniel Lyon (1818–61).* Graduated West Point 1841; Seminole War 1841–42; Mexican War 1846–47; captain 1851; commanded US arsenal at St. Louis; killed leading 1st Iowa Infantry at Battle of Wilson Creek, August 10, 1861.

Lyon   **Kansas**
Emporia   847 sq. mi.
33,690   35,935   34,732   35,108   32,071   26,928   26,576
August 30, 1855, as Breckenridge; organized February 17, 1857; name changed February 5, 1862. *Nathaniel Lyon.**

Lyon   **Kentucky**
Eddyville   214 sq. mi.
8,314   8,080   6,624   6,490   5,562   5,924   6,853
January 14, 1854. *Uncertain.* (1) *Chittenden Lyon (1787–1842);* Kentucky House of Representatives 1822–24; Kentucky Senate 1824–27; US representative 1827–35. (2) *Matthew Lyon (1749–1822);* Vermont legislature; US representative from Vermont 1797–1800, and from Kentucky 1803–11; father of Chittenden Lyon.

Lyon   **Minnesota**
Marshall   715 sq. mi.

25,857   25,425   24,789   25,207   24,273   22,655   22,253
November 2, 1869. *Nathaniel Lyon.**

Lyon   **Nevada**
Yerington   2,001 sq. mi.
51,980   34,501   20,001   13,594   8,221   6,143   3,679
November 25, 1861. *Uncertain.* (1) *Nathaniel Lyon.** (2) *Robert Lyon (?–?)*; Indian scout; Pyramid Lake Indian War 1860.

M

Mackinac   **Michigan**
Saint Ignance   1,022 sq. mi.
11,113   11,943   10,674   10,178   9,660   10,853   9,287
October 26, 1818, as Michilimackinac; name changed January 26, 1837. *Mackinac Island.* Ojibwa word for "place of the big injured [or lame] person"; name from a supposed extinct tribe applied to upper Great Lakes region.

Macomb   **Michigan**
Mount Clemens   479 sq. mi.
840,978   788,149   717,400   694,600   625,309   405,804   184,961
January 15, 1818. *Alexander Macomb (1782–1841).* Enlisted US Army 1799; appointed brigadier general 1814; commanded northern frontier on Lake Champlain, defeated British squadron at Plattsburgh 1814; received Thanks of Congress and gold metal for victory at Plattsburgh 1814; US Army commander in chief 1835–41.

Macon   **Alabama**
Tuskegee   609 sq. mi.
21,452   24,105   24,928   26,829   24,841   26,717   30,561
December 18, 1832. *Nathaniel Macon (1757–1837).* Revolutionary War; North Carolina Senate 1780–82 and 1784–85; US representative 1791–1815, speaker 1801–07; US senator 1815–28; president, North Carolina Constitutional Convention 1835.

Macon   **Georgia**
Oglethorpe   401 sq. mi.
14,740   14,074   13,114   14,003   12,933   13,170   14,213
December 14, 1837. *Nathaniel Macon.**

Macon   **Illinois**
Decatur   581 sq. mi.
110,768   114,706   117,206   131,375   125,010   118,257   98,853
January 19, 1829. *Nathaniel Macon.**

Macon   **Missouri**
Macon   801 sq. mi.
15,566   15,762   15,345   16,313   15,432   16,473   18,332
January 6, 1837. *Nathaniel Macon.**

Macon   **North Carolina**
Franklin   516 sq. mi.
33,922   29,811   23,499   20,178   15,788   14,935   16,174
1828. *Nathaniel Macon.**

Macon   **Tennessee**
Lafayette   307 sq. mi.
22,248   20,386   15,906   15,700   12,315   12,197   13,599
January 18, 1842. *Nathaniel Macon.**

Macoupin   **Illinois**
Carlinville   863 sq. mi.

| 47,765 | 49,019 | 47,679 | 49,384 | 44,557 | 43,524 | 44,210 |

January 17, 1829. *Macoupin Creek*. Miami word for "white potato" which grew in the area.

Madera   **California**
Madera   2,137 sq. mi.

| 150,865 | 123,109 | 88,090 | 63,116 | 41,519 | 40,468 | 36,964 |

March 11, 1893. *Town of Madera*. Spanish for "lumber" or "timber."

Madison   **Alabama**
Huntsville   802 sq. mi.

| 334,811 | 276,700 | 238,912 | 196,966 | 186,540 | 117,348 | 72,903 |

December 13, 1808. *James Madison (1751–1836)*. General Assembly of Virginia 1776; Continental Congress 1780–83 and 1786–88; federal Constitutional Convention 1787; co-author of *The Federalist* Papers 1787–88; US representative 1789–97; US secretary of state 1801–09; 4th president of the US 1809–17.

Madison   **Arkansas**
Huntsville   834 sq. mi.

| 15,717 | 14,243 | 11,618 | 11,373 | 9,453 | 9,068 | 11,734 |

September 30, 1836. *Madison County, Alabama*. Named for James Madison.* Early settlers were from Alabama.

Madison   **Florida**
Madison   696 sq. mi.

| 19,224 | 18,733 | 16,569 | 14,894 | 13,481 | 14,154 | 14,197 |

December 26, 1827. *James Madison.**

Madison   **Georgia**
Danielsville   282 sq. mi.

| 28,120 | 25,730 | 21,050 | 17,747 | 13,517 | 11,246 | 12,238 |

December 5, 1811. *James Madison.**

Madison   **Idaho**
Rexburg   469 sq. mi.

| 37,536 | 27,467 | 23,674 | 19,480 | 13,452 | 9,417 | 9,156 |

February 18, 1913. *James Madison.**

Madison   **Illinois**
Edwardsville   716 sq. mi.

| 269,282 | 258,941 | 249,238 | 247,691 | 250,934 | 224,689 | 182,307 |

September 14, 1812. *James Madison.**

Madison   **Indiana**
Anderson   452 sq. mi.

| 131,636 | 133,358 | 130,669 | 139,336 | 138,451 | 125,819 | 103,911 |

January 4, 1823; effective July 1, 1823. *James Madison.**

Madison   **Iowa**
Winterset   561 sq. mi.

| 15,679 | 14,019 | 12,483 | 12,597 | 11,558 | 12,295 | 13,131 |

January 13, 1846; organized February 19, 1849. *James Madison.**

Madison   **Kentucky**
Richmond   437 sq. mi.

| 82,916 | 70,872 | 57,508 | 53,352 | 42,730 | 33,482 | 31,179 |

December 15, 1785; effective August 1, 1788. *James Madison.**

Madison   **Louisiana**
Tallulah   624 sq. mi.

| 12,093 | 13,728 | 12,463 | 15,975 | 15,065 | 16,444 | 17,451 |

January 19, 1838. *James Madison.**

Madison   **Mississippi**
Canton   715 sq. mi.

| 95,203 | 74,674 | 53,794 | 41,613 | 29,737 | 32,904 | 33,860 |

January 29, 1828. *James Madison.**

Madison   **Missouri**
Fredericktown   494 sq. mi.

| 12,226 | 11,800 | 11,127 | 10,725 | 8,641 | 9,366 | 10,380 |

December 14, 1818. *James Madison.**

Madison   **Montana**
Virginia City   3,587 sq. mi.

| 7,691 | 6,851 | 5,989 | 5,448 | 5,014 | 5,211 | 5,998 |

February 2, 1865. *Madison River.* Named for James Madison* by Lewis and Clark 1805.

Madison   **Nebraska**
Madison   573 sq. mi.

| 34,876 | 35,226 | 32,655 | 31,382 | 27,402 | 25,145 | 24,338 |

January 26, 1856; organized April 6, 1868. *City of Madison, Wisconsin.* Named for James Madison* by settlers from Wisconsin.

Madison   **New York**
Wampsville   655 sq. mi.

| 73,442 | 69,441 | 69,120 | 65,150 | 62,864 | 54,635 | 46,214 |

March 21, 1806. *James Madison.**

Madison   **North Carolina**
Marshall   450 sq. mi.

| 20,764 | 19,635 | 16,953 | 16,827 | 16,003 | 17,217 | 20,522 |

January 27, 1851. *James Madison.**

Madison   **Ohio**
London   466 sq. mi.

| 43,435 | 40,213 | 37,068 | 33,004 | 28,318 | 26,454 | 22,300 |

February 16, 1810. *James Madison.**

Madison   **Tennessee**
Jackson   557 sq. mi.

| 98,294 | 91,837 | 77,982 | 74,546 | 65,727 | 60,655 | 60,128 |

November 7, 1821. *James Madison.**

Madison   **Texas**
Madisonville   466 sq. mi.

| 13,664 | 12,940 | 10,931 | 10,649 | 7,693 | 6,749 | 7,996 |

January 27, 1853; organized August 7, 1854. *James Madison.**

Madison   **Virginia**
Madison   321 sq. mi.

| 13,308 | 12,250 | 11,949 | 10,232 | 8,638 | 8,187 | 8,273 |

December 5, 1792; effective May 1, 1793. *James Madison.**

Magoffin   **Kentucky**
Salyersville   308 sq. mi.

| 13,333 | 13,332 | 13,077 | 13,515 | 10,443 | 11,156 | 13,839 |

February 22, 1860. *Beriah Magoffin (1815 85)*. Kentucky Senate 1850; governor of Kentucky 1859–62, resigned when legislature refused Kentucky's neutrality; Kentucky House of Representatives 1867–69.

Mahaska   **Iowa**
Oskaloosa   571 sq. mi.

| 22,381 | 22,335 | 21,522 | 22,867 | 22,177 | 23,602 | 24,672 |

February 17, 1843; organized February 5, 1844. *Mahaska (1784–1834)*. Iowa chief; signed treaties with US 1824, 1825 and 1830; killed by disgruntled Indian who Mahaska had turned over to US; name means "white cloud."

Mahnomen   **Minnesota**
Mahnomen   558 sq. mi.

| 5,413 | 5,190 | 5,044 | 5,535 | 5,638 | 6,341 | 7,059 |

December 27, 1906. *Descriptive*. Chippewa word for "wild rice" a major part of their diet.

Mahoning   **Ohio**
Youngstown   412 sq. mi.

| 238,823 | 257,555 | 264,806 | 289,487 | 303,424 | 300,840 | 257,629 |

February 16, 1846. *Mahoning River*. Delaware word for "salt lick."

Major   **Oklahoma**
Fairview   955 sq. mi.

| 7,527 | 7,545 | 8,055 | 8,772 | 7,529 | 7,808 | 10,279 |

July 16, 1907. *John C. Major (1863–1937)*. Oklahoma territorial legislature; Oklahoma Constitutional Convention 1907; Oklahoma legislature 1907–31.

Malheur   **Oregon**
Vale   9,888 sq. mi.

| 31,313 | 31,615 | 26,038 | 26,896 | 23,169 | 22,764 | 23,223 |

February 17, 1887. *Malheur River*. French for "misfortune" or "mishap;" named by French trappers who lost a cache of furs near the river.

Manassas   **Virginia**
(Independent City)   10 sq. mi.

| 37,821 | 35,135 | 27,957 | 15,438 | (a) | (a) | (a) |

May 1, 1975. *Manassas Junction*. Railroad hub named for Manassas Gap; from Mahahoac Indians. [(a) Part of Prince William County] (Associated county: Prince William)

Manassas Park   **Virginia**
(Independent City)   3 sq. mi.

| 14,273 | 10,290 | 6,734 | 6,524 | (a) | (a) | (a) |

June 1, 1975. *City of Manassas, Virginia*. [(a) Part of Prince William County] (Associated county: Prince William)

Manatee   **Florida**
Bradenton   743 sq. mi.

| 322,833 | 264,002 | 211,707 | 148,442 | 97,115 | 69,168 | 34,704 |

January 9, 1855. *Descriptive*. Refers to sea cows (manatees) in the area; Spanish corruption of Carib word for female breast, a distinguishing feature of manatees.

Manistee   **Michigan**
Manistee   542 sq. mi.

24,733   24,527   21,265   23,019   20,094   19,042   18,524
April 1, 1840; organized February 13, 1855. *Manistee River*. Ojibwa word possibly meaning "lost river" or "island in the river."

Manitowoc   **Wisconsin**
Manitowoc   589 sq. mi.
81,442   82,887   80,421   82,918   82,294   75,215   67,159
December 7, 1836; organized 1848. *Manitowoc River*. Algonquin word referring to "spirit world."

Marathon   **Wisconsin**
Wausau   1,545 sq. mi.
134,063   125,834   115,400   111,270   97,457   88,874   80,337
February 9, 1850. *Battle of Marathon*. Greeks defeated an invading Persian army 490 BCE.

Marengo   **Alabama**
Linden   977 sq. mi.
21,027   22,539   23,084   25,047   23,819   27,089   29,494
February 6, 1818. *Marengo, Italy*. Site of Napoleon's victory over Austria, June 14, 1800; county name chosen by early French settlers.

Maricopa   **Arizona**
Phoenix   9,200 sq. mi.
3,817,117 3,072,149 2,122,101   1,509,052   967,522   663,510   331,770
February 12, 1871. *Maricopa Indians*. Corruption of Spanish *mariposa* (butterfly) for their colorfully painted faces and hair.

Maries   **Missouri**
Vienna   527 sq. mi.
9,176   8,903   7,976   7,551   6,851   7,282   7,423
March 2, 1855. *Maries and Little Maries Rivers*. From French *marais* meaning "marsh" or "swamp."

Marin   **California**
San Rafael   520 sq. mi.
252,409   247,289   230,096   222,568   206,038   146,820   85,619
February 18, 1850. *Uncertain*. (1) *Marin Bay*; part of San Pablo Bay; from Spanish *Bahia de Nuestra Señora del Rosario la Marinera*. (2) *Marin (?–?)*; a San Rafael Mission Indian who lived on an island in Marin Bay.

Marinette   **Wisconsin**
Marinette   1,399 sq. mi.
41,749   43,384   40,548   39,314   35,810   34,660   35,748
February 27, 1879. *Town of Marinette*. Named for Marguerite Chevalier (1793–1865); daughter of Menominee chief; nick-named "Marinette" after Marie Antoinette; with husband, competed with American Fur Company.

Marion   **Alabama**
Hamilton   742 sq. mi.
30,776   31,214   29,830   30,041   23,788   21,837   27,264
February 13, 1818. *Francis Marion (1732–95)*. The "Swamp Fox"; lieutenant in French and Indian War 1761; brigadier general in American Revolution 1776–82; harassed British troops in South; South Carolina Senate 1782–90.

Marion   **Arkansas**
Yellville   597 sq. mi.
16,653   16,140   12,001   11,334   7,000   6,041   8,609
November 3, 1835, as Searcy; effective December 25, 1835; name changed September 29, 1836. *Francis Marion*.*

Marion   **Florida**
Ocala   1,585 sq. mi.

331,298   258,916   194,833   122,488   69,030   51,616   38,187
March 14, 1844. *Francis Marion.**

Marion   **Georgia**
Buena Vista   366 sq. mi.
8,742   7,144   5,590   5,297   5,099   5,477   6,521
December 14, 1827. *Francis Marion.**

Marion   **Illinois**
Salem   572 sq. mi.
39,437   41,691   41,561   43,523   38,986   39,349   41,700
January 24, 1823. *Francis Marion.**

Marion   **Indiana**
Indianapolis   396 sq. mi.
903,393   860,454   797,159   765,233   792,299   697,567   551,777
December 31, 1821; effective April 1, 1822. *Francis Marion.**

Marion   **Iowa**
Knoxville   555 sq. mi.
33,309   32,052   30,001   29,669   26,352   25,886   25,930
June 10, 1845. *Francis Marion.**

Marion   **Kansas**
Marion   944 sq. mi.
12,660   13,361   12,888   13,522   13,935   15,143   16,307
August 30, 1855; abolished 1857; recreated February 17, 1860; organized 1865. *Marion County, Ohio.* Named for Francis Marion.* Originally named for Francis Marion in 1855; at behest of a legislator from Ohio, the county was named to honor Marion County, Ohio, when the Kansas county was recreated in 1860.

Marion   **Kentucky**
Lebanon   343 sq. mi.
19,820   18,212   16,499   17,910   16,714   16,887   17,212
January 25, 1834. *Francis Marion.**

Marion   **Mississippi**
Columbia   542 sq. mi.
27,088   25,595   25,544   25,708   22,871   23,293   23,967
December 9, 1811. *Francis Marion.**

Marion   **Missouri**
Palmyra   437 sq. mi.
28,781   28,289   27,682   28,638   28,121   29,522   29,765
December 14, 1822; organized December 23, 1826. *Francis Marion.**

Marion   **Ohio**
Marion   404 sq. mi.
66,501   66,217   64,274   67,974   64,724   60,221   49,959
February 12, 1820; organized 1824. *Francis Marion.**

Marion   **Oregon**
Salem   1,182 sq. mi.
315,335   284,834   228,483   204,692   151,309   120,888   101,401
July 5, 1843, as Champoeg; name changed September 3, 1849. *Francis Marion.**

Marion   **South Carolina**
Marion   489 sq. mi.

33,062	35,466	33,899	34,179	30,270	32,014	33,110

March 12, 1785, as Liberty; name changed January 1, 1800; designated as county April 16, 1868. *Francis Marion.**

Marion   **Tennessee**
Jasper   498 sq. mi.

28,237	27,776	24,860	24,416	20,577	21,036	20,520

November 20, 1817. *Francis Marion.**

Marion   **Texas**
Jefferson   381 sq. mi.

10,546	10,941	9,984	10,360	8,517	8,049	10,172

February 8, 1860. *Francis Marion.**

Marion   **West Virginia**
Fairmont   309 sq. mi.

56,418	56,598	57,249	65,789	61,356	63,717	71,521

January 14, 1842. *Francis Marion.**

Mariposa   **California**
Mariposa   1,449 sq. mi.

18,251	17,130	14,302	11,108	6,015	5,064	5,145

February 18, 1850. *Mariposa River*. Spanish for "butterfly."

Marlboro   **South Carolina**
Bennettsville   480 sq. mi.

28,933	28,818	29,361	31,634	27,151	28,529	31,766

March 12, 1785; converted to judicial district January 1, 1800; redesignated as county April 16, 1868. *John Churchill, Duke of Marlboro (1650–1722)*. Supported William III during Glorious Revolution 1688; made Earl of Marlboro 1689; elevated by Queen Anne to Duke of Marlboro, a title rarely bestowed outside of royalty 1702; victorious at Blenheim (1704), Ramillies (1706), and Malplaquet (1709) during War of Spanish Succession against Napoleon.

Marquette   **Michigan**
Marquette   1,808 sq. mi.

67,077	64,634	70,887	74,101	64,686	56,154	47,654

March 9, 1843; organized December 1, 1851. *Jacques Marquette (1637–75)*. French explorer and Jesuit missionary; mission at Sault Sainte Marie was first settlement in Michigan 1668; accompanied Louis Joliet in exploring Mississippi River as far south as the Arkansas River; returned by way of Illinois River thereby opening the best water route between the Great Lakes and the Mississippi 1673–74.

Marquette   **Wisconsin**
Montello   456 sq. mi.

15,404	15,832	12,321	11,672	8,865	8,516	8,839

December 7, 1836; organized 1848. *Jacques Marquette.**

Marshall   **Alabama**
Guntersville   566 sq. mi.

93,019	82,231	70,832	65,622	54,211	48,018	45,090

January 9, 1836. *John Marshall (1755–1835)*. Officer in Virginia Militia 1777–81; Virginia House of Burgesses 1780 and 1782–88; federal Constitutional Convention 1788; US commissioner to France 1797–98; US representative 1799–1800; US secretary of state 1800; chief justice of the US 1801–35.

Marshall   **Illinois**
Lacon   387 sq. mi.

| 12,640 | 13,180 | 12,846 | 14,479 | 13,302 | 13,334 | 13,025 |

January 19, 1839. *John Marshall.**

Marshall   **Indiana**
Plymouth   444 sq. mi.

| 47,051 | 45,128 | 42,182 | 39,155 | 34,986 | 32,443 | 29,468 |

February 7, 1835; organized February 4, 1836; effective April 1, 1836. *John Marshall.**

Marshall   **Iowa**
Marshalltown   573 sq. mi.

| 40,648 | 39,311 | 38,276 | 41,652 | 41,076 | 37,984 | 35,611 |

January 13, 1846; organized October 1, 1849. *John Marshall.**

Marshall   **Kansas**
Marysville   900 sq. mi.

| 10,177 | 10,965 | 11,705 | 12,787 | 13,139 | 15,598 | 17,926 |

August 25, 1855. *Francis J. Marshall (1816–95).* Operated ferry across Big Blue River 1850; opened trading post for California emigrants 1851; Kansas territorial legislature 1855.

Marshall   **Kentucky**
Benton   301 sq. mi.

| 31,448 | 30,125 | 27,205 | 25,637 | 20,381 | 16,736 | 13,387 |

February 12, 1842. *John Marshall.**

Marshall   **Minnesota**
Warren   1,775 sq. mi.

| 9,439 | 10,155 | 10,993 | 13,027 | 13,060 | 14,262 | 16,125 |

February 25, 1879; organized March 11, 1881. *William Rainey Marshall (1825–96).* Surveyor; Wisconsin legislature 1848; banker 1855–57; established newspaper in St. Paul 1861; lieutenant colonel to brevet brigadier general 1862–65; governor of Minnesota 1866–70.

Marshall   **Mississippi**
Holly Springs   706 sq. mi.

| 37,144 | 34,993 | 30,361 | 29,296 | 24,027 | 24,503 | 25,106 |

February 9, 1836. *John Marshall.**

Marshall   **Oklahoma**
Madill   371 sq. mi.

| 15,840 | 13,184 | 10,829 | 10,550 | 7,682 | 7,263 | 8,177 |

July 16, 1907. *Elizabeth Ellen Marshall Henshaw (c1834–94).* Mother of George Henshaw, a delegate to the Oklahoma Constitutional Convention; Henshaw wanted the new county to be named after his mother's side of the family, which had links to John Marshall.*

Marshall   **South Dakota**
Britton   838 sq. mi.

| 4,656 | 4,576 | 4,844 | 5,404 | 5,965 | 6,663 | 7,835 |

March 10, 1885. *Marshall Vincent (?–?).* Homesteaded in Dakota Territory 1881; Day County commissioner when Marshall County was created from Day County.

Marshall   **Tennessee**
Lewisburg   375 sq. mi.

| 30,617 | 26,767 | 21,539 | 19,968 | 17,319 | 16,859 | 17,768 |

February 20, 1836. *John Marshall.**

Marshall   **West Virginia**
Moundsville   305 sq. mi.

33,107   35,519   37,356   41,608   37,598   38,041   36,893
March 12, 1835. *John Marshall.* *

Martin   **Florida**
Stuart   543 sq. mi.
146,318   126,731   100,900   64,014   28,035   16,932   7,807
May 30, 1925. *John Wellborn Martin (1884–1958)*. Mayor of Jacksonville 1917–24; governor of Florida 1925–29.

Martin   **Indiana**
Shoals   336 sq. mi.
10,334   10,369   10,369   11,001   10,969   10,608   10,678
January 17, 1820. *Uncertain.* (1) *Thomas Martin (?–1819)*; resident of Newport, Kentucky; major in continental army. (2) *Jeremiah Martin (?–?)*; Kentucky volunteer in War of 1812; Battle of the Thames. (3) *Tomas E. Martin (?–?)*; early settler.

Martin   **Kentucky**
Inez   230 sq. mi.
12,929   12,578   12,526   13,925   9,377   10,201   11,677
March 10, 1870. *John Preston Martin (1811–62)*. Kentucky House of Representatives 1841–43; US representative 1845–47; Kentucky Senate 1855–59.

Martin   **Minnesota**
Fairmont   712 sq. mi.
20,840   21,802   22,914   24,687   24,316   26,986   25,655
May 23, 1857; organized December 16, 1857. *Uncertain.* (1) *Henry Martin (1829–1908)*; Connecticut bank commissioner 1845–46; resident of Minnesota Territory 1856–57. (2) *Morgan L. Martin (1805–87)*; Wisconsin territorial delegate to Congress 1845–46; introduced legislation to create Minnesota Territory 1846. (3) *Martin McLeod* (see McLeod, Minnesota).

Martin   **North Carolina**
Williamston   461 sq. mi.
24,505   25,593   25,078   25,948   24,730   27,139   27,938
March 2, 1774. *Alexander Martin (1740–1807)*; governor of North Carolina 1782–85 and 1789–92; US senator 1793–98. Originally named for Josiah Martin (1737–86); officer in British Army 1757–69; royal governor of North Carolina 1771–75; forced to flee and rejoined British Army during American Revolution; served with Cornwallis in capture of Charleston 1780.

Martin   **Texas**
Stanton   915 sq. mi.
4,799   4,746   4,956   4,684   4,774   5,068   5,541
August 21, 1876; organized November 14, 1884. *Wyly Martin (1776–1842)*. 3rd lieutenant to captain 1813–23; resigned after killing a man in a duel; major in Texas Army; resigned after dispute with Sam Houston 1836; Republic of Texas legislature 1841.

Martinsville   **Virginia**
(Independent City)   11 sq. mi.
13,821   15,416   16,162   18,149   19,653   18,798   17,251
1928. *Joseph Martin (1740–1808)*. Early settler 1792. (Associated county: Henry.)

Mason   **Illinois**
Havana   539 sq. mi.
14,666   16,038   16,269   19,492   16,161   15,193   15,326
January 20, 1841, *Mason County, Kentucky*. Early settlers were from Kentucky.

Mason   **Kentucky**
Maysville   240 sq. mi.
17,490   16,800   16,666   17,765   17,273   18,454   18,486

November 5, 1788; effective May 1, 1789. *George Mason (1725–92)*. Virginia House of Burgesses 1759; Virginia Convention 1775; authored Virginia Declaration of Rights 1776; Virginia Assembly 1776–80 and 1786–88; federal Constitutional Convention 1787.

Mason   **Michigan**
Ludington   495 sq. mi.

28,705	28,274	25,537	26,365	22,612	21,929	20,474

April 1, 1840, as Notipekago; name changed March 8, 1843. *Stevens Thomson Mason (1811–43)*. Secretary and acting governor of Michigan Territory 1831–35; governor of Michigan Territory 1835–37; governor of Michigan 1837–40.

Mason   **Texas**
Mason   929 sq. mi.

4,012	3,738	3,423	3,683	3,356	3,780	4,945

January 22, 1858; organized August 2, 1858. *Fort Mason*. Established on Comanche Creek 1851; abandoned 1859. Name of uncertain origin: (1) George T. Mason (?–1846), 2nd lieutenant, 2nd US Dragoons, died near Brownsville in skirmish that precipitated Mexican War, April 25, 1846; (2) Richard B. Mason (1797–1850), Black Hawk War, brevet brigadier general in Mexican War, military governor of California 1847–49.

Mason   **Washington**
Shelton   959 sq. mi.

60,699	49,405	38,341	31,184	20,918	16,251	15,022

March 13, 1854, as Sawamish; name changed January 8, 1864. *Charles H. Mason (1830–59)*. Secretary of Washington Territory; acting governor during Yakima War 1855–58.

Mason   **West Virginia**
Point Pleasant   431 sq. mi.

27,324	25,957	25,178	27,045	24,306	24,459	23,537

January 2, 1804. *George Mason.**

Massac   **Illinois**
Metropolis   237 sq. mi.

15,429	15,161	14,752	14,990	13,889	14,341	13,594

February 8, 1843. *Fort Massac*. Grew from French trading post on Ohio River 1702. Name is of uncertain origin: (1) Most likely for Claude Louis, Marquis de Massaic (1686–1770), French minister of marine and colonies 1758, ordered conversion of the trading post to a fort 1758; (2) two Frenchmen associated with the fort whose names are similar to "Massac"; (3) corruption of French *massacre* for supposed slaughter of French soldiers by Indians.

Matagorda   **Texas**
Bay City   1,100 sq. mi.

36,702	37,957	36,928	37,828	27,913	25,744	21,559

March 17, 1836; organized 1837. *Matagorda Municipality*. Named for Matagorda Bay; Spanish for "canebrake."

Matanuska-Susitna   **Alaska**
Palmer   24,608 sq. mi.

88,995	59,322	39,683	17,816	6,509	5,188	(a)

January 1964. "Matanuska" from Russian *matanooski* for "Copper River people"; "Susitna" from Russian rendering of Tanaina name for "sandy river." [(a) Part of 3rd Judicial District.]

Mathews   **Virginia**
Mathews   86 sq. mi.

8,978	9,207	8,348	7,995	7,168	7,121	7,148

December 16, 1790. *Thomas Mathews (?–?)*; Captain in Continental Army; speaker, Virginia House of Delegates 1788–94.

Maui   **Hawaii**
Wailuku   1,162 sq. mi.

154,834   128,094   100,374   70,847   45,984   42,576   48,179
July 1905. *Island of Maui*. Named for Polynesian demi-god who brought the land out of the sea and separated the sky from the earth.

Maury   **Tennessee**
Columbia   613 sq. mi.
80,956   69,498   54,812   51,095   43,376   41,699   40,368
November 16, 1807. *Abram P. Maury (1766–1825)*. Tennessee Senate 1805 and 1819; commissioner to sell Cherokee lands.

Maverick   **Texas**
Eagle Pass   1,279 sq. mi.
54,258   47,297   36,378   31,398   18,093   14,508   12,292
February 2, 1856; organized July 13, 1871. *Samuel Augustus Maverick (1803–70)*. Signer, Texas Declaration of Independence 1836; Republic of Texas legislature 1843. Maverick did not brand his cattle and "maverick" became a synonym for unbranded cattle and "nonconformist."

Mayes   **Oklahoma**
Pryor   655 sq. mi.
41,259   38,369   33,366   32,261   23,302   20,073   19,743
July 16, 1907. *Uncertain*. (1) *Joel B. Mayes (1833–91)*; Cherokee; private in 1st Confederate Indian Brigade; principal chief of Cherokee Nation 1887–91. (2) *Samuel Houston Mayes (1845–1927)*; principal chief of Cherokee Nation 1895–99.

McClain   **Oklahoma**
Purcell   571 sq. mi.
34,506   27,740   22,795   20,291   14,157   12,740   14,681
July 16, 1907. *Charles M. McClain (1840–1915)*. Enlisted in Confederate Army 1861; moved to Chickasaw Nation, Indian Territory (Oklahoma) 1885; Oklahoma Constitutional Convention 1906–07.

McCone   **Montana**
Circle   2,643 sq. mi.
1,734   1,977   2,276   2,702   2,875   3,321   3,258
February 20, 1919. *George James McCone (1853–1929)*. Cattle and sheep rancher; Montana legislature 1900; Montana Senate; lobbied for creation of county.

McCook   **South Dakota**
Salem   574 sq. mi.
5,518   5,832   5,688   6,444   7,246   8,268   8,828
January 8, 1873; organized June 15, 1878. *Edwin Stanton McCook (1837–73)*. Graduated from Annapolis; Union Army, captain to brevet brigadier general 1861–64; secretary of Dakota Territory 1872–73; killed in saloon fight.

McCormick   **South Carolina**
McCormick   359 sq. mi.
10,233   9,958   8,868   7,797   7,955   8,629   9,577
February 19, 1916. *Cyrus Hall McCormick (1809–84)*. Perfected reaping machine 1834; owned large land holdings in county.

McCracken   **Kentucky**
Paducah   249 sq. mi.
65,565   65,514   62,879   61,310   58,281   57,306   49,137
December 17, 1824; organized 1825. *Virgil McCracken (?–1813)*. Kentucky legislature 1810–11; raised company of soldiers in War of 1812; captured and massacred at River Raisin.

McCreary   **Kentucky**
Whitley City   427 sq. mi.
18,306   17,080   15,603   15,634   12,548   12,463   16,660

March 12, 1912. *James B. McCreary (1838–1918).* Confederate Army, lieutenant colonel 1863; Kentucky House of Representatives 1869–73, speaker 1871 and 1873; governor of Kentucky 1875–79 and 1911–1915; US Representative 1885–97; US senator 1903–09.

McCulloch   **Texas**
Brady   1,066 sq. mi.

| 8,283 | 8,205 | 8,778 | 8,735 | 8,571 | 8,815 | 11,701 |

August 27, 1856; organized 1876. *Benjamin McCulloch (1811–62).* Battle of San Jacinto 1836; Texas Republic Congress 1839; Mexican War, Battles of Monterrey, Buena Vista, and Mexico City; US marshal 1853; brigadier general, Confederate Army; killed at Pea Ridge, March 7, 1862.

McCurtain   **Oklahoma**
Idabel   1,850 sq. mi.

| 33,151 | 34,402 | 33,433 | 36,151 | 28,642 | 25,851 | 31,588 |

July 16, 1907. *Green McCurtain (1848–1910).* Choctaw National Council 1874–80; treasurer, Choctaw Nation 1888–92; Choctaw national Senate 1892–94; chief, Choctaw Nation 1896–1900 and 1902–04.

McDonald   **Missouri**
Pineville   539 sq. mi.

| 23,083 | 21,681 | 16,938 | 14,917 | 12,357 | 11,798 | 14,144 |

March 3, 1849. *Alexander McDonald (?–?).* American Revolution; sergeant under General Francis Marion. One of three counties, with Jasper and Newton, in southwestern Missouri named for South Carolina soldiers who served with General Marion.

McDonough   **Illinois**
Macomb   589 sq. mi.

| 32,612 | 32,913 | 35,244 | 37,467 | 36,653 | 28,928 | 28,199 |

January 25, 1826; organized 1830. *Thomas McDonough (1783–1825).* Navy midshipman 1800; served on *Constellation* and *Philadelphia*; fought Barbary pirates 1801–05; captain, War of 1812; victorious in Battle of Lake Champlain 1814; received gold medal from Congress and an estate from Vermont legislature.

McDowell   **North Carolina**
Marion   441 sq. mi.

| 44,996 | 42,151 | 35,681 | 35,135 | 30,648 | 26,742 | 25,720 |

December 19, 1842. *Joseph McDowell (1756–1801).* Fought Cherokees 1776; major, North Carolina Militia, in command at Battle of King's Mountain 1780; North Carolina House of Commons 1785–88; federal Constitutional Convention 1788–89; North Carolina Senate 1791–95; US representative 1797–99.

McDowell   **West Virginia**
Welch   533 sq. mi.

| 22,113 | 27,329 | 35,233 | 49,899 | 50,666 | 71,358 | 98,887 |

February 20, 1858. *James McDowell (1795–1851).* Virginia House of Delegates 1830–35 and 1838; governor of Virginia 1842–46; US representative 1846–51.

McDuffie   **Georgia**
Thomson   257 sq. mi.

| 21,875 | 21,231 | 20,119 | 18,546 | 15,276 | 12,627 | 11,443 |

October 18, 1870. *George McDuffie (1790–1851).* Native of Georgia; South Carolina House of Representatives 1818–20; US representative from South Carolina 1821–34; governor of South Carolina 1834–36; US senator 1842–46.

McHenry   **Illinois**
Woodstock   603 sq. mi.

| 308,760 | 260,077 | 183,241 | 147,897 | 111,555 | 84,210 | 50,656 |

January 16, 1836; organized 1837. *William McHenry (?–1835).* War of 1812; Illinois Constitutional Convention 1818; major, Illinois Mounted Volunteers in Black Hawk War 1832; Illinois legislature 1832–35.

McHenry   **North Dakota**
Towner   1,874 sq. mi.
5,395   5,987   6,528   7,858   8,977   11,099   12,556
January 4, 1873; organized October 15, 1884. *James McHenry (?–?)*. Early settler in southern Dakota Territory; Dakota territorial legislature 1865; Vermillion postmaster 1867–69.

McIntosh   **Georgia**
Darien   424 sq. mi.
14,333   10,847   8,634   8,046   7,371   6,364   6,008
December 19, 1793. *Uncertain*. (1) *McIntosh family*; emigrated from Scotland to Georgia 1736. (2) *John Mohr McIntosh (1701–?)*; led family from Scotland to Georgia 1736; father of Lachlan McIntosh and grandfather of John McIntosh. (3) *Lachlan McIntosh (1727–1806)*; brigadier general on Washington's staff; established outposts that bolstered US claims to western lands following American Revolution; suspended from service for killing Button Gwinnett in a duel 1777 (see Gwinnett, Georgia); vindicated and promoted to major general. (4) *John McIntosh (?–1826)*; colonel during Revolutionary War and War of 1812.

McIntosh   **North Dakota**
Ashley   975 sq. mi.
2,089   3,390   4,021   4,800   5,545   6,702   7,590
March 9, 1883; organized October 4, 1884. *Edward H. McIntosh (c1822–1901)*. Dakota territorial legislature 1883; reportedly held up legislation creating counties until one was named for him.

McIntosh   **Oklahoma**
Eufaula   619 sq. mi.
20,252   19,456   16,779   15,562   12,472   12,371   17,829
July 16, 1907. *McIntosh Family*. Creek leaders; descendants of John Mohr McIntosh (see McIntosh [2], Georgia). Family includes: (1) William McIntosh (c1775–1825); tribal leader when Creeks were removed from Georgia; persuaded Lower Creeks (Cowetas) to cede lands to US; murdered by rival Creeks; (2) Chilly McIntosh (c1800–75); moved group of Creeks from Georgia to west of Mississippi River; 2nd Creek Regiment of volunteers in Confederate Army; (3) Roley McIntosh (c1790–?); led group of Creeks to Arkansas River; chief of Lower Creeks 1828–29; (4) Daniel N. McIntosh (1822–96); colonel, 1st Creek Regiment of mounted volunteers in Confederate Army.

McKean   **Pennsylvania**
Smethport   979 sq. mi.
43,450   45,936   47,131   50,635   51,915   54,517   56,607
March 26, 1804; organized 1826. *Thomas McKean (1734–1817)*. Delaware assembly 1752–59; Continental Congress 1774–83; signer, Declaration of Independence 1776; signer of Articles of Confederation 1778; Pennsylvania chief justice 1777–79; governor of Pennsylvania 1799–1808.

McKenzie   **North Dakota**
Watford City   2,760 sq. mi.
6,360   5,737   6,383   7,132   6,127   7,296   6,849
March 9, 1883; abolished 1896; recreated May 24, 1901; organized April 20, 1905. *Alexander McKenzie (1851–1922)*. Northern Pacific construction gang leader 1867–72; Burleigh County sheriff 1876–85; instrumental in moving Dakota territorial capital from Yankton to Bismarck.

McKinley   **New Mexico**
Gallup   5,450 sq. mi.
71,492   74,798   60,686   56,449   43,208   37,209   27,451
February 23, 1899. *William McKinley (1843–1901)*. Private to brevet major in Union Army 1861–65; US representative from Ohio 1877–84 and 1885–91; governor of Ohio 1892–96; 25th President of US 1897–1901; assassinated September 6, 1901; died September 14, 1901.

McLean   **Illinois**
Bloomington   1,183 sq. mi.

| 169,572 | 150,433 | 129,180 | 119,149 | 104,389 | 83,877 | 76,577 |

December 25, 1830. *John McLean (1791–1830)*. First US representative from Illinois 1817–18; Illinois House of Representatives 1820 and 1826–28; US senator 1829–30.

McLean   **Kentucky**
Calhoun   252 sq. mi.

| 9,531 | 9,938 | 9,628 | 10,090 | 9,062 | 9,355 | 10,021 |

February 6, 1854. *Alney McLean (1779–1841)*. Kentucky House of Representatives 1812–13; captain, War of 1812; US representative 1815–17 and 1819–21; Kentucky district judge 1821–41.

McLean   **North Dakota**
Washburn   2,111 sq. mi.

| 8,962 | 9,311 | 10,457 | 12,383 | 11,251 | 14,030 | 18,824 |

March 8, 1883; organized November 1, 1883. *John A. McLean (1849–1916)*. Construction supplier for Northern Pacific Railroad; mayor of Bismarck 1883; delegate to Washington to open Black Hills to mining.

McLennan   **Texas**
Waco   1,037 sq. mi.

| 234,906 | 213,517 | 189,123 | 170,755 | 147,553 | 150,091 | 130,194 |

January 22, 1850; organized August 5, 1850. *Neil McLennan (1777–1867)*. Surveyor; arrived in Texas 1835; settled near Waco 1845.

McLeod   **Minnesota**
Glencoe   491 sq. mi.

| 36,651 | 34,898 | 32,030 | 29,657 | 27,662 | 24,401 | 22,198 |

March 1, 1856. *Martin McLeod (1813–60)*. Fur trader; managed trading posts in western Wisconsin Territory (Minnesota); first Minnesota territorial legislature 1849–53.

McMinn   **Tennessee**
Athens   430 sq. mi.

| 52,266 | 49,015 | 42,383 | 41,878 | 35,462 | 33,662 | 32,024 |

November 13, 1819. *Joseph McMinn (1758–1824)*. Continental Army 1776; Tennessee Constitutional Convention 1796; Tennessee Senate 1796–1812, speaker 1805–11; governor of Tennessee 1815–21.

McMullen   **Texas**
Tilden   1,139 sq. mi.

| 707 | 851 | 817 | 789 | 1,095 | 1,116 | 1,187 |

February 1, 1858; organized 1877. *John McMullen (1785–1853)*. Established colony of Irish immigrants in Mexican Texas 1828; provisional government of Republic of Texas 1836; murdered January 20, 1853.

McNairy   **Tennessee**
Selmer   563 sq. mi.

| 26,075 | 24,653 | 22,422 | 22,525 | 18,396 | 18,085 | 20,390 |

October 8, 1823. *John McNairy (1762–1837)*. Judge, Territory South of the Ohio (Tennessee) 1790; Tennessee Constitutional Convention 1796; US judge in Tennessee 1797–1834.

McPherson   **Kansas**
McPherson   898 sq. mi.

| 29,180 | 29,554 | 27,268 | 26,855 | 24,778 | 24,285 | 23,670 |

February 26, 1867; organized March 1, 1870. *James Birdseye McPherson (1828–64)*. Graduated West Point 1849; 2nd lieutenant of engineers 1853; rose to brigadier general 1858–63; killed at Atlanta, July 22, 1864.

McPherson   **Nebraska**
Tryon   859 sq. mi.

| 539 | 533 | 546 | 593 | 623 | 735 | 825 |

March 31, 1887. *James Birdseye McPherson.**

McPherson   **South Dakota**
Leola   1,137 sq. mi.

2,459	2,904	3,228	4,027	5,022	5,821	7,071

January 8, 1873; organized March 6, 1884. *James Birdseye McPherson.**

Meade   **Kansas**
Meade   978 sq. mi.

4,575	4,631	4,247	4,788	4,912	5,505	5,710

March 20, 1873; abolished February 21, 1883; recreated March 7, 1885; organized November 4, 1885. *George Gordon Meade (1815–72)*. Graduated West Point 1835; Seminole War 1836; Mexican War, Battles of Reseca, Palo Alto, and Monterrey 1846; captain 1846; brigadier and major general of Union volunteers 1861–62; wounded at Glendale 1862; commanded Army of the Potomac; victorious at Gettysburg 1863.

Meade   **Kentucky**
Brandenburg   305 sq. mi.

28,602	26,349	24,170	22,854	18,796	18,938	9,422

December 17, 1823. *James M. Meade (?–1813)*. Battle of Tippecanoe 1811; captain 1812; killed at River Raisin, January 22, 1813.

Meade   **South Dakota**
Sturgis   3,471 sq. mi.

25,434	24,253	21,878	20,717	16,618	12,044	11,516

February 7, 1889. *Fort Meade*. Established in Black Hills 1878; named for George Gordon Meade.*

Meagher   **Montana**
White Sulphur Springs 2,392 sq. mi.

1,891	1,932	1,819	2,154	2,122	2,616	2,079

November 16, 1867. *Thomas Francis Meagher (1823–67)*. Banished by British to Tasmania for supporting Irish independence 1849; escaped to US 1852; brigadier general of Union volunteers 1862; secretary of Montana Territory 1865; acting governor of Montana Territory 1865–66; believed to have fallen from a steamboat on the Missouri River and drowned.

Mecklenburg   **North Carolina**
Charlotte   524 sq. mi.

919,628	695,454	511,433	404,270	354,656	272,111	197,052

1762; effective February 1, 1763. *Charlotte Sophia of Mecklenburg-Sterlitz*. (See Charlotte, Virginia.)

Mecklenburg   **Virginia**
Boydton   625 sq. mi.

32,727	32,380	29,241	29,444	29,426	31,428	33,497

November 27, 1764; effective March 1, 1765. *Charlotte Sophia of Mecklenburg-Sterlitz*. (See Charlotte, Virginia.)

Mecosta   **Michigan**
Big Rapids   555 sq. mi.

42,798	40,553	37,308	36,961	27,992	21,051	18,968

April 1, 1840; organized February 11, 1859. *Mecosta (?–?)*. Pottawatomie chief; signed treaty with US 1836; name is believed to refer to the word "bear" in some way.

Medina   **Ohio**
Medina   421 sq. mi.

172,332	151,095	122,354	113,150	82,717	65,315	40,417

February 18, 1812; organized 1818; *Medina, Saudi Arabia*. Holy city of Islam; association with Ohio is uncertain.

Medina   **Texas**
Hondo   1,325 sq. mi.

46,006	39,403	27,312	23,164	20,249	18,904	17,013

February 12, 1848; organized August 7, 1848. *Medina River*. Named for Pedro Medina (?–?), Spanish engineer and scholar; explorer Alonzo de León used charts published by Medina in mapping route through Texas, 1689.

Meeker	**Minnesota**					
Litchfield	608 sq. mi.					
23,300	22,644	20,846	20,594	18,810	18,887	18,966

February 23, 1856; organized 1866. *Bradley B. Meeker (1813–73)*. Supreme Court of Minnesota Territory 1849–53; Minnesota Constitutional Convention 1857.

Meigs	**Ohio**					
Pomeroy	430 sq. mi.					
23,770	23,072	22,987	23,641	19,799	22,159	23,227

January 21, 1819. *Return Jonathon Meigs (1764–1825)*. Indian fighter; Northwest Territory judge 1802–03; chief justice, Ohio Supreme Court 1803–04; judge, Louisiana Territory 1805–06; judge, Michigan Territory 1807–08; US senator from Ohio 1808–10; governor of Ohio 1810–14; US postmaster general 1814–23.

Meigs	**Tennessee**					
Decatur	195 sq. mi.					
11,753	11,086	8,033	7,431	5,219	5,160	6,080

January 20, 1836. *Return Jonathon Meigs*.*

Mellette	**South Dakota**					
White River	1,307 sq. mi.					
2,048	2,083	2,137	2,249	2,420	2,664	3,046

March 9, 1909; organized May 25, 1911. *Arthur Calvin Mellette (1842–96)*. Private, Company M, 9th Indiana Infantry; Indiana House of Representatives 1871–75; editor, *Muncie Times*; governor of Dakota Territory 1889; first governor of South Dakota 1889–93.

Menard	**Illinois**					
Petersburg	314 sq. mi.					
12,705	12,486	11,164	11,700	9,685	9,248	9,639

February 15, 1839. *Pierre Menard (1766–1844)*. Fur trader; lieutenant colonel, Indiana Militia; Indiana territorial legislature 1803–09; first lieutenant governor of Illinois 1818–22.

Menard	**Texas**					
Menard	902 sq. mi.					
2,242	2,360	2,252	2,346	2,646	2,964	4,175

January 22, 1858; organized May 8, 1871. *Michel Branaman Menard (1803–56)*. French Canadian trader; signer, Texas Declaration of Independence 1836; Republic of Texas legislature 1840–42.

Mendocino	**California**					
Ukiah	3,506 sq. mi.					
87,841	86,265	80,345	66,738	51,101	51,059	40,854

February 18, 1850; organized 1859. *Cape Mendocino*. Origin of name is of uncertain. (1) Antonio de Mendoza (1490–1552); first Viceroy of New Spain (Mexico) 1535–49; sent Coronado Expedition to Southwest US 1540–42; Viceroy of Peru 1551–52. (2) Lorenzo Suárez de Mendoza (c1518–83); Viceroy of New Spain 1580–83. Mendocino is adjectival form of Mendoza.

Menifee	**Kentucky**					
Frenchburg	204 sq. mi.					
6,306	6,566	5,092	5,117	4,050	4,276	4,789

March 10, 1869. *Richard Hickman Menifee (1809–41)*. Kentucky Commonwealth attorney 1832; Kentucky House of Representatives 1836–37; US representative 1837–39.

Menominee	**Michigan**					
Menominee	1,044 sq. mi.					
24,029	25,326	24,920	26,201	24,587	24,685	25,299

March 15, 1861, as Bleeker; name changed March 19, 1863. *Menominee River*. Named for Menominee Indians; Algonquin linguistic group; lived in northern Michigan and Wisconsin; name is Ojibwa for "wild rice people."

Menominee   **Wisconsin**
Keshena   358 sq. mi.
4,232   4,562   3,890   3,373   2,607   (a)   (a)
May 1, 1961. *Menominee Indians*. (See Menominee, Michigan.) County is coextensive with Menominee Reservation. [(a) Part of Oconto and Shawano Counties.]

Merced   **California**
Merced   1,935 sq. mi.
255,793   210,554   178,403   134,560   104,629   90,446   69,780
April 19, 1855. *Merced River*. Named *El Rio de Nuestra Señora de la Merced* (Our Lady of Mercy) by Spanish explorer Gabriel Moraga 1806.

Mercer   **Illinois**
Aledo   561 sq. mi.
16,434   16,957   17,290   19,286   17,294   17,149   17,374
January 13, 1825; organized 1835. *Hugh Mercer (1726–77)*. Physician; captain in Braddock's expedition to Fort Duquesne 1756; colonel, 3rd Battalion 1759; Virginia Militia 1775–76; colonel and brigadier general 1776; mortally wounded at Princeton, January 3, 1777.

Mercer   **Kentucky**
Harrodsburg   249 sq. mi.
21,331   20,817   19,148   19,011   15,960   14,596   14,643
August 1, 1785. *Hugh Mercer*.*

Mercer   **Missouri**
Princeton   454 sq. mi.
3,785   3,757   3,723   4,685   4,910   5,750   7,235
February 14, 1845. *Hugh Mercer*.*

Mercer   **New Jersey**
Trenton   225 sq. mi.
366,513   350,761   325,824   307,863   303,968   266,392   229,781
February 22, 1838. *Hugh Mercer*.*

Mercer   **North Dakota**
Stanton   1,043 sq. mi.
8,424   8,644   9,808   9,404   6,175   6,805   8,686
January 14, 1875; organized August 4, 1884. *William Henry Harrison Mercer (1844–1901)*. Union Army; early settler in Bismarck; Burleigh County commissioner.

Mercer   **Ohio**
Celina   462 sq. mi.
40,814   40,924   39,443   38,334   35,265   32,559   28,311
February 12, 1820; organized 1824. *Hugh Mercer*.*

Mercer   **Pennsylvania**
Mercer   673 sq. mi.
116,638   120,293   121,003   128,299   127,175   127,519   111,954
March 12, 1800; organized 1803. *Hugh Mercer*.*

Mercer   **West Virginia**
Princeton   419 sq. mi.

| 62,264 | 62,980 | 64,980 | 73,942 | 63,206 | 68,206 | 75,013 |

March 17, 1837. *Hugh Mercer.**

Meriwether   **Georgia**
Greenville   501 sq. mi.

| 21,992 | 22,534 | 22,411 | 21,229 | 19,461 | 19,756 | 21,055 |

December 14, 1827. *David Meriwether (1755–1822)*. Lieutenant, Continental Army; brigadier general, Georgia Militia; Georgia legislature, speaker 1797–1800; US representative 1802–07; commissioner to Creek Indians 1804.

Merrick   **Nebraska**
Central City   485 sq. mi.

| 7,845 | 8,204 | 8,024 | 8,945 | 8,751 | 8,363 | 8,812 |

November 4, 1858; organized October 12, 1859. *Elva Merrick De Puy (1828–?)*. Wife of Henry W. De Puy, member of Nebraska legislature, speaker 1860.

Merrimack   **New Hampshire**
Concord   934 sq. mi.

| 146,445 | 136,225 | 120,005 | 98,302 | 80,925 | 67,785 | 63,022 |

July 1, 1823. *Merrimack River*. Nipmuck word possibly meaning "swift water" or "sturgeon."

Mesa   **Colorado**
Grand Junction   3,329 sq. mi.

| 146,723 | 116,255 | 93,145 | 81,530 | 54,374 | 50,715 | 38,974 |

February 14, 1883. *Grand Mesa*. Reputably the largest mesa in the world; from Spanish word meaning "table," describing a plateau.

Metcalfe   **Kentucky**
Edmonton   290 sq. mi.

| 10,099 | 10,037 | 8,963 | 9,484 | 8,177 | 8,367 | 9,851 |

May 1, 1860. *Thomas Metcalfe (1780–1855)*. Captain, War of 1812; Kentucky House of Representatives 1812–16; US representative 1819–28; governor of Kentucky 1828–32; Kentucky Senate 1834; US senator 1848–49.

Miami   **Indiana**
Peru   374 sq. mi.

| 36,903 | 36,082 | 36,897 | 39,820 | 39,246 | 38,000 | 28,201 |

February 2, 1832; effective April 1, 1832; organized January 2, 1834. *Miami Indians*. Name is most likely from Delaware word *wemiamik* meaning "all friends," describing relationship between Miamis and Delawares. Originally lived in Midwest; later moved to Indian Territory (Oklahoma) via Kansas.

Miami   **Kansas**
Paola   576 sq. mi.

| 32,787 | 28,351 | 23,466 | 21,618 | 19,254 | 19,884 | 19,698 |

August 25, 1855, as Lykins; name changed June 3, 1861. *Miami Indians.**

Miami   **Ohio**
Troy   407 sq. mi.

| 102,506 | 98,868 | 93,182 | 90,381 | 84,342 | 72,901 | 61,309 |

January 16, 1807. *Uncertain*. (1) *Miami Indians.** (2) *Miami River*; named for Miami Indians.

Miami-Dade   **Florida**
Miami   1,898 sq. mi.

| 2,496,435 | 2,253,362 | 1,937,094 | 1,625,781 | 1,267,792 | 935,047 | 495,084 |

February 4, 1836, as Dade; Dade County and City of Miami merged November 12, 1997; name changed December 2, 1997. "Miami" from City of Miami; named for Miami River; Indian word for "very large." "Dade" from Francis Langhorne Dade (see Dade, Georgia).

Middlesex   **Connecticut**
Middletown   369 sq. mi.
165,676   155,071   143,196   129,017   114,816   88,865   67,332
1785. *Uncertain.* (1) *Middlesex County, England*; included London, a source of many colonists. (2) *Town of Middletown, Connecticut.*

Middlesex   **Massachusetts**
Cambridge   818 sq. mi.
1,503,085   1,465,396   1,398,468   1,367,034   1,397,268   1,238,742   1,064,569
May 10, 1643. *Middlesex County, England.**

Middlesex   **New Jersey**
New Brunswick   309 sq. mi.
809,858   750,162   671,780   595,893   583,813   433,856   264,872
March 7, 1683. *Middlesex County, England.**

Middlesex   **Virginia**
Saluda   130 sq. mi.
10,959   9,932   8,653   7,719   6,295   6,319   6,715
February 2, 1673. *Middlesex County, England.**

Midland   **Michigan**
Midland   516 sq. mi.
83,629   82,874   75,651   73,578   63,769   51,450   35,662
March 2, 1831; organized December 31, 1850; deorganized February 13, 1853; reorganized July 3, 1855. *Descriptive.* Refers to central location in Lower Peninsula.

Midland   **Texas**
Midland   900 sq. mi.
136,872   116,009   106,611   82,636   65,433   67,717   25,785
March 4, 1885. *Town of Midland.* Named for location midway between Fort Worth and El Paso on Texas & Pacific Railway.

Mifflin   **Pennsylvania**
Lewistown   411 sq. mi.
46,682   46,486   46,197   46,908   45,268   44,348   43,691
September 19, 1789. *Thomas Mifflin (1744–1800).* Continental Congress 1774–76 and 1782–84, president 1783; major general, Continental Army 1779; speaker, Pennsylvania House of Representatives 1785–88; federal Constitutional Convention 1787; governor of Pennsylvania 1790–99.

Milam   **Texas**
Cameron   1,017 sq. mi.
24,757   24,238   22,946   22,732   20,028   22,263   22,585
March 17, 1836; organized 1837. *Municipality of Milam.* Named for Benjamin R. Milam (1788–1835); War of 1812; traded with Comanches; active in obtaining Mexican independence from Spain and later Texas independence; killed during Siege of Bexar.

Millard   **Utah**
Fillmore   6,572 sq. mi.
12,503   12,405   11,333   8,970   6,988   7,866   9,387
October 4, 1851. *Millard Fillmore.* (See Fillmore, Minnesota.)

Mille Lacs   **Minnesota**
Milaca   572 sq. mi.
26,097   22,330   18,670   18,430   15,703   14,560   15,165

May 23, 1857; organized 1860. *Mille Lacs Lake*. French for "thousand lakes"; translation of lake's Ojibwa name meaning "all sorts" or "everywhere lake."

Miller   **Arkansas**
Texarkana   626 sq. mi.
43,462   40,443   38,467   37,766   33,385   31,686   32,614
December 22, 1874. *James Miller (1776–1851)*. Brevet colonel to brigadier general, US Army 1812–19; governor of Arkansas Territory 1819–25; Collector, Port of Salem, Massachusetts 1825–49.

Miller   **Georgia**
Colquitt   282 sq. mi.
6,125   6,383   6,280   7,038   6,397   6,908   9,023
February 26, 1856. *Andrew Jackson Miller (1806–56)*. Georgia House of Representatives 1836–38; Georgia Senate 1838–56; judge, Georgia Superior Court.

Miller   **Missouri**
Tuscumbia   593 sq. mi.
24,748   23,564   20,700   18,532   15,026   13,800   13,734
February 6, 1837. *John Miller (1781–1846)*. Lieutenant colonel, War of 1812; governor of Missouri 1826–32; US representative 1837–43.

Mills   **Iowa**
Glenwood   437 sq. mi.
15,059   14,547   13,202   13,406   11,606   13,050   14,064
January 15, 1851. *Frederick D. Mills (?–1847)*. Major, US Army 1846; organized company of Iowa volunteers 1847; died in Battle of Churubusco, August 20, 1847.

Mills   **Texas**
Goldthwaite   748 sq. mi.
4,936   5,151   4,531   4,477   4,212   4,467   5,999
March 15, 1887; organized September 12, 1887. *John T. Mills (1817–71)*. Established law practice in Texas 1837; Republic of Texas district judge 1839–46.

Milwaukee   **Wisconsin**
Milwaukee   241 sq. mi.
947,735   940,164   959,275   964,988   1,054,063   1,036,041   871,047
September 6, 1834; organized August 25, 1835. *Milwaukee River*. Uncertain Indian derivation; possibly from Potawatomi *meno* (good) and *aki* (land).

Miner   **South Dakota**
Howard   570 sq. mi.
2,389   2,884   3,272   3,739   4,454   5,398   6,268
January 8, 1873; organized December 2, 1880. *Brothers Nelson and Ephraim Miner*. (1) Nelson Miner (1827–79); organizer and captain of Dakota Cavalry 1862–65; Dakota territorial legislature 1869–79. (2) Ephraim Miner (1833–?); settled in Yankton 1867; Dakota territorial surveyor general 1867–70; Dakota territorial legislature 1872–73. Both were members of legislature at time of county's creation.

Mineral   **Colorado**
Creede   876 sq. mi.
712   831   558   804   786   424   698
March 27, 1893. *Descriptive*. Refers to mineral deposits in the area.

Mineral   **Montana**
Superior   1,219 sq. mi.

4,223	3,884	3,315	3,675	2,958	3,037	2,081

August 7, 1914. *Descriptive*. Refers to mineral deposits in the area.

Mineral   **Nevada**
Hawthorne   3,753 sq. mi.

4,772	5,071	6,475	6,217	7,051	6,329	5,560

February 10, 1911. *Descriptive*. Refers to mineral deposits in the area.

Mineral   **West Virginia**
Keyser   328 sq. mi.

28,212	27,078	26,697	27,234	23,109	22,354	22,333

February 1, 1866. *Descriptive*. Refers to coal and other mineral deposits in the area.

Mingo   **West Virginia**
Williamson   423 sq. mi.

26,839	28,253	33,739	37,336	32,780	39,742	47,409

January 30, 1895. *Mingo Indians*. Name is a corruption of Algonquin *mingwe*, referring to members of Iroquois language groups.

Minidoka   **Idaho**
Rupert   758 sq. mi.

20,069	20,174	19,361	19,718	15,731	14,394	9,785

January 28, 1913. *Uncertain*. (1) *Town of Minidoka*. (2) *Minidoka Reclamation Project*. Both are named from Shoshoni word meaning "broad expanse."

Minnehaha   **South Dakota**
Sioux Falls   807 sq. mi.

169,468	148,281	123,809	109,435	95,209	86,575	70,910

April 5, 1862; organized January 4, 1868. *Sioux River Falls*. From Santee Dakota word meaning "waterfall"; popularized as heroine in Longfellow's *Song of Hiawatha*, 1855.

Missaukee   **Michigan**
Lake City   565 sq. mi.

14,849	14,478	12,147	10,009	7,126	6,784	7,458

April 1, 1840; organized March 11, 1871. *Mesauke (?–?)*. Ottawa chief; signed treaties with US 1831 and 1833. Name may be from Ottawa *missi* (great) and *aukee* (world, earth, or country).

Mississippi   **Arkansas**
Blytheville   901 sq. mi.

46,480	51,979	57,525	59,517	62,060	70,174	82,375

November 1, 1833; effective January 1, 1834. *Mississippi River*. From *messipi*. French rendering of Chippewa name meaning "great water."

Mississippi   **Missouri**
Charleston   412 sq. mi.

14,358	13,427	14,442	15,726	16,647	20,695	22,551

February 14, 1845. *Mississippi River*.*

Missoula   **Montana**
Missoula   2,593 sq. mi.

109,299	95,802	78,687	76,016	58,263	44,663	35,493

December 14, 1860. *Town of Missoula Mills*. Salish word of uncertain origin; best guesses involve "water" and "awe." "Mills" referred to early industries.

Mitchell   **Georgia**
Camilla   512 sq. mi.

| 23,498 | 23,932 | 20,275 | 21,114 | 18,956 | 19,652 | 22,528 |

December 21, 1857. *Henry Mitchell (1760–1837).* Continental Army; wounded at Hanging Rock 1780; brigadier general, Georgia Militia; Georgia legislature.

Mitchell   **Iowa**
Osage   469 sq. mi.

| 10,776 | 10,874 | 10,928 | 12,329 | 13,108 | 14,043 | 13,945 |

January 15, 1851; organized October 2, 1854. *John Mitchel (1815–75).* Irish nationalist; arrested and sent to Tasmania 1848; escaped to US 1853; proslavery Richmond journalist during Civil War; returned to Ireland 1874. Second letter *l* most likely added to conform to more familiar spelling.

Mitchell   **Kansas**
Beloit   702 sq. mi.

| 6,373 | 6,932 | 7,203 | 8,117 | 8,010 | 8,866 | 10,320 |

February 26, 1867; organized 1870. *William D. Mitchell (c1841–1865).* Private, 2nd Kansas Cavalry, Union Army 1861; 1st lieutenant, Kentucky Cavalry; killed at Monroe's Crossroads, March 10, 1865.

Mitchell   **North Carolina**
Bakersville   221 sq. mi.

| 15,579 | 15,687 | 14,433 | 14,428 | 13,447 | 13,906 | 15,143 |

February 16, 1861. *Elisha Mitchell (1793–1857).* Professor, University of North Carolina; head of North Carolina geologic survey; determined Mount Mitchell as highest point in Eastern US 1835; killed from fall while verifying mountain's elevation. Mount Mitchell is named for him.

Mitchell   **Texas**
Colorado City   911 sq. mi.

| 9,403 | 9,698 | 8,016 | 9,088 | 9,073 | 11,255 | 14,357 |

August 21, 1876; organized January 10, 1881. *Brothers Asa and Eli Mitchell.* (1) Asa Mitchell (1795–1865); settled in Austin's colony 1822; Battle of Velasco 1832; sergeant, Battle of San Jacinto 1836. (2) Eli Mitchell (1797–1870); settled near Velasco 1824; fired first cannon shot at Battle of Gonzales, initiating Texas Revolution 1835.

Mobile   **Alabama**
Mobile   1,229 sq. mi.

| 412,992 | 399,843 | 378,643 | 364,980 | 317,308 | 314,301 | 231,105 |

December 18, 1812. *Mobile Bay, River, and Town.* From French Fort Louis de la Mobile named for Maubila Indians 1702; most likely from Choctaw word for "paddler."

Modoc   **California**
Alturas   3,918 sq. mi.

| 9,686 | 9,449 | 9,678 | 8,610 | 7,469 | 8,308 | 9,678 |

February 17, 1874. *Modoc Indians.* Lived in Southern Oregon and Northern California; Modoc War 1872–73; name may come from Klamath word for "south."

Moffat   **Colorado**
Craig   4,743 sq. mi.

| 13,795 | 13,184 | 11,357 | 13,133 | 6,525 | 7,061 | 5,946 |

February 17, 1911. *David Halliday Moffat (1839–1910).* Banker and railroad builder; president, Denver & Rio Grande Western Railroad 1884–91.

Mohave   **Arizona**
Kingman   13,311 sq. mi.

| 200,186 | 155,032 | 93,497 | 55,865 | 25,857 | 7,736 | 8,510 |

November 8, 1864. *Mojave Indians*. From *hamol* (three) and *avi* (mountain). Misspelling from clerical error also applied to Mohave Desert.

Moniteau   **Missouri**
California   415 sq. mi.
15,607   14,827   12,298   12,068   10,742   10,500   10,840
February 14, 1845. *Moniteau River*. French corruption of Algonquin word for "deity" or "god."

Monmouth   **New Jersey**
Freehold   469 sq. mi.
630,380   615,301   553,124   503,173   459,379   334,401   225,327
March 7, 1683. *Uncertain*. (1) *James Scott, Duke of Monmouth and Buccleuch (1649–85)*; eldest of Charles II's illegitimate children; fought against Dutch and French; claimed right to English throne; executed in Tower of London. (2) *Monmouthshire, Wales*; birthplace of an early settler.

Mono   **California**
Bridgeport   3,049 sq. mi.
14,202   12,853   9,956   8,577   4,016   2,213   2,115
April 24, 1861. *Mono Indians*. From Yokut word for "fly people"; Monos used fly pupae from Mono Lake for food and bartering.

Monona   **Iowa**
Onawa   694 sq. mi.
9,243   10,020   10,034   11,692   12,069   13,916   16,303
January 15, 1851; organized April 3, 1854. Variation of *We-no-nah* from Dakota legend (see Winona, Minnesota).

Monongalia   **West Virginia**
Morgantown   360 sq. mi.
96,189   81,866   75,509   75,024   63,714   55,617   60,797
November 6, 1776. *Monongahela River*. From Delaware word meaning "falling banks" referring to unstable river banks. Both spellings are European approximations of the Indian name for the river.

Monroe   **Alabama**
Monroeville   1,026 sq. mi.
23,068   24,324   23,968   22,651   20,883   22,372   25,732
June 29, 1815. *James Monroe (1758–1831)*. Lieutenant, Continental Army; wounded at Battle of Trenton 1776; Virginia Assembly 1782; Continental Congress 1783–86; US senator 1790–94; US minister to France 1794–96; governor of Virginia 1799–1802 and 1811; US secretary of state 1811–16; 5th US president 1817–25.

Monroe   **Arkansas**
Clarendon   607 sq. mi.
8,149   10,254   11,333   14,052   15,657   17,327   19,540
November 2, 1829; effective January 1, 1830. *James Monroe*.*

Monroe   **Florida**
Key West   983 sq. mi.
73,090   79,589   78,024   63,188   52,586   47,921   29,957
July 3, 1823; effective December 29, 1824. *James Monroe*.*

Monroe   **Georgia**
Forsyth   396 sq. mi.
26,424   21,757   17,113   14,610   10,991   10,495   10,523
May 15, 1821. *James Monroe*.*

Monroe   **Illinois**
Waterloo   385 sq. mi.
32,957   27,619   22,422   20,117   18,831   15,507   13,282
January 6, 1816. *James Monroe.**

Monroe   **Indiana**
Bloomington   395 sq. mi.
137,974   120,563   108,978   98,785   84,849   59,225   50,080
January 14, 1818; effective April 10, 1819. *James Monroe.**

Monroe   **Iowa**
Albia   434 sq. mi.
7,970   8,016   8,114   9,209   9,357   10,463   11,814
February 17, 1843, as Kishkekosh; organized July 1, 1845; name changed January 19, 1846. *James Monroe.**

Monroe   **Kentucky**
Tompkinsville   329 sq. mi.
10,963   11,756   11,401   12,353   11,642   11,799   13,770
January 19, 1820. *James Monroe.**

Monroe   **Michigan**
Monroe   549 sq. mi.
152,021   145,945   133,600   134,659   118,479   101,120   75,666
July 14, 1817. *James Monroe.**

Monroe   **Mississippi**
Aberdeen   765 sq. mi.
36,989   38,014   36,582   36,404   34,043   33,953   36,543
February 9, 1821. *James Monroe.**

Monroe   **Missouri**
Paris   648 sq. mi.
8,840   9,311   9,104   9,716   9,542   10,688   11,314
January 6, 1831. *James Monroe.**

Monroe   **New York**
Rochester   657 sq. mi.
744,344   735,343   713,968   702,238   711,917   586,387   487,632
February 23, 1821. *James Monroe.**

Monroe   **Ohio**
Woodsfield   456 sq. mi.
14,642   15,180   15,497   17,382   15,739   15,268   15,362
January 29, 1813; organized 1815. *James Monroe.**

Monroe   **Pennsylvania**
Stroudsburg   608 sq. mi.
169,842   138,687   95,709   69,409   45,422   39,567   33,773
April 1, 1836. *James Monroe.**

Monroe   **Tennessee**
Madisonville   636 sq. mi.
44,519   38,961   30,541   28,700   23,475   23,316   24,513
November 13, 1819. *James Monroe.**

Monroe   **West Virginia**
Union   473 sq. mi.
13,502   14,583   12,406   12,873   11,272   11,584   13,123
January 14, 1799. *James Monroe.**

Monroe   **Wisconsin**
Sparta   901 sq. mi.
44,673   40,899   36,633   35,074   31,610   31,241   31,378
March 21, 1854. *James Monroe.**

Montague   **Texas**
Montague   931 sq. mi.
19,719   19,117   17,274   17,410   15,326   14,893   17,070
December 24, 1857; organized August 2, 1858. *Daniel Montague (1798–1876).* Surveyor; captain, Texas Mounted Volunteers 1846–48; Texas Senate 1863; moved to Mexico following Civil War.

Montcalm   **Michigan**
Stanton   705 sq. mi.
63,342   61,266   53,059   47,555   39,660   35,795   31,013
March 2, 1831; organized March 20, 1850. *Louis-Joseph, Marquis de Montcalm-Gozon (1712–59).* Brigadier general in command of French troops in New France (Canada); defeated British at Oswego (1756) and Fort William Henry (1757); defeated and mortally wounded at Quebec September 13, 1759.

Monterey   **California**
Salinas   3,281 sq. mi.
415,057   401,762   355,660   290,444   250,071   198,351   130,498
February 18, 1850. *Monterey Bay and Town.* Named for Gaspar de Zuñiga y Azevedo, Count of Monterey (1560–1606); viceroy of New Spain (Mexico) 1595–1603; ordered Vizcaíno expedition which entered and named Monterey Bay 1602.

Montezuma   **Colorado**
Cortez   2,030 sq. mi.
25,535   23,830   18,672   16,510   12,952   14,024   9,991
April 16, 1889. *Montezuma II (1479–1520).* Aztec Emperor 1502–20; expanded empire to Honduras; defeated by Spanish under Cortez; executed June 30, 1520.

Montgomery   **Alabama**
Montgomery   784 sq. mi.
229,363   223,510   209,085   197,038   167,790   169,210   138,965
December 6, 1816. *Lemuel Purnell Montgomery (1786–1814).* Major, War of 1812; killed at Battle of Horseshoe Bend, March 27, 1814.

Montgomery   **Arkansas**
Mount Ida   780 sq. mi.
9,487   9,245   7,841   7,771   5,821   5,370   6,680
December 9, 1842. *Richard Montgomery (1738–75).* New York Provincial Congress 1775; brigadier general, Continental Army; captured Montreal 1775; killed in unsuccessful assault on Quebec, December 31, 1775.

Montgomery   **Georgia**
Mount Vernon   240 sq. mi.
9,123   8,270   7,163   7,011   6,099   6,284   7,901
December 19, 1793. *Richard Montgomery.**

Montgomery   **Illinois**
Hillsboro   704 sq. mi.
30,104   30,652   30,728   31,686   30,260   31,244   32,460
February 12, 1821. *Richard Montgomery.**

Montgomery   **Indiana**
Crawfordsville   505 sq. mi.

38,124	37,629	34,436	35,501	33,930	32,089	29,122

December 21, 1822; effective March 1, 1823. *Richard Montgomery.**

Montgomery   **Iowa**
Red Oak   424 sq. mi.

10,740	11,771	12,076	13,413	12,781	14,467	15,685

January 15, 1851; organized August 5, 1853. *Richard Montgomery.**

Montgomery   **Kansas**
Independence   644 sq. mi.

35,471	36,252	38,816	42,281	39,949	45,007	46,487

February 26, 1867; organized June 3, 1869. *Richard Montgomery.**

Montgomery   **Kentucky**
Mount Sterling   197 sq. mi.

26,499	22,554	19,561	20,046	15,364	13,461	13,025

December 14, 1796; effective March 1, 1797. *Richard Montgomery.**

Montgomery   **Maryland**
Rockville   491 sq. mi.

971,777	873,341	757,027	579,053	522,809	340,928	164,401

September 6, 1776. *Richard Montgomery.**

Montgomery   **Mississippi**
Winona   407 sq. mi.

10,925	12,189	12,388	13,366	12,918	13,320	14,470

May 13, 1871. *Richard Montgomery.**

Montgomery   **Missouri**
Montgomery City   536 sq. mi.

12,236	12,136	11,355	11,537	11,000	11,097	11,555

December 14, 1818. *Uncertain.* (1) *Montgomery County, Kentucky.* (2) *Richard Montgomery.**

Montgomery   **New York**
Fonda   403 sq. mi.

50,219	49,708	51,981	53,439	55,883	57,240	59,594

March 12, 1772, as Tryon; name changed April 2, 1784. *Richard Montgomery.**

Montgomery   **North Carolina**
Troy   492 sq. mi.

27,798	26,822	23,346	22,469	19,267	18,408	17,260

1779. *Richard Montgomery.**

Montgomery   **Ohio**
Dayton   462 sq. mi.

535,153	559,062	573,809	571,697	606,148	527,080	398,441

March 24, 1803. *Richard Montgomery.**

Montgomery   **Pennsylvania**
Norristown   483 sq. mi.

799,874	750,097	678,111	643,621	623,799	516,682	353,068

September 10, 1784. *Uncertain.* (1) *Richard Montgomery.** (2) *John Montgomery* (see Montgomery, Tennessee). (3) *Montgomeryshire, Wales.*

Montgomery   **Tennessee**
Clarksville   539 sq. mi.
172,331   134,768   100,498   83,342   62,721   55,645   44,186
April 9, 1796. *John Montgomery (1748–94)*; General, Pennsylvania Militia; battles of Brandywine and Germantown 1777; captain under George Rogers Clark 1778; founded Clarksville 1784; killed by Indians.

Montgomery   **Texas**
Conroe   1,042 sq. mi.
455,746   293,768   182,201   128,487   49,479   26,839   24,504
December 14, 1837. *Town of Montgomery*. Named for Richard Montgomery.*

Montgomery   **Virginia**
Christiansburg   387 sq. mi.
94,392   83,629   73,913   63,516   47,157   32,923   29,780
December 7, 1776. *Richard Montgomery*.* (Associated independent city: Radford.)

Montmorency   **Michigan**
Atlanta   547 sq. mi.
9,765   10,315   8,936   7,492   5,247   4,424   4,125
April 1, 1840, as Cheonoquet; name changed March 8, 1843; organized May 21, 1881. *Uncertain*. (1) *Francois de Laval-Montmorency (1621–1708)*; ordained as Jesuit priest 1647; first Roman Catholic Bishop of Quebec 1674; Quebec Council 1659. (2) *Henri, 2nd Duc de Montmorency (1595–1632)*; French military commander; purchased lieutenant-generalship of New France (Canada); never visited North America; engendered jealousy of Cardinal Richelieu; executed as traitor.

Montour   **Pennsylvania**
Danville   130 sq. mi.
18,267   18,236   17,735   16,675   16,508   16,730   16,001
May 3, 1850. *Uncertain*. (1) *Catherine (or Elizabeth or Isabelle) Montour (c1686–c1752)*; Indian interpreter for French and English; persuaded Iroquois not to attack settlers 1712. Given name is uncertain because she was always referred to as "Madame Montour." (2) *Montour Ridge*; mountain ridge named for Catherine Montour.

Montrose   **Colorado**
Montrose   2,241 sq. mi.
41,276   33,432   24,423   24,352   18,366   18,236   15,220
February 11, 1883. *Town of Montrose*. Named for Sir Walter Scott's *Legend of Montrose*; one of town's founders admired Scott.

Moody   **South Dakota**
Flandreau   519 sq. mi.
6,486   6,595   6,507   6,692   7,622   8,810   9,252
January 8, 1873. *Gideon Curtis Moody (1832–1904)*. Indiana House of Representatives 1861; Union Army, captain to colonel 1861–64; Dakota territorial legislature 1867–69 and 1874–75; Dakota Territory Supreme Court 1878–83; US senator from South Dakota 1889–91.

Moore   **North Carolina**
Carthage   698 sq. mi.
88,247   74,769   59,013   50,505   39,048   36,733   33,129
1784. *Alfred Moore (1755–1810)*. Captain to colonel, Continental Army 1775–77; attorney general of North Carolina 1782–91; led North Carolina ratification of US Constitution after initial rejection 1788; US Supreme Court 1800–04.

Moore   **Tennessee**
Lynchburg   129 sq. mi.
6.362   5,740   4,721   4,510   3,568   3,454   3,948
December 14, 1871. *William Moore (1786–1871)*. Officer, Tennessee Militia, Creek War and War of 1812; Tennessee House of Representatives 1825–29; Tennessee Senate 1833–37.

Moore **Texas**
Dumas 900 sq. mi.
21,904 20,121 17,865 16,575 14,060 14,773 13,349
August 21, 1876; organized July 6, 1892. *Edwin Ward Moore (1810–65)*. Lieutenant, US Navy; resigned to command Republic of Texas Navy 1839; raided and blockaded Mexican coast 1841.

Mora **New Mexico**
Mora 1,931 sq. mi.
4,881 5,180 4,264 4,205 4,673 6,028 8,720
February 1, 1860. *Town of Mora*. From Spanish *demora* meaning "delay" or "stop over."

Morehouse **Louisiana**
Bastrop 795 sq. mi.
27,979 31,021 31,938 34,803 32,463 33,709 32,038
March 25, 1844. *Abraham Morhouse (?–1813)*. Early settler in northern Louisiana; claimed to have been colonel in New York Militia. Letter *e* added to parish name by clerical error.

Morgan **Alabama**
Decatur 579 sq. mi.
119,490 111,064 100,043 90,231 77,306 60,454 52,924
February 6, 1818, as Cotaco; name changed June 14, 1821. *Daniel Morgan (1736–1802)*. Teamster under General Braddock 1755; lieutenant in Pontiac's War 1764; captain in Dunmore's War 1774; captain, Virginia Riflemen 1775; captured at Quebec 1775; colonel, Virginia Regiment 1776; brigadier general at Saratoga 1777; defeated British at Cowpens 1781; commanded troops at Whiskey Rebellion 1794; US representative from Virginia 1797–99.

Morgan **Colorado**
Fort Morgan 1,280 sq. mi.
28,159 27,171 21,939 22,513 20,105 21,192 18,074
February 19, 1889. *Fort Morgan*. Named for Christopher A. Morgan (?–1866); Private, 39th Ohio Volunteers 1861; rose to rank of colonel on General Pope's staff; inspector general at St. Louis.

Morgan **Georgia**
Madison 347 sq. mi.
17,868 15,457 12,883 11,572 9,904 10,280 11,899
December 10, 1807. *Daniel Morgan.**

Morgan **Illinois**
Jacksonville 569 sq. mi.
35,547 36,616 36,397 37,502 36,174 36,571 35,568
January 31, 1823. *Daniel Morgan.**

Morgan **Indiana**
Martinsville 404 sq. mi.
68,894 66,689 55,920 51,999 44,176 33,875 23,726
December 31, 1821; effective February 15, 1822. *Daniel Morgan.**

Morgan **Kentucky**
West Liberty 381 sq. mi.
13,923 13,948 11,648 12,103 10,019 11,056 13,624
December 7, 1822. *Daniel Morgan.**

Morgan **Missouri**
Versailles 598 sq. mi.
20,565 19,309 15,574 13,807 10,068 9,476 10,207
January 5, 1833. *Daniel Morgan.**

Morgan   **Ohio**
McConnelsville   416 sq. mi.
15,054   14,897   14,194   14,241   12,375   12,747   12,836
December 29, 1817; organized 1819. *Daniel Morgan.**

Morgan   **Tennessee**
Wartburg   522 sq. mi.
21,987   19,757   17,300   16,604   13,619   14,304   15,727
October 14, 1817. *Daniel Morgan.**

Morgan   **Utah**
Morgan   609 sq. mi.
9,469   7,129   5,528   4,917   3,983   2,837   2,519
January 17, 1862. *Jedediah Morgan Grant (1816–56)*. Baptized as Mormon 1833; ordained 1835; first mayor of Salt Lake City 1851–56; counselor to Brigham Young.

Morgan   **West Virginia**
Berkeley Springs   229 sq. mi.
17,541   14,943   12,128   10,711   8,547   8,376   8,276
February 9, 1820. *Daniel Morgan.**

Morrill   **Nebraska**
Bridgeport   1,424 sq. mi.
5,042   5,440   5,423   6,085   5,813   7,057   8,263
November 12, 1908. *Charles Henry Morrill (1843–1928)*. Private, Union Army 1863; private secretary to Nebraska Governor Nance 1879; University of Nebraska Board of Regents 1889–99, president 1892; financed geological expeditions throughout Nebraska.

Morris   **Kansas**
Council Grove   695 sq. mi.
5,923   6,104   6,198   6,419   6,432   7,392   8,485
August 25, 1855, as Wise; organized and name changed February 11, 1859. *Thomas Morris (1776–1844)*. Ohio House of Representatives intermittently 1806–21; Ohio Senate intermittently 1813–33; US senator 1833–39; abolitionist; Liberty Party vice presidential nominee 1844.

Morris   **New Jersey**
Morristown   460 sq. mi.
492,276   470,212   421,353   407,630   383,454   261,620   164,371
March 15, 1739. *Lewis Morris (1671–1746)*. Inherited estate of Morrisania (now southwest Bronx, New York) at age of one; Superior Court of New York and New Jersey 1692–1738, chief justice 1710–38; acting governor of New York 1731; governor of New Jersey 1738–46.

Morris   **Texas**
Daingerfield   252 sq. mi.
12,934   13,048   13,200   14,629   12,310   12,576   9,433
March 6, 1875. *William Wright Morris (1805–83)*. Republic of Texas legislature 1843; district court judge 1854; promoted railroads in East Texas.

Morrison   **Minnesota**
Little Falls   1,125 sq. mi.
33,198   31,712   29,604   29,311   26,949   26,641   25,832
February 25, 1856. *Brothers Allan and William Morrison*. Both operated trading posts. (1) William Morrison (1785–1866); first recorded visit to Lake Itasca, source of the Mississippi River 1804. (2) Allan Morrison (1803–77); first Minnesota territorial legislature.

Morrow   **Ohio**
Mount Gilead   406 sq. mi.

| 34,827 | 31,628 | 27,749 | 26,480 | 21,348 | 19,405 | 17,168 |

February 24, 1848. *Jeremiah Morrow (1771–1852).* Ohio territorial House of Representatives 1801–02; Ohio Senate 1803 and 1827–28; US representative 1803–13 and 1839–43; US senator 1813–19; governor of Ohio 1822–26; Ohio House of Representatives 1829 and 1835.

Morrow   **Oregon**
Heppner   2,032 sq. mi.

| 11,173 | 10,995 | 7,625 | 7,519 | 4,465 | 4,871 | 4,783 |

February 16, 1885. *Jackson L. Morrow (?–?).* Lieutenant in Western Indian Wars; merchant; Oregon legislature 1876 and 1885.

Morton   **Kansas**
Elkhart   730 sq. mi.

| 3,233 | 3,496 | 3,480 | 3,454 | 3,576 | 3,354 | 2,610 |

February 20, 1886; organized November 18, 1886. *Oliver Hazard Perry Throck Morton (1823–77).* Circuit judge 1852; governor of Indiana 1861–67; US senator 1867–77. Popular advocate for free soil policies.

Morton   **North Dakota**
Mandan   1,926 sq. mi.

| 27,471 | 25,303 | 23,700 | 25,177 | 20,310 | 20,992 | 19,295 |

January 8, 1873; organized February 18, 1881. *Oliver Morton.**

Motley   **Texas**
Matador   990 sq. mi.

| 1,210 | 1,426 | 1,532 | 1,950 | 2,178 | 2,870 | 3,963 |

August 21, 1876; organized February 25, 1891. *Junius William Mottley (1812–36).* Physician; signer, Texas Declaration of Independence 1836; killed at Battle of San Jacinto April 21, 1836. Clerical error caused misspelling of county name.

Moultrie   **Illinois**
Sullivan   336 sq. mi.

| 14,846 | 14,287 | 13,390 | 14,546 | 13,263 | 13,635 | 13,171 |

February 16, 1843. *William Moultrie (1730–1805).* South Carolina Militia during Creek War 1761; brigadier general, Continental Army; South Carolina legislature; governor of South Carolina 1785–87 and 1792–94.

Mountrail   **North Dakota**
Stanley   1,825 sq. mi.

| 7,673 | 6,631 | 7,021 | 7,679 | 8,437 | 10,077 | 9,418 |

January 4, 1873; abolished November 30, 1892; recreated January 25, 1909. *Joseph Mountraille (?–?).* French-Canadian fur trader; carried mail between Pembina and St. Paul. Name has various spellings including "Montreille."

Mower   **Minnesota**
Austin   711 sq. mi.

| 39,163 | 38,603 | 37,395 | 40,930 | 43,783 | 48,498 | 42,277 |

February 20, 1855; organized March 1, 1856. *John E. Mower (1815–79).* Minnesota territorial legislature 1854–55; Minnesota House of Representatives 1874–75.

Muhlenberg   **Kentucky**
Greenville   467 sq. mi.

| 31,449 | 31,839 | 31,318 | 32,238 | 27,537 | 27,971 | 32,501 |

December 14, 1798; effective May 15, 1799. *John Peter Gabriel Muhlenberg (1746–1807).* Virginia House of Burgesses 1774; Continental Army, colonel to major general 1777–83; US representative from Pennsylvania, intermittently 1789–1800; US senator 1801–02; collector, Port of Philadelphia 1802–07; extensive land holdings in Kentucky.

Multnomah   **Oregon**
Portland   431 sq. mi.
735,334   660,486   683,887   562,460   556,667   522,813   471,537
December 22, 1854. *Multnomah Indians*. Chinnokan tribe living on island in Columbia River; encountered by Lewis and Clark 1805; extinct from disease by 1835.

Murray   **Georgia**
Chatsworth   344 sq. mi.
39,628   36,506   26,147   19,685   12,986   10,447   10,676
December 3, 1832. *Thomas W. Murray (1790–1832)*. Georgia legislature 1818, speaker 1825; nominated for US Congress but died before election.

Murray   **Minnesota**
Slayton   705 sq. mi.
8,725   9,165   9,660   11,507   12,508   14,743   14,801
May 23, 1857; organized March 5, 1879. *William Pitt Murray (1825–1910)*. Minnesota territorial legislature 1852–53 and 1857; Minnesota House of Representatives 1863 and 1868; Minnesota Senate 1866–67 and 1875–76.

Murray   **Oklahoma**
Sulphur   416 sq. mi.
13,488   12,623   12,042   12,147   10,669   10,622   10,775
July 16, 1907. *William Henry "Alfalfa Bill" Murray (1869–1956)*. President, Oklahoma Constitutional Convention 1906; Oklahoma House of Representatives 1907–09; US representative 1913–17; governor of Oklahoma 1931–35.

Muscatine   **Iowa**
Muscatine   437 sq. mi.
42,745   41,722   39,907   40,436   37,181   33,840   32,148
December 7, 1836. *Muscatine Island*. Large island in Mississippi River; named from Fox word for "prairie."

Muscogee   **Georgia**
Columbus   216 sq. mi.
189,885   186,291   179,278   170,108   167,377   158,623   118,023
December 14, 1826; organized December 24, 1827. *Five Civilized Tribes*. Indian name applied to loose confederation in the southeastern US; included Cherokees, Chickasaws, Choctaws, Creeks, and Seminoles.

Muskegon   **Michigan**
Muskegon   499 sq. mi.
172,188   170,200   158,983   157,589   157,426   149,943   121,545
February 4, 1859. *Muskegon River*. From Chippewa name meaning "swampy place."

Muskingum   **Ohio**
Zanesville   665 sq. mi.
86,074   84,585   82,068   83,340   77,826   79,159   74,535
January 7, 1804. *Muskingum River*. From Delaware word meaning "swampy land."

Muskogee   **Oklahoma**
Muskogee   810 sq. mi.
70,990   69,451   68,078   66,939   59,542   61,866   65,573
July 16, 1907. *Five Civilized Tribes*. See Muscogee, Georgia.

Musselshell   **Montana**
Roundup   1,868 sq. mi.
4,538   4,497   4,106   4,428   3,734   4,888   5,408
February 11, 1911. *Musselshell River*. Descriptive of shells found along the river.

N

Nacogdoches   **Texas**
Nacogdoches   947 sq. mi.
64,524   59,203   54,753   46,786   36,362   28,046   30,326
March 17, 1836; organized 1837. *Department of Nacogdoches*. Mexican department named for Nacogdoches Indians. In Caddo language, the prefix *na* means "place of"; the root word may mean "persimmons" or "high placc."

Nance   **Nebraska**
Fullerton   442 sq. mi.
3,735   4,038   4,275   4,740   5,142   5,635   6,512
February 13, 1879; organized June 21, 1879. *Albinus Nance (1848–1911)*. Private, Illinois Cavalry 1864; Nebraska legislature 1874–78, speaker 1877; governor of Nebraska 1879–83.

Nantucket   **Massachusetts**
Nantucket   45 sq. mi.
10,172   9,520   6,012   5,087   3,774   3,559   3,484
June 22, 1695. *Nantucket Island*. Uncertain Wampagoan word; most suggestions refer to "water" or "island."

Napa   **California**
Napa   748 sq. mi.
136,484   124,279   110,765   99,199   79,140   65,890   46,603
February 18, 1850. *Napa Indians*. Uncertain derivation; possibly from Spanish rendering of Indian word meaning "house" or "habitat"; other possibilities include "fish harpoon."

Nash   **North Carolina**
Nashville   540 sq. mi.
95,840   87,420   76,677   67,153   59,122   61,002   59,919
1777. *Francis Nash (1742–77)*. North Carolina House of Commons 1764; Assembly 1771 and 1773–75; Provincial Council 1775; Continental Army, lieutenant colonel to brigadier general 1775–77; mortally wounded at Germantown October 4, 1777.

Nassau   **Florida**
Fernandina Beach   649 sq. mi.
73,314   57,663   43,941   32,894   20,626   17,189   12,811
December 29, 1824. *Nassau River*. Named for Nassau, capital of the Bahamas. Early settlers were from the Bahamas.

Nassau   **New York**
Mineola   285 sq. mi.
1,339,532   1,334,544   1,287,348   1,321,582   1,428,080   1,300,171   672,765
April 27, 1898; organized 1899. *William Nassau, Prince of Orange, King William III*. (See King William, Virginia.) Long Island was called Nassau Island during 17th Century.

Natchitoches   **Louisiana**
Natchitoches   1,252 sq. mi.
39,566   39,080   36,689   39,683   35,219   35,653   38,144
April 10, 1805. *Natchitoches Indians*. Uncertain derivation; most suggestions refer to "eaters" of local fruit.

Natrona   **Wyoming**
Casper   5,340 sq. mi.
75,450   66,533   61,226   71,856   51,264   49,623   31,437
March 9, 1888. *Descriptive*. Refers to local deposits of sodium carbonate or natron.

Navajo   **Arizona**
Holbrook   9,950 sq. mi.

107,449   97,470   77,658   67,629   47,715   37,994   29,446

March 21, 1895. *Navajo Indians*. Uncertain Spanish or Indian origin; possibilities include (1) Spanish *nava* (field) with suffix *ajo* (small); (2) pueblo of Navahu, New Mexico; (3) Spanish *navaja* meaning "knife."

Navarro   **Texas**
Corsicana   1,010 sq. mi.
47,735   45,124   39,926   35,323   31,150   34,423   39,916
April 25, 1846; organized July 13, 1846. *José Antonio Navarro (1795–1871)*. Mexican state legislator; supported slavery; signer, Texas Declaration of Independence 1836; Texas Congress; sole Hispanic delegate to Texas Constitutional Convention 1845. Supporter of Mexican independence from Spain; Texas independence from Mexico; Texas annexation to US; and Texas secession from US.

Nelson   **Kentucky**
Bardstown   418 sq. mi.
43,437   37,477   29,710   27,584   23,477   22,168   19,521
November 29, 1784; effective January 1, 1785. *Thomas Nelson (1738–89)*. Virginia House of Burgesses 1761 and 1774–75; Continental Congress 1775–77; signer, Declaration of Independence 1776; Virginia Assembly 1779–80; governor of Virginia 1781.

Nelson   **North Dakota**
Lakota   982 sq. mi.
3,126   3,715   4,410   5,233   5,776   7,034   8,090
March 2, 1883; organized June 9, 1883. *Nelson E. Nelson (1830–1913)*. One of first homesteaders in North Dakota; collector of customs at Pembina; territorial legislature 1883.

Nelson   **Virginia**
Lovingston   471 sq. mi.
15,020   14,445   12,778   12,204   11,702   12,752   14,042
December 25, 1807. *Thomas Nelson*.*

Nemaha   **Kansas**
Seneca   717 sq. mi.
10,178   10,717   10,446   11,211   11,825   12,897   14,341
August 25, 1855. *Nemaha River*. Dakota name of unknown origin; most translations refer to "river" or "stream."

Nemaha   **Nebraska**
Auburn   407 sq. mi.
7,248   7,576   7,980   8,367   8,976   9,099   10,973
November 23, 1854, as Forney; name changed March 7, 1855. *Nemaha River*.*

Neosho   **Kansas**
Erie   571 sq. mi.
16,512   16,997   17,035   18,967   18,812   19,455   20,348
August 25, 1855, as Dorn; name changed June 3, 1861; organized November 8, 1864. *Neosho River*. From Osage language; most translations refer to "river" or "stream."

Neshoba   **Mississippi**
Philadelphia   570 sq. mi.
29,676   28,684   24,800   23,789   20,802   20,927   25,730
December 23, 1833. *Choctaw word meaning "wolf."* Every source states that Neshoba means wolf, but none say why the name was given to the county.

Ness   **Kansas**
Ness City   1,075 sq. mi.
3,107   3,454   4,033   4,498   4,791   5,470   6,322

February 26, 1867; organized October 23, 1873; deorganized 1874; reorganized April 14, 1880. *Noah V. Ness (?–1864)*. Corporal, Company G, 7th Kansas Cavalry; mortally wounded at Abbeville, Mississippi, August 22, 1864.

Nevada **Arkansas**
Prescott 618 sq. mi.

8,997	9,955	10,101	11,097	10,111	10,700	14,781

March 20, 1871. *State of Nevada*. The shape of the county was thought to resemble that of Nevada; it roughly does when rotated 180°.

Nevada **California**
Nevada City 958 sq. mi.

98,764	92,033	78,510	51,645	26,346	20,911	19,888

April 25, 1851; organized May 28, 1851. *Town of Nevada City*. Spanish for "snow covered."

Newaygo **Michigan**
White Cloud 813 sq. mi.

48,460	47,874	38,202	34,917	27,992	24,160	21,567

April 1, 1840; organized January 27, 1851. *Uncertain*. One of two Chippewa chiefs, Nuwagon or Ningwegon, who signed treaties with US between 1819 and 1836.

Newberry **South Carolina**
Newberry 630 sq. mi.

37,508	36,108	33,172	31,242	29,273	29,416	31,771

March 12, 1785; converted to judicial district January 1, 1800; redesignated as county April 16, 1868. *Uncertain*. (1) *John Newberry (?–?)*; captain, served under General Sumter during Revolutionary War. (2) Family or families of early settlers named Newberry or Newbury. (3) Any one of towns in America or England named Newbury.

New Castle **Delaware**
Wilmington 426 sq. mi.

538,479	500,265	441,946	398,115	385,856	307,446	218,879

August 8, 1673. *Town of New Castle*. Name of uncertain origin. (1) Town of Newcastle, England. (2) William Cavendish, Duke of Newcastle (1592–1676); Earl of Newcastle 1628; governor to Prince of Wales (later Charles II); loyalist during English Civil War; elevated to duke by Charles II 1665.

New Hanover **North Carolina**
Wilmington 192 sq. mi.

202,667	160,307	120,284	103,471	82,996	71,742	63,272

1729. *House of Hanover*. English royal family beginning 1714. (See King George, Virginia.)

New Haven **Connecticut**
New Haven 605 sq. mi.

862,477	824,008	804,219	761,337	744,948	660,315	545,784

May 10, 1666. *Colony and town of New Haven*. Descriptive of harbor named Fayre Haven; symbolic of colonists' optimism.

New Kent **Virginia**
New Kent 210 sq. mi.

18,429	13,462	10,445	8,781	5,300	4,504	3,995

1654. *Uncertain*. (1) *Kent County, England*. (2) *Kent Island, Maryland*; named for Kent, England.

New London **Connecticut**
New London 665 sq. mi.

274,055	259,088	254,957	238,409	230,348	185,745	144,821

May 10, 1666. *Town of New London*. Named for London, England.

New Madrid **Missouri**
New Madrid 675 sq. mi.

18,956	19,760	20,928	22,945	23,420	31,350	39,444

October 1, 1812. *Spanish colonial district of New Madrid.* Named for Madrid, Spain.

Newport			**Rhode Island**
Newport			102 sq. mi.

82,888	85,433	87,194	81,383	94,559	81,891	61,539

June 22, 1703, as Rhode Island; name changed June 16, 1729. *Town of Newport.* Named for Newport, Isle of Wight, England.

Newport News		**Virginia**
(Independent City)		69 sq. mi.

180,719	180,150	170,045	144,903	138,177	113,662	82,233[a]

1634, as Warwick River; name changed to Warwick 1643; Newport News incorporated as independent city January 16, 1896; cities of Warwick and Newport News merged July 1, 1958. *Uncertain.* (1) *New Port Newce* after port of Newce, County Cork, Ireland. (2) *William Newce (?–1621)* and/or *Thomas Newce (?–1623)*; brothers; Thomas succeeded William as superintendent of the London Company's lands in Virginia. (3) *Combination* of William Newce with Christopher Newport (c1560–1621); British naval officer and privateer; commanded Jamestown expedition 1607; four subsequent voyages to Virginia 1608–11. [(a) Includes Warwick County (39,875).]

Newton			**Arkansas**
Jasper			821 sq. mi.

8,330	8,608	7,666	7,756	5,844	5,963	8,685

December 14, 1842. *Thomas Willoughby Newton (1804–53)*; US marshal for Arkansas; US representative 1845–46. (Sources agree that the county was named for Thomas Newton, however, the county seat's name of Jasper suggests a possible connection between William Jasper and John Newton who are linked together in other county names and seats [see Jasper, and Newton, Georgia]).

Newton			**Georgia**
Covington			272 sq. mi.

99,958	62,001	41,808	34,489	26,282	20,999	20,185

December 24, 1821. *John Newton (1752–80).* Sergeant under General Francis Marion; linked with friend William Jasper (see Jasper, Georgia) in a sensationalized story by Parson Weems of their exploits during Siege of Savannah 1775; captured at Charleston; died of small pox.

Newton			**Indiana**
Kentland			402 sq. mi.

14,244	14,566	13,551	14,844	11,606	11,502	11,006

February 7, 1835; abolished January 29, 1839; recreated December 8, 1859. *John Newton.**

Newton			**Mississippi**
Decatur			578 sq. mi.

21,720	21,838	20,291	19,944	18,983	19,517	22,681

February 25, 1836. *Isaac Newton (1642–1727).* English mathematician and philosopher; graduated from Cambridge University 1665; professor at Cambridge 1669–96; Royal Society 1671; knighted by Queen Anne 1705.

Newton			**Missouri**
Neosho			625 sq. mi.

58,1144	52,636	44,445	40,555	32,901	30,093	28,240

December 30, 1838. *John Newton.**

Newton			**Texas**
Newton			934 sq. mi.

14.445	15,072	13,569	13,254	11,657	10,372	10,832

April 22, 1846; organized July 13, 1846. *John Newton.**

New York　　　**New York**
New York　　　　23 sq. mi.
1,585,873　1,537,195　1,487,536　1,428,285　1,539,233　1,698,281　1,960,101
November 1, 1683. *King James II, Duke of York.* (See Albany, New York.)

Nez Perce　　　**Idaho**
Lewiston　　　　848 sq. mi.
39,265　　　37,410　　　33,754　　　33,220　　　30,376　　　27,006　　　22,658
February 4, 1864. *Nez Perce Indians.* Uncertain derivation. (1) French for "pierce ear" although the tribe did not pierce their ears. (2) From French *nez presse*, meaning "pressed nose" or "flattened nose" which was a tribal characteristic.

Niagara　　　**New York**
Lockport　　　　522 sq. mi.
216,469　　　219,846　　　220,756　　　227,354　　　235,720　　　242,269　　　189,992
March 11, 1808. *Niagara River.* European rendering of Iroquois name referring to "bisected bottom lands."

Nicholas　　　**Kentucky**
Carlisle　　　　195 sq. mi.
7,135　　　6,813　　　6,725　　　7,157　　　6,508　　　6,677　　　7,532
December 18, 1799; effective June 1, 1800. *George Nicholas (1754–99).* Captain to colonel in Continental Army; Virginia House of Delegates 1781; Virginia Constitutional Convention 1788; Kentucky Constitutional Convention 1792; first attorney general of Kentucky 1792.

Nicholas　　　**West Virginia**
Summersville　　　647 sq. mi.
26,233　　　26,562　　　26,775　　　28,126　　　22,552　　　25,414　　　27,696
January 30, 1818. *Wilson Cary Nicholas (1761–1820).* Commanded General Washington's Life Guard 1783; Virginia House of Delegates intermittently 1784–1800; US senator 1799–1804; collector of the Port of Norfolk 1804–07; US representative 1807–09; governor of Virginia 1814–16.

Nicollet　　　**Minnesota**
Saint Peter　　　448 sq. mi.
32,727　　　29,771　　　28,076　　　26,929　　　24,518　　　23,196　　　20,929
March 5, 1853. *Joseph Nicolas Nicollet (1786–1843).* French geographer and mathematician; emigrated to New Orleans 1832; explored upper Mississippi Valley on three expeditions 1836–39.

Niobrara　　　**Wyoming**
Lusk　　　　2,626 sq. mi.
2,484　　　2,407　　　2,499　　　2,924　　　2,924　　　3,750　　　4,701
February 14, 1911. *Niobrara River.* Omaha-Poncah name meaning "water spreading."

Noble　　　**Indiana**
Albion　　　　411 sq. mi.
47,536　　　46,275　　　37,877　　　35,443　　　31,382　　　28,162　　　25,075
February 7, 1835; effective June 1, 1835; organized February 6, 1836. *Uncertain.* (1) *James Noble (1785–1831)*; Indiana Constitutional Committee 1816; Indiana House of Representatives 1816; US senator 1816–31. (2) *Noah Noble (1794–1844)*; Indiana House of Representatives 1824; governor of Indiana 1831–37. James and Noah were brothers; it is generally agreed that the county was named for one or the other, but not both.

Noble　　　**Ohio**
Caldwell　　　398 sq. mi.
14,645　　　14,058　　　11,336　　　11,310　　　10,428　　　10,982　　　11,750
March 11, 1851. *Uncertain.* (1) *James Noble (?–?)*; pioneer settler. (2) *John Noble (?–1831)*; early settler. (3) *John Noble (1802–?)*; son of John Noble; county commissioner.

Noble   **Oklahoma**
Perry   732 sq. mi.

| 11,561 | 11,411 | 11,045 | 11,573 | 10,043 | 10,376 | 12,156 |

August 21, 1893, as County P; name changed November 6, 1894. *John Willock Noble (1831–1912).* 3rd Iowa Cavalry 1861; brevet brigadier general 1865; US district attorney for Eastern District of Missouri 1867; US secretary of interior 1889–93.

Nobles   **Minnesota**
Worthington   715 sq. mi.

| 21,378 | 20,832 | 20,098 | 21,840 | 23,208 | 23,365 | 22,435 |

May 23, 1857; organized October 19, 1870. *William H. Nobles (1816–76).* Discovered Nobles Pass through northern Sierra Nevada Mountains and developed Nobles Trail avoiding Donner Summit 1852; Minnesota territorial legislature 1854 and 1856; St. Paul city council 1855–56; surveyed wagon road intended to extend from Minnesota to Rocky Mountains 1856.

Nodaway   **Missouri**
Maryville   877 sq. mi.

| 23,370 | 21,912 | 21,709 | 21,996 | 22,467 | 22,215 | 24,033 |

January 2, 1843. *Nodaway River.* Pottawatomi word for "placid."

Nolan   **Texas**
Sweetwater   912 sq. mi.

| 15,216 | 15,802 | 16,594 | 17,359 | 16,220 | 18,963 | 19,808 |

August 21, 1876; organized January 10, 1881. *Philip Nolan (1771–1801).* American filibuster in New Spain (Mexico); was involved in James Wilkinson's schemes in southwestern US (see Wilkinson, Georgia); led four expeditions into Spanish Texas ostensibly to trade horses but may have been filibusters 1791–1801; built fort near Nacogdoches 1800; killed by Spanish forces 1801.

Nome   **Alaska**
(Census Area)   22,962 sq. mi.

| 9,492 | 9,196 | 8,288 | 6,537 | 5,749 | 6,091 | (a) |

City of Nome. Named for Cape Nome; name resulted from a transcription error when a draftsman wrote the notation "? Name" on a manuscript chart for an unnamed cape on the south side of Seward Peninsula; when transcribed to a British Admiralty chart in 1853, it was written as "C. Nome," which became Cape Nome. [(a) Part of 2nd Judicial Division.]

Norfolk   **Massachusetts**
Dedham   395 sq. mi.

| 670,850 | 650,306 | 616,087 | 606,587 | 605,051 | 510,256 | 392,308 |

March 26, 1793. *Norfolk County, Massachusetts Bay Colony.* Original Norfolk County, named for Norfolk County, England, was created May 10, 1643; it was abandoned when Massachusetts Bay Colony ceased to exist and most of the county became part of New Hampshire, February 4, 1680.

Norfolk   **Virginia**
(Independent City)   54 sq. mi.

| 242,803 | 234,403 | 261,229 | 266,979 | 307,951 | 305,872 | 213,513 |

February 11, 1845. *Norfolk County, England.* The city of Norfolk was first settled in 1622 and was incorporated as a city within Norfolk County in 1845; the city became independent of the county 1871.

Norman   **Minnesota**
Ada   873 sq. mi.

| 6,852 | 7,442 | 7,975 | 9,379 | 10,008 | 11,253 | 12,909 |

February 7, 1881. *Uncertain.* (1) *Norwegians.* Many early settlers were Norwegians (Normans). (2) *Norman W. Kittson* (see Kittson, Minnesota).

Northampton   **North Carolina**
Jackson   537 sq. mi.

| 22,099 | 22,086 | 20,798 | 22,584 | 24,009 | 26,811 | 28,432 |

1741. *James Compton, 5th Earl of Northampton (1687–1754)*. English House of Commons 1710; House of Lords 1711–54.

Northampton   **Pennsylvania**
Easton   370 sq. mi.

| 297,735 | 267,066 | 247,105 | 225,418 | 214,368 | 201,412 | 185,243 |

March 11, 1752. *Northamptonshire, England*. Name stipulated by Thomas Penn, son of William Penn, after his father-in-law's estate in Easton, Northamptonshire.

Northampton   **Virginia**
Eastville   212 sq. mi.

| 12,389 | 13,093 | 13,061 | 14,625 | 14,442 | 16,966 | 17,300 |

1634, as Accawmack; name changed 1643. *Uncertain*. (1) *Northamptonshire, England*. (2) *Spencer Compton, 2nd Earl of Northampton (1601–43)*; courtier of Charles I; made Earl of Northampton 1630; killed during English Civil War.

North Slope   **Alaska**
Barrow   88,695 sq. mi.

| 9,430 | 7,385 | 5,979 | 4,199 | 2,663 | 2,133 | (a) |

July 1, 1972. *Descriptive* of borough's location between Brooks Range and Arctic Ocean. [Part of 2nd and 4th Judicial Divisions.]

Northumberland   **Pennsylvania**
Sunbury   458 sq. mi.

| 94,528 | 94,556 | 96,771 | 100,381 | 99,190 | 104,138 | 117,115 |

March 22, 1772. *Northumberland County, England*. Name refers to area north of the Humber River in northern England.

Northumberland   **Virginia**
Heathsville   191 sq. mi.

| 12,330 | 12,259 | 10,524 | 9,828 | 9,239 | 10,185 | 10,012 |

1648. *Northumberland County, England*.*

Northwest Arctic   **Alaska**
Kotzebue   35,573 sq. mi.

| 7,523 | 7,208 | 6,113 | 4,831 | 4,434 | 3,560 | (a) |

June 2, 1986. *Descriptive* of borough's location in northwest Alaska. The Arctic Circle bisects the borough. [Part of 2nd Judicial Division.]

Norton   **Kansas**
Norton   878 sq. mi.

| 5,671 | 5,953 | 5,947 | 6,689 | 7,279 | 8,035 | 8,808 |

February 26, 1867, as Norton; organized August 22, 1872; name changed to Billings March 6, 1873; renamed Norton February 19, 1874. *Orloff Norton (1837–64)*. Private to captain in Kansas Volunteer Cavalry 1861–64; killed at Cave Hill, Arkansas, November 12, 1864.

Norton   **Virginia**
(Independent City)   7 sq. mi.

| 3,958 | 3,904 | 4,247 | 4,757 | 4,001 | 4,996 | (a) |

April 6, 1954. *Eckstein Norton (?–1893)*. President of Louisville & Nashville Railroad at time of opening of Clinch Valley branch 1891. [(a) Part of Wise County] (Associated county: Wise.)

Nottoway   **Virginia**
Nottoway   314 sq. mi.

| 15,853 | 15,725 | 14,993 | 14,666 | 14,260 | 15,141 | 15,479 |

December 22, 1788. *Uncertain*. (1) *Nottoway Indians*; Iroquoian tribe in southern Virginia; name given by neighboring Algonquins means "enemy" or "adder." (2) *Nottoway River*; named for Nottoways.

Nowata   **Oklahoma**
Nowata   566 sq. mi.
10,536   10,569   9,992   11,486   9,773   10,848   12,734
July 16, 1907. *Town of Nowata*. Name from Delaware word *noweta* or *noweeta* meaning "welcome."

Nuxobee   **Mississippi**
Macon   695 sq. mi.
11,545   12,548   12,604   13,212   14,288   16,826   20,022
December 23, 1833. *Nuxobee River*. From Choctaw word approximating "stinking water."

Nuckolls   **Nebraska**
Nelson   575 sq. mi.
4,500   5,057   5,786   6,726   7,404   8,217   9,609
January 13, 1860; organized June 27, 1871. *Uncertain*. (1) *Stephen Friel Nuckolls (1825–79)*; Nebraska territorial legislature 1859–60; congressional delegate from Wyoming Territory 1869–71; Wyoming territorial legislature 1871. (2) Both Stephen Nuckolls and his brother *Lafayette Nuckolls (1835–?)*; Nebraska territorial legislature at age nineteen 1854.

Nueces   **Texas**
Corpus Christi   838 sq. mi.
340,223   313,645   291,145   268,215   237,544   221,573   165,471
April 18, 1846; organized July 12, 1846. *Nueces River*. Spanish for "nut"; named in 1689 for pecan trees on its banks.

Nye   **Nevada**
Tonopah   18,182 sq. mi.
43,946   32,485   17,781   9,048   5,599   4,374   3,101
February 16, 1864. *James Warren Nye (1814–76)*. District Attorney, Madison County, New York, 1839; president, New York City Metropolitan Board of Police 1857–60; governor of Nevada Territory 1861–64; US senator from Nevada 1864–73.

O

Oakland   **Michigan**
Pontiac   868 sq. mi.
1,202,362   1,194,156   1,083,592   1,011,793   907,871   690,259   396,001
January 12, 1819; organized March 28, 1820. *Descriptive*. Refers to oak trees in the area.

Obion   **Tennessee**
Union City   545 sq. mi.
31,807   32,450   31,717   32,781   29,936   26,957   29,056
October 24, 1823. *Obion River*. From Indian word for "many prongs"; the river has four forks.

O'Brien   **Iowa**
Primghar   573 sq. mi.
14,398   15,102   15,444   16,972   17,522   18,840   18,970
January 15, 1851; organized April 7, 1860. *William Smith O'Brien (1803–64)*. English House of Commons 1826–39; leader of Irish independence movement 1848; sentenced to death for treason 1848; commuted to life imprisonment and transported to Tasmania 1849; fully pardoned and returned to Ireland 1856.

Ocean   **New Jersey**
Toms River   629 sq. mi.
576,567   510,916   433,203   346,038   208,470   108,241   56,622
February 15, 1850. *Atlantic Ocean*. The county fronts on the ocean.

Oceana   **Michigan**
Hart   512 sq. mi.

26,570   26,873   22,454   22,002   17,984   16,547   16,105

March 2, 1831; organized April 7, 1851. *Uncertain*. (1) *Descriptive* of location on "ocean" of Lake Michigan. (2) *The Commonwealth of Oceana*; utopian book by James Harrington 1656.

Ochiltree   **Texas**
Perryton   918 sq. mi.
10,223   9,006   9,128   9,588   9,704   9,380   6,024

August 21, 1876; organized February 21, 1889. *William Beck Ochiltree (1811–67)*. Judge, Texas Republic district court 1842; Republic of Texas secretary of treasury 1844; Texas attorney general 1845; Texas legislature 1855; Texas Constitutional Convention 1861; Provisional Congress of Confederate States 1861; colonel of infantry 1861, resigned commission due to ill health 1863.

Oconee   **Georgia**
Watkinsville   184 sq. mi.
32,808   26,225   17,618   12,427   7,915   6,304   7,009

February 25, 1875. *Oconee River*. Named for Indian village *Ukwunu* in central Georgia; Cherokee for "place of springs."

Oconee   **South Carolina**
Walhalla   626 sq. mi.
74,273   66,215   57,494   48,611   40,728   40,204   39,050

January 29, 1868. *Oconee Indians*. (See Oconee, Georgia.)

Oconto   **Wisconsin**
Oconto   998 sq. mi.
37,660   35,634   30,226   28,947   25,553   25,110   26,238

February 6, 1851; organized 1854. *Oconto River*. Uncertain origin: (1) Menominee name referring to fish; (2) Chippewa name derived from "watchful" or "ambush."

Ogemaw   **Michigan**
West Branch   563 sq. mi.
21,699   21,645   18,681   16,436   11,903   9,680   9,345

April 1, 1840; abolished March 7, 1867; recreated March 28, 1873; organized April 27, 1875. *Ogemakegato (1794–1840)*. Chief of Saginaw branch of Ojibwas; signed four treaties with US 1819–39; petitioned Congress to reimburse Indians for lands 1832.

Ogle   **Illinois**
Oregon   759 sq. mi.
53,497   51,032   45,957   46,338   42,867   38,106   33,429

January 16, 1836; organized 1839. *Joseph Ogle (1741–1821)*. Lieutenant and captain in Illinois Territorial Militia.

Oglethorpe   **Georgia**
Lexington   439 sq. mi.
14,899   12,635   9,763   8,929   7,598   7,926   9,958

December 19, 1793. *James Edward Oglethorpe (1696–1785)*. British Army 1710; House of Commons 1722; colonized Georgia near Savannah 1732; defeated Spanish force 1742; returned to England 1743.

Ohio   **Indiana**
Rising Sun   86 sq. mi.
6,128   5,623   5,315   5,114   4,289   4,165   4,223

January 4, 1844; effective May 1, 1844. *Ohio River*. French rendering of Iroquois *oheo*, *oyo*, or *oyoneri* meaning "beautiful."

Ohio   **Kentucky**
Hartford   587 sq. mi.
23,842   22,916   21,105   21,765   18,790   17,725   20,840

December 17, 1798; effective July 1, 1799. *Ohio River*.*

Ohio   **West Virginia**
Wheeling   106 sq. mi.
44,443   47,427   50,871   61,389   64,197   68,437   71,672
November 6, 1776. *Ohio River.**

Okaloosa   **Florida**
Crestview   930 sq. mi.
180,822   170,498   143,776   109,920   88,187   61,175   27,533
June 3, 1915. *Blackwater River*. From Choctaw name for river: *oka* (water) and *lusa* (black).

Okanogan   **Washington**
Okanogan   5,268 sq. mi.
41,120   39,564   33,350   30,639   25,867   25,520   29,131
February 2, 1888. *Uncertain*. (1) *Okanogan River*. (2) *Okanogan Lake or Mountains*. Name from Salish word for "rendezvous"; refers to a meeting place near US-Canadian border.

Okeechobee   **Florida**
Okeechobee   769 sq. mi.
39,996   35,910   29,627   20,264   11,233   6,424   3,454
May 8, 1917. *Lake Okeechobee*. From Hitchita words *oki* (water) and *chubi* (big).

Okfuskee   **Oklahoma**
Okemah   619 sq. mi.
12,191   11,814   11,551   11,125   10,683   11,706   16,948
July 16, 1907. *Okfuskee, Alabama*. Former Creek village; largest community in Creek Confederacy before Creek removal to Indian Territory (Oklahoma) 1834.

Oklahoma   **Oklahoma**
Oklahoma City   709 sq. mi.
718,633   660,448   599,611   568,933   526,805   439,506   325,352
May 2, 1890. *Oklahoma Territory*. From Choctaw words *okla* (people) and *humma* (red).

Okmulgee   **Oklahoma**
Okmulgee   697 sq. mi.
40,069   39,685   36,490   39,169   35,358   36,945   44,561
July 16, 1907. *Town of Okmulgee*. From Hitchita words *oki* (boiling) and *mulgi* (waters).

Oktibbeha   **Mississippi**
Starkville   458 sq. mi.
47,671   42,902   38,375   36,018   28,752   26,175   24,569
December 23, 1833. *Uncertain*. Either one of two streams named Oktibbeha; Choctaw name for "fighting water" or "icy water."

Oldham   **Kentucky**
La Grange   187 sq. mi.
60,316   46,178   33,263   27,795   14,687   13,388   11,018
December 15, 1823. *William Oldham (1753–91)*. 1st lieutenant in Nelsons Independent Rifle Company 1776; captain 1776; 5th Pennsylvania Regiment 1777; resigned 1779; member of Saint Clair's Militia; killed in Battle with Miamis.

Oldham   **Texas**
Vega   1,501 sq. mi.
2,052   2,185   2,278   2,283   2,258   1,928   1,672
August 21, 1876; organized June 12, 1881. *William Simpson Oldham (1813–68)*. Arkansas General Assembly 1838–42; speaker 1842; Arkansas Supreme Court 1844; moved to Texas 1849; Texas Secession Convention 1861; Confederate senator from Texas 1861–65.

Oliver   **North Dakota**
Center   723 sq. mi.

| 1,846 | 2,065 | 2,381 | 2,495 | 2,322 | 2,610 | 3,091 |

March 12, 1885; organized May 18, 1885. *Harry S. Oliver (1855–1909)*. Dakota territorial legislature, chairman, committee on county boundaries 1885; North Dakota legislature 1889–93.

Olmsted   **Minnesota**
Rochester   653 sq. mi.

| 144,248 | 124,277 | 106,470 | 92,006 | 84,104 | 65,532 | 48,228 |

February 20, 1855. *Uncertain*. (1) *David Olmsted (1822–61)*; Iowa Constitutional Convention 1846; settled in what became Minnesota Territory 1848; Minnesota territorial legislature 1849–50; proprietor of *Minnesota Democrat* 1853; first mayor of St. Paul 1854; (2) *Samuel Baldwin Olmsted (1810–78)*; Iowa Constitutional Convention 1844; Minnesota territorial legislature 1854.

Oneida   **Idaho**
Malad City   1,200 sq. mi.

| 4,286 | 4,125 | 3,492 | 3,258 | 2,864 | 3,603 | 4,387 |

January 22, 1864. *City of Oneida, New York*. Early settlers were from Oneida, New York.

Oneida   **New York**
Utica   1,212 sq. mi.

| 234,878 | 235,469 | 250,836 | 253,466 | 273,037 | 264,401 | 222,855 |

March 15, 1798. *Oneida Indians*. Name means "standing stone" or "stone people;" refers to a large stone in one of their villages. Lived in central New York State; smallest tribe of Iroquois Confederacy; sided with colonists during American Revolution.

Oneida   **Wisconsin**
Rhinelander   1,113 sq. mi.

| 35,998 | 36,776 | 31,679 | 31,216 | 24,427 | 22,112 | 20,648 |

April 11, 1885. *Oneida Indians*.* Many Oneidas moved from New York to northern Wisconsin.

Onondaga   **New York**
Syracuse   778 sq. mi.

| 467,026 | 458,336 | 468,973 | 463,920 | 472,476 | 423,028 | 341,719 |

March 5, 1794. *Onondaga Indians*. Name refers to "hill" or "mountain top." Member of Iroquois Confederation; main village was capital of the confederation.

Onslow   **North Carolina**
Jacksonville   763 sq. mi.

| 177,772 | 150,355 | 149,838 | 112,784 | 102,126 | 82,706 | 42,047 |

November 23, 1734. *Arthur Onslow (1691–1768)*. English statesman; House of Commons 1720–61, speaker 1728–61; chancellor to Queen Caroline (wife of George II) 1729; treasurer of the British Navy 1734–42.

Ontario   **New York**
Canandaigua   644 sq. mi.

| 107,931 | 100,224 | 95,101 | 88,909 | 78,849 | 68,070 | 60,172 |

January 27, 1789. *Lake Ontario*. Iroquois for "beautiful lake."

Ontonagon   **Michigan**
Ontonagon   1,311 sq. mi.

| 6,780 | 7,818 | 8,854 | 9,861 | 10,548 | 10,584 | 10,282 |

March 9, 1843; organized January 1, 1853. *Ontonagon River*. Uncertain Ojibwa word; possibilities include "bowl," "hunting river," or "fishing place."

Orange   **California**
Santa Ana   791 sq. mi.

3,010,232   2,846,289   2,410,556   1,932,709   1,420,386   703,925   216,224
March 11, 1889. *Descriptive*. Refers to local orange groves.

Orange   **Florida**
Orlando   903 sq. mi.
1,145,956   896,344   677,491   471,016   344,311   263,540   114,950
December 29, 1824, as Mosquito; name unofficially changed to Leigh Road 1842; name changed to Orange January 30, 1845. *Descriptive*. Refers to local orange groves.

Orange   **Indiana**
Paoli   398 sq. mi.
19,840   19,306   18,409   18,677   16,968   16,877   16,879
December 26, 1815; effective February 1, 1816. *Orange County, North Carolina*. Early settlers were from Orange County.

Orange   **New York**
Goshen   812 sq. mi.
372,813   341,367   307,647   259,603   221,657   183,734   152,255
November 1, 1683; organized 1698. *William Nassau, Prince of Orange, King William III* (see King William, Virginia). Title of "Orange" belonged to Nassau family from small territory in southern France.

Orange   **North Carolina**
Hillsborough   398 sq. mi.
133,801   118,227   93,851   77,055   57,707   42,970   34,435
1752. *Uncertain*. (1) *William Nassau, Prince of Orange, King William III*.* (2) *William V of Orange (1748–1806)*; grandson of King George II; Stadtholder (chief executive) of the Netherlands 1751; fled to England during French-supported revolution 1795.

Orange   **Texas**
Beaumont   334 sq. mi.
81,837   84,966   80,509   83,838   71,170   60,357   40,567
February 5, 1852. *Descriptive*. Refers to a specific orange grove near the Neches River.

Orange   **Vermont**
Chelsea   687 sq. mi.
28,936   28,226   26,149   22,739   17,676   16,014   17,027
February 22, 1781. *Uncertain*. (1) *Orange County, New York*. (2) *Town of Orange, Connecticut, or Orange, Massachusetts*. All of these possibilities derive from *William Nassau, Prince of Orange, King William III*.*

Orange   **Virginia**
Orange   341 sq. mi.
33,481   25,881   21,421   18,063   13,792   12,900   12,755
September 20, 1734. *William IV, Prince of Orange (1711–51)*. Stadtholder (chief executive) of the Netherlands 1729; married Princess Anne, eldest daughter of King George II 1734; father of William V (see Orange, North Carolina [2]).

Orangeburg   **South Carolina**
Orangeburg   1,106 sq. mi.
92,501   91,582   84,803   82,276   69,789   68,559   68,726
1769 as judicial district; designated as county April 16, 1868. *Town of Orangeburg*. Named for William IV, Prince of Orange.*

Oregon   **Missouri**
Alton   790 sq. mi.
10,881   10,344   9,470   10,238   9,180   9,845   11,978
February 14, 1845. *Oregon Country*. Dispute over Oregon between US and England was a major contemporary issue. Origin of name is uncertain; perhaps from careless transcription on an early North American map of "Ouisconsink River" to "Ouariconsint River."

Orleans **Louisiana**
New Orleans 169 sq. mi.
343,829 484,674 496,938 557,515 593,471 627,525 570,445
April 10, 1805. *Uncertain.* (1) *City of Orleans, France.* (2) *Phillippe II, Duc d'Orleans (1674–1723)*; regent of France during minority of Louis XV 1715–23; prime minister of France 1723.

Orleans **New York**
Albion 391 sq. mi.
42,883 44,171 41,846 38,496 37,305 34,159 29,832
November 12, 1824. *Uncertain.* (1) *City of Orleans, France.* (2) *French royal house of Orleans*; perhaps specifically Louis Phillippe Joseph, Duc d'Orleans (1747–93); supported colonists in American Revolution; father of King Louis-Phillippe.

Orleans **Vermont**
Newport 693 sq. mi.
27,231 26,277 24,053 23,440 20,153 20,143 21,190
November 5, 1792; organized 1799. *Uncertain.* (1) *City of Orleans, France.* (2) *Phillippe II, Duc d'Orleans* (see Orleans, Louisiana [2]).

Osage **Kansas**
Lyndon 706 sq. mi.
16,295 16,712 15,248 15,319 13,352 12,886 12,811
August 30, 1855, as Weller; organized and name changed February 11, 1859. *Marais des Cygnes River.* Formerly named Osage River; from Osage Indians (see Osage, Oklahoma).

Osage **Missouri**
Linn 604 sq. mi.
13,878 13,602 12,018 12,014 10,994 10,867 11,301
January 29, 1841; *Osage River.* From Osage Indians (see Osage, Oklahoma).

Osage **Oklahoma**
Pawhuska 2,246 sq. mi.
47,472 44,437 41,645 39,327 29,750 32,441 33,071
July 16, 1907. *Osage Indians.* French corruption of Algonquin *ouasash*, possibly meaning "bone men." Division of Dakotas; lived in Arkansas, Illinois, Kansas, and Missouri; removed to Indian Territory (Oklahoma) through a series of treaties with US 1808–70.

Osborne **Kansas**
Osborne 893 sq. mi.
3,858 4,452 4,867 5,959 6,416 7,506 8,558
February 26, 1867; organized September 12, 1871. *Vincent B. Osborne (1839–79).* Private, Kansas Volunteer Infantry, 1861; wounded at Wilson's Creek and discharged 1861; reenlisted as sergeant, Kansas Volunteer Cavalry, 1862; sutler at Fort Harker 1865; Kansas legislature 1872.

Osceola **Florida**
Kissimmee 1,327 sq. mi.
268,685 172,493 107,728 49,287 25,267 19,029 11,406
May 12, 1887. *Osceola (c1804–38).* Leader of Seminoles; resisted removal to Indian Territory (Oklahoma) 1835; captured under flag of truce 1837; died in Charleston prison.

Osceola **Iowa**
Sibley 399 sq. mi.
6,462 7,003 7,267 8,371 8,555 10,064 10,181
January 15, 1851; organized January 1, 1872. *Osceola.**

Osceola **Michigan**
Reed City 566 sq. mi.

| 23,528 | 23,197 | 20,146 | 18,928 | 14,838 | 11,395 | 13,797 |

April 1, 1840, as Unwattin; name changed March 8, 1843; organized March 17, 1869. *Osceola.**

Oscoda   **Michigan**
Mio   566 sq. mi.

| 8,640 | 9,418 | 7,842 | 6,858 | 4,726 | 3,447 | 3,134 |

April 1, 1804; organized March 10, 1881. *Coined word*. Word coined from Indian languages; *os* from *ossin* meaning "pebble"; and *coda* from *mushcoda* meaning "prairie." (See Schoolcraft, Michigan.)

Oswego   **New York**
Oswego   952 sq. mi.

| 122,109 | 122,377 | 121,771 | 113,901 | 100,897 | 86,118 | 77,181 |

March 1, 1816. *Oswego River*. Iroquois word for "flowing out" or "small water into large water" referring to Lake Ontario.

Otero   **Colorado**
La Junta   1,262 sq. mi.

| 18,831 | 20,311 | 20,185 | 22,567 | 23,523 | 24,128 | 25,275 |

March 25, 1889. *Miguel Antonio Otero (1829–82)*. New Mexico territorial legislature 1852–54; New Mexico Territory congressional delegate 1855–60; secretary of New Mexico Territory 1861–62; advocated transcontinental railroad through New Mexico; a founder of La Junta as a railhead 1875. Father of M. A. Otero (see Otero, New Mexico).

Otero   **New Mexico**
Alamogordo   6,613 sq. mi.

| 63,797 | 62,298 | 51,928 | 44,665 | 41,097 | 36,976 | 14,909 |

January 30, 1899. *Miguel Antonio Otero (1859–1944)*. City treasurer of Las Vegas, New Mexico; governor of New Mexico Territory 1897–1906; New Mexico territorial treasurer 1909–11. Son of M. A. Otero.*

Otoe   **Nebraska**
Nebraska City   616 sq. mi.

| 15,740 | 15,396 | 14,252 | 15,183 | 15,576 | 16,503 | 17,056 |

November 23, 1854, as Pierce; name changed 1855; organized December 1, 1856. *Otoe Indians*. Uncertain origin of name; possible shortened version of a place name. Migrated from Great Lakes region to Plains by 1700; various treaties with US 1830–54 led to resettlement in Indian Territory (Oklahoma) 1881.

Otsego   **Michigan**
Gaylord   515 sq. mi.

| 24,164 | 23,301 | 17,957 | 14,993 | 10,422 | 7,545 | 6,435 |

April 1, 1840, as Okkuddo; name changed March 8, 1843; organized March 12, 1875. *Otsego County, New York*. Many early settlers were from New York.

Otsego   **New York**
Cooperstown   1,002 sq. mi.

| 62,259 | 61,676 | 60,517 | 59,075 | 56,181 | 51,942 | 50,763 |

February 16, 1791. *Uncertain*. (1) *Otsego Lake*; one of the Finger Lakes. (2) *Town of Otsego*. Mohawk name for the lake; most likely means "place of the rock."

Ottawa   **Kansas**
Minneapolis   721 sq. mi.

| 6,091 | 6,163 | 5,634 | 5,971 | 6,183 | 6,779 | 7,265 |

February 27, 1860; organized November 1866. *Ottawa Indians*. Name means "trader" or "barterer." Algonquin linguistic family; lived between Ohio and Wisconsin; resettled in Kansas 1836; removed to Indian Territory (Oklahoma) 1870.

Ottawa   **Michigan**
Grand Haven   563 sq. mi.

263,801   238,314   187,768   157,174   128,181   98,719   73,751
March 2, 1831; organized December 29, 1837. *Ottawa Indians.**

Ottawa   **Ohio**
Port Clinton   255 sq. mi.
41,428   40,985   40,029   40,076   37,099   35,233   29,469
March 6, 1840. *Ottawa Indians.**

Ottawa   **Oklahoma**
Miami   471 sq. mi.
31,848   33,194   30,561   32,870   29,800   28,301   32,218
July 16, 1907. *Ottawa Indians.**

Otter Tail   **Minnesota**
Fergus Falls   1,972 sq. mi.
57,303   57,159   50,714   51,937   46,097   48,960   51,320
March 18, 1858; organized February 28, 1870. *Otter Tale Lake.* Translation of Indian name descriptive of long, narrow sandbar in the lake.

Ouachita   **Arkansas**
Camden   733 sq. mi.
26,120   38,790   30,574   30,541   30,896   31,641   33,051
November 29, 1842. *Ouachita River.* Named for Ouachita Indians (see Ouachita, Louisiana).

Ouachita   **Louisiana**
Monroe   610 sq. mi.
153,720   147,250   142,191   139,241   115,387   101,663   74,713
April 10, 1805. *Ouachita Indians.* Uncertain origins of name: (1) "black water" or "silver water"; (2) French rendering of Choctaw words meaning "big hunt." Clan of Caddoan family living in northeastern Louisiana.

Ouray   **Colorado**
Ouray   542 sq. mi.
4,436   3,742   2,295   1,925   1,546   1,601   2,103
January 18, 1877. *Ouray (c1833–80).* Succeeded father as chief of Ute Indians 1860; leader of Ute Confederacy; ceded lands to US through treaties 1863 and 1868; tried unsuccessfully to maintain peace with US following gold rush to Colorado 1878; persuaded Utes to settle on reservations 1880.

Outagamie   **Wisconsin**
Appleton   638 sq. mi.
176,695   160,971   140,510   128,799   119,356   101,794   81,722
February 17, 1851; organized 1852. *Fox Indians.* From Utugamig, Chippewa name for Fox Indians meaning "people of the other shore." Algonquin tribe related to Sauks; in constant fighting with surrounding tribes; the only Algonquin tribe to fight against the French.

Overton   **Tennessee**
Livingston   433 sq. mi.
22,083   20,118   17,636   17,575   14,866   14,661   17,566
September 11, 1806. *John Overton (1766–1833).* Tennessee Superior Court 1804–10; Tennessee Supreme Court 1811–16; a founder of Memphis 1819.

Owen   **Indiana**
Spencer   385 sq. mi.
21,575   21,786   17,281   15,841   12,163   11,400   11,763
December 21, 1818. *Abraham Owen (1769–1811).* Kentucky legislature; colonel, aide to General Harrison; killed in Battle of Tippecanoe, November 7, 1811.

Owen   **Kentucky**
Owenton   351 sq. mi.
10,841   10,547   9,035   8,924   7,470   8,237   9,755
February 6, 1819. *Abraham Owen.**

Owsley   **Kentucky**
Booneville   197 sq. mi.
4,755   4,858   5,036   5,709   5,023   5,369   7,324
January 23, 1843. *William Owsley (1782–1862)*. Kentucky House of Representatives 1809–11 and 1831; judge, Court of Appeals 1812–28; Kentucky Senate 1834–36; Kentucky secretary of state 1834–36; governor of Kentucky 1844–46.

Owyhee   **Idaho**
Murphy   7,666 sq. mi.
11,526   10,644   8,392   8,272   6,422   6,375   6,307
December 31, 1863. *Owyhee River*. Corruption of "Hawaii" in commemoration of Hawaiian trappers killed in the region.

Oxford   **Maine**
South Paris   2,077 sq. mi.
57,833   54,755   52,602   48,968   43,457   44,345   44,221
March 4, 1805. *Town of Oxford, Massachusetts*. Name chosen by an early settler born in Oxford, Massachusetts.

Ozark   **Missouri**
Gainesville   745 sq. mi.
9,723   9,542   8,598   7,961   6,226   6,744   8,856
January 29, 1841, as Ozark; name changed to Decatur, February 22, 1843; renamed Ozark March 24, 1845. *Ozark Mountains*. From French *aux arcs* (with bows); applied to local Indians.

Ozaukee   **Wisconsin**
Port Washington   233 sq. mi.
86,395   82,317   72,831   66,981   54,421   38,441   23,361
March 7, 1853. *Sauk Indians*. From complete name of Sauks, *Osauki-wug*, meaning "people of the yellow earth"; defeated with Fox allies in Black Hawk War 1832. (See Sauk, Wisconsin.)

P

Pacific   **Washington**
South Bend   933 sq. mi.
20,920   20,984   18,882   17,237   15,796   14,674   16,558
February 4, 1851. *Pacific Ocean*. County fronts on the ocean.

Page   **Iowa**
Clarinda   535 sq. mi.
15,932   16,976   16,870   19,063   18,507   21,023   23,921
February 24, 1847; organized March 22, 1852. *John Page (?–1846)*. 2nd lieutenant to captain 1818–31; killed at Battle of Palo Alto, May 8, 1846.

Page   **Virginia**
Luray   311 sq. mi.
24,042   23,177   21,690   19,401   16,581   15,572   15,152
March 30 1831. *John Page (1743–1808)*. Virginia Constitutional Convention 1776; lieutenant-governor of Virginia 1776–79; colonel, Continental Army; Virginia House of Delegates intermittently 1781–1801; US representative 1789–97; governor of Virginia 1802–05; US commissioner of loans 1805–08.

Palm Beach   **Florida**
West Palm Beach   1,970 sq. mi.

| 1,320,134 | 1,131,184 | 863,518 | 576,863 | 348,753 | 228,106 | 114,688 |

April 30, 1909. *Town of Palm Beach*. Descriptive of palm trees and ocean frontage.

Palo Alto   **Iowa**
Emmetsburg   564 sq. mi.

| 9,421 | 10,147 | 10,669 | 12,721 | 13,289 | 14,736 | 15,891 |

January 15, 1851; organized December 29, 1858. *Battle of Palo Alto*. First Battle of Mexican War, May 8, 1846; US commanded by Zachary Taylor defeated larger Mexican force.

Palo Pinto   **Texas**
Palo Pinto   952 sq. mi.

| 28,111 | 27,026 | 25,055 | 24,062 | 28,962 | 20,516 | 17,154 |

August 27, 1856; organized May 13, 1857. *Palo Pinto Creek*. Spanish for "painted stick"; may refer to mesquite trees covered with grey moss giving appearance of being painted.

Pamlico   **North Carolina**
Bayboro   337 sq. mi.

| 13,144 | 12,934 | 11,372 | 10,398 | 9,467 | 9,850 | 9,993 |

February 8, 1872. *Pamlico Sound*. Named for tribe of Algonquin Indians living in area; meaning of name is unknown.

Panola   **Mississippi**
Batesville   685 sq. mi.

| 34,707 | 34,274 | 29,996 | 28,164 | 26,829 | 28,791 | 31,271 |

February 9, 1836. *Cotton*. From Choctaw word for "cotton."

Panola   **Texas**
Carthage   802 sq. mi.

| 23,796 | 22,756 | 22,035 | 20,724 | 15,894 | 16,870 | 19,250 |

March 30, 1846; organized September 12, 1846. *Panola County, Mississippi*. One of the first county officials was from Panola County, Mississippi.

Park   **Colorado**
Fairplay   2,194 sq. mi.

| 16,206 | 14,523 | 7,174 | 5,333 | 2,185 | 1,822 | 1,870 |

November 1, 1861. *South Park*. A "park" is a large open valley between mountains.

Park   **Montana**
Livingston   2,803 sq. mi.

| 15,636 | 15,964 | 14,614[a] | 12,935[a] | 11,261[a] | 13,215[a] | 12,057[a] |

February 23, 1887. *Yellowstone National Park*. Named for Yellowstone River (see Yellowstone, Montana); first US national park 1872. [(a) Includes part of Yellowstone National Park: 1990 population, 52; 1980, 66; 1970, 64; 1960, 47; 1950, 58.]

Park   **Wyoming**
Cody   6,942 sq. mi.

| 28,205 | 25,786 | 23,178 | 21,639 | 17,752 | 17,294[a] | 15,535[a] |

February 15, 1909. *Yellowstone National Park*.* [(a) Includes part of Yellowstone National Park: 1960 population, 420; 1950, 353. Some of the park's population may have been in the portion included in Teton County, Wyoming.]

Parke   **Indiana**
Rockville   445 sq. mi.

| 17,339 | 17,241 | 15,410 | 16,372 | 14,600 | 14,804 | 15,674 |

January 9, 1821; effective April 2, 1821. *Benjamin Parke (1777–1835).* Attorney general of Indiana Territory 1804–08; Indiana territorial legislature 1805; Indiana Territory congressional delegate 1805–08; Indiana Territory judge 1808–17; judge, US District Court of Indiana 1817–35.

Parker   **Texas**
Weatherford   903 sq. mi.

116,927	88,495	64,785	44,609	33,888	22,880	21,528

December 12, 1855; organized March 11, 1856. *Uncertain.* (1) *Isaac Parker (1793–1883)*; served in Texas Revolution 1836; Republic of Texas legislature 1838–40 and 1841–43; Texas legislature 1846–53. (2) *Family of Cynthia Ann Parker (c1825–c1871)*; captured by Comanches as a child 1836; married Comanche chief Peta Nocona; mother of Quanah Parker, Comanche chief; refused pleas to return to white society. Isaac and Cynthia were uncle and niece.

Parmer   **Texas**
Farwell   881 sq. mi.

10,269	10,016	9,863	11,038	10,509	9,583	5,787

August 21, 1876; organized May 7, 1907. *Martin Parmer (1778–1850).* Fled to Louisiana after defeat of Fredonia Rebellion 1827; returned to Texas after pardon 1835; Republic of Texas legislature 1835; signer, Texas Declaration of Independence 1836; Texas Constitutional Convention 1836.

Pasco   **Florida**
Dade City   747 sq. mi.

464,697	344,765	281,131	193,643	75,955	36,785	20,529

June 2, 1887. *Samuel Pasco (1834–1917).* Private, Confederate Army 1861; captured at Mississippi Ridge 1863, paroled 1865; president, Florida Constitutional Convention 1885; Florida House of Representatives 1886–87, speaker 1887; US senator 1887–99.

Pasquotank   **North Carolina**
Elizabeth City   227 sq. mi.

40,661	34,897	31,298	28,462	26,824	25,630	24,347

1670. *Pasquotank Indians.* Algonquin tribe; name refers to "divided tidal water."

Passaic   **New Jersey**
Paterson   185 sq. mi.

501,226	489,049	453,060	447,585	460,782	406,618	337,093

February 7, 1837. *Passaic River.* From Lenape word referring to "valley."

Patrick   **Virginia**
Stuart   483 sq. mi.

18,490	19,407	17,473	17,647	15,282	15,282	15,642

November 26, 1790. *Patrick Henry.* (See Henry, Alabama.)

Paulding   **Georgia**
Dallas   312 sq. mi.

142,324	81,678	41,611	26,110	17,520	13,101	11,752

December 3, 1832. *John Paulding (1758–1818).* New York Militia; one of three New York militiamen who captured British Major André revealing Benedict Arnold's treason, September 23, 1780; all three received a silver medal and $200 pension from Congress. (See Van Wert, and Williams, Ohio.)

Paulding   **Ohio**
Paulding   416 sq. mi.

19,614	20,293	20,488	21,302	19,329	16,792	15,047

February 20, 1820; organized 1839. *John Paulding.**

Pawnee   **Kansas**
Larned   754 sq. mi.

6,973   7,233   7,555   8,065   8,484   10,254   11,041
February 26, 1867; organized November 4, 1872. *Pawnee River*. Named for Pawnee Indians (see Pawnee, Nebraska).

Pawnee   **Nebraska**
Pawnee City   431 sq. mi.
2,773   3,087   3,317   3,937   4,473   5,356   6,744
March 6, 1855; organized November 4, 1856. *Pawnee Indians*. Name may derive from Apache word for "slave" referring to Pawnees captured in Battle. Caddoan linguistic family; ranged from Nebraska to Texas; friendly to whites but fought with neighboring tribes; resettled in Indian Territory (Oklahoma) 1870s.

Pawnee   **Oklahoma**
Pawnee   568 sq. mi.
16,577   16,612   15,575   15,310   11,338   10,884   13,616
August 21, 1893, as County Q; organized and name changed 1895. *Pawnee Indians*.*

Payette   **Idaho**
Payette   407 sq. mi.
22,623   20,578   16,434   15,722   12,401   12,363   11,921
February 28, 1917. *Payette River*. Named for Francois Payette (?–?); trapper and explorer; postmaster of Hudson's Bay Company 1835; traded with emigrants on Oregon Trail.

Payne   **Oklahoma**
Stillwater   685 sq. mi.
77,350   68,190   61,507   62,435   50,654   44,231   46,430
May 2, 1890. *David Lewis Payne (1836–84)*. Kansas legislature 1864; leader of Boomer Movement which encouraged white settlers to move into Oklahoma's Unassigned Lands that had been reserved for Indian settlement 1880–84.

Peach   **Georgia**
Fort Valley   150 sq. mi.
27,695   23,668   21,189   19,151   15,990   13,846   11,705
July 18, 1924. *Descriptive*. Refers to peach orchards in the area.

Pearl River   **Mississippi**
Poplarville   811 sq. mi.
55,834   48,621   38,714   33,795   27,802   22,411   20,641
February 22, 1890. *Pearl River*. Translation of French *Riviere des Perles*; named after finding pearls in some mussels.

Pecos   **Texas**
Fort Stockton   4,764 sq. mi.
15,507   16,809   14,675   14,618   13,748   11,957   9,939
May 3, 1871; organized June 13, 1872. *Pecos River*. Keresan Indian word for "place where there is water."

Pembina   **North Dakota**
Cavalier   1,119 sq. mi.
7,413   8,585   9,238   10,399   10,728   12,946   13,990
January 9, 1867; organized August 12, 1867. *Pembina Trading Post*. Earliest settlement in Dakota Territory 1812; from corruption of Chippewa word meaning "high cranberry bush."

Pemiscot   **Missouri**
Caruthersville   493 sq. mi.
18,296   20,047   21,921   24,987   26,373   38,095   45,624
February 19, 1851. *Pemiscot Bayou*. From Fox word for "liquid mud."

Pender   **North Carolina**
Burgaw   870 sq. mi.

| 52,217 | 41,082 | 28,855 | 22,215 | 18,149 | 18,508 | 18,423 |

February 16, 1875. *William Dorsey Pender (1834–63)*. Graduated West Point 1854; resigned from US Army 1861; Confederate Army captain to major general 1861–63; mortally wounded at Gettysburg, July 1, 1863; died July 18.

Pendleton   **Kentucky**
Falmouth   277 sq. mi.

| 14,877 | 14,390 | 12,036 | 10,989 | 9,949 | 9,968 | 9,610 |

December 13, 1798; organized May 10, 1799. *Edmund Pendleton (1721–1803)*. Virginia House of Burgesses 1752–54; Continental Congress 1774–75; president, Committee of Safety 1775; Virginia House of Delegates 1776–77; president, Virginia Constitutional Convention 1788; president, Virginia Supreme Court of Appeals 1799–1803.

Pendleton   **West Virginia**
Franklin   696 sq. mi.

| 7,695 | 8,196 | 8,054 | 7,910 | 7,031 | 8,093 | 9,313 |

December 4, 1787; effective May 1, 1788. *Edmund Pendleton.* *

Pend Oreille   **Washington**
Newport   1,400 sq. mi.

| 13,001 | 11,732 | 8,915 | 8,580 | 6,025 | 6,914 | 7,413 |

March 1, 1911. *Pend d'Oreille Indians*. From French "hanging from the ear" for large shell ornaments the Pend d'Oreille wore on their ears.

Pennington   **Minnesota**
Thief River Falls   617 sq. mi.

| 13,930 | 13,584 | 13,306 | 15,258 | 13,266 | 12,468 | 12,965 |

November 23, 1910. *Edmund Pennington (1848–1926)*. Superintendent, Minneapolis, St. Paul & Sault Ste. Marie Railway Company 1888–89, general manager 1899–1905, president 1909.

Pennington   **South Dakota**
Rapid City   2,777 sq. mi.

| 100,948 | 88,565 | 81,343 | 70,361 | 59,349 | 58,195 | 34,053 |

January 11, 1875; organized April 19, 1877. *John L. Pennington (1821–1900)*. Alabama Senate 1866–70; governor of Dakota Territory 1874–78; US revenue collector for Dakota Territory 1878.

Penobscot   **Maine**
Bangor   3,397 sq. mi.

| 153,923 | 144,919 | 146,601 | 137,015 | 125,393 | 126,346 | 108,198 |

February 15, 1816; effective April 1, 1816. *Penobscot River*. Named for Penobscot Indians; name means "rocky place" or "rocky river." Tribe of Abnaki Confederacy; sided with French against English.

Peoria   **Illinois**
Peoria   619 sq. mi.

| 186,494 | 183,433 | 182,827 | 200,466 | 195,318 | 189,044 | 174,347 |

January 13, 1825. *Peoria Indians*. Origin of name is uncertain; possibly French rendering of Indian *piwarea*, meaning "carrier" or "packer."

Pepin   **Wisconsin**
Durand   232 sq. mi.

| 7,469 | 7,213 | 7,107 | 7,477 | 7,319 | 7,332 | 7,462 |

February 25, 1858. *Lake Pepin*. Uncertain origin; possibilities include: (1) Pepin brothers, 17th-century explorers; (2) Pepin le Bref (Pepin the Short) (714–68), king of the Franks, father of Charlemagne; (3) Stephen Pepin, Sieur de la Fond (?–?), explored Lake Superior 1679; (4) Jean Pepin (?–?), early settler.

Perkins   **Nebraska**
Grant   883 sq. mi.

2,970   3,200   3,367   3,637   3,423   4,189   4,809

November 8, 1887. *Charles Elliott Perkins (1840–1907)*. President of Chicago, Burlington & Quincy Railroad 1881–1901; developed railroad through Nebraska.

Perkins   **South Dakota**
Bison   2,870 sq. mi.
2,982   3,363   3,932   4,700   4,769   5,977   6,776

November 3, 1908; organized February 9, 1909. *Henry E. Perkins (1864–?)*. Mayor of Sturgis; South Dakota Senate, intermittently 1903–11.

Perquimans   **North Carolina**
Hertford   247 sq. mi.
13,453   11,368   10,447   9,486   8,351   9,178   9,602

1668, as Berkeley; name changed 1681. *Perquimans Indians*. Named by Yeopim Indians as "land of beautiful women." Algonquin tribe living on north side of Albemarle Sound.

Perry   **Alabama**
Marion   720 sq. mi.
10,591   11,861   12,759   15,012   15,388   17,358   20,439

December 13, 1819. *Oliver Hazard Perry (1785–1819)*. Midshipman 1799; lieutenant 1807; commanded schooner 1809; commanded squadron of gunboats 1812; constructed fleet of nine vessels on Lake Erie 1813; defeated British in Battle of Lake Erie, September 10, 1813; sent message to General Harrison "We have met the enemy and they are ours"; commodore 1819; died of yellow fever on diplomatic mission to Venezuela.

Perry   **Arkansas**
Perryville   551 sq. mi.
10,445   10,209   7,969   7,266   5,634   4,927   5,978

December 18, 1840. *Oliver Hazard Perry.**

Perry   **Illinois**
Pinckneyville   442 sq. mi.
22,350   23,094   21,412   21,714   19,757   19,184   21,684

January 29, 1827. *Oliver Hazard Perry.**

Perry   **Indiana**
Tell City   382 sq. mi.
19,338   18,899   19,107   19,346   19,075   17,232   17,367

September 7, 1814; effective November 1, 1814. *Oliver Hazard Perry.**

Perry   **Kentucky**
Hazard   340 sq. mi.
28,712   29,390   30,283   33,763   25,714   34,961   46,566

November 2, 1820. *Oliver Hazard Perry.**

Perry   **Mississippi**
New Augusta   647 sq. mi.
12,250   12,138   10,865   9,864   9,065   8,745   9,108

February 3, 1820. *Oliver Hazard Perry.**

Perry   **Missouri**
Perryville   474 sq. mi.
18,971   18,132   16,648   16,784   14,393   14,642   14,890

November 16, 1820. *Oliver Hazard Perry.**

Perry   **Ohio**
New Lexington   408 sq. mi.

36,058   34,078   31,557   31,032   27,434   27,864   28,999
December 26, 1817. *Oliver Hazard Perry.**

Perry   **Pennsylvania**
New Bloomfield   551 sq. mi.
45,969   43,602   41,172   35,718   28,615   26,582   24,782
March 22, 1820. *Oliver Hazard Perry.**

Perry   **Tennessee**
Linden   415 sq. mi.
7,915   7,631   6,612   6,111   5,238   5,273   6,462
November 14, 1819. *Oliver Hazard Perry.**

Pershing   **Nevada**
Lovelock   6,037 sq. mi.
6,753   6,693   4,336   3,408   2,670   3,199   3,103
March 18, 1919. *John Joseph Pershing (1860–1948)*. Graduated West Point 1886; various campaigns against Western Indians 1886–96; Spanish-American War in Cuba and Philippines 1898–99; punitive expedition into Mexico against Pancho Villa 1916; commanded World War I US expeditionary force to Europe 1917; Army chief of staff 1921.

Person   **North Carolina**
Roxboro   392 sq. mi.
39,464   35,623   30,180   29,164   25,914   26,394   24,361
February 1, 1792. *Thomas Person (1733–1800)*. North Carolina Assembly 1764; Provincial Council 1775; Council of Safety 1776; North Carolina House of Commons, intermittently 1777–97; North Carolina Senate 1787 and 1791; opposed ratification of Federal Constitution; benefactor of University of North Carolina.

Petersburg   **Alaska**
(Census Area)   3,282 sq. mi.
3,815   (a)   (a)   (a)   (a)   (a)   (b)
June 1, 2008. *Town of Petersburg*. Named for Peter Bushman (?–?); established salmon cannery and sawmill 1897–99. [(a) Part of Wrangell-Petersburg Census Area; (b) part of 1st Judicial District.]

Petersburg   **Virginia**
(Independent City)   23 sq. mi.
32,420   33,740   38,386   41,055   36,103   36,750   35,054
March 16, 1850. *Peter Jones (c1707–c1754)*. Established trading post named Peter's Point that grew into Petersburg. (Associated counties: Chesterfield, Dinwiddie, and Prince George.)

Petroleum   **Montana**
Winnett   1,655 sq. mi.
494   493   519   655   675   894   1,026
November 24, 1924. *Descriptive*. Refers to local oil fields.

Pettis   **Missouri**
Sedalia   682 sq. mi.
42,201   39,403   35,437   36,378   34,137   35,120   31,577
January 26, 1833. *Spencer Pettis (1802–31)*. Missouri secretary of state 1826–28; US representative 1829–31; controversy during reelection campaign led to duel with Major Tomas Biddle in which both men were killed.

Phelps   **Missouri**
Rolla   672 sq. mi.
45,156   39,825   35,248   33,633   29,481   25,396   21,504
November 13, 1857. *John Smith Phelps (1814–86)*. Missouri House of Representatives 1840; US representative 1845–63; lieutenant colonel to colonel in Union Army 1861; promoted to brigadier general in order to serve as military governor of Arkansas 1862; governor of Missouri 1877–81.

Phelps   **Nebraska**
Holdrege   540 sq. mi.
9,188   9,747   9,715   9,769   9,553   9,800   9,048
February 11, 1873. *William Phelps (1808–?)*. Steamboat captain on Missouri and Mississippi Rivers.

Philadelphia   **Pennsylvania**
Philadelphia   134 sq. mi.
1,526,006   1,517,550   1,585,577   1,688,210   1,948,609   2,002,512   2,071,605
March 10, 1682. *City of Philadelphia*. Named by William Penn for the site of ancient Christian church in Asia Minor; from Greek *philadelphos* meaning "brotherly love." City and county were established concurrently by Penn; merged February 2, 1854; county governmental functions assumed by city April 17, 1951.

Phillips   **Arkansas**
Helena   696 sq. mi.
21,757   26,445   28,838   34,772   40,046   43,997   46,254
May 1, 1820. *Sylvanus Phillips (1766–1831)*. Early settler; explored Arkansas River 1798; Arkansas territorial legislature 1820.

Phillips   **Colorado**
Holyoke   688 sq. mi.
4,442   4,480   4,189   4,542   4,131   4,440   4,924
March 27, 1889. *Rufus O. Phillips (1859–?)*. Secretary of Lincoln Land Company; active in railroad development.

Phillips   **Kansas**
Phillipsburg   886 sq. mi.
5,642   6,001   6,590   7,406   7,888   8,709   9,273
February 26, 1867; organized July 26, 1872. *William Phillips (?–1856)*. Free-state martyr; murdered at Leavenworth by proslavery mob, September 1, 1856.

Phillips   **Montana**
Malta   5,140 sq. mi.
4,253   4,601   5,163   5,367   5,386   6,027   6,334
February 5, 1915. *Benjamin D. Phillips (1857–?)*. Rancher and livestock man; Montana Senate 1898.

Piatt   **Illinois**
Monticello   439 sq. mi.
16,729   16,365   15,548   16,581   15,509   14,960   13,970
January 27, 1841. *Uncertain*. (1) *Piatt family*; early settlers. (2) *Benjamin Piatt (?–?)*; attorney general of Illinois Territory 1810–13. (3) *James A. Piatt (1789–1838)*; prominent member of Piatt family.

Pickaway   **Ohio**
Circleville   501 sq. mi.
55,698   52,727   48,225   43,662   40,071   35,855   29,352
January 12, 1810. *Piqua Indians*. Name of uncertain origin; may refer to "ashes." Allies of France during French and Indian War.

Pickens   **Alabama**
Carrollton   881 sq. mi.
19,746   20,949   20,699   21,481   29,326   21,882   24,349
December 19, 1820. *Andrew Pickens (1739–1817)*. Fought Cherokees 1760 and 1782; captain to brigadier general, Continental Army 1779–81; awarded sword by Congress for victory at Cowpens 1781; South Carolina House of Representatives 1781–94 and 1800–12; South Carolina Constitutional Convention 1790; US representative 1793–95; major general of militia 1795; declined nomination for governor 1812.

Pickens   **Georgia**
Jasper   232 sq. mi.

29,431   22,983   14,432   11,652   9,620   8,903   8,855
December 5, 1853. *Andrew Pickens.**

Pickens   **South Carolina**
Pickens   496 sq. mi.
119,224   110,757   93,894   79,292   58,956   46,030   40,058
December 20, 1826. *Andrew Pickens.**

Pickett   **Tennessee**
Byrdstown   163 sq. mi.
5,077   4,945   4,548   4,358   3,774   4,431   5,093
February 27, 1879. *Howard L. Pickett (1847–1914).* Tennessee legislature 1879; active in creation of county; moved to Arizona Territory 1882.

Pierce   **Georgia**
Blackshear   316 sq. mi.
18,758   15,636   13,328   11,897   9,281   9,678   11,112
December 18, 1857. *Franklin Pierce (1804–69).* New Hampshire House of Representatives 1829–33; US representative 1833–37; US senator 1837–42; colonel and brigadier general in Mexican War 1846–47; 14th President of US 1853–57.

Pierce   **Nebraska**
Pierce   573 sq. mi.
7,266   7,857   7,827   8,481   8,493   8,722   9,405
January 26, 1856; organized September 21, 1870. *Franklin Pierce.**

Pierce   **North Dakota**
Rugby   1,019 sq. mi.
4,357   4,675   5,052   6,166   6,323   7,394   8,326
March 11, 1887; organized April 6, 1889. *Gilbert Ashville Pierce (1839–1901).* 2nd lieutenant to colonel, Union Army 1861–64; Indiana House of Representatives 1868; assistant financial clerk, US Senate 1869–71; editor, Chicago *Inter-Ocean* newspaper 1871–83; governor of Dakota Territory 1884–87; US senator from North Dakota 1889–91; US minister to Portugal 1893.

Pierce   **Washington**
Tacoma   1,670 sq. mi.
795,225   700,820   586,203   485,643   411,027   321,590   275,876
December 22, 1852. *Franklin Pierce.**

Pierce   **Wisconsin**
Ellsworth   574 sq. mi.
41,019   36,804   32,765   31,149   26,652   22,503   21,448
March 14, 1853. *Franklin Pierce.**

Pike   **Alabama**
Troy   672 sq. mi.
32,899   29,605   27,595   28,050   25,038   25,987   30,608
December 17, 1821. *Zebulon Montgomery Pike (1779–1813).* Joined Army at age 15, 1794; 1st lieutenant to brigadier general 1799–1813; explored upper Mississippi River 1804; explored Arkansas River, attempted climb of Pikes Peak 1806; killed during War of 1812 in attack on York (Toronto), Canada, April 27, 1813.

Pike   **Arkansas**
Murfreesboro   601 sq. mi.
11,291   11,303   10,086   10,373   8,711   7,864   10,032
November 1, 1833. *Zebulon Montgomery Pike.**

Pike **Georgia**
Zebulon 216 sq. mi.
17,869 13,688 10,224 8,937 7,316 7,138 8,459
December 9, 1822; organized December 20, 1824. *Zebulon Montgomery Pike.**

Pike **Illinois**
Pittsfield 831 sq. mi.
16,430 17,384 17,577 18,896 19,185 20,552 22,155
January 31, 1821. *Zebulon Montgomery Pike.**

Pike **Indiana**
Petersburg 334 sq. mi.
12,845 12,837 12,509 13,465 12,281 12,797 14,995
December 21, 1816; effective February 1, 1817. *Zebulon Montgomery Pike.**

Pike **Kentucky**
Pikeville 787 sq. mi.
65,024 68,736 72,583 81,123 61,059 68,264 81,154
December 19, 1821. *Zebulon Montgomery Pike.**

Pike **Mississippi**
Magnolia 409 sq. mi.
40,404 38,940 36,882 36,173 31,756 35,063 35,137
December 9, 1815. *Zebulon Montgomery Pike.**

Pike **Missouri**
Bowling Green 670 sq. mi.
18,516 18,351 15,969 17,568 16,928 16,706 16,844
December 14, 1818. *Zebulon Montgomery Pike.**

Pike **Ohio**
Waverly 440 sq. mi.
28,709 27,695 24,249 22,802 19,114 19,380 14,607
January 3, 1815. *Zebulon Montgomery Pike.**

Pike **Pennsylvania**
Milford 545 sq. mi.
57,369 46,302 27,966 18,271 11,818 9,158 8,425
March 26, 1814. *Zebulon Montgomery Pike.**

Pima **Arizona**
Tucson 9,187 sq. mi.
980,263 843,746 666,880 531,443 351,667 265,660 141,216
November 8, 1864. *Pima Indians*. Spanish rendering of *pia* or *pim*, meaning "I don't know," the Pimas' repeated response to Spanish inquiries as to tribal name.

Pinal **Arizona**
Florence 5,366 sq. mi.
375,770 179,727 116,379 90,918 67,916 62,673 43,191
February 1, 1875. *Uncertain.* (1) *Pinal Apaches.* (2) *Pinal Mountains.* From Spanish word relating to "pine," or Apache word for "deer."

Pine **Minnesota**
Pine City 1,411 sq. mi.

29,750   26,530   21,264   19,871   16,821   17,004   18,223
March 1, 1856; organized April 1, 1857. *Descriptive*. Refers to extensive pine forests in the area.

Pinellas   **Florida**
Clearwater   274 sq. mi.
916,542   921,482   851,659   728,531   522,329   374,665   159,249
May 23, 1911. *Point Pinellas*. Southernmost point of Pinellas Peninsula. From Spanish *punta pinal*, meaning "point of pines."

Pipestone   **Minnesota**
Pipestone   465 sq. mi.
9,596   9,895   10,491   11,690   12,791   13,605   14,003
May 23, 1857, as Rock; exchanged name with Pipestone County, September 20, 1862; organized January 27, 1879. *Pipestone quarry*. Source of red pipestone (catlinite or steatite), a soft stone carved into Indian pipe bowls; quarry is sacred to local Indians. (See Rock, Minnesota.)

Piscataquis   **Maine**
Dover-Foxcroft   3,961 sq. mi.
17,535   17,235   18,653   17,634   16,285   17,379   18,617
March 23, 1838. *Piscataquis River*. Abnaki word for "river branch" or "little branch stream."

Pitkin   **Colorado**
Aspen   971 sq. mi.
17,148   14,872   12,661   10,338   6,185   2,381   1,646
February 23, 1881. *Frederick Walker Pitkin (1837–86)*. Moved to Colorado for his health; governor of Colorado 1879–83.

Pitt   **North Carolina**
Greenville   652 sq. mi.
168,148   133,798   107,924   90,146   73,900   69,942   63,789
November 25, 1760. *William Pitt, Earl of Chatham*. (See Chatham, Georgia.)

Pittsburg   **Oklahoma**
McAlester   1,305 sq. mi.
45,837   43,953   40,581   40,524   37,521   34,360   41,031
July 16, 1907. *City of Pittsburgh, Pennsylvania*. Former home of an early settler. The letter *h* was inadvertently omitted from the county name.

Pittsylvania   **Virginia**
Chatham   969 sq. mi.
63,506   61,745   55,655   66,147   58,789   58,296   66,096
December 15, 1766. *Combined word*. William Pitt, Earl of Chatham (see Chatham, Georgia) and Latin *sylva* meaning "woods." (Associated independent city: Danville.)

Piute   **Utah**
Junction   758 sq. mi.
1,556   1,435   1,277   1,329   1,164   1,436   1,911
January 16, 1865. *Paiute Indians*. From Indian *pai* (water) and *ute* (tribal name). Nomadic Indians of the Great Basin.

Placer   **California**
Auburn   1,407 sq. mi.
348,342   248,399   172,796   117,247   77,306   56,998   41,649
April 25, 1851; organized May 28, 1851. *Descriptive*. From Spanish word describing gold deposits on the surface or in streams.

Plaquemines   **Louisiana**
Pointe a la Hache   780 sq. mi.

| 23,042 | 26,757 | 25,575 | 26,049 | 25,225 | 22,545 | 14,329 |

March 31, 1807. *Persimmon trees.* Derived from Maubila word for persimmon trees in the area.

Platte   **Missouri**
Platte City   420 sq. mi.

| 89,322 | 73,781 | 57,867 | 46,341 | 32,081 | 23,350 | 14,973 |

December 31, 1838. *Platte Purchase.* Named for Platte River (see Platte, Nebraska). Northwest section of Missouri added to the state 1836.

Platte   **Nebraska**
Columbus   674 sq. mi.

| 32,237 | 31,662 | 29,820 | 28,852 | 26,508 | 23,992 | 19,910 |

January 26, 1856. *Platte River.* From French for "flat" or "shallow."

Platte   **Wyoming**
Wheatland   2,084 sq. mi.

| 8,667 | 8,807 | 8,145 | 11,975 | 6,486 | 7,195 | 7,925 |

February 9, 1911. *North Platte River.* Tributary of Platte River.*

Pleasants   **West Virginia**
Saint Marys   130 sq. mi.

| 7,605 | 7,514 | 7,546 | 8,236 | 7,274 | 7,124 | 6,369 |

March 29, 1851. *James Pleasants (1769–1836).* Virginia House of Delegates 1797–1802, clerk 1803–11; US representative 1811–19; US senator 1819–22; governor of Virginia 1822–25.

Plumas   **California**
Quincy   2,553 sq. mi.

| 20,007 | 20,824 | 19,739 | 17,340 | 11,707 | 11,620 | 13,519 |

March 18, 1854. *Feather River.* From Spanish name *Rio de las Plumas*, for the many feathers (plumas) floating on the surface.

Plymouth   **Iowa**
Le Mars   863 sq. mi.

| 24,986 | 24,849 | 23,388 | 24,743 | 24,312 | 23,906 | 23,352 |

January 15, 1851; organized October 27, 1858. *Plymouth Colony, Massachusetts.* First permanent English settlement in New England 1620; named for Plymouth, England, home of settlers.

Plymouth   **Massachusetts**
Plymouth   659 sq. mi.

| 494,919 | 472,822 | 435,276 | 405,437 | 333,314 | 248,449 | 189,468 |

June 2, 1685. *Town of Plymouth.* (See Plymouth, Iowa.)

Pocahontas   **Iowa**
Pocahontas   577 sq. mi.

| 7,310 | 8,662 | 9,525 | 11,369 | 12,729 | 14,234 | 15,496 |

January 15, 1851; organized May 11, 1859. *Pocahontas (c1595–1617).* Nickname meaning "playful girl"; actual name was Matoaka; daughter of Powhatan, chief of Powhatan Confederacy in southeastern Virginia (see Powhatan, Virginia); may have interceded with her father to save Captain John Smith; married John Rolfe 1614; died in England.

Pocahontas   **West Virginia**
Marlinton   940 sq. mi.

| 8,719 | 9,131 | 9,008 | 9,919 | 8,870 | 10,136 | 12,480 |

December 21, 1821. *Pocahontas.**

Poinsett   **Arkansas**
Harrisburg   758 sq. mi.

24,583   25,614   24,664   27,032   26,822   30,834   39,311

February 28, 1838. *Joel Roberts Poinsett (1779–1851)*. South Carolina House of Representatives 1816–20; US representative 1821–25; US minister to Mexico 1825–29; US secretary of war 1837–41. Amateur botanist; developed poinsettia from a Mexican flower.

Pointe Coupee   **Louisiana**
New Roads   557 sq. mi.
22,802   22,763   22,540   24,045   22,002   22,488   21,841

April 10, 1805. *Mississippi River cut point*. French for "cut point." A cut point is created when a river shortens its course by cutting across the neck of a loop forming an "ox bow."

Polk   **Arkansas**
Mena   858 sq. mi.
20,662   20,229   17,347   17,007   13,297   11,981   14,182

November 30, 1844. *James Knox Polk (1795–1849)*. Chief clerk of Tennessee Senate 1821–23; Tennessee House of Representatives 1823–25; US representative 1825–39, speaker 1835–39; governor of Tennessee 1839–41; 11th President of US 1845–49.

Polk   **Florida**
Bartow   1,798 sq. mi.
602,095   483,924   405,382   321,652   227,222   185,139   123,997

February 8, 1861. *James Knox Polk.**

Polk   **Georgia**
Cedartown   310 sq. mi.
41,475   38,127   33,815   32,386   29,656   28,015   30,976

December 20, 1851. *James Knox Polk.**

Polk   **Iowa**
Des Moines   574 sq. mi.
430,640   374,601   327,140   303,170   286,101   226,315   226,010

January 13, 1846; organized April 6, 1846. *James Knox Polk.**

Polk   **Minnesota**
Crookston   1,971 sq. mi.
31,600   31,369   32,498   34,844   34,435   36,182   35,900

July 20, 1858; organized February 27, 1879. *James Knox Polk.**

Polk   **Missouri**
Bolivar   636 sq. mi.
31,137   26,992   21,826   18,822   15,415   13,753   16,062

January 5, 1835. *James Knox Polk.**

Polk   **Nebraska**
Osceola   438 sq. mi.
5,406   5,639   5,675   6,320   6,468   7,210   8,044

January 26, 1856; organized August 6, 1870. *James Knox Polk.**

Polk   **North Carolina**
Columbus   238 sq. mi.
20,150   18,324   14,416   12,984   11,735   11,395   11,627

January 18, 1847. *William Polk (1758–1834)*. 2nd lieutenant, 4th South Carolina Mounted Infantry, wounded at Canebrake 1775; major of North Carolina troops at Germantown and Brandywine (1777), and Eutaw Springs (1781); lieutenant colonel 4th South Carolina Cavalry 1782; North Carolina House of Commons 1785–88 and 1790; North Carolina superintendent of internal revenue 1791–1808.

Polk   **Oregon**
Dallas   741 sq. mi.

75,403	62,380	49,541	45,203	35,349	26,523	26,317

December 22, 1845. *James Knox Polk.**

Polk   **Tennessee**
Benton   435 sq. mi.

16,825	16,050	13,643	13,602	11,669	12,160	14,074

November 28, 1839. *James Knox Polk.**

Polk   **Texas**
Livingston   1,057 sq. mi.

45,413	41,133	30,687	24,407	14,457	13,861	16,194

March 30, 1846; organized July 10, 1846. *James Knox Polk.**

Polk   **Wisconsin**
Balsam Lake   914 sq. mi.

44,205	41,319	34,773	32,351	26,666	24,968	24,944

March 14, 1853. *James Knox Polk.**

Pondera   **Montana**
Conrad   1,623 sq. mi.

6,153	6,424	6,433	6,731	6,611	7,653	6,392

February 17, 1919. *Uncertain.* (1) *Pend d'Oreille Indians*; phonetic rendering of French name; spelling used to avoid confusion for town and county in Idaho and Washington respectively (see Pend Oreille, Washington). (2) *Pondera River.*

Pontotoc   **Mississippi**
Pontotoc   498 sq. mi.

29,957	26,726	22,237	20,918	17,363	17,232	19,994

February 9, 1836. *Town of Pontotoc.* Rendering of Chickasaw word meaning "weed prairie."

Pontotoc   **Oklahoma**
Ada   720 sq. mi.

37,492	35,143	34,119	32,598	27,867	28,089	30,875

July 16, 1907. *Pontotoc County, Chickasaw Nation.* Name was brought to Oklahoma from Mississippi by Chickasaws 1832.

Pope   **Arkansas**
Russellville   813 sq. mi.

61,754	54,469	45,883	39,021	28,607	21,177	23,291

November 2, 1829; effective December 25, 1829. *John Pope (1770–1845).* Kentucky House of Representatives 1802 and 1806–07; US senator 1807–12; Kentucky Senate 1825–29; governor of Arkansas Territory 1829–35; US representative from Kentucky 1837–43.

Pope   **Illinois**
Golconda   369 sq. mi.

4,470	4,413	4,373	4,404	3,857	4,061	5,779

January 10, 1816. *Nathaniel Pope (1784–1850).* Secretary of Illinois Territory 1809–16; Illinois Territory congressional delegate 1816–18; US judge, District of Illinois 1819–50.

Pope   **Minnesota**
Glenwood   670 sq. mi.

10,995	11,236	10,745	11,657	11,107	11,914	12,862

February 20, 1862; organized February 28, 1866. *John Pope (1823–92).* Graduated West Point 1842; 2nd lieutenant in Mexican War, Battle of Buena Vista 1847; explored Red River of the North 1849; explored Rocky Mountains 1854–59; brigadier general 1861; defeated at 2nd Bull Run 1862; removed to command Department of the Northwest; led brutal defeat of Dakotas 1862; retired 1886.

Poquoson   **Virginia**
(Independent City)   15 sq. mi.
12,510   11,566   11,005   8,726   (a)   (a)   (a)
1975. From Algonquin word *pocosin* meaning "marsh" or "low, flat land." [Part of York County] (Associated county: York.)

Portage   **Ohio**
Ravenna   487 sq. mi.
161,419   152,061   142,585   135,856   125,868   91,798   63,954
February 10, 1807; effective June 7, 1807. *Descriptive.* Refers to portage between Cuyahoga and Tuscarawas Rivers.

Portage   **Wisconsin**
Stevens Point   801 sq. mi.
70,019   67,182   61,405   57,420   47,541   36,964   34,858
December 7, 1836; organized 1844. *Descriptive.* Refers to portage between Wisconsin and Fox Rivers.

Porter   **Indiana**
Valparaiso   418 sq. mi.
164,343   146,798   128,932   119,816   87,114   60,279   40,076
February 7, 1835; organized January 28, 1836. *David Porter (1780–1843).* Commanded frigate *Essex* in War of 1812; defeated by British off Valparaiso, Chile, 1813; commanded squadron against Caribbean pirates 1823–25; commander in chief of Mexican Navy 1826–29; US consul general to Algiers 1830; US minister to Turkey 1839.

Portsmouth   **Virginia**
(Independent City)   34 sq. mi.
95,535   100,565   103,907   104,577   110,963   114,773   80,039
March 1, 1858. *Portsmouth, England.* Named in hopes of becoming important seaport.

Posey   **Indiana**
Mount Vernon   410 sq. mi.
25,910   27,061   25,698   26,414   21,740   19,214   19,818
September 7, 1814; effective November 1, 1814. *Thomas Posey (1750–1818).* Continental Army, captain to brigadier general 1776–93; Louisiana Senate 1805–06; lieutenant governor of Kentucky; US senator from Louisiana 1812–13; governor of Indiana Territory 1813–16; Indian agent 1816–18.

Pottawatomie   **Kansas**
Westmoreland   841 sq. mi.
21,604   18,209   16,128   14,782   11,755   11,957   12,344
February 20, 1857. *Potawatomi Indians.* From Algonquin word *pottawatomink* which refers to "fire." Forced from Great Lakes region by Indians and Europeans; scattered throughout Midwest by 1800; ceded lands to US 1846; resettled in Indian Territory (Oklahoma). Added *e* is one of many variant spellings.

Pottawatomie   **Oklahoma**
Shawnee   788 sq. mi.
69,442   65,521   58,760   55,239   43,134   41,486   43,517
September 18, 1891. *Potawatomi Indians.**

Pottawattamie   **Iowa**
Council Bluffs   950 sq. mi.
93,158   87,704   82,628   86,561   86,991   83,102   69,682
September 27, 1848. *Potawatomi Indians.** One of many variable spellings.

Potter   **Pennsylvania**
Coudersport   1,081 sq. mi.

17,457	18,080	16,717	17,726	16,395	16,483	16,810

March 26, 1804; organized 1835. *James Potter (1729–89)*. Colonel, French and Indian War; colonel, Pennsylvania Militia 1776–77; wounded at Princeton 1777; brigadier to major general 1777–82.

Potter   **South Dakota**
Gettysburg   861 sq. mi.

2,329	2,693	3,190	3,674	4,449	4,926	4,688

January 8, 1873, as Ashmore; name changed January 14, 1875; organized December 27, 1883. *Joel A. Potter (1825–95)*. Physician; Dakota territorial legislature 1872; steward of South Dakota State Hospital.

Potter   **Texas**
Amarillo   908 sq. mi.

121,073	113,546	97,874	98,637	90,511	115,580	73,366

August 21, 1876; organized September 6, 1887. *Robert Potter (1799–1842)*. US Navy 1815–21; North Carolina House of Commons, intermittently 1826–35; emigrated to Texas 1835; signer, Texas Declaration of Independence 1836; Republic of Texas secretary of navy 1836; fought at San Jacinto 1836; Texas Congress 1837–41; killed in Regulator-Moderator War, a land feud in eastern Texas, March 2, 1842.

Powder River   **Montana**
Broadus   3,297 sq. mi.

1,743	1,858	2,090	2,520	2,862	2,485	2,693

March 7, 1919. *Powder River*. Named for gunpowder-colored sand along banks.

Powell   **Kentucky**
Stanton   179 sq. mi.

12,613	13,237	11,686	11,101	7,704	6,674	6,812

January 7, 1852. *Lazarus Powell (1812–67)*. Kentucky House of Representatives 1837–39; governor of Kentucky 1851–55; US commissioner to Utah 1858; US senator from Kentucky 1859–65.

Powell   **Montana**
Deer Lodge   2,326 sq. mi.

7,027	7,180	6,620	6,958	6,660	7,002	6,301

January 31, 1901. *John Wesley Powell (1834–1902)*. Private to brevet lieutenant colonel, Union Army 1861–65; lost right arm during Shiloh campaign 1862; explored Grand Canyon 1869; director, Smithsonian Institute Bureau of Ethnology 1880–1902; director, US Geological Survey 1880–94.

Power   **Idaho**
American Falls   1,404 sq. mi.

7,817	7,538	7,086	6,844	4,864	4,111	3,988

January 30, 1913. *Descriptive*. Refers to hydroelectric power generated at American Falls on Snake River.

Poweshiek   **Iowa**
Montezuma   585 sq. mi.

18,914	18,815	19,033	19,306	18,803	19,300	19,344

February 17, 1843; organized January 24, 1848; effective April 3, 1848. *Poweshiek (1797–?)*. Fox-Mesquaki chief; tried to prevent Black Hawk War 1832; moved Fox from Illinois to Iowa; ceded Indian lands 1832–42; expelled to Kansas 1846.

Powhatan   **Virginia**
Powhatan   260 sq. mi.

28,046	22,377	15,328	13,062	7,696	6,747	5,556

June 3, 1777. *Powhatan (c1550–1618)*. Named Wahunsonacook; called Powhatan by English after his village on James River; name is Algonquin for "falls in a river." Chief of Powhatan Confederacy in southeastern Virginia; maintained good relation with English settlers; father of Pocahontas (see Pocahontas, Iowa).

Prairie   **Arkansas**
Des Arc   648 sq. mi.
8,715   9,539   9,518   10,140   10,249   10,515   13,768
November 25, 1846. *Grand Prairie.* A large subregion of the Mississippi Delta.

Prairie   **Montana**
Terry   1,737 sq. mi.
1,179   1,199   1,383   1,836   1,752   3,318   2,377
February 5, 1915. *Descriptive.* Named for local geography.

Pratt   **Kansas**
Pratt   735 sq. mi.
9,656   9,647   9,702   10,275   10,056   12,122   12,156
February 26, 1867; organized July 25, 1879. *Caleb Pratt (c1832–61).* Auditor and county clerk of Douglas County; Union Army, 2nd lieutenant, Company D, 2nd Kansas 1861; killed at Wilson's Creek, August 10, 1861.

Preble   **Ohio**
Eaton   424 sq. mi.
42,270   42,337   40,113   38,223   34,719   32,498   27,081
February 15, 1808. *Edward Preble (1761–1807).* Privateer 1777; Massachusetts Navy aboard *Protector* 1779; lieutenant, US Navy 1798; commanded USS *Essex* (1799) and USS *Constitution* (1803); bombarded Tripoli against Barbary Pirates and forced renewal of treaty with Sultan of Morocco 1804; awarded gold medal by Congress 1805; declined appointment as navy secretary 1806.

Prentiss   **Mississippi**
Booneville   415 sq. mi.
25,276   25,556   23,278   24,025   20,133   17,949   19,810
April 15, 1870. *Seargeant Smith Prentiss (1808–50).* Mississippi House of Representatives 1836–37; US representative 1838–39. There are various spellings for the name "Seargeant."

Presidio   **Texas**
Marfa   3,855 sq. mi.
7,818   7,304   6,637   5,188   4,842   5,460   7,354
January 3, 1850; organized 1875. *Presidio del Norte.* Spanish military post (presidio); originally located at junction of Rio Grande and Conchos rivers in present-day Mexico 1759; abandoned and reestablished north of Rio Grande 1767; garrisoned by Spanish troops until 1814.

Presque Isle   **Michigan**
Rogers City   659 sq. mi.
13,376   14,411   13,743   14,267   12,836   13,117   11,996
April 1, 1840; organized March 31, 1871. *Presque Isle Peninsula.* Narrow spit into Lake Huron; French for "virtual island."

Preston   **West Virginia**
Kingwood   649 sq. mi.
33,520   29,334   29,037   30,460   25,455   27,233   31,399
January 19, 1818. *James Patton Preston (1774–1843).* Virginia Senate 1802–06; Lieutenant colonel and colonel of infantry 1812–13; wounded at Chrysler's Farm, Canada, November 11, 1813; governor of Virginia 1816–19.

Price   **Wisconsin**
Phillips   1,254 sq. mi.
14,159   15,822   15,600   15,788   14,520   14,370   16,344
March 3, 1879; organized February 18, 1882. *William Thompson Price (1824–86).* Wisconsin Assembly 1851 and 1882; Wisconsin Senate, intermittently 1857–81; US representative 1883–86.

Prince Edward   **Virginia**
Farmville   350 sq. mi.
23,368   19,720   17,320   16,456   14,379   14,121   15,398
November 17, 1753. *Prince Edward Augustus (1739–67)*. Grandson of King George II who reigned at time of county's creation; second son of Frederick Louis, Prince of Wales, and Princess Augusta (see Augusta, Virginia); brother of George III; made Duke of York and Albany 1760.

Prince George   **Virginia**
Prince George   265 sq. mi.
35,725   33,047   27,394   25,733   29,092   20,270   19,679
August 25, 1702. *Prince George (Jørgen) of Denmark and Norway (1653–1708)*. Son of King Frederick III of Denmark; married Princess Anne of England 1683; Duke of Cumberland 1689; lord high admiral of England 1702; denied title of king when wife became Queen Anne 1704. (Associated independent city: Hopewell.)

Prince George's   **Maryland**
Upper Marlboro   483 sq. mi.
863,420   801,515   729,268   665,071   660,567   357,395   194,182
May 20, 1695; organized April 23, 1696. *Prince George (Jørgen) of Denmark and Norway.**

Prince of Wales-Hyder   **Alaska**
(Census Area)   3,923 sq. mi.
5,559   6,146[a]   6,278[a]   3,822[a]   3,782[b]   1,772[b]   (c)
May 19, 2008. *Prince of Wales Island*; named by Captain Vancouver in 1793 for George, Prince of Wales, (1762–1830); regent during incapacity of George III 1810–20; King George IV 1820–30. *Hyder*; named for Frederick Hyder (?–?); Canadian mining engineer; predicted mineral wealth for area; Riverside Mine produced gold, silver, lead, zinc, and tungsten 1924–50. [(a) Prince of Wales-Outer Ketchikan Census Area. (b) Prince of Wales Census Area. (c) Part of First Judicial Division.]

Prince William   **Virginia**
Manassas   336 sq. mi.
402,002   280,813   215,686   144,703   111,102   50,164   22,612
June 19, 1730. *Prince William Augustus, Duke of Cumberland* (see Cumberland, Kentucky). (Associated independent cities: Manassas and Manassas Park.)

Providence   **Rhode Island**
Providence   410 sq. mi.
626,667   621,602   596,270   571,349   580,261   568,778   574,973
June 22, 1703, as Providence Plantations; name changed June 16, 1729. *Providence Plantations*. Roger Williams thanked "God's merciful providence" for delivering him to Narragansett Bay after fleeing Massachusetts 1636.

Prowers   **Colorado**
Lamar   1,638 sq. mi.
12,551   14,483   13,347   13,070   13,258   13,296   14,836
April 11, 1889. *John Wesley Prowers (1838–84)*. Worked at Bent's Fort 1856–63; freighted government supplies from Leavenworth, Kansas, to Fort Union, New Mexico, 1865–71; Colorado legislature 1873 and 1880; pioneer cattleman in southeastern Colorado.

Pueblo   **Colorado**
Pueblo   2,386 sq. mi.
159,063   141,472   123,051   125,972   118,238   118,707   90,188
November 1, 1861. *Town of Pueblo*. Spanish for "town" or "people." Named for original settlement of a fort and surrounding dwellings 1840.

Pulaski   **Arkansas**
Little Rock   760 sq. mi.

382,748   361,474   349,660   340,613   287,189   242,980   196,685

December 15, 1818; effective March 9, 1819. *Casimir (or Kasimierz) Pulaski (1748–79)*. Polish nobleman; came to America to aid colonists in during Revolution 1777; fought at Brandywine and Germantown 1777; mortally wounded at Siege of Savannah, October 9, 1779.

Pulaski   **Georgia**
Hawkinsville   249 sq. mi.
12,010   9,588   8,108   8,950   8,066   8,204   8,808
December 13, 1808. *Casimir Pulaski.**

Pulaski   **Illinois**
Mound City   199 sq. mi.
6,161   7,348   7,523   8,840   8,741   10,490   13,639
March 3, 1843. *Casimir Pulaski.**

Pulaski   **Indiana**
Winamac   434 sq. mi.
13,402   13,755   12,643   13,258   12,534   12,387   12,493
February 7, 1835; organized February 18, 1839; effective May 6, 1839. *Casimir Pulaski.**

Pulaski   **Kentucky**
Somerset   658 sq. mi.
63,063   56,217   49,489   45,803   35,234   34,403   38,452
December 10, 1798; effective June 1, 1799. *Casimir Pulaski.**

Pulaski   **Missouri**
Waynesville   547 sq. mi.
52,274   41,165   41,307   42,011   53,781   46,567   10,392
January 19, 1833. *Casimir Pulaski.**

Pulaski   **Virginia**
Pulaski   320 sq. mi.
34,872   35,127   34,496   35,229   29,564   27,258   27,758
March 30, 1839. *Casimir Pulaski.**

Pushmataha   **Oklahoma**
Antlers   1,396 sq. mi.
11,572   11,667   10,997   11,773   9,385   9,088   12,001
July 16, 1907. *Pushmataha District of Choctaw Nation*. Named for Chief Apushmataha (one of many spellings) (1764–1824); allied with US in War of 1812; given rank and uniform of brigadier general; negotiated treaties ceding Choctaw lands to US and eventually moving to Indian Territory (Oklahoma) 1805–20; died on mission to Washington to meet with President Monroe; buried in Congressional Cemetery.

Putnam   **Florida**
Palatka   728 sq. mi.
74,364   70,423   65,070   50,549   36,290   32,212   23,615
January 13, 1849. *Uncertain*. (1) *Benjamin Alexander Putnam (1801–69)*; officer in 2nd Seminole War 1835–42; Florida legislature; surveyor general of Florida 1849–54. (2) *Israel Putnam* (see Putnam, Georgia).

Putnam   **Georgia**
Eatonton   345 sq. mi.
21,218   18,812   14,137   10,295   8,394   7,798   7,731
December 10, 1807. *Israel Putnam (1718–90)*. British officer in French and Indian War 1754–63; Pontiac's War 1764; Connecticut legislature 1766; heard of Battle of Lexington while plowing his fields, hurried to Lexington without stopping to

change clothes 1775; Battle of Bunker Hill 1775; major general, Continental Army 1775–79; paralytic stroke ended military career 1779.

Putnam **Illinois**
Hennepin 160 sq. mi.

6,006	6,086	5,730	6,085	5,007	4,570	4,746

January 13, 1825; organized 1831. *Israel Putnam.**

Putnam **Indiana**
Greencastle 481 sq. mi.

37,963	36,019	30,315	29,163	26,932	24,927	22,950

December 31, 1821; effective April 1, 1822. *Israel Putnam.**

Putnam **Missouri**
Unionville 517 sq. mi.

4,979	5,223	5,079	6,092	5,916	6,999	9,166

February 22, 1843. *Israel Putnam.**

Putnam **New York**
Carmel 230 sq. mi.

99,710	95,745	83,941	77,193	56,696	31,722	20,307

June 12, 1812. *Israel Putnam.**

Putnam **Ohio**
Ottawa 483 sq. mi.

34,499	34,726	33,819	32,991	31,134	28,331	25,248

February 12, 1820; organized 1834. *Israel Putnam.**

Putnam **Tennessee**
Cookeville 401 sq. mi.

72,321	62,315	51,373	47,690	35,487	29,236	29,869

February 2, 1842; abolished March 1844; recreated February 11, 1854. *Israel Putnam.**

Putnam **West Virginia**
Winfield 346 sq. mi.

55,486	51,589	42,835	38,181	27,652	23,561	21,021

March 11, 1848. *Israel Putnam.**

Q

Quay **New Mexico**
Tucumcari 2,874 sq. mi.

9,041	10,155	10,823	10,577	10,903	12,279	13,971

February 28, 1903. *Matthew Stanley Quay (1833–1904).* Union Army lieutenant to colonel 1862–65; awarded Congressional Medal of Honor in 1888 for bravery at Fredericksburg 1862; Pennsylvania House of Representatives 1865–67; secretary of the commonwealth 1872–87 and 1879–82; Pennsylvania treasurer 1885–87; US senator 1887–99 and 1901–04; advocated New Mexico statehood.

Queen Anne's **Maryland**
Centreville 372 sq. mi.

47,798	40,563	33,953	25,508	18,422	16,569	14,579

April 18, 1706; organized May 1, 1707. *Queen Anne (1665–1714).* Second daughter of James II (see Albany, New York); sister of Mary II; married Prince George of Denmark (see Prince George, Virginia) 1683; Queen of England 1702–14. Unable to produce heir; of fifteen children only one, Prince William (1689–1700), survived infancy.

Queens   **New York**
Jamaica   109 sq. mi.
2,230,722   2,229,379   1,951,598   1,891,325   1,986,473   1,809,578   1,550,849
November 1, 1683. *Queen Catherine (1638–1703)*. Daughter of the Duke of Braganza who became King John IV of Portugal; wife of Charles II of England (see Charleston, South Carolina) 1662; tolerated Charles' many illegitimate children; remained in England following Charles' death (1685) until returning to Portugal 1692.

Quitman   **Georgia**
Georgetown   151 sq. mi.
2,513   2,598   2,209   2,357   2,180   2,432   3,015
December 10, 1858. *John Anthony Quitman (1799–1858)*. Mississippi House of Representatives 1826–27; chancellor of Mississippi 1828–35; Mississippi Constitutional Convention 1832; president, Mississippi Senate 1835–36; acting governor of Mississippi for five weeks 1835–36; brigadier general of volunteers 1846; Regular Army major general 1847–48; governor of Mississippi 1850–51; US representative 1855–58.

Quitman   **Mississippi**
Marks   405 sq. mi.
8,223   10,117   10,490   12,636   15,888   21,019   25,885
February 1, 1877. *John Anthony Quitman.**

R

Rabun   **Georgia**
Clayton   370 sq. mi.
16,276   15,050   11,648   10,466   8,327   7,456   7,424
December 21, 1819. *William Rabun (1771–1819)*. Captain of militia 1793; Georgia Assembly 1805–06; Georgia Senate 1810–16, president 1812–16; governor of Georgia 1817–19.

Racine   **Wisconsin**
Racine   333 sq. mi.
195,408   188,831   175,034   173,132   170,838   141,781   109,585
December 7, 1836. *Town of Racine*. French word for "root," prompted by numerous roots along banks of Racine River.

Radford   **Virginia**
(Independent City)   10 sq. mi.
16,408   15,859   15,940   13,225   11,596   9,371   9,026
January 22, 1892. *John Blair Radford (1813–72)*. Physician and landowner. (Associated county: Montgomery.)

Rains   **Texas**
Emory   229 sq. mi.
10,914   9,139   6,715   4,839   3,752   2,993   4,266
June 9, 1870; organized December 1, 1870. *Emory Rains (1800–78)*. Republic of Texas legislature 1837–38; Texas Constitutional Convention 1845; Texas legislature, intermittently 1847–59; surveyed area that became Rains County 1869.

Raleigh   **West Virginia**
Beckley   605 sq. mi.
78,859   79,220   76,819   86,821   70,080   77,826   96,273
January 23, 1850. *Sir Walter Ralegh (1552–1618)*. First lord proprietor of Virginia 1584–1603; voyage of discovery and piracy to America 1578; knighted 1585; attempted colonies on Roanoke Island 1585 and 1587; participated in victory over Spanish Armada 1588; fell from royal favor after marriage to one of queen's maids of honor 1592; stripped of all titles by James I and confined to Tower of London 1603–16; persuaded James I to allow expedition to Orinoco River in search of gold 1617–18, mission failed; beheaded, October 29, 1618. (American spelling includes letter *i*.)

Ralls	Missouri					
New London	470 sq. mi.					
10,167	9,626	8,476	8,911	7,764	8,078	8,686

November 16, 1820. *Daniel Ralls (c1785–1820)*. Missouri Assembly 1820; carried from sickbed to cast deciding vote for Thomas Hart Benton (see Benton, Arkansas) for US senator 1820; died one month later.

Ramsey	Minnesota					
Saint Paul	152 sq. mi.					
508,640	511,035	485,765	459,784	476,255	422,525	355,332

October 27, 1849; organized March 31, 1851; effective September 1, 1851. *Alexander Ramsey (1815–1903)*. US representative from Pennsylvania 1843–47; governor of Minnesota Territory 1849; governor of Minnesota 1860–63; US senator 1863–75; US secretary of war 1879–81.

Ramsey	North Dakota					
Devils Lake	1,187 sq. mi.					
11,451	12,066	12,681	13,048	12,915	13,443	14,373

January 4, 1873; organized January 25, 1883. *Alexander Ramsey.**

Randall	Texas					
Canyon	912 sq. mi.					
120,725	104,312	89,673	75,062	53,885	33,913	13,774

August 21, 1876; organized July 27, 1889. *Horace Randal (1833–64)*. Graduated West Point 1854; 2nd lieutenant, 8th US Infantry; resigned commission 1861; 1st lieutenant to colonel, Confederate Army 1861–62; appointed brigadier general but mortally wounded at Jenkin's Ferry before confirmed, April 30, 1864. (Clerical error added second letter *l* to county name.)

Randolph	Alabama					
Wedowee	581 sq. mi.					
22,913	22,380	19,881	20,075	18,331	19,477	22,513

December 18, 1832. *John Randolph (1773–1833)*. US representative from Virginia, intermittently 1799–1833; US senator 1825–27; fought a duel with Henry Clay (see Clay, Alabama) 1826; Virginia Constitutional Convention 1829; US minister to Russia 1830–33.

Randolph	Arkansas					
Pocahontas	652 sq. mi.					
17,969	18,195	16,558	16,834	12,645	12,520	15,982

October 29, 1835. *John Randolph.**

Randolph	Georgia					
Cuthbert	428 sq. mi.					
7,719	7,791	8,023	9,599	8,734	11,078	13,804

December 20, 1828. *John Randolph.**

Randolph	Illinois					
Chester	576 sq. mi.					
33,476	33,893	34,583	35,652	31,379	29,988	31,673

October 5, 1795. *Uncertain*. (1) *Beverly Randolph (1754–97)*; regimental officer during Revolutionary War; Virginia House of Delegates 1777 and 1779–81; governor of Virginia 1788–91. (2) *Edmund Jennings Randolph* (see Randolph, West Virginia).

Randolph	Indiana					
Winchester	452 sq. mi.					
26,171	27,401	27,148	29,997	28,915	28,434	27,141

January 10, 1818; effective August 10, 1818. *Uncertain*. (1) *Thomas Randolph (?–1811)*; Virginia legislature; attorney general of Indiana Territory; private, Indiana Militia; killed at Battle of Tippecanoe, November 7, 1811. (2) *Randolph County, North Carolina*; origin of early settlers.

Randolph   **Missouri**
Huntsville   483 sq. mi.
25,414   24,663   24,370   25,460   22,434   22,014   22,918
January 22, 1829. *John Randolph.**

Randolph   **North Carolina**
Asheboro   783 sq. mi.
141,752   130,454   106,546   91,728   76,358   61,497   50,804
February 26, 1779. *Peyton Randolph (1721–75)*. King's attorney for Virginia 1748; Virginia House of Burgesses 1764–74, speaker 1766; president, Continental Congress 1774–75.

Randolph   **West Virginia**
Elkins   1,040 sq. mi.
29,405   28,262   27,803   28,734   24,596   26,349   30,558
November 29, 1786; effective May 5, 1787. *Edmund Jennings Randolph (1753–1813)*. Aide-de-camp to General Washington 1775; Virginia attorney general 1776; Continental Congress 1779–82; governor of Virginia 1786–88; US Constitutional Convention 1788–89; first attorney general of US 1789–94; US secretary of state 1794–95.

Rankin   **Mississippi**
Brandon   775 sq. mi.
141,617   115,327   87,161   69,427   43,933   34,322   28,881
February 4, 1828. *Christopher Rankin (1788–1826)*. Mississippi territorial legislature 1813; Mississippi Constitutional Convention 1817; US representative 1819–26.

Ransom   **North Dakota**
Lisbon   862 sq. mi.
5,457   5,890   5,921   6,698   7,102   8,078   8,876
January 4, 1873; organized April 4, 1881. *Fort Ransom*. Established on Sheyenne River by General Terry 1867; abandoned 1872. Named for Tomas Edward Greenfield Ransom (1834–64); Union Army, captain to brigadier general 1861–64; received several combat wounds during campaigns of Fort Donelson, Shiloh, Vicksburg, and Atlanta; died from accumulated wounds.

Rapides   **Louisiana**
Alexandria   1,318 sq. mi.
131,613   126,337   131,556   135,282   118,078   111,351   90,648
April 10, 1805. *Rapids in the Red River*. French for "rapids." The specific rapids near Alexandria have disappeared.

Rappahannock   **Virginia**
Washington   266 sq. mi.
7,373   6,983   6,622   6,093   5,199   5,368   6,112
February 8, 1833. *Rappahannock River*. Algonquin name meaning "alternating river" or "river of quick-rising water"; refers to tidal flow of river's estuary at Chesapeake Bay.

Ravalli   **Montana**
Hamilton   2,391 sq. mi.
40,212   36,070   25,010   22,493   14,409   12,341   13,101
February 16, 1893. *Antonio Ravalli (1811–84)*. Jesuit missionary; arrived in North America 1844; worked among Kalispels at St. Ignatius Mission on the upper Columbia River 1845; missionary to Coeur d'Alenes 1854; St. Mary's mission among the Flatheads on the Bitter Root River 1866–84.

Rawlins   **Kansas**
Atwood   1,069 sq. mi.
2,519   2,966   3,404   4,105   4,393   5,279   5,728
March 20, 1873; organized March 11, 1881. *John Aaron Rawlins (1831–69)*. Union Army lieutenant to brigadier general 1861–65; aide-de-camp to General Grant; US secretary of war for six months 1869.

Ray   **Missouri**
Richmond   569 sq. mi.

23,494	23,354	21,971	21,378	17,599	16,075	15,932

November 16, 1820. *John Ray (?–1820)*. Missouri Constitutional Convention 1820; Missouri General Assembly 1820.

Reagan   **Texas**
Big Lake   1,175 sq. mi.

3,367	3,326	4,514	4,135	3,239	3,782	3,127

March 7, 1903. *John Henninger Reagan (1818–1905)*. Militia captain 1846; Texas House of Representatives 1846–47; postmaster general of the Confederacy 1861–64; US representative 1875–87; US senator 1887–91.

Real   **Texas**
Leakey   699 sq. mi.

3,309	3,047	2,412	2,469	2,013	2,079	2,479

April 3, 1913. *Julius Real (1860–1944)*. Rancher; Kerr County commissioner 1894–1902; Texas Senate 1908–14 and 1924–29.

Red Lake   **Minnesota**
Red Lake Falls   432 sq. mi.

4,089	4,299	4,525	5,471	5,388	5,830	6,806

December 24, 1896; organized April 6, 1897. *Red Lake River*. Name is translation of Chippewa name referring to red sunsets; river runs from Red Lake to the Red River of the North.

Red River   **Louisiana**
Coushatta   389 sq. mi.

9,091	9,622	9,387	10,433	9,226	9,978	12,113

March 7, 1871. *Red River*. Describes river's color from red clay and sandstone.

Red River   **Texas**
Clarksville   1,037 sq. mi.

12,860	14,314	14,317	16,101	14,298	15,682	21,851

March 17, 1836; organized December 14, 1837. *Red River.**

Red Willow   **Nebraska**
McCook   717 sq. mi.

11,055	11,448	11,705	12,615	12,191	12,940	12,977

February 27, 1873; organized May 27, 1873. *Red Willow Creek*. Mistranslation of Dakota *chahaska wakpala* meaning "Red Dogwood Creek"; tributary of Republican River.

Redwood   **Minnesota**
Redwood Falls   879 sq. mi.

16,059	16,815	17,254	19,341	20,024	21,718	22,127

February 6, 1862; organized February 23, 1865. *Redwood River*. Descriptive of red cedar trees or of red-barked bushes along river; tributary of Minnesota River.

Reeves   **Texas**
Pecos   2,635 sq. mi.

13,783	13,137	15,852	15,801	16,526	17,644	11,745

April 14, 1883; organized November 4, 1884. *George Robertson Reeves (1826–82)*. Sheriff of Grayson County 1848–50; Texas House of Representatives 1856–58 and intermittently 1870–82, speaker 1881–82; colonel, Confederate Cavalry 1861–64; died of hydrophobia following bite by rabid dog.

Refugio   **Texas**
Refugio   770 sq. mi.

7,383	7,828	7,976	9,289	9,494	10,975	10,113

March 17, 1836; organized 1837. *Our Lady of Refuge Mission.* From Spanish *Nuestra Señora del Refugio*; founded 1797, last Spanish mission in Texas; baptismal records maintained until 1828; buildings in ruins by 1835 from fighting during Texas Revolution.

Reno   **Kansas**
Hutchinson   1,255 sq. mi.
64,511   64,790   62,389   64,983   60,765   59,055   54,058
February 26, 1867; organized January 1, 1872. *Jesse Lee Reno (1823–62).* Graduated West Point 1846; 2nd lieutenant to major general 1847–62; brevetted for gallantry at Cerro Gordo and Chapultepec 1847; killed at South Mountain during Antietam campaign, September 14, 1862.

Rensselaer   **New York**
Troy   652 sq. mi.
159,429   152,538   154,429   151,966   152,510   142,585   132,607
February 7, 1791. *Renselaerwyck Manor.* Enormous land holdings along the Hudson River granted to the van Renselaer family by Dutch West India Company 1630; patroonship lasted until 1840. First van Renselaer patroon was Kiliaen van Renselaer (1580–1644); stockholder in Dutch West India Company; last patroon was Stephen van Rensselaer III (1764–1839); one of the wealthiest men in America. (Spelling of family name changed over time.)

Renville   **Minnesota**
Olivia   983 sq. mi.
15,730   17,154   17,673   20,401   21,139   23,249   23,954
February 20, 1855; organized July 31, 1866. *Joseph Renville (1779–1846).* Son of French father and Dakota mother; guide and interpreter for Zebulon Pike 1805–06 (see Pike, Alabama); British captain during War of 1812; established trading post at Lac qui Parle 1815; translated Bible into Dakota language.

Renville   **North Dakota**
Mohall   877 sq. mi.
2,470   2,610   3,160   3,608   3,828   4,698   5,405
January 4, 1873; abolished 1891; recreated July 20, 1910. *Uncertain.* (1) *Joseph Renville.** (2) *Gabriel Renville (1824–92)*; son of French-Canadian father and Dakota mother; Chief of Scouts for Minnesota Militia during Sioux War 1863–65; chief of Sisseton-Wahpeton Dakotas 1866–92.

Republic   **Kansas**
Belleville   717 sq. mi.
4,980   5,835   6,482   7,569   8,498   9,768   11,478
February 27, 1860; abolished 1865; recreated September 7, 1868; deorganized 1870; reorganized 1878. *Republican River.* Named for Republican Pawnees (Kitkehahki), one of four bands of Pawnees; called *Pahni Republique* by French; resettled to Indian Territory (Oklahoma) during 1870s.

Reynolds   **Missouri**
Centerville   808 sq. mi.
6,696   6,689   6,661   7,230   6,106   5,161   6,918
February 25, 1845. *Thomas Reynolds (1796–1844).* Clerk, Illinois House of Representatives 1818–22; chief justice, Illinois Supreme Court 1822–25; Illinois House of Representatives 1826–28; Missouri House of Representatives 1832; governor of Missouri 1840–44; committed suicide while governor.

Rhea   **Tennessee**
Dayton   315 sq. mi.
31,809   28,400   24,344   24,235   17,202   15,863   16,041
November 30, 1807. *John Rhea (1753–1832).* Ensign, 7th Virginia Regiment 1777; Battle of King's Mountain 1780; North Carolina House of Commons; delegate to North Carolina convention that ratified US Constitution 1789; Tennessee Constitutional Convention 1796; Tennessee House of Representatives 1796–97; US representative 1803–15 and 1817–23.

Rice   **Kansas**
Lyons   726 sq. mi.
10,083   10,761   10,610   11,900   12,320   13,909   15,635
February 26, 1867; organized August 18, 1871. *Samuel Allen Rice (1828–64)*. Colonel to brigadier general, Iowa Volunteers 1861–62; wounded at Jenkin's Ferry, April 30, 1864; died July 6.

Rice   **Minnesota**
Faribault   496 sq. mi.
64,142   56,665   49,183   46,087   41,582   38,988   36,235
March 5, 1853; organized October 9, 1855. *Henry Mower Rice (1817–94)*. Negotiated treaties with Indians ceding lands to US 1847; Minnesota Territory delegate to Congress 1853–57; US senator 1858–63; regent, University of Minnesota 1851–59; treasurer of Ramsey County 1878–84.

Rich   **Utah**
Randolph   1,029 sq. mi.
2,264   1,961   1,725   2,100   1,615   1,685   1,673
January 16, 1864, as Richland; name changed January 29, 1868. *Charles Coulson Rich (1809–83)*. Military leader during Mormon exodus to Utah 1847; apostle of church 1849; established Mormon colony in California 1851; Utah legislature 1864–72.

Richardson   **Nebraska**
Falls City   552 sq. mi.
8,363   9,531   9,937   11,315   12,277   13,903   16,886
November 23, 1854. *William Alexander Richardson (1811–75)*. Illinois House of Representatives 1836–38 and 1844–46, speaker 1844; Illinois Senate 1838–42; captain and major, Mexican War 1846–47; US representative 1847–56 and 1861–63; governor of Nebraska Territory 1858; US senator from Illinois 1863–65.

Richland   **Illinois**
Olney   360 sq. mi.
16,233   16,149   16,545   17,587   16,829   16,299   16,889
February 24, 1841. *Richland County, Ohio*. Origin of early settlers.

Richland   **Louisiana**
Rayville   559 sq. mi.
20,725   20,981   20,629   22,187   21,774   23,824   26,672
September 29, 1868. *Descriptive*. Refers to rich alluvial soils in the area.

Richland   **Montana**
Sidney   2,084 sq. mi.
9,746   9,667   10,716   12,243   9,837   10,504   10,366
May 27, 1914. *Descriptive*. Promotional name in hopes of attracting settlers.

Richland   **North Dakota**
Wahpeton   1,436 sq. mi.
16,321   17,998   18,148   19,207   18,089   18,824   19,865
January 4, 1873; organized November 25, 1875. *Morgan T. Rich (1832–98)*. Early settler; operated ferry across Bois de Sioux River 1869; ferry site became town of Wahpeton.

Richland   **Ohio**
Mansfield   495 sq. mi.
124,475   128,852   126,137   131,205   129,997   117,761   91,305
January 30, 1808; organized January 7, 1813. *Descriptive*. Refers to soils in the area.

Richland   **South Carolina**
Columbia   757 sq. mi.

384,504   320,677   285,720   269,735   233,868   200,102   142,565
March 12, 1785; converted to judicial district 1799; redesignated as county April 16, 1868. *Uncertain.* (1) *Descriptive.* Refers to rich soils in the area. (2) *Richland Plantation*; plantation of Thomas Taylor (1743–1833); captain to colonel 1780–82; South Carolina Senate 1790.

Richland   **Wisconsin**
Richland Center   586 sq. mi.
18,021   17,924   17,521   17,476   17,079   17,684   19,245
February 18, 1842; organized May 1, 1850. *Descriptive.* Promotional name in hopes of attracting settlers.

Richmond   **Georgia**
Augusta   324 sq. mi.
200,549   199,775   189,719   181,629   162,437   135,601   108,876
February 5, 1777. *Charles Lennox, 3rd Duke of Richmond (1735–1806).* Officer in British Army 1756–63; ambassador extraordinary and minister plenipotentiary to France 1766; member of Parliament; supported colonists in American Revolution; proposed withdrawal of British troops from America 1778; Knight of the Garter 1782.

Richmond   **New York**
Saint George   58 sq. mi.
468,730   443,728   378,977   352,121   295,443   221,991   191,555
November 1, 1683. *Charles Lennox, 1st Duke of Richmond (1672–1723).* Illegitimate son of King Charles II; created Duke of Richmond 1675; Knight of the Garter 1681; Lord High Admiral of Scotland 1701–05.

Richmond   **North Carolina**
Rockingham   474 sq. mi.
46,639   46,564   44,518   45,481   39,889   39,202   39,597
1779. *Charles Lennox, 3rd Duke of Richmond.**

Richmond   **Virginia**
Warsaw   191 sq. mi.
9,254   8,809   7,273   6,952   5,841   6,375   6,189
April 26, 1692. *Uncertain.* (1) *Richmond, England.* Site of British royal palace until 1780. (2) *Charles Lenox, 1st Duke of Richmond.**

Richmond   **Virginia**
(Independent City)   60 sq. mi.
204,214   197,790   203,056   219,214   249,621   219,958   230,310
July 17, 1782. *Richmond, England.* City site reminded founder, William Byrd II, of English town. (Associated counties: Chesterfield and Henrico.)

Riley   **Kansas**
Manhattan   610 sq. mi.
71,115   62,843   67,139   63,505   56,788   41,914   33,405
August 25, 1855. *Fort Riley.* Established 1853 to protect travelers on California, Oregon, and Santa Fe Trails. Named for Bennett Riley (1787–1853); ensign to captain 1813–18; served on frontier against Indians 1823; major to brevet major general 1837–47; military governor of California 1849; colonel, 1st Infantry 1850–53.

Ringgold   **Iowa**
Mount Ayr   536 sq. mi.
5,131   5,469   5,420   6,112   6,373   7,910   9,528
February 24, 1847; organized January 31, 1855. *Samuel Ringgold (1800–46).* Graduated West Point 1818; aide to General Winfield Scott; captain 1834; brevet major for service against Seminoles; mortally wounded at Palo Alto, May 8, 1846, died three days later.

Rio Arriba   **New Mexico**
Tierra Amarilla   5,861 sq. mi.

40,246	41,190	34,365	29,282	25,170	24,193	24,997

January 9, 1852. *Upper Rio Grande*. From Spanish for "upper river"; Spain divided colonial New Mexico into three areas: upper, middle, and lower.

Rio Blanco   **Colorado**
Meeker   3,221 sq. mi.

6,666	5,986	5,972	6,255	4,842	5,150	4,719

March 25, 1889. *White River*. Hispanicized name of White River.

Rio Grande   **Colorado**
Del Norte   912 sq. mi.

11,982	12,413	10,770	10,511	10,494	11,160	12,832

February 10, 1874. *Rio Grande*. Spanish for "large river"; largest river between Mississippi and Colorado Rivers.

Ripley   **Indiana**
Versailles   446 sq. mi.

28,818	26,523	24,616	24,398	21,138	20,641	18,763

December 27, 1816; organized January 14, 1818; effective April 10, 1818. *Eleazar Wheelock Ripley (1782–1839)*. Massachusetts House of Representatives 1807 and 1811; Massachusetts Senate 1812; lieutenant colonel to brevet major general 1812–14; received gold medal from Congress 1814; Louisiana Senate 1820; US representative from Louisiana 1835–39.

Ripley   **Missouri**
Doniphan   630 sq. mi.

14,100	13,509	12,303	12,458	9,803	9,096	11,414

January 5, 1833. *Eleazar Wheelock Ripley*.*

Ritchie   **West Virginia**
Harrisville   452 sq. mi.

10,449	10,343	10,233	11,442	10,145	10,877	12,535

February 18, 1843. *Thomas Ritchie (1778–1854)*. Founded *Richmond Enquirer* 1804; editor 1804–45; editorially supported public funding for schools and development of infrastructure.

Riverside   **California**
Riverside   7,206 sq. mi.

2,189,641	1,545,387	1,170,413	663,923	459,074	306,191	170,046

March 11, 1893. *Town of Riverside*. Named for location on Santa Ana River.

Roane   **Tennessee**
Kingston   361 sq. mi.

54,181	51,910	47,227	48,425	38,881	39,133	31,665

November 6, 1801. *Archibald Roane (1759–1819)*. Private at Yorktown 1781; Tennessee Constitutional Convention 1796; Tennessee Superior Court 1796–1801; governor of Tennessee 1801–03; Tennessee Supreme Court 1815–18.

Roane   **West Virginia**
Salem   484 sq. mi.

14,926	15,446	15,120	15,952	14,111	15,720	18,408

March 11, 1856. *Spencer Roane (1762–1822)*. Virginia House of Delegates 1783–84; judge, Virginia Supreme Court of Appeals 1794–1822; friend of Thomas Jefferson; son-in-law of Patrick Henry.

Roanoke   **Virginia**
Salem   251 sq. mi.

92,376	85,778	79,332	72,945	67,339	61,693	41,486

March 30, 1838. *Roanoke River*. Based on English misunderstanding of Algonquins' response to their questions; may mean anything from "white shells" to "tobacco." (Associated independent cities: Roanoke and Salem.)

Roanoke   **Virginia**
(Independent City)   43 sq. mi.
97,032   94,911   96,397   100,220   92,115   97,110   91,921
1884. *Roanoke River.** (Associated county: Roanoke)

Roberts   **South Dakota**
Sisseton   1,101 sq. mi.
10,149   10,016   9,914   10,911   11,678   13,190   14,929
March 8, 1883. *Samuel B. Roberts (1843–?)*. Union Army during Civil War; Fargo City Council; Dakota territorial legislature 1879–80 and 1883–84.

Roberts   **Texas**
Miami   924 sq. mi.
929   887   1,025   1,187   967   1,075   1,031
August 21, 1876; organized January 10, 1889. *Uncertain*. (1) *John S. Roberts (1797–1871)*; Battle of Nacogdoches, prelude to Texas Revolution 1832; signer, Texas Declaration of Independence 1836. (2) *Oran Milo Roberts (1815–98)*; Alabama legislature 1837; Texas Supreme Court 1857–61 and 1864–65; president, Secession Convention 1861; Texas Constitutional Convention 1866; chief justice, Texas Supreme Court 1874–78; governor of Texas 1879–83; professor of law, University of Texas 1883–93. (3) *Both John and Oran Roberts*.

Robertson   **Kentucky**
Mount Olivet   100 sq. mi.
2,282   2,266   2,124   2,265   2,163   2,443   2,881
February 11, 1867. *George Robertson (1790–1874)*. US representative from Kentucky 1817–21; Kentucky House of Representatives 1822–27 and 1848–52, speaker 1824–27 and 1851–52; Kentucky secretary of state 1824; law professor, Transylvania University 1834–57; Court of Appeals 1864–71.

Robertson   **Tennessee**
Springfield   476 sq. mi.
66,283   54,433   41,494   37,021   29,102   27,335   27,024
April 9, 1796. *James Robertson (1742–1814)*. Explored Watauga Valley 1770; settled future site of Nashville 1779; North Carolina legislature 1785; Tennessee Constitutional Convention 1796; Tennessee Senate 1798.

Robertson   **Texas**
Franklin   856 sq. mi.
16,622   16,000   15,511   14,653   14,389   16,157   19,908
December 14, 1837; organized 1838. *Sterling Clark Robertson (1785–1842)*. Major, War of 1812; Battle of New Orleans 1815; signer, Texas Declaration of Independence 1836; Republic of Texas Senate 1836 and 1840.

Robeson   **North Carolina**
Lumberton   949 sq. mi.
134,168   123,339   105,179   101,610   84,842   89,102   87,769
1787. *Thomas Robeson (1740–85)*. North Carolina legislature; North Carolina Provincial Convention 1775–76; colonel, paid troops out of own funds; Battle of Moore's Creek 1776; Battle of Elizabethtown 1781.

Rock   **Minnesota**
Luverne   482 sq. mi.
9,687   9,721   9,806   10,703   11,346   11,864   11,278
May 23, 1857, as Pipestone; exchanged names with Rock County February 20, 1862; organized February 7, 1874. *Pipestone deposit*. Large outcrop of pipestone rising above surrounding prairie. (See Pipestone, Minnesota.)

Rock   **Nebraska**
Bassett   1,008 sq. mi.
1,526   1,756   2,019   2,383   2,231   2,554   3,026
November 6, 1888; organized January 8, 1889. *Rock Creek*. Named for building-stone quarry adjacent to creek.

Rock   **Wisconsin**
Janesville   718 sq. mi.
160,331   152,307   139,510   139,240   131,970   113,913   92,778
December 7, 1836; organized February 19, 1839. *Uncertain*. (1) *Landmark rock*; large rock near Janesville marked safe fording site across the Rock River. (2) *Rock River*; named for the rock.

Rockbridge   **Virginia**
Lexington   598 sq. mi.
22,307   20,808   18,350   17,911   16,637   24,039   23,359
January 12, 1778. *Descriptive*. Refers to natural limestone bridge over Cedar Creek; once owned by Thomas Jefferson. (Associated independent cities: Buena Vista and Lexington.)

Rockcastle   **Kentucky**
Mount Vernon   317 sq. mi.
17,056   16,582   14,803   13,973   12,305   12,334   13,925
January 8, 1810. *Rockcastle River*. Named for large rock formations on river's banks.

Rockdale   **Georgia**
Conyers   130 sq. mi.
85,215   70,111   54,091   36,747   18,152   10,572   8,464
October 18, 1870. *Rockdale Church*. Named for large subterranean granite deposit underlying the area's red clay topsoil.

Rockingham   **New Hampshire**
Bentwood   695 sq. mi.
295,223   277,359   245,845   190,345   138,951   99,029   70,059
April 29, 1769. *Charles Watson-Wentworth, 2nd Marquess of Rockingham (1730–82)*. British Army; Knight of the Garter 1760; prime minister 1765–66 and 1782; repealed Stamp Act; sought to avoid armed conflict with American colonists even if it meant losing colonies; advocated recognition of US independence 1782.

Rockingham   **North Carolina**
Wentworth   566 sq. mi.
93,643   91,928   86,064   83,426   72,402   69,629   64,816
December 29, 1785. *Charles Watson-Wentworth, 2nd Marquess of Rockingham.**

Rockingham   **Virginia**
Harrisonburg   849 sq. mi.
76,314   67,725   57,842   57,038   47,890   40,485   35,079
January 12, 1778. *Charles Watson-Wentworth, 2nd Marquess of Rockingham.** (Associated independent city: Harrisonburg.)

Rock Island   **Illinois**
Rock Island   428 sq. mi.
147,546   149,374   148,723   165,968   166,734   150,991   133,558
February 9, 1831; organized July 5, 1833. *Rock Island*. Large island in the Mississippi River near mouth of Rock River; now named Arsenal Island.

Rockland   **New York**
New City   174 sq. mi.
311,687   286,753   265,475   259,530   229,903   136,803   89,276
February 23, 1798. *Descriptive*. Refers to rocky topography including Hudson Palisades.

Rockwall   **Texas**
Rockwall   127 sq. mi.
78,337   43,080   25,604   14,528   7,046   5,878   6,156
March 1, 1873. *Town of Rockwall*. Named for a subterranean rock formation discovered beneath the proposed town site.

Roger Mills   **Oklahoma**
Cheyenne   1,141 sq. mi.
3,647   3,436   4,147   4,799   4,452   5,090   7,395
April 19, 1892, as County F; name changed November 8, 1892. *Roger Quarles Mills (1832–1911)*. Texas House of Representatives 1859–60; private to colonel Confederate Army 1861–64; wounded at Missionary Ridge and Atlanta; US representative 1873–92; US senator 1892–99; advocated opening Indian Territory (Oklahoma) to white settlement.

Rogers   **Oklahoma**
Claremore   676 sq. mi.
86,905   70,641   55,170   46,436   28,425   20,614   19,532
July 16, 1907. *Clement V. Rogers (1839–1911)*. Rancher and stockman; Cherokee Senate 1862–63 and intermittently 1879–1903; Oklahoma Constitutional Convention 1907; father of humorist Will Rogers.

Rolette   **North Dakota**
Rolla   903 sq. mi.
13,937   13,674   12,772   12,177   11,549   10,641   11,102
January 4, 1873; October 14, 1884. *Joseph Rolette (1820–71)*. Operated American Fur Company trading post at Pembina; Minnesota territorial legislature 1853–57.

Rooks   **Kansas**
Stockton   891 sq. mi.
5,181   5,685   6,039   7,006   7,628   9,734   9,043
February 26, 1867; organized November 26, 1872. *John Calvin Rooks (1835–62)*. Enlisted as private, 11th Kansas Volunteer Cavalry Regiment 1862; mortally wounded at Battle of Prairie Grove, December 7, 1862; died four days later.

Roosevelt   **Montana**
Wolf Point   2,355 sq. mi.
10,425   10,620   10,999   10,467   10,365   11,731   9,580
February 18, 1919. *Theodore Roosevelt (1858–1919)*. New York Assembly 1882–84; US Civil Service Commission 1889–95; president, New York City Board of Police Commissioners; assistant secretary of the Navy 1897–98; colonel, Spanish-American War, commanded "Rough Riders"; governor of New York 1899–1900; vice president of US 1901; became president upon assassination of President McKinley 1901; 26th president of US 1901–09; Nobel Peace Prize for mediating Russian-Japanese conflict 1906; explored Amazon Basin 1913–14.

Roosevelt   **New Mexico**
Portales   2,447 sq. mi.
19,846   18,018   16,702   15,695   16,479   16,198   16,409
February 28, 1903. *Theodore Roosevelt.**

Roscommon   **Michigan**
Roscommon   520 sq. mi.
24,449   25,469   19,776   16,374   9,892   7,200   5,916
April 1, 1840, as Mikenauk; name changed March 8, 1843; organized March 20, 1875. *County Roscommon, Ireland*. Michigan legislature renamed several counties after Irish counties, March 8, 1843.

Roseau   **Minnesota**
Roseau   1,672 sq. mi.
15,629   16,338   15,026   12,574   11,569   12,154   14,505
February 28, 1894; organized April 6, 1896. *Roseau River and Roseau Lake*. French for "reed"; descriptive of reeds growing along lakes and streams.

Rosebud   **Montana**
Forsyth   5,010 sq. mi.
9,233   9,383   10,505   9,899   6,032   6,187   6,570
February 11, 1901. *Rosebud Creek.* Named for wild roses along banks.

Ross   **Ohio**
Chillicothe   689 sq. mi.
78,064   73,345   69,330   65,004   61,211   61,215   54,424
August 20, 1798. *James Ross (1762–1847).* Pennsylvania Constitutional Convention 1789–90; US senator 1794–1803; three times unsuccessful candidate for governor 1799–1808; friend of Northwest Territory Governor St. Clair, also from Pennsylvania.

Routt   **Colorado**
Steamboat Springs   2,362 sq. mi.
23,509   19,690   14,088   13,404   6,592   5,900   8,940
January 29, 1877. *John Long Routt (1826–1907).* Captain to colonel, 94th Illinois Volunteer Unit 1862–65, aide to General Grant; governor of Colorado Territory 1875–76; governor of Colorado 1876–79 and 1891–93; mayor of Denver 1883–85.

Rowan   **Kentucky**
Morehead   280 sq. mi.
23,333   22,094   20,353   19,049   17,010   12,808   12,708
March 15, 1856. *John Rowan (1773–1843).* Kentucky secretary of state 1804–06; US representative 1807–09; Kentucky House of Representatives, intermittently 1813–24; judge, Court of Appeals 1819–21; US senator 1825–31.

Rowan   **North Carolina**
Salisbury   511 sq. mi.
138,428   139,340   110,605   99,186   90,035   82,817   75,410
March 27, 1753. *Matthew Rowan (?–1760).* North Carolina General Assembly 1729; North Carolina Council 1734–60; surveyor general of North Carolina 1736; acting royal governor 1753–54.

Runnels   **Texas**
Ballinger   1,051 sq. mi.
10,501   11,495   11,294   11,872   12,108   15,016   16,771
February 1, 1858; organized February 16, 1880. *Uncertain.* (1) *Hardin Richard Runnels (1820–73);* Texas legislature 1847–54, speaker 1853–54; lieutenant governor 1855; governor of Texas 1857–59; Texas Secession Convention 1861; Texas Constitutional Convention 1866. (2) *Hiram George Runnels (1796–1857).* Mississippi legislature 1829–31 and 1840–41; governor of Mississippi 1833–35; fought duel with Volney Howard 1840 (see Howard, Texas); moved to Texas 1842; Texas Annexation Convention 1845; Texas Senate.

Rush   **Indiana**
Rushville   408 sq. mi.
17,392   18,261   18,129   19,604   20,352   20,393   19,799
December 31, 1821. *Benjamin Rush (1745–1813).* Physician; Continental Congress from Pennsylvania 1776–77; signer, Declaration of Independence 1776; participated in attempt to remove Washington from command of Continental Army 1777; surgeon general of the Army 1777–78; founder, Pennsylvania Hospital 1783; treasurer of US Mint at Philadelphia 1799–1813.

Rush   **Kansas**
La Crosse   718 sq. mi.
3,307   3,551   3,842   4,516   5,117   6,160   7,231
February 26, 1867; organized December 5, 1874. *Alexander Rush (?–1864).* Captain, Company H, 2nd Kansas Colored Cavalry; killed at Jenkin's Ferry, April 30, 1864.

Rusk   **Texas**
Henderson   924 sq. mi.

53,330   47,372   43,735   41,382   34,102   36,421   42,348

January 16, 1843. *Thomas Jefferson Rusk (1803–57)*. Signer, Texas Declaration of Independence 1836; Republic of Texas secretary of war 1836; Battle of San Jacinto 1836; Texas legislature 1837–38; major general Texas Militia 1838; chief justice of Texas 1838–40; US senator 1846–57, president pro tempore 1857.

Rusk   **Wisconsin**
Ladysmith   914 sq. mi.
14,755   15,347   15,079   15,589   14,238   14,794   16,790

May 15, 1901, as Gates; name changed June 19, 1905. *Jeremiah McLain Rusk (1830–93)*. Wisconsin Assembly 1862; major to brigadier general 1862–65; US representative 1871–77; governor of Wisconsin 1882–89; US secretary of agriculture 1889–93.

Russell   **Alabama**
Phenix City   641 sq. mi.
52,947   49,756   46,860   47,356   45,394   46,351   40,364

December 18, 1832. *Gilbert Christian Russell (1782–1861)*. Ensign to colonel, 3rd Infantry, US Army, 1803–14; fought against Creek Nation.

Russell   **Kansas**
Russell   886 sq. mi.
6,970   7,370   7,835   8,868   9,428   11,348   13,406

February 26, 1867; organized August 18, 1872. *Avra P. Russell (1833–62)*. Established express line from Leavenworth to Pikes Peak; captain, Company K, 2nd Kansas Volunteer Cavalry 1862; wounded at Battle of Prairie Grove, December 7, 1862, died five days later.

Russell   **Kentucky**
Jamestown   254 sq. mi.
17,565   16,315   14,716   13,708   10,542   11,076   13,717

December 14, 1825. *William Russell (1758–1825)*. Lieutenant, Continental Army; battles of Kings Mountain (1780) and Guilford Courthouse (1781); Virginia legislature 1790–91; Kentucky legislature, intermittently 1792–1823; lieutenant colonel, Kentucky Mounted Volunteers 1793; colonel 1808; Battle of Tippecanoe 1811.

Russell   **Virginia**
Lebanon   474 sq. mi.
28,897   30,308   28,667   31,761   24,533   26,290   26,818

January 6, 1786; effective May 1, 1786. *William Russell.**

Rutherford   **North Carolina**
Rutherfordton   564 sq. mi.
67,810   62,899   56,918   53,787   47,337   45,091   46,356

1779. *Griffith Rutherford (c1731–1805)*. British Army during French and Indian War; North Carolina Provincial Congress 1775; brigadier general, North Carolina Militia 1776; defeated Cherokees 1776; North Carolina Senate 1780; taken prisoner at Battle of Camden 1780, exchanged 1781; legislative council of Territory South of the Ohio (Tennessee) 1796.

Rutherford   **Tennessee**
Murfreesboro   619 sq. mi.
262,604   182,023   118,570   84,058   59,428   52,368   40,696

October 25, 1803, *Griffith Rutherford.**

Rutland   **Vermont**
Rutland   930 sq. mi.
61,642   63,400   62,142   58,347   52,637   46,719   45,905

February 22, 1781. *Town of Rutland*. Uncertain origin: (1) Rutland, Massachusetts; (2) John Manners, 3rd Duke of Rutland (1696–1779); courtier of George II and George III; privy councilor; lord justice of England; originated chess variant named for him.

S

Sabine   **Louisiana**
Many   867 sq. mi.
24,233   23,459   22,646   25,280   18,638   18,564   20,880
March 7, 1843. *Sabine River.* From Spanish name for the river *Rio Sabinas* meaning "River of Cypress Trees"; changed to "Sabine" by French.

Sabine   **Texas**
Hemphill   491 sq. mi.
10,834   10,469   9,586   8,702   7,187   7,302   8,568
March 17, 1836; organized December 14, 1837. *Sabine Municipality.* Former municipality within the Mexican Department of Nacogdoches; named for Sabine River.*

Sac   **Iowa**
Sac City   575 sq. mi.
10,350   11,529   12,234   14,118   15,573   17,007   17,518
January 15, 1851; organized April 7, 1856. *Sauk Indians.* Variant spelling. (See Sauk, Wisconsin.)

Sacramento   **California**
Sacramento   965 sq. mi.
1,418,788   1,223,499   1,041,219   783,381   631,498   502,778   277,140
February 18, 1850. *Sacramento River.* Spanish for "sacrament"; name originally given to Feather River, a tributary of the Sacramento 1808; name gradually became applied to the principal river.

Sagadahoc   **Maine**
Bath   254 sq. mi.
35,293   35,214   33,535   28,795   23,452   22,793   20,911
April 4, 1854. *Lower section of Kennebec River.* That part of the Kennebec River below the Androscoggin River was called *sagadahoc* (mouth of the river) by the Abnaki.

Saginaw   **Michigan**
Saginaw   800 sq. mi.
200,169   210,039   211,946   228,059   219,743   190,752   153,515
September 10, 1822; organized February 9, 1835. *Saginaw River.* From Ojibwa *saging*, meaning "at the mouth."

Saguache   **Colorado**
Saguache   3,169 sq. mi.
6,108   5,917   4,619   3,935   3,827   4,473   5,664
December 29, 1866. *Saguache Creek.* From Ute *sagaugauchipa*, meaning "blue earth" or "water at blue earth." Descriptive of blue clay deposits near the creek.

Saint Bernard   **Louisiana**
Chalmette   378 sq. mi.
35,897   67,229   66,631   64,097   51,185   32,186   11,087
March 31, 1807. *Ecclesiastical district of Saint Bernard Parish.* Named for St. Bernard of Clairvaux (1090–1153); entered monastery 1113; abbot 1115; drew up statutes for Knights Templar 1128; generated support for Second Crusade; canonized 1174.

Saint Charles   **Louisiana**
Hahnville   279 sq. mi.
52,780   48,072   42,437   37,259   29,550   21,219   13,363
March 31, 1807. *Ecclesiastical district of Saint Charles Parish.* Named for St. Carlo Borromeo (1538–84); nephew of Giovanni Angelo de Medici, Pope Pius IV; appointed by Pius IV as cardinal and archbishop of Milan before being ordained; Council of Trent 1545–63; ordained 1563; gave much of his personal fortune to philanthropy; canonized 1610.

Saint Charles   **Missouri**
Saint Charles   560 sq. mi.
360,485   283,883   212,907   144,107   92,954   52,970   29,834
October 1, 1812. *Spanish District of San Carlos*. Uncertain origin of name. (1) St. Carlo Borromeo.* (2) King Charles IV of Spain (1748–1819); became king 1788; invaded France 1794; retroceded Louisiana from Spain to France 1801; abdicated after Napoleon occupied Spain 1808; exiled in France and later in Rome 1808–19.

Saint Clair   **Alabama**
Ashville   632 sq. mi.
83,593   64,742   50,009   41,205   27,956   25,388   26,687
November 20, 1818. *Arthur Saint Clair (1734–1818)*. Served under General Wolfe at Quebec 1758; resigned from British Army 1762; colonel, Pennsylvania Militia 1776; brigadier general Continental Army 1776–83; surrendered Fort Ticonderoga to General Burgoyne 1777; Continental Congress 1785–87; governor of Northwest Territory 1788–1802; defeated by confederation of Miamis and Shawnees, "St. Clair's Defeat," at Fort Recovery 1791.

Saint Clair   **Illinois**
Belleville   658 sq. mi.
270,056   256,082   262,852   267,531   185,176   262,509   205,995
April 27, 1790. *Arthur Saint Clair*.*

Saint Clair   **Michigan**
Port Huron   721 sq. mi.
163,040   164,235   145,607   138,802   120,175   107,201   91,599
March 28, 1820; organized May 8, 1821. *Saint Clair Township*. Origin of name is uncertain. (1) Arthur St. Clair.* (2) Lake St. Clair; named for Clare of Assisi (see Santa Clara, California).

Saint Clair   **Missouri**
Osceola   670 sq. mi.
9,805   9,652   8,457   8,622   7,667   8,421   10,482
February 11, 1835; organized January 29, 1841. *Arthur Saint Clair*.*

Saint Croix   **Wisconsin**
Hudson   722 sq. mi.
84,345   63,155   50,251   43,262   34,354   29,164   25,905
January 9, 1840; deorganized 1843; reorganized February 28, 1849. *Saint Croix River*. Origin of name is uncertain. (1) A cross (French *croix*) was erected at the mouth of the river to memorialize a drowning victim. (2) Named by Father Hennepin (see Hennepin, Minnesota) for many burial markers in the area 1678.

Sainte Genevieve   **Missouri**
Sainte Genevieve   499 sq. mi.
18,145   17,842   16,037   15,180   12,867   12,116   11,237
October 1, 1812. *Town of Sainte Genevieve*. Named for Ste. Genevieve (422–500); given religious veil by bishop of Paris c437; rallied Parisians to resist Attila the Hun with faith in God; Attila spared Paris and besieged Orleans instead 451; patron saint of Paris.

Saint Francis   **Arkansas**
Forrest City   635 sq. mi.
28,258   29,329   28,497   30,858   30,799   33,303   36,841
October 13, 1827; effective December 1, 1827. *Saint Francis River*. Named for St. Francis of Assisi (1181–1226); abandoned family wealth to devote life of poverty to God; pilgrimage to Rome 1206; began to attract followers 1209; established Friars Minor which became Franciscan Order 1210; resigned as head of order because of poor administrative skills 1220; canonized 1228.

Saint Francois   **Missouri**
Farmington   452 sq. mi.

65,359	55,641	48,904	42,600	36,818	36,516	35,276

December 19, 1821. *Saint Francis River.** French spelling.

Saint Helena   **Louisiana**
Greensburg   408 sq. mi.

11,203	10,525	9,874	9,827	9,937	9,162	9,013

October 27, 1810. *Spanish parish of Santa Helena, West Florida.* Named for St. Helen (250–330); mother of Constantine the Great c272; converted to Christianity 313; made pilgrimage to Holy Land in search of the true cross c325. US claim to Spanish West Florida confirmed 1819.

Saint James   **Louisiana**
Convent   242 sq. mi.

22,102	21,216	20,879	21,495	19,733	18,369	15,334

March 31, 1807. *Ecclesiastical District of Saint James Parish.* Uncertain origin of name. (1) St. James the Greater (?–44); may have been cousin of Jesus; one of first four apostles; first apostle to be martyred when he was beheaded on orders of Herod Agrippa. (2) St. James the Less (?–c62); cousin of Jesus; one of twelve apostles; first bishop of Jerusalem; stoned to death by Pharisees after surviving being thrown from temple roof.

Saint Johns   **Florida**
Saint Augustine   601 sq. mi.

190,039	123,135	83,829	51,303	30,727	30,034	24,998

August 12, 1822. *Saint Johns River.* Named for a Spanish mission which was named for St. John the Baptist (see St. John the Baptist, Louisiana).

Saint John the Baptist   **Louisiana**
Laplace   213 sq. mi.

45,924	43,044	39,996	31,924	28,813	18,439	14,861

March 31, 1807. *Ecclesiastical District of Saint John the Baptist Parish.* Named for St. John the Baptist (c7 BCE–28 CE); lived in deserts of Judea; preached confession of sins and physical baptism; baptized Jesus; beheaded by Herod Antipas.

Saint Joseph   **Indiana**
South Bend   458 sq. mi.

266,931	265,559	247,052	241,617	245,045	238,614	205,058

January 29, 1830; effective April 1, 1830. *Saint Joseph River.* Named for French fort that was named for Mission St. Joseph founded by Father Allouez 1691. Origin of mission's name is uncertain: (1) St. Joseph, father of Jesus; (2) Father Joseph (?–?), French missionary who was an early settler in the area.

Saint Joseph   **Michigan**
Centreville   501 sq. mi.

61,295	62,422	58,913	56,083	47,392	42,332	35,071

October 29, 1829. *Saint Joseph River.**

Saint Landry   **Louisiana**
Opelousas   924 sq. mi.

83,384	87,700	80,331	84,128	80,364	81,493	78,476

March 31, 1807. *Ecclesiastical District of Saint Landry Parish.* Named for St. Landry (?–660); bishop of Paris 650; tradition of founding first hospital in Paris.

Saint Lawrence   **New York**
Canton   2,680 sq. mi.

111,944	111,931	111,974	114,254	111,911	111,239	98,897

March 3, 1802. *Saint Lawrence River.* Named for St. Lawrence (?–258); archdeacon and treasurer of Roman Catholic Church c257; tortured and put to death by Roman emperor Valerian.

Saint Louis   **Minnesota**
Duluth   6,247 sq. mi.
200,226   200,528   198,213   222,229   220,693   231,588   206,062
March 1, 1856; organized May 23, 1857. *Saint Louis River.* Named for King Louis IX of France (1214–70); became king of France 1226; Treaty of Paris with England by which Henry III retained some English lands in France but as a vassal to the king of France 1259; led crusade to Holy Land 1248; captured in Egypt and ransomed 1250; died of plague in Tunis on a second crusade; canonized 1297.

Saint Louis   **Missouri**
Clayton   508 sq. mi.
998,954   1,016,315   993,529   973,896   951,353   703,532   406,349
October 1, 1812. *Spanish district of San Luis.* Named for city of St. Louis which was named for French King Louis XV who was king at time of the city's settlement, and his patron saint, Louis IX (see Saint Louis, Minnesota).

Saint Louis   **Missouri**
(Independent City)   62 sq. mi.
319,294   348,189   396,685   453,085   622,236   750,026   856,796
March 5, 1877. *Spanish district of San Luis.**

Saint Lucie   **Florida**
Fort Pierce   572 sq. mi.
277,789   192,695   150,171   87,182   50,836   39,294   20,180
May 24, 1905. *Fort Santa Lucia.* Established by Spanish 1565; named for St. Lucy of Syracuse (c283–c304); according to legend took vow of chastity as a youth; a rejected suitor informed on her to Roman authorities; martyred by a sword thrust down her throat after unsuccessful attempts to burn her.

Saint Martin   **Louisiana**
Saint Martinville   738 sq. mi.
52,160   48,583   43,978   40,214   32,453   29,063   26,353
March 31, 1807. *Ecclesiastical District of Saint Martin Parish.* From St. Martin Church established 1765; named for St. Martin of Tours (316–97); converted to Christianity in early teens; served in Roman Army; arrested for refusing to fight; fled to France to avoid persecution 334; bishop of Tours 372; patron saint of France.

Saint Mary   **Louisiana**
Franklin   555 sq. mi.
54,650   53,500   58,086   64,253   60,752   48,833   35,848
April 17, 1811. *Ecclesiastical District of Saint Mary Parish.* Named for St. Mary (20 BCE–?); mother of Jesus; preeminent of all Roman Catholic saints.

Saint Mary's   **Maryland**
Leonardtown   357 sq. mi.
105,151   86,211   75,074   59,895   47,388   38,915   29,111
February 9, 1637; name changed to Potomac 1654; renamed St. Mary's 1658. *Saint Mary.**

Saint Tammany   **Louisiana**
Covington   846 sq. mi.
233,740   191,268   144,508   110,869   63,585   38,643   26,988
October 27, 1810. *Tamenend (c1628–98).* Delaware chief; name means "affable"; signed deed ceding land to William Penn 1683; popular with American colonists; called "patron saint" of colonists; not a saint of the Roman Catholic Church; had no known association with Louisiana.

Salem   **New Jersey**
Salem   332 sq. mi.
66,083   64,285   65,294   64,676   60,346   58,711   49,508
May 17, 1694. *Village of New Salem.* From Hebrew *shalom* meaning "peace"; settled by Quakers 1675.

Salem **Virginia**
(Independent City) 14 sq. mi.
24,802   24,747   23,756   23,958   21,982   (a)   (a)
December 31, 1967. *Salem, New Jersey*. Named in honor of a leading citizen from New Jersey. [(a) Part of Roanoke County] (Associated county: Roanoke.)

Saline **Arkansas**
Benton 724 sq. mi.
107,118   83,529   64,183   53,161   36,107   28,956   23,816
November 2, 1835. *Descriptive*. Refers to local salt works established 1827.

Saline **Illinois**
Harrisburg 380 sq. mi.
24,913   26,733   26,551   28,448   25,721   26,227   33,420
February 25, 1847; abolished 1851; recreated 1852. *Uncertain*. (1) *Saline Creek*. (2) *Descriptive* of salt springs and salt deposits in the area for which the creek is named.

Saline **Kansas**
Salina 720 sq. mi.
55,606   53,597   49,301   48,905   46,592   54,715   33,409
February 5, 1860. *Saline River*. French translation of Indian name, *ne miskua*, describing the river's salt content.

Saline **Missouri**
Marshall 756 sq. mi.
23,370   23,756   23,523   24,919   24,633   25,148   26,694
November 25, 1820; effective January 1, 1821. *Descriptive*. Refers to local salt springs.

Saline **Nebraska**
Wilber 574 sq. mi.
14,200   13,843   12,715   13,131   12,809   12,542   14,046
March 6, 1855; organized February 18, 1867. *Erroneous assumption*. Named for mistaken belief that there were salt deposits in the area.

Salt Lake **Utah**
Salt Lake City 742 sq. mi.
1,029,655   898,387   725,956   619,066   458,607   383,035   274,895
January 31, 1850, as Great Salt Lake; name changed January 29, 1868. *Great Salt Lake*. Largest body of water between Great Lakes and Pacific Ocean; high salt content from evaporation.

Saluda **South Carolina**
Saluda 453 sq. mi.
19,875   19,181   16,357   16,150   14,528   14,554   15,924
February 25, 1896. *Saluda River*. From Shawnee word for "corn river"; name also applied to local Shawnee tribe.

Sampson **North Carolina**
Clinton 946 sq. mi.
63,431   60,161   47,297   49,687   44,954   48,013   49,780
1784. *John Sampson (?–1784)*. Sheriff of New Hanover County 1742; North Carolina Governor's Council; lieutenant colonel of militia 1768.

San Augustine **Texas**
San Augustine 531 sq. mi.
8,865   8,946   7,999   8,785   7,858   7,722   8,837
March 17, 1836; organized 1837. *Municipality of San Augustine*. Named for *presidio* (fort) San Augustín de Ahumada; founded 1756; abandoned 1771. Presidio named for St. Augustine of Hippo (354–430); born Arelius Augustinius; converted to Christianity 386; ordained 391; bishop 396; wrote doctrines on faith and morals of the Roman Catholic Church.

San Benito   **California**
Hollister   1,389 sq. mi.
55,269   53,234   36,697   25,005   18,226   15,396   14,370
February 12, 1874. *San Benito Creek*. Named for St. Benedict of Nursia (c480–547); lived as hermit for three years; founded monastery at Monte Cassino c529; may have founded Benedictine Order; wrote rules for monastic life. "Benito" is Spanish diminutive of Benedicto. (San Juan Creek is modern name for San Benito Creek.)

San Bernardino   **California**
San Bernardino   20,057 sq. mi.
2,035,210   1,709,434   1,418,380   895,016   684,072   503,591   281,642
April 26, 1853. *San Bernardino Mountains*. Named for St. Bernardine (1380–1444); Franciscan preacher 1402; preached throughout Italy; declined three bishoprics.

Sanborn   **South Dakota**
Woonsocket   569 sq. mi.
2,355   2,675   2,833   3,213   3,697   4,641   5,142
March 9, 1883. *George W. Sanborn (1832–?)*. Brakeman for Chicago, Milwaukee & St. Paul Railroad; assistant superintendent of northern division 1869; superintendent of Iowa and Dakota Division 1870; extended railroad throughout eastern Dakota Territory.

Sanders   **Montana**
Thompson Falls   2,761 sq. mi.
11,413   10,227   8,669   8,675   7,093   6,880   6,983
February 7, 1905. *Wilbur Fiske Sanders (1834–1905)*. Recruited infantry company for Union Army 1861; 1st lieutenant, 64th Ohio Infantry; Montana Territory House of Representatives 1873–79; US senator from Montana 1890–93.

San Diego   **California**
San Diego   4,207 sq. mi.
3,095,313   2,813,833   2,498,016   1,861,846   1,357,854   1,033,011   556,808
February 18, 1850. *Town of San Diego*. Named for San Diego Bay and Mission San Diego de Alcalá, first mission in California 1769. Bay named for St. Didacus (Diego) (1400–63); lay brother in Order of Friars; guardian of Franciscan community on Canary Islands 1445–49; miraculous cures attributed to him; canonized 1588.

Sandoval   **New Mexico**
Bernalillo   3,711 sq. mi.
131,561   89,908   63,319   34,799   17,492   14,201   12,438
March 10, 1903. *Sandoval family*. Descendants of Juan de Diós Sandoval Martinez (?–1735); arrived in north central New Mexico 1692; had numerous children who in turn had numerous children. Prominent Sandovals in the area were Alejandro (1845–?) and José Pablo (1850–?); both were ranchers and members of New Mexico territorial legislature; other Sandovals were and are businessmen and ranchers in the county.

Sandusky   **Ohio**
Fremont   408 sq. mi.
60,944   61,792   61,963   63,267   60,983   56,486   46,114
February 12, 1820. *Sandusky River*. From Wyandot *otsaandosti* or *sandesti* meaning "water" or "cool water."

San Francisco   **California**
San Francisco   47 sq. mi.
805,235   776,733   723,959   678,974   715,674   740,316   775,357
February 18, 1850. *City of San Francisco*. Named for St. Francis of Assisi (see Saint Francis, Arkansas).

Sangamon   **Illinois**
Springfield   868 sq. mi.
197,465   188,951   178,386   176,089   161,335   146,539   131,484

January 20, 1821. *Sangamon River*. From Pottawatomie word of uncertain origin; most conjectures involve water, such as, "place of the outlet," "river mouth," or "he pours out."

Sanilac   **Michigan**
Sandusky   963 sq. mi.

43,114	44,547	39,928	40,789	34,889	32,314	30,837

September 10, 1822; organized December 31, 1849. *Sannilac*. Spirit warrior; from Wyandot legend that was basis of poem *Sannilac* by Henry Whiting 1831.

San Jacinto   **Texas**
Coldspring   569 sq. mi.

26,384	22,246	16,372	11,434	6,702	6,153	7,172

August 13, 1870; organized December 1, 1870. *Battle of San Jacinto*. Decisive battle of Texas Revolution, April 21, 1836; battle site named for San Jacinto River; origin of river's name is uncertain: (1) named for hyacinth plants that choked the river channel; (2) may have been discovered on St. Hyacinth's Day, August 17.

San Joaquin   **California**
Stockton   1,391 sq. mi.

685,306	563,598	480,628	347,342	290,208	249,989	200,750

February 18, 1850. *San Joaquin River*. Spanish name for St. Joachim (?–?); father of Mary, mother of Jesus.

San Juan   **Colorado**
Silverton   387 sq. mi.

699	558	745	833	831	849	1,471

January 31, 1876. *San Juan River*. Named for San Juan Pueblo which was named by Juan de Oñate for his patron saint, St. John the Baptist 1598. (See Saint John the Baptist, Louisiana.)

San Juan   **New Mexico**
Aztec   5,513 sq. mi.

130,044	113,801	91,605	81,433	52,517	53,306	18,292

February 24, 1887. *San Juan River*.*

San Juan   **Utah**
Monticello   7,820 sq. mi.

14,746	14,413	12,621	12,253	9,606	9,040	5,315

February 17, 1880. *San Juan River*.*

San Juan   **Washington**
Friday Harbor   174 sq. mi.

15,769	14,077	10,035	7,838	3,856	2,872	3,245

October 31, 1873. *San Juan Island*. Named for St. John the Baptist. (See Saint John the Baptist, Louisiana.)

San Luis Obispo   **California**
San Luis Obispo   3,299 sq. mi.

269,637	246,681	217,162	155,435	105,690	81,044	51,417

February 18, 1850. *Mission San Luis Obispo de Tolosa*. Founded by Junípero Serra 1772; named for St. Louis of Toulouse (1274–97); son of the King of Naples and Sicily; joined Friars Minor (Franciscans); bishop of Toulouse 1297; canonized 1317.

San Mateo   **California**
Redwood City   448 sq. mi.

718,451	707,161	649,623	587,329	556,234	444,387	235,659

April 19, 1856. *San Mateo Creek*. Named for St. Mathew (?–?); Roman tax collector; became one of Jesus' twelve disciples; author of first gospel of the Bible; preached in Ethiopia.

San Miguel   **Colorado**
Telluride   1,287 sq. mi.
7,359   6,594   3,653   3,192   1,949   2,944   2,693
November 1, 1883. *San Miguel River*. Spanish name for any one of many St. Michaels; most likely Archangel Michael; one of four great angels of the Old Testament; military leader in war between God and Satan in Book of Revelation.

San Miguel   **New Mexico**
Las Vegas   4,716 sq. mi.
29,393   30,126   25,743   22,751   21,951   23,468   26,512
January 9, 1852. *Town of San Miguel del Bado*. Named for Archangel Michael (see San Miguel, Colorado).

San Patricio   **Texas**
Sinton   693 sq. mi.
64,804   67,138   58,749   58,013   47,288   45,021   35,842
March 17, 1836; organized 1846. *Town of San Patricio*. Named for St. Patrick (389–461); born to Christian family in Roman Britain; kidnapped by pirates and taken to Ireland 405; escaped to Britain 411; returned to Ireland as missionary bishop 432; led conversion of Ireland to Christianity; patron saint of Ireland. County was settled by Irish families from New York 1828.

Sanpete   **Utah**
Manti   1,590 sq. mi.
27,822   22,763   16,259   14,620   10,976   11,053   13,891
January 31, 1850. *San Pitch Valley*. From division of Utes named *sampitches* or *sampichya*, among many variables; may also be name of a Ute chief.

San Saba   **Texas**
San Saba   1,135 sq. mi.
6,131   6,186   5,401   6,204   5,540   6,381   8,666
February 1, 1856; organized May 3, 1856. *San Saba River*. Named for St. Sabbas (439–532); preached in Judean wilderness; founded several monasteries and hospices; abbot of monastery near Jerusalem.

Santa Barbara   **California**
Santa Barbara   2,735 sq. mi.
423,895   399,347   369,608   298,694   264,324   168,962   98,220
February 18, 1850. *Town of Santa Barbara*. Named for Santa Barbara Channel and Mission which were named for St. Barbara (?–c235); daughter of Roman official, Dioscorus, whose duties included persecution of Christians; Barbara converted to Christianity and vowed to rule her life according to the gospels; refused to renounce Christianity to her father who then personally beheaded her.

Santa Clara   **California**
San Jose   1,290 sq. mi.
1,781,642   1,682,585   1,497,577   1,295,071   1,064,714   642,315   290,547
February 18, 1850. *Mission Santa Clara de Asís*. Founded 1777; named for St. Clare (1194–1253); born in Assisi; friend and follower of St. Francis of Assisi (see Saint Francis, Arkansas); entered Benedictine convent 1212; abbess of San Damiano Convent 1213–53; founded Order of Poor Ladies (Poor Clares); canonized 1255.

Santa Cruz   **Arizona**
Nogales   1,237 sq. mi.
47,420   38,381   29,676   20,459   13,966   10,808   9,344
March 15, 1899. *Santa Cruz River*. Spanish for "holy cross."

Santa Cruz   **California**
Santa Cruz   445 sq. mi.
262,382   255,602   229,734   188,141   123,790   84,219   66,534
February 18, 1850, as Branciforte; name changed April 5, 1850. *Mission Santa Cruz*. Founded 1791; named for Santa Cruz Creek; Spanish for "holy cross."

Santa Fe   **New Mexico**
Santa Fe   1,909 sq. mi.
144,170   129,292   98,928   75,360   53,756   44,970   38,153
January 9, 1852. *City of Santa Fe.* Established as *La Villa Real de Santa Fe* (Royal Town of the Holy Faith) 1609; named after town in Spain founded by Ferdinand and Isabella to celebrate Spain's victory over the Moors 1492.

Santa Rosa   **Florida**
Milton   1,012 sq. mi.
151,372   117,743   81,608   55,988   37,741   29,547   18,554
February 18, 1842. *Santa Rosa Island.* Named for St. Rose of Viterbo (1234–52); her life story is mostly legend; performed miracle at age three; began teaching at age ten; denounced Emperor Frederick II for harassing the pope; banished from Viterbo; canonized 1457.

Sarasota   **Florida**
Sarasota   556 sq. mi.
379,448   325,957   277,776   202,251   120,413   76,895   28,827
May 14, 1921. *Uncertain.* (1) *City of Sarasota*; (2) *Sarasota Bay.* Derivation of "Sarasota" is uncertain; conjectures include Indian or Spanish words ranging from "vegetation" to" dancing."

Saratoga   **New York**
Ballston Spa   810 sq. mi.
219,607   200,635   181,276   153,759   121,679   89,096   74,869
February 7, 1791. *Battle of Saratoga.* American General Gates (see Gates, North Carolina) defeated British General Burgoyne October 17, 1777. "Saratoga" is Mohawk name of uncertain meaning; leading contenders include "beaver place" or "side hill."

Sargent   **North Dakota**
Forman   859 sq. mi.
3,829   4,366   4,549   5,512   5,937   6,856   7,616
March 3, 1883; organized October 8, 1883. *Homer E. Sargent (1822–c1901).* General manager of Northern Pacific Railroad at time of county's creation.

Sarpy   **Nebraska**
Papillion   239 sq. mi.
158,840   122,595   102,583   86,015   63,696   31,281   15,693
February 7, 1857; organized June 19, 1857. *Peter A. Sarpy (1805–65).* Fur trader for American Fur Company on Platte River system; operated trading post at mouth of Platte River.

Sauk   **Wisconsin**
Baraboo   831 sq. mi.
61,976   55,225   46,975   43,469   39,057   36,179   38,120
January 11, 1840; organized March 10, 1844. *Sauk Indians.* Name means "yellow earth" from which Sauk believed they were created; also spelled "Sac." Originally in Great Lakes region; declared war against US under Chief Black Hawk; defeated at Bad Axe, August 2, 1832; united with Fox Indians; moved to Illinois and Iowa; resettled in Indian Territory (Oklahoma) 1870s.

Saunders   **Nebraska**
Wahoo   750 sq. mi.
20,780   19,830   18,285   18,716   17,018   17,720   16,923
January 26, 1856, as Calhoun; name changed January 8, 1862; organized November 10, 1866. *Alvin Saunders (1817–99).* Iowa Constitutional Convention 1846; Iowa Senate 1854–56 and 1858–60; governor of Nebraska Territory 1861–67; US senator from Nebraska 1877–83.

Sawyer   **Wisconsin**
Hayward   1,257 sq. mi.
16,557   16,196   14,181   12,843   9,670   9,475   10,323

March 10, 1883; organized 1885. *Philetus Sawyer (1816–1900).* Wisconsin Assembly 1857 and 1861; mayor of Oshkosh 1863–64; US representative 1865–78; US senator 1881–93.

Schenectady   **New York**
Schenectady   205 sq. mi.
154,727   146,555   149,285   149,946   160,979   152,896   142,497
March 7, 1809, *City of Schenectady.* Name from Dutch *skonowe,* meaning "flat land," or Dutch *schoonehetstede,* meaning "beautiful town."

Schleicher   **Texas**
Eldorado   1,311 sq. mi.
3,461   2,935   2,990   2,820   2,277   2,791   2,852
April 1, 1887; organized July 9, 1901. *Gustav Schleicher (1823–79).* Emigrated from Germany 1850; Texas House of Representatives 1853–54; Texas Senate 1859–61; captain of engineers, Confederate Army 1861–65; US representative 1875–79.

Schley   **Georgia**
Ellaville   167 sq. mi.
5,010   3,766   3,588   3,433   3,097   3,256   4,036
December 22, 1857. *William Schley (1786–1858).* Judge of superior court 1825–28; Georgia House of Representatives 1830; US representative 1833–35; governor of Georgia 1835–37.

Schoharie   **New York**
Schoharie   622 sq. mi.
32,749   31,582   31,859   29,710   24,750   22,616   22,703
April 6, 1795. *Town of Schoharie.* Derived from Mohawk name for Schoharie Creek, meaning "driftwood."

Schoolcraft   **Michigan**
Manistique   1,171 sq. mi.
8,485   8,903   8,302   8,575   8,226   8,953   9,148
March 9, 1843; organized March 23, 1871. *Henry Rowe Schoolcraft (1793–1864).* Explored Arkansas and Missouri 1818–20; explored upper Mississippi River and Lake Superior 1820–22; Michigan territorial legislature 1828–32; ethnologist and author of numerous books on Indians; Michigan superintendent of Indians affairs 1836–41; contrived the name of many Michigan counties by combining Indian words with unrelated Latin or Arabic words.

Schuyler   **Illinois**
Rushville   437 sq. mi.
7,544   7,189   7,498   8,365   8,135   8,746   9,613
January 13, 1825. *Philip John Schuyler (1733–1804).* British Army, captain to major 1755–58; worked in England to settle colonial claims 1758–63; Continental Congress from New York 1775–77 and 1778–81; major general Continental Army 1775, resigned 1779; New York Senate, intermittently 1780–97; US senator 1789–91 and 1797–98.

Schuyler   **Missouri**
Lancaster   307 sq. mi.
4,431   4,170   4,236   4,979   4,665   5,052   5,760
February 14, 1845. *Phillip John Schuyler.**

Schuyler   **New York**
Watkins Glen   328 sq. mi.
18,343   19,224   18,662   17,686   16,737   15,044   14,182
April 17, 1854. *Phillip John Schuyler.**

Schuylkill   **Pennsylvania**
Pottsville   779 sq. mi.
148,289   150,336   152,585   160,630   160,089   173,027   200,577
March 1, 1811. *Schuylkill River.* From Dutch *schuilplaats* meaning "hiding place."

Scioto   **Ohio**
Portsmouth   610 sq. mi.
79,499   79,195   80,327   84,545   76,951   84,216   82,910
March 24, 1803. *Scioto River*. From Wyandot *ochskonto*; first part refers to "deer," the second part is unknown but may refer to "river."

Scotland   **Missouri**
Memphis   437 sq. mi.
4,843   4,983   4,822   5,415   5,499   6,484   7,332
January 29, 1841. *Scotland, United Kingdom*. Suggested by settler with family ties to Scotland.

Scotland   **North Carolina**
Laurinburg   319 sq. mi.
36,157   35,998   33,754   23,273   26,929   25,183   26,336
February 20, 1899. *Scotland, United Kingdom*. Many early settlers were from Scotland.

Scott   **Arkansas**
Waldron   892 sq. mi.
11,233   10,996   10,205   9,685   8,207   7,297   10,057
November 5, 1833. *Andrew Scott (1788–1851)*. Judge, Superior Court of Arkansas Territory 1819–21; killed one man in a duel and another in a fight over an election defeat 1828; Arkansas Constitutional Convention 1836.

Scott   **Illinois**
Winchester   251 sq. mi.
5,355   5,537   5,644   6,142   6,096   6,377   7,245
February 16, 1839. *Scott County, Kentucky*. Early settlers were from Kentucky.

Scott   **Indiana**
Scottsburg   190 sq. mi.
24,181   22,960   20,991   20,422   17,144   14,643   11,519
January 12, 1820. *Charles Scott (1733–1813)*. British Army during French and Indian War; colonel to brevet major general, Continental Army 1776–77; captured 1780; released at end of war 1781; Virginia Assembly 1789–90; governor of Kentucky 1808–12.

Scott   **Iowa**
Davenport   458 sq. mi.
165,224   158,668   150,979   160,022   142,687   119,067   100,698
December 21, 1837. *Winfield Scott (1786–1866)*. Captain, Virginia Light Artillery 1808; lieutenant colonel to brigadier general 1812–14; brevet major general for bravery at Chippewa and Niagara Falls 1814; awarded gold medal by Congress 1814; supervised removal of Cherokees to Trans-Mississippi region 1838; commander in chief of US Army 1841–61; captured Vera Cruz 1847; occupied Mexico City 1848; lieutenant general 1852; unsuccessful Whig Party candidate for US president 1852.

Scott   **Kansas**
Scott City   718 sq. mi.
4,936   5,120   5,289   5,782   5,606   5,228   4,921
March 20, 1873; organized January 29, 1886. *Winfield Scott*.*

Scott   **Kentucky**
Georgetown   282 sq. mi.
47,173   33,061   23,867   21,813   17,948   15,376   15,141
June 1, 1792; effective September 1, 1792. *Charles Scott*.*

Scott   **Minnesota**
Shakopee   356 sq. mi.

129,928   89,498   57,846   43,784   32,423   21,909   16,486
March 5, 1853. *Winfield Scott.**

Scott   **Mississippi**
Forest   609 sq. mi.
28,264   28,423   24,137   24,556   21,369   21,187   21,681
December 23, 1833. *Abram Marshall Scott (1785–1833)*. Mississippi Constitutional Convention 1817; Mississippi Senate 1822 and 1826–27; lieutenant governor 1828–30; governor of Mississippi 1832–33.

Scott   **Missouri**
Benton   420 sq. mi.
39,191   40,422   39,376   39,647   33,250   32,748   32,842
December 28, 1821. *John Scott (1785–1861)*. Missouri territorial delegate to Congress 1815–20; US representative 1821–27.

Scott   **Tennessee**
Huntsville   532 sq. mi.
22,228   21,127   18,358   19,259   14,762   15,413   17,362
December 17, 1849. *Winfield Scott.**

Scott   **Virginia**
Gate City   536 sq. mi.
23,177   23,403   23,204   25,068   24,376   25,813   27,640
November 24, 1814. *Winfield Scott.**

Scotts Bluff   **Nebraska**
Gering   739 sq. mi.
36,970   36,951   36,025   38,344   36,432   33,809   33,939
November 6, 1888; organized January 28, 1889. *Scotts Bluff*. A landmark butte on the Oregon Trail; rises 800 feet above surrounding plain; named for Hiram Scott (c1805–28); became ill during a fur trading expedition and was left alone to die; bones found near Scotts Bluff were declared to be his.

Screven   **Georgia**
Sylvania   645 sq. mi.
14,593   15,374   13,842   14,043   12,591   14,919   18,000
December 14, 1793. *James Screven (c1744–78)*. Georgia Provincial Congress 1775; captain, 3rd Georgia Rangers 1776; brigadier general 1778; mortally wounded near Midway Church, Georgia, November 24, 1778.

Scurry   **Texas**
Snyder   905 sq. mi.
16,921   16,361   18,634   18,192   15,760   20,369   22,779
August 21, 1876; organized 1884. *William Read Scurry (1821–64)*. Republic of Texas legislature 1844–45; private to major during Mexican War 1846–48; owner and editor, *Austin Sate Gazette* 1848–54; Texas Secession Convention 1861; lieutenant colonel 4th Texas Cavalry 1861; commanded Confederate forces at Glorietta Pass 1862; mortally wounded at Jenkin's Ferry, April 30, 1864.

Searcy   **Arkansas**
Marshall   666 sq. mi.
8,195   8,261   7,841   8,847   7,731   8,124   10,424
December 13, 1838. *Richard Searcy (?–1832)*. Judge, Arkansas Territory 1823; twice unsuccessful candidate for territorial delegate to Congress 1828 and 1832.

Sebastian   **Arkansas**
Fort Smith   532 sq. mi.
125,744   115,071   99,590   95,172   79,237   66,685   64,202

January 6, 1851. *William King Sebastian (1812–65)*. Arkansas Circuit Court judge 1840–43; Arkansas Supreme Court 1843–45; Arkansas Senate 1846–47; US senator 1848–61; expelled from senate for supporting Confederacy 1861; senate posthumously revoked expulsion and compensated family 1877.

Sedgwick **Colorado**
Julesburg 548 sq. mi.

2,379	2,747	2,690	3,266	3,405	4,242	5,095

April 9, 1889. *Fort Sedgwick*. Founded near South Platte River 1864, as Camp Rankin; upgraded and name changed 1865. Named for John Sedgwick (see Sedgwick, Kansas).

Sedgwick **Kansas**
Wichita 998 sq. mi.

498,365	452, 869	403,662	366,531	350,694	343,231	222,290

February 26, 1867; organized April 27, 1870. *John Sedgwick (1813–64)*. Graduated West Point 1837; received two brevet promotions (captain and major) during Mexican War; colonel to major general 1861–64; killed at Spotsylvania, May 9, 1864.

Seminole **Florida**
Sanford 309 sq. mi.

422,718	365,196	287,529	179,752	83,692	54,947	26,883

April 25, 1913. *Seminole Indians*. Uncertain derivation of name: (1) Creek *simanole* or *siminole* meaning "runaways"; (2) Creek *ishi semoli* meaning "wild men"; (3) Spanish c*imarron* meaning "wild" or "runaway slave." Seminoles migrated to Florida during 18th century after separating from Oconees; combined with Florida Indians and runaway slaves; fiercely resisted removal to Indian Territory (Oklahoma) during 2nd Seminole War 1835–42 (see Osceola, Florida); about 3,800 Seminoles removed to Indian Territory; separate Seminole Nations are in Florida and Oklahoma.

Seminole **Georgia**
Donalsonville 235 sq. mi.

8,729	9,369	9,010	9,057	7,059	6,802	7,904

July 8, 1920. *Seminole Indians*.*

Seminole **Oklahoma**
Wewoka 633 sq. mi.

25,482	24,894	25,412	27,473	25,144	28,066	40,672

July 16, 1907. *Seminole Indians*.*

Seneca **New York**
Waterloo 324 sq. mi.

35,251	33,342	33,683	33,733	35,083	31,984	29,253

March 24, 1804. *Seneca Indians*. Various translations of "Seneca"; most involve "stone." Largest tribe in Iroquois confederation.

Seneca **Ohio**
Tiffin 551 sq. mi.

56,745	58,683	59,733	61,901	60,696	59,326	52,978

February 12, 1820; organized January 22, 1824. *Seneca Indians*.*

Sequatchie **Tennessee**
Dunlap 266 sq. mi.

14,112	11,370	8,863	8,605	6,331	5,915	5,685

December 9, 1857. *Sequatchie River Valley*. Named for Cherokee chief who signed treaties with Americans; nothing more is known of him.

Sequoyah **Oklahoma**
Sallisaw 673 sq. mi.

42,391   38,972   33,282   30,749   23,370   18,001   19,773

July 16, 1907. *Sequoyah (c1770–1843).* Developed a set of eighty-six syllables for writing Cherokee language; associated symbols were used to translate parts of the Bible into Cherokee and to print an Indian newspaper, *The Phoenix*; taught school in Indian Territory (Oklahoma).

Sevier   **Arkansas**
De Queen   565 sq. mi.
17,058   15,757   13,637   14,060   11,272   10,156   12,293

October 17, 1828. *Ambrose Hundley Sevier (1801–48).* Arkansas territorial legislature 1823–27; territorial delegate to Congress 1828–36; US senator 1836–48; US minister to Mexico 1848.

Sevier   **Tennessee**
Sevierville   593 sq. mi.
89,889   71,170   51,043   41,418   28,241   24,251   23,375

September 27, 1794. *John Sevier (1745–1815).* Served with Washington in Governor Dunmore's War 1773–74; only governor of proclaimed State of Franklin (Tennessee) 1785–88; US representative from North Carolina 1789–91; brigadier general of militia, Territory South of the Ohio 1791; governor of Tennessee 1796–1801 and 1803–09; Tennessee legislature 1810–11; US representative 1811–17.

Sevier   **Utah**
Richfield   1,911 sq. mi.
20,802   18,842   15,431   14,727   10,103   10,565   12,072

January 16, 1865. *Sevier River.* Named *Rio Severo* (Severe River) by Spanish; Americans later turned *severo* into a well-known popular name.

Seward   **Kansas**
Liberal   640 sq. mi.
22,952   22,510   18,743   17,071   15,744   15,930   9,972

March 20, 1873; organized February 18, 1886. *William Henry Seward (1801–72).* New York Senate 1830–34; governor of New York 1838–42; US senator 1849–61; US secretary of state 1861–69; negotiated treaty with Russia for purchase of Alaska 1867.

Seward   **Nebraska**
Seward   571 sq. mi.
16,750   16,496   15,450   15,789   14,460   13,581   13,155

March 6, 1855, as Greene; name changed January 3, 1862; organized February 9, 1866. *William Henry Seward.**

Shackelford   **Texas**
Albany   914 sq. mi.
3,378   3,302   3,316   3,915   3,323   3,990   5,001

February 1, 1858; organized September 12, 1874. *John Shackelford (1790–1857).* General Jackson's staff, War of 1812; Alabama Senate 1822–24; raised "Red Rovers," a company of Alabama volunteers for Texas Revolution 1835; Goliad campaign 1836; captured at Coleto; survived Goliad massacre because he was a physician tending to wounded; returned to Alabama 1836.

Shannon   **Missouri**
Eminence   1,004 sq. mi.
8,411   8,324   7,613   7,885   7,196   7,087   8,377

January 29, 1841. *George Shannon (1787–1836).* Youngest member of Lewis and Clark expedition 1804–06; leg amputated after attack by Arikaras 1807; Kentucky legislature 1820–23; US attorney for Missouri 1830–34; Missouri legislature 1834–36.

Shannon   **South Dakota**
(Unorganized)   2,094 sq. mi.
13,586   12,466   9,902   11,323   8,198   6,000   5,669

January 11, 1875; attached to Fall River County. *Peter Shannon (1821–99).* Pennsylvania legislature 1862–63; chief justice of Dakota Territory 1873–82.

Sharkey   **Mississippi**
Rolling Fork   432 sq. mi.

| 4,916 | 6,580 | 7,066 | 7,964 | 8,937 | 10,738 | 12,903 |

March 29, 1876. *William Lewis Sharkey (1798–1873)*. Mississippi House of Representatives 1828–29; Mississippi Supreme Court 1832; trustee, University of Mississippi 1844–65; provisional Reconstruction governor of Mississippi 1865; elected to US Senate but denied seat 1865.

Sharp   **Arkansas**
Ash Flat   604 sq. mi.

| 17,264 | 17,119 | 14,109 | 14,607 | 8,233 | 6,319 | 8,999 |

July 18, 1868. *Ephraim Sharp (1815–98)*. Arkansas General Assembly which supported Union as opposed to Confederate-leaning state legislature 1864; reputed to have participated in Underground Railroad; Arkansas legislature 1868.

Shasta   **California**
Redding   3,775 sq. mi.

| 177,223 | 163,256 | 147,036 | 115,715 | 77,640 | 59,468 | 36,413 |

February 18, 1850. *Mount Shasta*. Named Mount Sastise by Peter Ogden for Shastika Indians 1827.

Shawano   **Wisconsin**
Shawano   893 sq. mi.

| 41,949 | 40,664 | 37,157 | 35,928 | 32,650 | 34,351 | 35,249 |

February 16, 1853, as Shawanaw; organized 1860; spelling changed 1864. *Uncertain*. (1) *Lake Shawano*. (2) *Sawanoh (?–?)*; Chippewa chief; name may refer "south" or "southern."

Shawnee   **Kansas**
Topeka   544 sq. mi.

| 177,934 | 169,871 | 160,976 | 154,916 | 155,322 | 141,286 | 105,418 |

August 25, 1855. *Shawnee Indians*. From Algonquin *shawun* meaning "southern." First encountered by Europeans in Ohio River Valley; allied with French in French and Indian War; driven westward to Kansas; ceded lands and removed to Indian Territory (Oklahoma) 1854.

Sheboygan   **Wisconsin**
Sheboygan   511 sq. mi.

| 115,507 | 112,646 | 103,877 | 100,935 | 96,660 | 86,484 | 80,631 |

December 7, 1836; organized December 17, 1838. *Sheboygan River*. From Ojibwa words for "big pipe."

Shelby   **Alabama**
Columbiana   785 sq. mi.

| 195,085 | 143,293 | 99,358 | 66,298 | 38,037 | 32,132 | 30,362 |

February 7, 1818. *Isaac Shelby (1750–1826)*. Intermittent service during Revolutionary War 1774–80; awarded sword by North Carolina legislature for bravery at King's Mountain 1780; North Carolina legislature 1781–82; Kentucky Constitutional Convention 1792; governor of Kentucky 1792–96 and 1812–16; commanded Kentucky troops at Battle of the Thames 1813.

Shelby   **Illinois**
Shelbyville   759 sq. mi.

| 22,363 | 22,893 | 22,261 | 23,923 | 22,589 | 23,404 | 24,434 |

January 23, 1827. *Isaac Shelby.**

Shelby   **Indiana**
Shelbyville   411 sq. mi.

| 44,436 | 43,445 | 40,307 | 39,887 | 37,797 | 34,093 | 28,026 |

December 31, 1821; effective April 1, 1822. *Isaac Shelby.**

Shelby   **Iowa**
Harlan   591 sq. mi.

12,167   13,173   13,230   15,043   15,528   15,825   15,942
January 15, 1851; organized January 12, 1853; effective March 7, 1853. *Isaac Shelby.**

Shelby   **Kentucky**
Shelbyville   380 sq. mi.
42,074   33,337   24,824   23,328   18,999   18,493   17,912
June 23, 1792; effective September 1, 1792. *Isaac Shelby.**

Shelby   **Missouri**
Shelbyville   501 sq. mi.
6,373   6,799   6,942   7,826   7,906   9,063   9,730
January 2, 1835. *Isaac Shelby.**

Shelby   **Ohio**
Sidney   408 sq. mi.
49,423   47,910   44,915   43,089   37,748   33,586   28,488
January 7, 1819. *Isaac Shelby.**

Shelby   **Tennessee**
Memphis   763 sq. mi.
927,644   897,472   826,330   777,113   722,014   627,019   482,393
November 24, 1819. *Isaac Shelby.**

Shelby   **Texas**
Center   796 sq. mi.
25,448   25,224   22,034   23,084   19,672   20,479   23,479
March 17, 1836; organized 1837. *Isaac Shelby.**

Shenandoah   **Virginia**
Woodstock   509 sq. mi.
41,993   35,075   31,636   27,559   22,852   21,825   21,169
March 24, 1772, as Dunmore; name changed February 1, 1778. *Shenandoah River*. From Senedo word for "sprucey stream."

Sherburne   **Minnesota**
Elk River   433 sq. mi.
88,499   64,417   41,945   29,908   18,344   12,861   10,661
February 25, 1856; organized March 6, 1862. *Moses Sherburne (1808–68)*. Maine legislature; associate justice, Minnesota Territory Supreme Court 1853–57; Minnesota Constitutional Convention 1857.

Sheridan   **Kansas**
Hoxie   896 sq. mi.
2,556   2,813   3,043   3,544   3,859   4,267   4,607
March 20, 1873; organized June 2, 1880. *Philip Henry Sheridan (1831–88)*. Graduated West Point 1853; brevet 2nd lieutenant to lieutenant general 1853–69; Union cavalry officer during Civil War; blocked Lee's escape at Appomattox 1865; Army commander in chief 1884–88.

Sheridan   **Montana**
Plentywood   1,677 sq. mi.
3,384   4,105   4,732   5,414   5,779   6,458   6,674
March 24, 1913. *Philip Henry Sheridan.**

Sheridan   **Nebraska**
Rushville   2,441 sq. mi.
5,469   6,198   6,750   7,544   7,285   9,049   9,539
February 25, 1885; organized July 25, 1885. *Philip Henry Sheridan.**

Sheridan   **North Dakota**
McClusky   972 sq. mi.

1,321	1,710	2,148	2,819	3,232	4,350	5,253

January 4, 1873; abolished 1892; recreated December 24, 1908. *Philip Henry Sheridan.**

Sheridan   **Wyoming**
Sheridan   2,524 sq. mi.

29,116	26,560	23,562	25,048	17,852	18,989	20,185

March 9, 1888. *Town of Sheridan.* Named for Philip Henry Sheridan.*

Sherman   **Kansas**
Goodland   1,056 sq. mi.

6,010	6,760	6,926	7,759	7,792	6,682	7,373

March 20, 1873; organized September 20, 1886. *William Tecumseh Sherman (1820–91).* Graduated West Point 1840; 2nd lieutenant to captain 1840–53; resigned commission 1853; recommissioned 1861; colonel to major general 1861–65; March to the Sea across Georgia 1864; only person to receive Thanks of Congress twice during the Civil War for actions at Chattanooga and Atlanta; commander of the army 1869–83.

Sherman   **Nebraska**
Loup City   566 sq. mi.

3,152	3,318	3,718	4,226	4,725	5,382	6,421

March 1, 1871; organized April 1, 1873. *William Tecumseh Sherman.**

Sherman   **Oregon**
Moro   824 sq. mi.

1,765	1,934	1,918	2,172	2,139	2,446	2,271

February 25, 1889. *William Tecumseh Sherman.**

Sherman   **Texas**
Stratford   923 sq. mi.

3,034	3,186	2,858	3,174	3,657	2,605	2,443

August 21, 1876; organized June 13, 1889. *Sidney Sherman (1805–73).* Raised company of Kentucky volunteers for Texas Revolution 1835; colonel in Texas Army 1836; Battle of San Jacinto, credited with battle cry "Remember the Alamo," 1836; major general of Texas Militia; Republic of Texas legislature 1842; Texas legislature 1852–53.

Shiawassee   **Michigan**
Corunna   531 sq. mi.

70,648	71,687	69,770	71,140	63,075	53,446	45,967

September 10, 1822; organized March 13, 1837. *Shiawassee River.* Chippewa word of unknown origin; possibilities include both "twisting" and "straight."

Shoshone   **Idaho**
Wallace   2,630 sq. mi.

12,756	13,771	13,931	19,226	19,718	20,876	22,806

February 4, 1864. *Shoshoni Indians.* Name from *shawnt* meaning "abundance," and *shaw-nip* meaning "grass." Lived in Snake River region.

Sibley   **Minnesota**
Gaylord   589 sq. mi.

15,226	15,356	14,366	15,448	15,845	16,228	15,816

March 5, 1853; organized March 2, 1854. *Henry Hastings Sibley (1811–91).* American Fur Company agent in Minnesota 1834; congressional delegate from Wisconsin Territory 1848–49 and Minnesota Territory 1849–53; Minnesota territorial legislature 1855; Minnesota Constitutional Convention 1857; governor of Minnesota 1858–60; brigadier general of volunteers 1862–63; suppressed Dakota uprising 1862; brevet major general 1863; board of regents, University of Minnesota 1876–91.

Sierra   **California**
Downieville   953 sq. mi.
3,240   3,555   3,318   3,073   2,365   2,247   2,410
April 16, 1852. *Sierra Nevada Mountains*. From Spanish *sierra* meaning "saw"; applied to jagged mountain ranges, and *nevada* meaning "snow-covered." Named by Pedro Font after a mountain range in Spain 1776.

Sierra   **New Mexico**
Truth or Consequences   4,179 sq. mi.
11,988   13,270   9,912   8,454   7,189   6,409   7,186
April 3, 1884. *Uncertain*. (1) *Sierra Caballo*; Spanish for "horse"; ridge at north end of range resembles a horse's head. (2) *Sierra Negra*; from dark appearance caused by forested slopes. From Spanish *sierra* meaning "saw"; applied to jagged mountain ranges.

Silver Bow   **Montana**
Butte   718 sq. mi.
34,200   34,606   33,941   38,092   41,981   46,454   48,422
February 16, 1881. *Silver Bow Creek*. Named by miners; origin of name is lost in legend.

Simpson   **Kentucky**
Franklin   234 sq. mi.
17,327   16,405   15,145   14,673   13,054   11,548   11,678
January 28, 1819. *John Simpson (?–1813)*. Served under General Wayne at Battle of Fallen Timbers 1794; Kentucky House of Representatives 1807–11, speaker 1810–11; elected to US House of Representatives but was commissioned as captain at start of War of 1812; killed at Battle of River Raisin, January 22, 1813.

Simpson   **Mississippi**
Mendenhall   589 sq. mi.
27,503   27,639   23,953   23,441   19,947   20,454   21,819
January 23, 1824. *Josiah Simpson (?–1817)*. Mississippi territorial judge; Mississippi Constitutional Convention 1817.

Sioux   **Iowa**
Orange City   768 sq. mi.
33,704   31,589   29,903   30,813   27,996   26,375   26,381
January 15, 1851; organized January 1, 1860. *Sioux Indians*. From last syllable of *nadouaissiou*, a Chippewa-French word meaning "snakes" or "like adders"; derogatory name for Dakotas identifying them as enemies. (See Dakota, Minnesota.)

Sioux   **Nebraska**
Harrison   2,067 sq. mi.
1,311   1,475   1,549   1,845   2,034   2,575   3,124
February 19, 1877; organized September 20, 1886. *Sioux Indians*.*

Sioux   **North Dakota**
Fort Yates   1,094 sq. mi.
4,153   4,044   3,761   3,620   3,632   3,662   3,696
September 3, 1914. *Sioux Indians*.*

Siskiyou   **California**
Yreka   6,278 sq. mi.
44,900   44,301   43,531   39,732   33,225   32,885   30,733
March 22, 1852. *Siskiyou Mountains*. Uncertain derivation of name. (1) Chinook word meaning "bob-tailed horse"; name from an incident in which a bob-tailed horse was lost during a snow storm 1828. (2) Corruption of French *six cailloux* meaning "six stones" for a ford across the Umpqua River.

Sitka   **Alaska**
Sitka   2,870 sq. mi.

| 8,881 | 8,835 | 8,588 | 7,803 | 6,109 | 6,690 | (a) |

December 1971. *Town of Sitka*. Tlingit name believed to mean "by the sea" or "on Shi," the Tlingit name for Baranof Island. [(a) Part of 1st Judicial Division.]

Skagit   **Washington**
Mount Vernon   1,731 sq. mi.

| 116,901 | 102,979 | 79,555 | 64,138 | 53,281 | 51,350 | 43,273 |

November 28, 1883. *Skagit Indians*. Name means "place of refuge"; from tribe hiding in mountain valleys to avoid stronger enemies.

Skagway   **Alaska**
Skagway   452 sq. mi.

| 968 | (a) | (b) | (b) | (b) | (c) | (d) |

June 20, 2007. *Skagway River*. From Tlingit *schkagué* meaning "home of the north wind." [(a) Part of Skagway-Hoonah-Angoon Census Area; (b) part of Skagway-Yakutat-Angoon Census Area; (c) part of Lynn Canal-Icy Straits Census Area; (d) part of 1st Judicial Division.]

Skamania   **Washington**
Stevenson   1,656 sq. mi.

| 11,066 | 9,872 | 8,289 | 7,919 | 5,845 | 5,207 | 4,788 |

March 9, 1854. *Columbia River currents*. Chinook word describing swift currents in the river.

Slope   **North Dakota**
Amidon   1,215 sq. mi.

| 727 | 767 | 907 | 1,157 | 1,484 | 1,893 | 2,315 |

December 31, 1914. *Missouri Slope*. Local designation of area west of the Missouri River.

Smith   **Kansas**
Smith Center   895 sq. mi.

| 3,853 | 4,536 | 5,078 | 5,947 | 6,757 | 7,776 | 8,846 |

February 26, 1867; organized February 1, 1872. *James Nelson Smith (1837–64)*. Major, 2nd Colorado Volunteers; served in Arkansas and Missouri; killed at Battle of the Little Blue, October 23, 1864.

Smith   **Mississippi**
Raleigh   636 sq. mi.

| 16,491 | 16,182 | 14,798 | 15,077 | 13,561 | 14,303 | 16,740 |

December 23, 1833. *David Smith (1753–1835)*. Private in Revolutionary War; King's Mountain 1780; Cowpens and Eutaw Springs 1781; moved to Mississippi 1822. Father-in-law, Mississippi Governor Hiram Runnels, had the county named for Smith one month after becoming governor.

Smith   **Tennessee**
Carthage   314 sq. mi.

| 19,166 | 17,712 | 14,143 | 14,935 | 12,509 | 12,059 | 14,098 |

October 26, 1799. *Daniel Smith (1748–1818)*. Colonel in Revolutionary War; secretary of the Territory South of the Ohio River (Tennessee) 1790–96; Tennessee Constitutional Convention 1796; made first map of Tennessee; general, Tennessee Militia; US senator 1798–99 and 1805–09.

Smith   **Texas**
Tyler   921 sq. mi.

| 209,714 | 174,706 | 151,309 | 128,366 | 97,096 | 86,350 | 74,701 |

April 11, 1846; organized July 10, 1846. *James Smith (1792–1855)*. Volunteer in War of 1812; Texas Army, captain to brigadier general 1836–41; commanded Texas troops in suppressing Regulator-Moderator War 1844; Texas House of Representatives 1846–47.

Smyth   **Virginia**
Marion   451 sq. mi.

32,208 33,081 32,370 33,366 31,349 31,066 30,187

February 23, 1832. *Alexander Smyth (1765–1830)*. Virginia House of Delegates, intermittently 1792–1827; Virginia Senate 1808–09; colonel to brigadier general 1808–13; US representative 1817–24 and 1827–30.

Snohomish **Washington**
Everett 2,087 sq. mi.
713,335 606,024 465,642 337,720 265,236 172,199 111,580
January 14, 1861. *Snohomish Indians*. Unknown meaning; suffix *mish* means "people." Lived in lowlands along Puget Sound.

Snyder **Pennsylvania**
Middleburg 329 sq. mi.
39,702 37,546 36,680 33,584 29,269 25,922 22,912
March 2, 1855. *Simon Snyder (1759–1819)*. Pennsylvania Constitutional Convention 1789–90; Pennsylvania Assembly 1797–1807, speaker 1802–07; Pennsylvania Senate 1817.

Socorro **New Mexico**
Socorro 6,647 sq. mi.
17,866 18,078 14,764 12,566 9,763 10,168 9,670
January 9, 1852. *Town of Socorro*. Spanish for "succor"; name given to nearby Indian pueblo by Don Juan de Oñate for food given to starving colonists by Indians 1598.

Solano **California**
Fairfield 822 sq. mi.
413,344 394,542 340,421 235,203 169,941 134,597 104,833
February 18, 1850. *Francisco Solano (?–?)*. Chief of Suisun and Soscol Indians; defeated by Mexican general Vallejo 1835; given name of Solano when baptized at Mission San Francisco Solano; prevented Indian raid on the mission. County's name proposed by Vallejo.

Somerset **Maine**
Skowhegan 3,924 sq. mi.
52,228 50,888 49,767 45,028 40,597 39,749 39,785
March 1, 1809. *Somersetshire, England*. Home of Ferdinando Gorges, lord proprietor of Maine.

Somerset **Maryland**
Princess Anne 320 sq. mi.
26,470 24,747 23,440 19,188 18,924 19,623 20,745
August 26, 1666. *Mary Arundell Somerset (?–?)*. Wife of Sir John Somerset; sister of Anne Arundell Calvert (see Anne Arundel, Maryland); sister-in-law of Cecil Calvert (see Cecil and Calvert, Maryland).

Somerset **New Jersey**
Somerville 302 sq. mi.
323,444 297,490 240,279 203,129 198,372 143,913 99,052
May 14, 1688; organized April 23, 1714. *Somersetshire, England*. Assumed to be origin of early settlers or home of a prominent settler.

Somerset **Pennsylvania**
Somerset 1,074 sq. mi.
77,742 80,023 78,218 81,243 76,037 77,450 81,813
April 17, 1795. *Town of Somerset*. Named for Somersetshire, England; origin of early settlers.

Somervell **Texas**
Glen Rose 186 sq. mi.
8,490 6,809 5,360 4,154 2,793 2,577 2,542
March 13, 1875. *Alexander Somervell (1796–1854)*. Lieutenant colonel in Texas Army; Battle of San Jacinto 1836; Republic of Texas secretary of war 1836; brigadier general 1839; commanded Somervell Expedition, a punitive expedition into Mexico for Mexican Army raids into Texas 1842.

Sonoma   **California**
Santa Rosa   1,576 sq. mi.
483,878   458,614   388,222   299,681   204,885   147,375   103,405
February 18, 1850. *Town of Sonoma.* Name given by Spanish to Wintuns; *tso* is Wintun name for "earth," and *noma* means "village."

Southampton   **Virginia**
Courtland   599 sq. mi.
18,570   17,482   17,550   18,731   18,582   27,195   26,522
April 20, 1749. *Southampton Hundred.* Named for Henry Wriothesley, 3rd Earl of Southampton (1573–1624); patron of Shakespeare; imprisoned in Tower of London by Elizabeth I as ally of Earl of Essex 1601 (see Essex, Vermont); released by James I 1603; Virginia Company's council and treasurer 1609–24. A "hundred" was a political subdivision in early Virginia that contained 100 families or could produce 100 fighting men. [Associated independent city: Franklin.]

Southeast Fairbanks   **Alaska**
(Census Area)   24,769 sq. mi.
7,029   6,174   5,913   5,676   4,179   (a)   (b)
January 1, 1964. *City of Fairbanks.* Southeast section of Fairbanks Census Area left when the borough of Fairbanks North Star was created (see Fairbanks North Star, Alaska). [(a) Part of Fairbanks Census Area; (b) part of 4th Judicial Division.]

Spalding   **Georgia**
Griffin   196 sq. mi.
64,073   58,417   54,457   47,899   39,514   35,404   31,045
December 20, 1851. *Thomas Spalding (1774–1851).* Georgia House of Representatives 1794; Georgia Constitutional Convention 1798; Georgia Senate 1804; US representative 1805–06; Florida-Georgia Boundary Commission 1826; president of Milledgeville Convention which resolved that Georgia would resist any act of Congress abolishing slavery 1850.

Spartanburg   **South Carolina**
Spartanburg   808 sq. mi.
284,307   253,791   226,800   201,861   173,724   156,830   150,349
March 12, 1785; converted to judicial district January 1, 1800; redesignated as county April 16, 1868. *Spartan Regiment.* South Carolina Militia regiment; named for the military reputation of Sparta, Greece; fought at Cedar Springs and Musgrove's Mill 1780, and Cowpens 1781.

Spencer   **Indiana**
Rockport   397 sq. mi.
20,952   20,391   19,490   19,361   17,134   16,074   16,174
January 10, 1818. *Spear Spencer (?–1811);* also Spier Spencer. Sheriff of Harrison County, Indiana; captain of mounted riflemen; killed at Battle of Tippecanoe, November 7, 1811.

Spencer   **Kentucky**
Taylorsville   187 sq. mi.
17,061   11,766   6,801   5,929   5,488   5,680   6,157
January 7, 1824. *Spear Spencer.**

Spink   **South Dakota**
Redfield   1,504 sq. mi.
6,415   7,454   7,981   9,201   10,595   11,706   12,204
January 8, 1873; organized August 1, 1879. *Solomon Lewis Spink (1831–81).* Illinois House of Representatives 1864; secretary of Dakota Territory 1865–69; acting governor 1866–67; congressional delegate 1869–71.

Spokane   **Washington**
Spokane   1,764 sq. mi.
471,221   417,939   361,364   341,835   287,487   278,333   221,561
January 29, 1858; organized January 17, 1860; abolished January 19, 1864; recreated October 30, 1879. *Spokane Indians.* Name means "chief" or "child of the sun." Dominant tribe in a confederacy of Eastern Washington Indians.

Spotsylvania   **Virginia**
Spotsylvania   402 sq. mi.

122,397	90,395	57,403	34,435	16,424	13,819	11,920

December 17, 1720. *Alexander Spotswood (1676–1740)*. Ensign to lieutenant colonel, British Army 1693–1703; Battle of Blenheim 1704; lieutenant governor of Virginia 1710–22; deputy postmaster general of American colonies 1730–39. Name combined with Latin *sylva* meaning "woods." (Associated independent city: Fredericksburg.)

Stafford   **Kansas**
Saint John   792 sq. mi.

4,437	4,789	5,365	5,694	5,943	7,451	8,816

February 26, 1867; organized July 2, 1879. *Lewis Stafford (?–1863)*. Captain, Company E, 1st Kansas Volunteer Infantry, 1861; Battle of Wilson's Creek 1861; accidentally killed at Young's Point, Louisiana, January 31, 1863.

Stafford   **Virginia**
Stafford   269 sq. mi.

128,961	92,446	61,236	40,470	24,587	16,876	11,902

1664. *Staffordshire, England*. Most likely the origin of early settlers or home of a prominent settler.

Stanislaus   **California**
Modesto   1,495 sq. mi.

514,453	446,997	370,522	265,900	194,506	157,294	127,231

April 1, 1854. *Stanislaus River*. Named for Estanislao (?–?); Indian chief whose Christian name honored two Polish saints named Stanislaus; ran away from Mission San José c1828; led escaped neophytes in harassing settlements and missions; defeated by General Vallejo 1829 at a site near the river.

Stanley   **South Dakota**
Fort Pierre   1,444 sq. mi.

2,966	2,772	2,453	2,533	2,457	4,085	2,055

January 8, 1873; organized April 23, 1890. *David Sloan Stanley (1828–1902)*. Graduated West Point 1852; 2nd lieutenant to brevet major general 1852–65; Battle of Wilson's Creek 1861; Battle of Franklin 1864 (awarded Congressional Medal of Honor 1893); served in western Indian campaigns 1866–74; commandant of Fort Sully, Dakota Territory; brigadier general 1884; brevet major general 1892; governor of US Soldier's Home 1893–98.

Stanly   **North Carolina**
Albemarle   395 sq. mi.

60,585	58,100	51,765	48,517	42,822	40,873	37,130

January 11, 1841. *John Stanly (1774–1834)*. North Carolina House of Commons 1798–99 and intermittently 1812–26; US representative 1801–03 and 1809–11.

Stanton   **Kansas**
Johnson   680 sq. mi.

2,235	2,406	2,333	2,339	2,287	2,108	2,263

March 20, 1873; organized July 17, 1887. *Edwin McMasters Stanton (1814–69)*. Ohio lawyer; pioneered plea of temporary insanity as a murder defense; US attorney general 1860–61; US secretary of war 1862–68; died four days after being appointed to US Supreme Court.

Stanton   **Nebraska**
Stanton   428 sq. mi.

6,129	6,455	6,244	6,549	5,758	5,783	6,387

March 6, 1855, as Izard; name changed January 10, 1862; organized January 23, 1867. *Edwin McMasters Stanton.**

Stark   **Illinois**
Toulon   288 sq. mi.

5,994	6,332	6,534	7,389	7,510	8,152	8,721

March 2, 1839. *John Stark (1728–1822)*. Captured by Abenaki Indians 1752, ransomed 1753; lieutenant, French and Indian War 1755; colonel New Hampshire Regiment 1775; fought in Battles of Bunker Hill 1775, Trenton 1776, Bennington and Princeton 1777; brigadier general 1777; coined New Hampshire motto, "Live Free or Die" 1809.

Stark **North Dakota**
Dickinson 1,335 sq. mi.

24,199	22,636	22,832	23,697	19,613	18,451	16,317

February 10, 1879; organized May 30, 1883. *George Stark (?–?)*. Helped to reorganized Northern Pacific Railroad from bankruptcy 1873; vice president of Northern Pacific 1875–79; promoted settlement in Dakota Territory.

Stark **Ohio**
Canton 575 sq. mi.

375,586	378,098	367,585	378,823	372,210	340,345	283,194

February 13, 1808; organized January 1, 1809. *John Stark.**

Starke **Indiana**
Knox 309 sq. mi.

23,363	23,556	22,747	21,997	19,280	17,911	15,282

February 7, 1835; organized January 15, 1850. *John Stark.** Legislative error added letter *e* to county's name.

Starr **Texas**
Rio Grande City 1,223 sq. mi.

60,968	53,597	40,518	27,266	17,707	17,137	13,948

February 10, 1848; organized August 7, 1848. *James Harper Starr (1809–90)*. Physician and surgeon; Republic of Texas secretary of treasury 1837–39; promoted settlement in Texas; opposed secession but held various civilian positions in Confederate government 1861–65.

Staunton **Virginia**
(Independent City) 20 sq. mi.

23,746	23,853	24,461	21,857	24,504	22,232	19,927

1871. *Rebecca Staunton (c1690–1775)*. Wife of Sir William Gooch, governor of Virginia 1727–49 (see Goochland, Virginia). (Associated county: Augusta.)

Stearns **Minnesota**
Saint Cloud 1,343 sq. mi.

150,642	133,166	118,791	108,161	95,400	80,345	70,681

February 20, 1855. *Charles Thomas Stearns (1807–98)*. Minnesota territorial legislature 1849–58. Stearns was active in the creation of the county that was intended to be named for Isaac Stevens (see Stevens, Minnesota), but due to a clerical error was named after Stearns who was a member of the legislature at the time.

Steele **Minnesota**
Owatonna 430 sq. mi.

36,576	33,680	30,729	30,328	26,931	25,029	21,155

February 20, 1855; organized February 29, 1856. *Franklin Steele (1812–80)*. Made fortune in lumbering; acquired large land holdings in Minnesota and Dakota Territory; donated land for University of Minnesota 1851; built first bridge across Mississippi River between Minneapolis and St. Paul 1855.

Steele **North Dakota**
Finley 712 sq. mi.

1,975	2,258	2,420	3,106	3,749	4,719	5,145

March 8, 1883; organized June 13, 1883. *Uncertain*. (1) *Franklin Steele.** (2) *Edward H. Steele (1846–99)*; secretary-treasurer of Red River Land Company which had large holdings on area in and around county; advocated creation of the county.

Stephens **Georgia**
Toccoa 179 sq. mi.

26,175   25,435   23,257   21,763   29,331   18,391   16,647
August 18, 1905. *Alexander Hamilton Stephens (1812–83)*. Georgia House of Representatives 1836–41; Georgia Senate 1842; US representative 1843–59 and 1873–82; opposed secession but participated in Georgia Secession Convention 1861; Montgomery Convention 1861; vice president of Confederacy 1861–65; elected to US Senate but was denied seat 1866; governor of Georgia 1882–83.

Stephens   **Oklahoma**
Duncan   870 sq. mi.
45,048   43,182   42,299   43,419   35,902   37,900   34,071
July 16, 1907. *John Hall Stephens (1847–1924)*. Texas Senate 1886–88; US representative from Texas 1897–1917; promoted Oklahoma statehood.

Stephens   **Texas**
Breckenridge   897 sq. mi.
9,630   9,674   9,010   9,926   8,414   8,885   10,597
January 22, 1858, as Buchanan; name changed December 17, 1861; organized August 21, 1876. *Alexander Hamilton Stephens.**

Stephenson   **Illinois**
Freeport   565 sq. mi.
47,711   48,979   48,052   49,536   48,861   46,207   41,595
March 4, 1837. *Benjamin Stephenson (?–1822)*. Adjutant general of Illinois Territory 1813; colonel, War of 1812; congressional delegate 1814–16; Illinois Constitutional Convention 1818.

Sterling   **Texas**
Sterling City   923 sq. mi.
1,143   1,393   1,438   1,206   1,056   1,177   1,282
March 4, 1891; organized June 3, 1891. *W. S. Sterling (?–?)*. Buffalo hunter; first settler in area.

Steuben   **Indiana**
Angola   309 sq. mi.
34,185   32,214   27,446   24,694   20,159   17,184   17,087
February 7, 1835; organized January 18, 1837; effective May 1, 1837. *Friedrich Wilhelm Ludolf Gerhard Augustin von Steuben (1730–94)*. Prussian officer during Seven Years' War 1756–63; arrived in America to serve in Continental Army 1777; trained troops at Valley Forge 1778; major general at Monmouth (1778) and Yorktown (1781); became US citizen 1784.

Steuben   **New York**
Bath   1,391 sq. mi.
98,990   98,726   99,088   99,217   99,546   97,691   91,439
March 18, 1796. *Friedrich von Steuben.**

Stevens   **Kansas**
Hugoton   727 sq. mi.
5,724   5,463   5,048   4,736   4,198   4,400   4,516
March 20, 1873; organized August 3, 1886. *Thaddeus Stevens (1792–1868)*. Pennsylvania House of Representatives, intermittently 1833–41; Pennsylvania Constitutional Convention 1838; US representative 1849–53 and 1859–68; led Radical Republicans in imposing Reconstruction on the South following Civil War; led impeachment effort against President Andrew Johnson.

Stevens   **Minnesota**
Morris   564 sq. mi.
9,726   10,053   10,634   11,322   11,218   11,262   11,106
February 20, 1862; organized December 31, 1871. *Isaac Ingalls Stevens (1818–62)*. Graduated West Point at head of class 1839; staff of General Scott during Mexican War; wounded at Mexico City 1847; brevet captain and major 1847; initiated survey of railroad route between Minnesota and Washington Territory 1853; governor of Washington Territory 1853–57;

Washington Territory delegate to Congress 1857–61; reentered Union Army as colonel 1861; major general of volunteers 1862; killed at Chantilly, September 1, 1862.

Stevens	**Washington**					
Colville	2,478 sq. mi.					
43,531	40,066	30,948	28,979	17,405	17,884	18,850

January 20, 1863. *Isaac Ingalls Stevens.**

Stewart	**Georgia**					
Lumpkin	459 sq. mi.					
6,058	5,252	5,654	5,896	6,511	7,371	9,194

December 23, 1830. *Daniel Stewart (1759–1829)*. General, Continental Army; brigadier general of cavalry, War of 1812; Seminole War 1817–18.

Stewart	**Tennessee**					
Dover	459 sq. mi.					
13,324	12,370	9,479	8,665	7,319	7,851	9,175

November 1, 1803. *Duncan Stewart (1752–1815)*. North Carolina House of Commons 1789–90; Tennessee Senate 1801–07; moved to Mississippi c1808.

Stillwater	**Montana**					
Columbus	1,795 sq. mi.					
9,117	8,195	6,536	5,598	4,632	5,526	5,416

March 24, 1913. *Stillwater River*. Name is misleading; for most of its seventy miles the river is a fast-moving stream.

Stoddard	**Missouri**					
Bloomfield	823 sq. mi.					
29,968	29,705	28,895	29,009	25,771	29,490	33,463

January 2, 1835. *Amos Stoddard (1762–1813)*. Revolutionary War; Massachusetts legislature 1797; returned to Army as captain of artillery 1798; received formal transfer of Louisiana Purchase from France to US 1804; major 1807; killed during Siege of Fort Meigs, May 11, 1813.

Stokes	**North Carolina**					
Danbury	449 sq. mi.					
47,401	44,711	37,223	33,086	23,782	22,314	21,520

1789. *John Stokes (1756–90)*. Ensign to captain, 6th Virginia Regiment 1776–78; wounded and captured at Waxhaw Massacre 1780; exchanged 1783; North Carolina legislature 1786–87 and 1789; appointed US district judge, died on way to first court session.

Stone	**Arkansas**					
Mountain View	606 sq. mi.					
12,394	11,499	9,775	9,022	6,838	6,294	7,662

April 21, 1873. *Descriptive*. Refers to local stone formations.

Stone	**Mississippi**					
Wiggins	445 sq. mi.					
17,786	13,622	10,750	9,716	8,101	7,013	6,264

April 3, 1916. *John Marshall Stone (1830–1900)*. From captain to colonel, 2nd Mississippi Infantry 1861–65; Mississippi Senate 1870–76; governor of Mississippi 1876–82 and 1890–96.

Stone	**Missouri**					
Galena	464 sq. mi.					
32,202	28,658	19,078	15,587	9,921	8,176	9,748

February 10, 1851. *William Stone (?–?)*. Judge in Taney County from which Stone County was created.

Stonewall   **Texas**
Aspermont   916 sq. mi.
1,490   1,693   2,013   2,406   2,397   3,017   3,679
August 21, 1876; organized December 20, 1888. *Thomas Jonathon "Stonewall" Jackson (1824–63).* Graduated West Point 1846; brevet 2nd lieutenant to major 1846–47; Mexican War Battles of Vera Cruz, Chapultepec, and Contreras; resigned commission 1852; professor of artillery, Virginia Military Institute 1852–61; commissioned as colonel, Confederate Army, 1861; given nickname for standing firm at First Bull Run 1861; brigadier general to major general 1862; mortally wounded by own troops at Chancellorsville.

Storey   **Nevada**
Virginia City   263 sq. mi.
4,010   3,399   2,526   1,503   695   568   671
November 25, 1861. *Edward F. Storey (1828–60).* Lieutenant, Mexican War; miner, Comstock Lode 1859; raised rifle company to pursue marauding Paiutes 1860; killed in battle near Pyramid Lake.

Story   **Iowa**
Nevada   573 sq. mi.
89,542   79,981   74,252   72,326   62,783   49,327   44,294
January 13, 1846; organized June 1, 1853. *Joseph Story (1779–1845).* Massachusetts House of Representatives 1805–07 and 1811; US representative 1808–09; associate justice, US Supreme Court 1811–45; Massachusetts Constitutional Convention 1820. County's name suggested soon after Story's death.

Strafford   **New Hampshire**
Dover   369 sq. mi.
123,143   112,233   104,233   85,408   70,431   59,799   51,567
April 29, 1769; organized February 5, 1773. *Thomas Wentworth, Earl of Strafford (1593–1641).* British House of Commons 1614–41; court favorite of Charles I; Lord Deputy of Ireland 1632–40; made 1st Earl of Strafford 1640; impeached by enemies in Parliament and sent to Tower of London 1640; executed.

Stutsman   **North Dakota**
Jamestown   2,222 sq. mi.
21,100   21,908   22,241   24,154   23,550   25,137   24,158
January 4, 1873; organized June 20, 1873. *Enos Stutsman (1826–74).* Dakota territorial legislature, intermittently 1862–74, including when county was created; US customs agent 1866–67.

Sublette   **Wyoming**
Pinedale   4,887 sq. mi.
10,427   5,920   4,843   4,548   3,755   3,778   2,481
February 15, 1921. *William Lewis Sublette (1799–1845).* Fur trapper 1823–32; founder of Rocky Mountain Fur Company 1826; established trading post which became Fort Laramie 1834.

Suffolk   **Massachusetts**
Boston   58 sq. mi.
722,023   689,807   663,906   650,142   735,190   791,329   896,615
May 10, 1643. *Suffolk County, England.* Origin of early settlers.

Suffolk   **New York**
Riverhead   912 sq. mi.
1,493,350   1,419,369   1,321,864   1,284,231   1,124,950   666,784   276,129
November 1, 1683. *Suffolk County, England.* Origin of early settlers.

Suffolk   **Virginia**
(Independent City)   400 sq. mi.
84,585   63,677   52,141   47,621   45,024[a] 43,975[a] 37,577[a]

1637 as Upper Norfolk County; name changed to Nansemond 1642; incorporated into City of Nansemond, July 1972; merged with City of Suffolk, January 1, 1974. *Suffolk, England.* Origin of early settlers. [(a) Includes Nansemond County: 1970 population 35,166; 1960 31,366; 1950 25,238.]

Sullivan **Indiana**
Sullivan 447 sq. mi.

21,475	21,751	18,993	21,107	19,889	21,721	23,667

December 30, 1816. *Uncertain.* (1) *Daniel Sullivan (?–1790)*; settled near Vincennes 1786; conducted raids against local Indians; killed by Indians while traveling from Vincennes to Louisville. (2) *John Sullivan* (see Sullivan, New Hampshire).

Sullivan **Missouri**
Milan 648 sq. mi.

6,714	7,219	6,326	7,434	7,572	8,783	11,299

February 17, 1843, as Highland; name changed and organized February 14, 1845. *Sullivan County, Tennessee.* Name proposed by Missouri legislator from Tennessee.

Sullivan **New Hampshire**
Newport 537 sq. mi.

43,742	40,458	38,592	36,063	30,949	28,067	26,441

July 5, 1827. *John Sullivan (1740–95).* Continental Congress from New Hampshire 1774–75 and 1780–81; brigadier general and major general, Continental Army 1775–80; New Hampshire Constitutional Convention 1782; attorney general of New Hampshire 1782–86; president (governor) of New Hampshire 1786–88 and 1789–90; speaker, New Hampshire House of Representatives; judge, US District Court, 1789–95.

Sullivan **New York**
Monticello 968 sq. mi.

77,547	73,966	69,277	65,155	52,580	45,272	40,731

March 27, 1809. *John Sullivan.**

Sullivan **Pennsylvania**
Laporte 450 sq. mi.

6,428	6,556	6,104	6,349	5,961	6,251	6,745

March 15, 1847. *John Sullivan.**

Sullivan **Tennessee**
Blountsville 413 sq. mi.

156,823	153,048	143,596	143,968	127,329	114,139	95,063

1779; organized February 7, 1780. *John Sullivan.**

Sully **South Dakota**
Onida 1,007 sq. mi.

1,373	1,556	1,589	1,990	2,362	2,607	2,713

January 8, 1873; organized April 19, 1883. *Uncertain.* (1) *Alfred Sully (1821–79)*; graduated West Point 1841; 1st lieutenant to major general of volunteers 1847–1863; Battle of Antietam 1862; fought Indians in West 1863; mustered out of Volunteer Army and continued as colonel in Regular Army 1866; established Fort Sully 1866. (2) *Fort Sully*; named for Alfred Sully; established near Pierre 1863; relocated up Missouri River 1866; abandoned 1894.

Summers **West Virginia**
Hinton 360 sq. mi.

13,927	12,999	14,204	15,875	13,213	15,640	19,183

February 27, 1871. *George Summers (1804–68).* Virginia House of Delegates 1830–32 and 1834–36; US representative 1831–45; voted against Virginia secession 1861.

Summit **Colorado**
Breckinridge 608 sq. mi.

| 27,994 | 23,548 | 12,881 | 8,848 | 2,665 | 2,073 | 1,135 |

November 1, 1861. *Descriptive*. Refers to mountainous terrain; Continental Divide forms southeast boundary of county.

Summit   **Ohio**
Akron   413 sq. mi.

| 541,781 | 542,899 | 514,990 | 524,472 | 553,371 | 513,569 | 410,032 |

March 3, 1840. *Descriptive*. Located on divide between Lake Erie and Ohio River; highest point on Ohio Canal.

Summit   **Utah**
Coalville   1,872 sq. mi.

| 36,324 | 29,736 | 15,518 | 10,198 | 5,879 | 5,673 | 6,745 |

January 13, 1854. *Descriptive*. County is located on divide between Green River and the Great Basin.

Sumner   **Kansas**
Wellington   1,182 sq. mi.

| 24,132 | 25,946 | 25,841 | 24,928 | 23,553 | 25,316 | 23,646 |

February 26, 1867; organized February 7, 1871. *Charles Sumner (1811–74)*. US senator from Massachusetts 1851–74; ardent foe of extending slavery into Kansas; severely caned by South Carolina representative Preston Brooks (see Brooks, Georgia) on the floor of the Senate following speech "The Crime Against Kansas" 1856.

Sumner   **Tennessee**
Gallatin   529 sq. mi.

| 160,645 | 130,449 | 103,281 | 85,790 | 56,106 | 36,217 | 33,533 |

1786. *Jethro Sumner (1733–85)*. Virginia Militia, French and Indian War 1755–61; commanded Fort Bedford 1760; colonel, North Carolina 3rd Battalion 1776; brigadier general in Continental Army 1779–83; Battle of Camden 1780; Eutaw Springs 1781.

Sumter   **Alabama**
Livingston   904 sq. mi.

| 13,763 | 14,798 | 16,174 | 16,908 | 16,974 | 20,041 | 23,610 |

December 18, 1832. *Thomas Sumter (1734–1832)*. Lieutenant colonel, 6th Continental Regiment; brigadier general of militia 1780; South Carolina Senate 1781–82; US representative 1789–93 and 1797–1801; US senator 1801–10; last surviving officer of the American Revolution.

Sumter   **Florida**
Bushnell   547 sq. mi.

| 93,420 | 53,345 | 31,577 | 24,272 | 14,839 | 11,869 | 11,330 |

January 8, 1853. *Thomas Sumter*.*

Sumter   **Georgia**
Americus   483 sq. mi.

| 32,819 | 33,200 | 30,228 | 29,360 | 26,931 | 24,652 | 24,208 |

December 26, 1831. *Thomas Sumter*.*

Sumter   **South Carolina**
Sumter   665 sq. mi.

| 107,456 | 104,646 | 102,637 | 88,243 | 79,425 | 74,941 | 57,634 |

December 17, 1798, as judicial district; designated as county April 1, 1868. *Thomas Sumter*.*

Sunflower   **Mississippi**
Indianola   698 sq. mi.

| 29,450 | 34,369 | 32,867 | 34,844 | 37,047 | 45,750 | 56,031 |

February 15, 1844. *Sunflower River*. Named for the flower which is prevalent in the area.

Surry   **North Carolina**
Dobson   532 sq. mi.

73,673 71,219 61,704 59,449 51,415 48,205 45,593
January 1771; effective April 1, 1771. *Surrey, England*. Birthplace of then-Governor Tryon.

Surry   **Virginia**
Surry   279 sq. mi.
7,058 6,829 6,145 6,046 5,882 6,220 6,220
1652. *Surrey, England*. Name either proposed by a prominent citizen or for the origin of early settlers. (Letter *e* was dropped somewhere between England and America.)

Susquehanna **Pennsylvania**
Montrose   823 sq. mi.
43,356 42,238 40,380 37,876 34,344 33,137 31,970
February 21, 1810; organized 1812. *Susquehanna River*. Name is of uncertain Algonquin origin; may be from *sisku*, meaning "mud," and *hanne*, meaning "river."

Sussex   **Delaware**
Georgetown   936 sq. mi.
197,145 156,638 113,229 98,004 80,356 73,195 61,336
August 8, 1673, as Hoarkill; name changed to Deale 1681; name changed to Sussex, December 4, 1682. *Sussex County, England*. Named by William Penn for his home county in England.

Sussex   **New Jersey**
Newton   519 sq. mi.
149,265 144,166 130,943 116,119 77,528 49,255 34,423
June 8, 1753. *Sussex County, England*. Name either proposed by a prominent citizen or for the origin of early settlers.

Sussex   **Virginia**
Sussex   490 sq. mi.
12,087 12,504 10,248 10,874 11,464 12,411 12,785
November 28, 1753. *Sussex County, England*. Name either proposed by a prominent citizen or for the origin of early settlers.

Sutter   **California**
Yuba City   602 sq. mi.
94,737 78,930 64,415 52,246 41,935 33,380 26,239
February 18, 1850. *John Augustus Sutter (1803–80)*. Native of Switzerland; became Mexican citizen on arrival in California in order to own land 1839; received land grant; gold discovered on his property, leading to his financial ruin as workers deserted and squatters took over his land 1848; died in Washington while attempting to receive recompense for his losses.

Sutton   **Texas**
Sonora   1,454 sq. mi.
4,128 4,077 4,135 5,130 3,175 3,738 3,746
April 1, 1887; organized November 4, 1890. *John Schuyler Sutton (c1822–62)*. 2nd lieutenant, Republic of Texas Army 1839; captured on Santa Fe expedition 1841, released 1842; private, Texas Mounted Rifles during Mexican War, Monterrey and Mexico City campaigns; lieutenant colonel, 7th Texas Cavalry 1861; wounded at Battle of Valverde, February 21, 1862; died next day after refusing to have injured leg amputated.

Suwannee   **Florida**
Live Oak   689 sq. mi.
41,551 34,844 26,780 22,287 15,559 14,961 16,986
December 21, 1858. *Suwannee River*. Origin of name is unknown; possibilities include (1) Cherokee word *suwani*, meaning "echo"; (2) corruption of Spanish "San Juan" after a 17th Century mission in the area.

Swain   **North Carolina**
Bryson City   528 sq. mi.
13,981 12,968 11,268 10,283 7,861 8,387 9,921

February 24, 1871. *David Lowrie Swain (1801–68)*. North Carolina House of Commons 1824–30; governor of North Carolina 1832–35; president, University of North Carolina 1835–68; declined offer to serve in Confederate Senate 1863.

Sweet Grass   **Montana**
Big Timber   1,855 sq. mi.
3,651   3,609   3,154   3,216   2,980   3,290   3,621
March 5, 1895. *Uncertain*. (1) *Descriptive* of local vegetation. (2) *Sweet Grass Creek*; named for local vegetation. (3) *Sweet Grass Hills*; named for local vegetation.

Sweetwater   **Wyoming**
Green River   10,427 sq. mi.
43,806   37,613   38,823   41,723   18,391   17,920   22,017
December 27, 1867, as Carter; name changed December 13, 1869. *Sweetwater River*. Named for palatable water in contrast to most water found along the Oregon Trail.

Swift   **Minnesota**
Benson   742 sq. mi.
9,783   11,956   10,724   12,920   13,177   14,936   15,837
February 18, 1870; organized April 6, 1897. *Henry Adoniram Swift (1823–69)*. Minnesota Senate 1862–63 and 1864–65; governor of Minnesota 1863–64; registrar, US Land Office 1865–69.

Swisher   **Texas**
Tulia   890 sq. mi.
7,854   8,378   8,133   9,723   10,373   10,607   8,249
August 21, 1876; organized July 17, 1890. *James Gibson Swisher (1795–1864)*. Private, Tennessee Militia 1813–14; private, US Mounted Rangers 1814–15; moved to Texas 1833; repulsed Comanche raid 1834; captain in Texas Army 1835; Siege of Bexar (1835) and Battle of San Jacinto (1836); signer, Texas Declaration of Independence 1836.

Switzerland   **Indiana**
Vevay   221 sq. mi.
10,613   9,065   7,738   7,153   6,306   7,092   7,599
September 7, 1814; effective October 1, 1814. *Country of Switzerland*. County was settled by Swiss 1813.

T

Talbot   **Georgia**
Talbotton   391 sq. mi.
6,865   6,498   6,524   6,536   6,625   7,127   7,687
December 14, 1827. *Matthew Talbot (?–1827)*. Georgia Constitutional Conventions 1795 and 1798; Georgia Senate 1801–03 and 1808–23, president 1818–23; interim governor of Georgia 1819.

Talbot   **Maryland**
Easton   269 sq. mi.
37,782   33,182   30,549   25,604   23,682   21,578   19,428
February 18, 1662. *Uncertain*. (1) Either one of two women related to Cecilius Calvert (see Cecil, Maryland); (a) *Grace Calvert Talbot (1614–72)*; daughter of George Calvert, 1st Lord Baltimore (see Calvert, Maryland [1]) and sister of Cecilius; married Robert Talbott, 2nd Lord of Carlton (second *t* was dropped in America) 1630; (b) *Francis Arundell Talbot (?–?)*; sister-in-law of Cecilius Calvert through her sister Anne Arundell Calvert (see Anne Arundel, Maryland). (2) *Talbot family*; numerous members were related to Cecilius Calvert by blood or marriage.

Taliaferro   **Georgia**
Crawfordville   195 sq. mi.
1,717   2,077   1,915   2,032   2,423   3,370   4,515

December 24, 1825. *Benjamin Taliaferro (1750–1821)*. Lieutenant to captain, Revolutionary War 1776–80; captured at Charleston 1780; Georgia Assembly 1786; Georgia Senate, president 1792–96; Georgia Constitutional Convention 1798; US representative 1799–1802.

Talladega **Alabama**
Talladega 737 sq. mi.

82,291	80,321	74,107	73,826	65,280	65,495	63,639

December 18, 1832. *Battle of Talladega*. Andrew Jackson defeated Creeks, November 1813; name from Muskogee village of Talatigi; *talwa* or *talla* means "town," *atigi* or *teka* means "border"; village was near a tribal boundary.

Tallahatchie **Mississippi**
Charleston 645 sq. mi.

15,378	14,903	15,210	17,157	19,338	24,081	30,486

December 23, 1833. *Tallahatchie River*. Named from Choctaw *tali*, meaning "rock," and *hacha*, meaning "river."

Tallapoosa **Alabama**
Dadeville 717 sq. mi.

41,616	41,475	38,826	38,676	33,840	35,007	35,074

December 18, 1832. *Tallapoosa River*. Origin of name is unknown; disparate possibilities include Creek for "cat town," "swift river," or "newcomer."

Tama **Iowa**
Toledo 721 sq. mi.

17,767	18,103	17,419	19,533	20,147	21,413	21,688

February 17, 1843; organized July 4, 1853. *Tama (c1780–c1833)*. Fox chief; negotiated three treaties with US 1824–32; name believed to mean "sudden thunder crash."

Taney **Missouri**
Forsyth 632 sq. mi.

51,675	39,703	25,561	20,467	13,023	10,238	9,863

January 6, 1837. *Roger Brooke Taney (1777–1864)*. Maryland Senate 1816–21; US attorney general 1831–33; US treasurer 1833–34; chief justice of US 1836–64; presided over Dred Scott case 1857.

Tangipahoa **Louisiana**
Amite 791 sq. mi.

121,097	100,588	85,709	80,698	65,875	59,434	53,218

March 6, 1869. *Tangipahoa Indians*. Meaning of name is uncertain but most suggestions involve corn or maize in one way or another.

Taos **New Mexico**
Taos 2,203 sq. mi.

32,937	29,979	23,118	19,456	17,516	15,934	17,146

January 9, 1852. *Taos Pueblo*. Spanish attempt at Navajo name *Towi* or *Tuato*, meaning "village."

Tarrant **Texas**
Fort Worth 864 sq. mi.

1,809,034	1,446,219	1,170,103	860,880	716,317	538,495	361,253

December 20, 1849; organized August 5, 1850. *Edward H. Tarrant (1796–1858)*. Battle of New Orleans 1815; Texas Rangers 1835; Republic of Texas Congress 1837–38; brigadier general, Texas Army 1841; Battle of Village Creek 1841; Texas Constitutional Convention 1845; Texas legislature 1849–53.

Tate **Mississippi**
Senatobia 405 sq. mi.

28,886	25,370	21,432	20,119	18,544	18,138	18,011

December 23, 1873. *Uncertain.* (1) *Thomas Simpson Tate (?–c1881)*; trustee, Free Land and Colonization Company of De Soto County 1868; influential in creating Tate County from De Soto County; Mississippi legislature. (2) *Tate family*; prominent in northwestern Mississippi.

Tattnall   **Georgia**
Reidsville   479 sq. mi.
25,520   22,305   17,722   18,134   16,557   15,837   15,939
December 5, 1801. *Josiah Tattnall (1764–1803).* Continental Army under General Wayne 1782; Georgia Militia, colonel to brigadier general 1793–1801; Georgia House of Representatives 1795 and 1796; US senator 1796–99; governor of Georgia 1801–02.

Taylor   **Florida**
Perry   1,043 sq. mi.
22,570   19,256   17,111   16,532   13,641   13,168   10,416
December 23, 1856. *Zachary Taylor (1784–1850).* 1st lieutenant to brevet brigadier general 1808–37; defeated Seminoles at Lake Okeechobee 1837; Mexican War victories at Palo Alto, Reseca de la Palma, Matamoros, Monterrey, and Buena Vista 1846–47; 12th president of US 1849–50.

Taylor   **Georgia**
Butler   377 sq. mi.
8,906   8,815   7,642   7,902   7,865   8,311   9,113
January 15, 1852. *Zachary Taylor.**

Taylor   **Iowa**
Bedford   532 sq. mi.
6,317   6,958   7,114   8,353   8,790   10,288   12,420
February 24, 1847; organized February 26, 1851. *Zachary Taylor.**

Taylor   **Kentucky**
Campbellsville   266 sq. mi.
24,512   22,927   21,146   21,178   17,138   16,285   14,403
January 13, 1848. *Zachary Taylor.**

Taylor   **Texas**
Abilene   916 sq. mi.
131,506   126,555   119,655   110,932   97,853   101,078   63,370
February 1, 1858; organized July 3, 1878. *Taylor brothers.* In 1954 the Texas legislature declared the county to have been named for three Taylor brothers who died at the Alamo: Edward (1812–36), James (1814–36), and George (1816–36); all were privates serving as riflemen at the Alamo March 6, 1836. Before the legislature's action other eponymous contenders included a fourth Taylor at the Alamo and three Taylors who were members of the legislature at the time the county was created.

Taylor   **West Virginia**
Grafton   173 sq. mi.
16,895   16,089   15,144   16,584   13,878   15,010   18,422
January 19, 1844. *John Taylor (1753–1824).* Major to colonel in Revolutionary War; Virginia House of Delegates 1779–85 and 1796–1800; US senator, intermittently 1791–1824.

Taylor   **Wisconsin**
Medford   975 sq. mi.
20,689   19,680   18,901   18,817   16,958   17,843   18,456
March 4, 1875. *William Robert Taylor (1820–1909).* Served on various Dane County governing boards; Wisconsin legislature 1854–57; trustee, State Hospital for the Insane 1860–74; governor of Wisconsin 1874–76.

Tazewell   **Illinois**
Pekin   649 sq. mi.

135,394   128,485   123,692   132,078   118,649   90,789   76,165

January 31, 1827. *Littleton Waller Tazewell (1774–1860).* Virginia House of Delegates 1796–1800; US representative 1800–01; US senator 1824–32; governor of Virginia 1834–36. Member of US senate when county was created; may have advocated positions popular in Illinois, otherwise there is no discernible connection with Illinois.

Tazewell   **Virginia**
Tazewell   519 sq. mi.

45,078   44,598   45,960   50,511   39,816   44,791   47,512

December 20, 1799. *Henry Tazewell (1753–99).* Virginia House of Burgesses 1775; Virginia Constitutional Convention 1775–76; Virginia Supreme Court, chief justice, 1785–93; US senator 1794–99.

Tehama   **California**
Red Bluff   2,950 sq. mi.

63,463   56,039   49,625   38,888   29,517   25,305   19,276

April 9, 1856. *Village of Tehama.* Wintun Indian word of uncertain meaning; possibilities include: (1) "high water" or "low land"; (2) "salmon"; (3) a specific ford of the Sacramento River; (4) "plains" or "prairie."

Telfair   **Georgia**
McRae   437 sq. mi.

16,500   11,794   11,000   11,445   11,381   11,715   13,221

December 10, 1807. *Edward Telfair (1735–1807).* Georgia Council of Safety 1775–76; Georgia Provincial Congress 1776; Continental Congress 1777–79 and 1780–83; signer, Articles of Confederation 1781; governor of Georgia 1786 and 1790–93; federal Constitutional Convention 1787.

Teller   **Colorado**
Cripple Creek   557 sq. mi.

23,350   20,555   12,468   8,034   3,316   2,495   2,754

March 23, 1899. *Henry Moore Teller (1830–1914).* Major general, Colorado Militia 1862–64; US senator 1876–82 and 1885–1909; US secretary of interior 1882–85.

Tensas   **Louisiana**
Saint Joseph   603 sq. mi.

5,252   6,618   7,103   8,525   9,732   11,796   13,209

March 17, 1843. *Taensa Indians.* Unknown origin of name; may be for a tribal village; spelling is from French corruption.

Terrebonne   **Louisiana**
Houma   1,232 sq. mi.

111,860   104,503   96,982   94,393   76,049   60,771   43,328

March 22, 1822. *Uncertain.* French for "good earth." Possible sources include: (1) description of the area; (2) a parish in Canada; (3) Bayou Terrebonne; (4) Terrebonne Bay.

Terrell   **Georgia**
Dawson   335 sq. mi.

9,315   10,970   10,653   12,017   11,416   12,742   14,314

February 16, 1856. *William Terrell (1778–1855).* Physician; Georgia House of Representatives 1810–13; US representative 1817–21.

Terrell   **Texas**
Sanderson   2,358 sq. mi.

984   1,081   1,410   1,595   1,940   2,600   3,189

April 8, 1905. *Alexander Watkins Terrell (1827–1912).* District judge 1857–63; major to colonel, Confederate Army 1863–65; fled to Mexico after Civil War; served under Emperor Maximilian 1866; retuned to Texas 1866; Texas legislature 1875–82; US minister to Turkey 1893–97.

Terry   **Texas**
Brownfield   889 sq. mi.

12,651   12,761   13,218   14,581   14,118   16,286   13,107
August 21, 1876; organized July 5, 1904. *Benjamin Franklin Terry (1821–61)*. Delegate to Texas Secession Convention 1861; colonel, 8th Texas Cavalry; Battle of Bull Run 1861; killed in skirmish at Rowlett's Station, Kentucky, December 17, 1861.

Teton   **Idaho**
Driggs   449 sq. mi.
10,170   5,999   3,439   2,897   2,351   2,639   3,204
January 26, 1915. *Teton Mountains*. Three mountain peaks resembling female breasts; named *Les Trois Tetons* (The Three Breasts) by French trappers.

Teton   **Montana**
Choteau   2,272 sq. mi.
6,073   6,445   6,271   6,491   6,116   7,295   7,232
February 7, 1893. *Teton Peak*. Named for resemblance to female breast; this peak is not part of Teton Mountains Range (see Teton, Idaho).

Teton   **Wyoming**
Jackson   3,995 sq. mi.
21,294   18,251   11,172   9,355   4,823   3,062[a]   2,593[a]
February 15, 1921. *Teton Mountains*.* [(a) See note (a) at Park County, Wyoming.]

Texas   **Missouri**
Houston   1,177 sq. mi.
26,008   23,003   21,476   21,070   18,320   17,758   18,992
February 17, 1843, as Ashley; name changed February 14, 1845. *Republic of Texas*. From Tejas Indians whose greeting "Techas" was taken by early explorers as a tribal or regional name. Texas was popular in Missouri as a potential slave state.

Texas   **Oklahoma**
Guymon   2,041 sq. mi.
20,640   20,107   16,419   17,727   16,352   14,162   14,235
July 16, 1907. *State of Texas*. Named for proximity to Texas.

Thayer   **Nebraska**
Hebron   574 sq. mi.
5,228   6,055   6,635   7,582   7,779   9,118   10,563
January 26, 1856, as Jefferson; abolished 1867; recreated as Thayer, January 26, 1871; organized December 30, 1871. *John Milton Thayer (1820–1906)*. Brigadier general and major general, Nebraska Territorial Militia 1855–61; territorial senate 1860; Nebraska Constitutional Conventions 1860 and 1866; Union Army, colonel to major general of volunteers 1861–65; US senator 1867–71; governor of Wyoming Territory 1875–78; governor of Nebraska 1887–92.

Thomas   **Georgia**
Thomasville   545 sq. mi.
44,720   42,737   38,986   38,098   34,515   34,319   33,932
December 23, 1825. *Jett Thomas (1776–1817)*. Captain of artillery, War of 1812; major general, Georgia Militia; built state capitol at Milledgeville 1807.

Thomas   **Kansas**
Colby   1,075 sq. mi.
7,900   8,180   8,258   8,451   7,501   7,358   7,572
March 20, 1873; organized October 8, 1885. *George Henry Thomas (1816–70)*. Graduated West Point 1840; 2nd lieutenant to colonel 1840–61; native Virginian who remained in Union Army 1861; brigadier general and major general of volunteers 1861; commanded Army of the Tennessee 1862; brigadier general to major general, Regular Army 1863–64; drove Confederates from Tennessee at Battle of Nashville 1864; received Thanks of Congress 1865.

Thomas   **Nebraska**
Thedford   713 sq. mi.

647	729	851	973	954	1,078	1,206

March 31, 1887; organized October 7, 1887. *George Henry Thomas.**

Throckmorton   **Texas**
Throckmorton   913 sq. mi.

1,641	1,850	1,880	2,053	2,205	2,767	3,618

January 13, 1858; organized March 18, 1879. *William Edward Throckmorton (1795–1843)*. Physician; early settler in northern Texas; naming was compliment to his son, James Webb Throckmorton, governor of Texas and US senator.

Thurston   **Nebraska**
Pender   394 sq. mi.

6,940	7,171	6,936	7,186	6,942	7,237	8,590

March 7, 1855, as Blackbird; name changed and organized April 1, 1889. *John Mellen (also Mellon) Thurston (1847–1916)*. Omaha City Council 1872–74; Nebraska legislature 1875–77; attorney, Union Pacific Railroad 1877–88; US senator 1895–1901.

Thurston   **Washington**
Olympia   722 sq. mi.

252,264	207,355	161,238	124,264	76,894	55,049	44,884

January 12, 1852. *Samuel Royal Thurston (1816–51)*. Editor, *Iowa Gazette*; congressional delegate from Oregon Territory 1849–51; died at sea while returning from Washington, DC.

Tift   **Georgia**
Tifton   259 sq. mi.

40,118	38,407	34,998	32,862	27,288	23,487	22,645

August 17, 1905. *Nelson Tift (1810–77)*. Founder, city of Albany 1836; colonel, Baker County Militia 1840; Georgia House of Representatives, intermittently 1841–52; editor, *Albany Patriot* 1845–58; captain, Confederate Navy 1861–65; US representative 1868–69.

Tillamook   **Oregon**
Tillamook   1,103 sq. mi.

25,250	24,262	21,570	21,164	17,930	18,955	18,606

December 15, 1853. *Tillamook Indians*. From Salishan word believed to mean "land of many waters": name recorded as *Killamuch* by Lewis and Clark 1805.

Tillman   **Oklahoma**
Frederick   871 sq. mi.

7,992	9,287	10,384	12,398	12,901	14,654	17,598

July 16, 1907. *Benjamin Ryan Tillman (1847–1918)*. Governor of South Carolina 1890–94; founder of Clemson Agricultural and Mechanical College 1893; US senator 1895–1918. Tillman had no known connection with Oklahoma; name proposed by a South Carolinian member of the Oklahoma Constitutional Convention without consulting residents of the county.

Tioga   **New York**
Oswego   519 sq. mi.

51,125	51,784	52,337	49,812	46,513	37,802	30,166

February 16, 1791. *Tioga River*. From Iroquois word *tiagoa*, meaning "at the forks"; refers to a wedge of land at the confluence of Chemung and Susquehanna Rivers, an Indian meeting place.

Tioga   **Pennsylvania**
Wellsboro   1,134 sq. mi.

41,981	41,375	41,126	40,973	39,691	36,614	35,474

March 26, 1804; organized January 11, 1813. *Tioga River.**

Tippah   **Mississippi**
Ripley   458 sq. mi.
22,232   20,826   19,523   18,739   15,852   15,093   17,522
February 9, 1836. *Tippah Creek.* From Choctaw *bok tapa*, meaning "separated creek"; refers to the four branches of the creek.

Tippecanoe   **Indiana**
Lafayette   500 sq. mi.
172,780   148,955   130,598   121,702   109,378   89,122   74,473
January 20, 1826; effective March 1, 1826. *Uncertain.* (1) *Tippecanoe River*; uncertain origin of name; may be corruption of Potawatomie *ketapekonnong*, meaning "town" or "place." (2) *Battle of Tippecanoe*; fought near confluence of Tippecanoe and Wabash Rivers, November 7, 1811; General Harrison defeated Shawnees led by the Prophet.

Tipton   **Indiana**
Tipton   261 sq. mi.
15,936   16,577   16,119   16,819   16,650   15,856   15,566
January 15, 1844; effective May 1, 1844. *John Tipton (1786–1839).* Private, Indiana Militia 1807; promoted to captain during Battle of Tippecanoe 1811; Indiana House of Representatives 1819–23; commissioner to determine Indiana-Illinois boundary 1821; US senator 1832–39.

Tipton   **Tennessee**
Covington   458 sq. mi.
61,081   51,271   37,568   32,930   28,001   28,564   29,782
October 29, 1823. *Jacob Tipton (?–1791).* Captain of Tennessee company under General St. Clair fighting Indians on northwest frontier; killed in combat near Fort Wayne.

Tishomingo   **Mississippi**
Iuka   424 sq. mi.
19,593   19,163   17,683   18,434   14,940   13,889   15,544
February 9, 1836. *Tishomingo (1734–1838).* Chickasaw chief; served with General Wayne against Shawnees and with General Jackson during War of 1812; personally acquainted with Presidents Washington, Jefferson, Monroe, and Jackson; ceded Chickasaw lands east of Mississippi River 1832; forced to move to Indian Territory (Oklahoma) 1837; died on Trail of Tears near Little Rock.

Titus   **Texas**
Mount Pleasant   406 sq. mi.
32,334   28,118   24,009   21,442   16,702   16,785   17,302
May 11, 1846; organized July 13, 1846. *Andrew Jackson Titus (1814–55).* Texas legislature 1851–52; worked for annexation of Texas to US.

Todd   **Kentucky**
Elkton   375 sq. mi.
12,460   11,971   10,940   11,874   10,823   11,364   12,890
December 30, 1819. *John Todd (1750–82).* Lord Dunmore's War 1774; Virginia legislature 1777; acquired huge tracts of land in Kentucky and Tennessee; killed at Battle of Blue Licks, Kentucky, August 19, 1782.

Todd   **Minnesota**
Long Prairie   945 sq. mi.
24,895   24,426   23,363   24,991   22,114   23,119   25,420
February 20, 1855; organized March 1, 1856. *John Blair Smith Todd (1814–72).* Graduated West Point 1837; Seminole Wars 1837–42; Mexican War 1846–47; commander, Fort Riley, Minnesota Territory 1849–56; brigadier general of volunteers 1861–62; congressional delegate from Dakota Territory 1861–65; Dakota Territory legislature, speaker 1866–67.

Todd   **South Dakota**
(Unorganized)   1,389 sq. mi.

| 9,612 | 9,050 | 8,352 | 7,328 | 6,606 | 4,661 | 4,758 |

March 9, 1909; attached to Tripp County. *John Blair Smith Todd.**

Tolland   **Connecticut**
Rockville   410 sq. mi.

| 152,691 | 136,364 | 128,699 | 114,283 | 103,440 | 68,737 | 44,709 |

1785. *Town of Tolland*. Named for Tolland, Somersetshire, England; ancestral home of Governor Roger Wolcott, chief patentee of Tolland Township.

Tom Green   **Texas**
San Angelo   1,522 sq. mi.

| 110,224 | 104,010 | 98,458 | 84,784 | 71,047 | 64,630 | 58,929 |

March 13, 1874; organized January 5, 1875. *Thomas Green (1814–64)*. Private to major, Texas Army 1836; Battle of San Jacinto 1836; Republic of Texas legislature 1839; Texas Rangers 1846; colonel to brigadier general, Confederate Army 1861–63; killed at Battle of Blair's Landing, April 12, 1864.

Tompkins   **New York**
Ithaca   475 sq. mi.

| 101,564 | 96,501 | 94,097 | 87,085 | 76,879 | 66,164 | 59,122 |

April 7, 1817. *Daniel D. Tompkins (1774–1825)*. New York Constitutional Conventions 1801 and 1821; justice, New York Supreme Court 1804–07; governor of New York 1807–17; US vice president 1817–25.

Tooele   **Utah**
Tooele   6,941 sq. mi.

| 58,218 | 40,735 | 26,601 | 26,033 | 21,545 | 17,868 | 14,636 |

January 31, 1850. *Tooele Valley*. Origin of name is uncertain: (1) May be of Aztec origin, possibly for a chief; derived from "black bear" or "bear"; (2) descriptive of bulrushes or "tules" growing in the region.

Toole   **Montana**
Shelby   1,916 sq. mi.

| 5,324 | 5,267 | 5,046 | 5,559 | 5,839 | 7,904 | 6,867 |

May 7, 1914. *Joseph Kemp Toole (1851–1929)*. Montana Territory legislature 1879–81; president, Montana territorial council 1881–83; Montana Constitutional Conventions 1884 and 1889; congressional delegate 1885–89; governor of Montana 1889–93 and 1901–08.

Toombs   **Georgia**
Lyons   364 sq. mi.

| 27,223 | 20,067 | 24,072 | 22,592 | 19,151 | 16,837 | 17,382 |

August 18, 1905. *Robert Augustus Toombs (1810–85)*. Captain under General Scott in Creek War 1836; Georgia House of Representatives 1837–40 and 1841–44; US representative 1845–53; US senator 1853–61; Confederate secretary of state 1861; brigadier general in Confederate Army 1861–63.

Torrance   **New Mexico**
Estancia   3,345 sq. mi.

| 16,383 | 16,911 | 10,285 | 7,491 | 5,290 | 6,497 | 8,012 |

March 16, 1903. *Francis J. Torrance (?–?)*. Railroad developer; established New Mexico Central Railroad linking town of Torrance to transcontinental railroads.

Towner   **North Dakota**
Cando   1,025 sq. mi.

| 2,246 | 2,876 | 3,627 | 4,052 | 4,645 | 5,624 | 6,360 |

March 8, 1883; organized January 24, 1884. *Oscar M. Towner (1842–97)*. Some dispute as to whether or not Towner graduated from West Point and served in Confederate Army. It is known he was a cattleman and real estate promoter who served in Dakota territorial legislature at the time the county was created.

Towns   **Georgia**
Hiawassee   167 sq. mi.

10,471	9,319	6,754	5,638	4,565	4,538	4,803

March 6, 1856. *George Washington Bonaparte Towns (1801–54)*. Georgia House of Representatives 1829–30; Georgia Senate 1832–34; US representative 1835–39 and 1846–47; governor of Georgia 1847–51.

Traill   **North Dakota**
Hillsboro   862 sq. mi.

8,121	8,477	8,752	9,624	9,571	10,583	11,359

January 12, 1875. *Walter S. Traill (1847–1933)*. Clerk for Hudson's Bay Company 1866–75; supervised liquidation of Hudson's Bay Company in Red River region 1875; built trading post on Red River at Frog Point.

Transylvania   **North Carolina**
Brevard   379 sq. mi.

33,090	29,334	25,520	23,417	19,713	16,372	15,194

February 15, 1861. *Descriptive*. Derived from Latin *trans*, meaning "across," and *sylvan*, meaning "wooded" or "forested"; general name applied to area west of Appalachian Mountains.

Traverse   **Minnesota**
Wheaton   574 sq. mi.

3,558	4,134	4,463	5,542	6,254	7,503	8,053

February 20, 1862; organized February 14, 1881. *Lake Traverse*. Uncertain origin. (1) French translation of Dakota name into *Lac Travers*, meaning "crossways," referring to northeast-southwest orientation of the lake in relation to northwest-southeast orientation of Big Stone Lake and Lac qui Parle. (2) In early days of settlement, the Minnesota River would reverse direction during high floods, flowing northward into Lake Traverse and the drainage of the Red River of the North rather than its normal flow southward to the Mississippi River.

Travis   **Texas**
Austin   990 sq. mi.

1,024,266	812,280	576,407	419,573	295,516	212,136	160,980

January 25, 1840; organized April 8, 1843. *William Barret Travis (1809–36)*. Major and lieutenant colonel of artillery, Texas Army 1835; led expedition against Mexican fort at Anahuac 1835; commanded Texas garrison at the Alamo, March 6, 1836.

Treasure   **Montana**
Hysham   977 sq. mi.

718	861	874	981	1,069	1,345	1,402

February 7, 1919. *Promotional name*. Has had little effect in attracting settlers.

Trego   **Kansas**
WaKeeney   889 sq. mi.

3,001	3,319	3,694	4,165	4,436	5,473	5,868

February 26, 1867; organized June 21, 1879. *Edward P. Trego (?–1863)*. Captain, Company H, 8th Kansas Volunteer Infantry; killed at Chickamauga, September 19, 1863.

Trempealeau   **Wisconsin**
Whitehall   733 sq. mi.

28,816	27,010	25,263	26,158	23,344	23,377	23,730

January 27, 1854; organized January 1, 1855. *Trempealeau River*. Dakota name for river meaning "river soaked in water" was translated by French trappers into *la montagne qui trempe a l'eau*.

Treutlen   **Georgia**
Soperton   199 sq. mi.

6,885	6,854	5,994	6,087	5,647	5,874	6,522

August 21, 1917. *John Adam Treutlen (1726–83)*. Georgia Commons; Georgia Provincial Congress 1775; governor of Georgia 1777–78.

Trigg   **Kentucky**
Cadiz   441 sq. mi.
14,339   12,597   10,361   9,384   8,620   8,870   9,683
January 27, 1820. *Stephen Trigg (1742–82)*. Virginia legislature; trustee, Transylvania University; colonel of militia 1781; killed at Battle of Blue Licks, August 17, 1782.

Trimble   **Kentucky**
Bedford   152 sq. mi.
8,809   8,125   6,090   6,253   5,349   5,102   5,148
February 9, 1837. *Robert Trimble (1777–1828)*. Kentucky legislature 1803; judge, Court of Appeals 1808; chief justice of Kentucky 1810; US district judge 1816–26; US Supreme Court 1826–28.

Trinity   **California**
Weaverville   3,179 sq. mi.
13,786   13,022   13,063   11,858   7,615   9,706   5,087
February 18, 1850. *Trinity River*. Named in mistaken belief that the river flowed into Trinidad Bay on Pacific Ocean. Spanish *Trinidad* refers to the Holy Trinity of the Christian faith.

Trinity   **Texas**
Groveton   694 sq. mi.
14,585   13,779   11,445   9,450   7,628   7,539   10,040
February 11, 1850. *Trinity River*. Flows into Trinity Bay, an arm of Galveston Bay. Name from Spanish *Trinidad* which refers to the Holy Trinity of the Christian faith.

Tripp   **South Dakota**
Winner   1,612 sq. mi.
5,644   6,430   6,924   7,268   8,171   8,761   9,139
January 8, 1873; organized June 15, 1909. *Bartlett Tripp (1842–1911)*. President, South Dakota Constitutional Convention 1883; chief justice of Dakota Territory 1886–89; US minister to Austria-Hungary 1893–97.

Troup   **Georgia**
La Grange   414 sq. mi.
67,044   58,779   55,536   50,003   44,466   47,189   49,841
December 11, 1826. *George Michael Troup (1780–1856)*. Georgia House of Representatives 1803–05; US representative 1807–15; US senator 1816–18 and 1829–33; governor of Georgia 1823–27.

Trousdale   **Tennessee**
Hartsville   114 sq. mi.
7,870   7,259   5,920   6,137   5,155   4,914   5,520
September 5, 1870. *William Trousdale (1790–1872)*. Creek War 1813; lieutenant under General Jackson at New Orleans 1815; Tennessee legislature 1835; major general of volunteers in Seminole War 1836; colonel, Mexican War, wounded at Chapultepec 1847; governor of Tennessee 1849–51; US minister to Brazil 1852–57.

Trumbull   **Ohio**
Warren   618 sq. mi.
210,312   225,116   227,813   241,863   232,579   208,526   158,915
July 10, 1800. *Jonathon Trumbull (1740–1809)*. Connecticut legislature, intermittently 1774–88; paymaster, Continental Army 1776–80; secretary and aide-de-camp to General Washington 1780–83; US representative 1789–95, speaker 1791–93; US senator 1795–96; lieutenant governor 1796–97; governor of Connecticut 1797–1809; ceded Connecticut's Western Reserve lands in northeastern Ohio to US 1800.

Tucker   **West Virginia**
Parsons   419 sq. mi.
7,141   7,321   7,728   8,675   7,447   7,750   10,600

March 7, 1856. *Henry Saint George Tucker (1780–1848)*. Cavalry captain, War of 1812; US representative from Virginia 1815–19; chancellor of 4th Judicial District of Virginia 1824–31; president, Virginia Court of Appeals 1831–41; professor of law, University of Virginia 1841–45.

Tulare   **California**
Visalia   4,824 sq. mi.
442,179   368,021   311,921   245,738   188,322   168,403   149,264
April 20, 1852. *Tule marshlands*. From Aztec *tullin* (bulrushes) to Spanish *tule*. Descriptive of vast marshlands in southern San Joaquin Valley.

Tulsa   **Oklahoma**
Tulsa   570 sq. mi.
603,403   563,299   503,341   470,593   401,663   346,038   251,686
July 16, 1907. *City of Tulsa*. Name from "Tulsey Town" or "Tullahassee," a village in Alabama that had been the Creek's home before being removed to Indian Territory (Oklahoma) 1836.

Tunica   **Mississippi**
Tunica   455 sq. mi.
10,778   9,227   8,164   9,652   11,854   16,826   21,664
February 9, 1836. *Tunica Indians*. A small tribe living near the junction of the Yazoo and Mississippi Rivers. From Indian word for "the people."

Tuolumne   **California**
Sonora   2,221 sq. mi.
55,365   54,501   48,456   33,928   22,169   14,404   12,584
February 18, 1850. *Tuolumne Indians*. Corruption of Indian word *talmalamne* meaning "a cluster of stone wigwams" which refers to stone caves that some Indians lived in. The suffix *umne* is Miwok and Yokuts for "people."

Turner   **Georgia**
Ashburn   285 sq. mi.
8,930   9,504   8,703   9,510   8,790   8,439   10,479
August 18, 1905; effective January 1, 1906. *Henry Gray Turner (1839–1904)*. From private to captain in Confederate Army 1861–65; wounded at Gettysburg 1863; Georgia House of Representatives 1874–79; US representative 1881–97; justice, Georgia Supreme Court 1903.

Turner   **South Dakota**
Parker   617 sq. mi.
8,347   8,849   8,576   9,255   9,872   11,159   12,100
January 13, 1871. *John W. Turner (1800–83)*. Michigan General Assemble 1851; Dakota Territory legislature 1865–66 and 1872; superintendent of public instruction 1870–71.

Tuscaloosa   **Alabama**
Tuscaloosa   1,322 sq. mi.
194,656   164,875   150,522   137,541   116,029   109,047   94,092
February 6, 1818. *Tuscaloosa*. Choctaw name for their chiefs, meaning "black warrior," or may have been a particular chief.

Tuscarawas   **Ohio**
New Philadelphia   568 sq. mi.
92,582   90,914   84,090   84,614   77,211   76,789   70,320
February 13, 1808. *Tuscarawas River*. From Tuscarowa Indians; members of Iroquois Confederacy.

Tuscola   **Michigan**
Caro   803 sq. mi.
55,729   58,266   55,498   56,961   48,603   43,305   38,258

April 1, 1840; organized March 2, 1850. *Coined word.* Created from Indian words *dusinagon*, meaning "level," and *cola*, meaning "land." (See Schoolcraft, Michigan.)

Twiggs **Georgia**
Jeffersonville 358 sq. mi.
9,023 10,590 9,806 9,354 8,222 7,935 8,308
December 14, 1809. *John Twiggs (1750–1816).* Lieutenant to major general, in Georgia Militia 1774–91; Georgia Senate 1779–82; negotiated treaties with Creeks 1783.

Twin Falls **Idaho**
Twin Falls 1,921 sq. mi.
77,230 64,284 53,580 52,927 41,807 41,842 40,979
February 21, 1907. *Twin Falls of the Snake River.* The river is divided by a large rock formation that splits the falls.

Tyler **Texas**
Woodville 925 sq. mi.
21,766 20,871 16,646 16,223 12,417 10,666 11,292
April 3, 1846; organized July 13, 1846. *John Tyler (1790–1862).* Virginia House of Delegates 1811–16 and 1823–25; US representative 1823–25; governor of Virginia 1825–27; US senator 1827–36; US vice president 1841; 10th president of US 1841–45; Confederate Provisional Congress 1861.

Tyler **West Virginia**
Middlebourne 256 sq. mi.
9,208 9,592 9,796 11,320 9,929 10,026 10,535
December 6, 1814. *John Tyler (1747–1813).* Virginia House of Delegates 1777–85, speaker 1781–85; Virginia General Court 1789–1808; governor of Virginia 1808–11. Father of President John Tyler.*

Tyrrell **North Carolina**
Columbia 389 sq. mi.
4,407 4,149 3,856 3,975 3,806 4,520 5,048
1729. *John Tyrrell (1685–1729).* One of eight lords proprietor of Carolina; purchased proprietorship 1725.

U

Uinta **Wyoming**
Evanston 2,081 sq. mi.
21,118 19,742 18,705 13,021 7,100 7,484 7,331
December 1, 1869. *Uncertain.* (1) *Uinta Indians*; subtribe of Utes; dislocated by Mormon settlers. (2) *Uintah Mountains*; in Utah, immediately south of Wyoming; named for Uinta Utes (see Utah, Utah).

Uintah **Utah**
Vernal 4,480 sq. mi.
32,588 25,224 22,211 20,506 12,684 11,582 10,300
February 18, 1880. *Uinta Indians.**

Ulster **New York**
Kingston 1,124 sq. mi.
182,493 177,749 165,304 158,158 141,241 118,804 92,621
November 1, 1683. *James II.* Named Earl of Ulster for his Irish lands 1672 (see Albany, New York).

Umatilla **Oregon**
Pendleton 3,216 sq. mi.
75,889 70,548 59,249 58,861 44,923 44,352 41,703
September 27, 1862. *Umatilla River.* Named for Umatilla Indians, a group of tribes encountered by Lewis and Clark 1805.

Unicoi **Tennessee**
Erwin 186 sq. mi.
18,313 17,667 16,549 16,362 15,254 15,082 15,886
March 23, 1875. *Unicoi Mountains*. From Cherokee word *unega* meaning "white"; refers to low clouds and fog that frequently cover the mountains.

Union **Arkansas**
El Dorado 1,039 sq. mi.
41,639 45,629 46,719 48,573 45,428 49,518 49,686
November 2, 1829. *The United States*.

Union **Florida**
Lake Butler 244 sq. mi.
15,535 13,442 10,252 10,166 8,112 6,043 8,906
May 20, 1921. *Unity*. Named for unity of opinion that Bradford County should be split to form a new county.

Union **Georgia**
Blairsville 322 sq. mi.
21,356 17,289 11,993 9,390 6,811 6,510 7,318
December 3, 1832. *The United States*. Named to show local opposition to secession movement over Nullification issue.

Union **Illinois**
Jonesboro 413 sq. mi.
17,800 18,293 17,619 17,765 16,071 17,645 20,500
January 2, 1818. *Uncertain*. (1) Two rival denominations, Baptist and Dunker (German Baptist), held a joint revival locally known as the "union meeting" shortly before the county was formed. (2) The county was created the same year Illinois was admitted to the Union.

Union **Indiana**
Liberty 161 sq. mi.
7,516 7,349 6,976 6,860 6,582 6,457 6,412
January 5, 1821; effective February 1, 1821. *Uncertain*. (1) *The United States*. (2) *Town of Union*. (3) New county consisted of union of land from three counties. (4) Futile attempt to avoid a dispute over location of county seat.

Union **Iowa**
Creston 424 sq. mi.
12,534 12,309 12,750 13,858 13,557 13,712 15,651
January 15, 1851; organized January 12, 1853; effective May 1, 1853. *The Union*. Named for hopes to preserve the Union following Compromise of 1850.

Union **Kentucky**
Morganfield 343 sq. mi.
15,007 15,637 16,557 17,821 15,882 14,537 14,893
January 15, 1811. *The Union*. Named for desire to preserve the national union over sectional differences about issues leading to the War of 1812.

Union **Louisiana**
Farmerville 877 sq. mi.
22,721 22,803 20,690 21,167 18,447 17,624 19,141
May 13, 1839. *Uncertain*. (1) *The United States*. (2) Daniel Webster's oration "Liberty and Union, now and forever, one and inseparable," was popular in Louisiana at the time the parish was created.

Union **Mississippi**
New Albany 416 sq. mi.

27,134   25,362   22,085   21,741   19,096   18,904   20,262
July 7, 1870. *The United States.*

Union   **New Jersey**
Elizabeth   103 sq. mi.
536,499   522,541   493,819   504,094   543,116   504,255   398,138
March 19, 1857. *Uncertain.* (1) *Town of Union.* (2) Preservation of the Union in face of approaching Civil War. (3) United efforts of communities in establishing the new county.

Union   **New Mexico**
Clayton   3,824 sq. mi.
4,549   4,174   4,124   4,725   4,925   6,068   7,372
February 23, 1893. United opinion for creating county.

Union   **North Carolina**
Monroe   632 sq. mi.
201,292   123,677   84,211   70,380   54,714   44,670   42,034
December 19, 1842. *Uncertain.* (1) *American federal union.* (2) Compromise name instead of Clay or Jackson which were being advocated by Whigs and Democrats, respectively.

Union   **Ohio**
Marysville   432 sq. mi.
52,300   40,909   31,969   29,536   23,786   22,853   20,687
January 10, 1820. County was created from a union of territory from four counties.

Union   **Oregon**
La Grande   2,037 sq. mi.
25,748   24,530   23,598   23,921   19,377   18,180   17,962
October 14, 1864. *Town of Union.* Named for Union sentiment during Civil War.

Union   **Pennsylvania**
Lewisburg   316 sq. mi.
44,947   41,624   36,176   32,870   28,603   25,646   23,150
March 22, 1813. *The United States.*

Union   **South Carolina**
Union   514 sq. mi.
28,961   29,881   30,337   30,751   29,230   30,015   31,334
March 12, 1785; converted to judicial district January 1, 1800; redesignated as county April 16, 1868. *Union Church.* Unified congregation of Protestant denominations.

Union   **South Dakota**
Elk Point   461 sq. mi.
14,399   12,584   10,189   10,938   9,643   10,197   10,792
April 10, 1862, as Cole; name changed 1864. *Support for the Union in Civil War.*

Union   **Tennessee**
Maynardville   224 sq. mi.
19,109   17,808   13,694   11,707   9,072   8,498   8,670
January 3, 1850; organized February 6, 1854. *Uncertain.* (1) *The Union;* named out of concern for the federal union because of sectional differences leading to the Compromise of 1850. (2) County was created from a union of lands from five counties.

Upshur   **Texas**
Gilmer   583 sq. mi.
39,309   35,291   31,370   28,595   20,976   19,793   20,822

April 27, 1846; organized July 13, 1846. *Abel Parker Upshur (1791–1844)*. Virginia legislature 1825; judge, Virginia courts 1826–41; US secretary of navy 1841–43; US secretary of state 1843–44; killed by explosion of gun being demonstrated on USS *Princeton* in presence of President Tyler, February 28, 1844 (see Gilmer, West Virginia).

Upshur   **West Virginia**
Buckhannon   355 sq. mi.

| 24,254 | 23,404 | 22,867 | 23,427 | 19,092 | 18,292 | 19,242 |

March 25, 1851. *Abel Parker Upshur.**

Upson   **Georgia**
Thomaston   323 sq. mi.

| 27,153 | 27,597 | 26,300 | 25,998 | 23,505 | 23,800 | 25,078 |

December 15, 1824. *Stephen Upson (1784–1824)*. Trustee, University of Georgia; Georgia legislature 1820–24.

Upton   **Texas**
Rankin   1,241 sq. mi.

| 3,355 | 3,404 | 4,447 | 4,619 | 4,697 | 6,239 | 5,307 |

February 26, 1887; organized 1910. *Upton brothers*. Confederate officers. (1) *John Cunningham Upton (1828–62)*; lieutenant colonel, Hood's Texas Brigade; killed at 2nd Bull Run, August 30, 1862. (2) *William Felton Upton (1832–87)*; captain to lieutenant colonel 1861–65; Texas legislature 1866 and 1879–85.

Utah   **Utah**
Provo   2,003 sq. mi.

| 516,564 | 368,536 | 263,590 | 218,106 | 137,776 | 106,991 | 81,912 |

January 31, 1850. *Ute Indians*. From Apache and Navajo word for "hill dwellers"; Shoshone tribes of hunters and gatherers; tribal name written as "Yutta" by Spanish; current spelling is from Fremont 1844.

Uvalde   **Texas**
Uvalde   1,552 sq. mi.

| 26,405 | 25,926 | 23,340 | 22,441 | 17,348 | 16,814 | 16,015 |

February 8, 1850; organized April 21, 1856. *Uvalde Canyon*. Named for Juan de Ugalde (1729–1816); Spanish military officer; served in Europe and Peru; fought Apaches in Texas 1779–89.

V

Valdez-Cordova   **Alaska**
(Census Area)   34,240 sq. mi.

| 9,636 | 10,195 | 9,952 | 8,348 | 4,955[a] | 4,603[a] | (b) |

"Valdez" from *Port of Valdez*; named for Spanish naval officer Antonio Valdés y Basan; sponsored survey of Alaska's coast 1791. "Cordova" from *Town of Cordova*; named for Puerto Cordova (now Orca Bay); named by Spanish explorer Salvador Fidalgo in honor of Viceroy of New Spain (Mexico) Antonio Villacis y Cordova 1790. [(a) Includes Valdez-Chitina-Whittier Census Area. (b) Part of 3rd Judicial Division.]

Valencia   **New Mexico**
Los Lunas   1,066 sq. mi.

| 76,569 | 66,152 | 45,235 | 61,115 | 40,539 | 39,085 | 22,481 |

January 9, 1852. *Village of Valencia*. Named for several generations of Valencia families dating from the early 17th century. Prominent candidates for village name are (1) Francisco de Valencia (1607–84), Spanish lieutenant general in Rio Abajo area of New Mexico; (2) Juan de Valencia (?–?) whose hacienda became the site of Valencia village.

Valley   **Idaho**
Cascade   3,665 sq. mi.

| 9,862 | 7,651 | 6,109 | 5,604 | 3,609 | 3,663 | 4,270 |

February 26, 1917. *Long Valley*. Named for its length of 50 miles.

Valley   **Montana**
Glasgow   4,925 sq. mi.

7,369	7,675	8,239	10,250	11,471	17,080	11,353

February 6, 1893. *Milk River and Missouri River Valleys.*

Valley   **Nebraska**
Ord   568 sq. mi.

4,260	4,647	5,169	5,633	5,783	6,590	7,252

March 1, 1871; organized June 23, 1873. *Descriptive.* Refers to valleys and bottomlands in the area.

Val Verde   **Texas**
Del Rio   3,145 sq. mi.

48,879	44,856	38,721	35,910	27,471	24,461	16,635

February 20, 1885; organized May 2, 1885. *Battle of Val Verde.* Civil War battle in New Mexico Territory, February 21, 1862; secured the Far West for the Union. Spanish for "green valley."

Van Buren   **Arkansas**
Clinton   708 sq. mi.

17,295	16,192	14,008	13,357	8,275	7,228	9,687

November 11, 1833. *Martin Van Buren (1782–1862).* New York Senate 1813–20; attorney general of New York 1815–19; New York Constitutional Convention 1821; US senator 1828–29; US secretary of state 1829–31; US vice president 1833–37; 8th president of US 1837–1841.

Van Buren   **Iowa**
Keosauqua   485 sq. mi.

7,750	7,809	7,676	8,626	8,643	9,778	11,007

December 7, 1836. *Martin Van Buren.**

Van Buren   **Michigan**
Paw Paw   607 sq. mi.

76,258	76,263	70,060	66,814	56,173	48,395	39,184

October 29, 1829; organized April 3, 1837. *Martin Van Buren.** Michigan Territory named seven counties after members of Jackson's first cabinet in hopes of promoting statehood.

Van Buren   **Tennessee**
Spencer   273 sq. mi.

5,548	5,508	4,846	4,728	3,758	3,671	3,985

January 3, 1840. *Martin Van Buren.**

Vance   **North Carolina**
Henderson   254 sq. mi.

45,422	42,954	38,892	36,748	32,691	32,002	32,101

March 5, 1881. *Zebulon Baird Vance (1830–94).* North Carolina House of Commons 1854; US representative 1858–61; captain to colonel, Confederate Army 1861; governor of North Carolina 1862–65 and 1877–79, removed from office and imprisoned for Confederate activities 1865; elected to US Senate but denied seat 1870; US senator 1879–94.

Vanderburgh   **Indiana**
Evansville   233 sq. mi.

179,703	171,922	165,058	167,515	168,772	165,794	160,422

January 7, 1818. *Henry Vanderburgh (1760–1812).* Lieutenant to captain, Continental Army 1776; Northwest Territory legislative council; judge, Indiana Territory 1800–12.

Van Wert   **Ohio**
Van Wert   409 sq. mi.

28,744	29,659	30,464	30,458	29,194	28,840	26,971

February 12, 1820; organized March 18, 1837. *Isaac Van Wert (c1758–1828)*. One of three captors of British spy Major André 1780 (see Paulding, Georgia).

Van Zandt   **Texas**
Canton   843 sq. mi.
52,579   48,140   37,944   31,426   22,155   19,091   22,593
March 20, 1848. *Isaac Van Zandt (1813–47)*. Texas House of Representatives 1840–42; Republic of Texas charge d'affaires to US 1842; Texas Constitutional Convention 1842; died of yellow fever while campaigning for governor.

Venango   **Pennsylvania**
Franklin   674 sq. mi.
54,984   57,565   59,381   63,444   62,353   65,295   65,328
March 12, 1800; organized April 1, 1805. *Village of Venango*. Lenape village at the mouth of Venango River (now French Creek) at Allegheny River; from Lenape word for "otter" or, more colorfully, describing a specific "rude sculpture" on a tree near the river.

Ventura   **California**
Ventura   1,843 sq. mi.
823,318   753,197   669,016   529,174   376,430   199,138   114,647
March 22, 1872. *City of Ventura*. Named for Mission San Buenaventura (Spanish for "good fortune") which was named for St. Bonaventure (1221–74); member of Friars Minor (Franciscans) 1238; minister general 1257–74; declined bishopric 1265; compelled to become cardinal-bishop 1273; led reconciliation with Greek Church; canonized 1482.

Vermilion   **Illinois**
Danville   898 sq. mi.
81,625   83,919   88,257   95,222   97,047   96,176   87,079
January 18, 1826. *Vermilion River*. From French *vermeil* meaning "bright red"; named for reddish-orange color of river from red soils along the river. Tributary of Wabash River.

Vermilion   **Louisiana**
Abbeville   1,173 sq. mi.
57,999   53,807   50,055   48,458   43,071   38,855   36,929
March 25, 1844. *Vermilion River and Bay*. From French *vermeil* meaning "bright red"; descriptive of red color of water from river bluffs.

Vermillion   **Indiana**
Newport   257 sq. mi.
16,212   16,788   16,773   18,229   16,793   17,683   19,723
January 2, 1824; effective February 1, 1824. *Vermilion River, Illinois*.* (Second letter *l* is alternative spelling.)

Vernon   **Louisiana**
Leesville   1,328 sq. mi.
52,334   52,531   61,961   53,475   53,794   18,301   18,874
March 30, 1871. *Uncertain*. (1) *Mount Vernon*; home of George Washington (see Vernon, Wisconsin). More colorful possibilities include: (2) a popular teacher whose name was chosen as a compromise; (3) a local race horse; (4) a mule named Vernon that happened to wander by during a whiskey-inspired gathering discussing names for the parish.

Vernon   **Missouri**
Nevada   826 sq. mi.
21,159   20,454   19,041   19,806   19,065   20,540   22,685
February 27, 1855. *Miles Vernon (1786–1866)* War of 1812; Battle of New Orleans 1815; Tennessee legislature; Missouri Senate 1850–61; favored Missouri secession 1861.

Vernon   **Wisconsin**
Viroqua   792 sq. mi.

29,773   28,056   25,617   25,642   24,557   25,663   27,906

March 1, 1851, as Bad Axe; name changed March 22, 1862. *Mount Vernon*. Home of George Washington; named for British Admiral Edward Vernon, commanding officer of Washington's half-brother, Lawrence Washington.

Victoria   **Texas**
Victoria   882 sq. mi.
86,793   84,088   74,361   68,807   53,766   46,475   31,241

March 17, 1836; organized 1837. *Mexican Municipality of Victoria*. Named for Guadalupe Victoria (1786–1843); born Juan Manuel Felix Fernandez; changed name to "Guadalupe" to honor Mexico's patron saint and later to "Victoria" for hoped-for victory of Mexico over Spain; first president of Mexico 1825–29.

Vigo   **Indiana**
Terre Haute   403 sq. mi.
107,848   105,848   106,107   112,385   114,528   108,458   105,160

January 15, 1818. *Joseph María Francesco Vigo (1747–1836)*. Sardinian private in Spanish Army in New Orleans; fur trader 1772; merchant in Vincennes, provided supplies to George Rogers Clark; joined Clark in capture of British garrison at Vincennes 1779.

Vilas   **Wisconsin**
Eagle River   857 sq. mi.
21,430   21,033   17,707   16,535   10,958   9,332   9,363

April 12, 1893. *William Freeman Vilas (1840–1908)*. From captain to colonel, 23rd Wisconsin Volunteer Infantry 1861–65; law professor, University of Wisconsin 1868–85 and 1889–92, regent 1880–85 and 1898–1905; US postmaster general 1885–88; US secretary of interior 1888–89; US senator 1891–97.

Vinton   **Ohio**
McArthur   412 sq. mi.
13,435   12,806   11,098   11,584   9,420   10,274   10,759

March 23, 1850. *Samuel Finley Vinton (1792–1862)*. US representative from Ohio 1823–37 and 1843–51; president, Toledo & Cleveland Railroad 1853–54.

Virginia Beach   **Virginia**
(Independent City)   549 sq. mi.
437,994   425,257   393,069   262,199   172,106   84,215[a]   42,277[b]

May 16, 1691, as Princess Anne; city of Virginia Beach incorporated 1952; Princess Anne County annexed by Virginia Beach January 1, 1963. *Descriptive*. Refers to location on Atlantic Ocean. [(a) Includes Princess Anne County (76,124); (b) Princess Anne County.]

Volusia   **Florida**
DeLand   1,101 sq. mi.
494,593   443,343   370,712   258,762   169,487   125,319   74,229

December 29, 1854. *Volusia Landing*. Settlement on St. Johns River. Uncertain origin of name: (1) early settler named Volus; (2) Belgian or Frenchman named Veluche; (3) nearby plantation named Volusia.

W

Wabash   **Illinois**
Mount Carmel   223 sq. mi.
11,947   12,937   13,111   13,713   12,841   14,047   14,651

December 27, 1824. *Wabash River*. Uncertain origin of name. (1) French renderings *oubadhei* or *ouabachi* of Indian *wahbahshikki* meaning "pure white" or "white stone river"; (2) Miami *wabashkisibi* meaning "bog river."

Wabash   **Indiana**
Wabash   412 sq. mi.

32,888   34,960   35,069   36,640   35,553   32,605   29,047
February 2, 1832; organized January 22, 1835; effective March 1, 1835. *Wabash River.**

Wabasha   **Minnesota**
Wabasha   523 sq. mi.
21,676   21,610   19,744   19,335   17,224   17,007   16,878
October 27, 1849; organized March 5, 1853. *Town of Wabasha.* Named for hereditary line of Dakota chiefs named Wapasha, a title bestowed by French explorers meaning "red leaf" from oak trees in the area.

Wabaunsee   **Kansas**
Alma   794 sq. mi.
7,053   6,885   6,603   6,867   6,397   6,648   7,212
August 25, 1855, as Richardson; organized and name changed February 11, 1859. *Wabaunsee (?–?).* Potawatomie chief; led massacre of US troops at Fort Dearborn 1812; allied with Illinois Militia during Black Hawk War 1832; granted land in Illinois, later moved to Iowa. Translation of "Wabaunsee" is given as "dawn of day" or "foggy," supposedly related to conditions at the time of his more famous warrior exploits.

Wade Hampton   **Alaska**
(Census Area)   17,081 sq. mi.
7,459   7,028   5,791   4,665   3,917   3,128   (a)
Uncertain. (1) *Wade Hampton* (see Hampton, South Carolina); Hampton's son-in-law, John Randolph Tucker, judge of Alaska's 2nd Judicial Division, created a new recorder's district from Kuskokwim District and named it after his father-in-law 1913. (2) *Frederick Coate Wade (1860–1924) and Wade Hampton*; junior councilor and judge at 1903 Alaska Tribunal. Original spelling was "Wade-Hampton" with the hyphen suggesting separate components of the name. [(a) Part of 2nd Judicial Division.]

Wadena   **Minnesota**
Wadena   536 sq. mi.
13,843   13,713   13,154   14,192   12,412   12,199   12,806
June 11, 1858; organized February 17, 1881. *Wadena Trading Post.* Chippewa for "village" or "little round hill." Trading post was on the Crow Wing River on the road from Crow Wing to Otter Tail City and Pembina; abandoned 1899.

Wagoner   **Oklahoma**
Wagoner   562 sq. mi.
73,085   57,491   47,883   41,801   22,163   15,673   16,741
July 16, 1907. *Town of Wagoner.* Named for Henry Samuel "Bigfoot" Wagoner (?–?); dispatcher for Missouri, Kansas & Texas Railroad; ordered a switch be placed between Gibson Station and Lelietta which became known as "Wagoner's Switch" from which the town grew.

Wahkiakum   **Washington**
Cathlamet   263 sq. mi.
3,978   3,824   3,327   3,832   3,592   3,462   3,835
April 24, 1854. *Wahkiakum Indians.* Named for chief Wakaiyakam who led separation of Wahkiakums from Chinooks; traded with Lewis and Clark 1805. Name means "big timber."

Wake   **North Carolina**
Raleigh   635 sq. mi.
900,993   627,846   423,380   301,327   228,453   169,082   136,450
1771. *Margaret Wake Tryon (1733–1819).* Wife of Governor William Tyron who chose name to honor his wife.

Wakulla   **Florida**
Crawfordville   606 sq. mi.
30,776   22,863   14,202   10,887   6,308   5,257   5,258
March 11, 1843. *Wakulla Springs or River.* Spanish devised phonetic spelling "Guacara" from Indian name; Indians in turn corrupted Spanish name to Wakulla. Meaning of original Indian name is uncertain; best guess is that it means "mystery."

Waldo   **Maine**
Belfast   730 sq. mi.

38,786	36,280	33,018	28,414	23,382	22,632	21,687

February 7, 1827. *Samuel Waldo (1695–1759)*. Boston merchant and land speculator; mast agent for obtaining New England white pines for British Navy; opened Waldo Patent for settlers 1740; brigadier general in King George's War 1745.

Walker   **Alabama**
Jasper   791 sq. mi.

67,023	70,713	67,670	68,660	56,246	54,211	63,769

December 26, 1823. *John Williams Walker (1783–1823)*. Alabama territorial legislature 1817; Alabama Constitutional Convention 1819; US senator 1819–23.

Walker   **Georgia**
LaFayette   446 sq. mi.

68,756	61,053	58,340	56,470	50,691	45,264	38,198

December 8, 1833. *Freeman Walker (1780–1827)*. Georgia House of Representatives 1807–11; mayor of Augusta 1818–19 and 1823; US senator 1819–21.

Walker   **Texas**
Huntsville   784 sq. mi.

67,861	61,758	50,917	41,789	27,680	21,475	20,163

April 6, 1846; organized July 18, 1846. *Samuel Walker (1817–1847)*. Texas Ranger 1836; Walker-Colt revolver used in Texas was result of design suggestions offered to by Walker to Samuel Colt; served under General Taylor in Mexican War; killed at Huamantla, October 9, 1847. County originally named for Robert Walker but legislature changed honoree to Samuel Walker because of Robert's Union sympathies, December 10, 1863.

Wallace   **Kansas**
Sharon Springs   914 sq. mi.

1,485	1,749	1,821	2,045	2,215	2,069	2,508

March 11, 1868; abolished 1879; recreated and organized January 5, 1889. *William Harvey Lamb Wallace (1821–62)*. From private to 1st lieutenant, Illinois Infantry during Mexican War, mustered out 1847; recommissioned as colonel 1861; brigadier general 1862; died of wounds received at Shiloh, April 10, 1862

Walla Walla   **Washington**
Walla Walla   1,270 sq. mi.

58,781	55,180	48,439	47,435	42,176	42,195	40,135

April 25, 1854. *Walla Walla River*. Nez Perce word of uncertain meaning; all suggestions refer to some form of water.

Waller   **Texas**
Hempstead   513 sq. mi.

43,205	32,663	23,390	19,798	14,285	12,071	11,961

April 28, 1873; organized August 16, 1873. *Edwin Waller (1800–83)*. Signer, Texas Declaration of Independence 1836; Republic of Texas postmaster general for two days 1839; first mayor of Austin 1840; chief justice of Austin County 1844–56; Texas Secession Convention 1861; president, Texas Veterans Association 1873.

Wallowa   **Oregon**
Enterprise   3,146 sq. mi.

7,008	7,226	6,911	7,273	6,247	7,102	7,264

February 11, 1887. *Wallowa Lake and River*. From Nez Perce *lacallas*, a tripod structure for trapping fish.

Walsh   **North Dakota**
Grafton   1,282 sq. mi.

11,119	12,389	13,840	15,371	16,251	17,997	18,859

February 18, 1881; organized August 30, 1881. *George H. Walsh (1845–1913)*. Union army 1862–65; Dakota Territory legislature 1879–89; North Dakota legislature 1889–93.

Walthall   **Mississippi**
Tylertown   404 sq. mi.
15,443   15,156   14,352   13,761   12,500   13,512   15,563
March 16, 1910; organized March 16, 1914. *Edward Cary Walthall (1831–98)*. 1st lieutenant to major general, Confederate army 1861–65; wounded at Lookout Mountain 1863; US senator from Mississippi 1885–98.

Walton   **Florida**
De Funiak Springs   1,038 sq. mi.
55,043   40,601   27,760   21,300   16,087   15,576   14,725
December 29, 1824. *George Walton (?–?)*. Colonel and aide to General Jackson; governor of West Florida 1821–22; secretary of Florida Territory 1822–26.

Walton   **Georgia**
Monroe   326 sq. mi.
83,768   60,687   38,586   31,211   23,404   20,481   20,230
December 15, 1818. *George Walton (1750–1804)*. Continental Congress 1776–81; signer, Declaration of Independence 1776; colonel of militia, wounded and captured at Savannah 1779; governor of Georgia 1779–80 and 1783; chief justice of Georgia 1783–86 and 1793; US senator 1795–96; circuit court judge 1799–1804.

Walworth   **South Dakota**
Selby   709 sq. mi.
5,438   5,974   6,087   7,011   7,842   8,097   7,648
January 8, 1873; organized March 28, 1883. *Walworth County, Wisconsin*. Most likely named for the home of early settlers or on the suggestion of a prominent settler from Wisconsin.

Walworth   **Wisconsin**
Elkhorn   555 sq. mi.
102,228   93,759   75,000   71,507   63,444   52,368   41,584
December 7, 1836; organized 1838. *Reuben Hyde Walworth (1788–1867)*. Colonel, War of 1812; US representative from New York 1821–23; district judge 1823–28; nominated to US Supreme Court by President Tyler but not confirmed by Senate 1844; national leader of temperance movement.

Wapello   **Iowa**
Ottumwa   432 sq. mi.
35,625   36,051   35,687   40,241   42,149   46,126   47,397
February 17, 1843; organized February 13, 1844. *Wapello (1787–1842)*. Fox chief; led peaceful but ineffective resistance to European encroachment; moved village around Iowa several times; signed five treaties with US 1822–37.

Ward   **North Dakota**
Minot   2,013 sq. mi.
61,675   58,795   57,921   58,392   58,560   47,072   34,782
April 14, 1885; organized November 23, 1885. *Mark Ward (1844–1902)*. Dakota Territory legislature; chairman of Committee on Counties at time county was created 1885.

Ward   **Texas**
Monahans   836 sq. mi.
10,658   10,909   13,115   13,976   13,019   14,917   13,346
February 26, 1887; organized March 29, 1892. *Thomas William Ward (1807–72)*. Lost leg during Siege of Bexar 1835; commissioner, Texas Land Office 1841–48; mayor of Austin, intermittently 1840–65; lost right arm from misfired cannon celebrating San Jacinto Day 1841; opposed secession 1861; collector of customs at Corpus Christi 1865–69.

Ware   **Georgia**
Waycross   892 sq. mi.
36,312   35,483   35,471   37,180   33,525   34,219   30,289

December 15, 1824. *Nicholas Ware (1769–1824)*. Georgia legislature 1808–11 and 1814–15; mayor of Augusta 1819–21; US senator 1821–24.

Warren   **Georgia**
Warrenton   284 sq. mi.

5,834	6,336	6,078	6,583	6,669	7,360	8,779

December 19, 1793. *Joseph Warren (1741–75)*. Physician; president, Massachusetts Provisional Congress 1775; enlisted Paul Revere and Stephen Dawes to warn of British approach to Concord 1775; Battles of Lexington and Concord 1775; major general, Continental army 1775; killed at Battle of Bunker Hill, June 17, 1775.

Warren   **Illinois**
Monmouth   542 sq. mi.

17,707	18,735	19,181	21,943	21,595	21,587	21,981

January 13, 1825; organized July 1830. *Joseph Warren.**

Warren   **Indiana**
Williamsport   365 sq. mi.

8,508	8,419	8,176	8,976	8,705	8,545	8,535

January 19, 1827; effective March 1, 1827. *Joseph Warren.**

Warren   **Iowa**
Indianola   570 sq. mi.

46,225	40,671	36,033	34,878	27,432	20,829	17,758

January 13, 1846; organized February 10, 1849. *Joseph Warren.**

Warren   **Kentucky**
Bowling Green   542 sq. mi.

113,792	92,522	76,673	71,828	57,432	45,491	42,758

December 14, 1796; effective March 1, 1797. *Joseph Warren.**

Warren   **Mississippi**
Vicksburg   589 sq. mi.

48,773	49,644	47,880	51,627	44,981	42,206	39,616

October 22, 1809. *Joseph Warren.**

Warren   **Missouri**
Warrenton   429 sq. mi.

32,513	24,525	19,354	14,900	9,699	8,750	7,666

January 5, 1833. *Joseph Warren.**

Warren   **New Jersey**
Belvidere   357 sq. mi.

108,692	102,437	91,607	84,429	73,879	63,220	54,374

November 20, 1824. *Joseph Warren.**

Warren   **New York**
Lake George   867 sq. mi.

65,707	63,303	59,209	54,854	49,402	44,002	39,205

March 12, 1813. *Joseph Warren.**

Warren   **North Carolina**
Warrenton   428 sq. mi.

20,972	19,972	17,265	16,232	15,810	19,652	23,539

1779. *Joseph Warren.**

Warren   **Ohio**
Lebanon   401 sq. mi.

212,693	158,383	113,909	99,276	84,925	65,711	38,505

March 24, 1803. *Joseph Warren.**

Warren   **Pennsylvania**
Warren   884 sq. mi.

41,815	43,863	45,050	47,449	47,682	45,582	42,698

March 12, 1800; organized October 1, 1819. *Joseph Warren.**

Warren   **Tennessee**
McMinnville   433 sq. mi.

39,839	38,276	32,992	32,653	26,972	23,102	22,271

November 26, 1807. *Joseph Warren.**

Warren   **Virginia**
Front Royal   213 sq. mi.

37,575	31,584	26,142	21,200	15,301	14,655	14,801

March 9, 1836. *Joseph Warren.**

Warrick   **Indiana**
Boonville   385 sq. mi.

59,689	52,383	44,920	41,474	27,972	23,577	21,527

March 9, 1813. *Jacob Warrick (?–1811)*. Captain under General Harrison; mortally wounded at Battle of Tippecanoe November 7, 1811.

Wasatch   **Utah**
Heber City   1,176 sq. mi.

23,530	15,215	10,089	8,523	5,863	5,308	5,574

January 17, 1862. *Wasatch Mountains*. Derived from Ute word meaning "low pass over high range."

Wasco   **Oregon**
The Dalles   2,382 sq. mi.

25,213	23,791	21,683	21,732	20,133	20,205	15,552

January 11, 1854. *Wasco Indians*. Chinookan tribe living on Columbia River. Name is from Wasco word for "horn basin," from a cup-shaped rock near their village.

Waseca   **Minnesota**
Waseca   423 sq. mi.

19,136	19,526	18,079	18,448	16,663	16,041	14,957

February 27, 1857. *Descriptive*. Dakota word meaning "fertile"; refers to local soil.

Washakie   **Wyoming**
Worland   2,239 sq. mi.

8,533	8,289	8,388	9,496	7,569	8,883	7,252

February 9, 1911. *Washakie (c1804–1900)*. Shoshoni chief; assisted emigrants on Oregon Trail; US Army scout, advised General Crook not to pursue overwhelming Indian force that one week later defeated General Custer 1876; converted to Mormonism 1897; only Indian known to have received US military funeral. Name means "rawhide rattle" from a device used to scare enemy horses in battle.

Washburn   **Wisconsin**
Shell Lake   797 sq. mi.

15,911	16,036	13,772	13,174	10,601	10,301	11,665

March 27, 1883. *Cadwallader Colden Washburn (1818–82)*. US representative from Wisconsin 1855–61 and 1867–71; colonel to major general, 2nd Regiment Wisconsin Volunteer Cavalry 1862–65; governor of Wisconsin 1872–73.

Washington   **Alabama**
Chatom   1,080 sq. mi.

17,581	18,097	16,694	16,821	16,241	15,372	15,612

June 4, 1800. *George Washington (1732–99).* Surveyor; served with General Braddock in French and Indian War 1754–58; commanded Continental army during Revolutionary War 1775–83; defeated British at Yorktown 1781; resigned commission 1783; president, federal Constitutional Convention 1787; 1st president of US 1789–97; accepted commission as lieutenant general and commander in chief when war with France threatened 1798.

Washington   **Arkansas**
Fayetteville   942 sq. mi.

203,065	157,715	113,409	100,494	77,370	55,797	49,979

October 17, 1828; effective November 1, 1828. *George Washington.**

Washington   **Colorado**
Akron   2,518 sq. mi.

4,814	4,926	4,812	5,304	5,550	6,625	7,520

February 9, 1887. *George Washington.**

Washington   **Florida**
Chipley   583 sq. mi.

24,896	20,973	16,919	14,509	11,453	11,249	11,888

December 9, 1825. *George Washington.**

Washington   **Georgia**
Sandersville   678 sq. mi.

21,187	21,176	19,112	18,842	17,480	18,903	21,012

February 25, 1784. *George Washington.**

Washington   **Idaho**
Weiser   1,453 sq. mi.

10,198	9,977	8,550	8,803	7,633	8,378	8,576

February 20, 1879. *George Washington.**

Washington   **Illinois**
Nashville   563 sq. mi.

14,716	15,148	14,956	15,472	13,780	13,569	14,460

January 2, 1818. *George Washington.**

Washington   **Indiana**
Salem   514 sq. mi.

28,262	27,223	23,717	21,932	19,278	17,819	16,520

December 21, 1813; effective January 17, 1814. *George Washington.**

Washington   **Iowa**
Washington   569 sq. mi.

21,704	20,670	19,612	20,141	18,967	19,406	19,557

January 16, 1837, as Slaughter; organized January 18, 1838; name changed January 25, 1839. *George Washington.**

Washington   **Kansas**
Washington   895 sq. mi.

5,799	6,483	7,073	8,543	9,249	10,739	12,977

February 20, 1857. *George Washington.**

Washington   **Kentucky**
Springfield   297 sq. mi.

11,717   10,916   10,441   10,764   10,728   11,168   12,777
June 22, 1792. *George Washington.**

Washington   **Louisiana**
Franklinton   670 sq. mi.
47,168   43,926   43,185   44,207   41,987   44,015   38,371
March 6, 1819. *George Washington.**

Washington   **Maine**
Machias   2,563 sq. mi.
32,856   33,941   35,308   34,963   29,859   32,908   35,187
June 25, 1789; effective May 1, 1790. *George Washington.**

Washington   **Maryland**
Hagerstown   458 sq. mi.
147,430   131,923   121,393   113,086   103,829   91,219   78,886
September 6, 1776. *George Washington.**

Washington   **Minnesota**
Stillwater   384 sq. mi.
238,136   201,130   145,896   113,571   82,948   52,432   34,544
October 27, 1849; organized March 31, 1851; effective September 1, 1851. *George Washington.**

Washington   **Mississippi**
Greenville   725 sq. mi.
51,137   62,977   67,935   72,344   70,581   78,638   70,504
January 29, 1827. *George Washington.**

Washington   **Missouri**
Potosi   760 sq. mi.
25,195   23,344   20,380   17,983   15,086   14,346   14,689
August 21, 1813. *George Washington.**

Washington   **Nebraska**
Blair   390 sq. mi.
20,234   18,780   16,607   15,508   13,310   12,103   11,511
November 23, 1854. *George Washington.**

Washington   **New York**
Fort Edward   831 sq. mi.
63,216   61,042   59,330   54,795   52,725   48,746   47,144
March 12, 1772, as Charlotte; name changed April 2, 1784. *George Washington.**

Washington   **North Carolina**
Plymouth   348 sq. mi.
13,228   13,723   13,997   14,801   14,038   13,488   13,180
1799. *George Washington.**

Washington   **Ohio**
Marietta   632 sq. mi.
61,778   63,251   62,254   64,266   57,160   51,689   44,407
July 27, 1788. *George Washington.**

Washington   **Oklahoma**
Bartlesville   415 sq. mi.

| 50,976 | 48,996 | 48,066 | 48,113 | 42,277 | 42,347 | 32,880 |
July 16, 1907. *George Washington.**

Washington   **Oregon**
Hillsboro   724 sq. mi.

| 529,710 | 445,342 | 311,554 | 245,808 | 157,920 | 92,237 | 61,269 |
July 5, 1843, as Twality; name changed September 3, 1849. *George Washington.**

Washington   **Pennsylvania**
Washington   857 sq. mi.

| 207,820 | 202,897 | 204,584 | 217,074 | 210,876 | 217,271 | 209,628 |
March 28, 1781. *George Washington.**

Washington   **Rhode Island**
Wakefield   329 sq. mi.

| 126,979 | 123,546 | 110,006 | 93,317 | 83,586 | 59,054 | 48,542 |
June 3, 1729, as King's; name changed October 29, 1781. *George Washington.**

Washington   **Tennessee**
Jonesborough   326 sq. mi.

| 122,979 | 107,198 | 92,315 | 88,755 | 73,924 | 64,832 | 59,971 |
August 22, 1776. *George Washington.**

Washington   **Texas**
Brenham   604 sq. mi.

| 33,718 | 30,373 | 26,154 | 21,998 | 18,842 | 19,145 | 20,542 |
March 17, 1836; organized 1837. *Municipality of Washington on the Brazos*. Named for *George Washington.**

Washington   **Utah**
Saint George   2,426 sq. mi.

| 138,115 | 90,354 | 48,560 | 26,065 | 13,669 | 10,271 | 9,836 |
March 3, 1852. *George Washington.**

Washington   **Vermont**
Montpelier   687 sq. mi.

| 59,534 | 58,039 | 54,928 | 52,393 | 47,659 | 42,860 | 42,870 |
November 10, 1810, as Jefferson; organized October 16, 1811; effective December 1, 1811; name changed November 8, 1814. *George Washington.**

Washington   **Virginia**
Abingdon   561 sq. mi.

| 54,876 | 51,103 | 45,887 | 46,487 | 40,835 | 38,076 | 37,536 |
December 7, 1776. *George Washington.** (Associated independent city: Bristol.)

Washington   **Wisconsin**
West Bend   431 sq. mi.

| 131,887 | 117,493 | 95,328 | 84,848 | 63,839 | 46,119 | 33,902 |
December 7, 1836; organized August 13, 1840. *George Washington.**

Washita   **Oklahoma**
Cordell   1,003 sq. mi.

| 11,629 | 11,508 | 11,441 | 13,798 | 12,141 | 18,121 | 17,657 |
April 19, 1892, as County H; organized and name changed 1900. *Washita River*. Origin of name is uncertain. (1) From Indian word for "water with painted face"; a reference to the red silt in the river. (2) Anglicized rendering of Choctaw words for "big

hunt" (see Ouachita, Louisiana [2]). (3) From French *Faux Ouacita* meaning "False Ouachita" to distinguish this river from the Ouachita River in Arkansas and Louisiana.

Washoe   **Nevada**
Reno   6,302 sq. mi.
421,407   339,486   254,667   193,623   121,068   84,743   50,205
November 25, 1861. *Washoe Indians*. American rendering of tribal name *Washiu* meaning "people."

Washtenaw   **Michigan**
Ann Arbor   706 sq. mi.
344,791   322,895   282,937   264,748   234,103   172,440   134,606
September 10, 1822; organized November 20, 1826. *Grand River*. From *Washtenong*, Chippewa name for the Grand River. Name is of uncertain origin; may mean "river that is far off."

Watauga   **North Carolina**
Boone   313 sq. mi.
51,079   42,695   36,952   31,666   23,404   17,529   18,342
January 27, 1849. *Watauga River*. Uncertain origin; may be named for a Cherokee group or a village on the river.

Watonwan   **Minnesota**
Saint James   435 sq. mi.
11,211   11,876   11,682   12,361   13,298   14,460   13,881
February 25, 1860; organized June 15, 1871. *Watonwan Township*. County created from Watonwan Township, Blue Earth County; named for Watonwan River which is an anglicized version of Dakota word of unknown origin; most guesses refer to "fish" or "seeing."

Waukesha   **Wisconsin**
Waukesha   550 sq. mi.
389,891   360,767   304,715   280,326   231,365   158,249   85,901
January 31, 1846. *Uncertain*. (1) Fox Indians, (2) Fox River, or (3) the animal. From Indian word *wauk-tsha* meaning "fox."

Waupaca   **Wisconsin**
Waupaca   748 sq. mi.
52,410   51,731   46,104   42,831   37,780   35,340   35,056
February 17, 1851. *Waupaca River*. Indian name of uncertain origin; suggestions range from "white sand bottom" to "our brave young hero."

Waushara   **Wisconsin**
Wautoma   626 sq. mi.
24,496   23,154   19,385   18,526   14,795   13,497   13,920
February 15, 1851. *Contrived*. Pseudo-Indian name of unknown origin; best suggestion is "good land river."

Wayne   **Georgia**
Jesup   642 sq. mi.
30,099   26,565   22,356   20,750   17,858   17,921   14,248
May 11, 1803. *Anthony Wayne (1745–96)*. Pennsylvania House of Representatives 1774–75; colonel, 4th Pennsylvania Regiment; brigadier general 1777; Valley Forge 1777–78; captured Stony Point 1779; awarded Thanks of Congress and gold medal 1779; brevet major general 1783; retired from army 1784; Pennsylvania Assembly 1784; US representative from Georgia 1791–92; recommissioned as major general, defeated Indian confederacy at Battle of Fallen Timbers 1794; nicknamed "Mad Anthony" for daring military exploits.

Wayne   **Illinois**
Fairfield   714 sq. mi.
16,760   17,151   17,241   18,059   17,004   19,008   20,933
March 26, 1819. *Anthony Wayne.**

Wayne   **Indiana**
Richmond   402 sq. mi.

68,917	71,097	71,951	76,058	79,109	74,039	68,566

November 27, 1810; effective February 1, 1811. *Anthony Wayne.**

Wayne   **Iowa**
Corydon   525 sq. mi.

6,403	6,730	7,067	8,199	8,405	9,800	11,737

January 13, 1846; organized January 27, 1851. *Anthony Wayne.**

Wayne   **Kentucky**
Monticello   458 sq. mi.

20,813	19,923	17,468	17,022	14,268	14,700	16,475

December 18, 1800. *Anthony Wayne.**

Wayne   **Michigan**
Detroit   612 sq. mi.

1,820,584	2,061,162	2,111,687	2,337,891	2,666,751	2,666,297	2,435,235

November 21, 1815. *Anthony Wayne.**

Wayne   **Mississippi**
Waynesboro   811 sq. mi.

20,747	21,216	19,517	19,135	16,650	16,258	17,010

December 21, 1809. *Anthony Wayne.**

Wayne   **Missouri**
Greenville   759 sq. mi.

13,521	13,259	11,543	11,277	8,546	8,638	10,514

December 11, 1818. *Anthony Wayne.**

Wayne   **Nebraska**
Wayne   443 sq. mi.

9,595	9,851	9,364	9,858	10,400	9,959	10,129

March 4, 1871. *Anthony Wayne.**

Wayne   **New York**
Lyons   604 sq. mi.

93,772	93,765	89,123	84,581	79,404	67,989	57,323

April 11, 1823. *Anthony Wayne.**

Wayne   **North Carolina**
Goldsboro   553 sq. mi.

122,623	113,329	104,666	97,054	85,408	82,059	64,267

November 2, 1779. *Anthony Wayne.**

Wayne   **Ohio**
Wooster   555 sq. mi.

114,520	111,564	101,461	97,408	87,123	75,497	58,716

January 4, 1812. *Anthony Wayne.**

Wayne   **Pennsylvania**
Honesdale   726 sq. mi.

52,822	47,722	39,944	35,237	29,581	28,237	28,478

March 21, 1798. *Anthony Wayne.**

Wayne   **Tennessee**
Waynesboro   734 sq. mi.
17,021   16,842   13,935   13,946   12,365   11,908   13,864
November 24, 1817. *Anthony Wayne.**

Wayne   **Utah**
Loa   2,461 sq. mi.
2,778   2,509   2,177   1,911   1,483   1,728   2,205
March 10, 1892. *Wayne C. Robnison (1885–96).* Son of Utah legislator Willis Robison; killed in horsing accident at age eleven.

Wayne   **West Virginia**
Wayne   506 sq. mi.
42,481   42,903   41,636   46,021   37,581   38,977   38,696
January 18, 1842. *Anthony Wayne.**

Waynesboro   **Virginia**
(Independent City)   15 sq. mi.
21,006   19,520   18,549   15,329   16,707   15,694   12,357
December 31, 1947. *Anthony Wayne.** (Associated county: Augusta.)

Weakley   **Tennessee**
Dresden   580 sq. mi.
35,021   34,895   31,972   32,896   28,827   24,227   27,962
October 23, 1823. *Robert Weakley (1764–1845).* Continental Army 1870–83; North Carolina House of Representatives 1796; US representative from Tennessee 1809–11; Tennessee Senate 1823–24, speaker 1823; Tennessee Constitutional Convention 1834.

Webb   **Texas**
Laredo   3,361 sq. mi.
250,304   193,117   133,239   99,258   72,859   64,791   56,141
January 28, 1848; organized March 16, 1848. *James Webb (1792–1856).* War of 1812; US district judge, Florida Territory 1838; Republic of Texas attorney general 1839–41; Texas legislature 1841–44; Texas Constitutional Convention 1845; reporter, Texas supreme court 1846–49; Texas secretary of state 1850–51; district judge 1854–56.

Weber   **Utah**
Ogden   576 sq. mi.
231,236   196,533   158,330   144,616   126,278   110,744   83,319
January 31, 1850. *Weber River.* Named for John Weber (1779–1859); Danish sea captain; explorer and trapper in American West.

Webster   **Georgia**
Preston   209 sq. mi.
2,799   2,390   2,263   2,341   2,362   3,247   4,081
December 16, 1853, as Kinchafoonee; name changed February 21, 1856. *Daniel Webster (1782–1852).* US representative from New Hampshire 1813–17 and Massachusetts 1823–27; Massachusetts Constitutional Convention 1820; US senator 1827–41 and 1845–50; US secretary of state 1841–43 and 1850–52. Relatively moderate views on slavery had some support in South.

Webster   **Iowa**
Fort Dodge   716 sq. mi.
38,013   40,235   40,342   45,953   48,391   47,810   44,241
January 15, 1851, as Risley; organized and name changed January 12, 1853; effective March 1, 1853. *Daniel Webster.**

Webster   **Kentucky**
Dixon   332 sq. mi.

| 13,621 | 14,120 | 13,955 | 14,832 | 13,282 | 14,244 | 15,555 |

February 29, 1860. *Daniel Webster.**

Webster   **Louisiana**
Minden   593 sq. mi.

| 41,207 | 41,831 | 41,989 | 43,631 | 39,939 | 39,701 | 35,704 |

February 27, 1871. *Daniel Webster.**

Webster   **Mississippi**
Walthall   421 sq. mi.

| 10,253 | 10,294 | 10,222 | 10,300 | 10,047 | 10,580 | 11,607 |

April 6, 1874, as Sumner; name changed January 20, 1882. *Daniel Webster.**

Webster   **Missouri**
Marshfield   593 sq. mi.

| 36,202 | 31,045 | 23,753 | 20,414 | 15,562 | 13,753 | 15,072 |

March 3, 1855. *Daniel Webster.**

Webster   **Nebraska**
Red Cloud   575 sq. mi.

| 3,812 | 4,061 | 4,279 | 4,858 | 6,477 | 6,224 | 7,395 |

February 16, 1867; organized July 5, 1871. *Daniel Webster.**

Webster   **West Virginia**
Webster Springs   553 sq. mi.

| 9,154 | 9,719 | 10,729 | 12,245 | 9,809 | 13,719 | 17,888 |

January 10, 1860. *Daniel Webster.**

Weld   **Colorado**
Greeley   3,987 sq. mi.

| 252,825 | 180,936 | 131,821 | 123,438 | 89,297 | 72,344 | 67,504 |

November 1, 1861. *Lewis Ledyard Weld (1833–65)*. Ardent abolitionist in Kansas Territory; Secretary of Colorado Territory 1860; captain, 7th Colored Troops 1861; major and lieutenant colonel, 41st Colored Infantry; weakened physical condition exacerbated by conditions in trenches at Petersburg; died of illness.

Wells   **Indiana**
Bluffton   368 sq. mi.

| 27,636 | 27,600 | 25,948 | 25,401 | 23,821 | 21,220 | 19,564 |

February 7, 1835; organized February 2, 1837; effective May 1, 1837. *William Wells (c1766–1812)*. Kidnapped and raised by Miamis 1774; fought against Americans; interpreter during treaty negotiations; joined US Army after becoming concerned about possibility of killing Kentucky relatives in battle but maintained ties with Miamis; captain under Generals Wayne and Harrison; killed by Pottawatomies on mission with Miamis to rescue Fort Dearborn (Chicago).

Wells   **North Dakota**
Fessenden   1,271 sq. mi.

| 4,207 | 5,102 | 5,864 | 6,979 | 7,847 | 9,237 | 10,417 |

January 4, 1873, as Gingras; name changed February 26, 1881; organized August 28, 1884. *Edward P. Wells (1847–1936)*. Merchant in Milwaukee and Minneapolis 1864–78; banker in Jamestown, Dakota Territory 1880–1901; Dakota Territory legislature at time county's name was changed 1881.

West Baton Rouge   **Louisiana**
Port Allen   192 sq. mi.

| 23,788 | 21,601 | 19,419 | 19,086 | 16,864 | 14,796 | 11,738 |

March 31, 1807, as Baton Rouge; name changed 1812. *Baton Rouge Parish*. (See East Baton Rouge, Louisiana.)

West Carroll   **Louisiana**
Oak Grove   360 sq. mi.
11,604   12,314   12,093   12,922   13,028   14,177   17,248
March 28, 1877. *Carroll Parish.* (See East Carroll, Louisiana.)

Westchester   **New York**
White Plaines   431 sq. mi.
949,113   923,459   874,866   866,599   894,104   808,891   625,816
November 1, 1683. *Township of Westchester.* Named for Chester, England; most likely named for the home of a prominent settler or sponsor.

West Feliciana   **Louisiana**
Saint Francisville   403 sq. mi.
15,625   15,111   12,915   12,186   11,376   12,395   10,169
February 17, 1824. *Feliciana Parish.* (See East Feliciana, Louisiana.)

Westmoreland   **Pennsylvania**
Greensburg   1,028 sq. mi.
365,189   369,993   370,321   392,294   376,935   352,629   313,179
February 26, 1773. *Westmoreland County, England.* Named chosen because the county originally included all western Pennsylvania.

Westmoreland   **Virginia**
Montross   229 sq. mi.
17,454   16,718   15,480   14,041   12,142   11,042   10,148
July 1653. *Westmoreland County, England.* Most likely named for the home of a prominent settler or sponsor.

Weston   **Wyoming**
Newcastle   2,398 sq. mi.
7,208   6,644   6,518   7,106   6,307   7,929   6,733
March 12, 1890. *Uncertain.* (1) *John B. Weston (?–?)*; geologist and surveyor for Newcastle Coal Company; discovered rich anthracite coal deposits in the area 1878. (2) *Jefferson B. Weston (1831–95)*; Nebraska state auditor 1873–79; helped finance construction of Chicago, Burlington & Quincy Railroad in Wyoming.

Wetzel   **West Virginia**
New Martinsville   358 sq. mi.
16,583   17,693   19,258   21,874   20,314   19,347   20,154
January 10, 1846. *Lewis Wetzel (1764–1808).* Captured with his brother and taken to Ohio by Indians c1776; devoted his life to fighting Indians; known for excessive brutality even by frontier standards.

Wexford   **Michigan**
Cadillac   565 sq. mi.
32,735   30,484   26,360   25,102   19,717   18,466   18,628
April 1, 1840, as Kautawaubet; name changed March 8, 1843; organized March 30, 1869. *County Wexford, Ireland.* Michigan changed the names of many counties to honor Irish people or places.

Wharton   **Texas**
Wharton   1,086 sq. mi.
41,280   41,188   39,955   40,242   36,729   38,152   36,077
April 3, 1846. *Wharton brothers.* (1) *William Harris Wharton (1802–39)*; authored petition requesting Mexican statehood for Texas 1832; Siege of Bexar 1835; commissioner to seek aid from US 1835; Republic of Texas minister to US 1836–37; Texas Senate 1838. (2) *John Austin Wharton (1806–38)*; leader in Texas independence movement; adjutant general for General Houston; cited for bravery at Battle of San Jacinto 1836; Republic of Texas secretary of war 1836; Texas legislature 1836–37.

Whatcom   **Washington**
Bellingham   2,107 sq. mi.

| 201,140 | 166,814 | 127,780 | 106,701 | 81,950 | 70,317 | 66,733 |

March 9, 1854. *Whatcom Falls or Creek*. From Nooksack word meaning "noisy water."

Wheatland   **Montana**
Harlowton   1,423 sq. mi.

| 2,168 | 2,259 | 2,246 | 2,359 | 2,529 | 3,026 | 3,187 |

February 22, 1917. *Descriptive*. Refers to local wheat-producing farmland.

Wheeler   **Georgia**
Alamo   295 sq. mi.

| 7,421 | 6,179 | 4,903 | 5,155 | 4,496 | 5,342 | 6,712 |

August 14, 1912. *Joseph Wheeler (1836–1906)*. Graduated West Point 1859; 1st lieutenant to lieutenant general, Confederate Army 1861–65; senior cavalry general of Confederate Army; led ineffectual resistance to Sherman's March to the Sea 1864; US representative from Alabama 1881–82 and 1885–1900; major general of volunteers, Spanish-American War 1898; negotiated Spanish surrender of Cuba 1898; Tarlac campaign in Philippines 1899–1900; brigadier general, regular army 1900.

Wheeler   **Nebraska**
Bartlett   575 sq. mi.

| 818 | 886 | 948 | 1,060 | 1,054 | 1,297 | 1,526 |

February 17, 1877; organized April 11, 1881. *Daniel H. Wheeler (1834–1912)*. Merchant; Cass County clerk and judge 1864; secretary, Nebraska Board of Agriculture 1868–81; Nebraska Senate 1873–77.

Wheeler   **Oregon**
Fossil   1,715 sq. mi.

| 1,441 | 1,547 | 1,396 | 1,513 | 1,849 | 2,722 | 3,313 |

February 17, 1899. *Henry H. Wheeler (1826–1915)*. Owner and operator of stage line between The Dalles and Canyon City; rancher in Wheeler County area 1878–1904.

Wheeler   **Texas**
Wheeler   915 sq. mi.

| 5,410 | 5,284 | 5,879 | 7,137 | 6,434 | 7,947 | 10,317 |

April 21, 1876; organized April 12, 1879. *Royal Tyler Wheeler (1810–64)*. Republic of Texas district attorney 1842; district judge 1844; Texas Supreme Court 1854–64, chief justice 1857–64; professor of law, Austin College 1858.

White   **Arkansas**
Searcy   1,035 sq. mi.

| 77,076 | 67,165 | 54,676 | 50,835 | 39,253 | 32,745 | 38,040 |

October 23, 1835; effective December 1, 1835. *Uncertain*. (1) *Hugh Lawson White (1773–1840)*; Indian fighter; Tennessee Supreme Court 1801–07 and 1809–15; Tennessee Senate 1807–09 and 1817–25; US senator 1825–40. (2) *White River*; named for clear, transparent spring water.

White   **Georgia**
Cleveland   241 sq. mi.

| 27,144 | 19,944 | 13,006 | 10,120 | 7,742 | 6,935 | 5,951 |

December 22, 1857. *Uncertain*. (1) *David T. White (1812–71)*; Georgia legislature; revived stalled effort to create county. (2) *John White (?–?)*; British naval surgeon; Continental Army, from captain to colonel; during Siege of Savannah, captured over 100 British troops with six soldiers by convincing the British they were surrounded by a superior force 1779.

White   **Illinois**
Carmi   495 sq. mi.

| 14,665 | 15,371 | 16,522 | 17,864 | 17,312 | 19,373 | 20,935 |

December 9, 1815. *Uncertain*. (1) *Isaac White* (see White, Indiana). (2) *Leonard White (?–?)*; militia captain under Colonel Isaac White; colonel 1811; Illinois Constitutional Convention 1818; Illinois Senate 1820–36.

White   **Indiana**
Monticello   505 sq. mi.
24,643   25,267   23,265   23,867   20,995   19,709   18,042
February 1, 1834; effective April 1, 1834. *Isaac White (c1776–1811)*. Militia captain 1806; colonel 1809; killed at Battle of Tippecanoe, November 7, 1811.

White   **Tennessee**
Sparta   377 sq. mi.
25,841   23,102   20,090   19,567   17,088   15,577   16,204
September 11, 1806. *John White (?–1846)*. Continental army; Battles of Brandywine and Germantown 1777; early settler in central Tennessee.

White Pine   **Nevada**
Ely   8,876 sq. mi.
10,030   9,181   9,264   8,167   10,150   9,808   9,424
March 2, 1869. *White Pine Mining District*. Established after discoveries of silver, copper, and lead in White Pine Mountains 1865. Trees for which the White Pine Mountains are named are actually bristlecone pines.

Whiteside   **Illinois**
Morrison   684 sq. mi.
58,498   60,653   60,186   65,970   62,877   59,887   49,336
January 16, 1836; organized May 6, 1839. *Samuel Whiteside (1783–1866)*. Captain, Mounted Rifles 1812; captain of Rangers 1813; honorably discharged 1814; Illinois legislature 1819–21; brigadier general, Illinois Volunteers 1819; Black Hawk War 1832.

Whitfield   **Georgia**
Dalton   290 sq. mi.
102,599   83,525   72,462   65,789   55,108   42,109   34,432
December 30, 1851. *George Whitefield (1714–70)*. Clergyman, Church of England; missionary in America c1738; established Bethesda Orphanage, Savannah, 1740; resided in England but frequently visited America. (First letter *e* was omitted from county name.)

Whitley   **Indiana**
Columbia City   336 sq. mi.
33,292   30,707   27,651   26,215   23,395   20,954   18,828
February 7, 1835; organized February 17, 1838; effective April 1, 1838. *William Whitley (1749–1813)*. Explored Kentucky 1775–80; Indian fighter; referred to variously as captain, major, or colonel; volunteered as private in Kentucky Militia at age 63, 1812; killed at Battle of the Thames 1813.

Whitley   **Kentucky**
Williamsburg   438 sq. mi.
35,637   35,865   33,326   33,396   24,145   25,815   31,940
January 17, 1818. *William Whitley.**

Whitman   **Washington**
Colfax   2,159 sq. mi.
44,776   40,740   38,775   40,103   37,900   31,263   32,469
November 29, 1871. *Marcus Whitman (1802–47)*. Physician and missionary; with wife, Narcissa, established mission near Walla Walla 1836; encouraged American settlement of Oregon Country to counter British claims; the Whitmans and twelve others massacred by Cayuse Indians, November 29, 1847.

Wibaux   **Montana**
Wibaux   889 sq. mi.
1,017   1,068   1,191   1,476   1,465   1,698   1,907

August 17, 1914. *Uncertain.* (1) *Pierre Wibaux (1858–?)*; member of wealthy French family; settled in eastern Montana 1883; owned land throughout the West; invested in gold mines; built stockyards in Wibaux. (2) *Town of Wibaux*; named for Pierre Wibaux.

Wichita   **Kansas**
Leoti   719 sq. mi.

2,234	2,531	2,758	3,041	3,274	2,765	2,640

March 20, 1873; organized December 24, 1886. *Wichita Indians.* Meaning of name is uncertain; may refer to Wichita practice of painting their faces. Occupied southern plains; encountered by Coronado 1541; resettled in Indian Territory (Oklahoma) by 1870.

Wichita   **Texas**
Wichita Falls   628 sq. mi.

131,500	131,664	122,378	121,082	121,862	123,528	98,493

February 1, 1858; organized June 21, 1882. *Wichita River.* Named for Wichita Indians.*

Wicomico   **Maryland**
Salisbury   374 sq. mi.

98,733	84,644	74,339	64,540	54,236	49,050	39,641

August 17, 1867. *Wicomico River.* From Lenape word meaning "where houses are built"; rendered by English as *wicko-mekee.*

Wilbarger   **Texas**
Vernon   971 sq. mi.

13,535	14,676	15,121	15,931	15,355	17,748	29,552

February 1, 1858; organized October 10, 1881. *Wilbarger brothers.* (1) *Josiah Pugh Wilbarger (1801–44)*; teacher, surveyor, and farmer; survived scalping 1833. (2) *Mathias Wilbarger (c1807–53)*; settled near his brother Josiah in Austin Colony 1829.

Wilcox   **Alabama**
Camden   889 sq. mi.

11,670	13,183	13,568	14,755	16,303	18,739	23,476

December 13, 1819. *Joseph M. Wilcox (1791–1814).* Lieutenant in Creek War; captured and scalped 1814.

Wilcox   **Georgia**
Abbeville   378 sq. mi.

9,255	8,577	7,008	7,682	6,998	7,905	10,167

December 22, 1857. *Uncertain.* (1) *John Wilcox (?–?)*; captain, Georgia Militia; early settler in south-central Georgia. (2) *Mark Wilcox (c1800–50)*; sheriff, Telfair County; Georgia legislature; major general, Georgia Militia. John was father of Mark.

Wilkes   **Georgia**
Washington   469 sq. mi.

10,593	10,687	10,597	10,951	10,184	10,961	12,388

February 5, 1777. *John Wilkes (1725–97).* Member of British Parliament; imprisoned for his fervent opposition to George III; expelled from House of Commons 1769; reelected three times but was refused seat each time; Lord Mayor of London 1774; returned to Parliament 1774; opposed British colonial policies in America.

Wilkes   **North Carolina**
Wilkesboro   754 sq. mi.

69,340	65,632	59,393	58,657	49,524	45,269	45,243

1777; effective February 12, 1778. *John Wilkes.**

Wilkin   **Minnesota**
Breckenridge   751 sq. mi.

6,576	7,138	7,516	8,454	9,389	10,650	10,567

March 18, 1858, as Toombs; name changed to Andy Johnson March 18, 1862; name changed to Wilkin March 6, 1868; organized March 4, 1872. *Alexander Wilkin (1820–64)*. Infantry captain 1847, resigned 1848; secretary of Minnesota Territory 1851–53; US marshal for Minnesota; captain to colonel 1861–62; killed at Tupelo July 14, 1864.

Wilkinson   **Georgia**
Irwinton   447 sq. mi.
9,563   10,220   10,228   10,368   9,393   9,250   9,781
May 11, 1803; organized December 1805. *James Wilkinson (1757–1825)*. Captain, Continental Army; negotiated treaty with Creeks ceding land to Georgia; senior officer in US Army 1800–12; civil and military governor of Louisiana Territory 1805–07; involved in intrigue to make southwest US part of Spain; found innocent by court-martial 1811; brevet major general, led disastrous campaign against Canada in War of 1812; relieved of command for poor performance at Montreal; died in Mexico City seeking Spanish land grant in Texas.

Wilkinson   **Mississippi**
Woodville   678 sq. mi.
9,878   10,312   9,678   10,021   11,099   13,235   14,116
January 30, 1802. *James Wilkinson.**

Will   **Illinois**
Joliet   837 sq. mi.
677,560   502,266   357,313   324,460   249,498   191,617   134,336
January 12, 1836. *Conrad Will (c1778–1835)*. Physician; Illinois Constitutional Convention 1818; Illinois Senate 1818–19 and 1827–35; Illinois Assembly 1819–27.

Willacy   **Texas**
Raymondville   591 sq. mi.
22,134   20,082   17,705   17,495   15,570   20,084   20,920
March 11, 1911; organized 1912. *John G. Willacy (c1859–1943)*. Texas legislature 1899–1914; instrumental in creation of county; Texas tax commissioner 1921–25.

Williams   **North Dakota**
Williston   2,077 sq. mi.
22,398   19,761   21,129   22,237   19,301   22,051   16,442
November 30, 1892. *Erastus Appleman Williams (1850–1930)*. Involved in extension of Northern Pacific Railroad across Dakota Territory; Dakota Territory legislature 1872–89; North Dakota Constitutional Convention 1889; North Dakota legislature 1889–97, speaker 1897.

Williams   **Ohio**
Bryan   421 sq. mi.
37,642   39,188   36,956   36,369   33,669   29,968   26,202
February 12, 1820; organized 1824. *David Williams (1754–1831)*. One of three captors of British major André which revealed Benedict Arnold's treason (see Paulding, Georgia).

Williamsburg   **South Carolina**
Kingstree   934 sq. mi.
34,423   37,217   36,815   38,226   34,243   40,932   43,807
March 12, 1785; abolished January 1, 1800; recreated 1804 as judicial district; designated as county April 16, 1868. *Williamsburg Township*. Uncertain origin of township name; (1) King William III (see King William, Virginia); (2) William IV, Prince of Orange (see Orange, Virginia).

Williamsburg   **Virginia**
(Independent City)   9 sq. mi.
14,068   11,998   11,530   9,870   9,069   6,832   6,735
March 17, 1884. *King William III* (see King William, Virginia). (Associated counties: James City and York.)

Williamson   **Illinois**
Marion   420 sq. mi.

66,357	61,296	57,733	56,538	49,021	46,117	48,621

February 28, 1839. *Williamson County, Tennessee*. Origin of early settlers.

Williamson   **Tennessee**
Franklin   583 sq. mi.

183,182	126,638	81,021	58,108	34,330	25,267	24,307

October 26, 1799. *Hugh Williamson (1735–1819)*. Theologian, mathematician, astronomer, and physician; surgeon general to North Carolina troops 1779–82; North Carolina House of Commons 1782; Continental Congress, intermittently 1782–88; federal Constitution Convention 1787; US representative 1789–93.

Williamson   **Texas**
Georgetown   1,118 sq. mi.

422,679	249,967	139,551	76,521	37,305	35,044	38,853

March 13, 1848; organized August 7, 1848. *Robert McAlpin Williamson (c1806–59)*. Editor, *The Cotton Plant*; major, Texas army 1835; Battle of San Jacinto 1836; Republic of Texas Supreme Court 1836; Republic of Texas legislature 1841–44; Texas legislature 1845–50.

Wilson   **Kansas**
Fredonia   570 sq. mi.

9,409	10,332	10,289	12,128	11,317	13,077	14,815

August 30, 1855; organized September 9, 1864. *Hiero T. Wilson (1806–92)*. Merchant and Indian trader; sutler at Fort Scott 1843; Kansas Territory legislature 1855; Lecompton Constitutional Convention 1857.

Wilson   **North Carolina**
Wilson   368 sq. mi.

81,234	73,814	66,061	63,132	57,486	57,716	54,506

February 13, 1855. *Louis D. Wilson (1789–1847)*. North Carolina legislature 1815–46; resigned legislature and joined army at age 57 after being challenged to back up his ardent support of Mexican War; from captain to colonel 1846–47; died of fever at Vera Cruz.

Wilson   **Tennessee**
Lebanon   571 sq. mi.

113,993	88,809	67,675	56,064	36,999	27,668	26,318

October 26, 1799. *David Wilson (1752–c1804)*. Major in Revolutionary War; speaker, Territory South of the Ohio (Tennessee) Assembly 1794.

Wilson   **Texas**
Floresville   804 sq. mi.

42,918	32,408	22,650	16,756	13,041	13,267	14,672

February 13, 1860; organized August 6, 1860; name changed to Cibolo 1869; renamed Wilson 1874. *James Charles Wilson (1816–61)*. Somervell punitive mission into Mexico 1842; captured during Mier expedition into Mexico 1843; escaped execution 1843; Texas Senate 1851–52.

Winchester   **Virginia**
(Independent City)   9 sq. mi.

26,203	23,585	21,947	20,217	14,643	15,110	13,841

1874. *Winchester, England*. Birthplace of James Wood, one of city's founders. (Associated county: Frederick.)

Windham   **Connecticut**
Willimantic   513 sq. mi.

118,428	109,091	102,525	92,312	84,515	68,572	61,759

May 12, 1726. *Town of Windham*. Named for either of two towns in England: Windham, Sussex; or Wymondham (pronounced "Windham"), Norfolk.

Windham   **Vermont**
Newfane   785 sq. mi.
44,513   44,216   41,588   36,933   33,074   29,776   28,749
February 22, 1781. *Uncertain.* (1) Windham County, Connecticut; (2) Town of Windham, Connecticut.

Windsor   **Vermont**
Woodstock   969 sq. mi.
56,670   57,418   54,055   51,030   44,082   42,483   40,885
February 22, 1781. *Town of Windsor.* Uncertain origin of name. (1) John Stuart, Earl of Windsor (1713–92); Scottish peer; friend and virtual prime minister of George III; English secretary of state 1761. (2) Windsor, Connecticut. (3) Windsor Castle; residence of British sovereigns.

Winkler   **Texas**
Kermit   841 sq. mi.
7,110   7,173   8,626   9,944   9,640   13,652   10,064
February 26, 1887; organized April 5, 1910. *Clinton McKamy Winkler (1827–82).* Texas legislature 1848; captain to lieutenant colonel, Confederate Army, 1861–63; wounded at Gettysburg 1863; judge, Court of Civil Appeals 1876–82.

Winn   **Louisiana**
Winnfield   950 sq. mi.
15,313   16,894   16,269   17,253   16,369   16,034   16,119
February 24, 1852. *Walter O. Winn (?–?).* Founder of seminary that became Louisiana State University 1853; Louisiana legislature.

Winnebago   **Illinois**
Rockford   513 sq. mi.
295,266   278,418   252,913   250,884   246,623   209,765   152,385
January 16, 1836. *Winnebago Indians.* Uncertain derivation of name: (1) Algonquin word meaning "stinking water"; (2) reference to earlier home in Canada meaning "people of the sea." Lived in upper Midwest area; fought on British side in American Revolution and War of 1812; forced many times by treaties and warfare to relocate, winding up on reservations in Nebraska and Wisconsin 1862.

Winnebago   **Iowa**
Forest City   400 sq. mi.
10,866   11,723   12,122   13,010   12,990   13,099   13,450
February 20, 1847; organized November 1, 1857. *Winnebago Indians.**

Winnebago   **Wisconsin**
Oshkosh   434 sq. mi.
166,994   156,763   140,320   131,703   129,931   107,928   91,103
January 6, 1840; organized February 16, 1842. *Uncertain.* (1) *Winnebago Indians.** (2) *Lake Winnebago*; named for Winnebago Indians.*

Winneshiek   **Iowa**
Decorah   690 sq. mi.
21,056   21,310   20,847   21,876   21,758   21,651   21,639
February 20, 1847; organized January 5, 1851; effective March 1, 1851. *Winneshiek (1812–c1872).* Winnebago chief; supported Chief Black Hawk in Black Hawk War 1832; forced by US to move from Wisconsin to Iowa, Minnesota, South Dakota, and finally, Nebraska 1840–59.

Winona   **Minnesota**
Winona   626 sq. mi.
51,461   49,985   47,828   46,256   44,409   40,937   39,841
April 4, 1854. *Village of Winona.* Named for *We-no-nah*, name Dakotas gave to first-born daughters; also from a legendary We-no-nah who dove to her death in Lake Pepin rather than marry a man not of her choosing.

Winston   **Alabama**
Double Springs   613 sq. mi.

24,484	24,843	22,053	21,953	16,654	14,858	18,250

February 12, 1850, as Hancock; name changed January 22, 1858. *John Anthony Winston (1812–71)*. Alabama Assembly 1840–45; Alabama Senate, intermittently 1845–67; colonel, 1st Alabama Volunteers 1846; governor of Alabama 1853–57; Alabama Constitutional Convention 1865; elected to US Senate but not seated for refusing to take oath of allegiance 1867.

Winston   **Mississippi**
Louisville   607 sq. mi.

19,198	20,160	19,433	19,474	18,406	19,246	22,231

December 23, 1833. *Louis Winston (1784–1824)*. Militia colonel; secretary, Mississippi Constitutional Convention 1817; circuit court judge 1821–24.

Wirt   **West Virginia**
Elizabeth   233 sq. mi.

5,717	5,873	5,192	4,922	4,154	4,391	5,119

January 19, 1848. *William Wirt (1774–1838)*. Prosecuted case against Aaron Burr 1807; Virginia House of Delegates 1808; captain of artillery 1812; US attorney for Virginia 1816; US attorney general 1817–29; Anti-Masonic presidential candidate 1832.

Wise   **Texas**
Decatur   904 sq. mi.

59,127	48,793	34,679	26,575	19,687	17,012	16,141

January 23, 1856; organized May 5, 1856. *Henry Alexander Wise (1806–76)*. US representative from Virginia 1833–44; US minister to Brazil 1844–47; Virginia Constitutional Convention 1850; governor of Virginia 1856–60; Virginia Secession Convention 1861; brigadier general and major general, Confederate Army 1861–65.

Wise   **Virginia**
Wise   403 sq. mi.

41,452	40,123	39,573	43,863	35,947	43,579	56,336

February 16, 1856. *Henry Alexander Wise.** (Associated independent city: Norton.)

Wolfe   **Kentucky**
Campton   222 sq. mi.

7,355	7,065	6,503	6,698	5,669	6,534	7,615

March 5, 1860. *Nathaniel Wolfe (1810–65)*. Kentucky Senate 1853–55; Kentucky House of Representatives 1859–63; advocated Kentucky neutrality in Civil War.

Wood   **Ohio**
Bowling Green   617 sq. mi.

125,488	121,065	113,269	107,372	89,722	72,596	59,605

February 12, 1820. *Eleazer Derby Wood (1783–1814)*. Graduated West Point 1806; captain to lieutenant colonel 1812–13; built Fort Meigs 1813; Battle of the Thames 1813; killed during a sortie from Fort Erie September 17, 1814; first graduate of West Point to be killed in Battle.

Wood   **Texas**
Quitman   645 sq. mi.

41,964	36,752	29,380	24,697	18,859	17,653	21,308

February 5, 1850; organized August 5, 1850. *George Tyler Wood (1795–1856)*. Creek Indian War, Battle of Horseshoe Bend 1814; Georgia Assembly 1837–38; Texas Constitutional Convention 1845; colonel, Texas Mounted Volunteers, Battle of Monterrey 1846; Texas Senate 1846; governor of Texas 1847–49.

Wood   **West Virginia**
Parkersburg   368 sq. mi.

86,956	87,986	86,915	93,648	86,818	78,331	66,540

December 21, 1798. *James Wood (1741–1813)*. Captain, French and Indian War 1754; Virginia House of Burgesses 1775; colonel to brigadier general, Virginia Militia 1776–83; Battle of Brandywine 1777; Virginia Executive Council 1784; governor of Virginia 1796–99.

Wood   **Wisconsin**
Wisconsin Rapids   793 sq. mi.

74,749	75,555	73,605	72,799	65,362	59,105	50,500

March 29, 1856. *Joseph Wood (1811–90)*. Wisconsin commissioner of state lands 1848–52; Wisconsin legislature 1856; Wood County judge 1857–58.

Woodbury   **Iowa**
Sioux City   873 sq. mi.

102,172	103,877	98,276	100,884	103,052	107,849	103,917

January 15, 1851, as Wahkaw; name changed January 22, 1853; organized March 7, 1853. *Levi Woodbury (1789–1851)*. Governor of New Hampshire 1823–24; New Hampshire House of Representatives 1825; US senator 1825–31 and 1841–45; US secretary of navy 1831–34; US secretary of treasury 1834–41; US Supreme Court 1845–51.

Woodford   **Illinois**
Eureka   528 sq. mi.

38,664	35,469	32,653	33,320	28,012	24,579	21,335

February 27, 1841. *Woodford County, Kentucky*. Given the honor of naming the new county, Thomas Bullock named it for his home county in Kentucky.

Woodford   **Kentucky**
Versailles   189 sq. mi.

24,939	23,208	19,955	17,778	14,434	11,913	11,212

May 1, 1788. *William Woodford (1735–80)*. French and Indian War 1755; colonel, 2nd Virginia Regiment 1775; brigadier general, Continental army 1777; wounded at Brandywine 1777; captured at Charleston 1780; died in captivity 1780.

Woodruff   **Arkansas**
Augusta   587 sq. mi.

7,260	8,741	9,520	11,222	11,566	13,954	18,957

November 26, 1862. *William E. Woodruff (1795–1885)*. War of 1812; established *Arkansas Gazette* 1818; Arkansas treasurer 1836–38; Little Rock postmaster 1845; founded *Arkansas Democrat* 1850.

Woods   **Oklahoma**
Alva   1,286 sq. mi.

8,878	9,089	9,103	10,923	11,920	11,932	14,526

August 21, 1893, as County M; name changed November 6, 1894. *Samuel Newitt Wood (1825–91)*. Abolitionist in Kansas Territory 1854; part owner of *Kansas Tribune*; Kansas Territory legislature 1859–61; Kansas Senate 1861; although a Quaker, served in Union Army 1861–63, resigned as lieutenant colonel 1863; murdered in a dispute over the county seat for Stevens County 1891. (A clerical error added the letter *s* to the county's name.)

Woodson   **Kansas**
Yates Center   498 sq. mi.

3,309	3,788	4,116	4,600	4,789	5,423	6,711

August 30, 1855; organized May 22, 1858. *Daniel Woodson (1824–94)*. Secretary of Kansas Territory 1854–57, acting governor on numerous occasions; proslavery views were popular in territorial legislature.

Woodward   **Oklahoma**
Woodward   1,242 sq. mi.

20,081	18,486	18,976	21,172	15,537	13,902	14,383

August 21, 1893, as County N; name changed November 6, 1894. *Town of Woodward*. Named for Brinton W. Woodward (?–?); director of Santa Fe Railroad; town grew around train depot where railroad intersected an army road.

Worcester   **Maryland**
Snow Hill   468 sq. mi.

| 51,454 | 46,543 | 35,028 | 30,889 | 24,442 | 23,733 | 23,148 |

October 29, 1742. *Uncertain.* (1) *Edward Somerset, Earl of Worcester (1553–1628)*; court favorite of Elizabeth I and James I; became 4th Earl of Worcester 1589; great chamberlain at coronation of Charles I 1625. (2) *Edward Somerset, 6th Earl of Worcester (1601–67)*; became Earl of Worcester 1646; served Charles I in Wales and Ireland as general and admiral. (3) *Worcester, England.*

Worcester   **Massachusetts**
Worcester   1,511 sq. mi.

| 798,552 | 750,963 | 709,705 | 646,352 | 637,969 | 583,228 | 546,401 |

April 5, 1731. *Uncertain.* (1) *Worcester, England.* (2) *Town of Worcester Massachusetts*; named for Worcester, England.

Worth   **Georgia**
Sylvester   571 sq. mi.

| 21,679 | 21,967 | 19,745 | 18,064 | 14,770 | 16,682 | 19,357 |

December 20, 1853. *William Jenkins Worth (1794–1849).* 1st lieutenant to brevet major general 1813–46; brevet captain for bravery at Chippewa 1814; commandant of West Point cadets 1820–28; Seminole War 1838; brevet major general for heroism in Mexican War 1846; awarded sword by Congress 1847.

Worth   **Iowa**
Northwood   400 sq. mi.

| 7,598 | 7,909 | 7,991 | 9,075 | 8,968 | 10,259 | 11,068 |

January 15, 1851; organized October 13, 1857. *William Jenkins Worth.**

Worth   **Missouri**
Grant City   267 sq. mi.

| 2,171 | 2,382 | 2,440 | 3,008 | 3,359 | 3,936 | 5,120 |

February 6, 1861. *William Jenkins Worth.**

Wrangell   **Alaska**
Wrangle   2,541 sq. mi.

| 2,369 | 6,684 | 7,042 | 6,167 | 4,913 | 4,181 | (a) |

June 1, 2008. *Wrangell Island.* Named for Russian admiral Baron Ferdinand Petrovich Vrangelya (?–?); manager of Russian-American Fur Company 1830–36. [(a) Part of 1st Judicial Division.]

Wright   **Iowa**
Clarion   580 sq. mi.

| 13,229 | 14,334 | 14,269 | 16,319 | 17,294 | 19,447 | 19,652 |

January 15, 1851; organized October 1, 1855. *Joseph Albert Wright and Silas Wright*; legislature could not agree which one to name the county for; neither was closely associated with Iowa. (1) Joseph Wright (1810–67); Indiana House of Representatives 1833; Indiana Senate 1840; US representative 1843–45; governor of Indiana 1849–57; US minister to Prussia 1857–61 and 1865–67; US senator 1862–63. (2) Silas Wright (see Wright, Minnesota).

Wright   **Minnesota**
Buffalo   661 sq. mi.

| 124,700 | 89,986 | 68,710 | 58,681 | 38,933 | 29,935 | 27,716 |

February 20, 1855. *Silas Wright (1795–1847).* New York Senate 1824–27; brigadier general, New York Militia 1827; US representative 1827–29; New York comptroller 1829–33; US senator 1833–45; governor of New York 1844–46. County name suggested by a former resident of New York and friend of Wright.

Wright   **Missouri**
Hartville   682 sq. mi.

| 18,815 | 17,955 | 16,758 | 16,188 | 13,667 | 14,183 | 15,834 |

January 29, 1841. *Silas Wright.**

Wyandot   **Ohio**
Upper Sandusky   407 sq. mi.
22,615   22,908   22,254   22,651   21,826   21,648   19,785
February 3, 1845. *Wyandot Indians*. From Iroquoian word *Wendat*, possibly meaning "living near water"; the name Wyandots called themselves. Remnants of Huron tribes living north of Lake Ontario (see Huron, Michigan); Wyandots living in US Midwest removed to Kansas and Oklahoma 1840–67.

Wyandotte   **Kansas**
Kansas City   152 sq. mi.
157,505   157,882   161,993   172,335   186,845   185,495   165,318
January 29, 1859. *Wyandot Indians*.* (One of several alternate spellings.)

Wyoming   **New York**
Warsaw   593 sq. mi.
42,155   43,424   42,507   39,895   37,688   34,793   32,822
May 19, 1841. *Village of M'chewomink*. Delaware name meaning "on the broad plain"; rendered by English as "Wyoming," a name perpetuated by Thomas Campbell's poem *Gertrude of Wyoming* 1809.

Wyoming   **Pennsylvania**
Tunkhannock   397 sq. mi.
28,276   28,080   28,076   26,433   19,082   16,813   16,766
April 4, 1842. *Wyoming Valley*. Named for Indian village (see Wyoming, New York); site of massacre of settlers by Indian allies of British 1757.

Wyoming   **West Virginia**
Pineville   499 sq. mi.
23,796   25,708   28,990   35,993   30,095   34,836   37,540
January 26, 1850. *Wyoming Valley*.*

Wythe   **Virginia**
Wytheville   462 sq. mi.
29,235   27,599   25,466   25,522   22,139   21,975   23,327
December 1, 1789; effective May 1, 1790. *George Wythe (1726–1806)*. Virginia House of Burgesses 1758–68, clerk 1768–75; Continental Congress 1775–77; signer, Declaration of Independence 1776; professor of law, William & Mary College 1779–91; federal Constitutional Convention 1787.

Y

Yadkin   **North Carolina**
Yadkinville   335 sq. mi.
38,406   36,348   30,488   28,439   24,599   22,804   22,133
December 28, 1850. *Yadkin River*. Unknown Indian origin; possibly Siouan. Yadkin Valley was neutral territory in which a tribe's women, children, and elderly could be safely left during battles.

Yakima   **Washington**
Yakima   4,295 sq. mi.
243,231   222,581   188,823   172,508   144,971   145,112   135,723
January 21, 1865. *Yakima Indians*. From Indian word *Ya-ki-ná*, meaning "runaway." A Shahaptian tribe encountered by Lewis and Clark living on both sides of the Columbia River 1806.

Yakutat   **Alaska**
Yakutat   7,649 sq. mi.
662   808   (a)   (a)   (b)   (b)   (c)

September 22, 1992. *Town of Yakutat*. From Tlingit *yak* meaning "ocean" and *tat* meaning "saltwater estuary." [(a) Part of Skagway-Yakutat-Angoon and Valdez-Cordova Census Areas; (b) part of Skagway-Yakutat and Valdez-Chitina-Whitter Census Areas; (c) part of 1st and 3rd Judicial Divisions.]

Yalobusha   **Mississippi**
Water Valley   467 sq. mi.
12,678   13,051   12,033   13,139   11,915   12,502   15,191
December 23, 1833. *Yalobusha River*. From Choctaw words *yaluba* meaning "tadpoles" and *asha* meaning "to be there."

Yamhill   **Oregon**
McMinnville   716 sq. mi.
99,193   84,992   65,551   55,332   40,213   32,478   33,484
July 5, 1843. *Yamel Indians*. From Kalapuyan word for "ford" referring to a crossing of the Yamhill River.

Yancey   **North Carolina**
Burnsville   313 sq. mi.
17,818   17,774   15,419   14,934   12,629   14,008   16,306
December 1833. *Bartlett Yancey (1785–1828)*. US representative from North Carolina 1813–17; North Carolina Senate 1817–27; declined appointment as US minister to Peru 1826.

Yankton   **South Dakota**
Yankton   521 sq. mi.
22,438   21,652   19,252   18,952   19,039   17,551   16,804
April 10, 1862. *Town of Yankton*. Named for Yankton Indians; major division of Dakotas; from corruption of Dakota word *ihanktonwan* meaning "end village."

Yates   **New York**
Penn Yan   338 sq. mi.
25,348   24,621   22,810   21,459   19,831   18,614   17,615
February 5, 1823. *Joseph Christopher Yates (1768–1837)*. Mayor of Schenectady 1798–1808; New York Senate 1805–08; New York Supreme Court 1808–22; governor of New York 1823–24.

Yavapai   **Arizona**
Prescott   8,124 sq. mi.
211,033   167,517   107,714   68,145   36,733   28,912   24,991
November 8, 1864. *Yavapai Indians*. Apache-Mohave tribe; name of uncertain origin. (1) From their name for themselves, *enyaeva* meaning "sun" and *pai* meaning "people." (2) Apache *yava* meaning "hill" and Spanish *país* meaning "country." (3) From *ya mouth pai* meaning "talking people." (4) *Nya va pi* meaning "east" or "sun people."

Yazoo   **Mississippi**
Yazoo City   923 sq. mi.
28,065   28,149   25,506   27,349   27,304   31,653   35,712
January 21, 1823. *Uncertain* (1) *Yazoo River*; tributary of Mississippi River; named for Yazoo Indians. (2) *Yazoo Indians*; name means "to blow on an instrument."

Yell   **Arkansas**
Danville   930 sq. mi.
22,185   21,139   17,759   18,026   14,208   11,940   14,057
December 5, 1840. *Archibald Yell (1797–1847)*. Creek Indian wars; Battle of New Orleans 1815; Arkansas Territory judge 1832–35; US representative 1836–39 and 1845–46; governor of Arkansas 1840–44; colonel, 1st Arkansas Volunteer Cavalry 1846; killed at Battle of Buena Vista, February 22, 1847.

Yellow Medicine   **Minnesota**
Granite Falls   759 sq. mi.

10,438   11,080   11,684   13,653   14,418   15,523   16,279
March 6, 1871; organized February 25, 1874. *Yellow Medicine River*. Tributary of Minnesota River; local Indians used the yellow root of the moonseed vine as a medicine.

Yellowstone   **Montana**
Billings   2,633 sq. mi.
147,972   129,352   113,419   108,035   87,367   79,016   55,875
February 26, 1883; effective May 1, 1883. *Yellowstone River*. Named *Roche Jaune* (Yellow Rock) by French for yellow rocks along its banks.

Yoakum   **Texas**
Plains   800 sq. mi.
7,879   7,322   8,786   8,299   7,344   8,032   4,339
August 21, 1876; organized 1907. *Henderson King Yoakum (1810–56)*. Graduated West Point 1832; resigned commission 1833; captain, Tennessee Mounted Militia 1836; mayor of Murfreesboro 1837; colonel, Tennessee Infantry in Cherokee War 1838; Tennessee Senate 1839–45; private to 1st lieutenant, US Army 1846; Battle of Monterrey 1846; wrote *History of Texas* 1855.

Yolo   **California**
Woodland   1,015 sq. mi.
200,849   168,660   141,092   113,374   97,788   65,727   40,640
February 18, 1850. *Yolo Indians*. Corruption of Indian word *yoloy* or *yodoi* meaning "place abounding with rushes."

York   **Maine**
Alfred   991 sq. mi.
197,131   186,742   164,587   139,666   111,576   99,402   93,541
November 20, 1652; abolished and recreated twice 1664–1691. *Uncertain*. (1) *Town of York*; named for York, England. (2) *York and Yorkshire, England*. (3) *King James II*, Duke of York and Albany (see Albany, New York).

York   **Nebraska**
York   576 sq. mi.
13,665   14,598   14,428   14,798   13,685   13,724   14,346
March 13, 1855; organized January 4, 1870. *York County, Pennsylvania*. Most likely suggested by legislator from Pennsylvania.

York   **Pennsylvania**
York   904 sq. mi.
434,972   381,751   339,574   312,963   272,603   238,336   202,737
August 19, 1749. *Town of York*. Uncertain derivation: (1) York and Yorkshire, England; (2) King James II, Duke of York and Albany (see Albany, New York).

York   **South Carolina**
York   681 sq. mi.
226,073   164,614   131,497   106,720   85,216   78,760   71,596
March 12, 1785; converted to judicial district January 1, 1800; redesignated as county April 16, 1868. *York County, Pennsylvania*. Origin of early settlers.

York   **Virginia**
Yorktown   105 sq. mi.
65,464   56,297   42,422   35,463   33,203   21,583   11,750
1634 as Charles River; name changed 1643. *Uncertain*. (1) *King James II*, Duke of York and Albany (see Albany, New York). (2) *Yorkshire, England*. (Associated independent cities: Poquoson and part of Williamsburg.)

Young   **Texas**
Graham   914 sq. mi.
18,550   17,943   18,126   19,083   15,400   17,254   16,810

February 2, 1856; organized April 27, 1874. *William Cocke Young (1812–62)*. Texas Constitutional Convention 1845; Mexican War 1846; organized and commanded 11th Texas Cavalry, Confederate army 1861; murdered by outlaws October 16, 1862.

Yuba   **California**
Marysville   632 sq. mi.

72,155	60,219	58,228	49,733	44,736	33,859	24,420

February 18, 1850. *Yuba River*. Named from Maidu village *Yubu*, the tribe's name for itself.

Yukon-Koyukuk   **Alaska**
(Census Area)   145,505 sq. mi.

5,588	6,551	6,714	7,873	6,436[a]	5,716[a]	(b)

"Yukon"; from Yukon River; from Athabascan *yukonna* meaning "great river." "Koyukuk" from Koyukuk River; tributary of Yukon River; unknown origin: may be Russian adaptation of Athabascan word for "big mountain." [(a) Includes Upper Yukon Census Division: 1970, 1,684; 1960, 1,619. (b) Part of 4th Judicial Division.]

Yuma   **Arizona**
Yuma   5,514 sq. mi.

195,751	160,026	106,895	90,554	60,827	46,235	28,006

December 21, 1864. *Yuma Indians*. Unknown origin; best suggestion is from Spanish *humo* (smoke) from many fires noted by Spanish explorers to ward off cold during winter mornings and mosquitoes during the warmer months.

Yuma   **Colorado**
Wray   2,364 sq. mi.

10,043	9,841	8,954	9,682	8,544	8,912	10,827

March 15, 1889. *Town of Yuma*. From Yuma Switch railroad siding; named for Yuma Indian laborer from Arizona who died and was buried near the switch. (See Yuma, Arizona.)

Z

Zapata   **Texas**
Zapata   998 sq. mi.

14,018	12,182	9,279	6,628	4,352	4,393	4,405

January 22, 1858; organized April 26, 1858. *Antonio Zapata (c1800–40)*. Cattleman; led revolt against Mexican president Santa Anna 1838; one of proclaimers of Republic of Rio Grande, independent of Mexico 1840; captured and executed 1840; severed head displayed on a pole in Guerrero as warning to potential revolutionaries.

Zavala   **Texas**
Crystal City   1,297 sq. mi.

11,677	11,600	12,162	11,666	11,370	12,696	11,281

February 1, 1858; organized February 25, 1884. *Manuel Lorenzo Justiniano de Zavala y Sáenz (1788–1836)*. Political leader in Yucatán following Mexican independence from Spain; Mexican Congress 1823–24; Mexican Senate 1825–26; governor of State of Mexico 1826–28 and 1832–33; licensed to settle 500 families in Mexican Texas 1829; exiled in New York and Europe while Mexican Federalists lost power 1830–32; Mexican minister to France 1834; signer, Texas Declaration of Independence 1836; died of exposure following boating accident.

Ziebach   **South Dakota**
Dupree   1,961 sq. mi.

2,801	2,519	2,220	2,308	2,221	2,495	2,606

February 1, 1911. *Francis Marion Ziebach (1830–1929)*. Founded *Yankton Dakotaon* 1861; captain, Company A, Dakota Militia 1862; Dakota Territory legislature 1883–84; South Dakota Constitutional Convention 1883.

Appendix A: Counties by State

With County Seat and Date of Creation

This appendix lists counties alphabetically by state. The list includes the county seat and the date of the county's creation. The information provided at the beginning of each state's entry is meant to indicate the political entity under which the county was created. It is not intended to provide a political history of the state.

ALABAMA (67 COUNTIES)

Mississippi Territory April 7, 1798
Alabama Territory March 3, 1817
Admitted to Union December 14, 1819 (22nd)
Seceded January 11, 1861
Readmitted June 25, 1868

County	County Seat	Created
Autauga	Prattville	November 21, 1818
Baldwin	Bay Minette	December 21, 1809
Barbour	Clayton	December 18, 1832
Bibb[1]	Centreville	February 7, 1818
Blount	Oneonta	February 6, 1818
Bullock	Union Springs	December 5, 1866
Butler	Greenville	December 13, 1819
Calhoun[2]	Anniston	December 18, 1832
Chambers	Lafayette	December 18, 1832
Cherokee	Centre	January 9, 1836
Chilton[3]	Clanton	December 30, 1868
Choctaw	Butler	December 29, 1847
Clarke	Grove Hill	December 10, 1812
Clay	Ashland	December 7, 1866
Cleburne	Heflin	December 6, 1866
Coffee	Elba	December 29, 1841
Colbert	Tuscumbia	February 6, 1867
Conecuh	Evergreen	February 13, 1818
Coosa	Rockford	December 18, 1832
Covington[4]	Andalusia	December 7, 1821
Crenshaw	Luverne	November 24, 1866
Cullman	Cullman	January 24, 1877
Dale	Ozark	December 22, 1824
Dallas	Selma	February 9, 1818

DeKalb	Fort Payne	January 9, 1836
Elmore	Wetumpka	February 15, 1866
Escambia	Brewton	December 10, 1868
Etowah[5]	Gadsden	December 7, 1866
Fayette	Fayette	December 20, 1824
Franklin	Russellville	February 6, 1818
Geneva	Geneva	December 26, 1868
Greene	Eutaw	December 13, 1819
Hale	Greensboro	January 30, 1867
Henry	Abbeville	December 13, 1819
Houston	Dothan	February 6, 1903
Jackson	Scottsboro	December 13, 1819
Jefferson	Birmingham	December 13, 1819
Lamar[6]	Vernon	February 4, 1867
Lauderdale	Florence	February 6, 1818
Lawrence	Moulton	February 6, 1818
Lee	Opelika	December 5, 1866
Limestone	Athens	February 6, 1818
Lowndes	Haynesville	January 20, 1830
Macon	Tuskegee	December 18, 1832
Madison	Huntsville	December 13, 1808
Marengo	Linden	February 6, 1818
Marion	Hamilton	February 13, 1818
Marshall	Guntersville	January 9, 1836
Mobile	Mobile	December 18, 1812
Monroe	Monroeville	June 29, 1815
Montgomery	Montgomery	December 6, 1816
Morgan[7]	Decatur	February 6, 1818
Perry	Marion	December 13, 1819
Pickens	Carrollton	December 19, 1820
Pike	Troy	December 17, 1821
Randolph	Wedowee	December 18, 1832
Russell	Phenix City	December 18, 1832
Saint Clair	Ashville	November 20, 1818
Shelby	Columbiana	February 7, 1818
Sumter	Livingston	December 18, 1832
Talladega	Talladega	December 18, 1832
Tallapoosa	Dadeville	December 18, 1832
Tuscaloosa	Tuscaloosa	February 6, 1818
Walker	Jasper	December 26, 1823
Washington	Chatom	June 4, 1800
Wilcox	Camden	December 13, 1819
Winston[8]	Double Springs	February 12, 1850

Notes

1. Bibb created as Cahawba; name changed December 20, 1820
2. Calhoun created as Benton; name changed January 29, 1856
3. Chilton created as Baker; name changed December 17, 1874
4. Created as Covington; name changed to Jones August 6, 1868; renamed Covington October 10, 1868
5. Etowah created as Baine; name changed December 3, 1867
6. Lamar created as Jones; name changed February 8, 1877
7. Morgan created as Cotaco; name changed June 14, 1821
8. Winston created as Hancock; name changed January 22, 1858

ALASKA (16 BOROUGHS; 11 CENSUS AREAS; 2 MUNICIPALITIES)

Alaska District May 17, 1884
Alaska Territory August 24, 1912
Admitted to Union January 3, 1959 (49th)

County Equivalent[1]	Center	Created
Aleutians East (B)	Sand Point	October 23, 1987
Aleutians West (CA)		October 23, 1987
Anchorage (M)	Anchorage	September 13, 1963
Bethel (CA)		1957
Bristol Bay (B)	Naknek	October 1962
Denali (B)	Healy	December 1990
Dillingham		1963
Fairbanks North Star (B)	Fairbanks	January 1, 1964
Haines (B)	Haines	August 1968
Hoonah-Angoon (CA)		June 20, 2007
Juneau (B)	Juneau	December 1971
Kenai Peninsula (B)	Soldotna	September 13, 1963
Ketchikan Gateway (B)	Ketchikan	September 13, 1963
Kodiak Island (B)	Kodiak	September 1963
Lake and Peninsula (B)	King Salmon	April 1989
Matanuska-Susitna (B)	Palmer	January 1964
Nome (CA)		1961
North Slope (B)	Barrow	July 1, 1972
Northwest Arctic (B)	Kutzebue	June 1986
Petersburg (CA)		June 1, 2008
Prince of Wales-Hyder (CA)		June 1, 2008
Sitka (B)	Sitka	December 1971
Skagway (M)	Skagway	June 20, 2007
Southeast Fairbanks (CA)		January 1, 1964
Valdez-Cordova (CA)		1961
Wade Hampton (CA)		1961
Wrangell (B)	Wrangell	June 1, 2008
Yakutat (B)	Yakutat	September 1992
Yukon-Koyukuk (CA)		1961

Note

1. B = Borough; CA = Census Area; M = Municipality

ARIZONA (15 COUNTIES)

Arizona Territory February 24, 1863
Admitted to Union February 14, 1912 (48th)

County	County Seat	Created
Apache	Saint Johns	February 14, 1879
Cochise	Bisbee	February 1, 1881
Coconino	Flagstaff	February 19, 1891
Gila	Globe	February 8, 1881
Graham	Safford	March 10, 1881
Greenlee	Clifton	March 10, 1909

La Paz	Parker	November 2, 1983
Maricopa	Phoenix	February 14, 1871
Mohave	Kingman	December 21, 1864
Navajo	Holbrook	March 21, 1895
Pima	Tucson	December 15, 1864
Pinal	Florence	February 1, 1875
Santa Cruz	Nogales	March 15, 1899
Yavapai	Prescott	December 21, 1864
Yuma	Yuma	December 21, 1864

ARKANSAS (75 COUNTIES)

Missouri Territory June 14, 1812
Arkansas Territory March 2, 1819
Admitted to Union June 15, 1836 (25th)
Seceded May 6, 1861
Readmitted June 22, 1868

County	County Seat	Created
Arkansas	De Witt	December 31, 1813
Ashley	Hamburg	November 30, 1848
Baxter	Mountain Home	March 24, 1873
Benton	Bentonville	September 30, 1836
Boone	Harrison	April 9, 1869
Bradley	Warren	December 18, 1840
Calhoun	Hampton	December 6, 1850
Carroll	Berryville	November 1, 1833
Chicot	Lake Village	October 25, 1823
Clark	Arkadelphia	December 15, 1818
Clay[1]	Piggott	March 24, 1873
Cleburne	Heber Springs	February 20, 1883
Cleveland[2]	Rison	April 17, 1873
Columbia	Magnolia	December 17, 1852
Conway	Morrilton	October 20, 1825
Craighead	Jonesboro	February 19, 1859
Crawford	Van Buren	October 18, 1820
Crittenden	Marion	October 22, 1825
Cross	Wynne	November 15, 1862
Dallas	Fordyce	January 1, 1845
Desha	Arkansas City	December 12, 1838
Drew	Monticello	November 26, 1846
Faulkner	Conway	April 12, 1873
Franklin	Ozark	December 19, 1837
Fulton	Salem	December 21, 1842
Garland	Hot Springs	April 5, 1873
Grant	Sheridan	February 4, 1869
Greene	Paragould	November 5, 1833
Hempstead	Hope	December 15, 1818
Hot Spring	Malvern	November 2, 1829
Howard	Nashville	April 17, 1873
Independence	Batesville	October 23, 1820
Izard	Melbourne	October 27, 1825
Jackson	Newport	November 5, 1829

Jefferson	Pine Bluff	November 2, 1829
Johnson	Clarksville	November 16, 1833
Lafayette	Lewisville	October 15, 1827
Lawrence	Walnut Ridge	January 15, 1815
Lee	Marianna	April 17, 1873
Lincoln	Star City	March 28, 1871
Little River	Ashdown	March 5, 1867
Logan[3]	Paris	March 22, 1871
Lonoke	Lonoke	April 16, 1873
Madison	Huntsville	September 30, 1836
Marion[4]	Yellville	November 3, 1835
Miller	Texarkana	December 22, 1874
Mississippi	Blytheville	November 1, 1833
Monroe	Clarendon	November 2, 1829
Montgomery	Mount Ida	December 9, 1842
Nevada	Prescott	March 20, 1871
Newton	Jasper	December 14, 1842
Ouachita	Camden	November 29, 1842
Perry	Perryville	December 18, 1840
Phillips	Helena	May 1, 1820
Pike	Murfreesboro	November 1, 1833
Poinsett	Harrisburg	February 28, 1838
Polk	Mena	November 30, 1844
Pope	Russellville	November 2, 1829
Prairie	Des Arc	November 25, 1846
Pulaski	Little Rock	December 15, 1818
Randolph	Pocahontas	October 29, 1835
Saint Francis	Forrest City	October 13, 1827
Saline	Benton	November 2, 1835
Scott	Waldron	November 5, 1833
Searcy	Marshall	December 13, 1838
Sebastian	Fort Scott	January 6, 1851
Sevier	De Queen	October 17, 1828
Sharp	Ash Flat	July 18, 1868
Stone	Mountain View	April 21, 1873
Union	El Dorado	November 2, 1829
Van Buren	Clinton	November 11, 1833
Washington	Fayetteville	October 17, 1828
White	Searcy	October 23, 1835
Woodruff	Augusta	November 26, 1862
Yell	Danville	December 5, 1840

Notes

1. Clay created as Clayton; name changed December 6, 1875
2. Cleveland created as Dorsey; name changed March 5, 1885
3. Logan created as Sarber; name changed December 14, 1875
4. Marion created as Searcy; name changed September 29, 1836

CALIFORNIA (58 COUNTIES)

Constitutional Convention 1849–50
Admitted to Union September 9, 1850 (31st)

County	County Seat	Created
Alameda	Oakland	March 25, 1853
Alpine	Markleeville	March 16, 1864
Amador	Jackson	May 11, 1854
Butte	Oroville	February 18, 1850
Calaveras	San Andreas	February 18, 1850
Colusa[1]	Colusa	February 18, 1850
Contra Costa	Martinez	February 18, 1850
Del Norte	Crescent City	March 2, 1857
El Dorado	Placerville	February 18, 1850
Fresno	Fresno	April 19, 1856
Glenn	Willows	March 11, 1891
Humboldt	Eureka	May 12, 1853
Imperial	El Centro	August 6, 1907
Inyo	Independence	March 22, 1866
Kern	Bakersfield	April 2, 1866
Kings	Hanford	March 22, 1893
Lake	Lakeport	May 20, 1861
Lassen	Susanville	April 1, 1864
Los Angeles	Los Angeles	February 18, 1850
Madera	Madera	March 11, 1893
Marin	San Rafael	February 18, 1850
Mariposa	Mariposa	February 18, 1850
Mendocino	Ukiah	February 18, 1850
Merced	Merced	April 19, 1855
Modoc	Alturas	February 17, 1874
Mono	Bridgeport	April 24, 1861
Monterey	Salinas	February 18, 1850
Napa	Napa	February 18, 1850
Nevada	Nevada City	April 25, 1851
Orange	Santa Ana	March 11, 1889
Placer	Auburn	April 25, 1851
Plumas	Quincy	March 18, 1854
Riverside	Riverside	March 11, 1893
Sacramento	Sacramento	February 18, 1850
San Benito	Hollister	February 12, 1874
San Bernardino	San Bernardino	April 26, 1853
San Diego	San Diego	February 18, 1850
San Francisco	San Francisco	February 18, 1850
San Joaquin	Stockton	February 18, 1850
San Luis Obispo	San Luis Obispo	February 18, 1850
San Mateo	Redwood City	April 19, 1856
Santa Barbara	Santa Barbara	February 18, 1850
Santa Clara	San Jose	February 18, 1850
Santa Cruz[2]	Santa Cruz	February 18, 1850
Shasta	Redding	February 18, 1850
Sierra	Downieville	April 16, 1852
Siskiyou	Yreka	March 22, 1852
Solano	Fairfield	February 18, 1850
Sonoma	Santa Rosa	February 18, 1850
Stanislaus	Modesto	April 1, 1854
Sutter	Yuba City	February 18, 1850
Tehama	Red Bluff	April 9, 1856
Trinity	Weaverville	February 18, 1850

Tulare	Visalia	April 20, 1852
Tuolumne	Sonora	February 18, 1850
Ventura	Ventura	March 22, 1872
Yolo	Woodland	February 18, 1850
Yuba	Marysville	February 18, 1850

Notes

1. Colusa created as Colusi; spelling changed 1854
2. Santa Cruz created as Branciforte; name changed April 5, 1850

COLORADO (64 COUNTIES)

Colorado Territory February 28, 1861
Admitted to Union August 1, 1876 (38th)

County	County Seat	Created
Adams	Brighton	April 15, 1901
Alamosa	Alamosa	March 8, 1913
Arapahoe	Littleton	November 1, 1861
Archuleta	Pagosa Springs	April 15, 1885
Baca	Springfield	April 16, 1889
Bent	Las Animas	February 11, 1870
Boulder	Boulder	November 1, 1861
Broomfield	Broomfield	November 15, 2001
Chaffee[1]	Salida	November 1, 1861
Cheyenne	Cheyenne Wells	March 25, 1889
Clear Creek	Georgetown	November 1, 1861
Conejos[2]	Conejos	November 1, 1861
Costilla	San Luis	November 1, 1861
Crowley	Ordway	May 29, 1911
Custer	Westcliffe	March 9, 1877
Delta	Delta	February 11, 1883
Denver	Denver	March 18, 1901
Dolores	Dove Creek	February 19, 1881
Douglas	Castle Creek	November 1, 1861
Eagle	Eagle	February 11, 1883
Elbert	Kiowa	February 2, 1874
El Paso	Colorado Springs	November 1, 1861
Fremont	Canon City	November 1, 1861
Garfield	Glenwood Springs	February 10, 1883
Gilpin	Central City	November 1, 1861
Grand	Hot Sulphur Springs	February 2, 1874
Gunnison	Gunnison	February 9, 1877
Hinsdale	Lake City	February 10, 1874
Huerfano	Walsenburg	November 1, 1861
Jackson	Walden	May 5, 1909
Jefferson	Golden	November 1, 1861
Kiowa	Eads	April 11, 1889
Kit Carson	Burlington	April 11, 1889
Lake[3]	Leadville	November 1, 1861
La Plata	Durango	February 10, 1874
Larimer	Fort Collins	November 1, 1861

Las Animas	Trinidad	February 9, 1866
Lincoln	Hugo	April 11, 1889
Logan	Sterling	February 25, 1887
Mesa	Grand Junction	February 14, 1883
Mineral	Creede	March 27, 1893
Moffat	Craig	February 27, 1911
Montezuma	Cortez	April 16, 1889
Montrose	Montrose	February 11, 1883
Morgan	Fort Morgan	February 19, 1889
Otero	La Junta	March 25, 1889
Ouray[4]	Ouray	January 18, 1877
Park	Fairplay	November 1, 1861
Phillips	Holyoke	March 27, 1889
Pitkin	Aspen	February 23, 1881
Prowers	Lamar	April 11, 1889
Pueblo	Pueblo	November 1, 1861
Rio Blanco	Meeker	March 25, 1889
Rio Grande	Del Norte	February 10, 1874
Routt	Steamboat Springs	January 29, 1877
Saguache	Saguache	December 29, 1866
San Juan	Silverton	January 31, 1876
San Miguel	Telluride	November 1, 1883
Sedgwick	Julesburg	April 9, 1889
Summit	Breckenridge	November 1, 1861
Teller	Cripple Creek	March 23, 1899
Washington	Akron	February 9, 1887
Weld	Greeley	November 1, 1861
Yuma	Wray	March 15, 1889

Notes

1. Chaffee created as Lake; name changed February 10, 1879
2. Conejos created as Guadalupe; name changed November 7, 1861
3. Lake created as Carbonate; name changed February 10, 1879
4. Ouray created as Uncompahgre; name changed March 2, 1883

CONNECTICUT (8 COUNTIES)

Connecticut Colony established 1636
Connecticut and New Haven Colonies consolidated 1662
Independence Resolution June 14, 1776
Ratified Constitution January 9, 1788 (5th)

County	County Seat	Created
Fairfield	Bridgeport	1666
Hartford	Hartford	1666
Litchfield	Litchfield	October 9, 1751
Middlesex	Middletown	May 2, 1785
New Haven	New Haven	1666
New London	New London	1666
Tolland	Rockville	1785
Windham	Putnam	May 12, 1726

DELAWARE (3 COUNTIES)

Captured from Dutch by English 1664
Acquired by Pennsylvania 1682
Self-rule from Pennsylvania 1704
Declared independence July 4, 1776
Ratified Constitution December 7, 1787 (1st)

County	County Seat	Created
Kent[1]	Dover	June 21, 1680
New Castle	Wilmington	August 8, 1673
Sussex[2]	Georgetown	August 8, 1673

Notes

1. Kent created as Saint Johns; name changed December 31, 1683
2. Sussex created as Hoarkill; name changed to Deale 1681; name changed to Sussex December 4, 1682

DISTRICT OF COLUMBIA (1 FEDERAL DISTRICT)

County	County Seat	Created
	Washington	July 16, 1790

FLORIDA (67 COUNTIES)

Military government 1819
Florida Territory March 30, 1822
Admitted to Union March 3, 1845 (27th)
Seceded January 10, 1861
Readmitted June 25, 1868

County	County Seat	Created
Alachua	Gainesville	December 29, 1824
Baker	Macclenny	February 8, 1861
Bay	Panama City	April 24, 1913
Bradford[1]	Starke	December 21, 1858
Brevard[2]	Titusville	March 14, 1844
Broward	Fort Lauderdale	April 30, 1915
Calhoun	Blountstown	January 26, 1838
Charlotte	Port Charlotte	April 23, 1921
Citrus	Inverness	June 2, 1887
Clay	Green Cove Springs	December 31, 1858
Collier	Naples	May 8, 1923
Columbia	Lake City	February 4, 1832
DeSoto	Arcadia	May 19, 1887
Dixie	Cross City	April 25, 1921
Duval	Jacksonville	August 12, 1822
Escambia	Pensacola	July 21, 1821
Flagler	Bunnell	April 28, 1917
Franklin	Apalachicola	February 8, 1832
Gadsden	Quincy	June 24, 1823
Gilchrist	Trenton	December 4, 1925

Glades	Moore Haven	April 23, 1921
Gulf	Port Saint Joe	June 6, 1925
Hamilton	Jasper	December 26, 1827
Hardee	Wauchula	April 23, 1921
Hendry	LaBelle	May 11, 1923
Hernando[3]	Brooksville	February 24, 1843
Highlands	Sebring	April 23, 1921
Hillsborough	Tampa	January 25, 1834
Holmes	Bonifay	January 8, 1848
Indian River	Vero Beach	May 30, 1925
Jackson	Marianna	August 12, 1822
Jefferson	Monticello	January 6, 1827
Lafayette	Mayo	December 23, 1856
Lake	Tavares	May 27, 1887
Lee	Fort Myers	May 13, 1887
Leon	Tallahassee	December 29, 1824
Levy	Bronson	March 10, 1845
Liberty	Bristol	December 15, 1855
Madison	Madison	December 26, 1827
Manatee	Bradenton	January 9, 1855
Marion	Ocala	March 14, 1844
Martin	Stuart	May 30, 1925
Miami-Dade[4]	Miami	February 4, 1836
Monroe	Key West	July 3, 1823
Nassau	Fernandina Beach	December 29, 1824
Okaloosa	Crestview	June 3, 1915
Okeechobee	Okeechobee	May 8, 1917
Orange[5]	Orlando	December 29, 1824
Osceola	Kissimmee	May 12, 1887
Palm Beach	West Palm Beach	April 30, 1909
Pasco	Dade City	June 2, 1887
Pinellas	Clearwater	May 23, 1911
Polk	Bartow	February 8, 1861
Putnam	Palatka	January 13, 1849
Saint Johns	Saint Augustine	August 12, 1822
Saint Lucie	Fort Pierce	May 24, 1905
Santa Rosa	Milton	February 18, 1842
Sarasota	Sarasota	May 14, 1921
Seminole	Sanford	April 25, 1913
Sumter	Bushnell	January 8, 1853
Suwannee	Live Oak	December 21, 1858
Taylor	Perry	December 23, 1856
Union	Lake Butler	May 20, 1921
Volusia	DeLand	December 29, 1854
Wakulla	Crawfordville	March 11, 1843
Walton	De Funiak Springs	December 29, 1824
Washington	Chipley	December 9, 1825

Notes

1. Bradford created as New River; name changed December 6, 1861
2. Brevard created as Saint Lucie; name changed January 6, 1855
3. Created as Hernando; name changed to Benton March 6, 1844; renamed Hernando December 24, 1850
4. Miami-Dade created as Dade; name changed December 2, 1997
5. Orange created as Mosquito; name changed January 30, 1845

GEORGIA (159 COUNTIES)

British colony 1732
State constitution February 5, 1777
Ratified Constitution January 5, 1788 (4th)
Seceded January 19, 1861
Readmitted July 15, 1870

County	County Seat	Created
Appling	Baxley	December 15, 1818
Atkinson	Pearson	August 15, 1917
Bacon	Alma	July 27, 1914
Baker	Newton	December 12, 1825
Baldwin	Milledgeville	May 11, 1803
Banks	Homer	December 11, 1858
Barrow	Winder	July 7, 1914
Bartow[1]	Cartersville	December 3, 1832
Ben Hill	Fitzgerald	July 31, 1906
Berrien	Nashville	February 25, 1856
Bibb	Macon	December 9, 1822
Bleckley	Cochran	July 30, 1912
Brantley	Nahunta	August 14, 1920
Brooks	Quitman	December 11, 1858
Bryan	Pembroke	December 19, 1793
Bulloch	Statesboro	February 8, 1796
Burke	Waynesboro	February 5, 1777
Butts	Jackson	December 24, 1825
Calhoun	Morgan	February 20, 1854
Camden	Woodbine	February 5, 1777
Candler	Metter	July 17, 1914
Carroll	Carrollton	December 11, 1826
Catoosa	Ringgold	December 5, 1853
Charlton	Folkston	February 18, 1854
Chatham	Savannah	February 5, 1777
Chattahoochee	Cusseta	February 13, 1854
Chattooga	Summerville	December 28, 1838
Cherokee	Canton	December 26, 1831
Clarke	Athens	December 5, 1801
Clay	Fort Gaines	February 16, 1854
Clayton	Jonesboro	November 30, 1858
Clinch	Homerville	February 14, 1850
Cobb	Marietta	December 3, 1932
Coffee	Douglas	February 9, 1854
Colquitt	Moultrie	February 25, 1856
Columbia	Evans	December 10, 1790
Cook	Adel	July 30, 1918
Coweta	Newnan	December 11, 1826
Crawford	Knoxville	December 9, 1822
Crisp	Cordele	August 17, 1905
Dade	Trenton	December 25, 1837
Dawson	Dawsonville	December 3, 1957
Decatur	Bainbridge	December 8, 1823
DeKalb	Decatur	December 9, 1822
Dodge	Eastman	October 26, 1870
Dooly	Vienna	May 15, 1821

Dougherty	Albany	December 15, 1853
Douglas	Douglasville	October 17, 1870
Early	Blakely	December 15, 1818
Echols	Statenville	December 13, 1858
Effingham	Springfield	February 5, 1777
Elbert	Elberton	December 10, 1790
Emanuel	Swainsboro	December 10, 1812
Evans	Claxton	August 11, 1914
Fannin	Blue Ridge	January 21, 1854
Fayette	Fayetteville	May 15, 1821
Floyd	Rome	December 3, 1832
Forsyth	Cumming	December 3, 1832
Franklin	Carnesville	February 25, 1784
Fulton	Atlanta	December 20, 1853
Gilmer	Ellijay	December 3, 1832
Glascock	Gibson	December 19, 1857
Glynn	Brunswick	February 5, 1777
Gordon	Calhoun	February 13, 1850
Grady	Cairo	August 17, 1905
Greene	Greensboro	February 3, 1786
Gwinnett	Lawrenceville	December 15, 1818
Habersham	Clarkesville	December 15, 1818
Hall	Gainesville	December 15, 1818
Hancock	Sparta	December 17, 1793
Haralson	Buchanan	January 26, 1856
Harris	Hamilton	December 1, 1827
Hart	Hartwell	December 7, 1853
Heard	Franklin	December 22, 1830
Henry	McDonough	May 15, 1821
Houston	Perry	May 15, 1821
Irwin	Ocilla	December 15, 1818
Jackson	Jefferson	February 11, 1796
Jasper[2]	Monticello	December 10, 1807
Jeff Davis	Hazlehurst	August 18, 1905
Jefferson	Louisville	February 20, 1796
Jenkins	Millen	August 17, 1905
Johnson	Wrightsville	December 11, 1858
Jones	Gray	December 10, 1807
Lamar	Barnesville	August 17, 1920
Lanier	Lakeland	August 11, 1919
Laurens	Dublin	December 10, 1807
Lee	Leesburg	December 11, 1826
Liberty	Hinesville	February 5, 1777
Lincoln	Lincolnton	February 20, 1796
Long	Ludowici	August 14, 1920
Lowndes	Valdosta	December 23, 1825
Lumpkin	Dahlonega	December 3, 1832
Macon	Oglethorpe	December 14, 1837
Madison	Danielsville	December 5, 1811
Marion	Buena Vista	December 24, 1827
McDuffie	Thomson	October 18, 1870
McIntosh	Darien	December 19, 1793
Meriwether	Greenville	December 24, 1827
Miller	Colquitt	February 26, 1856
Mitchell	Camilla	December 21, 1857

Monroe	Forsyth	May 15, 1821
Montgomery	Mount Vernon	December 19, 1793
Morgan	Madison	December 10, 1807
Murray	Chatsworth	December 3, 1832
Muscogee	Columbus	December 11, 1826
Newton	Covington	December 24, 1821
Oconee	Watkinsville	February 25, 1875
Oglethorpe	Lexington	December 19, 1793
Paulding	Dallas	December 3, 1832
Peach	Fort Valley	July 18, 1924
Pickens	Jasper	December 5, 1853
Pierce	Blackshear	December 18, 1857
Pike	Zebulon	December 9, 1822
Polk	Cedartown	December 20, 1851
Pulaski	Hawkinsville	December 13, 1808
Putnam	Eatonton	December 10, 1807
Quitman	Georgetown	December 10, 1858
Rabun	Clayton	December 21, 1819
Randolph	Cuthbert	December 20, 1828
Richmond	Augusta	February 5, 1777
Rockdale	Conyers	October 18, 1870
Schley	Ellaville	December 22, 1857
Screven	Sylvania	December 14, 1793
Seminole	Donalsonville	July 8, 1920
Spalding	Griffin	December 20, 1851
Stephens	Toccoa	August 18, 1905
Stewart	Lumpkin	December 23, 1830
Sumter	Americus	December 26, 1831
Talbot	Talbotton	December 14, 1827
Taliaferro	Crawfordville	December 24, 1825
Tattnall	Reidsville	December 5, 1801
Taylor	Butler	January 15, 1852
Telfair	McRae	December 10, 1807
Terrell	Dawson	February 16, 1856
Thomas	Thomasville	December 23, 1825
Tift	Tifton	August 17, 1905
Toombs	Lyons	August 18, 1905
Towns	Hiawassee	March 6, 1856
Treutlen	Soperton	August 21, 1917
Troup	La Grange	December 11, 1826
Turner	Ashburn	August 18, 1905
Twiggs	Jeffersonville	December 14, 1809
Union	Blairsville	December 3, 1832
Upson	Thomaston	December 15, 1824
Walker	LaFayette	December 18, 1833
Walton	Monroe	December 15, 1818
Ware	Waycross	December 15, 1824
Warren	Warrenton	December 19, 1793
Washington	Sandersville	February 25, 1784
Wayne	Jesup	May 11, 1803
Webster[3]	Preston	December 16, 1853
Wheeler	Alamo	August 14, 1912
White	Cleveland	December 22, 1857
Whitfield	Dalton	December 30, 1851
Wilcox	Abbeville	December 22, 1857

Wilkes	Washington	February 5, 1777
Wilkinson	Irwinton	May 11, 1803
Worth	Sylvester	December 20, 1853

Notes

1. Bartow created as Cass; name changed December 6, 1861
2. Jasper created as Randolph; name changed December 10, 1812
3. Webster created as Kinchafoonee; name changed February 21, 1856

HAWAII (5 COUNTIES)

Territory of Hawaii April 30, 1900
Admitted to Union August 21, 1959 (50th)

County	County Seat	Created
Hawaii	Hilo	July 1905
Honolulu	Honolulu	July 1905
Kalawao[1]		July 1905
Kauai	Lihue	July 1905
Maui	Wailuku	July 1905

Note

1. Kalawao County has no county-level government. It is administered by the Health Department of the State of Hawaii. It is usually statistically included in Maui County.

IDAHO (44 COUNTIES)

Idaho Territory March 3, 1863
Admitted to Union July 3, 1890 (43rd)

County	County Seat	Created
Ada	Boise	December 22, 1864
Adams	Council	March 3, 1911
Bannock	Pocatello	March 6, 1893
Bear Lake	Paris	January 5, 1875
Benewah	Saint Maries	January 23, 1915
Bingham	Blackfoot	January 13, 1885
Blaine	Hailey	March 5, 1895
Boise	Idaho City	February 4, 1864
Bonner	Sandpoint	February 21, 1907
Bonneville	Idaho Falls	February 7, 1911
Boundary	Bonners Ferry	January 23, 1915
Butte	Arco	February 6, 1917
Camas	Fairfield	February 6, 1917
Canyon	Caldwell	May 7, 1891
Caribou	Soda Springs	February 11, 1919
Cassia	Burley	February 20, 1879
Clark	Dubois	February 1, 1919
Clearwater	Orofino	February 27, 1911
Custer	Challis	January 8, 1881
Elmore	Mountain Home	February 7, 1889

Franklin	Preston	January 20, 1913
Fremont	Saint Anthony	March 4, 1893
Gem	Emmett	March 19, 1915
Gooding	Gooding	January 28, 1913
Idaho	Grangeville	February 4, 1864
Jefferson	Rigby	February 18, 1913
Jerome	Jerome	February 8, 1919
Kootenai	Coeur d'Alene	December 22, 1864
Latah	Moscow	May 14, 1888
Lemhi	Salmon	January 9, 1869
Lewis	Nezperce	March 3, 1911
Lincoln	Shoshone	March 18, 1895
Madison	Rexburg	February 18, 1913
Minidoka	Rupert	January 28, 1913
Nez Perce	Lewiston	February 4, 1864
Oneida	Malad City	January 22, 1864
Owyhee	Murphy	December 31, 1863
Payette	Payette	February 28, 1917
Power	American Falls	January 30, 1913
Shoshone	Wallace	February 4, 1864
Teton	Driggs	January 26, 1915
Twin Falls	Twin Falls	February 21, 1907
Valley	Cascade	February 26, 1917
Washington	Weiser	February 20, 1879

ILLINOIS (102 COUNTIES)

Northwest Territory July 13, 1787
Indiana Territory May 7, 1800
Illinois Territory February 3, 1809
Admitted to Union December 3, 1818 (21st)

County	County Seat	Created
Adams	Quincy	January 13, 1825
Alexander	Cairo	March 4, 1819
Bond	Greenville	January 4, 1817
Boone	Belvidere	March 4, 1837
Brown	Mount Sterling	February 1, 1839
Bureau	Princeton	February 28, 1837
Calhoun	Hardin	January 10, 1825
Carroll	Mount Carroll	February 22, 1839
Cass	Virginia	March 3, 1837
Champaign	Urbana	February 20, 1833
Christian[1]	Taylorville	February 15, 1839
Clark	Marshall	March 22, 1819
Clay	Louisville	December 23, 1824
Clinton	Carlyle	December 27, 1824
Coles	Christian	December 25, 1830
Cook	Chicago	January 15, 1831
Crawford	Robinson	December 31, 1816
Cumberland	Toledo	March 2, 1843
DeKalb	Sycamore	March 4, 1837
De Witt	Clinton	March 1, 1839
Douglas	Tuscola	February 8, 1859

DuPage	Wheaton	February 9, 1839
Edgar	Paris	January 3, 1823
Edwards	Albion	November 28, 1814
Effingham	Effingham	February 15, 1831
Fayette	Vandalia	February 14, 1821
Ford	Paxton	February 17, 1859
Franklin	Benton	January 2, 1818
Fulton	Lewistown	January 28, 1823
Gallatin	Shawneetown	September 14, 1812
Greene	Carrollton	January 20, 1821
Grundy	Morris	February 7, 1841
Hamilton	McLeansboro	February 8, 1821
Hancock	Carthage	January 13, 1825
Hardin	Elizabethtown	March 2, 1839
Henderson	Oquawka	January 20, 1841
Henry	Cambridge	January 13, 1825
Iroquois	Watseka	February 26, 1833
Jackson	Murphysboro	January 10, 1816
Jasper	Newton	February 15, 1831
Jefferson	Mount Vernon	March 26, 1819
Jersey	Jerseyville	February 28, 1839
Jo Daviess	Galena	February 17, 1827
Johnson	Vienna	September 14, 1812
Kane	Geneva	January 16, 1836
Kankakee	Kankakee	February 11, 1853
Kendall	Yorkville	February 19, 1841
Knox	Galesburg	January 13, 1825
Lake	Waukegan	March 1, 1839
LaSalle	Ottawa	January 15, 1831
Lawrence	Lawrenceville	January 16, 1821
Lee	Dixon	February 27, 1839
Livingston	Pontiac	February 27, 1837
Logan	Lincoln	February 15, 1839
Macon	Decatur	January 19, 1829
Macoupin	Carlinville	January 17, 1829
Madison	Edwardsville	September 14, 1812
Marion	Salem	January 24, 1823
Marshall	Lacon	January 19, 1839
Mason	Havana	January 20, 1841
Massac	Metropolis	February 8, 1843
McDonough	Macomb	January 25, 1826
McHenry	Woodstock	January 16, 1836
McLean	Bloomington	December 25, 1830
Menard	Petersburg	February 15, 1839
Mercer	Aledo	January 13, 1825
Monroe	Waterloo	January 6, 1816
Montgomery	Hillsboro	February 12, 1821
Morgan	Jacksonville	January 31, 1823
Moultrie	Sullivan	February 16, 1843
Ogle	Oregon	January 16, 1836
Peoria	Peoria	January 13, 1825
Perry	Pinckneyville	January 29, 1827
Piatt	Monticello	January 27, 1841
Pike	Pittsfield	January 31, 1821
Pope	Golconda	January 10, 1816

Pulaski	Mound City	March 3, 1843
Putnam	Hennepin	January 13, 1825
Randolph	Chester	October 5, 1795
Richland	Olney	February 24, 1841
Rock Island	Rock Island	February 9, 1831
Saint Clair	Belleville	April 27, 1790
Saline	Harrisburg	February 25, 1847
Sangamon	Springfield	January 30, 1821
Schuyler	Rushville	January 13, 1825
Scott	Winchester	February 16, 1839
Shelby	Shelbyville	January 23, 1827
Stark	Toulon	March 2, 1839
Stephenson	Freeport	March 4, 1837
Tazewell	Pekin	January 31, 1827
Union	Jonesboro	January 2, 1818
Vermilion	Danville	January 18, 1826
Wabash	Mount Carmel	December 27, 1824
Warren	Monmouth	January 13, 1825
Washington	Nashville	January 2, 1818
Wayne	Fairfield	March 26, 1819
White	Carmi	December 9, 1815
Whiteside	Morrison	January 16, 1836
Will	Joliet	January 12, 1836
Williamson	Marion	February 28, 1839
Winnebago	Rockford	January 16, 1836
Woodford	Eureka	February 27, 1841

Note

1. Christian created as Dane; name changed February 1, 1840

INDIANA (92 COUNTIES)

Northwest Territory July 13, 1787
Indiana Territory May 7, 1800
Admitted to Union December 11, 1816 (19th)

County	County Seat	Created
Adams	Decatur	February 7, 1835
Allen	Fort Wayne	December 17, 1823
Bartholomew	Columbus	January 8, 1821
Benton	Fowler	February 18, 1840
Blackford	Hartford City	February 15, 1838
Boone	Lebanon	January 29, 1830
Brown	Nashville	February 4, 1836
Carroll	Delphi	January 7, 1828
Cass	Logansport	December 18, 1828
Clark	Jeffersonville	February 3, 1801
Clay	Brazil	February 12, 1825
Clinton	Frankfort	January 29, 1830
Crawford	English	January 29, 1818
Daviess	Washington	December 24, 1816
Dearborn	Lawrenceburg	March 7, 1803
Decatur	Greensburg	December 31, 1821

DeKalb	Auburn	February 7, 1835
Delaware	Muncie	January 26, 1827
Dubois	Jasper	December 20, 1817
Elkhart	Goshen	January 29, 1830
Fayette	Connersville	December 28, 1818
Floyd	New Albany	January 2, 1819
Fountain	Covington	December 20, 1825
Franklin	Brookville	November 27, 1810
Fulton	Rochester	February 7, 1835
Gibson	Princeton	March 9, 1813
Grant	Marion	February 10, 1831
Greene	Bloomfield	January 5, 1821
Hamilton	Noblesville	January 8, 1823
Hancock	Greenfield	January 26, 1827
Harrison	Corydon	October 11, 1808
Hendricks	Danville	December 20, 1823
Henry	New Castle	December 31, 1821
Howard[1]	Kokomo	January 15, 1844
Huntington	Huntington	February 2, 1832
Jackson	Brownstown	December 18, 1815
Jasper	Rensselaer	February 7, 1835
Jay	Portland	February 7, 1835
Jefferson	Madison	November 23, 1810
Jennings	Vernon	December 27, 1816
Johnson	Franklin	December 31, 1822
Knox	Vincennes	June 20, 1790
Kosciusko	Warsaw	February 7, 1835
LaGrange	Lagrange	February 2, 1832
Lake	Crown Point	January 28, 1836
LaPorte	LaPorte	January 9, 1832
Lawrence	Bedford	January 7, 1818
Madison	Anderson	January 4, 1823
Marion	Indianapolis	December 31, 1821
Marshall	Plymouth	February 7, 1835
Martin	Shoals	January 17, 1820
Miami	Peru	February 2, 1832
Monroe	Bloomington	January 14, 1818
Montgomery	Crawfordsville	December 21, 1822
Morgan	Martinsville	December 31, 1821
Newton	Kentland	February 7, 1835
Noble	Albion	February 7, 1835
Ohio	Rising Sun	January 4, 1844
Orange	Paoli	December 26, 1815
Owen	Spencer	December 21, 1818
Parke	Rockville	January 9, 1821
Perry	Tell City	September 7, 1814
Pike	Petersburg	December 21, 1816
Porter	Valparaiso	February 7, 1835
Posey	Mount Vernon	September 7, 1814
Pulaski	Winamac	February 7, 1835
Putnam	Greencastle	December 31, 1821
Randolph	Winchester	January 10, 1818
Ripley	Versailles	December 27, 1816
Rush	Rushville	December 31, 1821
Saint Joseph	South Bend	January 29, 1830

Scott	Scottsburg	January 12, 1820
Shelby	Shelbyville	December 31, 1821
Spencer	Rockport	January 10, 1818
Starke	Knox	February 7, 1835
Steuben	Angola	February 7, 1835
Sullivan	Sullivan	December 30, 1816
Switzerland	Vevay	September 7, 1814
Tippecanoe	Lafayette	January 20, 1826
Tipton	Tipton	January 15, 1844
Union	Liberty	January 5, 1821
Vanderburgh	Evansville	January 7, 1818
Vermillion	Newport	January 2, 1824
Vigo	Terre Haute	January 21, 1818
Wabash	Wabash	February 2, 1832
Warren	Williamsport	January 19, 1827
Warrick	Booneville	March 9, 1813
Washington	Salem	December 21, 1813
Wayne	Richmond	November 27, 1810
Wells	Bluffton	February 7, 1835
White	Monticello	February 1, 1834
Whitley	Columbia City	February 7, 1835

Note

1. Howard created as Richardville; name changed December 28, 1846

IOWA (99 COUNTIES)

Organized as part of Michigan Territory 1834
Wisconsin Territory July 3, 1836
Iowa Territory June 12, 1838
Admitted to Union December 28, 1846 (29th)

County	County Seat	Created
Adair	Greenfield	January 15, 1851
Adams	Corning	January 15, 1851
Allamakee	Waukon	February 20, 1847
Appanoose	Centerville	February 17, 1843
Audubon	Audubon	January 15, 1851
Benton	Vinton	December 21, 1837
Black Hawk	Waterloo	February 17, 1843
Boone	Boone	January 13, 1846
Bremer	Waverly	January 15, 1851
Buchanan	Independence	December 21, 1837
Buena Vista	Storm Lake	January 15, 1851
Butler	Allison	January 15, 1851
Calhoun[1]	Rockwell City	January 15, 1851
Carroll	Carroll	January 15, 1851
Cass	Atlantic	January 15, 1851
Cedar	Tipton	December 21, 1837
Cerro Gordo	Mason City	January 15, 1851
Cherokee	Cherokee	January 15, 1851
Chickasaw	New Hampton	January 15, 1851
Clarke	Osceola	January 13, 1846

Clay	Spencer	January 15, 1851
Clayton	Elkader	December 21, 1837
Clinton	Clinton	December 21, 1837
Crawford	Denison	January 15, 1851
Dallas	Adel	January 13, 1846
Davis	Bloomfield	February 17, 1843
Decatur	Leon	January 13, 1846
Delaware	Manchester	December 21, 1837
Des Moines	Burlington	September 6, 1834
Dickinson	Spirit Lake	January 15, 1851
Dubuque	Dubuque	September 6, 1834
Emmet	Estherville	January 15, 1851
Fayette	West Union	December 21, 1837
Floyd	Charles City	January 15, 1851
Franklin	Hampton	January 15, 1851
Fremont	Sidney	February 24, 1847
Greene	Jefferson	January 15, 1851
Grundy	Grundy Center	January 15, 1851
Guthrie	Guthrie Center	January 15, 1851
Hamilton	Webster City	December 22, 1856
Hancock	Garner	January 15, 1851
Hardin	Eldora	January 15, 1851
Harrison	Logan	January 15, 1851
Henry	Mount Pleasant	December 7, 1836
Howard	Cresco	January 15, 1851
Humboldt	Dakota City	January 15, 1851
Ida	Ida Grove	January 15, 1851
Iowa	Marengo	February 17, 1843
Jackson	Maquoketa	December 21, 1837
Jasper	Newton	January 13, 1846
Jefferson	Fairfield	January 21, 1839
Johnson	Iowa City	December 21, 1837
Jones	Anamosa	December 21, 1837
Keokuk	Sigourney	December 21, 1837
Kossuth	Algona	January 15, 1851
Lee	Fort Madison	December 7, 1836
Linn	Cedar Rapids	December 21, 1837
Louisa	Wapello	December 7, 1836
Lucas	Chariton	January 13, 1846
Lyon[2]	Rock Rapids	January 15, 1851
Madison	Winterset	January 13, 1846
Mahaska	Oskaloosa	February 17, 1843
Marion	Knoxville	June 10, 1845
Marshall	Marshalltown	January 13, 1846
Mills	Glenwood	January 15, 1851
Mitchell	Osage	January 15, 1851
Monona	Onawa	January 15, 1851
Monroe[3]	Albia	February 17, 1843
Montgomery	Red Oak	January 15, 1851
Muscatine	Muscatine	December 7, 1836
O'Brien	Primghar	January 15, 1851
Osceola	Sibley	January 15, 1851
Page	Clarinda	February 24, 1847
Palo Alto	Emmetsburg	January 15, 1851
Plymouth	Le Mars	January 15, 1851

Pocahontas	Pocahontas	January 15, 1851
Polk	Des Moines	January 13, 1846
Pottawattamie	Council Bluffs	January 15, 1851
Poweshiek	Montezuma	February 17, 1843
Ringgold	Mount Ayr	February 24, 1847
Sac	Sac City	January 15, 1851
Scott	Davenport	December 21, 1837
Shelby	Harlan	January 15, 1851
Sioux	Orange City	January 15, 1851
Story	Nevada	January 13, 1846
Tama	Toledo	February 17, 1843
Taylor	Bedford	February 24, 1847
Union	Creston	January 15, 1851
Van Buren	Keosauqua	December 7, 1836
Wapello	Ottumwa	February 17, 1843
Warren	Indianola	January 13, 1846
Washington[4]	Washington	January 16, 1837
Wayne	Corydon	January 13, 1846
Webster[5]	Fort Dodge	January 15, 1851
Winnebago	Forest City	January 15, 1851
Winneshiek	Decorah	February 20, 1847
Woodbury[6]	Sioux City	January 15, 1851
Worth	Northwood	January 15, 1851
Wright	Clarion	January 15, 1851

Notes

1. Calhoun created as Fox; name changed January 12, 1853
2. Lyon created as Buncombe; name changed September 11, 1862
3. Monroe created as Kishkikosh; name changed January 19, 1846
4. Washington created as Slaughter; name changed January 25, 1839
5. Webster created as Risley; name changed January 12, 1853
6. Woodbury created as Wahkaw; named changed January 12, 1853

KANSAS (105 COUNTIES)

Kansas Territory May 30, 1854
Admitted to Union January 29, 1861 (34th)

County	County Seat	Created
Allen	Iola	August 25, 1855
Anderson	Garnett	August 25, 1855
Atchison	Atchison	August 25, 1855
Barber[1]	Medicine Lodge	February 26, 1867
Barton	Great Bend	February 26, 1867
Bourbon	Fort Scott	August 25, 1855
Brown	Hiawatha	August 25, 1855
Butler	El Dorado	August 25, 1855
Chase	Cottonwood Falls	February 11, 1859
Chautauqua	Sedan	March 20, 1875
Cherokee[2]	Columbus	August 25, 1855
Cheyenne	Saint Francis	March 20, 1873
Clark	Ashland	February 26, 1867
Clay	Clay Center	February 20, 1857

Cloud[3]	Concordia	February 27, 1860
Coffey	Burlington	August 25, 1855
Comanche	Coldwater	February 26, 1867
Cowley	Winfield	February 26, 1867
Crawford	Girard	February 13, 1867
Decatur	Oberlin	March 20, 1873
Dickinson	Abilene	February 20, 1857
Doniphan	Troy	August 25, 1855
Douglas	Lawrence	August 25, 1855
Edwards	Kinsley	March 18, 1874
Elk	Howard	March 25, 1875
Ellis	Hays	February 26, 1867
Ellsworth	Ellsworth	February 26, 1867
Finney[4]	Garden City	March 20, 1873
Ford	Dodge City	February 26, 1867
Franklin	Ottawa	August 25, 1855
Geary[5]	Junction City	August 30, 1855
Gove	Gove City	March 11, 1868
Graham	Hill City	February 26, 1867
Grant	Ulysses	March 20, 1873
Gray	Cimarron	March 13, 1881
Greeley	Tribune	March 20, 1873
Greenwood	Eureka	August 25, 1855
Hamilton	Syracuse	March 20, 1873
Harper	Anthony	February 26, 1867
Harvey	Newton	March 7, 1872
Haskell	Sublette	March 23, 1887
Hodgeman[6]	Jetmore	February 26 1867
Jackson[7]	Holton	August 25, 1855
Jefferson	Oskaloosa	August 25, 1855
Jewell	Mankato	February 26, 1867
Johnson	Olathe	August 25, 1855
Kearny[8]	Lakin	March 20, 1873
Kingman	Kingman	March 7, 1872
Kiowa	Comanche	February 26, 1867
Labette	Oswego	February 26, 1867
Lane	Dighton	March 20, 1873
Leavenworth	Leavenworth	August 25, 1855
Lincoln	Lincoln	February 26, 1867
Linn	Mound City	August 25, 1855
Logan[9]	Oakley	March 13, 1881
Lyon[10]	Emporia	August 25, 1855
Marion	Marion	August 25, 1855
Marshall	Marysville	August 25, 1855
McPherson	McPherson	February 26, 1867
Meade	Meade	March 20, 1873
Miami[11]	Paola	August 25, 1855
Mitchell	Beloit	February 26, 1867
Montgomery	Independence	February 26, 1867
Morris[12]	Council Grove	August 25, 1855
Morton	Elkhart	February 20, 1886
Nemaha	Seneca	August 25, 1855
Neosho[13]	Erie	August 25, 1855
Ness	Ness City	February 26, 1867
Norton[14]	Norton	February 26, 1867

Osage[15]	Lyndon	August 30, 1855
Osborne	Osborne	February 26, 1867
Ottawa	Minneapolis	February 27, 1860
Pawnee	Larned	February 26, 1867
Phillips	Phillipsburg	February 26, 1867
Pottawatomie	Westmoreland	February 20, 1857
Pratt	Pratt	February 26, 1867
Rawlins	Atwood	March 20, 1873
Reno	Hutchinson	February 26, 1867
Republic	Belleville	February 27, 1860
Rice	Lyons	February 26, 1867
Riley	Manhattan	August 25, 1855
Rooks	Stockton	February 26, 1867
Rush	La Crosse	February 26, 1867
Russell	Russell	February 26, 1867
Saline	Salina	February 15, 1860
Scott	Scott City	March 20, 1873
Sedgwick	Wichita	February 26, 1867
Seward	Liberal	March 20, 1873
Shawnee	Topeka	August 25, 1855
Sheridan	Hoxie	March 20, 1873
Sherman	Goodland	March 20, 1873
Smith	Smith Center	February 26, 1867
Stafford	Saint John	February 26, 1867
Stanton	Johnson	March 20, 1873
Stevens	Hugoton	March 20, 1873
Sumner	Wellington	February 26, 1867
Thomas	Colby	March 20, 1873
Trego	WaKeeney	February 26, 1867
Wabaunsee[16]	Alma	August 25, 1855
Wallace	Sharon Springs	March 11, 1868
Washington	Washington	February 20, 1857
Wichita	Leoti	March 20, 1873
Wilson	Fredonia	August 25, 1855
Woodson	Yates Center	August 25, 1855
Wyandotte	Kansas City	January 29, 1859

Notes

1. Barber created as Barbour; spelling corrected March 1, 1883
2. Cherokee created as McGee; name changed February 18, 1860
3. Cloud created as Shirley; named changed February 26, 1867
4. Finney created as Sequoyah; name changed February 21, 1883
5. Geary created as Davis; name changed February 28, 1889
6. Hodgeman created as Hageman; name corrected 1868
7. Jackson created as Calhoun; name changed February 11, 1859
8. Kearny created as Kearney; spelling corrected March 5, 1887
9. Logan created as Saint John; name changed February 24, 1887
10. Lyon created as Breckenridge; name changed February 5, 1862
11. Miami created as Lykins; name changed June 3, 1861
12. Morris created as Wise; name changed February 11, 1859
13. Neosho created as Dorn; name changed June 3, 1861
14. Created as Norton; name changed to Billings March 6, 1873; renamed Norton February 19, 1874
15. Osage created as Weller; name changed February 11, 1859
16. Wabaunsee created as Richardson; name changed February 11, 1859

KENTUCKY (120 COUNTIES)

Part of Virginia 1780–92
Admitted to Union June 1, 1792 (15th)

County	County Seat	Created
Adair	Columbia	December 11, 1801
Allen	Scottsville	January 11, 1815
Anderson	Lawrenceburg	January 16, 1827
Ballard	Wickliffe	February 15, 1842
Barren	Glasgow	December 20, 1798
Bath	Owingsville	January 15, 1811
Bell[1]	Pineville	February 28, 1867
Boone	Burlington	December 13, 1798
Bourbon	Paris	December 29, 1785
Boyd	Catlettsburg	February 16, 1860
Boyle	Danville	February 15, 1842
Bracken	Brooksville	December 14, 1796
Breathitt	Jackson	February 8, 1839
Breckinridge	Hardinsburg	December 9, 1799
Bullitt	Shepherdsville	December 13, 1796
Butler	Morgantown	January 18, 1810
Caldwell	Princeton	January 13, 1809
Calloway	Murray	December 19, 1821
Campbell	Newport	December 17, 1794
Carlisle	Bardwell	April 3, 1886
Carroll	Carrollton	February 9, 1838
Carter	Grayson	February 9, 1838
Casey	Liberty	November 14, 1806
Christian	Hopkinsville	December 13, 1796
Clark	Winchester	December 6, 1792
Clay	Manchester	December 2, 1806
Clinton	Albany	February 20, 1836
Crittenden	Marion	January 26, 1842
Cumberland	Burkesville	December 14, 1798
Daviess	Owensboro	January 14, 1815
Edmonson	Brownsville	January 12, 1825
Elliott	Sandy Hook	January 26, 1869
Estill	Irvine	January 27, 1808
Fayette	Lexington	June 30, 1780
Fleming	Flemingsburg	February 10, 1798
Floyd	Prestonsburg	December 13, 1799
Franklin	Frankfort	December 7, 1794
Fulton	Hickman	January 15, 1845
Gallatin	Warsaw	December 14, 1798
Garrard	Lancaster	December 17, 1796
Grant	Williamstown	February 12, 1820
Graves	Mayfield	December 19, 1821
Grayson	Leitchfield	January 25, 1810
Green	Greensburg	December 20, 1792
Greenup	Greenup	December 12, 1803
Hancock	Hawesville	January 3, 1829
Hardin	Elizabethtown	December 15, 1792
Harlan	Harlan	January 28, 1819
Harrison	Cynthiana	December 21, 1793

Hart	Munfordville	January 28, 1819
Henderson	Henderson	December 21, 1798
Henry	New Castle	December 14, 1798
Hickman	Clinton	December 19, 1821
Hopkins	Madisonville	December 9, 1806
Jackson	McKee	February 2, 1858
Jefferson	Louisville	June 30, 1780
Jessamine	Nicholasville	December 19, 1798
Johnson	Paintsville	February 24, 1843
Kenton	Covington	January 29, 1840
Knott	Hindman	May 5, 1884
Knox	Barbourville	December 19, 1799
Larue	Hodgenville	March 4, 1843
Laurel	London	December 12, 1825
Lawrence	Louisa	December 14, 1821
Lee	Beattyville	January 29, 1870
Leslie	Hyden	March 29, 1878
Letcher	Whitesburg	March 3, 1842
Lewis	Vanceburg	December 2, 1806
Lincoln	Stanford	June 30, 1780
Livingston	Smithland	December 13, 1798
Logan	Russellville	September 1, 1792
Lyon	Eddyville	January 14, 1854
Madison	Richmond	December 15, 1785
Magoffin	Salyersville	February 22, 1860
Marion	Lebanon	January 25, 1834
Marshall	Benton	February 12, 1842
Martin	Inez	March 10, 1870
Mason	Maysville	November 5, 1788
McCracken	Paducah	December 17, 1824
McCreary	Whitley City	March 12, 1912
McLean	Calhoun	February 6, 1854
Meade	Brandenburg	December 17, 1823
Menifee	Frenchburg	March 10, 1869
Mercer	Harrodsburg	December 15, 1785
Metcalfe	Edmonton	February 1, 1860
Monroe	Tompkinsville	January 19, 1820
Montgomery	Mount Sterling	December 14, 1796
Morgan	West Liberty	December 7, 1822
Muhlenberg	Greenville	December 14, 1798
Nelson	Bardstown	November 12, 1784
Nicholas	Carlisle	December 18, 1799
Ohio	Hartford	December 17, 1798
Oldham	La Grange	December 15, 1823
Owen	Owenton	February 6, 1819
Owsley	Booneville	January 23, 1843
Pendleton	Falmouth	December 13, 1798
Perry	Hazard	November 2, 1820
Pike	Pikeville	December 19, 1821
Powell	Stanton	January 7, 1852
Pulaski	Somerset	December 10, 1798
Robertson	Mount Olivet	February 11, 1867
Rockcastle	Mount Vernon	January 8, 1810
Rowan	Morehead	March 15, 1856
Russell	Jamestown	December 14, 1825

Scott	Georgetown	June 22, 1792
Shelby	Shelbyville	June 23, 1792
Simpson	Franklin	January 28, 1819
Spencer	Taylorsville	January 7, 1824
Taylor	Campbellsville	January 13, 1848
Todd	Elkton	December 30, 1819
Trigg	Cadiz	January 27, 1820
Trimble	Bedford	February 9, 1837
Union	Morganfield	January 15, 1811
Warren	Bowling Green	December 4, 1796
Washington	Springfield	June 22, 1792
Wayne	Monticello	December 18, 1800
Webster	Dixon	February 29, 1860
Whitley	Williamsburg	January 17, 1818
Wolfe	Campton	March 5, 1860
Woodford	Versailles	November 12, 1788

Note

1. Bell created as Josh Bell; name changed 1873

LOUISIANA (64 PARISHES)

Louisiana Territory March 3, 1805
Admitted to Union April 30, 1812 (18th)
Seceded January 26, 1861
Readmitted July 9, 1868

County	**County Seat**	**Created**
Acadia	Crowley	October 2, 1886
Allen	Oberlin	June 12, 1912
Ascension	Donaldsonville	March 31, 1807
Assumption	Napoleonville	March 31, 1807
Avoyelles	Marksville	March 31, 1807
Beauregard	DeRidder	June 12, 1912
Bienville	Arcadia	March 14, 1848
Bossier	Benton	February 24, 1843
Caddo	Shreveport	January 18, 1838
Calcasieu	Lake Charles	March 24, 1840
Caldwell	Columbia	March 6, 1838
Cameron	Cameron	March 15, 1870
Catahoula	Harrisonburg	March 23, 1808
Claiborne	Homer	March 13, 1828
Concordia	Vidalia	March 31, 1807
De Soto	Mansfield	April 1, 1843
East Baton Rouge	Baton Rouge	December 22, 1810
East Carroll	Lake Providence	March 28, 1877
East Feliciana	Clinton	February 17, 1824
Evangeline	Ville Platte	June 15, 1910
Franklin	Winnsboro	March 1, 1843
Grant	Colfax	March 4, 1869
Iberia	New Iberia	October 30, 1868
Iberville	Plaquemine	March 31, 1807

Jackson	Jonesboro	February 27, 1845
Jefferson	Gretna	February 11, 1825
Jefferson Davis	Jennings	June 12, 1912
Lafayette	Lafayette	January 17, 1823
Lafourche[1]	Thibodaux	March 31, 1807
La Salle	Jena	July 3, 1908
Lincoln	Ruston	February 27, 1873
Livingston	Livingston	February 10, 1832
Madison	Tallulah	January 19, 1838
Morehouse	Bastrop	March 25, 1844
Natchitoches	Natchitoches	March 31, 1807
Orleans	New Orleans	March 31, 1807
Ouachita	Monroe	March 31, 1807
Plaquemines	Point a la Hache	March 31, 1807
Pointe Coupee	New Roads	March 31, 1807
Rapides	Alexandria	March 31, 1807
Red River	Coushatta	March 7, 1871
Richland	Rayville	September 29, 1868
Sabine	Many	March 7, 1843
Saint Bernard	Chalmette	March 31, 1807
Saint Charles	Hahnville	March 31, 1807
Saint Helena	Greensburg	October 27, 1810
Saint James	Convent	March 31, 1807
Saint John the Baptist	Laplace	March 31, 1807
Saint Landry	Opelousas	March 31, 1807
Saint Martin	Saint Martinsville	March 31, 1807
Saint Mary	Franklin	April 17, 1811
Saint Tammany	Covington	October 27, 1810
Tangipahoa	Amite	March 6, 1869
Tensas	Saint Joseph	March 17, 1843
Terrebonne	Houma	March 22, 1822
Union	Farmerville	March 13, 1839
Vermillion	Abbeville	March 25, 1844
Vernon	Leesville	March 30, 1871
Washington	Franklinton	March 6, 1819
Webster	Minden	February 27, 1871
West Baton Rouge[2]	Port Allen	March 31, 1807
West Carroll	Oak Grove	March 28, 1877
West Feliciana	Saint Francisville	February 17, 1824
Winn	Winnfield	February 24, 1852

Notes

1. Lafourche created as Interior; name changed to Lafourche Interior 1812; name changed to Lafourche 1853
2. West Baton Rouge created as Baton Rouge; name changed 1812

MAINE (16 COUNTIES)

Part of Massachusetts 1652–1820
Admitted to Union March 15, 1820 (23rd)

County	County Seat	Created
Androscoggin	Auburn	March 18, 1854
Aroostook	Caribou	March 16, 1830

Cumberland	Portland	June 19, 1760
Franklin	Farmington	March 20, 1838
Hancock	Ellsworth	June 25, 1789
Kennebec	Augusta	February 20, 1799
Knox	Rockland	March 9, 1860
Lincoln	Wiscasset	June 19, 1760
Oxford	South Paris	March 4, 1805
Penobscot	Bangor	February 15, 1816
Piscataquis	Dover-Foxcroft	March 23, 1838
Sagadahoc	Bath	April 4, 1854
Somerset	Skowhegan	March 1, 1809
Waldo	Belfast	February 7, 1827
Washington	Machias	June 25, 1789
York	Alfred	November 20, 1652

MARYLAND (23 COUNTIES; 1 INDEPENDENT CITY)

Colony granted to Lord Baltimore 1632
Independence declared July 4, 1776
Ratified Constitution April 28, 1788 (7th)

County	County Seat	Created
Allegany	Cumberland	December 25, 1789
Anne Arundel[1]	Annapolis	April 9, 1650
Baltimore	Towson	June 30, 1695
Baltimore	(Independent City)	July 4, 1851
Calvert[2]	Prince Frederick	July 3, 1654
Caroline	Denton	December 5, 1773
Carroll	Westminster	January 19, 1837
Cecil	Elkton	December 31, 1674
Charles	La Plata	July 10, 1658
Dorchester	Cambridge	February 16, 1669
Frederick	Frederick	June 10, 1748
Garrett	Oakland	April 1, 1872
Harford	Bel Air	March 2, 1774
Howard	Ellicott City	July 4, 1851
Kent	Chestertown	August 2, 1642
Montgomery	Rockville	September 6, 1776
Prince George's	Upper Marlboro	May 20, 1695
Queen Anne's	Centreville	April 18, 1706
Saint Mary's[3]	Leonardtown	February 9, 1637
Somerset	Princess Anne	August 22, 1666
Talbot	Easton	February 18, 1662
Washington	Hagerstown	September 6, 1776
Wicomico	Salisbury	August 17, 1867
Worcester	Snow Hill	October 29, 1742

Notes

1. Created as Anne Arundel; name changed to Providence 1654; renamed Anne Arundel 1658
2. Created as Calvert; name changed to Patuxent October 31, 1654; renamed Calvert December 31, 1658
3. Created as Saint Mary's; name changed to Potomac 1654; renamed Saint Mary's 1658

MASSACHUSETTS (14 COUNTIES)

Massachusetts Bay Colony 1628
Declared independence July 4, 1776
Ratified Constitution February 6, 1788 (6th)

County	County Seat	Created
Barnstable	Barnstable	June 2, 1685
Berkshire	Pittsfield	April 24, 1761
Bristol	Taunton	June 2, 1685
Dukes	Edgartown	June 22, 1695
Essex	Salem	May 10, 1643
Franklin	Greenfield	June 24, 1811
Hampden	Springfield	February 25, 1812
Hampshire	Northampton	May 7, 1662
Middlesex	Cambridge	May 10, 1643
Nantucket	Nantucket	June 22, 1695
Norfolk	Dedham	March 26, 1793
Plymouth	Plymouth	June 2, 1685
Suffolk	Boston	May 10, 1643
Worcester	Worcester	April 5, 1731

MICHIGAN (83 COUNTIES)

Michigan Territory January 30, 1805
Admitted to Union January 26, 1837 (26th)

County	County Seat	Created
Alcona[1]	Harrisville	April 1, 1840
Alger	Munising	March 17, 1885
Allegan	Allegan	March 2, 1831
Alpena[2]	Alpena	April 1, 1840
Antrim[3]	Bellaire	April 1, 1840
Arenac	Standish	March 2, 1831
Baraga	L'Anse	February 19, 1875
Barry	Hastings	October 29, 1829
Bay	Bay City	April 20, 1857
Benzie	Beulah	February 27, 1863
Berrien	Saint Joseph	October 29, 1829
Branch	Coldwater	October 29, 1829
Calhoun	Marshall	October 29, 1829
Cass	Cassopolis	October 29, 1829
Charlevoix[4]	Charlevoix	April 1, 1840
Cheboygan	Cheboygan	April 1, 1840
Chippewa	Sault Sainte Marie	December 22, 1826
Clare[5]	Harrison	April 1, 1840
Clinton	Saint Johns	March 2, 1831
Crawford[6]	Grayling	April 1, 1840
Delta	Escanaba	March 9, 1843
Dickinson	Iron Mountain	May 21, 1891
Eaton	Charlotte	October 29, 1829
Emmet[7]	Petoskey	April 1, 1840
Genesee	Flint	March 28, 1835

Gladwin	Gladwin	March 2, 1831
Gogebic	Bessemer	February 7, 1887
Grand Traverse	Traverse City	April 7, 1851
Gratiot	Ithaca	March 2, 1831
Hillsdale	Hillsdale	October 29, 1829
Houghton	Houghton	March 19, 1845
Huron	Bad Axe	April 1, 1840
Ingham	Mason	October 29, 1829
Ionia	Ionia	March 2, 1831
Iosco[8]	Tawas City	April 1, 1840
Iron	Crystal Falls	April 3, 1885
Isabella	Mount Pleasant	March 2, 1831
Jackson	Jackson	October 29, 1829
Kalamazoo	Kalamazoo	October 29, 1829
Kalkaska[9]	Kalkaska	April 1, 1840
Kent	Grand Rapids	March 2, 1831
Keweenaw	Eagle River	March 11, 1861
Lake[10]	Baldwin	April 1, 1840
Lapeer	Lapeer	September 10, 1822
Leelanau	Suttons Bay	April 1, 1840
Lenawee	Adrian	September 10, 1822
Livingston	Howell	March 21, 1833
Luce	Newberry	March 1, 1887
Mackinac[11]	Saint Ignance	October 26, 1818
Macomb	Mount Clemens	January 15, 1818
Manistee	Manistee	April 1, 1840
Marquette	Marquette	March 9, 1843
Mason[12]	Ludington	April 1, 1840
Mecosta	Big Rapids	April 1, 1840
Menominee[13]	Menominee	March 15, 1861
Midland	Midland	March 2, 1831
Missaukee	Lake City	April 1, 1840
Monroe	Monroe	July 14, 1817
Montcalm	Stanton	March 2, 1831
Montmorency[14]	Atlanta	April 1, 1840
Muskegon	Muskegon	February 4, 1859
Newaygo	White Cloud	April 1, 1840
Oakland	Pontiac	January 12, 1819
Oceana	Hart	March 2, 1831
Ogemaw	West Branch	April 1, 1840
Ontonagon	Ontonagon	March 9, 1843
Osceola[15]	Reed City	April 1, 1840
Oscoda	Mio	April 1, 1840
Otsego[16]	Gaylord	April 1, 1840
Ottawa	Grand Haven	March 2, 1831
Presque Isle	Rogers City	April 1, 1840
Roscommon[17]	Roscommon	April 1, 1840
Saginaw	Saginaw	September 10, 1822
Saint Clair	Port Huron	March 28, 1820
Saint Joseph	Centreville	October 29, 1829
Sanilac	Sandusky	September 10, 1822
Schoolcraft	Manistique	March 9, 1843
Shiawassee	Corunna	September 10, 1822
Tuscola	Caro	April 1, 1840
Van Buren	Paw Paw	October 29, 1829

Washtenaw	Ann Arbor	September 10, 1822
Wayne	Detroit	November 21, 1815
Wexford[18]	Cadillac	April 1, 1840

Notes

1. Alcona created as Negwegon (or Newago); name changed March 8, 1843
2. Alpena created as Anamickee; name changed March 8, 1843
3. Antrim created as Megisee; name changed March 8, 1843
4. Charlevoix created as Reshkauko (or Keshkauko); name changed March 8, 1843
5. Clare created as Kaykakee; name changed March 8, 1843
6. Crawford created as Shawano; name changed March 8, 1843
7. Emmett created as Tonedagana; name changed March 8, 1843
8. Iosco created as Kanotin; name changed March 8, 1843
9. Kalkaska created as Wabassee; name changed to Kalcasca March 8, 1843; spelling changed January 27, 1871
10. Lake created as Aishcum; name changed March 8, 1843
11. Mackinac created as Michilimackinac; name shortened January 26, 1837
12. Mason created as Notipekago; name changed March 8, 1843
13. Menominee created as Blecker; name changed March 19, 1863
14. Montmorency created as Cheonoquet; name changed March 8, 1843
15. Osceola created as Unwattin; name changed March 8, 1843
16. Otsego created as Okkuddo; name changed March 8, 1843
17. Roscommon created as Mikenauk; name changed March 8, 1843
18. Wexford created as Kautawaubet; name changed March 8, 1843

MINNESOTA (87 COUNTIES)

Minnesota Territory May 3, 1849
Admitted to Union May 11, 1858 (32nd)

County	County Seat	Created
Aiktin[1]	Aitkin	May 23, 1857
Anoka	Anoka	May 23, 1857
Becker	Detroit Lakes	March 18, 1858
Beltrami	Bemidji	February 28, 1866
Benton	Foley	October 27, 1849
Big Stone	Ortonville	February 20, 1862
Blue Earth	Mankato	March 5, 1853
Brown	New Ulm	February 20, 1855
Carlton	Carlton	May 23, 1857
Carver	Chaska	February 20, 1855
Cass	Walker	March 31, 1851
Chippewa	Montevideo	February 20, 1862
Chisago	Center City	March 31, 1851
Clay[2]	Moorhead	March 18, 1858
Clearwater	Bagley	December 20, 1902
Cook	Grand Marais	March 9, 1874
Cottonwood	Windom	May 23, 1857
Crow Wing	Brainerd	May 23, 1857
Dakota	Hastings	October 27, 1849
Dodge	Mantorville	February 20, 1855
Douglas	Alexandria	March 8, 1858
Faribault	Blue Earth	February 20, 1855
Fillmore	Preston	March 5, 1853
Freeborn	Albert Lea	February 20, 1855

Goodhue	Red Wing	March 5, 1853
Grant	Elbow Lake	March 6, 1868
Hennepin	Minneapolis	March 6, 1852
Houston	Caledonia	February 23, 1854
Hubbard	Park Rapids	February 26, 1883
Isanti	Cambridge	February 13, 1857
Itasca	Grand Rapids	October 27, 1849
Jackson	Jackson	May 23, 1857
Kanabec	Mora	March 13, 1858
Kandiyohi	Willmar	March 20, 1858
Kittson[3]	Hallock	October 27, 1849
Koochiching	International Falls	December 19, 1906
Lac qui Parle	Madison	March 6, 1871
Lake[4]	Two Harbors	February 20, 1855
Lake of the Woods	Baudette	November 28, 1922
Le Sueur	Le Center	March 5, 1853
Lincoln	Ivanhoe	November 4, 1873
Lyon	Marshall	March 6, 1868
Mahnomen	Mahnomen	December 27, 1906
Marshall	Warren	February 25, 1879
Martin	Fairmont	May 23, 1857
McLeod	Glencoe	March 1, 1856
Meeker	Litchfield	February 23, 1856
Mille Lacs	Milaca	May 23, 1857
Morrison	Little Falls	February 25, 1856
Mower	Austin	February 20, 1855
Murray	Slayton	May 23, 1857
Nicollet	Saint Peter	March 5, 1853
Nobles	Worthington	May 23, 1857
Norman	Ada	February 17, 1881
Olmsted	Rochester	February 20, 1855
Otter Tail	Fergus Falls	March 18, 1858
Pennington	Thief River Falls	November 23, 1910
Pine	Pine City	March 1, 1856
Pipestone[5]	Pipestone	May 23, 1857
Polk	Crookston	July 20, 1858
Pope	Glenwood	February 20, 1862
Ramsey	Saint Paul	October 27, 1849
Red Lake	Red Lake Falls	December 24, 1896
Redwood	Redwood Falls	February 6, 1862
Renville	Olivia	February 20, 1855
Rice	Faribault	March 5, 1853
Rock[6]	Luverne	May 23, 1857
Roseau	Roseau	February 28, 1894
Saint Louis	Duluth	May 23, 1857
Scott	Shakopee	March 5, 1853
Sherburne	Elk River	February 25, 1856
Sibley	Gaylord	March 5, 1853
Stearns	Saint Cloud	February 20, 1855
Steel	Owatonna	February 20, 1855
Stevens	Morris	February 20, 1855
Swift	Benson	February 18, 1870
Todd	Long Prairie	February 20, 1855
Traverse	Wheaton	February 20, 1862
Wabasha	Wabasha	October 27, 1849

Wadena	Wadena	June 11, 1858
Waseca	Waseca	February 27, 1857
Washington	Stillwater	October 27, 1849
Watonwan	Saint James	February 25, 1860
Wilkin[7]	Breckenridge	March 18, 1858
Winona	Winona	February 23, 1854
Wright	Buffalo	February 20, 1855
Yellow Medicine	Granite Falls	March 6, 1871

Notes

1. Aitkin created as Aiken; spelling changed 1872
2. Clay created as Breckinridge; name changed March 6, 1862
3. Kittson created as Pembina; name changed March 9, 1878
4. Lake created as Superior; name changed to Saint Louis March 3, 1855; name changed March 1, 1856
5. Pipestone created as Rock; name changed September 20, 1862
6. Rock created as Pipestone; name changed September 20, 1862
7. Wilkins created as Toombs; name changed to Andy Johnson March 18, 1862; name changed March 6, 1868

MISSISSIPPI (82 COUNTIES)

Mississippi Territory April 7, 1798
Admitted to Union December 10, 1817 (20th)
Seceded January 9, 1861
Readmitted February 23, 1870

County	County Seat	Created
Adams	Natchez	April 2, 1799
Alcorn	Corinth	April 15, 1870
Amite	Liberty	February 24, 1809
Attala	Kosciusko	December 23, 1833
Benton	Ashland	July 21, 1870
Bolivar	Cleveland	February 9, 1836
Calhoun	Pittsboro	March 8, 1852
Carroll	Carrollton	December 23, 1833
Chickasaw	Houston	February 9, 1836
Choctaw	Ackerman	December 23, 1833
Claiborne	Port Gibson	January 27, 1802
Clarke	Quitman	December 23, 1833
Clay[1]	West Point	May 12, 1871
Coahoma	Clarksdale	February 9, 1836
Copiah	Hazlehurst	January 21, 1823
Covington	Collins	February 5, 1819
DeSoto	Hernando	February 9, 1826
Forrest	Hattiesburg	April 19, 1906
Franklin	Meadville	December 21, 1809
George	Lucedale	March 16, 1910
Greene	Leakesville	December 9, 1811
Grenada	Grenada	May 9, 1870
Hancock	Bay Saint Louis	December 18, 1812
Harrison	Gulfport	February 5, 1841
Hinds	Jackson	February 12, 1821
Holmes	Lexington	February 19, 1833
Humphreys	Belzoni	March 28, 1918

Issaquena	Mayersville	January 23, 1844
Itawamba	Fulton	February 9, 1836
Jackson	Pascagoula	December 18, 1812
Jasper	Bay Springs	December 23, 1833
Jefferson[2]	Fayette	April 2, 1799
Jefferson Davis	Prentiss	March 31, 1906
Jones[3]	Laurel	January 23, 1833
Kemper	De Kalb	December 23, 1833
Lafayette	Oxford	February 9, 1836
Lamar	Purvis	February 19, 1904
Lauderdale	Meridian	December 23, 1833
Lawrence	Monticello	December 22, 1814
Leake	Carthage	December 23, 1833
Lee	Tupelo	October 26, 1866
Leflore	Greenwood	March 15, 1871
Lincoln	Brookhaven	April 7, 1870
Lowndes	Columbus	January 30, 1830
Madison	Canton	January 29, 1828
Marion	Columbia	December 9, 1811
Marshall	Holly Springs	February 9, 1836
Monroe	Aberdeen	February 9, 1821
Montgomery	Winona	May 13, 1871
Neshoba	Philadelphia	December 23, 1833
Newton	Decatur	February 25, 1836
Noxubee	Macon	December 23, 1833
Oktibbeha	Starkville	December 23, 1833
Panola	Batesville	February 9, 1836
Pearl River	Poplarville	February 22, 1890
Perry	New Augusta	February 3, 1820
Pike	Magnolia	December 9, 1815
Pontotoc	Pontotoc	February 9, 1836
Prentiss	Booneville	April 15, 1870
Quitman	Marks	February 1, 1877
Rankin	Brandon	February 4, 1828
Scott	Forest	December 23, 1833
Sharkey	Rolling Fork	March 29, 1876
Simpson	Mendenhall	January 23, 1824
Smith	Raleigh	December 23, 1833
Stone	Wiggins	April 3, 1916
Sunflower	Indianola	February 15, 1844
Tallahatchie	Charleston	December 23, 1833
Tate	Senatobia	April 15, 1873
Tippah	Ripley	February 9, 1836
Tishomingo	Iuka	February 9, 1836
Tunica	Tunica	February 9, 1836
Union	New Albany	July 7, 1870
Walthall	Tylertown	March 16, 1910
Warren	Vicksburg	December 22, 1809
Washington	Greenville	January 29, 1827
Wayne	Waynesboro	December 21, 1809
Webster[4]	Walthall	April 6, 1874
Wilkinson	Woodville	January 30, 1802
Winston	Louisville	December 23, 1833
Yalobusha	Water Valley	December 23, 1833
Yazoo	Yazoo City	January 21, 1823

Notes

1. Clay created as Colfax; name changed April 10, 1876
2. Jefferson created as Pickering; name changed January 11, 1802
3. Created as Jones; name changed to Davis 1865; renamed Jones 1869
4. Webster created as Sumner; name changed January 20, 1882

MISSOURI (114 COUNTIES; 1 INDEPENDENT CITY)

Missouri Territory March 3, 1805
Admitted to Union August 10, 1821 (24th)

County	County Seat	Created
Adair	Kirksville	January 29, 1841
Andrew	Savannah	January 29, 1841
Atchison[1]	Rock Port	February 23, 1843
Audrain	Mexico	January 12, 1831
Barry	Cassville	January 5, 1835
Barton	Lamar	December 12, 1835
Bates	Butler	January 29, 1841
Benton	Warsaw	January 3, 1835
Bollinger	Marble Hill	March 1, 1851
Boone	Columbia	November 16, 1820
Buchanan	Saint Joseph	December 31, 1838
Butler	Poplar Bluff	February 27, 1849
Caldwell	Kingston	December 29, 1836
Callaway	Fulton	November 25, 1820
Camden[2]	Camdenton	January 29, 1841
Cape Girardeau	Jackson	October 1, 1812
Carroll	Carrollton	January 2, 1833
Carter	Van Buren	March 10, 1859
Cass[3]	Harrisonville	March 3, 1835
Cedar	Stockton	February 14, 1845
Chariton	Keytesville	November 16, 1820
Christian	Ozark	March 8, 1859
Clark	Kahoka	December 16, 1836
Clay	Liberty	January 2, 1822
Clinton	Plattsburg	January 2, 1833
Cole	Jefferson City	November 16, 1820
Cooper	Boonville	December 17, 1818
Crawford	Steelville	January 23, 1829
Dade	Greenfield	January 29, 1841
Dallas[4]	Buffalo	January 29, 1841
Daviess	Gallatin	December 29, 1836
DeKalb	Maysville	February 25, 1845
Dent	Salem	February 10, 1851
Douglas	Ava	October 29, 1857
Dunklin	Kennett	February 14, 1845
Franklin	Union	December 11, 1818
Gasconade	Hermann	November 25, 1820
Gentry	Albany	February 12, 1841
Greene	Springfield	January 2, 1833
Grundy	Trenton	January 29, 1841
Harrison	Bethany	February 14, 1845
Henry[5]	Clinton	December 13, 1834

Hickory	Hermitage	February 14, 1845
Holt[6]	Oregon	January 29, 1841
Howard	Fayette	January 13, 1816
Howell	West Plains	March 2, 1857
Iron	Ironton	February 17, 1857
Jackson	Kansas City	December 15, 1826
Jasper	Carthage	January 29, 1841
Jefferson	Hillsboro	December 8, 1818
Johnson	Warrensburg	December 13, 1834
Knox	Edina	February 14, 1845
Laclede	Lebanon	February 24, 1849
Lafayette[7]	Lexington	November 16, 1820
Lawrence	Mount Vernon	February 14, 1845
Lewis	Monticello	January 2, 1833
Lincoln	Troy	December 14, 1818
Linn	Linneus	January 6, 1837
Livingston	Chillicothe	January 6, 1837
Macon	Macon	January 6, 1837
Madison	Fredericktown	December 14, 1818
Maries	Vienna	March 2, 1855
Marion	Palmyra	December 14, 1822
McDonald	Pineville	March 3, 1849
Mercer	Princeton	February 14, 1845
Miller	Tuscumbia	February 6, 1837
Mississippi	Charleston	February 14, 1845
Moniteau	California	February 14, 1845
Monroe	Paris	January 6, 1831
Montgomery	Montgomery City	December 14, 1818
Morgan	Versailles	January 5, 1833
New Madrid	New Madrid	October 1, 1812
Newton	Neosho	December 30, 1838
Nodaway	Maryville	January 2, 1843
Oregon	Alton	February 14, 1845
Osage	Linn	January 29, 1841
Ozark[8]	Gainesville	January 29, 1841
Pemiscot	Caruthersville	February 19, 1851
Perry	Perryville	November 16, 1820
Pettis	Sedalia	January 26, 1833
Phelps	Rolla	November 13, 1857
Pike	Bowling Green	December 14, 1818
Platte	Platte City	December 31, 1818
Polk	Bolivar	January 5, 1835
Pulaski	Waynesville	January 19, 1833
Putnam	Unionville	February 22, 1843
Ralls	New London	November 16, 1820
Randolph	Huntsville	January 22, 1829
Ray	Richmond	November 16, 1820
Reynolds	Centerville	February 25, 1845
Ripley	Doniphan	January 5, 1833
Saint Charles	Saint Charles	October 1, 1812
Saint Clair	Osceola	January 16, 1833
Sainte Genevieve	Sainte Genevieve	October 1, 1812
Saint Francois	Farmington	December 19, 1821
Saint Louis	Clayton	October 1, 1812
Saint Louis	(Independent City)	March 5, 1877

Saline	Marshall	November 25, 1820
Schuyler	Lancaster	February 14, 1845
Scotland	Memphis	January 29, 1841
Scott	Benton	December 28, 1821
Shannon	Eminence	January 29, 1841
Shelby	Shelbyville	January 2, 1835
Stoddard	Bloomfield	January 2, 1835
Stone	Galena	February 10, 1851
Sullivan[9]	Milan	February 17, 1843
Taney	Forsyth	January 6, 1837
Texas[10]	Houston	February 17, 1843
Vernon	Nevada	February 7, 1851
Warren	Warrenton	January 5, 1833
Washington	Potosi	August 21, 1813
Wayne	Greenville	December 11, 1818
Webster	Marshfield	March 3, 1855
Worth	Grant City	February 6, 1861
Wright	Hartville	January 29, 1841

Notes

1. Atchison created as Allen; named changed February 14, 1845
2. Camden created as Kinderhook; name changed February 23, 1843
3. Cass created as Van Buren; name changed February 19, 1849
4. Dallas created as Niangaua; name changed December 14, 1844
5. Henry created as Rives; name changed February 15, 1841
6. Holt created as Nodaway; name changed February 15 1841
7. Lafayette created as Lillard; name changed February 16, 1825
8. Created as Ozark; name changed to Decatur February 22, 1843; renamed Ozark March 24, 1845
9. Sullivan created as Highland; name changed February 14, 1845
10. Texas created as Ashley; name changed February 14, 1845

MONTANA (56 COUNTIES)

Washington Territory March 2, 1853
Idaho Territory March 3, 1863
Montana Territory May 26, 1864
Admitted to Union November 8, 1889 (41st)

County	County Seat	Created
Beaverhead	Dillon	February 2, 1865
Big Horn	Hardin	January 13, 1913
Blaine	Chinook	February 29, 1912
Broadwater	Townsend	February 9, 1897
Carbon	Red Lodge	March 4, 1895
Carter	Ekalaka	February 22, 1917
Cascade	Great Falls	September 12, 1887
Chouteau	Fort Benton	February 2, 1865
Custer[1]	Miles City	February 2, 1865
Daniels	Scobey	August 30, 1920
Dawson	Glendive	January 15, 1869
Deer Lodge	Anaconda	February 2, 1865
Fallon	Baker	December 9, 1913
Fergus	Lewistown	March 12, 1885
Flathead	Kalispell	February 6, 1893

Gallatin	Bozeman	February 2, 1865
Garfield	Jordan	February 7, 1919
Glacier	Cut Bank	February 17, 1919
Golden Valley	Ryegate	October 4, 1920
Granite	Philipsburg	March 2, 1893
Hill	Havre	February 28, 1912
Jefferson	Boulder	February 2, 1865
Judith Basin	Sanford	December 10, 1920
Lake	Polson	May 11, 1923
Lewis and Clark[2]	Helena	February 2, 1865
Liberty	Chester	February 11, 1920
Lincoln	Libby	March 9, 1909
Madison	Virginia City	February 2, 1865
McCone	Circle	February 20, 1919
Meagher	White Sulphur Springs	November 16, 1867
Mineral	Superior	August 7, 1914
Missoula	Missoula	December 14, 1860
Musselshell	Roundup	February 11, 1911
Park	Livingston	February 23, 1887
Petroleum	Winnett	November 24, 1924
Phillips	Malta	February 5, 1915
Pondera	Conrad	February 17, 1919
Powder River	Broadus	March 7, 1919
Powell	Deer Lodge	January 31, 1901
Prairie	Terry	February 5, 1915
Ravalli	Hamilton	February 16, 1893
Richland	Sidney	May 27, 1914
Roosevelt	Wolf Point	February 18, 1919
Rosebud	Forsyth	February 11, 1901
Sanders	Thompson Falls	February 7, 1903
Sheridan	Plentywood	March 24, 1913
Silver Bow	Butte	February 16, 1881
Stillwater	Columbus	March 24, 1913
Sweet Grass	Big Timber	March 5, 1895
Teton	Choteau	February 7, 1893
Toole	Shelby	May 14, 1914
Treasure	Hysham	February 7, 1919
Valley	Glasgow	February 6, 1893
Wheatland	Harlowton	February 22, 1917
Wibaux	Wibaux	August 17, 1914
Yellowstone	Billings	February 26, 1883

Notes

1. Custer created as Big Horn; name changed April 1, 1882
2. Lewis and Clark created as Edgerton; name changed December 20, 1867

NEBRASKA (93 COUNTIES)

Nebraska Territory May 30, 1854
Admitted to Union March 1, 1867 (37th)

County	County Seat	Created
Adams	Hastings	February 16, 1867
Antelope	Neligh	March 1, 1874

Arthur	Arthur	March 31, 1887
Banner	Harrisburg	November 6, 1888
Blaine	Brewster	March 5, 1885
Boone	Albion	March 1, 1871
Box Butte	Alliance	November 2, 1886
Boyd	Butte	March 20, 1891
Brown	Ainsworth	February 19, 1883
Buffalo	Kearney	March 14, 1855
Burt	Tekamah	November 23, 1854
Butler	David City	January 26, 1856
Cass	Plattsmouth	November 23, 1854
Cedar	Hartington	February 12, 1857
Chase	Imperial	February 27, 1873
Cherry	Valentine	February 23, 1883
Cheyenne	Sidney	June 22, 1867
Clay	Clay Center	February 16, 1867
Colfax	Schuyler	February 5, 1869
Cuming	West Point	March 10, 1855
Custer	Broken Bow	February 17, 1877
Dakota	Dakota City	March 7, 1855
Dawes	Chadron	February 19, 1885
Dawson	Lexington	January 11, 1860
Deuel	Chappell	November 6, 1888
Dixon	Ponca	January 26, 1856
Dodge	Fremont	November 23, 1854
Douglas	Omaha	November 23, 1854
Dundy	Benkelman	February 27, 1873
Fillmore	Geneva	January 26, 1856
Franklin	Franklin	February 16, 1867
Frontier	Stockville	January 17, 1872
Furnas	Beaver City	February 27, 1873
Gage	Beatrice	March 16, 1855
Garden	Oshkosh	November 2, 1909
Garfield	Burwell	November 8, 1884
Gosper	Elwood	November 26, 1873
Grant	Hyannis	March 31, 1887
Greeley	Greeley	March 1, 1871
Hall	Grand Island	November 4, 1858
Hamilton	Aurora	February 16, 1867
Harlan	Alma	June 3, 1871
Hayes	Hayes Center	February 19, 1877
Hitchcock	Trenton	February 27, 1873
Holt[1]	O'Neill	January 13, 1860
Hooker	Mullen	March 29, 1889
Howard	Saint Paul	March 1, 1871
Jefferson[2]	Fairbury	January 26, 1856
Johnson	Tecumseh	March 2, 1855
Kearney	Minden	January 10, 1860
Keith	Ogallala	February 27, 1873
Keya Paha	Springview	November 4, 1884
Kimball	Kimball	November 6, 1888
Knox[3]	Center	February 10, 1857
Lancaster	Lincoln	March 6, 1855
Lincoln[4]	North Platte	January 7, 1860
Logan	Stapleton	February 24, 1885

Loup	Taylor	February 25, 1883
Madison	Madison	January 26, 1856
McPherson	Tryon	March 31, 1887
Merrick	Central City	November 4, 1858
Morrill	Bridgeport	November 12, 1908
Nance	Fullerton	February 13, 1879
Nemaha[5]	Auburn	November 23, 1854
Nuckolls	Nelson	January 13, 1860
Otoe[6]	Nebraska City	November 23, 1854
Pawnee	Pawnee City	March 6, 1855
Perkins	Grant	November 8, 1887
Phelps	Holdrege	February 11, 1873
Pierce[7]	Pierce	January 26, 1856
Platte	Columbus	January 26, 1856
Polk	Osceola	January 26, 1856
Red Willow	McCook	February 27, 1873
Richardson	Falls City	November 23, 1854
Rock	Bassett	November 6, 1888
Saline	Wilbur	March 6, 1855
Sarpy	Papillion	February 7, 1857
Saunders[7]	Wahoo	January 26, 1856
Scotts Bluff	Gering	November 6, 1888
Seward[8]	Seward	March 6, 1855
Sheridan	Rushville	February 25, 1885
Sherman	Loup City	March 1, 1871
Sioux	Harrison	February 19, 1877
Stanton[9]	Stanton	March 6, 1855
Thayer	Hebron	January 26, 1871
Thomas	Thedford	March 31, 1887
Thurston[10]	Pender	March 7, 1855
Valley	Ord	March 1, 1871
Washington	Blair	November 23, 1854
Wayne	Wayne	March 4, 1871
Webster	Red Cloud	February 16, 1867
Wheeler	Bartlett	February 17, 1877
York	York	March 13, 1855

Notes

1. Holt created as West; name changed January 9, 1862
2. Jefferson created as Jones; name changed 1867
3. Knox created as L'eau qui Court; name changed to Emmett February 18, 1867; name changed February 21, 1873
4. Lincoln created as Shorter; name changed December 11, 1861
5. Nemaha created as Forney; name changed March 17, 1855
6. Otoe created as Pierce; name changed 1855
7. Saunders created as Calhoun; name changed January 8, 1862
8. Seward created as Greene; name changed January 3, 1862
9. Stanton created as Izard; name changed January 10, 1862
10. Thurston created as Blackbird; name changed March 28, 1889

NEVADA (16 COUNTIES; 1 INDEPENDENT CITY)

Nevada Territory March 2, 1861
Admitted to Union October 31, 1864 (36th)

County	County Seat	Created
Carson City[1]	(Independent City)	November 25, 1861
Churchill	Fallon	November 25, 1861
Clark	Las Vegas	February 9, 1909
Douglas	Minden	November 25, 1861
Elko	Elko	March 5, 1869
Esmeralda	Goldfield	November 25, 1861
Eureka	Eureka	March 1, 1873
Humboldt	Winnemucca	November 25, 1861
Lander	Battle Mountain	December 19, 1862
Lincoln	Pioche	February 26, 1866
Lyon	Yerington	November 25, 1861
Mineral	Hawthorne	February 10, 1911
Nye	Tonopah	February 16, 1864
Pershing	Lovelock	March 18, 1919
Storey	Virginia City	November 25, 1861
Washoe	Reno	November 25, 1861
White Pine	Ely	March 2, 1869

Note

1. Carson City created as Ormsby County; consolidated into Carson City 1969

NEW HAMPSHIRE (10 COUNTIES)

Separated from Massachusetts Colony 1680
Declared independence July 4, 1776
Ratified Constitution June 21, 1788 (9th)

County	County Seat	Created
Belknap	Laconia	December 22, 1840
Carroll	Ossipee	December 22, 1840
Cheshire	Keene	April 29, 1769
Coos	Lancaster	December 24, 1803
Grafton	North Haverhill	April 29, 1769
Hillsborough	Nashua	April 29, 1769
Merrimack	Concord	July 1, 1823
Rockingham	Brentwood	April 29, 1769
Strafford	Dover	April 29, 1769
Sullivan	Newport	July 5, 1827

NEW JERSEY (21 COUNTIES)

Provinces of East Jersey and West Jersey 1675–1702
East and West Jersey merged into New Jersey 1702
Declared Independence July 4, 1776
Ratified Constitution December 18, 1787 (3rd)

County	County Seat	Created
Atlantic	Mays Landing	February 7, 1837
Bergen[1]	Hackensack	March 1, 1683
Burlington[2]	Mount Holly	May 17, 1694
Camden	Camden	March 13, 1844

Cape May[2]	Cape May Court House	November 12, 1692
Cumberland	Bridgeton	January 19, 1748
Essex[1]	Newark	March 1, 1683
Gloucester[2]	Woodbury	May 28, 1686
Hudson	Jersey City	February 22, 1840
Hunterdon	Flemington	March 13, 1714
Mercer	Trenton	February 22, 1838
Middlesex[1]	New Brunswick	March 1, 1683
Monmouth[1]	Freehold	March 1, 1683
Morris	Morristown	March 15, 1739
Ocean	Toms River	February 15, 1850
Passaic	Paterson	February 7, 1837
Salem[2]	Salem	May 17, 1694
Somerset[1]	Somerville	May 14, 1688
Sussex	Newton	June 8, 1753
Union	Elizabeth	March 19, 1857
Warren	Belvidere	November 20, 1824

Notes

1. East Jersey
2. West Jersey

NEW MEXICO (33 COUNTIES)

New Mexico Territory September 9, 1850
Admitted to Union January 6, 1912 (47th)

County	County Seat	Created
Bernalillo	Albuquerque	January 9, 1852
Catron	Reserve	February 25, 1921
Chaves	Roswell	February 25, 1889
Cibola	Grants	January 19, 1981
Colfax	Raton	January 25, 1869
Curry	Clovis	February 25, 1909
De Baca	Fort Sumner	February 28, 1917
Dona Ana	Las Cruces	January 9, 1852
Eddy	Carlsbad	February 25, 1889
Grant	Silver City	January 30, 1868
Guadalupe	Santa Rosa	February 26, 1891
Harding	Mosquero	March 4, 1921
Hidalgo	Lordsburg	February 25, 1919
Lea	Lovington	March 7, 1917
Lincoln	Carrizozo	January 16, 1869
Los Alamos	Los Alamos	March 16, 1949
Luna	Deming	March 16, 1901
McKinley	Gallup	February 23, 1899
Mora	Mora	February 1, 1860
Otero	Alamogordo	January 30, 1899
Quay	Tucumcari	February 28, 1903
Rio Arriba	Tierra Amarillo	January 9, 1852
Roosevelt	Portales	February 28, 1903
Sandoval	Bernalillo	March 10, 1903
San Juan	Aztec	February 24, 1997

San Miguel	Las Vegas	January 9, 1852
Santa Fe	Santa Fe	January 9, 1852
Sierra	Truth or Consequences	April 3, 1884
Socorro	Socorro	January 9, 1852
Taos	Taos	January 9, 1852
Torrance	Estancia	March 16, 1903
Union	Clayton	February 23, 1893
Valencia	Los Lunas	January 9, 1852

NEW YORK (62 COUNTIES)

Surrendered to England by Dutch August 27, 1664
Declared independence July 4, 1776
Ratified Constitution July 26, 1788 (11th)

County	County Seat	Created
Albany	Albany	November 1, 1683
Allegany	Belmont	April 7, 1806
Bronx	Bronx	April 19, 1912
Broome	Binghamton	March 28, 1806
Cattaraugus	Little Valley	March 11, 1808
Cayuga	Auburn	March 8, 1799
Chautauqua	Mayville	March 11, 1808
Chemung	Elmira	March 29, 1836
Chenango	Norwich	March 15, 1798
Clinton	Plattsburgh	March 17, 1788
Columbia	Hudson	April 4, 1786
Cortland	Cortland	April 8, 1808
Delaware	Delhi	March 10, 1797
Dutchess	Poughkeepsie	November 1, 1683
Erie	Buffalo	April 2, 1821
Essex	Elizabethtown	March 1, 1799
Franklin	Malone	March 11, 1808
Fulton	Johnstown	April 18, 1838
Genesee	Batavia	March 30, 1802
Greene	Catskill	March 25, 1800
Hamilton	Lake Pleasant	April 12, 1816
Herkimer	Herkimer	February 16, 1791
Jefferson	Watertown	March 28, 1805
Kings	Brooklyn	November 1, 1683
Lewis	Lowville	March 28, 1805
Livingston	Geneseo	February 23, 1821
Madison	Wampsville	March 21, 1806
Monroe	Rochester	February 23, 1821
Montgomery[1]	Fonda	March 12, 1772
Nassau	Mineola	April 27, 1898
New York	New York	November 1, 1683
Niagara	Lockport	March 11, 1808
Oneida	Utica	March 15, 1798
Onondaga	Syracuse	March 5, 1794
Ontario	Canandaigua	January 27, 1789
Orange	Goshen	November 1, 1683
Orleans	Albion	November 12, 1824
Oswego	Oswego	March 1, 1816

Otsego	Cooperstown	February 16, 1791
Putnam	Carmel	June 12, 1812
Queens	Jamaica	November 1, 1683
Rensselaer	Troy	February 7, 1791
Richmond	Saint George	November 1, 1683
Rockland	New City	February 23, 1798
Saint Lawrence	Canton	March 3, 1802
Saratoga	Ballston Spa	February 7, 1791
Schenectady	Schenectady	March 7, 1809
Schoharie	Schoharie	April 6, 1795
Schuyler	Watkins Glen	April 17, 1854
Seneca	Waterloo	March 24, 1804
Steuben	Bath	March 18, 1796
Suffolk	Riverhead	November 1, 1683
Sullivan	Monticello	March 27, 1809
Tioga	Owego	February 16, 1791
Tompkins	Ithaca	April 7, 1817
Ulster	Kingston	November 1, 1693
Warren	Lake George	March 12, 1813
Washington[2]	Fort Edward	March 12, 1772
Wayne	Lyons	April 11, 1823
Westchester	White Plaines	November 1, 1683
Wyoming	Warsaw	May 19, 1841
Yates	Penn Yan	February 5, 1823

Notes

1. Montgomery created as Tryon; name changed April 2, 1784
2. Washington created as Charlotte; name changed April 2, 1784

NORTH CAROLINA (100 COUNTIES)

Carolina proprietary colony 1663
North and South Carolina made separate provinces 1710
Declared independence July 4, 1776
Ratified Constitution November 21, 1789 (12th)
Seceded May 20, 1861
Readmitted July 4, 1868

County	County Seat	Created
Alamance	Graham	January 9, 1849
Alexander	Taylorsville	January 15, 1847
Alleghany	Sparta	1859
Anson	Wadesboro	1750
Ashe	Jefferson	1799
Avery	Newland	February 23, 1911
Beaufort[1]	Washington	December 3, 1705
Bertie	Windsor	1722
Bladen	Elizabethtown	November 11, 1734
Brunswick	Bolivia	March 9, 1764
Buncombe	Asheville	January 14, 1792
Burke	Morganton	April 8, 1777
Cabarrus	Concord	1792

Caldwell	Lenoir	January 11, 1841
Camden	Camden	April 8, 1777
Carteret	Beaufort	August 8, 1722
Caswell	Yanceyville	April 8, 1777
Catawba	Newton	December 12, 1842
Chatham	Pittsboro	April 1, 1771
Cherokee	Murphy	January 4, 1839
Chowan	Edenton	1671
Clay	Hayesville	February 20, 1861
Cleveland[2]	Shelby	January 11, 1841
Columbus	Whiteville	December 15, 1808
Craven[3]	New Bern	December 3, 1705
Cumberland	Fayetteville	1754
Currituck	Currituck	1684
Dare	Manteo	February 2, 1870
Davidson	Lexington	December 9, 1822
Davie	Mocksville	December 20, 1836
Duplin	Kenansville	April 7, 1750
Durham	Durham	February 28, 1881
Edgecombe	Tarboro	1741
Forsyth	Winston-Salem	January 16, 1849
Franklin	Louisburg	1779
Gaston	Gastonia	December 21, 1846
Gates	Gatesville	1779
Graham	Robbinsville	January 30, 1872
Granville	Oxford	1746
Greene	Snow Hill	1799
Guilford	Greensboro	April 1, 1771
Halifax	Halifax	January 1, 1759
Harnett	Lillington	February 7, 1855
Haywood	Waynesville	December 15, 1808
Henderson	Hendersonville	December 15, 1838
Hertford	Winton	May 1, 1760
Hoke	Raeford	February 1, 1911
Hyde[4]	Swanquarter	December 3, 1705
Iredell	Statesville	1788
Jackson	Sylva	January 29, 1851
Johnston	Smithfield	1746
Jones	Trenton	January 19, 1779
Lee	Sanford	March 6, 1907
Lenoir	Kinston	1791
Lincoln	Lincolnton	1779
Macon	Franklin	1828
Madison	Marshall	January 27, 1851
Martin	Williamston	March 2, 1774
McDowell	Marion	December 19, 1842
Mecklenburg	Charlotte	1762
Mitchell	Bakersville	February 16, 1861
Montgomery	Troy	1779
Moore	Carthage	1784
Nash	Nashville	1777
New Hanover	Wilmington	1729
Northampton	Jackson	1741
Onslow	Jacksonville	November 23, 1731

Orange	Hillsborough	1752
Pamlico	Bayboro	February 8, 1872
Pasquotank	Elizabeth City	1670
Pender	Burgaw	February 16, 1875
Perquimans[5]	Hertford	1671
Person	Roxboro	February 1, 1792
Pitt	Greenville	November 25, 1760
Polk	Columbus	January 18, 1847
Randolph	Asheboro	February 26, 1779
Richmond	Rockingham	October 1779
Robeson	Lumberton	1787
Rockingham	Wentworth	December 29, 1735
Rowan	Salisbury	March 27, 1753
Rutherford	Rutherfordton	1779
Sampson	Clinton	1784
Scotland	Laurinburg	February 20, 1899
Stanly	Albemarle	January 11, 1841
Stokes	Danbury	1789
Surry	Dobson	January 1771
Swain	Bryson City	February 24, 1871
Transylvania	Brevard	February 15, 1861
Tyrrell	Columbia	1729
Union	Monroe	December 19, 1842
Vance	Henderson	March 5, 1881
Wake	Raleigh	1771
Warren	Warrenton	1779
Washington	Plymouth	1799
Watauga	Boone	January 27, 1849
Wayne	Goldsboro	November 7, 1779
Wilkes	Wilkesboro	1777
Wilson	Wilson	February 13, 1855
Yadkin	Yadkinville	December 28, 1850
Yancey	Burnsville	1833

Notes

1. Beaufort created as Pamptecough; name changed 1712
2. Cleveland created as Cleaveland; spelling changed 1885
3. Craven created as Archdale; name changed 1712
4. Hyde created as Wickham; name changed 1712
5. Perquimans created as Berkeley; name changed 1681

NORTH DAKOTA (53 COUNTIES)

Dakota Territory March 2, 1861
Admitted to Union November 2, 1889 (39th)

County	County Seat	Created
Adams	Hettinger	April 17, 1907
Barnes[1]	Valley City	January 4, 1873
Benson	Minnewaukan	March 9, 1883
Billings	Medora	February 10, 1879
Bottineau	Bottineau	January 4, 1873

Bowman	Bowman	March 8, 1883
Burke	Bowbells	February 8, 1910
Burleigh	Bismarck	January 4, 1873
Cass	Fargo	January 4, 1873
Cavalier	Langdon	January 4, 1873
Dickey	Ellendale	March 5, 1881
Divide	Crosby	December 9, 1910
Dunn	Manning	March 9, 1883
Eddy	New Rockford	March 31, 1885
Emmons	Linton	February 10, 1879
Foster	Carrington	January 4, 1873
Golden Valley	Beach	November 19, 1912
Grand Forks	Grand Forks	January 4, 1873
Grant	Carson	November 25, 1916
Griggs	Cooperstown	February 18, 1881
Hettinger	Mott	March 9, 1883
Kidder	Steele	January 4, 1873
LaMoure	LaMoure	January 4, 1873
Logan	Napoleon	January 4, 1873
McHenry	Towner	January 4, 1873
McIntosh	Ashley	March 9, 1883
McKenzie	Watford City	March 9, 1883
McLean	Washburn	March 8, 1883
Mercer	Stanton	January 14, 1875
Morton	Mandan	January 8, 1873
Mountrail	Stanley	January 4, 1873
Nelson	Lakota	March 2, 1883
Oliver	Center	March 12, 1885
Pembina	Cavalier	January 9, 1867
Pierce	Rugby	March 11, 1887
Ramsey	Devils Lake	January 4, 1873
Ransom	Lisbon	January 4, 1873
Renville	Mohall	January 4, 1873
Richland	Wahpeton	January 4, 1873
Rolette	Rolla	January 4, 1873
Sargent	Forman	March 3, 1883
Sheridan	McClusky	January 4, 1873
Sioux	Fort Yates	September 3, 1914
Slope	Amidon	December 31, 1914
Stark	Dickinson	February 10, 1879
Steele	Finley	March 8, 1883
Stutsman	Jamestown	January 4, 1873
Towner	Cando	March 8, 1883
Traill	Hillsboro	January 12, 1875
Walsh	Grafton	February 18, 1881
Ward	Minot	April 14, 1885
Wells[2]	Fessenden	January 4, 1873
Williams	Williston	November 30, 1892

Notes

1. Barnes created as Burbank; name changed January 14, 1875
2. Wells created as Gingras; name changed February 26, 1881

OHIO (88 COUNTIES)

Northwest Territory July 13, 1787
Admitted to Union March 1, 1803 (17th)

County	County Seat	Created
Adams	West Union	July 10, 1797
Allen	Lima	February 12, 1820
Ashland	Ashland	February 24, 1846
Ashtabula	Jefferson	February 10, 1807
Athens	Athens	February 20, 1805
Auglaize	Wapakoneta	February 14, 1848
Belmont	Saint Clairsville	September 7, 1801
Brown	Georgetown	December 27, 1817
Butler	Hamilton	March 24, 1803
Carroll	Carrollton	December 25, 1832
Champaign	Urbana	February 20, 1805
Clark	Springfield	December 26, 1817
Clermont	Batavia	December 6, 1800
Clinton	Wilmington	February 19, 1810
Columbiana	Lisbon	March 25, 1803
Coshocton	Coshocton	January 31, 1810
Crawford	Bucyrus	February 12, 1820
Cuyahoga	Cleveland	February 10, 1807
Darke	Greenville	January 3, 1809
Defiance	Defiance	March 4, 1845
Delaware	Delaware	February 10, 1808
Erie	Sandusky	March 15, 1838
Fairfield	Lancaster	December 9, 1800
Fayette	Washington Court House	February 19, 1810
Franklin	Columbus	March 30, 1803
Fulton	Wauseon	February 28, 1850
Gallia	Gallipolis	March 25, 1803
Geauga	Chardon	December 31, 1805
Greene	Xenia	March 24, 1803
Guernsey	Cambridge	January 31, 1810
Hamilton	Cincinnati	January 2, 1790
Hancock	Findlay	February 12, 1820
Hardin	Kenton	February 12, 1820
Harrison	Cadiz	January 12, 1813
Henry	Napoleon	February 12, 1820
Highland	Hillsboro	February 18, 1805
Hocking	Logan	January 3, 1818
Holmes	Millersburg	January 20, 1824
Huron	Norwalk	February 7, 1809
Jackson	Jackson	January 12, 1816
Jefferson	Steubenville	July 27, 1797
Knox	Mount Vernon	January 30, 1808
Lake	Painesville	March 6, 1840
Lawrence	Ironton	December 21, 1815
Licking	Newark	January 30, 1808
Logan	Bellefontaine	December 30, 1817
Lorain	Elyria	December 26, 1822
Lucas	Toledo	June 20, 1835
Madison	London	February 16, 1810

Mahoning	Youngstown	February 16, 1846
Marion	Marion	February 12, 1820
Medina	Medina	February 18, 1812
Meigs	Pomeroy	January 21, 1819
Mercer	Celina	February 12, 1820
Miami	Troy	January 16, 1807
Monroc	Woodsfield	January 29, 1813
Montgomery	Dayton	March 24, 1803
Morgan	McConnelsville	December 29, 1817
Morrow	Mount Gilead	February 24, 1848
Muskingum	Zanesville	January 7, 1804
Noble	Caldwell	March 11, 1851
Ottawa	Port Clinton	March 6, 1840
Paulding	Paulding	February 12, 1820
Perry	New Lexington	December 26, 1817
Pickaway	Circleville	January 12, 1810
Pike	Waverly	January 4, 1815
Portage	Ravenna	February 10, 1807
Preble	Eaton	February 15, 1808
Putnam	Ottawa	February 12, 1820
Richland	Mansfield	January 30, 1808
Ross	Chillicothe	August 20, 1798
Sandusky	Fremont	February 12, 1820
Scioto	Portsmouth	March 24, 1803
Seneca	Tiffin	February 12, 1820
Shelby	Sidney	January 7, 1819
Stark	Canton	February 13, 1808
Summit	Akron	March 3, 1840
Trumbull	Warren	July 10, 1800
Tuscarawas	New Philadelphia	February 13, 1808
Union	Marysville	January 10, 1820
Van Wert	Van Wert	February 12, 1820
Vinton	McArthur	March 23, 1850
Warren	Lebanon	March 24, 1803
Washington	Marietta	July 27, 1788
Wayne	Wooster	February 13, 1808
Williams	Bryan	February 12, 1820
Wood	Bowling Green	February 12, 1820
Wyandot	Upper Sandusky	February 3, 1845

OKLAHOMA (77 COUNTIES)

Indian Lands 1819–1890
Oklahoma Territory May 2, 1890
Admitted to Union November 16, 1907 (46th)

County	County Seat	Created
Adair	Stillwell	July 16, 1907
Alfalfa	Cherokee	July 16, 1907
Atoka	Atoka	July 16, 1907
Beaver[1]	Beaver	May 2, 1890
Beckham	Sayre	July 16, 1907
Blaine[2]	Watonga	April 19, 1892
Bryan	Durant	July 16, 1907

Caddo[3]	Anadarko	July 4, 1901
Canadian	El Reno	May 2, 1890
Carter	Ardmore	July 16, 1907
Cherokee	Tahlequah	July 16, 1907
Choctaw	Hugo	July 16, 1907
Cimarron	Boise City	July 16, 1907
Cleveland	Norman	May 2, 1890
Coal	Coalgate	July 16, 1907
Comanche	Lawton	July 4, 1901
Cotton	Walters	August 27, 1912
Craig	Vinita	July 16, 1907
Creek	Sapulpa	July 16, 1907
Custer[4]	Arapahoe	April 19, 1892
Delaware	Jay	July 16, 1907
Dewey[5]	Taloga	April 19, 1892
Ellis	Arnett	July 16, 1907
Garfield[6]	Enid	August 21, 1893
Garvin	Pauls Valley	July 16, 1907
Grady	Chickasha	July 16, 1907
Grant[7]	Medford	August 21, 1893
Greer	Mangum	February 8, 1860
Harmon	Hollis	June 2, 1909
Harper	Buffalo	July 16, 1907
Haskell	Stigler	July 16, 1907
Hughes	Holdenville	July 16, 1907
Jackson	Altus	July 16, 1907
Jefferson	Waurika	July 16, 1907
Johnston	Tishomingo	July 16, 1907
Kay[8]	Newkirk	August 21, 1893
Kingfisher	Kingfisher	May 2, 1890
Kiowa	Hobart	July 4, 1901
Latimer	Wilburton	July 16, 1907
Le Flore	Poteau	July 16, 1907
Lincoln	Chandler	September 18, 1891
Logan	Guthrie	May 2, 1890
Love	Marietta	July 16, 1907
Major	Fairview	July 16, 1907
Marshall	Madill	July 16, 1907
Mayes	Pryor	July 16, 1907
McClain	Purcell	July 16, 1907
McCurtain	Idabel	July 16, 1907
McIntosh	Eufaula	July 16, 1907
Murray	Sulphur	July 16, 1907
Muskogee	Muskogee	July 16, 1907
Noble[9]	Perry	August 21, 1893
Nowata	Nowata	July 16, 1907
Okfuskee	Okemah	July 16, 1907
Oklahoma	Oklahoma City	May 2, 1890
Okmulgee	Okmulgee	July 16, 1907
Osage	Pawhuska	July 16, 1907
Ottawa	Miami	July 16, 1907
Pawnee[10]	Pawnee	August 21, 1893
Payne	Stillwater	May 2, 1890
Pittsburg	McAlester	July 16, 1907

Pontotoc	Ada	July 16, 1907
Pottawatomie	Shawnee	September 8, 1891
Pushmataha	Antlers	July 16, 1907
Roger Mills[11]	Cheyenne	April 19, 1892
Rogers	Claremore	July 16, 1907
Seminole	Wewoka	July 16, 1907
Sequoyah	Sallisaw	July 16, 1907
Stephens	Duncan	July 16, 1907
Texas	Guymon	July 16, 1907
Tillman	Frederick	July 16, 1907
Tulsa	Tulsa	July 16, 1907
Wagoner	Wagoner	July 16, 1907
Washington	Bartlesville	July 16, 1907
Washita[12]	Cordell	April 19, 1892
Woods[13]	Alva	August 21, 1893
Woodward[14]	Woodward	August 21, 1893

Notes

1. Beaver created as County 7; name changed July 16, 1907
2. Blaine created as County C; name changed July 16, 1907
3. Caddo created as County I; name changed November 8, 1902
4. Custer created as County G; name changed November 8, 1892
5. Dewey created as County D; name changed November 8, 1898
6. Garfield created as County O; name changed November 6, 1894
7. Grant created as County O; name changed November 6, 1894
8. Kay created as County K; name changed 1895
9. Noble created as County P; name changed November 6, 1894
10. Pawnee created as County Q; name changed 1895
11. Roger Mills created as County F; name changed November 8, 1892
12. Washita created as County H; name changed 1900
13. Woods created as County M; name changed November 6, 1894
14. Woodward created as County N; name changed November 6, 1894

OREGON (36 COUNTIES)

Provisional government 1843
Oregon Territory August 14, 1848
Admitted to Union February 14, 1859 (33rd)

County	County Seat	Created
Baker	Baker City	September 22, 1862
Benton	Corvallis	December 23, 1847
Clackamas	Oregon City	July 5, 1843
Clatsop	Astoria	June 22, 1844
Columbia	Saint Helens	January 16, 1854
Coos	Coquille	December 22, 1853
Crook	Prineville	October 24, 1882
Curry	Gold Beach	December 18, 1855
Deschutes	Bend	December 13, 1916
Douglas	Roseburg	January 7, 1852
Gilliam	Condon	February 25, 1885
Grant	Canyon City	October 14, 1864
Harney	Burns	February 25, 1889

Hood River	Hood River	June 23, 1908
Jackson	Medford	January 12, 1852
Jefferson	Madras	December 12, 1914
Josephine	Grants Pass	January 22, 1856
Klamath	Klamath	October 17, 1882
Lake	Lakeview	October 24, 1874
Lane	Eugene	January 28, 1851
Lincoln	Newport	February 20, 1893
Linn	Albany	December 28, 1847
Malheur	Vale	February 17, 1887
Marion[1]	Salem	July 5, 1843
Morrow	Heppner	February 16, 1885
Multnomah	Portland	December 22, 1854
Polk	Dallas	December 22, 1845
Sherman	Moro	February 25, 1889
Tillamook	Tillamook	December 15, 1853
Umatilla	Pendleton	September 27, 1862
Union	La Grande	October 14, 1864
Wallowa	Enterprise	February 11, 1887
Wasco	The Dalles	January 11, 1854
Washington[2]	Hillsboro	July 5, 1843
Wheeler	Fossil	February 17, 1899
Yamhill	McMinnville	July 5, 1843

Notes

1. Marion created as Champoeg; name changed September 3, 1849
2. Washington created as Twality; name changed September 3, 1849

PENNSYLVANIA (67 COUNTIES)

Colony established March 4, 1681
Declared independence July 4, 1776
Ratified Constitution December 12, 1787 (2nd)

County	County Seat	Created
Adams	Gettysburg	January 22, 1800
Allegheny	Pittsburgh	September 24, 1788
Armstrong	Kittanning	March 12, 1800
Beaver	Beaver	March 12, 1800
Bedford	Bedford	March 9, 1771
Berks	Reading	March 11, 1752
Blair	Hollidaysburg	February 26, 1846
Bradford[1]	Towanda	February 21, 1810
Bucks	Doylestown	March 10, 1682
Butler	Butler	March 12, 1800
Cambria	Ebensburg	March 26, 1804
Cameron	Emporium	March 29, 1860
Carbon	Jim Thorpe	March 13, 1843
Centre	Bellefonte	February 13, 1800
Chester	West Chester	March 10, 1682
Clarion	Clarion	March 11, 1839
Clearfield	Clearfield	March 26, 1804

Clinton	Lock Haven	June 21, 1839
Columbia	Bloomsburg	March 22, 1813
Crawford	Meadville	March 12, 1800
Cumberland	Carlisle	January 27, 1750
Dauphin	Harrisburg	March 4, 1785
Delaware	Media	September 26, 1789
Elk	Ridgway	April 18, 1843
Erie	Erie	March 12, 1800
Fayette	Uniontown	September 26, 1783
Forest	Tionesta	April 11, 1848
Franklin	Chambersburg	September 9, 1784
Fulton	McConnellsburg	April 19, 1850
Greene	Waynesburg	February 9, 1796
Huntingdon	Huntingdon	September 20, 1787
Indiana	Indiana	March 30, 1803
Jefferson	Brookville	March 26, 1804
Juniata	Mifflintown	March 2, 1831
Lackawanna	Scranton	August 21, 1878
Lancaster	Lancaster	May 10, 1729
Lawrence	New Castle	March 20, 1849
Lebanon	Lebanon	February 16, 1813
Lehigh	Allentown	March 6, 1812
Luzerne	Wilkes-Barre	September 25, 1786
Lycoming	Williamsport	April 13, 1795
McKean	Smethport	March 26, 1804
Mercer	Mercer	March 12, 1800
Mifflin	Lewistown	September 19, 1789
Monroe	Stroudsburg	April 1, 1836
Montgomery	Norristown	September 10, 1784
Montour	Danville	May 3, 1850
Northampton	Easton	March 11, 1752
Northumberland	Sunbury	March 21, 1772
Perry	New Bloomfield	March 22, 1820
Philadelphia	Philadelphia	March 10, 1682
Pike	Milford	March 26, 1814
Potter	Coudersport	March 26, 1804
Schuylkill	Pottsville	March 1, 1811
Snyder	Middleburg	March 2, 1855
Somerset	Somerset	April 17, 1795
Sullivan	Laporte	March 15, 1847
Susquehanna	Montrose	February 21, 1810
Tioga	Wellsburg	March 26, 1804
Union	Lewisburg	March 22, 1813
Venango	Franklin	March 12, 1800
Warren	Warren	March 12, 1800
Washington	Washington	March 28, 1781
Wayne	Honesdale	March 21, 1798
Westmoreland	Greensburg	February 26, 1773
Wyoming	Tunkhannock	April 4, 1842
York	York	August 19, 1749

Note

1. Bradford created as Ontario; name changed March 24, 1812

RHODE ISLAND (5 COUNTIES)

Chartered 1663
Renounced allegiance to England May 14, 1776
Ratified Constitution May 29, 1790 (13th)

County	County Seat	Created
Bristol	Bristol	February 17, 1747
Kent	Warwick	June 11, 1750
Newport[1]	Newport	June 22, 1703
Providence[2]	Providence	June 22, 1703
Washington[3]	West Kingston	June 23, 1729

Notes

1. Kent created as Rhode Island; name changed June 16, 1729
2. Providence created as Providence Plantations; name changed June 16, 1729
3. Washington created as King's; named changed October 29, 1781

SOUTH CAROLINA (46 COUNTIES)

Carolina proprietary colony 1663
North and South Carolina made separate provinces 1710
Declared independence July 4, 1776
Ratified Constitution May 23, 1788 (8th)
Seceded December 20, 1860
Readmitted December 20, 1868

County	County Seat	Created
Abbeville	Abbeville	March 12, 1785
Aiken	Aiken	March 10, 1871
Allendale	Allendale	February 6, 1919
Anderson	Anderson	December 20, 1826
Bamberg	Bamberg	February 25, 1897
Barnwell[1]	Barnwell	March 12, 1785
Beaufort	Beaufort	1769
Berkeley	Moncks Corner	January 31, 1882
Calhoun	Saint Matthews	February 14, 1908
Charleston	Charleston	1769
Cherokee	Gaffney	February 25, 1897
Chester	Chester	March 12, 1785
Chesterfield	Chesterfield	March 12, 1785
Clarendon	Manning	March 12, 1785
Colleton	Walterboro	1682
Darlington	Darlington	March 12, 1785
Dillon	Dillon	February 15, 1910
Dorchester	Saint George	February 25, 1897
Edgefield	Edgefield	March 12, 1785
Fairfield	Winnsboro	March 12, 1785
Florence	Florence	December 22, 1888
Georgetown	Georgetown	1769
Greenville	Greenville	March 22, 1786
Greenwood	Greenwood	March 2, 1897

Hampton	Hampton	February 18, 1878
Horry	Conway	December 19, 1801
Jasper	Ridgeland	January 30, 1912
Kershaw	Camden	February 19, 1791
Lancaster	Lancaster	March 12, 1785
Laurens	Laurens	March 12, 1785
Lee	Bishopville	February 25, 1902
Lexington	Lexington	March 12, 1785
Marion[2]	Marion	March 12, 1785
Marlboro	Bennettsville	March 12, 1785
McCormick	McCormick	February 19, 1916
Newberry	Newberry	March 12, 1785
Oconee	Walhalla	January 29, 1868
Orangeburg	Orangeburg	1769
Pickens	Pickens	December 20, 1826
Richland	Columbia	March 12, 1785
Saluda	Saluda	February 25, 1896
Spartanburg	Spartanburg	March 12, 1785
Sumter	Sumter	December 17, 1798
Union	Union	March 12, 1785
Williamsburg	Kingstree	March 12, 1785
York	York	March 12, 1785

Notes

1. Barnwell created as Winton; name changed January 1, 1800
2. Marion created as Liberty; name changed January 1, 1800

SOUTH DAKOTA (66 COUNTIES)

Dakota Territory March 2, 1861
Admitted to Union November 2, 1889 (40th)

County	County Seat	Created
Aurora	Plankinton	February 22, 1879
Beadle	Huron	February 22, 1879
Bennett	Martin	March 9, 1909
Bon Homme	Tyndall	April 5, 1862
Brookings	Brookings	April 5, 1862
Brown	Aberdeen	February 22, 1879
Brule	Chamberlain	January 14, 1875
Buffalo	Gannvalley	January 6, 1864
Butte	Belle Fourche	March 2, 1883
Campbell	Mound City	January 8, 1873
Charles Mix	Lake Andes	May 8, 1862
Clark	Clark	January 8, 1873
Clay	Vermillion	April 10, 1862
Codington	Watertown	February 15, 1877
Corson	McIntosh	March 2, 1909
Custer	Custer	January 11, 1875
Davison	Mitchell	January 8, 1873
Day	Webster	October 1, 1879
Deuel	Clear Lake	April 5, 1862

Dewey[1]	Timber Lake	January 8, 1873
Douglas	Armour	January 8, 1873
Edmunds	Ipswich	January 8, 1873
Fall River	Hot Springs	April 3, 1883
Faulk	Faulkton	January 8, 1873
Grant	Milbank	January 8, 1873
Gregory	Burke	May 8, 1862
Haakon	Phillip	November 3, 1914
Hamlin	Hayti	January 8, 1873
Hand	Miller	January 8, 1873
Hanson	Alexandria	January 13, 1871
Harding	Buffalo	March 5, 1881
Hughes	Pierre	January 8, 1873
Hutchinson	Olivet	May 8, 1862
Hyde	Highmore	January 8, 1873
Jackson	Kadoka	March 8, 1883
Jerauld	Wessington Springs	March 9, 1883
Jones	Murdo	January 15, 1916
Kingsbury	De Smet	January 8, 1873
Lake	Madison	January 8, 1873
Lawrence	Deadwood	January 11, 1875
Lincoln	Canton	April 5, 1862
Lyman	Kennebec	January 8, 1873
Marshall	Britton	March 10, 1885
McCook	Salem	January 8, 1873
McPherson	Leola	January 8, 1873
Meade	Sturgis	February 7, 1889
Mellette	White River	March 9, 1909
Miner	Howard	January 8, 1873
Minnehaha	Sioux Falls	April 5, 1862
Moody	Flandreau	January 8, 1873
Pennington	Rapid City	January 11, 1875
Perkins	Bison	November 3, 1908
Potter[2]	Gettysburg	January 8, 1873
Roberts	Sisseton	March 8, 1883
Sanborn	Woonsocket	March 9, 1883
Shannon	(Unorganized)[3]	January 11, 1875
Spink	Redfield	January 8, 1873
Stanley	Fort Pierre	January 8, 1873
Sully	Onida	January 8, 1873
Todd	(Unorganized)[4]	March 9, 1909
Tripp	Winner	January 8, 1873
Turner	Parker	January 13, 1871
Union[5]	Elk Point	April 10, 1862
Walworth	Selby	January 8, 1873
Yankton	Yankton	April 10, 1862
Ziebach	Dupree	February 1, 1911

Notes

1. Dewey created as Rush; name changed March 9, 1883
2. Potter created as Ashmore; name changed January 14, 1875
3. Shannon attached to Fall River County
4. Todd attached to Tripp County
5. Union created as Cole; name changed January 7, 1864

TENNESSEE (95 COUNTIES)

Part of North Carolina until April 2, 1790
Territory South of the Ohio River May 26, 1790
Admitted to Union June 1, 1796 (16th)
Seceded June 8, 1861
Readmitted July 24, 1866

County	County Seat	Created
Anderson	Clinton	November 6, 1801
Bedford	Shelbyville	December 3, 1807
Benton	Camden	December 19, 1835
Bledsoe	Pikeville	November 30, 1807
Blount	Maryville	July 11, 1795
Bradley	Cleveland	February 10, 1836
Campbell	Jacksboro	September 11, 1806
Cannon	Woodbury	January 31, 1836
Carroll	Huntingdon	November 7, 1821
Carter	Elizabethtown	April 9, 1796
Cheatham	Ashland	February 28, 1856
Chester	Henderson	March 4, 1879
Claiborne	Tazewell	October 29, 1801
Clay	Celina	June 24, 1870
Cocke[1]	Newport	October 9, 6797
Coffee	Manchester	January 8, 1836
Crockett	Alamo	December 20, 1845
Cumberland	Crossville	November 16, 1855
Davidson	Nashville	April 14, 1783
Decatur	Decaturville	November 1845
DeKalb	Smithville	December 11, 1837
Dickson	Charlotte	October 25, 1803
Dyer	Dyersburg	October 16, 1823
Fayette	Somerville	September 29, 1824
Fentress	Jamestown	November 28, 1823
Franklin	Winchester	December 3, 1807
Gibson	Trenton	October 21, 1823
Giles	Pulaski	November 14, 1809
Grainger	Rutledge	April 22, 1796
Greene	Greeneville	1783
Grundy	Altamont	January 29, 1844
Hamblen	Morristown	June 8, 1870
Hamilton	Chattanooga	October 25, 1819
Hancock	Sneedville	January 7, 1844
Hardeman	Bolivar	October 16, 1823
Hardin	Savannah	November 13, 1819
Hawkins	Rogersville	January 6, 1787
Haywood	Brownsville	November 3, 1823
Henderson	Lexington	November 7, 1821
Henry	Paris	November 7, 1821
Hickman	Centerville	December 3, 1807
Houston	Erin	January 23, 1871
Humphreys	Waverly	October 19, 1809
Jackson	Gainesboro	November 6, 1801
Jefferson	Dandridge	June 11, 1792
Johnson	Mountain City	January 2, 1836

Knox	Knoxville	June 11, 1792
Lake	Tiptonville	June 24, 1870
Lauderdale	Ripley	November 24, 1835
Lawrence	Lawrenceburg	October 21, 1817
Lewis	Hohenwald	December 23, 1843
Lincoln	Fayetteville	November 14, 1809
Loudon[2]	Loudon	June 2, 1809
Macon	Lafayette	January 18, 1842
Madison	Jackson	November 7, 1821
Marion	Jasper	November 20, 1817
Marshall	Lewisburg	February 20, 1836
Maury	Columbia	November 16, 1807
McMinn	Athens	November 13, 1819
McNairy	Selmer	October 8, 1823
Meigs	Decatur	January 20, 1836
Monroe	Madisonville	November 13, 1819
Montgomery	Clarksville	April 9, 1796
Moore	Lynchburg	December 14, 1871
Morgan	Wartburg	October 15, 1817
Obion	Union City	October 24, 1823
Overton	Livingston	September 11, 1806
Perry	Linden	November 14, 1818
Pickett	Byrdstown	February 27, 1879
Polk	Benton	November 28, 1839
Putnam	Cookeville	February 2, 1842
Rhea	Dayton	November 30, 1807
Roane	Kingston	November 6, 1801
Robertson	Springfield	April 9, 1796
Rutherford	Murfreesboro	October 25, 1803
Scott	Huntsville	December 17, 1849
Sequatchie	Dunlap	December 9, 1857
Sevier	Sevierville	September 27, 1794
Shelby	Memphis	November 24, 1819
Smith	Carthage	October 26, 1799
Stewart	Dover	November 1, 1803
Sullivan	Blountsville	1779
Sumner	Gallatin	November 17, 1786
Tipton	Covington	October 29, 1823
Trousdale	Hartsville	June 21, 1870
Unicoi	Erwin	March 23, 1875
Union	Maynardville	January 3, 1850
Van Buren	Spencer	January 3, 1840
Warren	McMinnville	November 26, 1807
Washington	Jonesborough	August 22, 1776
Wayne	Waynesboro	November 24, 1817
Weakley	Dresden	October 21, 1823
White	Sparta	September 11, 1806
Williamson	Franklin	October 26, 1799
Wilson	Lebanon	October 26, 1799

Notes

1. Created as Cocke; name changed to Union January 28, 1846; renamed Cocke January 3, 1850
2. Loudon created as Christiana; name changed July 7, 1870

TEXAS (254 COUNTIES)

Republic of Texas March 2, 1836
Admitted to Union December 29, 1845 (28th)
Seceded March 2, 1861
Readmitted March 30, 1870

County	County Seat	Created
Anderson	Palestine	March 24, 1846
Andrews	Andrews	August 21, 1876
Angelina	Lufkin	April 22, 1846
Aransas	Rockport	September 18, 1871
Archer	Archer City	January 22, 1858
Armstrong	Claude	August 21, 1876
Atascosa	Jourdanton	January 25, 1856
Austin	Bellville	March 17, 1836
Bailey	Muleshoe	August 21, 1876
Bandera	Bandera	January 26, 1856
Bastrop[1]	Bastrop	March 17, 1836
Baylor	Seymour	February 1, 1858
Bee	Beeville	December 8, 1857
Bell	Belton	January 22, 1850
Bexar	San Antonio	March 17, 1836
Blanco	Johnson City	February 12, 1858
Borden	Gail	August 21, 1876
Bosque	Meridian	February 4, 1854
Bowie	New Boston	December 17, 1840
Brazoria	Angleton	March 17, 1836
Brazos[2]	Bryan	January 30, 1841
Brewster	Alpine	February 2, 1887
Briscoe	Silverton	August 21, 1876
Brooks	Falfurrias	March 11, 1911
Brown	Brownwood	August 27, 1856
Burleson	Caldwell	March 24, 1846
Burnet	Burnet	February 5, 1852
Caldwell	Lockhart	March 6, 1848
Calhoun	Port Lavaca	April 4, 1846
Callahan	Baird	February 1, 1858
Cameron	Brownsville	February 12, 1848
Camp	Pittsburg	April 6, 1874
Carson	Panhandle	August 21, 1876
Cass[3]	Linden	April 25, 1846
Castro	Dimmitt	August 21, 1876
Chambers	Anahuac	February 12, 1858
Cherokee	Rusk	April 11, 1846
Childress	Childress	August 21, 1876
Clay	Henrietta	December 24, 1857
Cochran	Morton	August 21, 1876
Coke	Robert Lee	March 13, 1889
Coleman	Coleman	February 1, 1858
Collin	McKinney	April 3, 1846
Collingsworth	Wellington	August 21, 1876
Colorado	Columbus	March 17, 1836
Comal	New Braunfels	March 24, 1846

Comanche	Comanche	January 25, 1856
Concho	Paint Rock	February 1, 1858
Cooke	Gainesville	March 20, 1848
Coryell	Gatesville	February 4, 1854
Cottle	Paducah	August 21, 1876
Crane	Crane	February 26, 1887
Crocket	Ozona	January 22, 1875
Crosby	Crosbyton	August 21, 1876
Culberson	Van Horn	March 10, 1911
Dallam	Dalhart	August 21, 1876
Dallas	Dallas	March 30, 1846
Dawson	Lamesa	August 21, 1876
Deaf Smith	Hereford	August 21, 1876
Delta	Cooper	July 29, 1870
Denton	Denton	April 11, 1846
DeWitt	Cuero	March 24, 1846
Dickens	Dickens	August 21, 1876
Dimmitt	Carrizo Springs	February 1, 1858
Donley	Clarendon	August 21, 1876
Duval	San Diego	February 1, 1858
Eastland	Eastland	February 1, 1858
Ector	Odessa	February 26, 1887
Edwards	Rocksprings	February 1, 1858
Ellis	Waxahachie	December 20, 1849
El Paso	El Paso	January 3, 1850
Erath	Stephenville	January 25, 1856
Falls	Marlin	January 28, 1850
Fannin	Bonham	December 14, 1837
Fayette	La Grange	December 14, 1837
Fisher	Roby	August 21, 1876
Floyd	Floydada	August 21, 1876
Foard	Crowell	March 3, 1891
Fort Bend	Richmond	December 29, 1837
Franklin	Mount Vernon	March 6, 1873
Freestone	Fairfield	September 6, 1850
Frio	Pearsall	February 1, 1858
Gaines	Seminole	August 21, 1876
Galveston	Galveston	May 15, 1838
Garza	Post	August 21, 1876
Gillespie	Fredericksburg	February 23, 1848
Glasscock	Garden City	April 4, 1887
Goliad	Goliad	March 17, 1836
Gonzales	Gonzales	March 17, 1836
Gray	Pampa	August 21, 1876
Grayson	Sherman	March 17, 1846
Gregg	Longview	April 12, 1873
Grimes	Anderson	April 6, 1846
Guadalupe	Seguin	March 30, 1846
Hale	Plainview	August 21, 1876
Hall	Memphis	August 21, 1876
Hamilton	Hamilton	January 22, 1858
Hansford	Spearman	August 21, 1876
Hardeman	Quanah	February 1, 1858
Hardin	Kountze	January 22, 1858

Harris[4]	Houston	March 17, 1836
Harrison	Marshall	January 28, 1839
Hartley	Channing	August 21, 1876
Haskell	Haskell	February 1, 1858
Hays	San Marcos	March 1, 1848
Hemphill	Canadian	August 21, 1876
Henderson	Athens	April 27, 1846
Hidalgo	Edinburg	January 24, 1852
Hill	Hillsboro	February 7, 1853
Hockley	Levelland	August 21, 1876
Hood	Granbury	November 2, 1866
Hopkins	Sulphur Springs	March 25, 1846
Houston	Crockett	June 12, 1837
Howard	Big Spring	August 21, 1876
Hudspeth	Sierra Blanca	February 16, 1917
Hunt	Greenville	April 11, 1846
Hutchinson	Stinnett	August 21, 1876
Irion	Mertzon	March 7, 1889
Jack	Jacksboro	August 21, 1876
Jackson	Edna	March 17, 1836
Jasper	Jasper	March 17, 1836
Jeff Davis	Fort Davis	March 15, 1887
Jefferson	Beaumont	March 17, 1836
Jim Hogg	Hebbronville	March 31, 1913
Jim Wells	Alice	March 25, 1911
Johnson	Cleburne	February 13, 1854
Jones	Anson	February 1, 1858
Karnes	Karnes City	February 4, 1854
Kaufman	Kaufman	February 26, 1848
Kendall	Boerne	January 10, 1862
Kenedy	Sarita	April 2, 1921
Kent	Jayton	August 21, 1876
Kerr	Kerrville	January 26, 1856
Kimble	Junction	January 22, 1858
King	Guthrie	August 21, 1876
Kinney	Brackettville	January 28, 1850
Kleberg	Kingsville	February 27, 1913
Knox	Benjamin	February 1, 1858
Lamar	Paris	December 17, 1840
Lamb	Littlefield	August 21, 1876
Lampasas	Lampasas	February 1, 1858
La Salle	Cotulla	February 1, 1858
Lavaca	Hallettsville	April 6, 1846
Lee	Giddings	April 14, 1874
Leon	Centerville	March 17, 1846
Liberty	Liberty	March 17, 1836
Limestone	Groesbeck	April 11, 1846
Lipscomb	Lipscomb	August 21, 1876
Live Oak	George West	February 2, 1856
Llano	Llano	February 1, 1856
Loving	Mentone	February 26, 1887
Lubbock	Lubbock	August 21, 1876
Lynn	Tahoka	August 21, 1876
Madison	Madisonville	January 27, 1853

Marion	Jefferson	February 8, 1860
Martin	Stanton	August 21, 1876
Mason	Mason	January 22, 1858
Matagorda	Bay City	March 17, 1836
Maverick	Eagle Pass	February 2, 1856
McCulloch	Brady	August 27, 1856
McLennan	Waco	January 22, 1850
McMullen	Tilden	February 1, 1858
Medina	Hondo	February 12, 1848
Menard	Menard	January 22, 1858
Midland	Midland	March 4, 1885
Milan	Cameron	March 17, 1836
Mills	Goldthwaite	March 15, 1887
Mitchell	Colorado City	August 21, 1876
Montague	Montague	December 24, 1857
Montgomery	Conroe	December 14, 1837
Moore	Dumas	August 21, 1876
Morris	Daingerfield	March 6, 1875
Motley	Matador	August 21, 1876
Nacogdoches	Nacogdoches	March 17, 1836
Navarro	Corsicana	April 25, 1846
Newton	Newton	April 22, 1846
Nolan	Sweetwater	August 21, 1876
Nueces	Corpus Christi	April 18, 1846
Ochiltree	Perryton	August 21, 1876
Oldham	Vega	August 21, 1876
Orange	Orange	February 5, 1852
Palo Pinto	Palo Pinto	August 27, 1856
Panola	Carthage	March 30, 1846
Parker	Weatherford	December 12, 1855
Parmer	Farwell	August 21, 1876
Pecos	Fort Stockton	May 3, 1871
Polk	Livingston	March 30, 1846
Potter	Amarillo	August 21, 1876
Presidio	Marfa	January 3, 1850
Rains	Emory	June 9, 1870
Randall	Canyon	August 21, 1876
Reagan	Big Lake	March 7, 1903
Real	Leakey	April 3, 1913
Red River	Clarksville	March 17, 1836
Reeves	Pecos	April 14, 1883
Refugio	Refugio	March 17, 1836
Roberts	Miami	August 21, 1876
Robertson	Franklin	December 14, 1837
Rockwall	Rockwall	March 1, 1873
Runnels	Ballinger	February 1, 1858
Rusk	Henderson	January 16, 1843
Sabine	Hemphill	March 17, 1836
San Augustine	San Augustine	March 17, 1836
San Jacinto	Coldspring	August 13, 1870
San Patricio	Sinton	March 17, 1836
San Saba	San Saba	February 1, 1856
Schleicher	Eldorado	April 1, 1887
Scurry	Snyder	August 21, 1876

Shackelford	Albany	February 1, 1858
Shelby	Center	March 17, 1836
Sherman	Stratford	August 21, 1876
Smith	Tyler	April 11, 1846
Somervell	Glen Rose	March 13, 1875
Starr	Rio Grande City	February 10, 1848
Stephens[5]	Breckenridge	January 22, 1858
Sterling	Sterling City	March 4, 1891
Stonewall	Aspermont	August 21, 1876
Sutton	Sonora	April 1, 1887
Swisher	Tulia	August 21, 1876
Tarrant	Fort Worth	December 20, 1849
Taylor	Abilene	February 1, 1858
Terrell	Sanderson	April 8, 1905
Terry	Brownfield	August 21, 1876
Throckmorton	Throckmorton	January 13, 1858
Titus	Mount Pleasant	May 11, 1846
Tom Green	San Angelo	March 13, 1874
Travis	Austin	January 25, 1840
Trinity	Groveton	February 11, 1850
Tyler	Woodville	April 3, 1846
Upshur	Gilmer	April 27, 1846
Upton	Rankin	February 26, 1887
Uvalde	Uvalde	February 8, 1850
Val Verde	Del Rio	February 20, 1885
Van Zandt	Canton	March 20, 1848
Victoria	Victoria	March 17, 1836
Walker	Huntsville	April 6, 1846
Waller	Hempstead	April 28, 1873
Ward	Monahans	February 26, 1887
Washington	Brenham	March 17, 1836
Webb	Laredo	January 28, 1848
Wharton	Wharton	April 3, 1846
Wheeler	Wheeler	August 21, 1876
Wichita	Wichita Falls	February 1, 1858
Wilbarger	Vernon	February 1, 1858
Willacy	Raymondville	March 11, 1911
Williamson	Georgetown	March 13, 1848
Wilson	Floresville	February 13, 1860
Winkler	Kermit	February 26, 1887
Wise	Decatur	January 23, 1856
Wood	Quitman	February 5, 1850
Yoakum	Plains	August 21, 1876
Young	Graham	February 2, 1856
Zapata	Zapata	January 22, 1858
Zavala	Crystal City	February 1, 1858

Notes

1. Bastrop created as Mina; name changed December 18, 1837
2. Brazos created as Navasota; name changed January 30, 1841
3. Created as Cass; name changed to Davis December 17, 1861; renamed Cass May 16, 1871
4. Harris created as Harrisburg; name changed December 28, 1839
5. Stephens created as Buchanan; name changed December 17, 1861

UTAH (29 COUNTIES)

State of Deseret March 10, 1849
Utah Territory September 9, 1850
Admitted to Union January 4, 1896 (45th)

County	County Seat	Created
Beaver	Beaver	January 5, 1856
Box Elder	Brigham City	January 5, 1856
Cache	Logan	January 5, 1856
Carbon	Price	March 8, 1894
Daggett	Manila	March 4, 1917
Davis	Farmington	January 31, 1850
Duchesne	Duchesne	March 3, 1913
Emery	Castle Dale	February 12, 1880
Garfield	Panguitch	March 9, 1882
Grand	Moab	March 13, 1890
Iron[1]	Parowan	January 31, 1850
Juab	Nephi	March 3, 1852
Kane	Kanab	January 16, 1864
Millard	Fillmore	October 4, 1851
Morgan	Morgan	January 17, 1862
Piute	Junction	January 16, 1865
Rich[2]	Randolph	January 16, 1864
Salt Lake[3]	Salt Lake City	January 31, 1850
San Juan	Monticello	February 17, 1880
Sanpete	Manti	January 31, 1850
Sevier	Richfield	January 16, 1865
Summit	Coalville	January 13, 1854
Tooele	Tooele	January 31, 1850
Uintah	Vernal	February 18, 1880
Utah	Provo	January 31, 1850
Wasatch	Heber City	January 17, 1862
Washington	Saint George	March 3, 1852
Wayne	Loa	March 10, 1892
Weber	Ogden	January 31, 1850

Notes

1. Iron created as Little Salt Lake; name changed December 3, 1850
2. Rich created as Richland; name changed January 29, 1868
3. Salt Lake created as Great Salt Lake; name changed January 29, 1868

VERMONT (14 COUNTIES)

Declared independence from New York January 15, 1777
Admitted to Union March 4, 1791 (14th)

County	County Seat	Created
Addison	Addison	October 18, 1785
Bennington	Bennington	1779
Caledonia	Saint Johnsbury	November 5, 1792
Chittenden	Burlington	October 22, 1787
Essex	Guildhall	November 5, 1792

Franklin	Saint Albans	November 5, 1792
Grand Isle	North Hero	November 9, 1802
Lamoille	Hyde Park	October 26, 1835
Orange	Orange	February 22, 1781
Orleans	Newport	November 5, 1792
Rutland	Rutland	February 22, 1781
Washington[1]	Montpelier	November 1, 1810
Windham	Newfane	February 22, 1781
Windsor	Woodstock	February 22, 1781

Note

1. Washington created as Jefferson; name changed November 4, 1814

VIRGINIA (95 COUNTIES; 39 INDEPENDENT CITIES)

Royal colony 1624
Declared independence July 4, 1776
Ratified Constitution June 25, 1788 (10th)
Seceded April 17, 1861
Readmitted January 26, 1870

County	County Seat	Created
Accomack	Accomac	1661
Albemarle	Charlottesville	October 6, 1744
Alexandria	(Independent City)	March 13, 1852
Alleghany	Covington	January 5, 1822
Amelia	Amelia Court House	September 9, 1734
Amherst	Amherst	April 7, 1761
Appomattox	Appomattox	February 8, 1845
Arlington[1]	Arlington	March 13, 1847
Augusta	Staunton	December 15, 1738
Bath	Warm Springs	December 14, 1790
Bedford	Bedford	December 13, 1753
Bedford	(Independent City)	August 30, 1968
Bland	Bland	March 30, 1861
Botetourt	Fincastle	November 28, 1769
Bristol	(Independent City)	February 12, 1890
Brunswick	Lawrenceville	December 17, 1720
Buchanan	Grundy	February 13, 1858
Buckingham	Buckingham	April 7, 1761
Buena Vista	(Independent City)	1892
Campbell	Rustburg	December 15, 1781
Caroline	Bowling Green	March 15, 1727
Carroll	Hillsville	January 17, 1842
Charles City	Charles City	1634
Charlotte	Charlotte Court House	November 27, 1764
Charlottesville	(Independent City)	1888
Chesapeake[2]	(Independent City)	May 16, 1691
Chesterfield	Chesterfield	May 1, 1749
Clarke	Berryville	March 8, 1836
Colonial Heights	(Independent City)	1961
Covington	(Independent City)	1952
Craig	New Castle	March 21, 1851

Culpeper	Culpeper	March 23, 1748
Cumberland	Cumberland	March 23, 1749
Danville	(Independent City)	1890
Dickenson	Clintwood	March 3, 1880
Dinwiddie	Dinwiddie	March 9, 1752
Emporia	(Independent City)	July 31, 1967
Essex	Tappahannock	April 26, 1692
Fairfax	Fairfax	May 27, 1742
Fairfax	(Independent City)	June 30, 1961
Falls Church	(Independent City)	1948
Fauquier	Warrenton	April 5, 1759
Floyd	Floyd	January 15, 1831
Fluvanna	Palmyra	June 3, 1777
Franklin	Rocky Mount	November 29, 1785
Franklin	(Independent City)	December 21, 1961
Frederick	Winchester	December 15, 1738
Fredericksburg	(Independent City)	1879
Galax	(Independent City)	November 30, 1953
Giles	Pearisburg	January 6, 1806
Gloucester	Gloucester	1651
Goochland	Goochland	March 6, 1777
Grayson	Independence	November 7, 1792
Greene	Stanardsville	January 24, 1838
Greensville	Emporia	November 28, 1780
Halifax	Halifax	April 17, 1752
Hampton[3]	(Independent City)	March 19, 1849
Hanover	Hanover	November 26, 1720
Harrisonburg	(Independent City)	1916
Henrico	Richmond	1634
Henry	Martinsville	October 23, 1776
Highland	Monterey	March 19, 1847
Hopewell	(Independent City)	1916
Isle of Wight[4]	Isle of Wight	1634
James City	Williamsburg	1634
King and Queen	King and Queen Court House	April 16, 1691
King George	King George	November 20, 1720
King William	King William	September 12, 1701
Lancaster	Lancaster	1651
Lee	Jonesville	October 25, 1792
Lexington	(Independent City)	December 31, 1965
Loudoun	Leesburg	May 17, 1757
Louisa	Louisa	June 2, 1742
Lunenburg	Lunenburg	April 1, 1746
Lynchburg	(Independent City)	1895
Madison	Madison	December 5, 1792
Manassas	(Independent City)	May 1, 1975
Manassas Park	(Independent City)	June 1, 1975
Martinsville	(Independent City)	1928
Mathews	Mathews	December 16, 1790
Mecklenburg	Boydton	November 27, 1764
Middlesex	Saluda	February 2, 1768
Montgomery	Christiansburg	December 7, 1776
Nelson	Lovingston	December 25, 1807
New Kent	New Kent	1654
Newport News[5]	(Independent City)	July 1, 1958

Norfolk	(Independent City)	February 11, 1845
Northampton[6]	Eastville	1634
Northumberland	Heathsville	1648
Norton	(Independent City)	1954
Nottoway	Nottaway	December 22, 1788
Orange	Orange	September 30, 1734
Page	Luray	March 30, 1831
Patrick	Stuart	November 26, 1790
Petersburg	(Independent City)	March 16, 1850
Pittsylvania	Chatham	December 15, 1766
Poquoson	(Independent City)	1976
Portsmouth	(Independent City)	March 1, 1858
Powhatan	Powhatan	June 3, 1777
Prince Edward	Farmville	November 17, 1753
Prince George	Prince George	August 25, 1702
Prince William	Manassas	June 19, 1730
Pulaski	Pulaski	March 30, 1839
Radford	(Independent City)	1892
Rappahannock	Washington	February 8, 1833
Richmond	Warsaw	April 26, 1692
Richmond	(Independent City)	July 17, 1782
Roanoke	Salem	March 30, 1838
Roanoke	(Independent City)	1884
Rockbridge	Lexington	January 12, 1778
Rockingham	Harrisonburg	January 12, 1778
Russell	Lebanon	January 6, 1786
Salem	(Independent City)	December 31, 1967
Scott	Gate City	November 24, 1814
Shenandoah	Woodstock	March 24, 1772
Smyth	Marion	February 23, 1832
Southampton	Courtland	April 30, 1749
Spotsylvania	Spotsylvania	December 17, 1720
Stafford	Stafford	1664
Staunton	(Independent City)	June 16, 1908
Suffolk[8]	(Independent City)	1637
Surry	Surry	1652
Sussex	Sussex	November 28, 1753
Tazewell	Tazewell	December 20, 1799
Virginia Beach[9]	(Independent City)	May 16, 1691
Warren	Front Royal	March 9, 1836
Washington	Abingdon	December 7, 1776
Waynesboro	(Independent City)	February 1948
Westmoreland	Montross	July 1653
Williamsburg	(Independent City)	1884
Winchester	(Independent City)	1874
Wise	Wise	February 16, 1856
Wythe	Wytheville	December 1, 1789
York[10]	Yorktown	1634

Notes

1. Arlington created as Alexandria; name changed March 16, 1920
2. Chesapeake created as Norfolk 1691; consolidated with City of South Norfolk January 1, 1963
3. Hampton created as Elizabeth City 1634; merged with City of Hampton July 1, 1952
4. Isle of Wight created as Warrosquyoake; name changed 1637

5. Newport News created as Warwick River 1634; name changed to Warrick 1643; merged with City of Newport News July 1, 1958
6. Northampton created as Accawmack; name changed 1643
7. Shenandoah created as Dunmore; name changed February 1, 1778
8. Suffolk created as Upper Norfolk March 1645; name changed to Nansemond 1642; merged with City of Suffolk 1874
9. Virginia Beach created as Princess Anne 1691; merged with City of Virginia Beach January 1, 1963
10. York created as Charles River; name changed 1643

WASHINGTON (39 COUNTIES)

Champeog provisional government May 2, 1843
Oregon Territory August 14, 1848
Washington Territory March 2, 1853
Admitted to Union November 11, 1889 (42nd)

County	County Seat	Created
Adams	Ritzville	November 28, 1883
Asotin	Asotin	October 27, 1883
Benton	Prosser	March 8, 1905
Chelan	Wenatchee	March 13, 1899
Clallam	Port Angeles	April 26, 1854
Clark[1]	Vancouver	June 27, 1844
Columbia	Dayton	November 11, 1875
Cowlitz	Kelso	April 21, 1854
Douglas	Waterville	November 28, 1883
Ferry	Republic	February 18, 1899
Franklin	Pasco	November 28, 1883
Garfield	Pomeroy	November 29, 1881
Grant	Ephrata	February 24, 1909
Grays Harbor[2]	Montesano	April 14, 1854
Island	Coupeville	January 6, 1853
Jefferson	Port Townsend	December 22, 1852
King	Seattle	December 22, 1852
Kitsap[3]	Port Orchard	January 16, 1857
Kittitas	Ellensburg	November 24, 1883
Klickitat	Goldendale	December 20, 1859
Lewis	Chehalis	December 21, 1845
Lincoln	Davenport	November 24, 1883
Mason[4]	Shelton	March 13, 1854
Okanogan	Okanogan	February 2, 1888
Pacific	South Bend	February 4, 1851
Pend Oreille	Newport	March 1, 1911
Pierce	Tacoma	December 22, 1852
San Juan	Friday Harbor	October 31, 1873
Skagit	Mount Vernon	November 28, 1883
Skamania	Stevenson	March 9, 1854
Snohomish	Everett	January 14, 1861
Spokane[5]	Spokane	January 29, 1858
Stevens	Colville	January 20, 1863
Thurston	Olympia	January 12, 1852
Wahkiakum	Cathlamet	April 24, 1854
Walla Walla	Walla Walla	April 25, 1854
Whatcom	Bellingham	March 9, 1854
Whitman	Colfax	November 29, 1871
Yakima	Yakima	January 21, 1865

Notes

1. Clark created as Vancouver; name changed September 3, 1849
2. Grays Harbor created as Chehalis; name changed March 15, 1915
3. Kitsap created as Slaughter; name changed July 13, 1857
4. Mason created as Sawamish; name changed January 8, 1864
5. Spokane created as Shoshone; name changed 1860

WEST VIRGINIA (55 COUNTIES)

Part of Virginia until June 11, 1861
Admitted to Union June 20, 1863 (35th)

County	County Seat	Created
Barbour	Philippi	March 3, 1843
Berkeley	Martinsburg	March 24, 1772
Boone	Madison	March 11, 1847
Braxton	Sutton	January 15, 1836
Brooke	Wellsburg	November 30, 1796
Cabell	Huntington	January 2, 1809
Calhoun	Grantsville	March 5, 1856
Clay	Clay	March 29, 1858
Doddridge	West Union	February 4, 1845
Fayette	Fayetteville	February 28, 1831
Gilmer	Glenville	February 3, 1845
Grant	Petersburg	February 14, 1866
Greenbrier	Lewisburg	January 12, 1778
Hampshire	Romney	December 13, 1753
Hancock	New Cumberland	January 15, 1848
Hardy	Moorefield	December 10, 1785
Harrison	Clarksburg	June 4, 1784
Jackson	Ripley	March 1, 1831
Jefferson	Charles Town	January 8, 1801
Kanawha	Charleston	November 14, 1788
Lewis	Weston	December 18, 1816
Lincoln	Hamlin	February 23, 1867
Logan	Logan	January 12, 1824
Marion	Fairmont	January 14, 1842
Marshall	Moundsville	March 12, 1835
Mason	Point Pleasant	January 2, 1804
McDowell	Welch	February 20, 1858
Mercer	Princeton	March 17, 1837
Mineral	Keyser	February 1, 1866
Mingo	Williamson	January 30, 1895
Monongalia	Morgantown	November 6, 1776
Monroe	Union	January 14, 1799
Morgan	Berkeley Springs	February 9, 1820
Nicholas	Summersville	January 30, 1818
Ohio	Wheeling	November 6, 1776
Pendleton	Franklin	December 4, 1787
Pleasants	Saint Marys	March 29, 1851
Pocahontas	Marlinton	December 21, 1821
Preston	Kingwood	January 19, 1818
Putnam	Winfield	March 11, 1848

Raleigh	Beckley	January 23, 1850
Randolph	Elkins	November 29, 1786
Ritchie	Harrisville	February 18, 1843
Roane	Spencer	March 11, 1856
Summers	Hinton	February 27, 1871
Taylor	Grafton	January 19, 1844
Tucker	Parsons	March 7, 1856
Tyler	Middlebourne	December 6, 1814
Upshur	Buckhannon	March 26, 1851
Wayne	Wayne	January 18, 1842
Webster	Webster Springs	January 10, 1860
Wetzel	New Martinsville	January 10, 1846
Wirt	Elizabeth	January 19, 1848
Wood	Parkersburg	December 21, 1798
Wyoming	Pineville	January 26, 1850

WISCONSIN (72 COUNTIES)

Michigan Territory January 11, 1805
Wisconsin Territory April 20, 1836
Admitted to Union May 29, 1848 (30th)

County	County Seat	Created
Adams	Friendship	March 11, 1848
Ashland	Ashland	March 27, 1860
Barron[1]	Barron	March 19, 1859
Bayfield[2]	Washburn	February 19, 1845
Brown	Green Bay	October 26, 1818
Buffalo	Alma	July 6, 1853
Burnett	Siren	March 31, 1856
Calumet	Chilton	December 7, 1836
Chippewa	Chippewa Falls	February 3, 1845
Clark	Neillsville	July 6, 1853
Columbia	Portage	February 3, 1846
Crawford	Prairie du Chien	October 26, 1818
Dane	Madison	December 7, 1836
Dodge	Juneau	December 7, 1836
Door	Sturgeon Bay	February 11, 1851
Douglas	Superior	February 9, 1854
Dunn	Menominee	February 3, 1854
Eau Claire	Eau Claire	October 6, 1856
Florence	Florence	March 18, 1882
Fond du Lac	Fond du Lac	December 7, 1836
Forest	Crandon	April 11, 1885
Grant	Lancaster	December 8, 1836
Green	Monroe	December 8, 1836
Green Lake	Green Lake	March 5, 1858
Iowa	Dodgeville	October 9, 1829
Iron	Hurley	March 1, 1893
Jackson	Black River Falls	February 11, 1853
Jefferson	Jefferson	December 7, 1836
Juneau	Mauston	October 13, 1856
Kenosha	Kenosha	January 30, 1850
Kewaunee	Kewaunee	April 16, 1852
La Crosse	La Crosse	March 1, 1851

Lafayette	Darlington	January 31, 1846
Langlade[3]	Antigo	February 27, 1879
Lincoln	Merrill	March 4, 1874
Manitowoc	Manitowoc	December 7, 1836
Marathon	Wausau	February 9, 1850
Marinette	Marinette	February 27, 1879
Marquette	Marquette	December 7, 1836
Menominee	Keshena	May 1, 1961
Milwaukee	Milwaukee	September 6, 1834
Monroe	Sparta	March 21, 1854
Oconto	Oconto	February 6, 1851
Oneida	Rhinelander	April 11, 1885
Outagamie	Appleton	February 17, 1851
Ozaukee	Port Washington	March 7, 1853
Pepin	Durand	February 25, 1858
Pierce	Ellsworth	March 14, 1853
Polk	Balsam Lake	March 14, 1853
Portage	Stevens Point	December 7, 1836
Price	Phillips	March 3, 1879
Racine	Racine	December 7, 1836
Richland	Richland Center	February 18, 1842
Rock	Janesville	December 7, 1836
Rusk[4]	Ladysmith	May 15, 1901
Saint Croix	Hudson	January 9, 1840
Sauk	Baraboo	January 11, 1840
Sawyer	Hayward	March 10, 1883
Shawano[5]	Shawano	February 16, 1853
Sheboygan	Sheboygan	December 7, 1836
Taylor	Medford	March 4, 1875
Trempealeau	Whitehall	January 27, 1854
Vernon[6]	Viroqua	March 1, 1851
Vilas	Eagle River	April 12, 1893
Walworth	Elkhorn	December 7, 1836
Washburn	Shell Lake	March 27, 1883
Washington	West Bend	December 7, 1836
Waukesha	Waukesha	January 31, 1846
Waupaca	Waupaca	February 17, 1851
Waushara	Wautoma	February 15, 1851
Winnebago	Oshkosh	January 6, 1840
Wood	Wisconsin Rapids	March 29, 1856

Notes

1. Barron created as Dallas; name changed March 4, 1869
2. Bayfield created as La Pointe; name changed April 12, 1866
3. Langlade created as New; named changed February 19, 1880
4. Rusk created as Gates; name changed June 19, 1905
5. Shawano created as Shawanaw; spelling changed 1864
6. Vernon created as Bad Axe; name changed March 22, 1862

WYOMING (23 COUNTIES)

Dakota Territory March 2, 1861
Wyoming Territory July 25, 1868
Admitted to Union July 10, 1890 (44th)

County	County Seat	Created
Albany	Laramie	December 16, 1868
Big Horn	Basin	March 12, 1890
Campbell	Gillette	February 13, 1911
Carbon	Rawlins	December 16, 1868
Converse	Douglas	March 9, 1888
Crook	Sundance	December 8, 1875
Fremont	Lander	March 5, 1884
Goshen	Torrington	February 9, 1911
Hot Springs	Thermopolis	February 9, 1911
Johnson[1]	Buffalo	December 8, 1875
Laramie	Cheyenne	January 9, 1867
Lincoln	Kemmerer	February 20, 1911
Natrona	Casper	March 9, 1888
Niobrara	Lusk	February 14, 1911
Park	Cody	February 15, 1909
Platte	Wheatland	February 9, 1911
Sheridan	Sheridan	March 9, 1888
Sublette	Pinedale	February 15, 1921
Sweetwater[2]	Green River	December 27, 1867
Teton	Jackson	February 15, 1921
Uinta	Evanston	December 1, 1869
Washakie	Worland	February 9, 1911
Weston	Newcastle	March 12, 1890

Notes

1. Johnson created as Pease; name changed December 13, 1879
2. Sweetwater created as Carter; name changed December 13, 1869

Appendix B: Counties in Order of Creation

A number of variables are involved in determining the date a county was created. Is it the date the county was created by legislation? Is it the date the legislation was signed by the governor or, in the case of colonial counties, by the king or viceroy? Is it the date the county government began to function? Was such functioning a meeting or an election? All of these scenarios have been used to establish the date a county was created. In some cases, usually colonial counties, only the year or possibly the month is all that can be positively ascertained.

The date given for an independent city (indicated by IC) is not the date the city was founded but the date the city achieved independent status. An exception to this is in Virginia where the independent cities of Chesapeake, Hampton, Newport News, Suffolk, and Virginia Beach were merged with the counties of Norfolk, Elizabeth City, Warwick, Nansemond, and Princess Anne respectively. The date given for these five Virginia independent cities is the date its predecessor county was created. The same exception applies to Carson City, Nevada, which was merged with Ormsby County.

In this listing, there is no attempt to rank the creation of counties in numerical order. The exact date of the creation of a county in colonial America is often difficult, if not impossible, to determine.

COUNTY	STATE	CREATED
Charles City	Virginia	1634
Henrico	Virginia	1634
Isle of Wight	Virginia	1634
James City	Virginia	1634
Newport News (IC)	Virginia	1634
Northampton	Virginia	1634
York	Virginia	1634
Saint Mary's	Maryland	February 9, 1637
Suffolk (IC)	Virginia	1637
Kent	Maryland	August 2, 1642
Essex	Massachusetts	May 10, 1643
Middlesex	Massachusetts	May 10, 1643
Suffolk	Massachusetts	May 10, 1643
Northumberland	Virginia	1648
Anne Arundel	Maryland	July 30, 1650
Gloucester	Virginia	1651
Lancaster	Virginia	1651
York	Maine	November 20, 1652
Surry	Virginia	1652
Westmoreland	Virginia	July 1653
Calvert	Maryland	July 3, 1654
New Kent	Virginia	1654
Charles	Maryland	July 10, 1658
Accomack	Virginia	1661

Talbot	Maryland	February 18, 1662
Hampshire	Massachusetts	May 7, 1662
Stafford	Virginia	1664
Somerset	Maryland	August 22, 1666
Fairfield	Connecticut	1666
Hartford	Connecticut	1666
New Haven	Connecticut	1666
New London	Connecticut	1666
Currituck	North Carolina	1668
Perquimans	North Carolina	1668
Dorchester	Maryland	February 16, 1669
Pasquotank	North Carolina	1670
Chowan	North Carolina	1671
Middlesex	Virginia	February 2, 1673
New Castle	Delaware	August 8, 1673
Sussex	Delaware	August 8, 1673
Cecil	Maryland	December 31, 1674
Kent	Delaware	June 21, 1680
Bucks	Pennsylvania	March 10, 1682
Chester	Pennsylvania	March 10, 1682
Philadelphia	Pennsylvania	March 10, 1682
Colleton	South Carolina	1682
Essex	New Jersey	March 1, 1683
Bergen	New Jersey	March 7, 1683
Middlesex	New Jersey	March 7, 1683
Monmouth	New Jersey	March 7, 1683
Albany	New York	November 1, 1683
Dutchess	New York	November 1, 1683
Kings	New York	November 1, 1683
New York	New York	November 1, 1683
Orange	New York	November 1, 1683
Queens	New York	November 1, 1683
Richmond	New York	November 1, 1683
Suffolk	New York	November 1, 1683
Ulster	New York	November 1, 1683
Westchester	New York	November 1, 1683
Barnstable	Massachusetts	June 2, 1685
Bristol	Massachusetts	June 2, 1685
Plymouth	Massachusetts	June 2, 1685
Gloucester	New Jersey	May 26, 1686
Somerset	New Jersey	May 14, 1688
King and Queen	Virginia	May 12, 1691
Chesapeake (IC)	Virginia	May 16, 1691
Virginia Beach (IC)	Virginia	May 16, 1691
Essex	Virginia	April 26, 1692
Richmond	Virginia	April 26, 1692
Cape May	New Jersey	November 12, 1692
Burlington	New Jersey	May 17, 1694
Salem	New Jersey	May 17, 1694
Prince George's	Maryland	May 20, 1695
Dukes	Massachusetts	June 22, 1695
Nantucket	Massachusetts	June 22, 1695
Baltimore	Maryland	June 30, 1695
King William	Virginia	September 12, 1701
Prince George	Virginia	August 25, 1702

Newport	Rhode Island	June 22, 1703
Providence	Rhode Island	June 22, 1703
Craven	North Carolina	December 5, 1703
Beaufort	North Carolina	December 3, 1705
Hyde	North Carolina	December 3, 1705
Queen Anne's	Maryland	April 18, 1706
Hunterdon	New Jersey	March 11, 1714
King George	Virginia	November 24, 1720
Hanover	Virginia	November 26, 1720
Brunswick	Virginia	December 17, 1720
Spotsylvania	Virginia	December 17, 1720
Bertie	North Carolina	August 2, 1722
Carteret	North Carolina	August 8, 1722
Windham	Connecticut	May 12, 1726
Goochland	Virginia	March 6, 1727
Caroline	Virginia	March 15, 1727
Lancaster	Pennsylvania	May 10, 1729
Washington	Rhode Island	June 3, 1729
New Hanover	North Carolina	1729
Tyrrell	North Carolina	1729
Prince William	Virginia	June 19, 1730
Worcester	Massachusetts	April 5, 1731
Orange	Virginia	September 20, 1734
Amelia	Virginia	September 30, 1734
Bladen	North Carolina	November 11, 1734
Onslow	North Carolina	November 23, 1734
Augusta	Virginia	December 15, 1738
Frederick	Virginia	December 15, 1738
Morris	New Jersey	March 15, 1739
Edgecombe	North Carolina	April 4, 1741
Northampton	North Carolina	1741
Fairfax	Virginia	May 27, 1742
Louisa	Virginia	June 2, 1742
Worcester	Maryland	October 29, 1742
Albemarle	Virginia	October 16, 1744
Lunenburg	Virginia	April 1, 1746
Granville	North Carolina	1746
Johnston	North Carolina	1746
Bristol	Rhode Island	February 17, 1747
Cumberland	New Jersey	January 19, 1748
Culpeper	Virginia	March 23, 1748
Cumberland	Virginia	March 23, 1748
Frederick	Maryland	June 10, 1748
Southampton	Virginia	April 20, 1749
Chesterfield	Virginia	May 1, 1749
York	Pennsylvania	August 19, 1749
Cumberland	Pennsylvania	January 27, 1750
Duplin	North Carolina	April 7, 1750
Kent	Rhode Island	June 11, 1750
Anson	North Carolina	1750
Litchfield	Connecticut	October 9, 1751
Dinwiddie	Virginia	March 9, 1752
Berks	Pennsylvania	March 11, 1752
Northampton	Pennsylvania	March 11, 1752
Halifax	Virginia	April 17, 1752

Orange	North Carolina	1752
Rowan	North Carolina	March 27, 1753
Sussex	New Jersey	June 8, 1753
Prince Edward	Virginia	November 17, 1753
Sussex	Virginia	November 28, 1753
Bedford	Virginia	December 13, 1753
Hampshire	West Virginia	December 13, 1753
Cumberland	North Carolina	1754
Loudoun	Virginia	May 17, 1757
Halifax	North Carolina	January 1, 1759
Fauquier	Virginia	April 5, 1759
Hertford	North Carolina	May 1, 1760
Cumberland	Maine	June 19, 1760
Lincoln	Maine	June 19, 1760
Pitt	North Carolina	November 25, 1760
Amherst	Virginia	April 7, 1761
Buckingham	Virginia	April 7, 1761
Berkshire	Massachusetts	April 24, 1761
Mecklenburg	North Carolina	1762
Brunswick	North Carolina	March 9, 1764
Charlotte	Virginia	November 27, 1764
Mecklenburg	Virginia	November 27, 1764
Pittsylvania	Virginia	December 15, 1766
Cheshire	New Hampshire	April 29, 1769
Grafton	New Hampshire	April 29, 1769
Hillsborough	New Hampshire	April 29, 1769
Rockingham	New Hampshire	April 29, 1769
Strafford	New Hampshire	April 29, 1769
Botetourt	Virginia	November 28, 1769
Beaufort	South Carolina	1769
Charleston	South Carolina	1769
Georgetown	South Carolina	1769
Orangeburg	South Carolina	1769
Surry	North Carolina	January 1771
Bedford	Pennsylvania	March 9, 1771
Chatham	North Carolina	April 1, 1771
Guilford	North Carolina	April 1, 1771
Wake	North Carolina	1771
Montgomery	New York	March 12, 1772
Washington	New York	March 12, 1772
Northumberland	Pennsylvania	March 22, 1772
Shenandoah	Virginia	March 24, 1772
Berkeley	West Virginia	March 24, 1772
Westmoreland	Pennsylvania	February 26, 1773
Caroline	Maryland	December 5, 1773
Harford	Maryland	March 2, 1774
Martin	North Carolina	March 2, 1774
Washington	Tennessee	August 22, 1776
Montgomery	Maryland	September 6, 1776
Washington	Maryland	September 6, 1776
Henry	Virginia	October 23, 1776
Monongalia	West Virginia	November 6, 1776
Ohio	West Virginia	November 7, 1776
Montgomery	Virginia	December 7, 1776
Washington	Virginia	December 7, 1776

Burke	Georgia	February 5, 1777
Camden	Georgia	February 5, 1777
Chatham	Georgia	February 5, 1777
Effingham	Georgia	February 5, 1777
Glynn	Georgia	February 5, 1777
Liberty	Georgia	February 5, 1777
Richmond	Georgia	February 5, 1777
Wilkes	Georgia	February 5, 1777
Burke	North Carolina	April 8, 1777
Camden	North Carolina	April 8, 1777
Caswell	North Carolina	April 8, 1777
Fluvanna	Virginia	June 3, 1777
Powhatan	Virginia	June 3, 1777
Nash	North Carolina	1777
Wilkes	North Carolina	1777
Greenbrier	West Virginia	January 12, 1778
Rockbridge	Virginia	January 12, 1778
Rockingham	Virginia	January 12, 1778
Jones	North Carolina	January 19, 1779
Randolph	North Carolina	February 26, 1779
Wayne	North Carolina	November 2, 1779
Bennington	Vermont	1779
Franklin	North Carolina	1779
Gates	North Carolina	1779
Lincoln	North Carolina	1779
Montgomery	North Carolina	1779
Richmond	North Carolina	1779
Rutherford	North Carolina	1779
Sullivan	Tennessee	1779
Warren	North Carolina	1779
Fayette	Kentucky	June 30, 1780
Jefferson	Kentucky	June 30, 1780
Lincoln	Kentucky	June 30, 1780
Greensville	Virginia	November 28, 1780
Rutland	Vermont	February 22, 1781
Windham	Vermont	February 22, 1781
Windsor	Vermont	February 22, 1781
Washington	Pennsylvania	March 28, 1781
Campbell	Virginia	December 15, 1781
Richmond (IC)	Virginia	July 17, 1782
Fayette	Pennsylvania	September 26, 1783
Davidson	Tennessee	October 6, 1783
Greene	Tennessee	1783
Franklin	Georgia	February 25, 1784
Washington	Georgia	February 25, 1784
Harrison	West Virginia	June 4, 1784
Franklin	Pennsylvania	September 9, 1784
Montgomery	Pennsylvania	September 10, 1784
Nelson	Kentucky	November 29, 1784
Moore	North Carolina	1784
Sampson	North Carolina	1784
Dauphin	Pennsylvania	March 4, 1785
Abbeville	South Carolina	March 12, 1785
Barnwell	South Carolina	March 12, 1785
Chester	South Carolina	March 12, 1785

Chesterfield	South Carolina	March 12, 1785
Clarendon	South Carolina	March 12, 1785
Darlington	South Carolina	March 12, 1785
Edgefield	South Carolina	March 12, 1785
Fairfield	South Carolina	March 12, 1785
Lancaster	South Carolina	March 12, 1785
Laurens	South Carolina	March 12, 1785
Lexington	South Carolina	March 12, 1785
Marion	South Carolina	March 12, 1785
Marlboro	South Carolina	March 12, 1785
Newberry	South Carolina	March 12, 1785
Richland	South Carolina	March 12, 1785
Spartanburg	South Carolina	March 12, 1785
Union	South Carolina	March 12, 1785
Williamsburg	South Carolina	March 12, 1785
York	South Carolina	March 12, 1785
Mercer	Kentucky	August 1, 1785
Addison	Vermont	October 18, 1785
Franklin	Virginia	November 29, 1785
Hardy	West Virginia	December 10, 1785
Madison	Kentucky	December 15, 1785
Bourbon	Kentucky	December 29, 1785
Rockingham	North Carolina	December 29, 1785
Middlesex	Connecticut	1785
Tolland	Connecticut	1785
Russell	Virginia	January 6, 1786
Greene	Georgia	February 3, 1786
Greenville	South Carolina	March 22, 1786
Columbia	New York	April 4, 1786
Luzerne	Pennsylvania	September 25, 1786
Randolph	West Virginia	November 29, 1786
Sumner	Tennessee	1786
Hawkins	Tennessee	January 6, 1787
Huntingdon	Pennsylvania	September 20, 1787
Chittenden	Vermont	October 22, 1787
Pendleton	West Virginia	December 4, 1787
Robeson	North Carolina	1787
Clinton	New York	March 7, 1788
Woodford	Kentucky	May 1, 1788
Washington	Ohio	July 27, 1788
Allegheny	Pennsylvania	September 24, 1788
Mason	Kentucky	November 5, 1788
Kanawha	West Virginia	November 14, 1788
Nottoway	Virginia	December 22, 1788
Iredell	North Carolina	1788
Ontario	New York	January 27, 1789
Hancock	Maine	June 25, 1789
Washington	Maine	June 25, 1789
Mifflin	Pennsylvania	September 19, 1789
Delaware	Pennsylvania	September 26, 1789
Wythe	Virginia	December 1, 1789
Allegany	Maryland	December 25, 1789
Stokes	North Carolina	1789
Hamilton	Ohio	January 2, 1790
Saint Clair	Illinois	April 27, 1790

Knox	Indiana	June 20, 1790
District of Columbia		July 16, 1790
Patrick	Virginia	November 26, 1790
Columbia	Georgia	December 10, 1790
Elbert	Georgia	December 10, 1790
Bath	Virginia	December 14, 1790
Mathews	Virginia	December 16, 1790
Rensselaer	New York	February 7, 1791
Saratoga	New York	February 7, 1791
Herkimer	New York	February 16, 1791
Otsego	New York	February 16, 1791
Tioga	New York	February 16, 1791
Kershaw	South Carolina	February 19, 1791
Lenoir	North Carolina	1791
Buncombe	North Carolina	January 14, 1792
Person	North Carolina	February 1, 1792
Scott	Kentucky	June 1, 1792
Jefferson	Tennessee	June 11, 1792
Knox	Tennessee	June 11, 1792
Washington	Kentucky	June 22, 1792
Shelby	Kentucky	June 23, 1792
Logan	Kentucky	September 1, 1792
Lee	Virginia	October 25, 1792
Caledonia	Vermont	November 5, 1792
Essex	Vermont	November 5, 1792
Franklin	Vermont	November 5, 1792
Orleans	Vermont	November 5, 1792
Grayson	Virginia	November 7, 1792
Madison	Virginia	December 5, 1792
Clark	Kentucky	December 6, 1792
Hardin	Kentucky	December 15, 1792
Green	Kentucky	December 20, 1792
Cabarrus	North Carolina	1792
Norfolk	Massachusetts	March 26, 1793
Screven	Georgia	December 14, 1793
Hancock	Georgia	December 17, 1793
Bryan	Georgia	December 19, 1793
McIntosh	Georgia	December 19, 1793
Montgomery	Georgia	December 19, 1793
Oglethorpe	Georgia	December 19, 1793
Warren	Georgia	December 19, 1793
Harrison	Kentucky	December 21, 1793
Onondaga	New York	March 5, 1794
Sevier	Tennessee	September 27, 1794
Franklin	Kentucky	December 7, 1794
Campbell	Kentucky	December 17, 1794
Schoharie	New York	April 6, 1795
Lycoming	Pennsylvania	April 13, 1795
Somerset	Pennsylvania	April 17, 1795
Blount	Tennessee	July 11, 1795
Randolph	Illinois	October 5, 1795
Bulloch	Georgia	February 8, 1796
Greene	Pennsylvania	February 9, 1796
Jackson	Georgia	February 11, 1796
Jefferson	Georgia	February 20, 1796

Lincoln	Georgia	February 20, 1796
Steuben	New York	March 18, 1796
Carter	Tennessee	April 9, 1796
Montgomery	Tennessee	April 9, 1796
Robertson	Tennessee	April 9, 1796
Grainger	Tennessee	April 22, 1796
Bracken	Kentucky	June 1, 1796
Brooke	West Virginia	November 30, 1796
Bullitt	Kentucky	December 13, 1796
Christian	Kentucky	December 13, 1796
Montgomery	Kentucky	December 14, 1796
Warren	Kentucky	December 14, 1796
Garrard	Kentucky	December 17, 1796
Delaware	New York	March 10, 1797
Adams	Ohio	July 10, 1797
Jefferson	Ohio	July 29, 1797
Cocke	Tennessee	October 9, 1797
Fleming	Kentucky	February 10, 1798
Rockland	New York	February 23, 1798
Chenango	New York	March 15, 1798
Oneida	New York	March 15, 1798
Wayne	Pennsylvania	March 21, 1798
Ross	Ohio	August 20, 1798
Pulaski	Kentucky	December 10, 1798
Boone	Kentucky	December 13, 1798
Livingston	Kentucky	December 13, 1798
Pendleton	Kentucky	December 13, 1798
Cumberland	Kentucky	December 14, 1798
Gallatin	Kentucky	December 14, 1798
Henry	Kentucky	December 14, 1798
Muhlenberg	Kentucky	December 14, 1798
Ohio	Kentucky	December 17, 1798
Sumter	South Carolina	December 17, 1798
Jessamine	Kentucky	December 19, 1798
Barren	Kentucky	December 20, 1798
Henderson	Kentucky	December 21, 1798
Wood	West Virginia	December 21, 1798
Monroe	West Virginia	January 14, 1799
Kennebec	Maine	February 20, 1799
Essex	New York	March 1, 1799
Cayuga	New York	March 8, 1799
Adams	Mississippi	April 2, 1799
Jefferson	Mississippi	April 2, 1799
Smith	Tennessee	October 26, 1799
Williamson	Tennessee	October 26, 1799
Wilson	Tennessee	October 26, 1799
Breckinridge	Kentucky	December 9, 1799
Floyd	Kentucky	December 13, 1799
Nicholas	Kentucky	December 18, 1799
Knox	Kentucky	December 19, 1799
Tazewell	Virginia	December 20, 1799
Ashe	North Carolina	1799
Greene	North Carolina	1799
Washington	North Carolina	1799
Adams	Pennsylvania	January 22, 1800

Centre	Pennsylvania	February 13, 1800
Armstrong	Pennsylvania	March 12, 1800
Beaver	Pennsylvania	March 12, 1800
Butler	Pennsylvania	March 12, 1800
Crawford	Pennsylvania	March 12, 1800
Erie	Pennsylvania	March 12, 1800
Mercer	Pennsylvania	March 12, 1800
Venango	Pennsylvania	March 12, 1800
Warren	Pennsylvania	March 12, 1800
Greene	New York	March 25, 1800
Washington	Alabama	June 4, 1800
Trumbull	Ohio	July 10, 1800
Clermont	Ohio	December 6, 1800
Fairfield	Ohio	December 9, 1800
Wayne	Kentucky	December 18, 1800
Jefferson	West Virginia	January 8, 1801
Clark	Indiana	February 3, 1801
Belmont	Ohio	September 7, 1801
Claiborne	Tennessee	October 29, 1801
Anderson	Tennessee	November 6, 1801
Jackson	Tennessee	November 6, 1801
Roane	Tennessee	November 6, 1801
Clarke	Georgia	December 5, 1801
Tattnall	Georgia	December 5, 1801
Adair	Kentucky	December 11, 1801
Horry	South Carolina	December 19, 1801
Claiborne	Mississippi	January 27, 1802
Wilkinson	Mississippi	January 30, 1802
Saint Lawrence	New York	March 3, 1802
Genesee	New York	March 30, 1802
Grand Isle	Vermont	November 9, 1802
Dearborn	Indiana	March 7, 1803
Butler	Ohio	March 24, 1803
Greene	Ohio	March 24, 1803
Montgomery	Ohio	March 24, 1803
Scioto	Ohio	March 24, 1803
Warren	Ohio	March 24, 1803
Columbiana	Ohio	March 25, 1803
Gallia	Ohio	March 25, 1803
Franklin	Ohio	March 30, 1803
Indiana	Pennsylvania	March 30, 1803
Baldwin	Georgia	May 11, 1803
Wayne	Georgia	May 11, 1803
Wilkinson	Georgia	May 11, 1803
Dickson	Tennessee	October 25, 1803
Rutherford	Tennessee	October 25, 1803
Stewart	Tennessee	November 1, 1803
Greenup	Kentucky	December 12, 1803
Coos	New Hampshire	December 24, 1803
Mason	West Virginia	January 2, 1804
Muskingum	Ohio	January 7, 1804
Seneca	New York	March 24, 1804
Cambria	Pennsylvania	March 26, 1804
Clearfield	Pennsylvania	March 26, 1804
Jefferson	Pennsylvania	March 26, 1804

McKean	Pennsylvania	March 26, 1804
Potter	Pennsylvania	March 26, 1804
Tioga	Pennsylvania	March 26, 1804
Highland	Ohio	February 18, 1805
Athens	Ohio	February 20, 1805
Champaign	Ohio	February 20, 1805
Oxford	Maine	March 4, 1805
Jefferson	New York	March 28, 1805
Lewis	New York	March 28, 1805
Concordia	Louisiana	April 10, 1805
Iberville	Louisiana	April 10, 1805
Lafourche	Louisiana	April 10, 1805
Natchitoches	Louisiana	April 10, 1805
Orleans	Louisiana	April 10, 1805
Ouachita	Louisiana	April 10, 1805
Pointe Coupee	Louisiana	April 10, 1805
Rapides	Louisiana	April 10, 1805
Geauga	Ohio	December 31, 1805
Giles	Virginia	January 6, 1806
Madison	New York	March 21, 1806
Broome	New York	March 28, 1806
Allegany	New York	April 7, 1806
Campbell	Tennessee	September 11, 1806
Overton	Tennessee	September 11, 1806
White	Tennessee	September 11, 1806
Casey	Kentucky	November 14, 1806
Clay	Kentucky	December 2, 1806
Lewis	Kentucky	December 2, 1806
Hopkins	Kentucky	December 9, 1806
Miami	Ohio	January 16, 1807
Ashtabula	Ohio	February 10, 1807
Cuyahoga	Ohio	February 10, 1807
Portage	Ohio	February 10, 1807
Ascension	Louisiana	March 31, 1807
Assumption	Louisiana	March 31, 1807
Avoyelles	Louisiana	March 31, 1807
Plaquemines	Louisiana	March 31, 1807
Saint Bernard	Louisiana	March 31, 1807
Saint Charles	Louisiana	March 31, 1807
Saint James	Louisiana	March 31, 1807
Saint John the Bap.	Louisiana	March 31, 1807
Saint Landry	Louisiana	March 31, 1807
Saint Martin	Louisiana	March 31, 1807
West Baton Rouge	Louisiana	March 31, 1807
Maury	Tennessee	November 16, 1807
Warren	Tennessee	November 26, 1807
Bledsoe	Tennessee	November 30, 1807
Rhea	Tennessee	November 30, 1807
Bedford	Tennessee	December 3, 1807
Franklin	Tennessee	December 3, 1807
Hickman	Tennessee	December 3, 1807
Jasper	Georgia	December 10, 1807
Jones	Georgia	December 10, 1807
Laurens	Georgia	December 10, 1807
Morgan	Georgia	December 10, 1807

Putnam	Georgia	December 10, 1807
Telfair	Georgia	December 10, 1807
Nelson	Virginia	December 25, 1807
Knox	Ohio	January 30, 1808
Licking	Ohio	January 30, 1808
Richland	Ohio	January 30, 1808
Delaware	Ohio	February 10, 1808
Stark	Ohio	February 13, 1808
Tuscarawas	Ohio	February 13, 1808
Preble	Ohio	February 15, 1808
Estill	Kentucky	February 19, 1808
Cattaraugus	New York	March 11, 1808
Chautauqua	New York	March 11, 1808
Franklin	New York	March 11, 1808
Niagara	New York	March 11, 1808
Catahoula	Louisiana	March 23, 1808
Cortland	New York	April 8, 1808
Harrison	Indiana	October 11, 1808
Madison	Alabama	December 13, 1808
Pulaski	Georgia	December 13, 1808
Columbus	North Carolina	December 15, 1808
Haywood	North Carolina	December 15, 1808
Cabell	West Virginia	January 2, 1809
Darke	Ohio	January 3, 1809
Caldwell	Kentucky	January 13, 1809
Huron	Ohio	February 7, 1809
Amite	Mississippi	February 24, 1809
Somerset	Maine	March 1, 1809
Schenectady	New York	March 7, 1809
Sullivan	New York	March 27, 1809
Humphreys	Tennessee	October 19, 1809
Giles	Tennessee	November 14, 1809
Lincoln	Tennessee	November 14, 1809
Twiggs	Georgia	December 14, 1809
Baldwin	Alabama	December 21, 1809
Franklin	Mississippi	December 21, 1809
Wayne	Mississippi	December 21, 1809
Warren	Mississippi	December 22, 1809
Rockcastle	Kentucky	January 8, 1810
Pickaway	Ohio	January 12, 1810
Butler	Kentucky	January 18, 1810
Grayson	Kentucky	January 25, 1810
Coshocton	Ohio	January 31, 1810
Guernsey	Ohio	January 31, 1810
Madison	Ohio	February 16, 1810
Clinton	Ohio	February 19, 1810
Fayette	Ohio	February 19, 1810
Bradford	Pennsylvania	February 21, 1810
Susquehanna	Pennsylvania	February 21, 1810
Saint Helena	Louisiana	October 27, 1810
Saint Tammany	Louisiana	October 27, 1810
Washington	Vermont	November 10, 1810
Jefferson	Indiana	November 23, 1810
Wayne	Indiana	November 27, 1810
East Baton Rouge	Louisiana	December 22, 1810

Bath	Kentucky	January 15, 1811
Union	Kentucky	January 15, 1811
Franklin	Indiana	February 1, 1811
Schuylkill	Pennsylvania	March 1, 1811
Saint Mary	Louisiana	April 17, 1811
Franklin	Massachusetts	June 24, 1811
Madison	Georgia	December 5, 1811
Greene	Mississippi	December 9, 1811
Marion	Mississippi	December 9, 1811
Wayne	Ohio	January 4, 1812
Hampden	Massachusetts	February 12, 1812
Medina	Ohio	February 18, 1812
Lehigh	Pennsylvania	March 6, 1812
Putnam	New York	June 12, 1812
Gallatin	Illinois	September 14, 1812
Johnson	Illinois	September 14, 1812
Madison	Illinois	September 14, 1812
Cape Girardeau	Missouri	October 1, 1812
New Madrid	Missouri	October 1, 1812
Saint Charles	Missouri	October 1, 1812
Sainte Genevieve	Missouri	October 1, 1812
Saint Louis	Missouri	October 1, 1812
Clarke	Alabama	December 10, 1812
Emanuel	Georgia	December 10, 1812
Hancock	Mississippi	December 14, 1812
Jackson	Mississippi	December 14, 1812
Mobile	Alabama	December 18, 1812
Harrison	Ohio	January 2, 1813
Monroe	Ohio	January 29, 1813
Lebanon	Pennsylvania	February 16, 1813
Gibson	Indiana	March 9, 1813
Warrick	Indiana	March 9, 1813
Warren	New York	March 12, 1813
Columbia	Pennsylvania	March 22, 1813
Union	Pennsylvania	March 22, 1813
Washington	Missouri	August 21, 1813
Washington	Indiana	December 21, 1813
Arkansas	Arkansas	December 31, 1813
Pike	Pennsylvania	March 26, 1814
Perry	Indiana	September 7, 1814
Posey	Indiana	September 7, 1814
Switzerland	Indiana	September 7, 1814
Scott	Virginia	November 24, 1814
Edwards	Illinois	November 28, 1814
Tyler	West Virginia	December 6, 1814
Lawrence	Mississippi	December 22, 1814
Pike	Ohio	January 3, 1815
Allen	Kentucky	January 11, 1815
Daviess	Kentucky	January 14, 1815
Lawrence	Arkansas	January 15, 1815
Penobscot	Maine	February 16, 1815
Monroe	Alabama	June 29, 1815
Wayne	Michigan	November 21, 1815
Pike	Mississippi	December 9, 1815
White	Illinois	December 9, 1815

Jackson	Indiana	December 18, 1815
Lawrence	Ohio	December 21, 1815
Orange	Indiana	December 26, 1815
Monroe	Illinois	January 6, 1816
Jackson	Illinois	January 10, 1816
Pope	Illinois	January 10, 1816
Jackson	Ohio	January 12, 1816
Howard	Missouri	January 13, 1816
Hamilton	New York	February 12, 1816
Oswego	New York	March 1, 1816
Montgomery	Alabama	December 6, 1816
Lewis	West Virginia	December 18, 1816
Pike	Indiana	December 21, 1816
Daviess	Indiana	December 24, 1816
Jennings	Indiana	December 27, 1816
Ripley	Indiana	December 27, 1816
Sullivan	Indiana	December 30, 1816
Crawford	Illinois	December 31, 1816
Bond	Illinois	January 4, 1817
Tompkins	New York	April 7, 1817
Monroe	Michigan	July 14, 1817
Morgan	Tennessee	October 14, 1817
Lawrence	Tennessee	October 21, 1817
Marion	Tennessee	November 20, 1817
Wayne	Tennessee	November 24, 1817
Brown	Ohio	December 17, 1817
Dubois	Indiana	December 20, 1817
Clark	Ohio	December 26, 1817
Perry	Ohio	December 26, 1817
Morgan	Ohio	December 29, 1817
Logan	Ohio	December 30, 1817
Franklin	Illinois	January 2, 1818
Union	Illinois	January 2, 1818
Washington	Illinois	January 2, 1818
Hocking	Ohio	January 3, 1818
Lawrence	Indiana	January 7, 1818
Vanderburgh	Indiana	January 7, 1818
Randolph	Indiana	January 10, 1818
Spencer	Indiana	January 10, 1818
Monroe	Indiana	January 14, 1818
Macomb	Michigan	January 15, 1818
Whitley	Kentucky	January 17, 1818
Preston	West Virginia	January 19, 1818
Vigo	Indiana	January 21, 1818
Crawford	Indiana	January 29, 1818
Nicholas	West Virginia	January 30, 1818
Blount	Alabama	February 6, 1818
Franklin	Alabama	February 6, 1818
Lauderdale	Alabama	February 6, 1818
Lawrence	Alabama	February 6, 1818
Limestone	Alabama	February 6, 1818
Marengo	Alabama	February 6, 1818
Morgan	Alabama	February 6, 1818
Tuscaloosa	Alabama	February 6, 1818
Bibb	Alabama	February 7, 1818

Shelby	Alabama	February 7, 1818
Dallas	Alabama	February 9, 1818
Conecuh	Alabama	February 13, 1818
Marion	Alabama	February 13, 1818
Mackinac	Michigan	October 26, 1818
Brown	Wisconsin	October 26, 1818
Crawford	Wisconsin	October 26, 1818
Saint Clair	Alabama	November 20, 1818
Autauga	Alabama	November 21, 1818
Jefferson	Missouri	December 8, 1818
Franklin	Missouri	December 11, 1818
Wayne	Missouri	December 11, 1818
Lincoln	Missouri	December 14, 1818
Madison	Missouri	December 14, 1818
Montgomery	Missouri	December 14, 1818
Pike	Missouri	December 14, 1818
Appling	Georgia	December 15, 1818
Clark	Arkansas	December 15, 1818
Early	Georgia	December 15, 1818
Gwinnett	Georgia	December 15, 1818
Habersham	Georgia	December 15, 1818
Hall	Georgia	December 15, 1818
Hempstead	Arkansas	December 15, 1818
Irwin	Georgia	December 15, 1818
Pulaski	Arkansas	December 15, 1818
Walton	Georgia	December 15, 1818
Cooper	Missouri	December 17, 1818
Owen	Indiana	December 21, 1818
Fayette	Indiana	December 28, 1818
Floyd	Indiana	January 2, 1819
Covington	Mississippi	January 5, 1819
Shelby	Ohio	January 7, 1819
Oakland	Michigan	January 12, 1819
Meigs	Ohio	January 21, 1819
Harlan	Kentucky	January 28, 1819
Hart	Kentucky	January 28, 1819
Simpson	Kentucky	January 28, 1819
Owen	Kentucky	February 6, 1819
Alexander	Illinois	March 4, 1819
Washington	Louisiana	March 6, 1819
Clark	Illinois	March 22, 1819
Jefferson	Illinois	March 26, 1819
Wayne	Illinois	March 26, 1819
Hamilton	Tennessee	October 25, 1819
Hardin	Tennessee	November 13, 1819
McMinn	Tennessee	November 13, 1819
Monroe	Tennessee	November 13, 1819
Perry	Tennessee	November 14, 1819
Shelby	Tennessee	November 24, 1819
Butler	Alabama	December 3, 1819
Greene	Alabama	December 13, 1819
Henry	Alabama	December 13, 1819
Jackson	Alabama	December 13, 1819
Jefferson	Alabama	December 13, 1819
Perry	Alabama	December 13, 1819

Wilcox	Alabama	December 13, 1819
Rabun	Georgia	December 21, 1819
Todd	Kentucky	December 30, 1819
Union	Ohio	January 10, 1820
Scott	Indiana	January 12, 1820
Martin	Indiana	January 17, 1820
Monroe	Kentucky	January 19, 1820
Trigg	Kentucky	January 27, 1820
Perry	Mississippi	February 3, 1820
Morgan	West Virginia	February 9, 1820
Allen	Ohio	February 12, 1820
Crawford	Ohio	February 12, 1820
Grant	Kentucky	February 12, 1820
Hancock	Ohio	February 12, 1820
Hardin	Ohio	February 12, 1820
Henry	Ohio	February 12, 1820
Marion	Ohio	February 12, 1820
Mercer	Ohio	February 12, 1820
Paulding	Ohio	February 12, 1820
Putnam	Ohio	February 12, 1820
Sandusky	Ohio	February 12, 1820
Seneca	Ohio	February 12, 1820
Van Wert	Ohio	February 12, 1820
Williams	Ohio	February 12, 1820
Wood	Ohio	February 12, 1820
Perry	Pennsylvania	March 22, 1820
Saint Clair	Michigan	March 28, 1820
Phillips	Arkansas	May 1, 1820
Crawford	Arkansas	October 18, 1820
Independence	Arkansas	October 23, 1820
Perry	Kentucky	November 2, 1820
Boone	Missouri	November 16, 1820
Chariton	Missouri	November 16, 1820
Cole	Missouri	November 16, 1820
Lafayette	Missouri	November 16, 1820
Perry	Missouri	November 16, 1820
Ralls	Missouri	November 16, 1820
Ray	Missouri	November 16, 1820
Callaway	Missouri	November 25, 1820
Gasconade	Missouri	November 25, 1820
Saline	Missouri	November 25, 1820
Pickens	Alabama	December 19, 1820
Greene	Indiana	January 5, 1821
Union	Indiana	January 5, 1821
Bartholomew	Indiana	January 8, 1821
Parke	Indiana	January 9, 1821
Lawrence	Illinois	January 16, 1821
Greene	Illinois	January 20, 1821
Sangamon	Illinois	January 20, 1821
Pike	Illinois	January 31, 1821
Hamilton	Illinois	February 8, 1821
Monroe	Mississippi	February 9, 1821
Hinds	Mississippi	February 12, 1821
Montgomery	Illinois	February 12, 1821
Fayette	Illinois	February 14, 1821

Livingston	New York	February 23, 1821
Monroe	New York	February 23, 1821
Erie	New York	April 2, 1821
Dooly	Georgia	May 15, 1821
Fayette	Georgia	May 15, 1821
Henry	Georgia	May 15, 1821
Houston	Georgia	May 15, 1821
Monroe	Georgia	May 15, 1821
Escambia	Florida	July 21, 1821
Carroll	Tennessee	November 7, 1821
Henderson	Tennessee	November 7, 1821
Henry	Tennessee	November 7, 1821
Madison	Tennessee	November 7, 1821
Lawrence	Kentucky	December 14, 1821
Covington	Alabama	December 17, 1821
Pike	Alabama	December 17, 1821
Calloway	Kentucky	December 19, 1821
Graves	Kentucky	December 19, 1821
Hickman	Kentucky	December 19, 1821
Pike	Kentucky	December 19, 1821
Saint Francois	Missouri	December 19, 1821
Pocahontas	West Virginia	December 21, 1821
Newton	Georgia	December 24, 1821
Scott	Missouri	December 28, 1821
Decatur	Indiana	December 31, 1821
Henry	Indiana	December 31, 1821
Marion	Indiana	December 31, 1821
Morgan	Indiana	December 31, 1831
Putnam	Indiana	December 31, 1821
Rush	Indiana	December 31, 1821
Shelby	Indiana	December 31, 1821
Clay	Missouri	January 2, 1822
Alleghany	Virginia	January 5, 1822
Terrebonne	Louisiana	March 22, 1822
Duval	Florida	August 12, 1822
Jackson	Florida	August 12, 1822
Saint Johns	Florida	August 12, 1822
Lapeer	Michigan	September 10, 1822
Lenawee	Michigan	September 10, 1822
Saginaw	Michigan	September 10, 1822
Sanilac	Michigan	September 10, 1822
Shiawassee	Michigan	September 10, 1822
Washtenaw	Michigan	September 10, 1822
Morgan	Kentucky	December 7, 1822
Bibb	Georgia	December 9, 1822
Crawford	Georgia	December 9, 1822
DeKalb	Georgia	December 9, 1822
Pike	Georgia	December 9, 1822
Davidson	North Carolina	December 9, 1822
Marion	Missouri	December 14, 1822
Montgomery	Indiana	December 21, 1822
Lorain	Ohio	December 26, 1822
Johnson	Indiana	December 31, 1822
Edgar	Illinois	January 3, 1823
Madison	Indiana	January 4, 1823

Hamilton	Indiana	January 8, 1823
Lafayette	Louisiana	January 17, 1823
Copiah	Mississippi	January 21, 1823
Yazoo	Mississippi	January 21, 1823
Marion	Illinois	January 24, 1823
Fulton	Illinois	January 28, 1823
Morgan	Illinois	January 31, 1823
Yates	New York	February 5, 1823
Wayne	New York	April 11, 1823
Gadsden	Florida	June 24, 1823
Merrimack	New Hampshire	July 1, 1823
Monroe	Florida	July 3, 1823
McNairy	Tennessee	October 8, 1823
Dyer	Tennessee	October 16, 1823
Hardeman	Tennessee	October 16, 1823
Gibson	Tennessee	October 21, 1823
Weakley	Tennessee	October 23, 1823
Obion	Tennessee	October 24, 1823
Chicot	Arkansas	October 25, 1823
Tipton	Tennessee	October 29, 1823
Haywood	Tennessee	November 3, 1823
Fentress	Tennessee	November 28, 1823
Decatur	Georgia	December 8, 1823
Oldham	Kentucky	December 15, 1823
Allen	Indiana	December 17, 1823
Meade	Kentucky	December 17, 1823
Hendricks	Indiana	December 20, 1823
Walker	Alabama	December 26, 1823
Vermillion	Indiana	January 2, 1824
Spencer	Kentucky	January 7, 1824
Logan	West Virginia	January 12, 1824
Holmes	Ohio	January 20, 1824
Simpson	Mississippi	January 23, 1824
East Feliciana	Louisiana	February 17, 1824
West Feliciana	Louisiana	February 17, 1824
Fayette	Tennessee	September 29, 1824
Orleans	New York	November 12, 1824
Warren	New Jersey	November 20, 1824
Upson	Georgia	December 15, 1824
Ware	Georgia	December 15, 1824
McCracken	Kentucky	December 17, 1824
Fayette	Alabama	December 20, 1824
Dale	Alabama	December 22, 1824
Clay	Illinois	December 23, 1824
Clinton	Illinois	December 27, 1824
Wabash	Illinois	December 27, 1824
Alachua	Florida	December 29, 1824
Leon	Florida	December 29, 1824
Nassau	Florida	December 29, 1824
Orange	Florida	December 29, 1824
Walton	Florida	December 29, 1824
Calhoun	Illinois	January 10, 1825
Edmonson	Kentucky	January 12, 1825
Adams	Illinois	January 13, 1825
Hancock	Illinois	January 13, 1825

Henry	Illinois	January 13, 1825
Knox	Illinois	January 13, 1825
Mercer	Illinois	January 13, 1825
Peoria	Illinois	January 13, 1825
Putnam	Illinois	January 13, 1825
Schuyler	Illinois	January 13. 1825
Warren	Illinois	January 13, 1825
Jefferson	Louisiana	February 11, 1825
Clay	Indiana	February 12, 1825
Conway	Arkansas	October 20, 1825
Crittenden	Arkansas	October 22, 1825
Izard	Arkansas	October 27, 1825
Washington	Florida	December 9, 1825
Baker	Georgia	December 12, 1825
Laurel	Kentucky	December 12, 1825
Russell	Kentucky	December 14, 1825
Lowndes	Georgia	December 23, 1825
Thomas	Georgia	December 23, 1825
Butts	Georgia	December 24, 1825
Taliaferro	Georgia	December 24, 1825
Fountain	Indiana	December 30, 1825
Vermilion	Illinois	January 18, 1826
Tippecanoe	Indiana	January 20, 1826
Jones	Mississippi	January 24, 1826
McDonough	Illinois	January 25, 1826
Tishomingo	Mississippi	February 9, 1826
Tunica	Mississippi	February 9, 1826
Newton	Mississippi	February 25, 1826
Coweta	Georgia	June 9, 1826
Carroll	Georgia	December 11, 1826
Lee	Georgia	December 11, 1826
Troup	Georgia	December 11, 1826
Muscogee	Georgia	December 14, 1826
Jackson	Missouri	December 15, 1826
Anderson	South Carolina	December 20, 1826
Pickens	South Carolina	December 20, 1826
Chippewa	Michigan	December 22, 1826
Jefferson	Florida	January 6, 1827
Anderson	Kentucky	January 16, 1827
Warren	Indiana	January 19, 1827
Shelby	Illinois	January 23, 1827
Delaware	Indiana	January 26, 1827
Hancock	Indiana	January 26, 1827
Perry	Illinois	January 29, 1827
Washington	Mississippi	January 29, 1827
Tazewell	Illinois	January 31, 1827
Waldo	Maine	February 7, 1827
Jo Daviess	Illinois	February 17, 1827
Sullivan	New Hampshire	July 5, 1827
Saint Francis	Arkansas	October 13, 1827
Lafayette	Arkansas	October 15, 1827
Harris	Georgia	December 14, 1827
Marion	Georgia	December 14, 1827
Meriwether	Georgia	December 14, 1827
Talbot	Georgia	December 14, 1827

Hamilton	Florida	December 26, 1827
Madison	Florida	December 26, 1827
Carroll	Indiana	January 7, 1828
Madison	Mississippi	January 29, 1828
Rankin	Mississippi	February 4, 1828
Claiborne	Louisiana	March 13, 1828
Sevier	Arkansas	October 17, 1828
Washington	Arkansas	October 17, 1828
Cass	Indiana	December 18, 1828
Randolph	Georgia	December 20, 1828
Macon	North Carolina	1828
Hancock	Kentucky	January 3, 1829
Macoupin	Illinois	January 17, 1829
Macon	Illinois	January 19, 1829
Randolph	Missouri	January 22, 1829
Crawford	Missouri	January 23, 1829
Iowa	Wisconsin	October 9, 1829
Barry	Michigan	October 29, 1829
Berrien	Michigan	October 29, 1829
Branch	Michigan	October 29, 1829
Calhoun	Michigan	October 29, 1829
Cass	Michigan	October 29, 1829
Eaton	Michigan	October 29, 1829
Hillsdale	Michigan	October 29, 1829
Ingham	Michigan	October 29, 1829
Jackson	Michigan	October 29, 1829
Kalamazoo	Michigan	October 29, 1829
Saint Joseph	Michigan	October 29, 1829
Van Buren	Michigan	October 29, 1829
Hot Spring	Arkansas	November 2, 1829
Jefferson	Arkansas	November 2, 1829
Monroe	Arkansas	November 2, 1829
Pope	Arkansas	November 2, 1829
Union	Arkansas	November 2, 1829
Jackson	Arkansas	November 5, 1829
Lowndes	Alabama	January 20, 1830
Boone	Indiana	January 29, 1830
Clinton	Indiana	January 29, 1830
Elkhart	Indiana	January 29, 1830
Saint Joseph	Indiana	January 29, 1830
Lowndes	Mississippi	January 30, 1830
Heard	Georgia	December 22, 1830
Stewart	Georgia	December 23, 1830
Coles	Illinois	December 25, 1830
McLean	Illinois	December 25, 1830
Monroe	Missouri	January 6, 1831
Audrain	Missouri	January 12, 1831
Cook	Illinois	January 15, 1831
La Salle	Illinois	January 15, 1831
Floyd	Virginia	January 15, 1831
Rock Island	Illinois	February 9, 1831
Grant	Indiana	February 10, 1831
Effingham	Illinois	February 15, 1831
Jasper	Illinois	February 15, 1831
Fayette	West Virginia	February 28, 1831

Jackson	West Virginia	March 1, 1831
Allegan	Michigan	March 2, 1831
Arenac	Michigan	March 2, 1831
Clinton	Michigan	March 2, 1831
Gladwin	Michigan	March 2, 1831
Gratiot	Michigan	March 2, 1831
Ionia	Michigan	March 2, 1831
Isabella	Michigan	March 2, 1831
Juniata	Pennsylvania	March 2, 1831
Kent	Michigan	March 2, 1831
Midland	Michigan	March 2, 1831
Montcalm	Michigan	March 2, 1831
Oceana	Michigan	March 2, 1831
Ottawa	Michigan	March 2, 1831
Page	Virginia	March 30, 1831
Cherokee	Georgia	December 26, 1831
Sumter	Georgia	December 26, 1831
LaPorte	Indiana	January 9, 1832
Huntington	Indiana	February 2, 1832
LaGrange	Indiana	February 2, 1832
Miami	Indiana	February 2, 1832
Wabash	Indiana	February 2, 1832
Columbia	Florida	February 4, 1832
Franklin	Florida	February 8, 1832
Livingston	Louisiana	February 10, 1832
Smyth	Virginia	February 23, 1832
Bartow	Georgia	December 3, 1832
Cobb	Georgia	December 3, 1832
Floyd	Georgia	December 3, 1832
Forsyth	Georgia	December 3, 1832
Gilmer	Georgia	December 3, 1832
Lumpkin	Georgia	December 3, 1832
Murray	Georgia	December 3, 1832
Paulding	Georgia	December 3, 1832
Union	Georgia	December 3, 1832
Barbour	Alabama	December 18, 1832
Calhoun	Alabama	December 18, 1832
Chambers	Alabama	December 18, 1832
Coosa	Alabama	December 18, 1832
Macon	Alabama	December 18, 1832
Randolph	Alabama	December 18, 1832
Russell	Alabama	December 18, 1832
Sumter	Alabama	December 18, 1832
Talladega	Alabama	December 18, 1832
Tallapoosa	Alabama	December 18, 1832
Carroll	Ohio	December 25, 1832
Carroll	Missouri	January 2, 1833
Clinton	Missouri	January 2, 1833
Greene	Missouri	January 2, 1833
Lewis	Missouri	January 2, 1833
Morgan	Missouri	January 5, 1833
Ripley	Missouri	January 5, 1833
Warren	Missouri	January 5, 1833
Pulaski	Missouri	January 19, 1833
Pettis	Missouri	January 26, 1833

Rappahannock	Virginia	February 8, 1833
Holmes	Mississippi	February 19, 1833
Champaign	Illinois	February 20, 1833
Iroquois	Illinois	February 26, 1833
Livingston	Michigan	March 21, 1833
Carroll	Arkansas	November 1, 1833
Mississippi	Arkansas	November 1, 1833
Pike	Arkansas	November 1, 1833
Greene	Arkansas	November 5, 1833
Scott	Arkansas	November 5, 1833
Van Buren	Arkansas	November 11, 1833
Johnson	Arkansas	November 16, 1833
Walker	Georgia	December 18, 1833
Attala	Mississippi	December 23, 1833
Carroll	Mississippi	December 23, 1833
Choctaw	Mississippi	December 23, 1833
Clarke	Mississippi	December 23, 1833
Jasper	Mississippi	December 23, 1833
Kemper	Mississippi	December 23, 1833
Lauderdale	Mississippi	December 23, 1833
Leake	Mississippi	December 23, 1833
Neshoba	Mississippi	December 23, 1833
Noxubee	Mississippi	December 23, 1833
Oktibbeha	Mississippi	December 23, 1833
Scott	Mississippi	December 23, 1833
Smith	Mississippi	December 23, 1833
Tallahatchie	Mississippi	December 23, 1833
Winston	Mississippi	December 23, 1833
Yalobusha	Mississippi	December 23, 1833
Yancey	North Carolina	December 1833
Hillsborough	Florida	January 25, 1834
Marion	Kentucky	January 25, 1834
White	Indiana	February 1, 1834
Des Moines	Iowa	September 6, 1834
Dubuque	Iowa	September 6, 1834
Milwaukee	Wisconsin	September 6, 1834
Henry	Missouri	December 13, 1834
Johnson	Missouri	December 13, 1834
Shelby	Missouri	January 2, 1835
Stoddard	Missouri	January 2, 1835
Benton	Missouri	January 3, 1835
Barry	Missouri	January 5, 1835
Polk	Missouri	January 5, 1835
Adams	Indiana	February 7, 1835
DeKalb	Indiana	February 7, 1835
Fulton	Indiana	February 7, 1835
Jasper	Indiana	February 7, 1835
Jay	Indiana	February 7, 1835
Kosciusko	Indiana	February 7, 1835
Marshall	Indiana	February 7, 1835
Newton	Indiana	February 7, 1835
Noble	Indiana	February 7, 1835
Porter	Indiana	February 7, 1835
Pulaski	Indiana	February 7, 1835
Starke	Indiana	February 7, 1835

Steuben	Indiana	February 7, 1835
Wells	Indiana	February 7, 1835
Whitley	Indiana	February 7, 1835
Saint Clair	Missouri	February 11, 1835
Cass	Missouri	March 3, 1835
Marshall	West Virginia	March 12, 1835
Genesee	Michigan	March 28, 1835
Lucas	Ohio	June 20, 1835
White	Arkansas	October 23, 1835
Lamoille	Vermont	October 26, 1835
Randolph	Arkansas	October 29, 1835
Saline	Arkansas	November 2, 1835
Marion	Arkansas	November 3, 1835
Lauderdale	Tennessee	November 24, 1835
Benton	Tennessee	December 19, 1835
Johnson	Tennessee	January 2, 1836
Coffee	Tennessee	January 8, 1836
Cherokee	Alabama	January 9, 1836
DeKalb	Alabama	January 9, 1836
Marshall	Alabama	January 9, 1836
Will	Illinois	January 12, 1836
Braxton	West Virginia	January 15, 1836
Kane	Illinois	January 16, 1836
McHenry	Illinois	January 16, 1836
Ogle	Illinois	January 16, 1836
Whiteside	Illinois	January 16, 1836
Winnebago	Illinois	January 16, 1836
Meigs	Tennessee	January 20, 1836
Lake	Indiana	January 28, 1836
Cannon	Tennessee	January 31, 1836
Brown	Indiana	February 4, 1836
Miami-Dade	Florida	February 4, 1836
Bolivar	Mississippi	February 9, 1836
Chickasaw	Mississippi	February 9, 1836
Coahoma	Mississippi	February 9, 1836
DeSoto	Mississippi	February 9, 1836
Itawamba	Mississippi	February 9, 1836
Lafayette	Mississippi	February 9, 1836
Marshall	Mississippi	February 9, 1836
Panola	Mississippi	February 9, 1836
Pontotoc	Mississippi	February 9, 1836
Tippah	Mississippi	February 9, 1836
Bradley	Tennessee	February 10, 1836
Clinton	Kentucky	February 20, 1836
Marshall	Tennessee	February 20, 1836
Clarke	Virginia	March 8, 1836
Warren	Virginia	March 9, 1836
Austin	Texas	March 17, 1836
Bastrop	Texas	March 17, 1836
Bexar	Texas	March 17, 1836
Brazoria	Texas	March 17, 1836
Colorado	Texas	March 17, 1836
Goliad	Texas	March 17, 1836
Gonzales	Texas	March 17, 1836
Harris	Texas	March 17, 1836

Jackson	Texas	March 17, 1836
Jasper	Texas	March 17, 1836
Jefferson	Texas	March 17, 1836
Liberty	Texas	March 17, 1836
Matagorda	Texas	March 17, 1836
Milam	Texas	March 17, 1836
Nacogdoches	Texas	March 17, 1836
Red River	Texas	March 17, 1836
Refugio	Texas	March 17, 1836
Sabine	Texas	March 17, 1836
San Augustine	Texas	March 17, 1836
San Patricio	Texas	March 17, 1836
Shelby	Texas	March 17, 1836
Victoria	Texas	March 17, 1836
Washington	Texas	March 17, 1836
Chemung	New York	March 29, 1836
Monroe	Pennsylvania	April 1, 1836
Madison	Arkansas	September 29, 1836
Benton	Arkansas	September 30, 1836
Calumet	Wisconsin	December 7, 1836
Dane	Wisconsin	December 7, 1836
Dodge	Wisconsin	December 7, 1836
Fond du Lac	Wisconsin	December 7, 1836
Henry	Iowa	December 7, 1836
Jefferson	Wisconsin	December 7, 1836
Lee	Iowa	December 7, 1836
Louisa	Iowa	December 7, 1836
Manitowoc	Wisconsin	December 7, 1836
Marquette	Wisconsin	December 7, 1836
Muscatine	Iowa	December 7, 1836
Portage	Wisconsin	December 7, 1836
Racine	Wisconsin	December 7, 1836
Rock	Wisconsin	December 7, 1836
Sheboygan	Wisconsin	December 7, 1836
Van Buren	Iowa	December 7, 1836
Walworth	Wisconsin	December 7, 1836
Washington	Wisconsin	December 7, 1836
Grant	Wisconsin	December 8, 1836
Green	Wisconsin	December 8, 1836
Clark	Missouri	December 16, 1836
Davie	North Carolina	December 20, 1836
Caldwell	Missouri	December 29, 1836
Daviess	Missouri	December 29, 1836
Linn	Missouri	January 6, 1837
Livingston	Missouri	January 6, 1837
Macon	Missouri	January 6, 1837
Taney	Missouri	January 6, 1837
Carroll	Maryland	January 19, 1837
Miller	Missouri	February 6, 1837
Passaic	New Jersey	February 7, 1837
Trimble	Kentucky	February 9, 1837
Atlantic	New Jersey	February 17, 1837
Livingston	Illinois	February 27, 1837
Bureau	Illinois	February 28, 1837
Cass	Illinois	March 3, 1837

Boone	Illinois	March 4, 1837
DeKalb	Illinois	March 4, 1837
Stephenson	Illinois	March 4, 1837
Mercer	West Virginia	March 17, 1837
Houston	Texas	June 12, 1837
DeKalb	Tennessee	December 11, 1837
Macon	Georgia	December 14, 1837
Fannin	Texas	December 14, 1837
Fayette	Texas	December 14, 1837
Montgomery	Texas	December 14, 1837
Robertson	Texas	December 14, 1837
Franklin	Arkansas	December 19, 1837
Benton	Iowa	December 21, 1837
Buchanan	Iowa	December 21, 1837
Cedar	Iowa	December 21, 1837
Clayton	Iowa	December 21, 1837
Clinton	Iowa	December 21, 1837
Delaware	Iowa	December 21, 1837
Fayette	Iowa	December 21, 1837
Jackson	Iowa	December 21, 1837
Johnson	Iowa	December 21, 1837
Jones	Iowa	December 21, 1837
Keokuk	Iowa	December 21, 1837
Linn	Iowa	December 21, 1837
Scott	Iowa	December 21, 1837
Dade	Georgia	December 25, 1837
Fort Bend	Texas	December 29, 1837
Washington	Iowa	January 18, 1838
Caddo	Louisiana	January 18, 1838
Madison	Louisiana	January 19, 1838
Greene	Virginia	January 24, 1838
Calhoun	Florida	January 26, 1838
Carroll	Kentucky	February 9, 1838
Carter	Kentucky	February 9, 1838
Blackford	Indiana	February 15, 1838
Mercer	New Jersey	February 22, 1838
Poinsett	Arkansas	February 28, 1838
Caldwell	Louisiana	March 6, 1838
Erie	Ohio	March 15, 1838
Franklin	Maine	March 20, 1838
Piscataquis	Maine	March 23, 1838
Roanoke	Virginia	March 30, 1838
Fulton	New York	April 18, 1838
Desha	Arkansas	December 12, 1838
Searcy	Arkansas	December 13, 1838
Henderson	North Carolina	December 15, 1838
Chattooga	Georgia	December 28, 1838
Newton	Missouri	December 30, 1838
Buchanan	Missouri	December 31, 1838
Platte	Missouri	December 31, 1838
Cherokee	North Carolina	January 4, 1839
Marshall	Illinois	January 19, 1839
Jefferson	Iowa	January 21, 1839
Harrison	Texas	January 28, 1839
Brown	Illinois	February 1, 1839

Breathitt	Kentucky	February 8, 1839
DuPage	Illinois	February 9, 1839
Christian	Illinois	February 15, 1839
Logan	Illinois	February 15, 1839
Menard	Illinois	February 15, 1839
Scott	Illinois	February 16, 1839
Carroll	Illinois	February 22, 1839
Lee	Illinois	February 27, 1839
Jersey	Illinois	February 28, 1839
Williamson	Illinois	February 28, 1839
De Witt	Illinois	March 1, 1839
Lake	Illinois	March 1, 1839
Hardin	Illinois	March 2, 1839
Stark	Illinois	March 2, 1839
Clarion	Pennsylvania	March 11, 1839
Union	Louisiana	March 13, 1839
Aroostook	Maine	March 16, 1839
Pulaski	Virginia	March 30, 1839
Clinton	Pennsylvania	June 21, 1839
Polk	Tennessee	November 28, 1839
Van Buren	Tennessee	January 3, 1840
Winnebago	Wisconsin	January 6, 1840
Saint Croix	Wisconsin	January 9, 1840
Sauk	Wisconsin	January 11, 1840
Travis	Texas	January 25, 1840
Kenton	Kentucky	January 29, 1840
Benton	Indiana	February 18, 1840
Hudson	New Jersey	February 22, 1840
Summit	Ohio	March 3, 1840
Lake	Ohio	March 6, 1840
Ottawa	Ohio	March 6, 1840
Calcasieu	Louisiana	March 24, 1840
Alcona	Michigan	April 1, 1840
Alpena	Michigan	April 1, 1840
Antrim	Michigan	April 1, 1840
Charlevoix	Michigan	April 1, 1840
Cheboygan	Michigan	April 1, 1840
Clare	Michigan	April 1, 1840
Crawford	Michigan	April 1, 1840
Emmet	Michigan	April 1, 1840
Huron	Michigan	April 1, 1840
Iosco	Michigan	April 1, 1840
Kalkaska	Michigan	April 1, 1840
Lake	Michigan	April 1, 1840
Leelanau	Michigan	April 1, 1840
Manistee	Michigan	April 1, 1840
Mason	Michigan	April 1, 1840
Mecosta	Michigan	April 1, 1840
Missaukee	Michigan	April 1, 1840
Montmorency	Michigan	April 1, 1840
Newaygo	Michigan	April 1, 1840
Ogemaw	Michigan	April 1, 1840
Osceola	Michigan	April 1, 1840
Oscoda	Michigan	April 1, 1840
Otsego	Michigan	April 1, 1840

Presque Isle	Michigan	April 1, 1840
Roscommon	Michigan	April 1, 1840
Tuscola	Michigan	April 1, 1840
Wexford	Michigan	April 1, 1840
Yell	Arkansas	December 5, 1840
Bowie	Texas	December 17, 1840
Lamar	Texas	December 17, 1840
Bradley	Arkansas	December 18, 1840
Perry	Arkansas	December 18, 1840
Belknap	New Hampshire	December 22, 1840
Carroll	New Hampshire	December 22, 1840
Caldwell	North Carolina	January 11, 1841
Cleveland	North Carolina	January 11, 1841
Stanly	North Carolina	January 11, 1841
Henderson	Illinois	January 20, 1841
Mason	Illinois	January 20, 1841
Piatt	Illinois	January 27, 1841
Adair	Missouri	January 29, 1841
Andrew	Missouri	January 29, 1841
Bates	Missouri	January 29, 1841
Camden	Missouri	January 29, 1841
Dade	Missouri	January 29, 1841
Dallas	Missouri	January 29, 1841
Grundy	Missouri	January 29, 1841
Holt	Missouri	January 29, 1841
Jasper	Missouri	January 29, 1841
Osage	Missouri	January 29, 1841
Ozark	Missouri	January 29, 1841
Scotland	Missouri	January 29, 1841
Shannon	Missouri	January 29, 1841
Wright	Missouri	January 29, 1841
Brazos	Texas	January 30, 1841
Harrison	Mississippi	February 5, 1841
Gentry	Missouri	February 12, 1841
Grundy	Illinois	February 17, 1841
Kendall	Illinois	February 19, 1841
Richland	Illinois	February 24, 1841
Woodford	Illinois	February 27, 1841
Wyoming	New York	May 19, 1841
Coffee	Alabama	December 29, 1841
Marion	West Virginia	January 14, 1842
Carroll	Virginia	January 17, 1842
Macon	Tennessee	January 18, 1842
Wayne	West Virginia	January 18, 1842
Owsley	Kentucky	January 23, 1842
Crittenden	Kentucky	January 26, 1842
Putnam	Tennessee	February 2, 1842
Marshall	Kentucky	February 12, 1842
Ballard	Kentucky	February 15, 1842
Boyle	Kentucky	February 15, 1842
Richland	Wisconsin	February 18, 1842
Santa Rosa	Florida	February 18, 1842
Letcher	Kentucky	March 3, 1842
Wyoming	Pennsylvania	April 4, 1842
Ouachita	Arkansas	November 29, 1842

Montgomery	Arkansas	December 9, 1842
Catawba	North Carolina	December 12, 1842
Newton	Arkansas	December 14, 1842
McDowell	North Carolina	December 19, 1842
Union	North Carolina	December 19, 1842
Fulton	Arkansas	December 21, 1842
Nodaway	Missouri	January 2, 1843
Rusk	Texas	January 16, 1843
Massac	Illinois	February 8, 1843
Atchison	Missouri	February 14, 1843
Moultrie	Illinois	February 16, 1843
Appanoose	Iowa	February 17, 1843
Black Hawk	Iowa	February 17, 1843
Davis	Iowa	February 17, 1843
Iowa	Iowa	February 17, 1843
Mahaska	Iowa	February 17, 1843
Monroe	Iowa	February 17, 1843
Poweshiek	Iowa	February 17, 1843
Sullivan	Missouri	February 17, 1843
Tama	Iowa	February 17, 1843
Texas	Missouri	February 17, 1843
Wapello	Iowa	February 17, 1843
Ritchie	West Virginia	February 18, 1843
Putnam	Missouri	February 22, 1843
Bossier	Louisiana	February 24, 1843
Hernando	Florida	February 24, 1843
Johnson	Kentucky	February 24, 1843
Franklin	Louisiana	March 1, 1843
Larue	Kentucky	March 1, 1843
Cumberland	Illinois	March 2, 1843
Barbour	West Virginia	March 3, 1843
Pulaski	Illinois	March 3, 1843
Sabine	Louisiana	March 7, 1843
Delta	Michigan	March 9, 1843
Marquette	Michigan	March 9, 1843
Ontonagon	Michigan	March 9, 1843
Schoolcraft	Michigan	March 9, 1843
Wakulla	Florida	March 11, 1843
Carbon	Pennsylvania	March 13, 1843
Tensas	Louisiana	March 17, 1843
De Soto	Louisiana	April 1, 1843
Elk	Pennsylvania	April 18, 1843
Clackamas	Oregon	July 5, 1843
Marion	Oregon	July 5, 1843
Washington	Oregon	July 5, 1843
Yamhill	Oregon	July 5, 1843
Lewis	Tennessee	December 23, 1843
Ohio	Indiana	January 4, 1844
Hancock	Tennessee	January 7, 1844
Howard	Indiana	January 15, 1844
Tipton	Indiana	January 15, 1844
Taylor	West Virginia	January 19, 1844
Issaquena	Mississippi	January 23, 1844
Grundy	Tennessee	January 29, 1844
Sunflower	Mississippi	February 15, 1844

Camden	New Jersey	March 13, 1844
Brevard	Florida	March 14, 1844
Marion	Florida	March 14, 1844
Morehouse	Louisiana	March 25, 1844
Vermilion	Louisiana	March 25, 1844
Clatsop	Oregon	June 22, 1844
Clark	Washington	June 27, 1844
Polk	Arkansas	November 30, 1844
Dallas	Arkansas	January 1, 1845
Fulton	Kentucky	January 15, 1845
Chippewa	Wisconsin	February 3, 1845
Gilmer	West Virginia	February 3, 1845
Wyandot	Ohio	February 3, 1845
Doddridge	West Virginia	February 4, 1845
Appomattox	Virginia	February 8, 1845
Norfolk	Virginia	February 11, 1845
Cedar	Missouri	February 14, 1845
Dunklin	Missouri	February 14, 1845
Harrison	Missouri	February 14, 1845
Hickory	Missouri	February 14, 1845
Knox	Missouri	February 14, 1845
Lawrence	Missouri	February 14, 1845
Mercer	Missouri	February 14, 1845
Mississippi	Missouri	February 14, 1845
Moniteau	Missouri	February 14, 1845
Oregon	Missouri	February 14, 1845
Schuyler	Missouri	February 14, 1845
Bayfield	Wisconsin	February 19, 1845
DeKalb	Missouri	February 25, 1845
Reynolds	Missouri	February 25, 1845
Jackson	Louisiana	February 27, 1845
Defiance	Ohio	March 4, 1845
Levy	Florida	March 10, 1845
Houghton	Michigan	March 19, 1845
Marion	Iowa	June 10, 1845
Decatur	Tennessee	November 1845
Crockett	Tennessee	December 20, 1845
Lewis	Washington	December 21, 1845
Polk	Oregon	December 22, 1845
Wetzel	West Virginia	January 10, 1846
Boone	Iowa	January 13, 1846
Clarke	Iowa	January 13, 1846
Dallas	Iowa	January 13, 1846
Decatur	Iowa	January 13, 1846
Jasper	Iowa	January 13, 1846
Lucas	Iowa	January 13, 1846
Madison	Iowa	January 13, 1846
Marshall	Iowa	January 13, 1846
Polk	Iowa	January 13, 1846
Story	Iowa	January 13, 1846
Warren	Iowa	January 13, 1846
Wayne	Iowa	January 13, 1846
Lafayette	Wisconsin	January 31, 1846
Waukesha	Wisconsin	January 31, 1846
Columbia	Wisconsin	February 3, 1846

Mahoning	Ohio	February 16, 1846
Ashland	Ohio	February 24, 1846
Blair	Pennsylvania	February 26, 1846
Grayson	Texas	March 17, 1846
Leon	Texas	March 17, 1846
Anderson	Texas	March 24, 1846
Burleson	Texas	March 24, 1846
Comal	Texas	March 24, 1846
DeWitt	Texas	March 24, 1846
Hopkins	Texas	March 25, 1846
Dallas	Texas	March 30, 1846
Guadalupe	Texas	March 30, 1846
Panola	Texas	March 30, 1846
Polk	Texas	March 30, 1846
Collin	Texas	April 3, 1846
Tyler	Texas	April 3, 1846
Wharton	Texas	April 3, 1846
Calhoun	Texas	April 4, 1846
Lavaca	Texas	April 6, 1846
Walker	Texas	April 6, 1846
Cherokee	Texas	April 11, 1846
Denton	Texas	April 11, 1846
Hunt	Texas	April 11, 1846
Limestone	Texas	April 11, 1846
Smith	Texas	April 11, 1846
Nueces	Texas	April 18, 1846
Angelina	Texas	April 22, 1846
Newton	Texas	April 22, 1846
Cass	Texas	April 25, 1846
Navarro	Texas	April 25, 1846
Henderson	Texas	April 27, 1846
Upshur	Texas	April 27, 1846
Titus	Texas	May 11, 1846
Prairie	Arkansas	November 25, 1846
Drew	Arkansas	November 26, 1846
Gaston	North Carolina	December 21, 1846
Alexander	North Carolina	January 15, 1847
Polk	North Carolina	January 18, 1847
Allamakee	Iowa	February 20, 1847
Winneshiek	Iowa	February 20, 1847
Fremont	Iowa	February 24, 1847
Page	Iowa	February 24, 1847
Pottawattamie	Iowa	February 24, 1847
Ringgold	Iowa	February 24, 1847
Taylor	Iowa	February 24, 1847
Saline	Illinois	February 25, 1847
Boone	West Virginia	March 11, 1847
Arlington	Virginia	March 13, 1847
Sullivan	Pennsylvania	March 15, 1847
Highland	Virginia	March 19, 1847
Benton	Oregon	December 23, 1847
Linn	Oregon	December 28, 1847
Choctaw	Alabama	December 29, 1847
Holmes	Florida	January 8, 1848
Taylor	Kentucky	January 13, 1848

Hancock	West Virginia	January 15, 1848
Wirt	West Virginia	January 19, 1848
Webb	Texas	January 28, 1848
Starr	Texas	February 10, 1848
Cameron	Texas	February 12, 1848
Medina	Texas	February 12, 1848
Auglaize	Ohio	February 14, 1848
Gillespie	Texas	February 23, 1848
Morrow	Ohio	February 24, 1848
Kaufman	Texas	February 26, 1848
Hays	Texas	March 1, 1848
Caldwell	Texas	March 6, 1848
Adams	Wisconsin	March 11, 1848
Putnam	West Virginia	March 11, 1848
Williamson	Texas	March 13, 1848
Bienville	Louisiana	March 14, 1848
Cooke	Texas	March 20, 1848
Van Zandt	Texas	March 20, 1848
Grimes	Texas	April 6, 1848
Forest	Pennsylvania	April 11, 1848
Ashley	Arkansas	November 30, 1848
Putnam	Florida	January 13, 1849
Forsyth	North Carolina	January 16, 1849
Watauga	North Carolina	January 27, 1849
Alamance	North Carolina	January 29, 1849
Laclede	Missouri	February 24, 1849
Butler	Missouri	February 27, 1849
McDonald	Missouri	March 3, 1849
Hampton (IC)	Virginia	March 19, 1849
Lawrence	Pennsylvania	March 20, 1849
Benton	Minnesota	October 27, 1849
Dakota	Minnesota	October 27, 1849
Itasca	Minnesota	October 27, 1849
Kittson	Minnesota	October 27, 1849
Ramsey	Minnesota	October 27, 1849
Wabasha	Minnesota	October 27, 1849
Washington	Minnesota	October 27, 1849
Scott	Tennessee	December 17, 1849
Ellis	Texas	December 20, 1849
Tarrant	Texas	December 20, 1849
El Paso	Texas	January 3, 1850
Presidio	Texas	January 3, 1850
Union	Tennessee	January 3, 1850
Bell	Texas	January 22, 1850
McLennan	Texas	January 22, 1850
Raleigh	West Virginia	January 23, 1850
Wyoming	West Virginia	January 26, 1850
Falls	Texas	January 28, 1850
Kinney	Texas	January 28, 1850
Kenosha	Wisconsin	January 30, 1850
Iron	Utah	January 31, 1850
Salt Lake	Utah	January 31, 1850
Sanpete	Utah	January 31, 1850
Tooele	Utah	January 31, 1850
Utah	Utah	January 31, 1850

Weber	Utah	January 31, 1850
Wood	Texas	February 5, 1850
Uvalde	Texas	February 8, 1850
Marathon	Wisconsin	February 9, 1850
Trinity	Texas	February 11, 1850
Winston	Alabama	February 12, 1850
Gordon	Georgia	February 13, 1850
Clinch	Georgia	February 14, 1850
Ocean	New Jersey	February 15, 1850
Butte	California	February 18, 1850
Calaveras	California	February 18, 1850
Colusa	California	February 18, 1850
Contra Costa	California	February 18, 1850
El Dorado	California	February 18, 1850
Los Angeles	California	February 18, 1850
Marin	California	February 18, 1850
Mariposa	California	February 18, 1850
Mendocino	California	February 18, 1850
Monterey	California	February 18, 1850
Napa	California	February 18, 1850
Sacramento	California	February 18, 1850
San Diego	California	February 18, 1850
San Francisco	California	February 18, 1850
San Joaquin	California	February 18, 1850
San Luis Obispo	California	February 18, 1850
Santa Barbara	California	February 18, 1850
Santa Clara	California	February 18, 1850
Santa Cruz	California	February 18, 1850
Shasta	California	February 18, 1850
Solano	California	February 18, 1850
Sonoma	California	February 18, 1850
Sutter	California	February 18, 1850
Trinity	California	February 18, 1850
Tuolumne	California	February 18, 1850
Yolo	California	February 18, 1850
Yuba	California	February 18, 1850
Fulton	Ohio	February 20, 1850
Petersburg (IC)	Virginia	March 16, 1850
Vinton	Ohio	March 23, 1850
Fulton	Pennsylvania	April 19, 1850
Montour	Pennsylvania	May 3, 1850
Freestone	Texas	September 6, 1850
Davis	Utah	October 5, 1850
Calhoun	Arkansas	December 6, 1850
Yadkin	North Carolina	December 28, 1850
Sebastian	Arkansas	January 6, 1851
Adair	Iowa	January 15, 1851
Adams	Iowa	January 15, 1851
Audubon	Iowa	January 15, 1851
Bremer	Iowa	January 15, 1851
Buena Vista	Iowa	January 15, 1851
Butler	Iowa	January 15, 1851
Calhoun	Iowa	January 15, 1851
Carroll	Iowa	January 15, 1851
Cass	Iowa	January 15, 1851

Cerro Gordo	Iowa	January 15, 1851
Cherokee	Iowa	January 15, 1851
Chickasaw	Iowa	January 15, 1851
Clay	Iowa	January 15, 1851
Crawford	Iowa	January 15, 1851
Dickinson	Iowa	January 15, 1851
Emmet	Iowa	January 15, 1851
Floyd	Iowa	January 15, 1851
Franklin	Iowa	January 15, 1851
Greene	Iowa	January 15, 1851
Grundy	Iowa	January 15, 1851
Guthrie	Iowa	January 15, 1851
Hancock	Iowa	January 15, 1851
Hardin	Iowa	January 15, 1851
Harrison	Iowa	January 15, 1851
Howard	Iowa	January 15, 1851
Ida	Iowa	January 15, 1851
Kossuth	Iowa	January 15, 1851
Lyon	Iowa	January 15, 1851
Mills	Iowa	January 15, 1851
Mitchell	Iowa	January 15, 1851
Monona	Iowa	January 15, 1851
Montgomery	Iowa	January 15, 1851
O'Brien	Iowa	January 15, 1851
Osceola	Iowa	January 15, 1851
Palo Alto	Iowa	January 15, 1851
Plymouth	Iowa	January 15, 1851
Pocahontas	Iowa	January 15, 1851
Sac	Iowa	January 15, 1851
Shelby	Iowa	January 15, 1851
Sioux	Iowa	January 15, 1851
Union	Iowa	January 15, 1851
Webster	Iowa	January 15, 1851
Winnebago	Iowa	January 15, 1851
Woodbury	Iowa	January 15, 1851
Worth	Iowa	January 15, 1851
Wright	Iowa	January 15, 1851
Madison	North Carolina	January 27, 1851
Lane	Oregon	January 28, 1851
Jackson	North Carolina	January 29, 1851
Pacific	Washington	February 4, 1851
Oconto	Wisconsin	February 6, 1851
Dent	Missouri	February 10, 1851
Stone	Missouri	February 10, 1851
Door	Wisconsin	February 11, 1851
Waushara	Wisconsin	February 15, 1851
Outagamie	Wisconsin	February 17, 1851
Waupaca	Wisconsin	February 17, 1851
Pemiscot	Missouri	February 19, 1851
Bollinger	Missouri	March 1, 1851
La Crosse	Wisconsin	March 1, 1851
Vernon	Wisconsin	March 1, 1851
Noble	Ohio	March 11, 1851
Craig	Virginia	March 21, 1851
Upshur	West Virginia	March 26, 1851

Pleasants	West Virginia	March 29, 1851
Cass	Minnesota	March 31, 1851
Chisago	Minnesota	March 31, 1851
Grand Traverse	Michigan	April 7, 1851
Nevada	California	April 25, 1851
Placer	California	April 25, 1851
Baltimore (IC)	Maryland	July 4, 1851
Howard	Maryland	July 4, 1851
Millard	Utah	October 4, 1851
Polk	Georgia	December 20, 1851
Spalding	Georgia	December 20, 1851
Whitfield	Georgia	December 30, 1851
Douglas	Oregon	January 7, 1852
Powell	Kentucky	January 7, 1852
Bernalillo	New Mexico	January 9, 1852
Dona Ana	New Mexico	January 9, 1852
Rio Arriba	New Mexico	January 9, 1852
San Miguel	New Mexico	January 9, 1852
Santa Fe	New Mexico	January 9, 1852
Socorro	New Mexico	January 9, 1852
Taos	New Mexico	January 9, 1852
Valencia	New Mexico	January 9, 1852
Jackson	Oregon	January 12, 1852
Thurston	Washington	January 12, 1852
Taylor	Georgia	January 15, 1852
Hidalgo	Texas	January 24, 1852
Burnet	Texas	February 5, 1852
Orange	Texas	February 5, 1852
Winn	Louisiana	February 24, 1852
Juab	Utah	March 3, 1852
Washington	Utah	March 3, 1852
Hennepin	Minnesota	March 6, 1852
Calhoun	Mississippi	March 8, 1852
Siskiyou	California	March 22, 1852
Kewaunee	Wisconsin	April 16, 1852
Sierra	California	April 16, 1852
Tulare	California	April 20, 1852
Columbia	Arkansas	December 17, 1852
Jefferson	Washington	December 22, 1852
King	Washington	December 22, 1852
Pierce	Washington	December 22, 1852
Island	Washington	January 6, 1853
Sumter	Florida	January 8, 1853
Madison	Texas	January 27, 1853
Hill	Texas	February 7, 1853
Jackson	Wisconsin	February 11, 1853
Kankakee	Illinois	February 11, 1853
Shawano	Wisconsin	February 16, 1853
Blue Earth	Minnesota	March 5, 1853
Fillmore	Minnesota	March 5, 1853
Goodhue	Minnesota	March 5, 1853
Le Sueur	Minnesota	March 5, 1853
Nicollet	Minnesota	March 5, 1853
Rice	Minnesota	March 5, 1853
Scott	Minnesota	March 5, 1853

Sibley	Minnesota	March 5, 1853
Ozaukee	Wisconsin	March 7, 1853
Pierce	Wisconsin	March 14, 1853
Polk	Wisconsin	March 14, 1853
Alameda	California	March 25, 1853
San Bernardino	California	April 26, 1853
Humboldt	California	May 22, 1853
Buffalo	Wisconsin	July 6, 1853
Clark	Wisconsin	July 6, 1853
Catoosa	Georgia	December 5, 1853
Pickens	Georgia	December 5, 1853
Hart	Georgia	December 7, 1853
Dougherty	Georgia	December 15, 1853
Tillamook	Oregon	December 15, 1853
Webster	Georgia	December 16, 1853
Fulton	Georgia	December 20, 1853
Worth	Georgia	December 20, 1853
Coos	Oregon	December 22, 1853
Wasco	Oregon	January 11, 1854
Summit	Utah	January 13, 1854
Lyon	Kentucky	January 14, 1854
Columbia	Oregon	January 16, 1854
Fannin	Georgia	January 21, 1854
Trempealeau	Wisconsin	January 27, 1854
Dunn	Wisconsin	February 3, 1854
Bosque	Texas	February 4, 1854
Coryell	Texas	February 4, 1854
Karnes	Texas	February 4, 1854
McLean	Kentucky	February 6, 1854
Coffee	Georgia	February 9, 1854
Douglas	Wisconsin	February 9, 1854
Chattahoochee	Georgia	February 13, 1854
Johnson	Texas	February 13, 1854
Clay	Georgia	February 16, 1854
Charlton	Georgia	February 18, 1854
Calhoun	Georgia	February 20, 1854
Skamania	Washington	March 9, 1854
Whatcom	Washington	March 9, 1854
Mason	Washington	March 13, 1854
Androscoggin	Maine	March 18, 1854
Plumas	California	March 18, 1854
Monroe	Wisconsin	March 21, 1854
Stanislaus	California	April 1, 1854
Houston	Minnesota	April 4, 1854
Sagadahoc	Maine	April 4, 1854
Winona	Minnesota	April 4, 1854
Grays Harbor	Washington	April 14, 1854
Schuyler	New York	April 17, 1854
Cowlitz	Washington	April 21, 1854
Wahkiakum	Washington	April 24, 1854
Walla Walla	Washington	April 25, 1854
Clallam	Washington	April 26, 1854
Amador	California	May 10, 1854
Burt	Nebraska	November 23, 1854
Cass	Nebraska	November 23, 1854

Dodge	Nebraska	November 23, 1854
Douglas	Nebraska	November 23, 1854
Nemaha	Nebraska	November 23, 1854
Otoe	Nebraska	November 23, 1854
Richardson	Nebraska	November 23, 1854
Washington	Nebraska	November 23, 1854
Multnomah	Oregon	December 22, 1854
Volusia	Florida	December 29, 1854
Manatee	Florida	January 9, 1855
Harnett	North Carolina	February 7, 1855
Wilson	North Carolina	February 13, 1855
Brown	Minnesota	February 20, 1855
Carver	Minnesota	February 20, 1855
Dodge	Minnesota	February 20, 1855
Faribault	Minnesota	February 20, 1855
Freeborn	Minnesota	February 20, 1855
Lake	Minnesota	February 20, 1855
Mower	Minnesota	February 20, 1855
Olmsted	Minnesota	February 20, 1855
Renville	Minnesota	February 20, 1855
Stearns	Minnesota	February 20, 1855
Steele	Minnesota	February 20, 1855
Todd	Minnesota	February 20, 1855
Wright	Minnesota	February 20, 1855
Vernon	Missouri	February 27, 1855
Johnson	Nebraska	March 2, 1855
Maries	Missouri	March 2, 1855
Snyder	Pennsylvania	March 2, 1855
Webster	Missouri	March 3, 1855
Lancaster	Nebraska	March 6, 1855
Pawnee	Nebraska	March 6, 1855
Saline	Nebraska	March 6, 1855
Seward	Nebraska	March 6, 1855
Stanton	Nebraska	March 6, 1855
Dakota	Nebraska	March 7, 1855
Thurston	Nebraska	March 7, 1855
York	Nebraska	March 13, 1855
Buffalo	Nebraska	March 14, 1855
Cuming	Nebraska	March 16, 1855
Gage	Nebraska	March 16, 1855
Merced	California	April 19, 1855
Allen	Kansas	August 25, 1855
Anderson	Kansas	August 25, 1855
Atchison	Kansas	August 25, 1855
Bourbon	Kansas	August 25, 1855
Brown	Kansas	August 25, 1855
Butler	Kansas	August 25, 1855
Cherokee	Kansas	August 25, 1855
Coffey	Kansas	August 25, 1855
Doniphan	Kansas	August 25, 1855
Douglas	Kansas	August 25, 1855
Franklin	Kansas	August 25, 1855
Geary	Kansas	August 25, 1855
Greenwood	Kansas	August 25, 1855
Jackson	Kansas	August 25, 1855

Jefferson	Kansas	August 25, 1855
Johnson	Kansas	August 25, 1855
Leavenworth	Kansas	August 25, 1855
Linn	Kansas	August 25, 1855
Lyon	Kansas	August 25, 1855
Marshall	Kansas	August 25, 1855
Miami	Kansas	August 25, 1855
Morris	Kansas	August 25, 1855
Nemaha	Kansas	August 25, 1855
Neosho	Kansas	August 25, 1855
Osage	Kansas	August 25, 1855
Riley	Kansas	August 25, 1855
Shawnee	Kansas	August 25, 1855
Wabaunsee	Kansas	August 25, 1855
Wilson	Kansas	August 25, 1855
Woodson	Kansas	August 25, 1855
Marion	Kansas	August 30, 1855
Cumberland	Tennessee	November 16, 1855
Barton	Missouri	December 12, 1855
Parker	Texas	December 12, 1855
Liberty	Florida	December 15, 1855
Curry	Oregon	December 18, 1855
Beaver	Utah	January 5, 1856
Box Elder	Utah	January 5, 1856
Cache	Utah	January 5, 1856
Josephine	Oregon	January 22, 1856
Wise	Texas	January 23, 1856
Atascosa	Texas	January 25, 1856
Bandera	Texas	January 25, 1856
Comanche	Texas	January 25, 1856
Erath	Texas	January 25, 1856
Haralson	Georgia	January 26, 1856
Butler	Nebraska	January 26, 1856
Dixon	Nebraska	January 26, 1856
Fillmore	Nebraska	January 26, 1856
Jefferson	Nebraska	January 26, 1856
Kerr	Texas	January 26, 1856
Madison	Nebraska	January 26, 1856
Pierce	Nebraska	January 26, 1856
Platte	Nebraska	January 26, 1856
Polk	Nebraska	January 26, 1856
Saunders	Nebraska	January 26, 1856
Thayer	Nebraska	January 26, 1856
Lampasas	Texas	February 1, 1856
Llano	Texas	February 1, 1856
San Saba	Texas	February 1, 1856
Live Oak	Texas	February 2, 1856
Maverick	Texas	February 2, 1856
Young	Texas	February 2, 1856
Terrell	Georgia	February 16, 1856
Wise	Virginia	February 16, 1856
Meeker	Minnesota	February 23, 1856
Berrien	Georgia	February 25, 1856
Colquitt	Georgia	February 25, 1856
Morrison	Minnesota	February 25, 1856

Sherburne	Minnesota	February 25, 1856
Miller	Georgia	February 26, 1856
Cheatham	Tennessee	February 28, 1856
McLeod	Minnesota	March 1, 1856
Pine	Minnesota	March 1, 1856
Saint Louis	Minnesota	March 1, 1856
Calhoun	West Virginia	March 5, 1856
Towns	Georgia	March 6, 1856
Tucker	West Virginia	March 7, 1856
Roane	West Virginia	March 11, 1856
Rowan	Kentucky	March 15, 1856
Wood	Wisconsin	March 29, 1856
Burnett	Wisconsin	March 31, 1856
Tehama	California	April 9, 1856
Fresno	California	April 19, 1856
San Mateo	California	April 19, 1856
Brown	Texas	August 27, 1856
Jack	Texas	August 27, 1856
McCulloch	Texas	August 27, 1856
Palo Pinto	Texas	August 27, 1856
Eau Claire	Wisconsin	October 6, 1856
Juneau	Wisconsin	October 13, 1856
Hamilton	Iowa	December 22, 1856
Lafayette	Florida	December 23, 1856
Taylor	Florida	December 23, 1856
Kitsap	Washington	January 16, 1857
Sarpy	Nebraska	February 7, 1857
Knox	Nebraska	February 10, 1857
Cedar	Nebraska	February 12, 1857
Isanti	Minnesota	February 13, 1857
Iron	Missouri	February 17, 1857
Clay	Kansas	February 20, 1857
Dickinson	Kansas	February 20, 1857
Pottawatomie	Kansas	February 20, 1857
Washington	Kansas	February 20, 1857
Humboldt	Iowa	February 26, 1857
Waseca	Minnesota	February 27, 1857
Del Norte	California	March 2, 1857
Howell	Missouri	March 2, 1857
Union	New Jersey	March 19, 1857
Bay	Michigan	April 20, 1875
Aitkin	Minnesota	May 23, 1857
Anoka	Minnesota	May 23, 1857
Carlton	Minnesota	May 23, 1857
Cottonwood	Minnesota	May 23, 1857
Crow Wing	Minnesota	May 23, 1857
Jackson	Minnesota	May 23, 1857
Martin	Minnesota	May 23, 1857
Mille Lacs	Minnesota	May 23, 1857
Murray	Minnesota	May 23, 1857
Nobles	Minnesota	May 23, 1857
Pipestone	Minnesota	May 23, 1857
Rock	Minnesota	May 23, 1857
Douglas	Missouri	October 29, 1857
Phelps	Missouri	November 13, 1857

Dawson	Georgia	December 3, 1857
Bee	Texas	December 8, 1857
Sequatchie	Tennessee	December 9, 1857
Pierce	Georgia	December 18, 1857
Glascock	Georgia	December 19, 1857
Mitchell	Georgia	December 21, 1857
Schley	Georgia	December 22, 1857
White	Georgia	December 22, 1857
Wilcox	Georgia	December 22, 1857
Clay	Texas	December 24, 1857
Montague	Texas	December 24, 1857
Throckmorton	Texas	January 13, 1858
Archer	Texas	January 22, 1858
Hamilton	Texas	January 22, 1858
Hardin	Texas	January 22, 1858
Kimble	Texas	January 22, 1858
Mason	Texas	January 22, 1858
Menard	Texas	January 22, 1858
Stephens	Texas	January 22, 1858
Zapata	Texas	January 22, 1858
Spokane	Washington	January 29, 1858
Baylor	Texas	February 1, 1858
Callahan	Texas	February 1, 1858
Coleman	Texas	February 1, 1858
Concho	Texas	February 1, 1858
Dimmitt	Texas	February 1, 1858
Duval	Texas	February 1, 1858
Eastland	Texas	February 1, 1858
Edwards	Texas	February 1, 1858
Frio	Texas	February 1, 1858
Hardeman	Texas	February 1, 1858
Haskell	Texas	February 1, 1858
Jones	Texas	February 1, 1858
Knox	Texas	February 1, 1858
La Salle	Texas	February 1, 1858
McMullen	Texas	February 1, 1858
Runnels	Texas	February 1, 1858
Shackelford	Texas	February 1, 1858
Taylor	Texas	February 1, 1858
Wichita	Texas	February 1, 1858
Wilbarger	Texas	February 1, 1858
Zavala	Texas	February 1, 1858
Jackson	Kentucky	February 2, 1858
Blanco	Texas	February 12, 1858
Chambers	Texas	February 12, 1858
Buchanan	Virginia	February 13, 1858
McDowell	West Virginia	February 20, 1858
Pepin	Wisconsin	February 25, 1858
Portsmouth (IC)	Virginia	March 1, 1858
Green Lake	Wisconsin	March 5, 1858
Douglas	Minnesota	March 8, 1858
Becker	Minnesota	March 18, 1858
Clay	Minnesota	March 18, 1858
Otter Tail	Minnesota	March 18, 1858
Wilkin	Minnesota	March 18, 1858

Kandiyohi	Minnesota	March 20, 1858
Clay	West Virginia	March 29, 1858
Galveston	Texas	May 15, 1858
Wadena	Minnesota	June 11, 1858
Polk	Minnesota	July 20, 1858
Kanabec	Minnesota	October 12, 1858
Hall	Nebraska	November 4, 1858
Merrick	Nebraska	November 4, 1858
Clayton	Georgia	November 30, 1858
Quitman	Georgia	December 10, 1858
Banks	Georgia	December 11, 1858
Brooks	Georgia	December 11, 1858
Johnson	Georgia	December 11, 1858
Echols	Georgia	December 13, 1858
Bradford	Florida	December 21, 1858
Suwannee	Florida	December 21, 1858
Clay	Florida	December 31, 1858
Wyandotte	Kansas	January 29, 1859
Muskegon	Michigan	February 4, 1859
Douglas	Illinois	February 8, 1859
Chase	Kansas	February 11, 1859
Ford	Illinois	February 17, 1859
Craighead	Arkansas	February 19, 1859
Christian	Missouri	March 8, 1859
Carter	Missouri	March 10, 1859
Barron	Wisconsin	March 19, 1859
Klickitat	Washington	December 20, 1859
Alleghany	North Carolina	1859
Lincoln	Nebraska	January 7, 1860
Kearney	Nebraska	January 10, 1860
Webster	West Virginia	January 10, 1860
Holt	Nebraska	January 13, 1860
Nuckolls	Nebraska	January 13, 1860
Mora	New Mexico	February 1, 1860
Greer	Oklahoma	February 8, 1860
Marion	Texas	February 8, 1860
Wilson	Texas	February 13, 1860
Saline	Kansas	February 15, 1860
Magoffin	Kentucky	February 22, 1860
Watonwan	Minnesota	February 25, 1860
Cloud	Kansas	February 27, 1860
Ottawa	Kansas	February 27, 1860
Republic	Kansas	February 27, 1860
Webster	Kentucky	February 29, 1860
Wolfe	Kentucky	March 5, 1860
Knox	Maine	March 9, 1860
Ashland	Wisconsin	March 27, 1860
Cameron	Pennsylvania	March 29, 1860
Boyd	Kentucky	April 25, 1860
Metcalfe	Kentucky	May 1, 1860
Dawson	Nebraska	June 11, 1860
Missoula	Montana	December 14, 1860
Snohomish	Washington	January 14, 1861
Worth	Missouri	February 6, 1861
Baker	Florida	February 8, 1861

Polk	Florida	February 8, 1861
Transylvania	North Carolina	February 15, 1861
Mitchell	North Carolina	February 16, 1861
Clay	North Carolina	February 20, 1861
Keweenaw	Michigan	March 11, 1861
Menominee	Michigan	March 15, 1861
Bland	Virginia	March 30, 1861
Mono	California	April 24, 1861
Lake	California	May 20, 1861
Arapahoe	Colorado	November 1, 1861
Boulder	Colorado	November 1, 1861
Clear Creek	Colorado	November 1, 1861
Conejos	Colorado	November 1, 1861
Costilla	Colorado	November 1, 1861
Douglas	Colorado	November 1, 1861
El Paso	Colorado	November 1, 1861
Fremont	Colorado	November 1, 1861
Gilpin	Colorado	November 1, 1861
Huerfano	Colorado	November 1, 1861
Jefferson	Colorado	November 1, 1861
Lake	Colorado	November 1, 1861
Larimer	Colorado	November 1, 1861
Park	Colorado	November 1, 1861
Pueblo	Colorado	November 1, 1861
Summit	Colorado	November 1, 1861
Weld	Colorado	November 1, 1861
Carson City (IC)	Nevada	November 25, 1861
Churchill	Nevada	November 25, 1861
Douglas	Nevada	November 25, 1861
Esmeralda	Nevada	November 25, 1861
Humboldt	Nevada	November 25, 1861
Lyon	Nevada	November 25, 1861
Storey	Nevada	November 25, 1861
Washoe	Nevada	November 25, 1861
Kendall	Texas	January 10, 1862
Morgan	Utah	January 17, 1862
Wasatch	Utah	January 17, 1862
Redwood	Minnesota	February 6, 1862
Big Stone	Minnesota	February 20, 1862
Chippewa	Minnesota	February 20, 1862
Pope	Minnesota	February 20, 1862
Stevens	Minnesota	February 20, 1862
Traverse	Minnesota	February 20, 1862
Bon Homme	South Dakota	April 5, 1862
Brookings	South Dakota	April 5, 1862
Deuel	South Dakota	April 5, 1862
Lincoln	South Dakota	April 5, 1862
Minnehaha	South Dakota	April 5, 1862
Clay	South Dakota	April 10, 1862
Union	South Dakota	April 10, 1862
Yankton	South Dakota	April 10, 1862
Charles Mix	South Dakota	May 8, 1862
Gregory	South Dakota	May 8, 1862
Hutchinson	South Dakota	May 8, 1862
Baker	Oregon	September 22, 1862

Umatilla	Oregon	September 27, 1862
Cross	Arkansas	November 15, 1862
Woodruff	Arkansas	November 26, 1862
Lander	Nevada	December 19, 1862
Stevens	Washington	January 20, 1863
Benzie	Michigan	February 27, 1863
Owyhee	Idaho	December 31, 1863
Buffalo	South Dakota	January 6, 1864
Kane	Utah	January 16, 1864
Rich	Utah	January 16, 1864
Oneida	Idaho	January 22, 1864
Boise	Idaho	February 4, 1864
Idaho	Idaho	February 4, 1864
Nez Perce	Idaho	February 4, 1864
Shoshone	Idaho	February 4, 1864
Nye	Nevada	February 16, 1864
Alpine	California	March 16, 1864
Lassen	California	April 1, 1864
Grant	Oregon	October 14, 1864
Union	Oregon	October 14, 1864
Mohave	Arizona	November 8, 1864
Pima	Arizona	November 8, 1864
Yavapai	Arizona	November 8, 1864
Yuma	Arizona	November 8, 1864
Ada	Idaho	December 22, 1864
Kootenai	Idaho	December 22, 1864
Piute	Utah	January 16, 1865
Sevier	Utah	January 16, 1865
Yakima	Washington	January 21, 1865
Beaverhead	Montana	February 2, 1865
Chouteau	Montana	February 2, 1865
Custer	Montana	February 2, 1865
Deer Lodge	Montana	February 2, 1865
Gallatin	Montana	February 2, 1865
Jefferson	Montana	February 2, 1865
Lewis and Clark	Montana	February 2, 1865
Madison	Montana	February 2, 1865
Mineral	West Virginia	February 1, 1866
Las Animas	Colorado	February 9, 1866
Grant	West Virginia	February 14, 1866
Elmore	Alabama	February 15, 1866
Lincoln	Nevada	February 25, 1866
Beltrami	Minnesota	February 28, 1866
Inyo	California	March 22, 1866
Kern	California	April 2, 1866
Lee	Mississippi	October 26, 1866
Hood	Texas	November 2, 1866
Crenshaw	Alabama	November 24, 1866
Bullock	Alabama	December 5, 1866
Lee	Alabama	December 5, 1866
Cleburne	Alabama	December 6, 1866
Clay	Alabama	December 7, 1866
Etowah	Alabama	December 7, 1866
Saguache	Colorado	December 29, 1866
Laramie	Wyoming	January 9, 1867

Pembina	North Dakota	January 9, 1867
Hale	Alabama	January 30, 1867
Lamar	Alabama	February 4, 1867
Colbert	Alabama	February 6, 1867
Robertson	Kentucky	February 11, 1867
Crawford	Kansas	February 13, 1867
Adams	Nebraska	February 16, 1867
Clay	Nebraska	February 16, 1867
Franklin	Nebraska	February 16, 1867
Hamilton	Nebraska	February 16, 1867
Webster	Nebraska	February 16, 1867
Lincoln	West Virginia	February 23, 1867
Barber	Kansas	February 26, 1867
Barton	Kansas	February 26, 1867
Clark	Kansas	February 26, 1867
Comanche	Kansas	February 26, 1867
Cowley	Kansas	February 26, 1867
Ellis	Kansas	February 26, 1867
Ellsworth	Kansas	February 26, 1867
Ford	Kansas	February 26, 1867
Graham	Kansas	February 26, 1867
Harper	Kansas	February 26, 1867
Hodgeman	Kansas	February 26, 1867
Jewell	Kansas	February 26, 1867
Kiowa	Kansas	February 26, 1867
Labette	Kansas	February 26, 1867
Lincoln	Kansas	February 26, 1867
McPherson	Kansas	February 26, 1867
Mitchell	Kansas	February 26, 1867
Montgomery	Kansas	February 26, 1867
Ness	Kansas	February 26, 1867
Norton	Kansas	February 26, 1867
Osborne	Kansas	February 26, 1867
Pawnee	Kansas	February 26, 1867
Phillips	Kansas	February 26, 1867
Pratt	Kansas	February 26, 1867
Reno	Kansas	February 26, 1867
Rice	Kansas	February 26, 1867
Rooks	Kansas	February 26, 1867
Rush	Kansas	February 26, 1867
Russell	Kansas	February 26, 1867
Sedgwick	Kansas	February 26, 1867
Smith	Kansas	February 26, 1867
Stafford	Kansas	February 26, 1867
Sumner	Kansas	February 26, 1867
Trego	Kansas	February 26, 1867
Bell	Kentucky	February 28, 1867
Little River	Arkansas	March 5, 1867
Cheyenne	Nebraska	June 22, 1867
Wicomico	Maryland	August 17, 1867
Meagher	Montana	November 16, 1867
Sweetwater	Wyoming	December 27, 1867
Oconee	South Carolina	January 29, 1868
Grant	New Mexico	January 30, 1868
Grant	Minnesota	March 6, 1868

Gove	Kansas	March 11, 1868
Wallace	Kansas	March 11, 1868
Sharp	Arkansas	July 18, 1868
Richland	Louisiana	September 29, 1868
Iberia	Louisiana	October 30, 1868
Escambia	Alabama	December 10, 1868
Albany	Wyoming	December 16, 1868
Carbon	Wyoming	December 16, 1868
Geneva	Alabama	December 26, 1868
Chilton	Alabama	December 30, 1868
Lemhi	Idaho	January 9, 1869
Dawson	Montana	January 15, 1869
Lincoln	New Mexico	January 16, 1869
Colfax	New Mexico	January 25, 1869
Grant	Arkansas	February 4, 1869
Colfax	Nebraska	February 15, 1869
White Pine	Nevada	March 2, 1869
Grant	Louisiana	March 4, 1869
Elko	Nevada	March 5, 1869
Tangipahoa	Louisiana	March 6, 1869
Menifee	Kentucky	March 10, 1869
Elliott	Kentucky	April 1, 1869
Boone	Arkansas	April 9, 1869
Lyon	Minnesota	November 2, 1869
Uinta	Wyoming	December 1, 1869
Lee	Kentucky	January 29, 1870
Dare	North Carolina	February 2, 1870
Bent	Colorado	February 11, 1870
Swift	Minnesota	February 18, 1870
Martin	Kentucky	March 10, 1870
Cameron	Louisiana	March 15, 1870
Lincoln	Mississippi	April 7, 1870
Alcorn	Mississippi	April 15, 1870
Prentiss	Mississippi	April 15, 1870
Grenada	Mississippi	May 9, 1870
Loudon	Tennessee	June 2, 1870
Hamblen	Tennessee	June 8, 1870
Rains	Texas	June 9, 1870
Clay	Tennessee	June 16, 1870
Union	Mississippi	July 7, 1870
Benton	Mississippi	July 21, 1870
Delta	Texas	July 29, 1870
San Jacinto	Texas	August 13, 1870
Trousdale	Tennessee	September 5, 1870
Douglas	Georgia	October 17, 1870
McDuffie	Georgia	October 18, 1870
Rockdale	Georgia	October 18, 1870
Dodge	Georgia	October 26, 1870
Alexandria (IC)	Virginia	1870
Hanson	South Dakota	January 13, 1871
Turner	South Dakota	January 13, 1871
Houston	Tennessee	January 21, 1871
Maricopa	Arizona	February 12, 1871
Orange	Vermont	February 22, 1871
Swain	North Carolina	February 24, 1871

Webster	Louisiana	February 27, 1871
Summers	West Virginia	February 27, 1871
Antelope	Nebraska	March 1, 1871
Boone	Nebraska	March 1, 1871
Greeley	Nebraska	March 1, 1871
Howard	Nebraska	March 1, 1871
Sherman	Nebraska	March 1, 1871
Valley	Nebraska	March 1, 1871
Wayne	Nebraska	March 4, 1871
Yellow Medicine	Minnesota	March 6, 1871
Red River	Louisiana	March 7, 1871
Aiken	South Carolina	March 10, 1871
Leflore	Mississippi	March 15, 1871
Nevada	Arkansas	March 20, 1871
Logan	Arkansas	March 22, 1871
Lincoln	Arkansas	March 28, 1871
Vernon	Louisiana	March 30, 1871
Pecos	Texas	May 3, 1871
Clay	Mississippi	May 12, 1871
Montgomery	Mississippi	May 13, 1871
Harlan	Nebraska	June 3, 1871
Aransas	Texas	September 18, 1871
Lac qui Parle	Minnesota	November 7, 1871
Whitman	Washington	November 29, 1871
Moore	Tennessee	December 14, 1871
Staunton (IC)	Virginia	1871
Frontier	Nebraska	January 17, 1872
Graham	North Carolina	January 30, 1872
Pamlico	North Carolina	February 8, 1872
Harvey	Kansas	March 7, 1872
Kingman	Kansas	March 7, 1872
Ventura	California	March 22, 1872
Garrett	Maryland	April 1, 1872
Barnes	North Dakota	January 4, 1873
Bottineau	North Dakota	January 4, 1873
Burleigh	North Dakota	January 4, 1873
Cass	North Dakota	January 4, 1873
Cavalier	North Dakota	January 4, 1873
Foster	North Dakota	January 4, 1873
Grand Forks	North Dakota	January 4, 1873
Kidder	North Dakota	January 4, 1873
LaMoure	North Dakota	January 4, 1873
Logan	North Dakota	January 4, 1873
McHenry	North Dakota	January 4, 1873
Mountrail	North Dakota	January 4, 1873
Ramsey	North Dakota	January 4, 1873
Ransom	North Dakota	January 4, 1873
Renville	North Dakota	January 4, 1873
Richland	North Dakota	January 4, 1873
Rolette	North Dakota	January 4, 1873
Sheridan	North Dakota	January 4, 1873
Stutsman	North Dakota	January 4, 1873
Wells	North Dakota	January 4, 1873
Campbell	South Dakota	January 8, 1873
Clark	South Dakota	January 8, 1873

Davison	South Dakota	January 8, 1873
Dewey	South Dakota	January 8, 1873
Douglas	South Dakota	January 8, 1873
Edmunds	South Dakota	January 8, 1873
Faulk	South Dakota	January 8, 1873
Grant	South Dakota	January 8, 1873
Hamlin	South Dakota	January 8, 1873
Hand	South Dakota	January 8, 1873
Hughes	South Dakota	January 8, 1873
Hyde	South Dakota	January 8, 1873
Kingsbury	South Dakota	January 8, 1873
Lake	South Dakota	January 8, 1873
Lyman	South Dakota	January 8, 1873
McCook	South Dakota	January 8, 1873
McPherson	South Dakota	January 8, 1873
Miner	South Dakota	January 8, 1873
Moody	South Dakota	January 8, 1873
Morton	North Dakota	January 8, 1873
Potter	South Dakota	January 8, 1873
Spink	South Dakota	January 8, 1873
Stanley	South Dakota	January 8, 1873
Sully	South Dakota	January 8, 1873
Tripp	South Dakota	January 8, 1873
Walworth	South Dakota	January 8, 1873
Furnas	Nebraska	January 27, 1873
Phelps	Nebraska	February 11, 1873
Chase	Nebraska	February 27, 1873
Dundy	Nebraska	February 27, 1873
Hitchcock	Nebraska	February 27, 1873
Keith	Nebraska	February 27, 1873
Lincoln	Louisiana	February 27, 1873
Eureka	Nevada	March 1, 1873
Rockwall	Texas	March 1, 1873
Stanton	Kansas	March 20, 1873
Cheyenne	Kansas	March 20, 1873
Decatur	Kansas	March 20, 1873
Finney	Kansas	March 20, 1873
Grant	Kansas	March 20, 1873
Greeley	Kansas	March 20, 1873
Hamilton	Kansas	March 20, 1873
Kearny	Kansas	March 20, 1873
Lane	Kansas	March 20, 1873
Meade	Kansas	March 20, 1873
Rawlins	Kansas	March 20, 1873
Scott	Kansas	March 20, 1873
Seward	Kansas	March 20, 1873
Sheridan	Kansas	March 20, 1873
Sherman	Kansas	March 20, 1873
Stevens	Kansas	March 20, 1873
Thomas	Kansas	March 20, 1873
Wichita	Kansas	March 20, 1873
Baxter	Arkansas	March 24, 1873
Clay	Arkansas	March 24, 1873
Garland	Arkansas	April 5, 1873
Faulkner	Arkansas	April 12, 1873

Gregg	Texas	April 12, 1873
Lonoke	Arkansas	April 16, 1873
Cleveland	Arkansas	April 17, 1873
Howard	Arkansas	April 17, 1873
Lee	Arkansas	April 17, 1873
Stone	Arkansas	April 21, 1873
Waller	Texas	April 28, 1873
Red Willow	Nebraska	May 27, 1873
San Juan	Washington	October 31, 1873
Lincoln	Minnesota	November 4, 1873
Gosper	Nebraska	November 26, 1873
Tate	Mississippi	December 23, 1873
Elbert	Colorado	February 2, 1874
Grand	Colorado	February 2, 1874
Hinsdale	Colorado	February 10, 1874
La Plata	Colorado	February 10, 1874
Rio Grande	Colorado	February 10, 1874
San Benito	California	February 12, 1874
Modoc	California	February 17, 1874
Lincoln	Wisconsin	March 4, 1874
Tom Green	Texas	March 13, 1874
Edwards	Kansas	March 18, 1874
Camp	Texas	April 6, 1874
Webster	Mississippi	April 6, 1874
Lee	Texas	April 14, 1874
Lake	Tennessee	June 24, 1874
Lake	Oregon	October 24, 1874
Cook	Minnesota	November 3, 1874
Miller	Arkansas	December 22, 1874
Winchester (IC)	Virginia	1874
Bear Lake	Idaho	January 5, 1875
Custer	South Dakota	January 11, 1875
Lawrence	South Dakota	January 11, 1875
Pennington	South Dakota	January 11, 1875
Shannon	South Dakota	January 11, 1875
Traill	North Dakota	January 12, 1875
Mercer	North Dakota	January 14, 1875
Brule	South Dakota	January 14, 1875
Crockett	Texas	January 22, 1875
Pinal	Arizona	February 1, 1875
Pender	North Carolina	February 16, 1875
Baraga	Michigan	February 19, 1875
Oconee	Georgia	February 25, 1875
Taylor	Wisconsin	March 4, 1875
Franklin	Texas	March 6, 1875
Morris	Texas	March 6, 1875
Somervell	Texas	March 13, 1875
Unicoi	Tennessee	March 23, 1875
Chautauqua	Kansas	March 25, 1875
Elk	Kansas	March 3, 1875
Columbia	Washington	November 11, 1875
Crook	Wyoming	December 8, 1875
Johnson	Wyoming	December 8, 1875
San Juan	Colorado	January 31, 1876
Sharkey	Mississippi	March 29, 1876

Andrews	Texas	August 21, 1876
Armstrong	Texas	August 21, 1876
Bailey	Texas	August 21, 1876
Borden	Texas	August 21, 1876
Briscoe	Texas	August 21, 1876
Carson	Texas	August 21, 1876
Castro	Texas	August 21, 1876
Childress	Texas	August 21, 1876
Cochran	Texas	August 21, 1876
Collingsworth	Texas	August 21, 1876
Cottle	Texas	August 21, 1876
Crosby	Texas	August 21, 1876
Dallam	Texas	August 21, 1876
Dawson	Texas	August 21, 1876
Deaf Smith	Texas	August 21, 1876
Dickens	Texas	August 21, 1876
Donley	Texas	August 21, 1876
Fisher	Texas	August 21, 1876
Floyd	Texas	August 21, 1876
Gaines	Texas	August 21, 1876
Garza	Texas	August 21, 1876
Gray	Texas	August 21, 1876
Hale	Texas	August 21, 1876
Hall	Texas	August 21, 1876
Hansford	Texas	August 21, 1876
Hartley	Texas	August 21, 1876
Hemphill	Texas	August 21, 1876
Hockley	Texas	August 21, 1876
Howard	Texas	August 21, 1876
Hutchinson	Texas	August 21, 1876
Kent	Texas	August 21, 1876
King	Texas	August 21, 1876
Lamb	Texas	August 21, 1876
Lipscomb	Texas	August 21, 1876
Lubbock	Texas	August 21, 1876
Lynn	Texas	August 21, 1876
Martin	Texas	August 21, 1876
Mitchell	Texas	August 21, 1876
Moore	Texas	August 21, 1876
Motley	Texas	August 21, 1876
Nolan	Texas	August 21, 1876
Ochiltree	Texas	August 21, 1876
Oldham	Texas	August 21, 1876
Parmer	Texas	August 21, 1876
Potter	Texas	August 21, 1876
Randall	Texas	August 21, 1876
Roberts	Texas	August 21, 1876
Scurry	Texas	August 21, 1876
Sherman	Texas	August 21, 1876
Stonewall	Texas	August 21, 1876
Swisher	Texas	August 21, 1876
Terry	Texas	August 21, 1876
Wheeler	Texas	August 21, 1876
Yoakum	Texas	August 21, 1876
Ouray	Colorado	January 18, 1877

Cullman	Alabama	January 24, 1877
Routt	Colorado	January 29, 1877
Quitman	Mississippi	February 1, 1877
Washington	Colorado	February 9, 1877
Codington	South Dakota	February 15, 1877
Custer	Nebraska	February 17, 1877
Wheeler	Nebraska	February 17, 1877
Hayes	Nebraska	February 19, 1877
Sioux	Nebraska	February 19, 1877
Saint Louis (IC)	Missouri	March 5, 1877
Custer	Colorado	March 9, 1877
Gunnison	Colorado	March 9, 1877
East Carroll	Louisiana	March 28, 1877
West Carroll	Louisiana	March 28, 1877
Hampton	South Carolina	February 18, 1878
Leslie	Kentucky	March 29, 1878
Lackawanna	Pennsylvania	August 21, 1878
Billings	North Dakota	February 10, 1879
Chaffee	Colorado	February 10, 1879
Emmons	North Dakota	February 10, 1879
Stark	North Dakota	February 10, 1879
Nance	Nebraska	February 13, 1879
Cassia	Idaho	February 20, 1879
Washington	Idaho	February 20, 1879
Aurora	South Dakota	February 22, 1879
Beadle	South Dakota	February 22, 1879
Brown	South Dakota	February 22, 1879
Apache	Arizona	February 24, 1879
Marshall	Minnesota	February 25, 1879
Langlade	Wisconsin	February 27, 1879
Marinette	Wisconsin	February 27, 1879
Pickett	Tennessee	February 27, 1879
Price	Wisconsin	March 3, 1879
Chester	Tennessee	March 4, 1879
Day	South Dakota	October 1, 1879
Fredericksburg (IC)	Virginia	1879
Emery	Utah	February 12, 1880
San Juan	Utah	February 17, 1880
Uintah	Utah	February 18, 1880
Dickenson	Virginia	March 3, 1880
Custer	Idaho	January 8, 1881
Cochise	Arizona	February 1, 1881
Norman	Minnesota	February 7, 1881
Gila	Arizona	February 8, 1881
Silver Bow	Montana	February 16, 1881
Griggs	North Dakota	February 18, 1881
Walsh	North Dakota	February 18, 1881
Dolores	Colorado	February 19, 1881
Pitkin	Colorado	February 23, 1881
Durham	North Carolina	February 28, 1881
Dickey	North Dakota	March 5, 1881
Harding	South Dakota	March 5, 1881
Vance	North Carolina	March 5, 1881
Graham	Arizona	March 10, 1881
Gray	Kansas	March 13, 1881

Logan	Kansas	March 13, 1881
Garfield	Washington	November 29, 1881
Berkeley	South Carolina	January 31, 1882
Garfield	Utah	March 9, 1882
Florence	Wisconsin	March 18, 1882
Klamath	Oregon	October 17, 1882
Crook	Oregon	October 24, 1882
Garfield	Colorado	February 10, 1883
Delta	Colorado	February 11, 1883
Eagle	Colorado	February 11, 1883
Montrose	Colorado	February 11, 1883
Mesa	Colorado	February 14, 1883
Brown	Nebraska	February 19, 1883
Cleburne	Arkansas	February 20, 1883
Cherry	Nebraska	February 23, 1883
Loup	Nebraska	February 23, 1883
Hubbard	Minnesota	February 26, 1883
Yellowstone	Montana	February 26, 1883
Nelson	North Dakota	March 2, 1883
Butte	South Dakota	March 2, 1883
Sargent	North Dakota	March 3, 1883
Bowman	North Dakota	March 8, 1883
Jackson	South Dakota	March 8, 1883
McLean	North Dakota	March 8, 1883
Roberts	South Dakota	March 8, 1883
Steele	North Dakota	March 8, 1883
Towner	North Dakota	March 8, 1883
Benson	North Dakota	March 9, 1883
Dunn	North Dakota	March 9, 1883
Hettinger	North Dakota	March 9, 1883
Jerauld	South Dakota	March 9, 1883
McIntosh	North Dakota	March 9, 1883
McKenzie	North Dakota	March 9, 1883
Sanborn	South Dakota	March 9, 1883
Sawyer	Wisconsin	March 10, 1883
Washburn	Wisconsin	March 27, 1883
Fall River	South Dakota	April 3, 1883
Reeves	Texas	April 14, 1883
Asotin	Washington	October 27, 1883
San Miguel	Colorado	November 1, 1883
Kittitas	Washington	November 24, 1883
Lincoln	Washington	November 24, 1883
Adams	Washington	November 28, 1883
Douglas	Washington	November 28, 1883
Franklin	Washington	November 28, 1883
Skagit	Washington	November 28, 1883
Fremont	Wyoming	March 5, 1884
Williamsburg (IC)	Virginia	March 17, 1884
Sierra	New Mexico	April 3, 1884
Knott	Kentucky	May 5, 1884
Keya Paha	Nebraska	November 4, 1884
Garfield	Nebraska	November 8, 1884
Roanoke (IC)	Virginia	1884
Bingham	Idaho	January 13, 1885
Morrow	Oregon	February 16, 1885

Dawes	Nebraska	February 19, 1885
Val Verde	Texas	February 20, 1885
Logan	Nebraska	February 24, 1885
Gilliam	Oregon	February 25, 1885
Sheridan	Nebraska	February 25, 1885
Midland	Texas	March 4, 1885
Blaine	Nebraska	March 5, 1885
Marshall	South Dakota	March 10, 1885
Fergus	Montana	March 12, 1885
Oliver	North Dakota	March 12, 1885
Alger	Michigan	March 17, 1885
Eddy	North Dakota	March 31, 1885
Iron	Michigan	April 3, 1885
Forest	Wisconsin	April 11, 1885
Oneida	Wisconsin	April 11, 1885
Archuleta	Colorado	April 14, 1885
Ward	North Dakota	April 14, 1885
Morton	Kansas	February 20, 1886
Carlisle	Kentucky	April 3, 1886
Acadia	Louisiana	October 2, 1886
Box Butte	Nebraska	November 2, 1886
Brewster	Texas	February 2, 1887
Gogebic	Michigan	February 7, 1887
Wallowa	Oregon	February 11, 1887
Malheur	Oregon	February 17, 1887
Park	Montana	February 23, 1887
San Juan	New Mexico	February 24, 1887
Logan	Colorado	February 25, 1887
Crane	Texas	February 26, 1887
Ector	Texas	February 26, 1887
Loving	Texas	February 26, 1887
Upton	Texas	February 26, 1887
Ward	Texas	February 26, 1887
Winkler	Texas	February 26, 1887
Luce	Michigan	March 1, 1887
Pierce	North Dakota	March 11, 1887
Jeff Davis	Texas	March 15, 1887
Mills	Texas	March 15, 1887
Haskell	Kansas	March 23, 1887
Arthur	Nebraska	March 31, 1887
Grant	Nebraska	March 31, 1887
McPherson	Nebraska	March 31, 1887
Thomas	Nebraska	March 31, 1887
Schleicher	Texas	April 1, 1887
Sutton	Texas	April 1, 1887
Glasscock	Texas	April 4, 1887
Osceola	Florida	May 12, 1887
Lee	Florida	May 13, 1887
DeSoto	Florida	May 19, 1887
Lake	Florida	May 27, 1887
Citrus	Florida	June 2, 1887
Pasco	Florida	June 2, 1887
Cascade	Montana	September 12, 1887
Perkins	Nebraska	November 8, 1887
Okanogan	Washington	February 2, 1888

Charlottesville (IC)	Virginia	March 2, 1888
Converse	Wyoming	March 9, 1888
Natrona	Wyoming	March 9, 1888
Sheridan	Wyoming	March 9, 1888
Latah	Idaho	May 14, 1888
Banner	Nebraska	November 6, 1888
Deuel	Nebraska	November 6, 1888
Kimball	Nebraska	November 6, 1888
Rock	Nebraska	November 6, 1888
Scotts Bluff	Nebraska	November 6, 1888
Florence	South Carolina	December 22, 1888
Elmore	Idaho	February 7, 1889
Meade	South Dakota	February 7, 1889
Morgan	Colorado	February 19, 1889
Chaves	New Mexico	February 25, 1889
Eddy	New Mexico	February 25, 1889
Harney	Oregon	February 25, 1889
Sherman	Oregon	February 25, 1889
Irion	Texas	March 7, 1889
Orange	California	March 11, 1889
Coke	Texas	March 13, 1889
Yuma	Colorado	March 15, 1889
Cheyenne	Colorado	March 25, 1889
Otero	Colorado	March 25, 1889
Rio Blanco	Colorado	March 25, 1889
Phillips	Colorado	March 27, 1889
Hooker	Nebraska	March 29, 1889
Sedgwick	Colorado	April 9, 1889
Kiowa	Colorado	April 11, 1889
Kit Carson	Colorado	April 11, 1889
Lincoln	Colorado	April 11, 1889
Prowers	Colorado	April 11, 1889
Baca	Colorado	April 16, 1889
Montezuma	Colorado	April 16, 1889
Bristol (IC)	Virginia	February 12, 1890
Pearl River	Mississippi	February 22, 1890
Big Horn	Wyoming	March 12, 1890
Weston	Wyoming	March 12, 1890
Grand	Utah	March 13, 1890
Beaver	Oklahoma	May 2, 1890
Canadian	Oklahoma	May 2, 1890
Cleveland	Oklahoma	May 2, 1890
Kingfisher	Oklahoma	May 2, 1890
Logan	Oklahoma	May 2, 1890
Oklahoma	Oklahoma	May 2, 1890
Payne	Oklahoma	May 2, 1890
Danville (IC)	Virginia	1890
Coconino	Arizona	February 19, 1891
Guadalupe	New Mexico	February 26, 1891
Foard	Texas	March 3, 1891
Sterling	Texas	March 4, 1891
Canyon	Idaho	March 7, 1891
Glenn	California	March 11, 1891
Boyd	Nebraska	March 20, 1891
Dickinson	Michigan	May 21, 1891

Lincoln	Oklahoma	September 18, 1891
Pottawatomie	Oklahoma	September 18, 1891
Radford (IC)	Virginia	January 22, 1892
Buena Vista (IC)	Virginia	February 15, 1892
Wayne	Utah	March 10, 1892
Blaine	Oklahoma	April 19, 1892
Custer	Oklahoma	April 19, 1892
Dewey	Oklahoma	April 19, 1892
Roger Mills	Oklahoma	April 19, 1892
Washita	Oklahoma	April 19, 1892
Williams	North Dakota	November 30, 1892
Flathead	Montana	February 6, 1893
Valley	Montana	February 6, 1893
Teton	Montana	February 7, 1893
Ravalli	Montana	February 16, 1893
Lincoln	Oregon	February 20, 1893
Union	New Mexico	February 23, 1893
Iron	Wisconsin	March 1, 1893
Granite	Montana	March 2, 1893
Fremont	Idaho	March 4, 1893
Bannock	Idaho	March 6, 1893
Madera	California	March 11, 1893
Riverside	California	March 11, 1893
Kings	California	March 22, 1893
Mineral	Colorado	March 27, 1893
Vilas	Wisconsin	April 12, 1893
Kay	Oklahoma	April 21, 1893
Garfield	Oklahoma	August 21, 1893
Grant	Oklahoma	August 21, 1893
Noble	Oklahoma	August 21, 1893
Pawnee	Oklahoma	August 21, 1893
Woods	Oklahoma	August 21, 1893
Woodward	Oklahoma	August 21, 1893
Roseau	Minnesota	February 28, 1894
Carbon	Utah	March 8, 1894
Mingo	West Virginia	January 30, 1895
Carbon	Montana	March 4, 1895
Blaine	Idaho	March 5, 1895
Sweet Grass	Montana	March 5, 1895
Lincoln	Idaho	March 18, 1895
Navajo	Arizona	March 21, 1895
Lynchburg (IC)	Virginia	1895
Saluda	South Carolina	February 25, 1896
Red Lake	Minnesota	December 24, 1896
Broadwater	Montana	February 9, 1897
Bamberg	South Carolina	February 25, 1897
Cherokee	South Carolina	February 25, 1897
Dorchester	South Carolina	February 25, 1897
Greenwood	South Carolina	March 2, 1897
Nassau	New York	April 27, 1898
Otero	New Mexico	January 30, 1899
Wheeler	Oregon	February 17, 1899
Ferry	Washington	February 18, 1899
Scotland	North Carolina	February 20, 1899
McKinley	New Mexico	February 23, 1899

Chelan	Washington	March 13, 1899
Santa Cruz	Arizona	March 15, 1899
Teller	Colorado	March 23, 1899
Powell	Montana	January 31, 1901
Rosebud	Montana	February 11, 1901
Luna	New Mexico	March 16, 1901
Denver	Colorado	March 18, 1901
Adams	Colorado	April 15, 1901
Rusk	Wisconsin	May 15, 1901
Caddo	Oklahoma	July 4, 1901
Comanche	Oklahoma	August 6, 1901
Kiowa	Oklahoma	1901
Lee	South Carolina	February 25, 1902
Clearwater	Minnesota	December 20, 1902
Houston	Alabama	February 9, 1903
Quay	New Mexico	February 28, 1903
Roosevelt	New Mexico	February 28, 1903
Reagan	Texas	March 7, 1903
Sandoval	New Mexico	March 10, 1903
Torrance	New Mexico	March 16, 1903
Lamar	Mississippi	March 13, 1904
Sanders	Montana	February 7, 1905
Benton	Washington	March 8, 1905
Terrell	Texas	April 8, 1905
Saint Lucie	Florida	July 1, 1905
Hawaii	Hawaii	July 1905
Honolulu	Hawaii	July 1905
Kauai	Hawaii	July 1905
Maui	Hawaii	July 1905
Kalawao	Hawaii	July 1905
Crisp	Georgia	August 17, 1905
Grady	Georgia	August 17, 1905
Jenkins	Georgia	August 17, 1905
Tift	Georgia	August 17, 1905
Jeff Davis	Georgia	August 18, 1905
Stephens	Georgia	August 18, 1905
Toombs	Georgia	August 18, 1905
Turner	Georgia	August 18, 1905
Forrest	Mississippi	April 19, 1906
Ben Hill	Georgia	July 31, 1906
Koochiching	Minnesota	December 19, 1906
Mahnomen	Minnesota	December 27, 1906
Bonner	Idaho	February 21, 1907
Twin Falls	Idaho	February 21, 1907
Lee	North Carolina	March 6, 1907
Adams	North Dakota	April 17, 1907
Adair	Oklahoma	July 16, 1907
Alfalfa	Oklahoma	July 16, 1907
Atoka	Oklahoma	July 16, 1907
Beckham	Oklahoma	July 16, 1907
Bryan	Oklahoma	July 16, 1907
Carter	Oklahoma	July 16, 1907
Cherokee	Oklahoma	July 16, 1907
Choctaw	Oklahoma	July 16, 1907
Cimarron	Oklahoma	July 16, 1907

Coal	Oklahoma	July 16, 1907
Craig	Oklahoma	July 16, 1907
Creek	Oklahoma	July 16, 1907
Delaware	Oklahoma	July 16, 1907
Ellis	Oklahoma	July 16, 1907
Garvin	Oklahoma	July 16, 1907
Grady	Oklahoma	July 16, 1907
Harper	Oklahoma	July 16, 1907
Haskell	Oklahoma	July 16, 1907
Hughes	Oklahoma	July 16, 1907
Jackson	Oklahoma	July 16, 1907
Jefferson	Oklahoma	July 16, 1907
Johnston	Oklahoma	July 16, 1907
Latimer	Oklahoma	July 16, 1907
Le Flore	Oklahoma	July 16, 1907
Love	Oklahoma	July 16, 1907
Major	Oklahoma	July 16, 1907
Marshall	Oklahoma	July 16, 1907
Mayes	Oklahoma	July 16, 1907
McClain	Oklahoma	July 16, 1907
McCurtain	Oklahoma	July 16, 1907
McIntosh	Oklahoma	July 16, 1907
Murray	Oklahoma	July 16, 1907
Muskogee	Oklahoma	July 16, 1907
Nowata	Oklahoma	July 16, 1907
Okfuskee	Oklahoma	July 16, 1907
Okmulgee	Oklahoma	July 16, 1907
Osage	Oklahoma	July 16, 1907
Ottawa	Oklahoma	July 16, 1907
Pittsburg	Oklahoma	July 16, 1907
Pontotoc	Oklahoma	July 16, 1907
Pushmataha	Oklahoma	July 16, 1907
Rogers	Oklahoma	July 16, 1907
Seminole	Oklahoma	July 16, 1907
Sequoyah	Oklahoma	July 16, 1907
Stephens	Oklahoma	July 16, 1907
Texas	Oklahoma	July 16, 1907
Tillman	Oklahoma	July 16, 1907
Tulsa	Oklahoma	July 16, 1907
Wagoner	Oklahoma	July 16, 1907
Washington	Oklahoma	July 16, 1907
Imperial	California	August 6, 1907
Calhoun	South Carolina	February 14, 1908
Hood River	Oregon	June 23, 1908
La Salle	Louisiana	July 3, 1908
Perkins	South Dakota	November 3, 1908
Morrill	Nebraska	November 12, 1908
Clark	Nevada	February 9, 1909
Park	Wyoming	February 15, 1909
Grant	Washington	February 24, 1909
Curry	New Mexico	February 25, 1909
Corson	South Dakota	March 2, 1909
Bennett	South Dakota	March 9, 1909
Lincoln	Montana	March 9, 1909
Mellette	South Dakota	March 9, 1909

Todd	South Dakota	March 9, 1909
Greenlee	Arizona	March 10, 1909
Palm Beach	Florida	April 30, 1909
Jackson	Colorado	May 5, 1909
Harmon	Oklahoma	June 2, 1909
Garden	Nebraska	November 2, 1909
Dillon	South Carolina	February 15, 1910
George	Mississippi	March 16, 1910
Walthall	Mississippi	March 16, 1910
Evangeline	Louisiana	June 15, 1910
Burke	North Dakota	July 12, 1910
Pennington	Minnesota	November 23, 1910
Divide	North Dakota	December 6, 1910
Ziebach	South Dakota	February 1, 1911
Bonneville	Idaho	February 7, 1911
Hoke	North Carolina	February 7, 1911
Goshen	Wyoming	February 9, 1911
Hot Springs	Wyoming	February 9, 1911
Platte	Wyoming	February 9, 1911
Washakie	Wyoming	February 9, 1911
Mineral	Nevada	February 10, 1911
Avery	North Carolina	February 11, 1911
Musselshell	Montana	February 11, 1911
Campbell	Wyoming	February 13, 1911
Niobrara	Wyoming	February 14, 1911
Lincoln	Wyoming	February 20, 1911
Clearwater	Idaho	February 27, 1911
Moffat	Colorado	February 27, 1911
Pend Oreille	Washington	March 1, 1911
Adams	Idaho	March 3, 1911
Lewis	Idaho	March 3, 1911
Culberson	Texas	March 10, 1911
Brooks	Texas	March 11, 1911
Willacy	Texas	March 11, 1911
Jim Wells	Texas	March 25, 1911
Pinellas	Florida	May 23, 1911
Crowley	Colorado	May 29, 1911
Jasper	South Carolina	January 30, 1912
Hill	Montana	February 28, 1912
Blaine	Montana	February 29, 1912
McCreary	Kentucky	March 12, 1912
Bronx	New York	April 19, 1912
Allen	Louisiana	June 12, 1912
Beauregard	Louisiana	June 12, 1912
Jefferson Davis	Louisiana	June 12, 1912
Bleckley	Georgia	July 30, 1912
Cotton	Oklahoma	August 27, 1912
Wheeler	Georgia	August 12, 1912
Golden Valley	North Dakota	November 11, 1912
Big Horn	Montana	January 13, 1913
Franklin	Idaho	January 20, 1913
Gooding	Idaho	January 28, 1913
Minidoka	Idaho	January 28, 1913
Power	Idaho	January 30, 1913
Jefferson	Idaho	February 18, 1913

Madison	Idaho	February 18, 1913
Kleberg	Texas	February 27, 1913
Duchesne	Utah	March 3, 1913
Alamosa	Colorado	March 8, 1913
Sheridan	Montana	March 24, 1913
Stillwater	Montana	March 24, 1913
Jim Hogg	Texas	March 31, 1913
Real	Texas	April 3, 1913
Bay	Florida	April 24, 1913
Seminole	Florida	April 25, 1913
Fallon	Montana	December 9, 1913
Toole	Montana	May 7, 1914
Richland	Montana	May 27, 1914
Barrow	Georgia	July 7, 1914
Bacon	Georgia	July 27, 1914
Mineral	Montana	August 7, 1914
Evans	Georgia	August 11, 1914
Wibaux	Montana	August 17, 1914
Sioux	North Dakota	September 3, 1914
Candler	Georgia	November 3, 1914
Haakon	South Dakota	November 3, 1914
Jefferson	Oregon	December 12, 1914
Slope	North Dakota	December 31, 1914
Benewah	Idaho	January 23, 1915
Boundary	Idaho	January 23, 1915
Teton	Idaho	January 26, 1915
Phillips	Montana	February 5, 1915
Prairie	Montana	February 5, 1915
Gem	Idaho	March 15, 1915
Broward	Florida	April 30, 1915
Okaloosa	Florida	June 3, 1915
Jones	South Dakota	January 15, 1916
McCormick	South Carolina	February 19, 1916
Jefferson Davis	Mississippi	March 31, 1916
Stone	Mississippi	April 3, 1916
Hopewell (IC)	Virginia	July 1, 1916
Grant	North Dakota	November 25, 1916
Deschutes	Oregon	December 13, 1916
Harrisonburg (IC)	Virginia	1916
Butte	Idaho	February 6, 1917
Camas	Idaho	February 6, 1917
Hudspeth	Texas	February 16, 1917
Carter	Montana	February 22, 1917
Wheatland	Montana	February 22, 1917
Valley	Idaho	February 26, 1917
De Baca	New Mexico	February 28, 1917
Payette	Idaho	February 28, 1917
Daggett	Utah	March 4, 1917
Lea	New Mexico	March 7, 1917
Flagler	Florida	April 28, 1917
Okeechobee	Florida	May 8, 1917
Atkinson	Georgia	August 15, 1917
Treutlen	Georgia	August 21, 1917
Humphreys	Mississippi	March 28, 1918
Cook	Georgia	July 30, 1918

Clark	Idaho	February 1, 1919
Allendale	South Carolina	February 6, 1919
Garfield	Montana	February 7, 1919
Treasure	Montana	February 7, 1919
Jerome	Idaho	February 8, 1919
Caribou	Idaho	February 11, 1919
Glacier	Montana	February 17, 1919
Pondera	Montana	February 17, 1919
Roosevelt	Montana	February 18, 1919
McCone	Montana	February 20, 1919
Hidalgo	New Mexico	February 25, 1919
Powder River	Montana	March 7, 1919
Pershing	Nevada	March 18, 1919
Liberty	Montana	February 11, 1920
Seminole	Georgia	July 8, 1920
Brantley	Georgia	August 14, 1920
Long	Georgia	August 14, 1920
Lamar	Georgia	August 17, 1920
Daniels	Montana	August 30, 1920
Golden Valley	Montana	October 4, 1920
Lanier	Georgia	November 2, 1920
Judith Basin	Montana	December 10, 1920
Sublette	Wyoming	February 15, 1921
Teton	Wyoming	February 15, 1921
Catron	New Mexico	February 25, 1921
Harding	New Mexico	March 4, 1921
Kenedy	Texas	April 2, 1921
Charlotte	Florida	April 23, 1921
Glades	Florida	April 23, 1921
Hardee	Florida	April 23, 1921
Highlands	Florida	April 23, 1921
Dixie	Florida	April 25, 1921
Sarasota	Florida	May 14, 1921
Union	Florida	May 20, 1921
Lake of the Woods	Minnesota	November 28, 1922
Collier	Florida	May 8, 1923
Hendry	Florida	May 11, 1923
Lake	Montana	May 11, 1923
Peach	Georgia	July 18, 1924
Petroleum	Montana	November 24, 1924
Indian River	Florida	May 30, 1925
Martin	Florida	May 30, 1925
Gulf	Florida	June 6, 1925
Gilchrist	Florida	December 4, 1925
Martinsville (IC)	Virginia	1928
Waynesboro (IC)	Virginia	December 31, 1947
Colonial Heights (IC)	Virginia	1948
Falls Church (IC)	Virginia	1948
Los Alamos	New Mexico	March 16, 1949
Covington (IC)	Virginia	1952
Galax (IC)	Virginia	November 30, 1953
Norton (IC)	Virginia	April 6, 1954
Bethel (CA)	Alaska	1957
Menominee	Wisconsin	May 1, 1961
Fairfax (IC)	Virginia	July 30, 1961

Franklin (IC)	Virginia	December 21, 1961
Nome (CA)	Alaska	1961
Valdez-Cordova (CA)	Alaska	1961
Wade Hampton (CA)	Alaska	1961
Yukon-Koyukuk (CA)	Alaska	1961
Bristol Bay (B)	Alaska	October 1962
Anchorage (B)	Alaska	September 13, 1963
Kenai Peninsula (B)	Alaska	September 13, 1963
Ketchikan Gateway (B)	Alaska	September 13, 1963
Kodiak Island (B)	Alaska	September 1963
Dillingham (CA)	Alaska	1963
Fairbanks North Star (B)	Alaska	January 1, 1964
Southeast Fairbanks (CA)	Alaska	January 1, 1964
Matanuska-Susitna (B)	Alaska	January 1964
Lexington (IC)	Virginia	January 1, 1966
Emporia (IC)	Virginia	July 31, 1967
Salem (IC)	Virginia	December 31, 1967
Bedford (IC)	Virginia	August 30, 1968
Haines (B)	Alaska	August 1968
Juneau (B)	Alaska	December 1971
Sitka (B)	Alaska	December 1971
North Slope (B)	Alaska	July 1, 1972
Manassas (IC)	Virginia	May 1, 1975
Manassas Park (IC)	Virginia	June 1, 1975
Poquoson (IC)	Virginia	1975
Cibola	New Mexico	June 19, 1981
La Paz	Arizona	November 2, 1982
Northwest Arctic (B)	Alaska	June 1986
Aleutians East (B)	Alaska	October 23, 1987
Aleutians West (CA)	Alaska	October 23, 1987
Lake and Peninsula (B)	Alaska	April 1989
Denali (B)	Alaska	December 1990
Yakutat (B)	Alaska	September 1992
Broomfield	Colorado	November 15, 2001
Skagway (B)	Alaska	June 20, 2007
Hoonah-Angoon (CA)	Alaska	June 20, 2007
Prince of Wales-Hyder (CA)	Alaska	May 19, 2008
Petersburg (CA)	Alaska	June 1, 2008
Wrangell (B)	Alaska	June 1, 2008

Appendix C: Rank by 2010 Population

This appendix lists the 100 counties with the greatest populations and the 100 with the smallest populations. Space considerations make it impractical to include all 3,143 counties in this list. Listing the top and bottom 100 counties provides an idea of the variations in county populations. Readers are certainly welcome to compile their own all-inclusive rankings.

Sixty-one of the top 100 counties in population are in states east of the Mississippi River. Fifteen of the 39 counties in states west of the Mississippi are in California.

TOP 100 COUNTIES RANKED BY POPULATION

Rank	County	County Seat	State	Population	State Rank
1.	Los Angeles	Los Angeles	California	9,818,605	1/58
2.	Cook	Chicago	Illinois	5,194,675	1/102
3.	Harris	Houston	Texas	4,092,459	1/254
4.	Maricopa	Phoenix	Arizona	3,817,117	1/15
5.	San Diego	San Diego	California	3,095,313	2/58
6.	Orange	Santa Ana	California	3,010,232	3/58
7.	Kings	Brooklyn	New York	2,504,700	1/62
8.	Miami-Dade	Miami	Florida	2,496,435	1/67
9.	Dallas	Dallas	Texas	2,368,139	2/254
10.	Queens	Jamaica	New York	2,230,722	2/62
11.	Riverside	Riverside	California	2,189,641	4/58
12.	San Bernardino	San Bernardino	California	2,035,210	5/58
13.	Clark	Las Vegas	Nevada	1,951,269	1/17
14.	King	Seattle	Washington	1,931,249	1/39
15.	Wayne	Detroit	Michigan	1,820,584	1/83
16.	Tarrant	Fort Worth	Texas	1,809,034	3/254
17.	Santa Clara	San Jose	California	1,781,642	6/58
18.	Broward	Fort Lauderdale	Florida	1,748,066	2/67
19.	Bexar	San Antonio	Texas	1,714,773	4/254
20.	New York	New York	New York	1,585,873	3/62
21.	Philadelphia	Philadelphia	Pennsylvania	1,526,006	1/67
22.	Alameda	Oakland	California	1,510,271	7/58
23.	Middlesex	Cambridge	Massachusetts	1,503,085	1/14
24.	Suffolk	Riverhead	New York	1,493,350	4/62
25.	Sacramento	Sacramento	California	1,418,788	8/58
26.	Bronx	Bronx	New York	1,385,108	5/62
27.	Nassau	Mineola	New York	1,339,532	6/62
28.	Palm Beach	West Palm Beach	Florida	1,320,134	3/67

29.	Cuyahoga	Cleveland	Ohio	1,280,122	1/88
30.	Hillsborough	Tampa	Florida	1,229,226	4/67
31.	Allegheny	Pittsburgh	Pennsylvania	1,223,348	2/67
32.	Oakland	Pontiac	Michigan	1,202,362	2/63
33.	Franklin	Columbus	Ohio	1,163,414	2/88
34.	Hennepin	Minneapolis	Minnesota	1,152,425	1/87
35.	Orange	Orlando	Florida	1,145,856	5/67
36.	Fairfax	Fairfax	Virginia	1,081,726	1/134
37.	Contra Costa	Martinez	California	1,049,025	9/58
38.	Salt Lake	Salt Lake City	Utah	1,029,655	1/29
39.	Travis	Austin	Texas	1,024,266	5/254
40.	Saint Louis	Clayton	Missouri	998,954	1/115
41.	Pima	Tucson	Arizona	980,263	2/15
42.	Montgomery	Rockville	Maryland	971,777	1/24
43.	Honolulu	Honolulu	Hawaii	953,207	1/5
44.	Westchester	White Plains	New York	949,113	7/62
45.	Milwaukee	Milwaukee	Wisconsin	947,735	1/72
46.	Fresno	Fresno	California	930,450	10/58
47.	Shelby	Memphis	Tennessee	927,644	1/95
48.	Fulton	Atlanta	Georgia	920,581	1/159
49.	Mecklenburg	Charlotte	North Carolina	919,628	1/100
50.	Erie	Buffalo	New York	919,040	8/62
51.	DuPage	Wheaton	Illinois	916,924	2/102
52.	Fairfield	Bridgeport	Connecticut	916,829	1/8
53.	Pinellas	Clearwater	Florida	916,542	6/67
54.	Bergen	Hackensack	New Jersey	905,116	1/21
55.	Marion	Indianapolis	Indiana	903,393	1/92
56.	Wake	Raleigh	North Carolina	900,993	2/100
57.	Hartford	Hartford	Connecticut	894,014	2/8
58.	Duval	Jacksonville	Florida	864,263	7/67
59.	Prince George's	Upper Marlboro	Maryland	863,420	2/24
60.	New Haven	New Haven	Connecticut	862,477	3/8
61.	Macomb	Mount Clemens	Michigan	840,978	3/83
62.	Kern	Bakersfield	California	839,631	11/58
63.	Ventura	Ventura	California	823,318	12/58
64.	Middlesex	New Brunswick	New Jersey	809,858	2/21
65.	Gwinnett	Lawrenceville	Georgia	805,321	2/159
66.	San Francisco	San Francisco	California	805,235	13/58
67.	Baltimore	Towson	Maryland	805,029	3/24
68.	Hamilton	Cincinnati	Ohio	802,374	3/88
69.	El Paso	El Paso	Texas	800,647	6/254
70.	Montgomery	Norristown	Pennsylvania	799,874	3/67
71.	Worcester	Worcester	Massachusetts	798,552	2/14
72.	Pierce	Tacoma	Washington	795,225	2/39
73.	Essex	Newark	New Jersey	783,969	3/21
74.	Collin	McKinney	Texas	782,341	7/254
75.	Hidalgo	Edinburg	Texas	774,769	8/254
76.	Monroe	Rochester	New York	744,344	9/62
77.	Essex	Salem	Massachusetts	743,159	3/14
78.	Jefferson	Louisville	Kentucky	741,096	1/120
79.	Multnomah	Portland	Oregon	735,334	1/36
80.	Suffolk	Boston	Massachusetts	722,023	4/14
81.	Oklahoma	Oklahoma City	Oklahoma	718,633	1/77
82.	San Mateo	Redwood City	California	718,451	14/58
83.	Snohomish	Everett	Washington	713,335	3/39

84.	Lake	Waukegan	Illinois	703,462	3/102
85.	DeKalb	Decatur	Georgia	691,893	3/159
86.	Cobb	Marietta	Georgia	688,078	4/159
87.	San Joaquin	Stockton	California	685,306	15/58
88.	Will	Joliet	Illinois	677,560	4/102
89.	Jackson	Independence	Missouri	674,158	2/115
90.	Norfolk	Dedham	Massachusetts	670,850	5/14
91.	Denton	Denton	Texas	662,614	9/254
92.	Bernalillo	Albuquerque	New Mexico	662,564	1/33
93.	Jefferson	Birmingham	Alabama	658,466	1/67
94.	Hudson	Jersey City	New Jersey	634,266	4/21
95.	Monmouth	Freehold	New Jersey	630,380	5/21
96.	Davidson	Nashville	Tennessee	626,681	2/95
97.	Providence	Providence	Rhode Island	626,667	1/5
98.	Bucks	Doylestown	Pennsylvania	625,249	4/67
99.	El Paso	Colorado Springs	Colorado	622,263	1/64
100.	Baltimore	(Independent City)	Maryland	620,961	4/24

The counties listed below have the smallest populations. Ninety-eight of the smallest 100 counties in population are in states west of the Mississippi. One of the exceptions, Issaquena County, Mississippi, borders on the Mississippi River. The other exception is Taliaferro County, Georgia.

BOTTOM 100 COUNTIES RANKED BY POPULATION

Rank	County	County Seat	State	Population	State Rank
3044.	Divide	Crosby	North Dakota	2,071	45/53
3045.	Jerauld	Wessington Springs	South Dakota	2,071	58/66
3046.	Dolores	Dove Creek	Colorado	2,064	58/64
3047.	Garden	Oshkosh	Nebraska	2,057	75/93
3048.	Oldham	Vega	Texas	2,052	235/254
3049.	Garfield	Burwell	Nebraska	2,049	76/93
3050.	Mellette	White River	South Dakota	2,048	59/66
3051.	Gosper	Elwood	Nebraska	2,044	77/93
3052.	De Baca	Fort Sumner	New Mexico	2,022	32/33
3053.	Dundy	Benkelman	Nebraska	2,008	78/93
3054.	Edwards	Rocksprings	Texas	2,002	236/254
3055.	Logan	Napoleon	North Dakota	1,990	46/53
3056.	Eureka	Eureka	Nevada	1,987	16/17
3057.	Steele	Finley	North Dakota	1,975	47/53
3058.	Burke	Bowbells	North Dakota	1,968	48/53
3059.	Deuel	Chappell	Nebraska	1,941	79/93
3060.	Haakon	Phillip	South Dakota	1,937	60/66
3061.	Hodgeman	Jetmore	Kansas	1,916	101/105
3062.	Buffalo	Gannvalley	South Dakota	1,912	61/66
3063.	Armstrong	Claude	Texas	1,901	237/254
3064.	Comanche	Coldwater	Kansas	1,891	102/105
3065.	Meagher	White Sulphur Springs	Montana	1,891	46/56
3066.	Gilliam	Condon	Oregon	1,871	34/36
3067.	Oliver	Center	North Dakota	1,846	49/53
3068.	Cheyenne	Cheyenne Wells	Colorado	1,836	59/64
3069.	Denali	Healy	Alaska	1,826	25/29
3070.	Sherman	Moro	Oregon	1,765	35/36
3071.	Daniels	Scobey	Montana	1,751	47/56
3072.	Lane	Dighton	Kansas	1,750	103/105

3073.	Powder River	Broadus	Montana	1,743	48/56
3074.	McCone	Circle	Montana	1,734	49/56
3075.	Taliaferro	Crawfordville	Georgia	1,717	159/159
3076.	Golden Valley	Beach	North Dakota	1,680	50/53
3077.	Throckmorton	Throckmorton	Texas	1,641	238/254
3078.	Briscoe	Silverton	Texas	1,637	239/254
3079.	Lake and Peninsula	King Salmon	Alaska	1,631	26/29
3080.	Irion	Mertzon	Texas	1,599	240/254
3081.	Piute	Junction	Utah	1,556	28/29
3082.	Rock	Bassett	Nebraska	1,526	80/93
3083.	Cottle	Paducah	Texas	1,505	241/254
3084.	Stonewall	Aspermont	Texas	1,490	242/254
3085.	Wallace	Sharon Springs	Kansas	1,485	104/105
3086.	Campbell	Mound City	South Dakota	1,466	62/66
3087.	Wheeler	Fossil	Oregon	1,441	36/36
3088.	Hyde	Highmore	South Dakota	1,420	63/66
3089.	Issaquena	Mayersville	Mississippi	1,406	82/82
3090.	Kiowa	Eads	Colorado	1,398	60/64
3091.	Jackson	Walden	Colorado	1,394	61/64
3092.	Sully	Onida	South Dakota	1,373	64/66
3093.	Foard	Crowell	Texas	1,336	243/254
3094.	Sheridan	McClusky	North Dakota	1,321	51/53
3095.	Sioux	Harrison	Nebraska	1,311	81/93
3096.	Harding	Buffalo	South Dakota	1,255	65/66
3097.	Greeley	Tribune	Kansas	1,247	105/105
3098.	Glasscock	Garden City	Texas	1,226	244/254
3099.	Motley	Matador	Texas	1,210	245/254
3100.	Garfield	Jordan	Montana	1,206	50/56
3101.	Prairie	Terry	Montana	1,179	51/56
3102.	Alpine	Markleeville	California	1,175	58/58
3103.	Carter	Ekalaka	Montana	1,160	52/56
3104.	Sterling	Sterling City	Texas	1,143	246/254
3105.	Camas	Fairfield	Idaho	1,117	43/44
3106.	Daggett	Manila	Utah	1,059	29/29
3107.	Wibaux	Wibaux	Montana	1,017	53/56
3108.	Jones	Murdo	South Dakota	1,006	66/66
3109.	Bristol Bay	Naknek	Alaska	997	27/29
3110.	Terrell	Sanderson	Texas	984	247/254
3111.	Clark	Dubois	Idaho	982	44/44
3112.	Skagway	Skagway	Alaska	968	28/29
3113.	Hayes	Hayes Center	Nebraska	967	82/93
3114.	Roberts	Miami	Texas	929	248/254
3115.	Golden Valley	Ryegate	Montana	884	54/56
3116.	Hinsdale	Lake City	Colorado	843	62/64
3117.	Keya Paha	Springview	Nebraska	824	83/93
3118.	Wheeler	Bartlett	Nebraska	818	84/93
3119.	Kent	Jayton	Texas	808	249/254
3120.	Billings	Medora	North Dakota	783	52/53
3121.	Esmeralda	Goldfield	Nevada	783	17/17
3122.	Logan	Stapleton	Nebraska	763	85/93
3123.	Hooker	Mullen	Nebraska	736	86/93
3124.	Slope	Amidon	North Dakota	727	53/53
3125.	Treasure	Hysham	Montana	718	55/56
3126.	Mineral	Creede	Colorado	712	63/64
3127.	McMullen	Tilden	Texas	707	250/254

3128.	San Juan	Silverton	Colorado	699	64/64
3129.	Harding	Mosquero	New Mexico	695	33/33
3130.	Banner	Harrisburg	Nebraska	690	87/93
3131.	Yakutat	Yakutat	Alaska	662	29/29
3132.	Thomas	Thedford	Nebraska	647	88/93
3133.	Borden	Gail	Texas	641	251/254
3134.	Loup	Taylor	Nebraska	632	89/93
3135.	Grant	Hyannis	Nebraska	614	90/93
3136.	McPherson	Tryon	Nebraska	539	91/93
3137.	Petroleum	Winnett	Montana	494	56/56
3138.	Blaine	Brewster	Nebraska	478	92/93
3139.	Arthur	Arthur	Nebraska	460	93/93
3140.	Kenedy	Sarita	Texas	416	252/254
3141.	King	Guthrie	Texas	286	253/254
3142.	Kalawao	Kalaupapa	Hawaii	90	5/5
3143.	Loving	Mentone	Texas	82	254/254

Appendix D: County Rank by Area

This appendix lists the 100 counties with the largest areas and the 100 counties with the smallest areas. Space considerations make it impractical to include all 3,143 counties in this appendix. Listing the top and bottom 100 counties provides an idea of the variations in county areas. Readers are certainly welcome to compile their own all-inclusive rankings.

The ranking of counties and county equivalents by area is skewed by the enormous areas of Alaska's boroughs and census areas and the relatively miniscule areas of Virginia's independent cities. The Alaskan census area of Yukon-Koyukuk tops the list at 145,505 square miles. Yukon-Koyukuk is larger than every state except Alaska, Texas, California, and Montana. The smallest is the independent city of Falls Church, Virginia, at two square miles. Since this book includes all county equivalents, the areas of Alaska's subdivisions and Virginia's independent cities are included in this list.

The nine largest counties in area and thirteen of the largest eighteen are in Alaska. Ninety-eight of the top 100 counties in area are west of the Mississippi River. The two exceptions are Aroostook, Maine, and Saint Louis, Minnesota.

TOP 100 COUNTIES ARRANGED BY AREA SIZE

Rank	County	County Seat	State	Area	State Rank
1.	Yukon-Koyukuk	(Census Area)	Alaska	145,505	1/29
2.	North Slope	(Census Area	Alaska	88,695	2/29
3.	Bethel	(Census Area)	Alaska	40,570	3/29
4.	Northwest Arctic	Kotzebue	Alaska	35,573	4/29
5.	Valdez-Cordova	(Census Area)	Alaska	34,240	5/29
6.	Southeast Fairbanks	(Census Area)	Alaska	24,769	6/29
7.	Matanuska-Susitna	Palmer	Alaska	24,608	7/29
8.	Lake and Peninsula	King Salmon	Alaska	23,652	8/29
9.	Nome	(Census Area)	Alaska	22,962	9/29
10.	San Bernardino	San Bernardino	California	20,057	1/58
11.	Coconino	Flagstaff	Arizona	18,619	1/15
12.	Dillingham	(Census Area)	Alaska	18,569	10/29
13.	Nye	Tonopah	Nevada	18,182	1/17
14.	Elko	Elko	Nevada	17,170	2/17
15.	Wade Hampton	(Census Area)	Alaska	17,081	11/29
16.	Kenai Peninsula	Soldotna	Alaska	16,075	12/29
17.	Mohave	Kingman	Arizona	13,311	2/15
18.	Denali	Healy	Alaska	12,751	13/29
19.	Apache	Saint Johns	Arizona	11,198	3/15
20.	Lincoln	Pioche	Nevada	10,633	3/17
21.	Sweetwater	Green River	Wyoming	10,427	1/23
22.	Inyo	Independence	California	10,181	2/58
23.	Harney	Burns	Oregon	10,133	1/36

24.	Navajo	Holbrook	Arizona	9,950	4/15
25.	Malheur	Vale	Oregon	9,888	2/36
26.	Humboldt	Winnemucca	Nevada	9,641	4/17
27.	Maricopa	Phoenix	Arizona	9,200	5/15
28.	Pima	Tucson	Arizona	9,187	6/15
29.	Fremont	Lander	Wyoming	9,184	2/23
30.	White Pine	Ely	Nevada	8,876	5/17
31.	Idaho	Grangeville	Idaho	8,477	1/44
32.	Lake	Lakeview	Oregon	8,139	3/36
33.	Kern	Bakersfield	California	8,132	3/58
34.	Yavapai	Prescott	Arizona	8,124	7/15
35.	Carbon	Rawlins	Wyoming	7,898	3/23
36.	Clark	Las Vegas	Nevada	7,891	6/17
37.	San Juan	Monticello	Utah	7,820	1/29
38.	Owyhee	Murphy	Idaho	7,666	2/44
39.	Yakutat	Yakutat	Alaska	7,649	14/29
40.	Hoonah-Angoon	(Census Area)	Alaska	7,525	15/29
41.	Fairbanks North Star	Fairbanks	Alaska	7,338	16/29
42.	Riverside	Riverside	California	7,206	4/58
43.	Aleutians East	Sand Point	Alaska	6,982	17/29
44.	Park	Cody	Wyoming	6,942	4/23
45.	Tooele	Tooele	Utah	6,941	2/29
46.	Catron	Reserve	New Mexico	6,924	1/33
47.	Aroostook	Caribou	Maine	6,671	1/16
48.	Socorro	Socorro	New Mexico	6,647	2/33
49.	Otero	Alamogordo	New Mexico	6,613	3/33
50.	Millard	Fillmore	Utah	6,572	3/29
51.	Kodiak Island	Kodiak	Alaska	6,550	18/29
52.	Washoe	Reno	Nevada	6,302	7/17
53.	Siskiyou	Yreka	California	6,278	5/58
54.	Saint Louis	Duluth	Minnesota	6,247	1/87
55.	Brewster	Alpine	Texas	6,184	1/254
56.	Cochise	Bisbee	Arizona	6,166	8/15
57.	Chaves	Roswell	New Mexico	6,065	4/33
58.	Pershing	Lovelock	Nevada	6,037	8/17
59.	Cherry	Valentine	Nebraska	5,960	1/93
60.	Fresno	Fresno	California	5,958	6/58
61.	Klamath	Klamath Falls	Oregon	5,941	4/36
62.	Rio Arriba	Tierra Amarilla	New Mexico	5,861	5/33
63.	Box Elder	Brigham City	Utah	5,746	4/29
64.	Beaverhead	Dillon	Montana	5,542	1/56
65.	Yuma	Yuma	Arizona	5,514	9/15
66.	San Juan	Aztec	New Mexico	5,513	6/33
67.	Lander	Battle Mountain	Nevada	5,490	9/17
68.	McKinley	Gallup	New Mexico	5,450	7/33
69.	Pinal	Florence	Arizona	5,366	10/15
70.	Natrona	Casper	Wyoming	5,340	5/23
71.	Okanogan	Okanogan	Washington	5,268	1/39
72.	Garfield	Panguitch	Utah	5,175	5/29
73.	Phillips	Malta	Montana	5,140	2/56
74.	Flathead	Kalispell	Montana	5,088	3/56
75.	Douglas	Roseburg	Oregon	5,036	5/36
76.	Rosebud	Forsyth	Montana	5,010	4/56
77.	Big Horn	Basin	Montana	4,995	5/56
78.	Churchill	Fallon	Nevada	4,930	10/17

79.	Valley	Glasgow	Montana	4,926	6/56
80.	Custer	Challis	Idaho	4,921	3/44
81.	Sublette	Pinedale	Wyoming	4,887	6/23
82.	Ketchikan Gateway	Ketchikan	Alaska	4,858	19/29
83.	Lincoln	Carrizozo	New Mexico	4,831	8/33
84.	Tulare	Visalia	California	4,824	7/58
85.	Campbell	Gillette	Wyoming	4,803	7/23
86.	Las Animas	Trinidad	Colorado	4,773	1/64
87.	Pecos	Fort Stockton	Texas	4,764	2/254
88.	Gila	Globe	Arizona	4,758	11/15
89.	Moffat	Craig	Colorado	4,743	2/64
90.	San Miguel	Las Vegas	New Mexico	4,716	9/33
91.	Garfield	Jordan	Montana	4,675	7/56
92.	Graham	Safford	Arizona	4,623	12/15
93.	Hudspeth	Sierra Blanca	Texas	4,571	3/254
94.	Lemhi	Salmon	Idaho	4,563	4/44
95.	Lane	Eugene	Oregon	4,553	6/36
96.	Lassen	Susanville	California	4,541	8/58
97.	Cibola	Grants	New Mexico	4,539	10/33
98.	Grant	Canyon City	Oregon	4,529	7/36
99.	La Paz	Parker	Arizona	4,500	13/15
100.	Uintah	Vernal	Utah	4,480	6/29

The following list gives the smallest 100 counties in area. Of the 100 counties with the smallest areas, 91 are east of the Mississippi River. Forty of the smallest counties are independent cities and the District of Columbia. Thirty-six of the smallest independent cities are in Virginia.

BOTTOM 100 COUNTIES ARRANGED BY AREA SIZE

Rank	County	County Seat	State	Area	State Rank
3044.	Blackford	Hartford City	Indiana	165	89/92
3045.	Pickett	Byrdstown	Tennessee	163	92/95
3046.	Catoosa	Ringgold	Georgia	162	152/159
3047.	Hamblen	Morristown	Tennessee	161	93/95
3048.	Union	Liberty	Indiana	161	90/92
3049.	Barrow	Winder	Georgia	160	153/159
3050.	Boyd	Catlettsburg	Kentucky	160	114/120
3051.	Kenton	Covington	Kentucky	160	114/120
3052.	Putnam	Hennepin	Illinois	160	102/102
3053.	Greene	Stanardsville	Virginia	156	92/134
3054.	Denver	Denver	Colorado	153	62/64
3055.	Ramsey	Saint Paul	Minnesota	152	87/87
3056.	Trimble	Bedford	Kentucky	152	116/120
3057.	Wyandotte	Kansas City	Kansas	152	105/105
3058.	Campbell	Newport	Kentucky	151	117/120
3059.	Quitman	Georgetown	Georgia	151	154/159
3060.	Gilpin	Central City	Colorado	150	63/64
3061.	Peach	Fort Valley	Georgia	150	155/159
3062.	Floyd	New Albany	Indiana	148	91/92
3063.	Carson City	(Independent City)	Nevada	145	17/17
3064.	Glascock	Gibson	Georgia	144	156/159
3065.	Clayton	Jonesboro	Georgia	142	157/159
3066.	James City	Williamsburg	Virginia	142	93/134
3067.	Philadelphia	Philadelphia	Pennsylvania	134	66/67

3068.	Lancaster	Lancaster	Virginia	133	94/134
3069.	Middlesex	Saluda	Virginia	130	95/134
3070.	Montour	Danville	Pennsylvania	130	67/67
3071.	Pleasants	Saint Marys	West Virginia	130	52/55
3072.	Rockdale	Conyers	Georgia	130	158/159
3073.	Carroll	Carrollton	Kentucky	129	118/129
3074.	Moore	Lynchburg	Tennessee	129	94/95
3075.	Rockwall	Rockwall	Texas	127	254/254
3076.	Essex	Newark	New Jersey	126	19/21
3077.	Clarke	Athens	Georgia	119	159/159
3078.	Trousdale	Hartsville	Tennessee	114	95/95
3079.	Los Alamos	Los Alamos	New Mexico	109	33/33
3080.	Queens	Jamaica	New York	109	58/62
3081.	Ohio	Wheeling	West Virginia	106	53/55
3082.	York	Yorktown	Virginia	105	96/134
3083.	Dukes	Edgartown	Massachusetts	103	12/14
3084.	Union	Elizabeth	New Jersey	103	20/21
3085.	Newport	Newport	Rhode Island	102	4/5
3086.	Gallatin	Warsaw	Kentucky	101	119/120
3087.	Robertson	Mount Olivet	Kentucky	100	120/120
3088.	Brooke	Wellsburg	West Virginia	89	54/55
3089.	Mathews	Mathews	Virginia	86	97/134
3090.	Ohio	Rising Sun	Indiana	86	92/92
3091.	Hancock	New Cumberland	West Virginia	83	55/55
3092.	Grand Isle	North Hero	Vermont	82	14/14
3093.	Baltimore	(Independent City)	Maryland	81	24/24
3094.	Kings	Brooklyn	New York	71	59/62
3095.	Newport News	(Independent City)	Virginia	69	98/134
3096.	Saint Louis	(Independent City)	Missouri	62	115/115
3097.	District of Columbia	Washington	(Federal District)	61	1/1
3098.	Richmond	(Independent City)	Virginia	60	99/134
3099.	Richmond	Saint George	New York	58	60/62
3100.	Suffolk	Boston	Massachusetts	58	13/14
3101.	Norfolk	(Independent City)	Virginia	54	100/134
3102.	Hampton	(Independent City)	Virginia	51	101/134
3103.	Lynchburg	(Independent City)	Virginia	49	102/134
3104.	San Francisco	San Francisco	California	47	58/58
3105.	Hudson	Jersey City	New Jersey	46	21/21
3106.	Nantucket	Nantucket	Massachusetts	45	14/14
3107.	Danville	(Independent City)	Virginia	43	103/134
3108.	Roanoke	(Independent City)	Virginia	43	103/134
3109.	Bronx	Bronx	New York	42	61/62
3110.	Portsmouth	(Independent City)	Virginia	34	105/134
3111.	Broomfield	Broomfield	Colorado	33	64/64
3112.	Arlington	Arlington	Virginia	26	106/134
3113.	Bristol	Bristol	Rhode Island	24	5/5
3114.	New York	New York	New York	23	62/62
3115.	Petersburg	(Independent City)	Virginia	23	107/134
3116.	Staunton	(Independent City)	Virginia	20	108/134
3117.	Harrisonburg	(Independent City)	Virginia	17	109/134
3118.	Alexandria	(Independent City)	Virginia	15	110/134
3119.	Poquoson	(Independent City)	Virginia	15	110/134
3120.	Waynesboro	(Independent City)	Virginia	15	110/134
3121.	Salem	(Independent City)	Virginia	14	113/134
3122.	Bristol	(Independent City)	Virginia	13	114/134

3123	Kalawao	Kalaupapa	Hawaii	12	5/5
3124.	Martinsville	(Independent City)	Virginia	11	115/134
3125.	Charlottesville	(Independent City)	Virginia	10	116/134
3126.	Fredericksburg	(Independent City)	Virginia	10	116/134
3127.	Hopewell	(Independent City)	Virginia	10	116/134
3128.	Manassas	(Independent City)	Virginia	10	116/134
3129.	Radford	(Independent City)	Virginia	10	116/134
3130.	Williamsburg	(Independent City)	Virginia	9	121/134
3131.	Winchester	(Independent City)	Virginia	9	121/134
3132.	Colonial Heights	(Independent City)	Virginia	8	123/134
3133.	Franklin	(Independent City)	Virginia	8	123/134
3134.	Galax	(Independent City)	Virginia	8	123/134
3135.	Bedford	(Independent City)	Virginia	7	126/134
3136.	Buena Vista	(Independent City)	Virginia	7	126/134
3137.	Emporia	(Independent City)	Virginia	7	126/134
3138.	Norton	(Independent City)	Virginia	7	126/134
3139.	Fairfax	(Independent City)	Virginia	6	130/134
3140.	Covington	(Independent City)	Virginia	5	131/134
3141.	Lexington	(Independent City)	Virginia	3	132/134
3142.	Manassas Park	(Independent City)	Virginia	3	132/134
3143.	Falls Church	(Independent City)	Virginia	2	134/134

Appendix E: Eliminated Counties

Listed here are counties that were eliminated for various reasons. These counties were absorbed, merged, annexed, or gradually whittled away by the creation of surrounding counties. Often the action listed under "Cause of Elimination" is just the last act of the county's gradual demise. Eliminated counties did not cease to exist simply because of a name change—such counties are listed with their states in Appendix A. These counties were eliminated by legislative or court action.

The location of these counties can be roughly determined by noting the name of the county that caused their abandonment. Counties enclosed in brackets were themselves eliminated later. In some instances, the name of an eliminated county was given to a later county created in a different location. These counties are indicated by an asterisk (*).

COUNTY	YEARS	CAUSE OF ELIMINATION
ALABAMA		
Decatur	1821–25	Merged into Jackson

ALASKA

From 1869 to 1910 Alaska had two political subdivisions. The Northern District roughly corresponded to Judicial Divisions 2 and 4 given below. The Southern District corresponded to Judicial Districts 1 and 3.

In 1910 four judicial divisions were established. The First Judicial Division included Haines, Hoonah-Angoon, Juneau, Ketchikan Gateway, Petersburg, Prince of Wales-Hyder, Sitka, Skagway, Wrangell, and Yakutat. The Second Judicial Division included Nome, North Slope, Northwest Arctic, and Wade Hampton. The Third Judicial Division included Aleutians East, Aleutians West, Anchorage, Bristol Bay, Dillingham, Kenai Peninsula, Kodiak Island, Lake and Peninsula, and Valdez-Cordova. The Fourth Judicial Division included Bethel, Denali, Fairbanks North Star, Matanuska-Susitna, Southeast Fairbanks, and Yukon-Koyukuk. These judicial divisions had little local government and were administered by the State.

Beginning in 1963, Alaska's political subdivisions began to be created as boroughs whose governmental structure is similar to cities. Areas outside of boroughs are classified as census areas. These are unorganized areas administered by the State of Alaska. Since 1963 Alaska's political subdivisions have continuously evolved with boroughs growing at the expense of census areas. See Appendix A for a listing of Alaska's current boroughs and census areas.

ARIZONA		
Arizona	1860–62	Created and eliminated by New Mexico Territory
Pah-Ute	1865–71	Merged into Mohave
ARKANSAS		
Lovely	1827–28	Abolished by creation of Washington
Miller*	1820–36	Became part of Texas
CALIFORNIA		
Coso	1864–66	Abolished by creation of Inyo
Klamath	1851–75	Merged into Humboldt and Siskiyou
Pautah	1852–59	Created in Utah Territory; abolished by California

COLORADO
| Greenwood | 1870–74 | Abolished by creation of Elbert |
| Platte | 1872–74 | Merged into Weld |

FLORIDA
| Bloxham | 1915–16 | Absorbed by Levy and Marion |
| Fayette | 1832–34 | Merged into Jackson |

GEORGIA
| Campbell | 1828–1932 | Annexed by Fulton |
| Milton | 1857–1932 | Annexed by Fulton |

IDAHO
| Alturas | 1864–95 | Abolished by creation of Blaine |
| Logan | 1889–95 | Abolished by creation of Blaine and Lincoln |

ILLINOIS
| Highland | 1847–48 | Merged into Adams |
| Marquette | 1843–47 | Abolished by creation of [Highland] |

IOWA
Bancroft	1851–55	Merged into Kossuth
Cook	1836–38	Absorbed by Muscatine
Crocker	1870–71	Merged into Kossuth
Yell	1851–53	Merged into Webster

KANSAS
Arapahoe	1873–83	Abolished by creation of Finney
Buffalo	1873–81	Merged into Gray
Foote	1873–81	Merged into Gray
Garfield	1887–93	Merged into Finney
Howard	1867–75	Abolished by creation of Chautauqua and Elk
Hunter	1855–64	Merged into Butler
Irving	1860–64	Merged into Butler
Kansas	1873–83	Absorbed by Seward
Madison	1855–61	Merged into Greenwood and Lyon
Otoe	1860–64	Merged into Butler
Peketon	1860–64	Absorbed by non-county area in southwest Kansas
Sequoyah	1873–83	Abolished by creation of Finney
Seward*	1855–67	Abolished by creation of [Howard]
Washington*	1855–57	Absorbed by non-county area in southwest Kansas

KENTUCKY
| Kentucky | 1776–80 | Abolished by creation of Fayette, Jefferson, and Lincoln |

LOUISIANA
	1805–45	Counties of Acadia, Attakapas, Concordia, German Coast, Iberville, La-fourche, Natchitoches Opelousas, Orleans, Ouachita, Pointe Coupee, and Rapides abolished in favor of parishes
Carroll	1838–77	Divided into East and West Carroll
Warren	1811–14	Merged into Concordia and Ouachita

MARYLAND
| Charles* | 1650–54 | Abolished by creation of Calvert |
| Durham | 1669–72 | Abolished by creation of Worcester |

MICHIGAN

Isle Royal	1875–97	Annexed to Keweenaw
Manitou	1855–95	Annexed to Charlevoix and Leelanau
Omeena	1840–53	Annexed to Grand Traverse
Wyandot	1840–53	Annexed to Cheboygan

MINNESOTA

Big Sioux	1857–58	Lost to Dakota Territory
Buchanan	1857–61	Merged into Pine
Davis	1855–62	Abolished by creation of Chippewa and [Lac qui Parle]
Lac qui Parle*	1862–68	Absorbed by Chippewa and Stevens
Lincoln*	1861–68	Absorbed by Renville
Mahkahto	1849–51	Abolished by creation of Cass
Manomin	1857–69	Merged into Anoka
Monongalia	1861–70	Merged into Kandiyohi
Newton	1855–56	Abolished by creation of Saint Louis
Saint Louis*	1855–56	Abolished by creation of Lake
Wahnata	1849–51	Abolished by creation of Cass

MISSISSIPPI

Bainbridge	1823–24	Merged into Covington
Baldwin	1809–17	Became part of Alabama Territory
Clarke*	1812–17	Became part of Alabama Territory
Mobile	1812–17	Became part of Alabama Territory
Pearl	1872–78	Merged into Hancock and Marion
Washington*	1800–17	Became part of Alabama Territory

MISSOURI

Dodge	1846–53	Annexed to Putnam
Donaldson	1847–49	Merged into Cass, Jackson, Johnson, and Lafayette
Lawrence*	1815–25	Merged into Wayne
White	1835–37	Absorbed by non-county area in south central Missouri

NEBRASKA

Blackbird	1855–89	Abolished by creation of Thurston
Clay*	1855–64	Merged into Gage and Lancaster
Jackson	1855–56	Abolished by creation of Fillmore
Jones	1856–67	Merged into Jefferson
Loup*	1855–56	Abolished by creation of Madison, [Monroe], and Platte
McNeal	1855–56	Abolished by creation of Madison and Pierce
Monroe	1856–60	Merged into Platte

NEVADA

| Roop | 1861–83 | Merged into Washoe |

NEW MEXICO

| San Juan* | 1861–62 | Merged into Taos |
| Santa Ana | 1852–76 | Merged into Bernalillo and Santa Fe |

NEW YORK

| Cornwall | 1683–86 | Transferred to Massachusetts |

NORTH CAROLINA

| Albemarle | 1664–89 | Abolished by creation of Chowan, Currituck, Pasquotank, and Perquimans |
| Bath | 1696–1705 | Abolished by creation of Beaufort, Craven, and Hyde |

Bute	1764–79	Abolished by creation of Franklin and Warren
Clarendon	1664–67	Eliminated by abandonment of only settlement
Dobbs	1758–91	Abolished by creation of Greene and Lenoir
Tryon	1768–79	Abolished by creation of Lincoln and Rutherford

NORTH DAKOTA

Allred	1883–1905	Merged into McKenzie
Boreman	1873–89	Absorbed by non-county area in South Dakota
Buffalo	1871–73	Abolished by creation of Bottineau, Burleigh, [De Smet], Kidder, Logan, McHenry, Mountrail, Renville, Rolette, Sheridan, [Stevens], Stutsman, [Wallette], and Wells
Buford	1883–92	Abolished by creation of Williams
Church	1887–92	Absorbed by McHenry, McLean, and Pierce
De Smet	1873–87	Abolished by creation of Pierce
Flannery	1883–92	Abolished by creation of Williams
Garfield	1885–92	Absorbed by McLean and Ward
Howard	1873–83	Abolished by creation of [Allred], Dunn, McKenzie, and [Wallace]
Stevens	1873–92	Absorbed by McLean and Ward
Villard	1883–87	Absorbed by Billings, Stark, and non-county area
Wallace	1883–1905	Merged into McKenzie
Wallette	1873–83	Abolished by creation of [Buford] and [Flannery]
Williams	1873–92	Merged into Mercer
Wynn	1883–87	Absorbed by Bottineau, McHenry, Renville, and Ward

OHIO

| Wayne* | 1796–1803 | Absorbed by Greene, Franklin, and Montgomery |

OKLAHOMA

| Day | 1892–1907 | Abolished by creation of Ellis and Roger Mills |
| Swanson | 1918–19 | Absorbed by Comanche, Kiowa, and Tillman |

OREGON

| Umpqua | 1851–62 | Merged into Douglas |

SOUTH CAROLINA

In 1868 South Carolina designated its political subdivisions as counties. Prior to 1868, the subdivisions had been designated as counties (1682), parishes (1706), townships (1731), and judicial districts (1769). Some, but not all, judicial districts were eliminated in 1785 and some others in 1800. The boundaries of these subdivisions often overlapped each other. Beginning in 1785, some counties were created and later eliminated within judicial districts. It is beyond the purview of this appendix to untangle this subdivisional history.

SOUTH DAKOTA

Armstrong	1873–79	Merged into Hutchinson
Armstrong	1883–1952	Merged into Dewey
Beadle*	1873–79	Abolished by creation of Brown
Boreman	1873–1909	Abolished by creation of Corson
Bramble	1873–79	Merged into Miner
Bruguier	1862–64	Absorbed by Charles Mix
Burchard	1873–79	Absorbed by Hand
Burdick	1883–89	Merged into Harding
Cheyenne	1875–83	Abolished by creation of Jackson, [Nowlin], [Armstrong], and [Sterling]
Choteau	1883–98	Absorbed by Butte and Meade
Cragin	1873–79	Abolished by creation of Aurora
Delano	1875–98	Merged into Meade
Ewing	1883–94	Merged into Harding

Forsythe	1875–81	Merged into Custer
Greeley	1873–79	Abolished by creation of Day
Jayne	1862–71	Absorbed by Hutchinson
Lugenbeel	1875–1909	Abolished by creation of Bennett and Todd
Mandan	1875–87	Merged into Lawrence
Martin	1881–98	Merged into Butte
Meyer	1873–1909	Abolished by creation of Mellette and Todd
Mills	1873–79	Abolished by creation of Brown
Nowlin	1883–98	Absorbed by Lyman and Stanley
Pratt	1873–1909	Abolished by creation of Mellette
Presho	1873–1907	Merged into Tripp
Rinehart	1883–98	Absorbed by Butte and Meade
Schnasse	1883–1911	Abolished by creation of Ziebach
Scobey	1883–98	Merged into Meade
Sterling	1883–1911	Abolished by creation of Ziebach
Stone	1873–79	Abolished by creation of Day
Thompson	1873–79	Merged into Spink
Todd*	1862–97	Merged into Gregory
Wagner	1883–98	Merged into Butte
Washabaugh	1883–1979	Merged into Jackson
Washington	1883–1943	Merged into Shannon
Wetmore	1873–79	Abolished by creation of Aurora
White River	1875–83	Abolished by creation of Jackson and [Nowlin]
Wood	1873–79	Merged into Kingsbury
Ziebach*	1875–98	Merged into Pennington

TENNESSEE

Bell	1870–71	Absorbed by Fayette, Hardeman, and McNairy
Christian	1852–53	Absorbed by Carroll, Gibson, Henderson, and Madison
Cumberland	1837–45	Absorbed by Davidson, Dickson, Montgomery, and Robertson
Erthridge	1870–71	Absorbed by Carroll, Gibson, Henry, and Weakley
Grant	1869–70	Absorbed by Carroll, Gibson, Henderson, and Madison
Hanes	1877–78	Absorbed by Benton, Carroll, Decatur, and Henderson
Hanover	1844–45	Absorbed by Fayette and Shelby
Hatchie	1846–47	Absorbed by Hardeman and McNairy
James	1870–1920	Merged into Hamilton
Jones	1844–45	Absorbed by Blount and Monroe
Nashoba	1871–73	Absorbed by Fayette and Shelby
Powell	1835–36	Absorbed by Greene, Hawkins, Jefferson, Sullivan, and Washington
Taylor	1852–53	Absorbed by Hardin and Wayne
Tennessee	1788–96	Divided into Montgomery and Robertson
Webster	1873–74	Absorbed by Campbell, Claiborne, and Union
Wisdom	1875–76	Absorbed by Hardeman, Henderson, Madison, and McNairy

TEXAS

Dawson*	1858–66	Divided into Kinney and Uvalde
Encinal	1858–99	Merged into Webb
Foley	1887–97	Merged into Brewster
Greer	1860–96	Awarded to Oklahoma by US Supreme Court

UTAH

Carson	1855–61	Became part of Nevada Territory
Cedar	1857–62	Merged into Utah County
Desert	1852–62	Absorbed by Box Elder and Tooele
Greasewood	1857–62	Merged into Box Elder

Green River	1852–68	Absorbed by Summit, Rich, and Wyoming Territory
Malad	1857–62	Merged into Box Elder
Rio Virgin	1869–72	Merged into Washington
Shambip	1857–62	Merged into Tooele

VERMONT

Cumberland	1779–81	Abolished by creation of Orange, Windham, and Windsor

VIRGINIA

Clifton Forge †	1906–2001	Merged into Alleghany
Elizabeth City	1634–1952	Merged into City of Hampton
Fincastle	1772–76	Divided into [Kentucky], Montgomery, and Washington
Kentucky	1776–80	Divided into Fayette, Jefferson, and Lincoln
Lower Norfolk	1637–91	Divided into [Norfolk] and [Princess Anne]
Manchester †	1900–10	Merged into City of Richmond
Nansemond	1637–1974	Merged into City of Suffolk
New Norfolk	1636–37	Divided into [Lower Norfolk] and [Nansemond]
Norfolk	1691–1963	Merged into City of Chesapeake
Princess Anne	1691–1963	Merged into City of Virginia Beach
Rappahannock*	1656–92	Divided into Essex and Richmond
South Boston †	1960–95	Merged into Halifax
South Norfolk †	1921–63	Merged into City of Chesapeake
Warwick	1634–1952	Merged into City of Newport News

(† Independent City)

WASHINGTON

Ferguson	1863–65	Merged into Klickitat

Bibliography

The primary source used in the compilation of this book was, of course, previous editions of Kane's *The American Counties*. A close second was Michael Beatty's *County Name Origins of the United States* (Jefferson, North Carolina: McFarland & Co., Inc., 2001). This is a huge book listing the name origin of every county and parish in the U.S. It does not, however, address independent cities and Alaska. The book is divided into sections by states. At the end of each state's section is a bibliography for counties in that state. The bibliographies are extensive but rather difficult to use because they are arranged in proper bibliographic form by author or title rather than by county. Nonetheless, this is an excellent resource devoted to narrative discussions of the how and why of county name origins.

In the first four editions of the *American Counties*, Kane included bibliographic entries for most counties. Many of Kane's references, however, are by now over one hundred years old having been published during the heyday of county histories, roughly from 1880 to 1920. Many of the county histories of this era were prone to boosterism. Prominent local citizens would often subscribe to these histories and would receive individual biographies in the book extolling their virtues. Reference to these bibliographies are omitted because any researcher of a county will eventually be led to the county's local or state library, or historical society which should have these early county histories. Also, most US counties have their own websites with links to myriad sources of information including these older histories.

Population figures given in Kane's previous editions were checked against data compiled and edited by Richard L. Forstall, *Population of States and Counties of the United States: 1790 to 1990* (US Bureau of the Census, Washington, DC, 1996). The Census Bureau's website was the source for the 2000 and 2010 county populations and county. Access the Census Bureau's American Factfinder at http://www.census.gov.

There is an overwhelming amount of information available on the Internet. The problem is deciding when to end the search. Google was used to initiate most searches for individuals for whom counties were named. Google led into county histories or genealogical sites with varying degrees of success in finding the sought after information.

The Department of Commerce's definition of "first order subdivision" used to define counties and other entities listed in this book is from the National Institute of Standards and Technology's website at: http://www.itl.nist.gov/fipspubs/fip6-4.htm. Disputed spellings of counties and county seats were resolved by two websites: (1) the US Geological Survey's Geographic Names Information System at: http://geonames.usgs.gov and (2) the National Association of Counties (NACo) at: http://www.naco.org. NACo's website provides the names and address of county officials who could be contacted if necessary.

There are numerous Internet sites that provide information about individuals. Information on any person who has served in Congress is available at "The Biographical Directory of the United States Congress, 1774–Present" at: http://bioguide.congress.gov/biosearch/biosearch.asp. An interesting website that includes almost all politicians who have served at national, state, and local levels is the "Political Graveyard" at: http://politicalgraveyard.com/index.html. The biographies of saints for whom counties have been named were found at the Catholic Forum's patron saint index at: http://www.catholic-forum.com/saints/patron02.htm. A good starting point for exploring Indian tribal names is http://www.native-languages.org/languages.htm. Most states have websites providing historical data. One of the most extensive is the "The Handbook of Texas Online" at http://www.tsha.utexas.edu/handbook/online/index.html.

Information on the dates of county creation was supported by "AniMap Plus," a compact disc available from The Gold Bug, Alamo, California (http//goldbug.com/store). This is a fascinating collection of maps for each state showing the boundary changes for all counties from 1634 to the present. Another source for county creation dates, as well as spellings and county seats, is *The Handybook for Genealogists: United States of America*, 10th edition (Everton Publishers, Draper, Utah,

2002). Because of their reliance on county records, genealogical books and websites are excellent sources of information on counties.

By now, virtually every county in the United States has its own website. Some sites are certainly better than others but they all provide a point of departure for exploring counties. Some provide county histories and other categories of information. Listing all the county sites checked in compiling this book would essentially be a list of all the counties in the US. It is left to the readers to track down the ones of interest to them. Happy hunting.

About the Authors

Charles Curry Aiken is a native of San Diego, California. He attended San Diego State College (now University), graduating in 1966 with a Bachelor's Degree in Latin American Studies and a California Secondary Teaching Credential. He taught junior high school history in Los Angeles for one year before going to work for the Army at Sierra Army Depot, Herlong, California, as a civilian safety officer. While with the Army, he received a Master's Degree in Liberal Studies from Oklahoma University. In 1972 Aiken transferred to an army activity in Philadelphia, Pennsylvania. The following year, he went to work for the Navy Safety School in Bloomington, Indiana, where he now lives as a retired safety training consultant.

Aiken's interest in counties is an avocation. His lifelong interest in geography focused on counties when as an adolescent he discovered Joseph Kane's *The American Counties*. His job as a safety instructor with the Navy gave him the opportunity to travel throughout the United States which led to the hobby of photographing county courthouses. Over the span of 30 years, Aiken visited and photographed all 3,114 county courthouses in the 48 contiguous states and Hawaii.

When Kane stopped writing *The American Counties* in 1983, Aiken offered to write the 5th edition which was published in 2003.

Joseph Nathan Kane was the originator of *The American Counties* books. His life spanned the twentieth century from 1899 to 2002. Kane lived in New York City for most of his life. After graduating from Columbia University, he began work writing for trade journals. This led to an interest in little-known inventors which in turn led to an interest in facts and trivia. He wrote over 50 books of minutia on various subjects from US presidents to dogs, including American counties. Kane's command of trivia led him to be a contributor of questions for "The $64,000 Question" and "Break the $250,000 Bank." He was not involved in the TV quiz show scandals of the 1950s, but the demise of these shows ended this pursuit. However, he continued to write. There are a number of websites devoted to Kane. A simple web search could lead a reader to the type of minutia that Kane so loved.